WITHDRAWN

FOUNDATIONS OF THE NINETEENTH CENTURY
VOL. I

FOUNDATIONS OF THE NINETEENTH CENTURY

BY HOUSTON STEWART CHAMBERLAIN

Translated from the German by John Lees

With an Introduction
by
GEORGE L. MOSSE

VOLUME I

HOWARD FERTIG

New York · 1968

First published in English in 1910
by John Lane The Bodley Head Ltd.

HOWARD FERTIG, INC. EDITION 1968
Published by arrangement with The Bodley Head Ltd.

Introduction to the 1968 Edition copyright © 1968 by George L. Mosse

Library of Congress Catalog Card Number: 67-29735

Printed in the United States of America
by Noble Offset Printers, Inc.

INTRODUCTION
TO THE 1968 EDITION

Houston Stewart Chamberlain

Why republish Houston Stewart Chamberlain's *Foundations of the Nineteenth Century*? This ponderous book is not a work of scholarship nor even a discussion of recognizable historical facts. Yet after its first appearance in 1899, the *Foundations* enjoyed great popularity, passing through twenty-eight editions until 1942, and such popularity must count for something. And, in fact, the ideas and prejudices that fill this work aroused considerable sympathy in the minds of many German-speaking readers. If we find the arguments tortured and their logic fallacious, this was not the impression Chamberlain's hundreds of thousands of readers came away with. The *Foundations of the Nineteenth Century* is a historical document of great importance; it is a vital part of that German ideology which influenced not only the educated classes but filtered down to the rest of the population as well.

Edmond Vermeil has called Chamberlain "the best known of the Nazi doctrinaires."[1] This simplifies the problem with which his philosophy confronts us today. To be sure, Alfred Rosenberg, the Nazi ideologue, saw his own *Mythos of the Twentieth Century* (1930) as a continuation of Chamberlain's work, and believed that Chamberlain was the first to state clearly all the conse-

[1] Edmond Vermeil, "The Origin, Nature and Development of German Nationalist Ideology in the 19th and 20th Centuries," *The Third Reich* (London, 1955), p. 67.

v

quences of the supposed Germanic superiority over all other peoples and races.[2] But the *Foundations* is a more important work than the *Mythos of the Twentieth Century*. A great number of copies of Rosenberg's book were sold but it was read by few, while Chamberlain's work pioneered a "meta-history" that was of vast importance both for its content and style. Chamberlain praises the dilettante over the specialist in the introduction to the *Foundations*. The dilettante, unlike the specialist, is willing to construct a synthesis of all historical events and trends of the past—and on the basis of such a truly cosmic construct to form his own dogmatic conclusions about the future of man and his world. These conclusions must then have a general validity. They must not only be descriptive of the whole human past but must also be prophetic and illuminate the future of mankind. Others had written "universal history," but here such writing played a primary role in the construction of the final synthesis within a historical framework of philosophy, religion, and science. However different his conclusions, Oswald Spengler's *Decline of the West* also belongs to this genre.

Such histories attempted to reconcile divergent forces like religion, philosophy, and science, and Chamberlain confidently undertook this task in his book. The result was a picture of civilization which saw in the German the savior and therefore the leading power of the world. The basis of German greatness was the Aryan race, which

[2] Alfred Rosenberg, *Der Mythus des 20. Jahrhunderts* (Munich, 1935), p. 81. Hans F. K. Guenther, perhaps the most important theoretician of race, in the 1930's praised Chamberlain's *Foundations* for having brought racial thought to the attention of a wide circle of Germans for the first time. *Rassenkunde des Deutschen Volkes* (Munich, 1935), p. 20.

drew unto itself all the qualities of creativity and organizational genius that other races lacked. But this is to put the argument too simply, because what impressed the readers was precisely the pretentiousness with which the argument was put forth. They were swept away by the show of broad learning in history and philosophy as well as science. These disciplines became part of the overall world view and were distorted in the process; but the way in which they suffered at Chamberlain's hands was to determine the view of history, philosophy, and science of a whole generation committed to this Germanic ideology as a way out of the dilemmas of modernity.

Chamberlain did not shirk the central issue: science and religion did seem opposed to each other. In order to construct his synthesis he turned to the philosophy of Immanuel Kant, which became basic to his thought and about which he was to write a two-volume work (1905). His reading of Kant can be summarized as follows: on the one hand, there was a Germanic science, which determined with the utmost accuracy that which existed empirically; on the other hand, there was a Germanic religion founded by Luther, which opened infinite vistas to the German soul. This religion took priority, for it alone could fathom the "essence of things" (Kant's *Ding an Sich*) and keep science within its proper bounds while, at the same time, appropriating empirical evidence in support of itself.[3] Race was both an established fact of science and a part of the essence of things.

What was this religion that Luther had founded? If Kant was decisive in forming Chamberlain's synthesis of

[3] I.e., George L. Mosse, *The Crisis of German Ideology* (New York, 1964), pp. 93–5.

civilization, Richard Wagner was equally important in determining his view of religion. Wagner became the "sun of his life," and the composer's ideals of the "new music" were the "firm center" and "resting point" of his own spirit.[4] In Wagner's work he found a synthesis of music, visual art (staging), and Germanic ideology—"the highest flight of Aryan consciousness," as he described it later in life.[5] Chamberlain's religion was the mysterious union of musical ecstacy, worship of nature, and the Germanic heritage. Such a religion was for Aryans only. Christ himself became, in Chamberlain's hands, the archetype of this faith—a non-Jewish Christ who, as an Aryan, reacted against supposed Jewish formalism and hardheaded rationalism. The *Foundations* reflects this religion : it is the measuring rod against which the supposedly materialistic Greeks and Jews are measured in the light of history. The natural sciences were sucked into this mystique while, at the same time, giving added respectability to Chamberlain's thought in the minds of his vast number of captivated readers.

Yet there was actually little new in this thought. A few years earlier Paul de Lagarde had already preached a similar "Germanic religion" and there were others who followed suit. But this is just the point—Chamberlain's book took its place within an already present stream of thought, while having enough unique twists and turns to make it stand out from the rest. Reading the *Foundations* means acquiring familiarity with a mainstream of Germanic thought and pondering on how such ideas could

[4] Houston Stewart Chamberlain, *Lebenswege Meines Denkens* (Munich, 1919), p. 163.
[5] *Ibid.,* p. 242.

have appealed to so many people over such a long span of time.

A brief review of Chamberlain's life helps one to understand how he could relate himself to this German national mystique and indeed become one of its chief prophets. He was born in Portsmouth (1855), where his father was a captain (later admiral) in the English navy. Chamberlain was educated first in France and then at Cheltenham College, an English public school (or "private school," as we would call it in the United States). There he seems to have rebelled against the "sober emphasis" upon traditional subject matter and the exclusion of all creative arts from the curriculum. The harsh discipline of Cheltenham and its unimaginative teachers turned him toward the arts, especially music.[6] Chamberlain wrote in later years that he had always been a compulsive dreamer, leading a vigorous dream life side by side with his waking hours. Such a person would have responded badly to the discipline and curriculum of an English public school, and we know of many other boys in this *milieu* who turned to cultivating their inner lives, the "soul" which proved so receptive to an emotion-centered mystique. Moreover, Chamberlain's dreams focused not only upon people but especially upon a romantic nature replete with mysterious mountains and deep-running streams.[7] Here the search for a religion that was close to nature and the race may have found its first encouragement.

Illness forced him to leave the school and take cures in Germany, which was destined to become his spiritual home from 1870 on. Germany gave him a feeling of liber-

[6] *Ibid.*, pp. 163 ff.
[7] *Ibid.*, p. 169.

ation. He was no longer imprisoned within the discipline of a school but was taught by his own sympathetic tutors. Chamberlain began studying science, especially the structure of plants and their roots. Eventually he wrote a long dissertation on this subject, which was accepted by the University of Vienna in 1889.

Chamberlain belonged to the class of "private scholars," men who had advanced degrees but who never entered the academic, or indeed any other profession. There was not enough room in the academic world for all those who took higher degrees, many taking them for the status they afforded, rather than as a guarantee of university employment. We do not really know why, in his youth, Chamberlain never tried for such a career; perhaps it was his ill health, or the fear of being rejected—in all likelihood his contempt for the specialist played a part. The class of "private scholars" existed in Europe as a whole, but in Germany, with its undue emphasis upon academic prestige, it was apt to further a group of disgruntled outsiders who were constantly knocking at the door of university recognition. The majority of the prophets of the Germanic race belonged to this class, many of whom formed what has been called the "academic proletariat."

Unable or unwilling to use their learning in accepted channels of academic reward and prestige, they sought instead to become critics and prophets. As disgruntled outsiders with little money at their disposal (like Chamberlain who suffered chronic poverty) such men opposed present society, indeed all of modernity, and sought to connect their knowledge to the glorious future of the race to which they did belong (as many professors did not). Some, like Paul de Lagarde, eventually obtained univer-

sity chairs after having spent half a lifetime condemning
sterile academic knowledge. There is as we have seen no
evidence that Chamberlain ever wanted to become part of
the academic establishment; eventually the Wagner circle
at Bayreuth sufficed to give him a place in the sun. He
shared the attitudes of the "academic proletariat": Chamberlain could have been a professor of botany but he became a prophet whose condemnation of specialists in the
introduction of the *Foundations* is identical to the condemnation of professors that runs through the works of
his fellow Germanic writers. Academic knowledge was
swamped by the ambition to remake the world as a whole
in order that the Aryan might dominate it.

Chamberlain's pursuit of scientific research did not
mean that he led a tranquil life confined to a laboratory.
He traveled a lot, living for a time in Geneva and Dres-
den, visiting watering places in search of good health,
which eluded him most of his life. Eventually he settled
in Vienna for twenty years (1889–1909); then he moved
to Bayreuth, where he spent the rest of his days (1909–
27). It could be hazarded that his search for a spiritual
"resting place" had its foundation in his early restless
life. Moreover, Chamberlain's constant ill health may
well be connected with his admiration for vigorous and
dominating heroes: whether it be Wagner's *Nibelungen*
or the young Hitler. There is a similar connection between ill health and admiration for Germanic heroes in
the philosophy of one of his famous older contemporaries, the historian Heinrich von Treitschke. These facts
should complete the psychological picture which, whatever
weight one may choose to give it, made Chamberlain
receptive to the mystique of race and Germanism, en-

couraging his search for a spiritual resting place.

Chamberlain's "path towards Bayreuth" began in 1872, shortly after his arrival in Germany. But study and listening to Wagner's works for many years had to take the place of the pilgrimage to Bayreuth. Finally, in 1882, Chamberlain had saved enough money to attend the Festival and see the master in person. Bayreuth became not only the "home of his soul" but eventually his physical home as well. Chamberlain's personal connections with Bayreuth came about, not through friendship with Richard Wagner (who died in 1883) but through an increasingly close relationship with Wagner's wife, Cosima, the daughter of the composer Franz von Liszt. Cosima Wagner devoted herself to her husband's heritage and made Bayreuth the center of the Wagner cult. She encouraged works like Leopold von Schroeder's *The Completion of the Aryan Mysteries at Bayreuth*,[8] which reflected her own view of her husband's place in history. Small wonder that she found a soulmate in Chamberlain, who in 1895 published a long book on Richard Wagner with similar content. Cosima Wagner actively encouraged the writing of the *Foundations* and received the work with admiration. A convinced racist, she singled out the passages dealing with the Jews, Germans, and their relation to religion as the most inspirational.[9] After Chamberlain's death Wagner's ninety-two-year-old widow reminisced (1930) that his settling in Bayreuth was of such importance in

[8] I.e., Leopold von Schroeder, *Die Vollendung des arischen mysteriums in Bayreuth* (Munich, 1911). Schroeder was a Munich professor who was interested in Indian literature and religion.

[9] *Cosima Wagner und Houston Stewart Chamberlain im Briefwechsel,* ed. Paul Pretzsch (Leipzig, 1934), pp. 552, 556.

her life that he continued to speak to her in the quiet of her soul.[10]

Chamberlain's friendship with Cosima Wagner was climaxed by his marriage to her daughter Eva in 1908. Now he was a member of the "master's" family as well as the propagandist for Cosima's concept of Wagner's work and thought. No doubt his close association with Bayreuth contributed to the popularity of the *Foundations*. Reading this book can give one an idea of the kind of ideology that was current among Wagner's admirers, whom Cosima had gathered at Bayreuth—the "Wagner circle" through which many of the prophets of Aryan predominance passed.

To be sure, Chamberlain himself asserted that Darwin, not Wagner, provided the primary inspiration for his racial theories. He interpreted Darwin's concept of the struggle for the survival of the species as proof that race determined the course of all life. Typically enough, he faulted Darwin for not realizing the full consequences of this truth, but he praised him for providing the empirical proof that inevitably led to such a conclusion.[11] However, it seems clear that Chamberlain had acquired the concept of race before he happened upon Darwin, and that the *Origin of Species* was used to provide his doctrine with the kind of scientific respectability for which he longed so much. Science was distorted as he integrated it within his total world view; a synthesis which was based, in the last resort, upon a Germanic mystique closer to Wagner than to Darwin. The *Foundations* reflects the "ultra

[10] *Ibid.*, p. 12.

[11] Houston Stewart Chamberlain, *Briefe, 1882–1924* (Munich, 1928), Vol. I, pp. 83–5.

Wagnerian nonsense"[12] which Cosima cultivated so carefully and which, in turn, became a part of the mainstream of Germanic nationalism. The *Foundations* is, without doubt, the most important work that reflected this dubious inspiration. As Chamberlain put it on another occasion: eventually the ideals of Bayreuth will show their strength in a way hardly dreamt of at present—the strongest will win and the strongest is he whose thought is "mythical."[13]

Nothing Chamberlain undertook during the rest of his life could rival the influence of this book. He was now accepted as a Germanic prophet and corresponded with the young Emperor William II who, admiring Bayreuth, was himself attracted to Chamberlain's work. During the First World War he became a busy propagandist for the German cause, until his delicate health finally collapsed. From then until his death in 1927, he remained a semi-paralyzed invalid. Others of his persuasion became pessimists as Germany lost the war and a republic seemed to endanger the very existence of the Aryan race, but not Chamberlain, for he had always been optimistic about the Aryans' future. Once Chamberlain had found a resting place in his ideology, there was little that could sap the strength of his convictions. This the more so since in the midst of German collapse he discovered the prophet who would lead the Aryans to victory. At the Bayreuth Festival of 1923 he had been introduced to Adolf Hitler.

Hitler met Chamberlain at Wagner's house and was

[12] The phrase is Ernst Newman's, from *A Study of Wagner* (London, 1899), p. 241.

[13] Houston Stewart Chamberlain, *Richard Wagner* (London and Philadelphia, 1900), p. 374.

greatly impressed.[14] There is little doubt that Hitler knew the *Foundations,* but Chamberlain did not play an essential role in the formation of his thought. Hitler later criticized Chamberlain for believing that Christianity could have any reality on a spiritual level—even as an Aryan religion.[15] It is interesting to note that the one major criticism which Cosima Wagner made to her friend about the *Foundations* concerned Chamberlain's apparent denial that Christ could be known through prayer.[16] Nor, as a matter of fact, was Chamberlain quite as single-minded on the Jewish question as the future Führer. Chamberlain belonged to a school of racial thought that distinguished between the evil of "Judaism" and the individual Jew. He wrote to Leopold von Schroeder about his friendship for many "wonderful" Jews. Yet Jews must be eradicated from German cultural life because in the last analysis their Jewishness is bound to the evil and materialistic principles of Judaism. We must neither hate the Jew nor apply humanitarian principles in order to allow his participation in German life. the Jewish question can only be solved through meeting the Jew as a foreigner.[17]

Many others made such a differentiation between the individual Jew and Judaism as an evil principle, but there is no evidence that Hitler ever permitted himself such fine distinctions. Hitler hailed Chamberlain as a famous Ger-

---

[14] He is only mentioned once in *Mein Kampf* (Munich, 1934), p. 296, to the effect that the German government then and now was "unfortunately" not interested in Chamberlain's insights.

[15] *Hitler's Secret Conversations, 1941–1944* (New York, 1953), p. 119.

[16] *Cosima Wagner und Houston Stewart Chamberlain,* p. 564.

[17] Chamberlain, *Briefe, 1882–1924,* Vol. I, pp. 169–71.

manic prophet, but there is no evidence that he helped to determine the course of his life. In any case, the literature of both racism and Germanic thought has a basic similarity that makes it difficult to venture which particular work was decisive in forming Hitler's ideology. To be sure, some may have joined the Nazi party because their hero Chamberlain admired the Führer.[18]

Much more important, in the long run, was the academic respectability which the *Foundations*, as a supposedly learned tract, gave to Nazi racism and the Germanic cult. The book could be used both on the Nazi road to power, and to consolidate control over the German mind once power had been achieved. The German longing for academic respectability plays an important role, not only in the *Foundations'* reception, but also in the use that could be made of the work by racist-oriented political movements. This German trait is unique; nowhere else in Europe did rightist and nationalist movements feel such a need to bolster their ideologies by a show of learning. Even in German popular literature the hero—strong, kind, and courageous—was apt to combine such praiseworthy traits with an exhibition of encyclopedic knowledge.[19] In Germany ideologies had to show themselves as "true" through a combination of philosophical, historical, and scientific analysis—producing the meta-history of which the *Foundations* is an important example. The German scholarship of the nineteenth century that all Europe

[18] One such case is reported by William Sheridan Allen, *The Nazi Seizure of Power* (Chicago, 1965), p. 26.

[19] Viktor Böhm makes this remark about a typical hero in one of Karl May's novels. May was probably one of the most popular writers during Chamberlain's lifetime. *Karl May* (Vienna, 1955), p. 58.

rightly admired had this attitude as one of its byproducts. Men saw the prestige of this scholarship and greedily grasped the meta-history that was put before them, but they failed to separate true from pseudo learning.

If the meeting at Bayreuth did not markedly influence the development of Hitler's own thought, it acted as a catalyst upon Chamberlain. Here, Chamberlain wrote, was a man who was all heart, who loved his people and who showed a courage reminiscent of Martin Luther.[20] Chamberlain described the future Führer as "the true awakener [of souls] and at the same time the giver of rest."[21]

This phrase can symbolize the trend of the whole Germanic ideology, that national mystique which was to be so fateful to the world and so attractive to many in the German-speaking regions of Europe. The Aryan and his religion were to be awakened by a messiah who would purge their nation of its ills and reconquer its rightful place in the world. But at the same time, this awakening meant a new restfulness: for the Aryan had now discovered his own inner nature and his soul. This concept of life echoes throughout the *Foundations,* and Adolf Hitler, who gave this feeling of restfulness to the aged and infirm Chamberlain, would eventually provide it to the nation itself.

This appeal was common to both National Socialists and to those conservatives who regarded the Nazis as a dangerous mass movement. Chamberlain's influence

[20] Houston Stewart Chamberlain, "Adolf Hitler zu seinem Geburtstag am 20. April, 1924," *Auswahl aus seinen Werken* (Breslau, 1934), pp. 65–6.
[21] "Ein Brief Chamberlains an Adolf Hitler" (October 7, 1923), *Auswahl,* p. 68.

touched many conservatives more directly than Adolf
Hitler, even though they were at times ambivalent about
the racial theories in the *Foundations*. Such a leading conservative of the nineteen twenties as Moeller van den
Bruck could proudly list Chamberlain as one of his intellectual ancestors.[22] Within a certain circle of German
youth before, during, and after the First World War,
Chamberlain's work also attained important influence.
Members of the German Youth Movement, which contained some of the nation's most articulate youth, liked
the combination of a Germanic religion with racial superiority which the *Foundations* ascribed to the Aryan.[23]
Longing for a "true" integration with the *Volk* was made
easier through such a meta-history, which gave supposed
depth and scholarly respectability to this idealism.

Here again, the *Foundations* could be counted in the
mainstream of the German nationalist mystique and its
influence could radiate widely across the whole spectrum
of the population, whatever the individual's party or
group affiliation. Chamberlain himself never joined in
active politics; he merely counseled such nationalist pressure groups as the Pan-German League.[24] Yet the book

[22] Fritz Stern, *The Politics of Cultural Despair* (Berkeley
and Los Angeles, 1961), p. 187; Klemens von Klemperer, *Germany's New Conservatism* (Princeton, 1957), p. 196.

[23] For this see Walter Laqueur, *Young Germany* (New York,
1962) and the remarks on Chamberlain by Hans Blüher, the
contemporary historian of the Youth Movement, in *Der Jud ist
Schuld* (Vienna, 1932), pp. 69–81.

[24] I.e., Heinrich Class, *Wider den Strom* (Leipzig, 1932),
pp. 87 ff. Class, the leader of the Pan Germans, was Chamberlain's lawyer. Chamberlain also endorsed the most racist group
of the German Youth Movement, *Die Greifen* (The Hawks),
George L. Mosse, *op cit.*, p. 226.

he wrote typifies an attitude and trend of thought that not only ate deeply into the nation but eventually became an awesome reality. There is an intimate connection between the popularity of this book and the bloody history of our times.

Madison, Wisconsin   George L. Mosse
May 1967

AUTHOR'S INTRODUCTION

Alles beruht auf Inhalt, Gehalt und Tüchtigkeit eines zuerst
aufgestellten Grundsatzes und auf der Reinheit des Vorsatzes.
GOETHE.

PLAN OF THE WORK

THE work of which this is the first Book is one
that is not to be made up of fragments patched
together, but one that has been conceived
and planned out from the beginning as a
complete and finished whole. The object, therefore, of
this general introduction must be to give an idea of the
scheme of the whole work when it shall have been brought
to an end. It is true that this first book is, in form,
complete in itself; yet it would not be what it is if it
had not come into existence as a part of a greater conception. It is this greater conception that must be the
subject of the preface to the " part which, in the first
instance, is the whole."

There is no need to dwell in detail upon the limitations which the individual must admit, when he stands
face to face with an immeasurable world of facts. The
mastery of such a task, scientifically, is impossible;
it is only artistic power, aided by those secret parallels
which exist between the world of vision and of thought,
by that tissue which—like ether—fills and connects
the whole world, that can, if fortune is favourable, produce a unity here which is complete, and that, too,
though only fragments be employed to make it. If
the artist does succeed in this, then his work has not

xxi

been superfluous : the immeasurable has been brought
within the scope of vision, the shapeless has acquired a
form. In such a task the individual has an advantage
over a combination of men, however capable they may
be, for a homogeneous whole can be the work only of
an individual mind. But he must know how to turn
this advantage to good account, for it is his only one.
Art appears only as a whole, as something perfect in
itself ; science, on the other hand, is bound to be fragmentary. Art unites and science disconnects. Art
gives form to things, science dissects forms. The man
of science stands on an Archimedean point outside the
world : therein lies his greatness, his so-called objectivity ;
but this very fact is also the cause of his manifest in-
sufficiency ; for no sooner does he leave the sphere of
actual observation, to reduce the manifoldness of experience to the unity of conception and idea, than he
finds himself hanging by the thin thread of abstraction in
empty space. The artist, on the contrary, stands at the
world's centre (that is, at the centre of his own world),
and his creative power takes him as far as his senses can
reach ; for this creative power is but the manifestation
of the individual mind acting and reacting upon its
surroundings. But for that reason also he cannot be
reproached for his "subjectivity" : that is the fundamental condition of his creative work. In the case
before us the subject has definite historical boundaries
and is immutably fixed for ever. Untruth would be
ridiculous, caprice unbearable ; the author cannot say,
like Michael Angelo, " Into this stone there comes nothing
but what I put there " :

> in pietra od in candido foglio
> che nulla ha dentro, et evvi ci ch'io voglio!

On the contrary, unconditional respect for facts must
be his guiding star. He must be artist, not in the sense
of the creative genius, but only in the limited sense of one

who employs the methods of the artist. He should give shape, but only to that which is already there, not to that which his fancy may mirror. Philosophical history is a desert; fanciful history an idiot asylum. We must therefore demand that the artistic designer should have a positive tendency of mind and a strictly scientific conscience. Before he reasons, he must know: before he gives shape to a thing, he must test it. He cannot look upon himself as master, he is but a servant, the servant of truth.

These remarks will probably suffice to give the reader some notion of the general principles which have been followed in planning this work. We must leave the airy heights of philosophic speculation and descend to the earth. If in such undertakings the moulding and shaping of the materials at hand is the only task which the individual can entrust to himself, how is he to set about it in the present case?

The *Nineteenth Century!* It seems an inexhaustible theme, and so it really is; and yet it is only by including more that it becomes comprehensible and possible of achievement. This appears paradoxical, but it is nevertheless true. As soon as our gaze rests long and lovingly upon the past, out of which the present age developed amid so much suffering, as soon as the great fundamental facts of history are brought vividly home to us and rouse in our hearts violent and conflicting emotions with regard to the present, fear and hope, loathing and enthusiasm, all pointing to a future which it must be our work to shape, towards which too we must henceforth look with longing and impatience— then the great immeasurable nineteenth century shrivels up to relatively insignificant dimensions; we have no time to linger over details, we wish to keep nothing but the important features vividly and clearly before our minds, in order that we may know who we are and whither we are tending. This gives a definite aim with a fair prospect of attaining it : the individual can venture now to begin the undertaking. The lines of his work are so clearly traced for him that he only requires to follow them faithfully.

The following is the outline of my work. In the " Foundations " I discuss the first eighteen centuries of the Christian era with frequent reference to times more remote ; I do not profess to give a history of the past, but merely of that past which is still living ; as a matter of fact this involves so much, and an accurate and critical knowledge of it is so indispensable to every one who wishes to form an estimate of the present, that I am inclined to regard the study of the " Foundations " of the nineteenth century as almost the most important part of the whole undertaking. A second book would be devoted to this century itself : naturally only the leading ideas could be treated in such a work, and the task of doing so would be very much lightened and simplified by the " Foundations," in which our attention had been continually directed to the nineteenth century. A supplement might serve to form an approximate idea of the importance of the century ; that can only be done by comparing it with the past, and here the " Foundations " would have prepared the ground ; by this procedure, moreover, we should be able to fore-shadow the future—no capricious and fanciful picture, but a shadow cast by the present in the light of the past. Then at last the century would stand out before our eyes clearly shaped and defined—not in the form of a chronicle or an encyclopædia, but as a living " cor-poreal " thing.

So much for the general outline. But as I do not wish it to remain as shadowy as the future, I shall give some more detailed information concerning the execution of my plan. As regards the results at which I arrive, I do not feel called upon to anticipate them here, as they can only carry conviction after consideration of all the arguments which I shall have to bring forward in their support.

The Foundations

In this first book it has been my task to endeavour to reveal the bases upon which the nineteenth century rests; this seemed to me, as I have said, the most difficult and important part of the whole scheme; for this reason I have devoted two volumes to it. In the sphere of history understanding means seeing the evolution of the present from the past; even when we are face to face with a fact which cannot be explained further, as happens in the case of every pre-eminent personality and every nation of strong individuality at its first appearance on the stage of history, we see that these are linked with the past, and it is from this point of connection that we must start, if we wish to form a correct estimate of their significance. If we draw an imaginary line separating the nineteenth from all preceding centuries, we destroy at one stroke all possibility of understanding it critically. The nineteenth century is not the child of the former ages —for a child begins life afresh—rather it is their direct product; mathematically considered, a sum; physiologically, a stage of life. We have inherited a certain amount of knowledge, accomplishments, thoughts, &c., we have further inherited a definite distribution of economic forces, we have inherited errors and truths, conceptions, ideals, superstitions: many of these things have grown so familiar that any other conditions would be inconceivable; many which promised well have become stunted, many have shot up so suddenly that they have almost broken their connection with the aggregate life, and while the roots of these new flowers reach down to forgotten generations, their fantastic blossoms are taken for something absolutely new. Above all we have inherited the blood and the body by which and in which we live.

Whoever takes the admonition " Know thyself" seriously will soon recognise that at least nine-tenths of this " self " do not really belong to himself. And this is true also of the spirit of a century. The pre-eminent individual, who is able to realise his physical position in the universe and to analyse his intellectual inheritance, can attain to a relative freedom ; he then becomes at least conscious of his own conditional position, and though he cannot transform himself, he can at least exercise some influence upon the course of further development ; a whole century, on the other hand, hurries unconsciously on as fate impels it : its human equipment is the fruit of departed generations, its intellectual treasure—corn and chaff, gold, silver, ore and clay—is inherited, its tendencies and deviations result with mathematical necessity from movements that have gone before. Not only, therefore, is it impossible to compare or to determine the characteristic features, the special attributes and the achievements of our century, without knowledge of the past, but we are not even able to make any precise statement about it, if we have not first of all become clear with regard to the material of which we are physically and intellectually composed. This is, I repeat, the most important problem.

The Turning-point

My object in this book being to connect the present with the past, I have been compelled to sketch in outline the history of that past. But, inasmuch as my history has to deal with the present, that is to say, with a period of time which has no fixed limit, there is no case for a strictly defined beginning. The

nineteenth century points onward into the future, it
points also back into the past : in both cases a limitation is allowable only for the sake of convenience, it
does not lie in the facts.   In general I have regarded
the year I of the Christian era as the beginning of our
history and have given a fuller justification of this view
in the introduction to the first part : but it will be seen
that I have not kept slavishly to this scheme.   Should
we ever become true Christians, then certainly that
which is here merely suggested, without being worked
out, would become an historical actuality, for it would
mean the birth of a new race : perhaps the twenty-fourth
century, into which, roughly speaking, the nineteenth
throws faint shadows, will be able to draw more definite
outlines.   Compelled as I have been to let the beginning
and the end merge into an undefined penumbra, a clearly
drawn middle line becomes all the more indispensable
to me, and as a date chosen at random could not be satisfactory in this case, the important thing has been to fix the
turning-point of the history of Europe.   The awakening
of the Teutonic peoples to the consciousness of their
all-important vocation as the founders of a completely
new civilisation and culture forms this turning-point ;
the year 1200 can be designated the central moment of
this awakening.

Scarcely any one will have the hardihood to deny
that the inhabitants of Northern Europe have become the
makers of the world's history.   At no time indeed have
they stood alone, either in the past or in the present ; on
the contrary, from the very beginning their individuality
has developed in conflict with other individualities, first
of all in conflict with that human chaos composed of
the ruins of fallen Rome, then with all the races of the
world in turn ;   others, too, have exercised influence—
indeed great influence—upon the destinies of mankind,
but then always merely as opponents of the men from

the north. What was fought out sword in hand was of but little account ; the real struggle, as I have attempted to show in chaps. vii. and viii. of this work, was one of ideas ; this struggle still goes on to-day. If, however, the Teutons were not the only peoples who moulded the world's history, they unquestionably deserve the first place : all those who from the sixth century onwards appear as genuine shapers of the destinies of mankind, whether as builders of States or as discoverers of new thoughts and of original art, belong to the Teutonic race. The impulse given by the Arabs is short-lived ; the Mongolians destroy, but do not create anything ; the great Italians of the *rinascimento* were all born either in the north saturated with Lombardic, Gothic and Frankish blood, or in the extreme Germano-Hellenic south ; in Spain it was the Western Goths who formed the element of life ; the Jews are working out their " Renaissance " of to-day by following in every sphere as closely as possible the example of the Teutonic peoples. From the moment the Teuton awakes, a new world begins to open out, a world which of course we shall not be able to call purely Teutonic—one in which, in the nineteenth century especially, there have appeared new elements, or at least elements which formerly had a lesser share in the process of development, as, for example, the Jews and the formerly pure Teutonic Slavs, who by mixture of blood have now become " un-Teutonised "—a world which will yet perhaps assimilate great racial complexes and so lay itself open to new influences from all the different types, but at any rate a new world and a new civilisation, essentially different from the Helleno-Roman, the Turanian, the Egyptian, the Chinese and all other former or contemporaneous ones. As the " beginning " of this new civilisation, that is, as the moment when it began to leave its peculiar impress on the world, we can, I think, fix the thirteenth century. Individuals such as Alfred the Great, Charlemagne, Scotus Erigena and others had long ago proved their Teutonic individuality by their civilising activity. It is, however, not individuals, but communities, that make history; these individuals had been only pioneers. In order to become a civilising power the Teuton had to awaken and grow strong in the exercise far and wide of his individual will in opposition to the will of others forced upon him from outside. This did not take place all at once, neither did it happen at the same time in all the spheres of life; the choice of the year 1200 as turning-point is therefore arbitrary, but I hope, in what follows, to be able to justify it, and my purpose will be gained if I in this way succeed in doing away with those two absurdities—the idea of Middle Ages and that of a Renaissance—by which more than by anything else an understanding of our present age is not only obscured, but rendered directly impossible.

Abandoning these formulæ which have but served to give rise to endless errors, we are left with the simple and clear view that our whole civilisation and culture of to-day is the work of one definite race of men, the Teutonic.* It is untrue that the Teutonic barbarian conjured up the so-called " Night of the Middle Ages "; this night followed rather upon the intellectual and moral bankruptcy of the raceless chaos of humanity which the dying Roman Empire had nurtured; but for the Teuton everlasting night would have settled upon the world; but for the unceasing opposition of the non-Teutonic peoples, but for that unrelenting hostility to everything Teutonic which has not yet died down among the racial chaos which has never been exterminated, we should have reached a stage of culture quite different

* Under this designation I embrace the various portions of the one great North European race, whether " Teutonic " in the narrower Tacitean meaning of the word, or Celts or genuine Slavs—*see* chap. vi. for further particulars.

from that witnessed by the nineteenth century. It is equally untrue that our culture is a renaissance of the Hellenic and the Roman : it was only after the birth of the Teutonic peoples that the renaissance of past achievements was possible and not *vice versâ;* and this *rinascimento,* to which we are beyond doubt eternally indebted for the enriching of our life, retarded nevertheless just as much as it promoted, and threw us for a long time out of our safe course. The mightiest creators of that epoch—a Shakespeare, a Michael Angelo—do not know a word of Greek or Latin. Economic advance —the basis of our civilisation—takes place in opposition to classical traditions and in a bloody struggle against false imperial doctrines. But the greatest mistake of all is the assumption that our civilisation and culture are but the expression of a general progress of mankind ; not a single fact in history supports this popular belief (as I think I have conclusively proved in the ninth chapter of this book) ; and in the meantime this empty phrase strikes us blind, and we lose sight of the self-evident fact — that our civilisation and culture, as in every previous and every other contemporary case, are the work of a definite, individual racial type, a type possessing, like everything individual, great gifts but also insurmountable limitations. And so our thoughts float around in limitless space, in a hypothetical "humanity," and we pass by unnoticed that which is concretely presented and which alone effects any-thing in history, the definite individuality. Hence the obscurity of our historical groupings. For if we draw one line through the year 500, and a second through the year 1500, and call these thousand years the Middle Ages, we have not dissected the organic body of history as a skilled anatomist, but hacked it in two like a butcher. The capture of Rome by Odoacer and by Dietrich of Berne are only episodes in that entry of the Teutonic peoples into the history of the world, which went on for a thousand years : the decisive thing, namely; the idea of the unnational world-empire, far from receiving its death-blow thereby, for a long time drew new life from the intervention of the Teutonic races. While, therefore, the year 1—the (approximate) date of the birth of Christ—is a date which is ever memorable in the history of mankind and even in the mere annals of events, the year 500 has no importance whatever. Still worse is the year 1500, for if we draw a line through it we draw it right through the middle of all conscious and unconscious efforts and developments—economic, political, artistic, scientific—which enrich our lives to-day and are moving onward to a still distant goal. If, however, we insist on retaining the idea of " Middle Ages " there is an easy way out of the difficulty : it will suffice if we recognise that we Teutons ourselves, together with our proud nineteenth century, are floundering in what the old historians used to call a " Middle Age "—a genuine " Middle Age." For the predominance of the Provisional and the Transitional, the almost total absence of the Definite, the Complete and the Balanced, are marks of our time ; we are in the " midst " of a development, already far from the starting-point and presumably still far from the goal.

What has been said may in the meantime justify the rejection of other divisions ; the conviction that I have not chosen arbitrarily, but have sought to recognise the one great fundamental fact of all modern history, will be established by the study of the whole work. Yet I cannot refrain from briefly adducing some reasons to account for my choice of the year 1200 as a convenient central date.

THE YEAR 1200

If we ask ourselves when it is that we have the first sure indications that something new is coming into being, a new form of the world in place of the old shattered ruin, and of the prevailing chaos, we must admit that they are already to be met with in many places in the twelfth century (in Northern Italy even in the eleventh), they multiply rapidly in the thirteenth—the glorious century, as Fiske calls it—attain to a glorious early full bloom in the social and industrial centres in the fourteenth and fifteenth centuries, in art in the fifteenth and sixteenth, in science in the sixteenth and seventeenth, and in philosophy in the seventeenth and eighteenth. This movement does not advance in a straight line ; in State and Church fundamental principles are at war with each other, and in the other spheres of life there is far too little consciousness to prevent men from ever and anon straying from the right path ; but the all-important question we have to ask ourselves is, whether it is only interests that clash, or whether ideals, suggested by a definite individuality, are floating before the eyes of men ; these ideals we do possess approximately since the thirteenth century ; but we have not yet attained them, they are floating before us in the distance, and to this fact is due the feeling that we are still very deficient in the moral equilibrium and the æsthetic harmony of the ancients, but it is at the same time the basis of our hope for better things. When we glance backwards we are indeed entitled to cherish high hopes. And, I repeat, if when looking back we try to discover when the first shimmer of those rays of hope can be clearly seen, we find the time to be about the year 1200. In Italy the movement to found cities had begun in the eleventh century, that movement which aimed at the same time at the furtherance of trade and industry and

the granting of far-reaching rights of freedom to whole
classes of the population, which had hitherto pined under
the double yoke of Church and State ; in the twelfth
century this strengthening of the core of the European
population had become so widely spread and intensified
that at the beginning of the thirteenth century the
powerful Hansa and the Rhenish Alliance of Cities could
be formed. Concerning this movement Ranke writes
(*Weltgeschichte*, iv. 238) : " It is a splendid, vigorous
development, which is thus initiated . . . the cities
constitute a world power, paving the way for civic
liberty and the formation of powerful States." Even
before the final founding of the Hansa, the Magna Charta
had been proclaimed in England, in the year 1215, a
solemn proclamation of the inviolability of the great
principle of personal freedom and personal security.
" No one may be condemned except in accordance with
the laws of the land. Right and justice may not be bought
nor refused." In some countries of Europe this first
guarantee for the dignity of man has not to this day
become law ; but since that June 15, 1215, a general
law of conscience has gradually grown out of it, and
whoever runs counter to this is a criminal, even though
he wear a crown. I may mention another important point
in which Teutonic civilisation showed itself essentially
different from all others : in the course of the thirteenth
century slavery and the slave trade disappeared from
European countries (with the exception of Spain). In
the thirteenth century money begins to take the place
of natural products in buying and selling ; almost exactly
in the year 1200 we see in Europe the first manufacture
of paper—without doubt the most momentous industrial achievement till the invention of the locomotive.
It would, however, be erroneous to regard the advance
of trade and the stirring of instincts of freedom as the
only indications of the dawn of a new day. Perhaps

the great movement of religious feeling, the most powerful representative of which was Francis of Assisi (*b.* 1182)
is a factor of deeper and more lasting influence ; in it
a genuinely democratic impulse makes itself apparent ;
the faith and life of men like Francis call in question the
tyranny of Church as of State, and deal a death-blow
to the despotism of money. " This movement," one of
the authorities * on Francis of Assisi writes, " gives men
the first forewarning of universal freedom of thought."
At the same moment the avowedly anti-Catholic movement, that of the Albigenses, came into dangerous prominence in Western Europe.   In another sphere of religious
life some equally important steps were taken at the same
time : after Peter Abelard (*d.* 1142) had unconsciously
defended the Indo-European conception of religion
against the Semitic, especially by emphasising the sym-
bolic character of all religious ideas, two orthodox schoolmen, Thomas Aquinas and Duns Scotus, made in the
thirteenth century an admission which was just as
dangerous for the church dogma by conceding, in agreement with each other (though they were otherwise
opponents), the right of existence to a philosophy which
differed from theology.   And while theoretical thinking
here began to assert itself, other scholars, among whom
Albertus Magnus (*b.* 1193) and Roger Bacon (*b.* 1214) are
especially conspicuous, laid the foundations of modern
natural science by turning the attention of men from
logical disputes to mathematics, physics, astronomy and
chemistry. Cantor (*Vorlesungen über Geschichte der
Mathematik*, 2 Aufl. ii. 3) says that in the thirteenth
century " a new era in the history of mathematical
science " began ; this was especially the work of Leonardo
of Pisa, who was the first to introduce to us the Indian
(falsely called Arabian) numerical signs, and of Jordanus
Saxo, of the family of Count Eberstein, who initiated

* Thode, *Franz von Assisi*, p. 4.

us into the art of algebraic calculation (also originally
invented by the Hindoos). The first dissection of a
human body—which was of course the first step towards
scientific medicine—took place towards the end of the
thirteenth century, after an interval of one thousand
six hundred years, and it was carried out by Mondino
de' Luzzi, of Northern Italy. Dante, likewise a child
of the thirteenth century, also deserves mention here
—indeed very special mention. "Nel mezzo del cam-
min di nostra vita" is the first line of his great poem,
and he himself, the first artistic genius of world-wide
importance in the new Teutonic epoch of culture, is
the typical figure at this turning-point of history, the
point at which she has left behind her "the half of her
way," and, after having travelled at break-neck speed
downhill for centuries, sets herself to climb the steep,
difficult path on the opposite slope Many of Dante's
sentiments in the *Divina Comedia* and in his *Tractatus
de monarchia* appear to us like the longing glance of the
man of great experience out of the social and political
chaos surrounding him, towards a harmoniously ordered
world; and such a glance was possible as a sure sign
that the movement had already begun; the eye of
genius is a ray of light that shows the way to
others.*

But long before Dante—this point must not be overlooked—a poetical creative power had manifested itself

* I am not here thinking of the details of his proofs, coloured as they
are by scholasticism, but of such things as his views on the relation
of men to one another (*Monarchia*, I. chaps. iii. and iv.) or on the
federation of States, each of which he says shall retain its own individuality and its own legislature, while the Emperor, as "peace-
maker" and judge in matters that are "common and becoming to all,"
shall form the bond of union (I. chap. xiv.). In other things Dante
himself, as genuine "middle" figure, allows himself to be very much
influenced by the conceptions of his time and dwells in poetical Utopias.
This point is more fully discussed in chap. vii., and especially in
the introduction to chap. viii. of this book.

in the heart of the most genuine Teutonic life, in the
north, a fact in itself sufficient to prove how little need
we had of a classical revival to enable us to create incomparable masterpieces of art : in the year 1200,
Chrestien de Troyes, Hartmann von Aue, Wolfram von
Eschenbach, Walther von der Vogelweide, Gottfried von
Strassburg were writing their poems, and I mention
only some of the most famous names, for, as Gottfried
says, "of the nightingales there are many more." And
up to this time the questionable separation of poetry and
music (which originated from the worship of the dead
letters) had not taken place : the poet was at the same
time singer ; when he invented the "word" he invented
for it at the same time the particular "tone" and the
particular "melody." And so we see music too, the
most original art of the new culture, develop just at the
moment when the peculiar individuality of this culture
began to show itself in a perfectly new form as polyphonic
harmonious art.   The first master of note in the treatment
of counterpoint is the poet and dramatist Adam de la
Halle (*b.* 1240).   With him—and so with a genuinely
Teutonic word- and sound-creator—begins the development of music in the strict sense, so that the musical
authority Gevaert can write : " Désormais l'on peut
considérer ce treizième siècle, si décrié jadis, comme le
siècle initiateur de tout l'art moderne." Likewise in
the thirteenth century those inspired artists Niccolo
Pisano, Cimabue and Giotto revealed their talents, and to
them we are indebted, in the first place, not merely for
a "Renaissance" of the plastic and graphic arts, but
above all for the birth of a perfectly new art, that of
modern painting.   It was also in the thirteenth century
that Gothic architecture came into prominence (the
"Teutonic style" as Rumohr rightly wished to call it) :
almost all masterpieces of church architecture, the incomparable beauty of which we to-day admire but cannot

imitate, originate in that one century. In the meantime (shortly before 1200), the first purely secular university had been founded in Bologna, at which only jurisprudence, philosophy and medicine were taught.* We see in how many ways a new life began to manifest itself about the year 1200. A few names would prove nothing ; but the fact that a movement embraces all lands and grades of society, that the most contradictory phenomena point backwards to a similar cause and forwards to a common goal, proves that we have here to deal not with an accidental and individual thing but with a great, general process which is maturing with unconscious imperativeness in the inmost heart of society. And that peculiar " decline in historical sense and historical understanding about the middle of the thirteenth century," to which different scholars have wonderingly called attention,† should be taken also, I think, in this connection : under the guidance of the Teutonic peoples men have just begun a new life ; they have, so to speak, turned a corner in their course and even the nearest past has completely vanished from their sight : henceforth they belong to the future.

It is most surprising to have to chronicle the fact that exactly at this moment, when the new European world was arising out of chaos, the discovery of the remaining parts of the world also began, without which our blossoming Teutonic culture could never have developed its own peculiar power of expansion : in the second half of the thirteenth century Marco Polo made expeditions of discovery and thereby laid the foundations of our still incomplete knowledge of the surface of our planet. What is gained by this is, in the first place

---

* The theological faculty was not established till towards the end of the fourteenth century (Savigny).

† See Döllinger, *Das Kaisertum Karls des Grossen* (Akad. Vorträge iii. 156).

and apart from the widening of the horizon, the capability of expansion ; this, however, denotes only something relative ; the most important thing is that European authority may hope within a measurable space of time to encompass the earth and thereby no longer be exposed, like former civilisations, to the plundering raids of unlooked for and unbridled barbaric Powers.

So much to justify my choice of the thirteenth century as separating-line.

That there is, nevertheless, something artificial in such a choice I have admitted at the very beginning and I repeat it now ; in particular one must not think that I attribute a special fateful importance to the year 1200 : the ferment of the first twelve centuries of the Christian era has of course not yet ceased, it still confuses thousands and thousands of intellects, and on the other hand we may cheerfully assert that the new harmonious world began to dawn in the minds of individuals long before 1200. The rightness or wrongness of such a scheme is revealed only by its use. As Goethe says : " Everything depends on the fundamental truth, the development of which reveals itself not so easily in speculation as in practice : this is the touch-stone of what has been admitted by the intellect."

Division into Two Parts

In consequence of this fixing of the turning-point of our history, this book, which treats of the period up to the year 1800, falls naturally into two parts : the one deals with the period previous to the year 1200, the other the period subsequent to that year.

In the first part—the origins—I have discussed first the legacy of the old world, then the heirs and lastly the fight of the heirs for their inheritance. As everything new is attached to something already in existence, something older, the first fundamental question is, " What component parts of our intellectual capital are inherited ? " the second, no less important, is, " Who are we ? " Though the answering of these questions may take us back into the distant past, the interest remains always a present interest, because in the whole construction of every chapter, as well as in every detail of the discussion, the one all-absorbing consideration is that of the nineteenth century. The legacy of the old world forms still an important—often quite inadequately digested—portion of the very youngest world : the heirs with their different natures stand opposed to one another to-day as they did a thousand years ago ; the struggle is as bitter, as confused as ever ; the investigation of the past means therefore at the same time an examination of the too abundant material of the present. Let no one, however, regard my remarks on Hellenic art and philosophy, on Roman history and Roman law, on the teaching of Christ, or, again, on the Teutonic peoples and the Jews, &c., as independent academic treatises and apply to them the corresponding standard. I have not approached these subjects as a learned authority, but as a child of to-day that desires to understand the living present world ; and I have formed my judgments, not from the Aristophanic cloud-cuckoo-land of a supernatural objectivity, but from that of a conscious Teuton whom Goethe not in vain has warned :

> Was euch nicht angehört,
> Müsset ihr meiden ;
> Was euch das Inn're stört,
> Dürft ihr nicht leiden !

In the eyes of God all men, indeed all creatures, may be equal : but the divine law of the individual is to maintain and to defend his individuality. I have formed my idea of Teutonicism on a scale quite as large ; which means in this case " as large-heartedly as possible," and have not pleaded the cause of any particularism whatever. I have, on the other hand, vigorously attacked whatever is un-Teutonic, but—as I hope—nowhere in an unchivalrous manner.

The fact that the chapter on the entry of the Jews into western history has been made so long may perhaps demand explanation. For the subject of this book, so diffuse a treatment would not have been indispensable ; but the prominent position of the Jews in the nineteenth century, as also the great importance for the history of our time of the philo- and anti-semitic currents and controversies, made an answer to the question, " Who is the Jew ? " absolutely imperative. Nowhere could I find a clear and exhaustive answer to this question, so I was compelled to seek and to give it myself. The essential point here is the question of religion ; and so I have treated this very point at considerable length, not merely in the fifth, but also in the third and in the seventh chapters. For I have become convinced that the usual treatment of the " Jewish question " is altogether and always superficial ; the Jew is no enemy of Teutonic civilisation and culture ; Herder may be right in his assertion that the Jew is always alien to us, and consequently we to him, and no one will deny that this is to the detriment of our work of culture ; yet I think that we are inclined to under-estimate our own powers in this respect and, on the other hand, to exaggerate the importance of the Jewish influence. Hand in hand with this goes the perfectly ridiculous and revolting tendency to make the Jew the general scapegoat for all the vices of our time. In reality the " Jewish peril " lies much deeper ; the Jew is not responsible for it ; we have given rise to it ourselves and must overcome it ourselves. No souls thirst more after religion than the Slavs, the Celts and the Teutons : their history proves it ; it is because of the lack of a true religion that our whole Teutonic culture is sick unto death (as I show in the ninth chapter), and this will mean its ruin if timely help does not come. We have stopped up the spring that welled up in our own hearts and made ourselves dependent upon the scanty, brackish water which the Bedouins of the desert draw from their wells. No people in the world is so beggarly-poor in religion as the Semites and their half-brothers the Jews; and we, who were chosen to develop the profoundest and sublimest religious conception of the world as the light, life and vitalising force of our whole culture, have with our own hands firmly tied up the veins of life and limp along like crippled Jewish slaves behind Jehovah's Ark of the Covenant! Hence my exhaustive treatment of the Jewish question: my object was to find a broad and strong foundation for so important a judgment.

The second part—the gradual rise of a new world—has in these "Foundations" only one chapter devoted to it, "from the year 1200 to the year 1800." Here I found myself in a sphere which is pretty familiar even to the unlearned reader, and it would have been altogether superfluous to copy from histories of politics and of culture which are within the reach of all. My task was accordingly limited to shaping and bringing into clearer range than is usually the case the too abundant material which I could presume to be known—as material; and here again my one consideration was of course the nineteenth century, the subject of my work. This chapter stands on the border-line between the two parts, that now published and what is to follow; many things which in the preceding chapters could only be alluded to, not fully and systematically discussed, such for instance as the fundamental importance of Teutonicism for our new world and the value of our conceptions of progress and degeneration for the understanding of history, find complete treatment here; on the other hand, the short

sketch of development in the various spheres of life
brings us hurriedly to the nineteenth century, and the
tabular statement concerning knowledge, civilisation
and culture, and their various elements points to the
work of comparison which forms the plan of the supplement and gives occasion for many an instructive parallel :
at the same moment as we see the Teuton blossom forth
in his full strength, as though nothing had been denied
him, and he were hurrying to a limitless goal, we behold
also his limitations ; and this is very important, for
it is upon these last characteristics that his individuality
depends.

In view of certain prejudices I shall probably have to
justify myself for treating State and Church in this chapter as subordinate matters—or, more properly speaking,
as phenomena among others, and not the most important.
State and Church form henceforth, as it were, only the
skeleton : the Church is an inner bone structure in which,
as is usual, with advancing age an always stronger tendency to chronic anchylosis shows itself ; the State
develops more and more into the peripheric bone-cuirass,
so well known in zoology, the so-called dermatoskeleton ;
its structure becomes always massier, it stretches over
the " soft parts." until at last in the nineteenth century
it has grown to truly megalotheric dimensions and sets
apart from the true course of life and, if I may say so,
" ossifies " an extremely large percentage of the effective
powers of humanity as military and civil officials. This
is not meant as criticism ; the boneless and invertebrate
animals have never, as is well known, played a great
part in the world ; it is besides far from my purpose
to wish to moralise in this book ; I wish merely to explain
why in the second part I have not felt obliged to lay
special stress upon the further development of Church
and State. The impulse to their development had already
been given in the thirteenth century, when nationalism

having prevailed over imperialism, the latter was scheming how to win back what was lost ; nothing essentially new was added later ; even the movements against the all too prevalent violation of individual freedom by Church and State had already begun to make themselves felt very forcibly and frequently. Church and State serve from now onwards, as I have said, as the skeleton—now and then suffering from fractures in arms and legs but nevertheless a firm skeleton—yet take comparatively little share in the gradual rise of a new world ; henceforth they follow rather than lead. On the other hand, in all European countries in the most widely different spheres of free human activity there arises from about the year 1200 onwards a really recreative movement. The Church schism and the revolt against State decrees are in reality rather the mechanical side of this movement ; they spring from the deeply felt need, experienced by newly awakening powers, of making room for themselves ; the creative element, strictly speaking, has to be sought elsewhere. I have already indicated where, when I sought to justify my choice of the year 1200 as turning-point : the advance in things technical and industrial, the founding of commerce on a large scale on the thoroughly Teutonic basis of stainless uprightness, the rise of busy towns, the discovery of the earth (as we may daringly call it), the study of nature which begins diffidently but soon extends its horizon over the whole cosmos, the sounding of the deepest depths of human thought, from Roger Bacon to Kant, the soaring of the spirit up to heaven, from Dante to Beethoven : it is in all this that we may recognise the rise of a new world.

THE CONTINUATION

With this study of the gradual rise of a new world, approximately from the year 1200 to the year 1800, these " Foundations " come to a close. The detailed plan of the " Nineteenth Century " lies before me. In it I carefully avoid all artificial theorising and all attempts to find an immediate connection between the two parts. It is quite sufficient that the explanatory account of the first eighteen centuries has been already given ; even though frequent and express reference to it be not necessary, it will prove itself as the indispensable introduction ; the supplement will then be devoted to drawing parallels and to the calculation of comparative values. Here I shall confine myself to considering one by one the most important phenomena of the century ; the principal features of political, religious and social organisation, the course of development of the technical arts, the progress of natural science and the humanities, and, lastly, the history of the human mind as a thinking and creative power ; everywhere, of course, only the principal currents will be emphasised and nothing but the highest achievements mentioned.

The consideration of these points is led up to by an introductory chapter on the " New Forces " which have asserted themselves in this century and have given to it its characteristic physiognomy, but which could not be treated adequately within the limits of one of the general chapters. The press, for instance, is at the same time a political and a social power of the very first rank ; its stupendous development in the nineteenth century it owes primarily to industry and art. I do not refer so much to the production of newspapers by time-saving machinery, &c., as to telegraphy, which supplies the papers with news, and to railways, which spread printed matter everywhere. The press is the most powerful ally of capitalism ; on art, philosophy and science it cannot really exercise a distinct determining influence, but even here it can hasten or delay, and so exercise in a high degree a formative influence upon

the age.   This is a power unknown to previous centuries.
In the same way technical developments, the invention
and perfection of the railway and the steamboat, as
also of the electric telegraph, have exercised no small influence upon all spheres of human activity and wrought
a great change in the face of our earth and in the
conditions of life upon it : quite direct is the influence
on strategy and consequently upon politics, as well as
on trade and industry, while science and even art have
also been indirectly affected : the astronomers of all
lands can with comparative ease betake themselves to
the North Cape or the Fiji Islands to observe a total
eclipse of the sun, and the German festival plays in
Bayreuth have, towards the end of the century, thanks
to the railway and the steamboat, become a living centre
of dramatic art for the whole world.   Among these
forces I likewise reckon the emancipation of the Jews.
Like every power that has newly dropped its fetters,
like the press and quick transit, this sudden inroad of
the Jews upon the life of the European races, who
mould the history of the world, has certainly not brought
good alone in its train ; the so-called Classical Renaissance
was after all merely a new birth of ideas, the Jewish
Renaissance is the resurrection of a Lazarus long considered dead, who introduces into the Teutonic world the
customs and modes of thought of the Oriental, and who
at the same time seems to receive a new lease of life
thereby, like the vine-pest which, after leading in America
the humble life of an innocent little beetle, was introduced
into Europe and suddenly attained to a world-wide
fame of serious import.   We have, however, reason
to hope and believe that the Jews, like the Americans,
have brought us not only a new pest but also a new
vine.   Certain it is that they have left a peculiar impress upon our time, and that the " new world " which
is arising will require a very great exercise of its strength

for the work of assimilating this fragment of the " old world." There are still other " new forces " which will have to be discussed in their proper place. The founding of modern chemistry, for example, is the starting-point of a new natural science; and the perfecting of a new artistic language by Beethoven is beyond doubt one of the most pregnant achievements in the sphere of art since the days of Homer; it gave men a new organ of speech, that is to say, a new power.

The supplement is intended, as I have said, to furnish a comparison between the " Foundations " and the book which is to follow. This comparison I shall carry out point by point in several chapters, using the scheme of the first part; this method will, I think, be found to lead to many suggestive discoveries and interesting distinctions. Besides, it paves the way splendidly for the somewhat bold but indispensable glance into the future, without which our conception would not acquire complete plasticity; it is only in this way that we can hope to gain a bird's-eye view of the nineteenth century and so be able to judge it with perfect objectivity; this will be the end of my task.

Such then is the extremely simple and unartificial plan of the continuation. It is a plan which, perhaps, I may not live to carry out, yet I am obliged to mention it here, as it has to no small degree influenced the form of the present book.

ANONYMOUS FORCES

In this general introduction I must also discuss briefly some specially important points, so that later we may not be detained by out-of-place theoretical discussions.

Almost all men are by nature " hero-worshippers "; and no valid objection can be urged against this healthy instinct. Simplification is a necessity of the human mind ; we find ourselves involuntarily setting up a single name in place of the many names representative of a movement ; further, the personality is something given, individual, definite, while everything that lies beyond is an abstraction and an ever-varying circle of ideas.

We might therefore put together the history of a century by a mere list of names : it seems to me, however, that a different procedure is necessary to bring out what is really essential. For it is remarkable how slightly the separate individualities stand out in relief from each other. Men form inside their racial individualities an atomic but nevertheless very homogeneous mass. If a great spirit were to lean out from among the stars and, bending in contemplation over our earth, were capable of seeing not only our bodies but also our souls, the human population of any part of the world would certainly appear to him as uniform as an ant-heap does to us : he would of course distinguish warriors, workers, idlers and monarchs, he would notice that the one runs hither, the other thither, but on the whole his impression would be that all individuals obey, and must obey, a common impersonal impulse. Extremely narrow limits are set to the influence as well as to the arbitrariness of the great personality. All great and lasting revolutions in the life of society have taken place " blindly." A remarkable personality, as, for example, that of Napoleon, can lead us astray on this point, and yet even his, when closely examined, appears as a blindly working Fate. Its possibility is explained by previous events : had there been no Richelieu, no Louis XIV., no Louis XV., no Voltaire, no Rousseau, no French Revolution—there would have been no Napoleon ! How closely linked, moreover, is the life-achievement of such a man with the national character of the whole people, with its virtues and its failings : without a French people, no Napoleon ! The activity of this commander is directed in particular towards the outside world, and here again we must say : but for the irresolution of Friedrich Wilhelm III., but for the want of principle in the House of Habsburg, but for the troubles in Spain, but for the criminal treatment of Poland just previously, no Napoleon had been possible ! And if, in order to be quite clear on this point, we consult the biographies and correspondence of Napoleon, to see what were his aims and aspirations, we shall find that all of them remained unrealised, and that he sank back into the indistinguishable homogeneous mass, as clouds dissipate after a storm, as soon as the community rose to oppose the predominance of individual will. On the other hand, the radical change of our whole economic conditions of life, which no power on earth could prevent, the passing of a considerable portion of the property of nations into new hands, and further, the thorough remodelling of the relations of all parts of the earth, and so of all men, to one another, which we read of in the history of the world, took place in the course of the nineteenth century as the result of a series of technical discoveries in the sphere of quick transit and of industry, the importance of which no one even suspected. We need only read in this connection the masterly exposition in the fifth volume of Treitschke's *Deutsche Geschichte*. The depreciation of landed property, the progressive impoverishment of the peasant, the advance of industry, the rise of an incalculable army of industrial proletarians, and consequently of a new form of Socialism, a radical change of all political conditions : all this is a result of changed conditions of traffic and has been brought about, if I may so express it, anonymously, like the building of an ant's nest, in which each ant only sees the individual grains which it laboriously drags to the heap. The same, however, is true of ideas : they hold man in a tyrannical grasp, they clutch his mind as a bird of prey its quarry and no one can resist them ; so long as any particular

conception is dominant, nothing can be accomplished outside the sphere of its magic influence ; whoever cannot feel as it dictates is condemned to sterility, however talented he may be. This we have seen in the second half of the nineteenth century in connection with Darwin's theory of evolution. This idea had already begun to appear in the eighteenth century, as a natural reaction from the old theory of the immutability of species, which Linnæus had brought to formal perfection. In Herder, Kant and Goethe we meet with the idea of evolution in characteristic colouring ; it is the revolt of great minds against dogma : in the case of the first, because he, following the course of Teutonic philosophy, endeavoured to find in the development of the idea " nature " an entity embracing man ; in the case of the second, because he as metaphysician and moralist could not bear to lose the conception of perfectibility, while the third, with the eye of the poet, discovered on all sides phenomena which seemed to him to point to a primary relationship between all living organisms, and feared lest his discovery should evaporate into abstract nothingness if this relationship were not viewed as resting upon direct descent. This is how such thoughts arise. In minds of such phenomenal breadth as Goethe's, Herder's and Kant's there is room for very different conceptions side by side ; they are to be compared with Spinoza's God, whose one substance manifests itself simultaneously in various forms ; in their ideas on metamorphosis, affinities and development, I can find nothing contrary to other views, and I believe that they would have rejected our present dogma of evolution, as they did that of immutability.*
I return to this point in another place. The overwhelming

* Compare in this connection Kant's extremely complete exposition which forms the concluding portion of the division " On the regulative use of ideas of pure reason " in his *Critique of pure Reason*. The great thinker here points to the fact that the idea of a " continuous gradation of creatures " did not and cannot originate from observation

majority of men with their display of ant-like activity
are quite incapable of viewing things in such an original
manner ; productive power can be generated only by
simple healthy specialisation. A manifestly unsound
system like that of Darwin exercises a much more powerful
influence than the deepest speculations, just because of its
" practicability."   And so we have seen the idea of evolution develop itself till it spread from biology and geology
to all spheres of thought and investigation, and, intoxicated by its success, exercised such a tyranny that any
one who did not swear by it was to be looked upon as
a simpleton.   I am not here concerned with the philosophy
of all these phenomena ; I have no doubt that the spirit
of man as a whole expresses itself appropriately.   I may,
however, appropriate Goethe's remark, " what especially
impresses me is the people, a great mass, a necessary
inevitable existence " and thus establish and explain
my conviction, that great men are in reality the flower
of history and not its roots.   And so I consider it
proper to portray a century not so much by an enumeration of its leading men as by an emphasising of the
anonymous currents, from which it has derived its
peculiar and characteristic stamp in the various centres
of social. industrial and scientific life.

but from an interest of reason. " The steps of such a ladder, as experience can supply them to us, are far, too far, removed from one
another, and what we suppose to be little distinctions are commonly
in nature itself such wide clefts that on such observations as intentions
of nature we can lay no stress whatever (especially when things are
so manifold, since it must always be easy to find certain resemblances
and approximations)."   In his criticism of Herder he reproaches the
hypothesis of evolution with being one of those ideas "in the case of
which one cannot think anything at all."   Kant, whom even Haeckel
calls the most important predecessor of Darwin, had thus gone so far as
to supply the antidote to the dogmatic abuse of such a hypothesis.

GENIUS

There is, however, one exception. When we are dealing not with the mere power of observation, of comparison, of calculation, or with the inventive, industrial or intellectual activity struggling for existence, but with a purely creative activity, then Personality is everything. The history of art and philosophy is the history of individual men, the history of the really creative men of genius. Here nothing else counts. Whatever outside this is achieved within the sphere of philosophy—and much of importance is so achieved—belongs to science ; in art it belongs to mechanical art, that is, to industry.

I lay all the more stress on this point, because at the present day regrettable confusion prevails with regard to it. The idea and consequently the word " Genius " originated in the eighteenth century ; they arose from the necessity of possessing a particular defining expression for " specifically creative minds." No less a thinker than Kant calls our attention to the fact that " the greatest discoverer in the sphere of science differs only in degree from the ordinary man, the Genius, on the other hand, differs specifically." This remark of Kant's is beyond doubt just, but we make the one reservation, that of extending—as we cannot help doing—the term " work of genius " to every creation, in which the imagination plays a formative and predominant part, and in this connection the philosophic genius deserves the same place as the poetic or the plastic. Here let me say that I give to the word philosophy its old, wide signification, which embraced not only the abstract philosophy of reason, but natural philosophy, the philosophy of religion, and all thought which rises to the dignity of a philosophy of life. If the word genius is to retain a sense, we must employ it only of men who have everlastingly enriched our intellectual store by powerful creations of their imagination, but it must be applicable to all such without exception. Not only the *Iliad* and *Prometheus Bound*, the *Adoration of the Cross* and *Hamlet*, but also Plato's *World of Ideas* and Democritus' *World of Atoms*, the Chandogya's *tat-twam-asi* and Copernicus' *System of the Heavens* are works of immortal genius; for just as indestructible as matter and power are the flashes of light which radiate from the brains of men endowed with creative power; they never cease to reflect for each other the generations and the nations, and if they sometimes pale for a time, they shine out brightly once more when they strike a creative eye. In recent years it has been discovered that in the depths of the ocean, to which the sunlight does not penetrate, there are fishes which light up this world of darkness electrically; even thus is the dark night of human knowledge lighted up by the torch of genius. Goethe lit a torch with his *Faust*, Kant another with his conception of the transcendental ideality of time and space: both were creators of great imaginative power, both were men of genius. The scholastic strife about the Königsberg thinker, the battles between Kantians and anti-Kantians seem to me of just as much moment as the work of the zealous *Faust* critics: what is the use of logical hair-splitting here? What in such a case is the meaning of the phrase, " to be right "? Blessed are they who have eyes to see and ears to hear! If the study of the stone, the moss, the microscopic infusorium fills us with wonder and admiration, with what reverence must we look up to the greatest phenomenon that nature presents to us—Genius!

GENERALISATIONS

I must here add a remark of some importance. Though we are to concern ourselves particularly with general tendencies, not with events and personages, still the danger of too wide generalisations must not be overlooked. We are but too prone to sum up prematurely. It is this tendency that makes men so often hang, as it were, a ticket round the neck of the nineteenth century, even though they must know that it is utterly impossible by means of a single word to be just both to ourselves and to the past. A fixed idea of this kind is quite sufficient to render a clear comprehension of historical development impossible.

Quite commonly, for example, the nineteenth century is called the "century of natural science." When we remember what the sixteenth, seventeenth, and eighteenth centuries have achieved in this very sphere, we must surely hesitate before bestowing any such title on the nineteenth. We have but continued to build and by our industry have discovered much, but whether we can point to a Copernicus and a Galileo, to a Kepler and a Newton, to a Lavoisier and a Bichat * appears to me at least doubtful. Cuvier's activity attains indeed to the dignity of philosophical importance, and the powers of observation and invention of men like Bunsen (the chemist) and Pasteur come remarkably near genius; of imperishable fame are men like Louis Agassiz, Michael Faraday, Julius Robert Mayer, Heinrich Hertz and perhaps some few others; but we must at least admit that their achievements do not surpass those of their predecessors. Some years ago a University teacher of the medical faculty with a fine reputation for theoretical as well as practical work remarked to me, " In the case of us scholars nowadays it is not so much a question of brain convolutions as of perseverance." It would indeed be false modesty, and an emphasising of the unimportant, to designate the nineteenth century the "century of perseverance." All the more so, since the

* He died in 1802.

designation of " the century of the rolling wheel " would
certainly be quite as justifiable for an epoch which has
produced the railway and the bicycle. Better, certainly,
would be the general term " the century of science,"
by which would be understood that the spirit of accurate
investigation which received its first encouragement from
Roger Bacon had put all departments of study under its
yoke. This spirit, however, if the matter be fully considered, will be found to have brought about less surprising results in the sphere of natural science, in which
since earliest times the exact observation of the heavenly
bodies formed the basis of all knowledge, than in other
spheres, in which arbitrary methods had hitherto been the
order of the day. Perhaps it would be a true and apt
characterisation of the nineteenth century—though at the
same time an unfamiliar one to most educated people—
to style it the " century of philology." First called into
being towards the end of the eighteenth century by
such men as Jones, Anquetil du Perron, the brothers
Schlegel and Grimm, Karadžić and others, comparative
philology has in the course of a single century made
quite extraordinary progress. To establish the organism
and the history of language means not merely to throw
light upon anthropology, ethnology and history, but
particularly to strengthen human minds for new achievements. And while the philology of the nineteenth
century thus laboured for the future, it unearthed buried
treasures of the past, which are among the most valuable
possessions of mankind. It is not necessary to feel
sympathy for the pseudo-Buddhistical sport of half-
educated idlers in order to recognise clearly that the discovery of the divine doctrine of understanding of the ancient
Indians is one of the greatest achievements of the nineteenth century, destined to exercise an enduring influence upon distant ages. To this has been added the
knowledge of old Teutonic poetry and mythology. Every-

thing that tends to strengthen genuine individuality
is a real safety anchor.   The brilliant series of Teutonic
and Indian scholars has, half unconsciously, accomplished a great work at the right moment ; now we too
possess our " holy books," and what they teach is more
beautiful and nobler than what the Old Testament
sets forth.   The belief in our strength, which the history
of the nineteenth century gives us, has been intensified
to an incalculable extent by this discovery of our independent capacity for much that is of the highest,
and to which our relation was hitherto one of subjection : in particular the myth of the peculiar aptitude
of the Jew for religion is finally exploded ; for this
later generations will owe a debt of gratitude to the
nineteenth century.   This is one of the greatest and
most far-reaching achievements of our time, and so
the title " the century of philology " would be in a certain
sense justified.   In this connection we have mentioned
another of the characteristic phenomena of the nineteenth
century.   Ranke had prophesied that our century would
be a century of nationality ; that was a correct political
prognostic, for never before have the nations stood
opposed to each other so clearly and definitely as antagonistic unities.   It has, however, also become a century of
races, and that indeed is in the first instance a necessary
and direct consequence of science and scientific thinking.
I have already said at the beginning of this introduction
that science does not unite but dissects.   That statement has not contradicted itself here.   Scientific anatomy
has furnished such conclusive proofs of the existence of
physical characteristics distinguishing the races from
each other that they can no longer be denied ; scientific
philology has discovered between the various languages
fundamental differences which cannot be bridged over ;
the scientific study of history in its various branches
has brought about similar results, especially by the

exact determination of the religious history of each race, in which only the most general of general ideas can raise the illusion of similarity, while the further development has always followed and still follows definite, sharply divergent lines. The so-called unity of the human race is indeed still honoured as a hypothesis, but only as a personal, subjective conviction lacking every material foundation. The ideas of the eighteenth century with regard to the brotherhood of nations were certainly very noble but purely sentimental in their origin; and in contrast to these ideas to which the Socialists still cling, limping on like reserves in the battle, stern reality has gradually asserted itself as the necessary result of the events and investigations of our time. There are many other titles for which much might be said: Rousseau had already spoken prophetically of a " siècle des révolutions," others speak of a century of Jewish emancipation, century of electricity, century of national armies, century of colonies, century of music, century of advertisement, century of the proclamation of infallibility. Lately I found the nineteenth century described in an English book as *the religious century*, and could not quite dispute the statement; for Beer, the author of the *Geschichte des Welthandels*, the nineteenth century is the " economic " century, whereas Professor Paulsen in his *Geschichte des gelehrten Unterrichts* (2 Aufl. ii. 206) calls it the *sæculum historicum* in contrast to the preceding *sæculum philosophicum*, and Goethe's expression " ein aberweises Jahrhundert " could be applied quite as well to the nineteenth century as to the eighteenth. No such generalisation possesses any real value.

THE NINETEENTH CENTURY

These remarks bring me to the close of this general introduction. But before I write the last line I should like to place myself, according to an old custom, under the protection of highly honoured men.

Lessing writes in his *Briefe, die neueste Litteratur betreffend*, that "history should not trouble with unimportant facts, should not burden the memory, but enlighten the understanding." Taken generally, this is saying too much. But in the case of a book which is directed not to historians but to the educated layman, the remark is perfectly justified. To enlighten the understanding, not to teach in the real sense of the word, but to suggest, to stimulate thoughts and conclusions, that is my aim.

Goethe differs somewhat from Lessing in his conception of the task of the historian. He says, " The best thing that we get from history is the enthusiasm it arouses." These words, too, I have kept in mind in the course of my work, for I am convinced that understanding, however well enlightened, avails little, if not united to enthusiasm. The understanding is the machine ; the more perfect every detail in it, the more neatly every part fits into the other, the more efficient will it be, but only potentially, for, in order to be driven, it requires the motive-power, and the motive-power is enthusiasm. Perhaps, however, it is difficult to take Goethe's hint and wax enthusiastic over the nineteenth century, simply for this reason, that self-love is so contemptible ; we wish to test ourselves strictly, and tend to under-estimate rather than over-estimate ; may future ages judge us more leniently. I find it difficult to grow enthusiastic because the material element is so predominant in this century. Just as our battles have generally been won not by the personal superiority of individuals but by the number of the soldiers, or to put it more simply by the amount of food for powder, so in the very same way have treasures in gold and knowledge and discoveries been piled up. Things have increased in numbers and in bulk, men have collected but not sifted ; such, at any rate, has been the general tendency.   The nineteenth century is essentially a century of accumulation, an age of transition and of the provisional; in other respects it is neither fish nor flesh ; it dangles between empiricism and spiritism, between *liberalismus vulgaris*, as it has been wittily called, and the impotent efforts of senile conservatism, between autocracy and anarchism, doctrines of infallibility and the most stupid materialism, worship of the Jew and Anti-Semitism, the rule of the millionaire and proletarian government.   Not ideas, but material gains, are the characteristic feature of the nineteenth century.   The great thoughts that have cropped up here and there, the mighty creations of art, from *Faust*, Part II., to *Parsifal*, have brought undying fame to the German people, but they are for future times.   After the great social revolutions and the momentous intellectual achievements (at the close of the eighteenth and the early dawn of the nineteenth century) material for further development had again to be collected.   And so this too great preoccupation with the material banished the beautiful almost entirely from life ; at the present moment there exists perhaps no savage, at least no half-civilised people, which does not to my mind possess more beauty in its surroundings and more harmony in its existence as a whole than the great mass of so-called civilised Europeans. It is therefore, I think, necessary to be moderate in our enthusiastic admiration for the nineteenth century.   On the other hand it is easy to feel the enthusiasm spoken of by Goethe, as soon as our glance rests not upon the one century alone but embraces all that " new world " which has been slowly unfolding for centuries.   Certainly the commonly accepted idea of " progress " has by no means a sound philosophical foundation ; under this flag sail almost all the refuse wares of our time ; Goethe, who never tires of pointing to enthusiasm as the motive element in our nature, declares his conviction nevertheless to be that " Men become wiser and more discerning, but not better, happier and more vigorous, or if they do become so, it is only for a time." * But what could be more elevating than consciously to work towards such an epoch, in which, if only for a time, mankind will be better, happier and more vigorous ? And when we regard the nineteenth century not as something isolated but as part of a much greater period of time, we discover soon that out of the barbarism which followed upon the downfall of the old world, and out of the wild ferment called forth by the shock of opposing forces, some centuries ago a perfectly new organisation of human society began to develop, and that our world of to-day —far from being the summit of this evolution—simply represents a transition stage, a " middle point " in the long and weary journey. If the nineteenth century were really a summit, then the pessimistic view of life would be the only justifiable one : to see, after all the great achievements in the intellectual and material spheres, bestial wickedness still so widespread, and misery increased a thousandfold, could cause us only to repeat Jean Jacques Rousseau's prayer : " Almighty God, deliver us from the sciences and the pernicious arts of our fathers ! Grant us ignorance, innocence and poverty once more as the only things which can bring happiness and which are of value in Thine eyes ! " If, however, as I have said, we see in the nineteenth century a stage in the journey, if we do not let ourselves be blinded by visions of " golden ages," or by delusions of the future and the past, if we do not allow ourselves to be led astray in our sound judgment by Utopian conceptions of a gradual improvement of mankind as a whole, and of political machinery working ideally, then we are justified in the hope and belief that we Teutonic peoples, and the

* Eckerman   October 23, 1828.

peoples under our influence, are advancing towards a new harmonious culture, incomparably more beautiful than any of which history has to tell, a culture in which men should really be "better and happier" than they are at present. It may be that the tendency of modern education to direct the glance so unceasingly to the past is regrettable, but it has the advantage that one does not require to be a Schiller to feel with him that "no single modern man can vie with the individual Athenian for the prize of manhood." * For that reason we now direct our glance to the future, to that future the character of which is beginning to dawn upon us, as we are gradually becoming aware of the real significance of the present era which embraces the last seven hundred years. We will vie with the Athenian. We will form a world in which beauty and harmony of existence do not, as in their case, depend upon the employment of slaves, upon eunuchs, and the seclusion of women! We may confidently hope to do so, for we see this world slowly and with difficulty rising up around our brief span of life. And the fact that it does so unconsciously does not matter; even the half-fabulous Phœnician historian Sanchuniathon says in the first part of his first book, when speaking of the creation of the world: "Things themselves, however, knew nothing of their own origin." The same holds true to-day; history endlessly illustrates Mephisto's words, "Du glaubst zu schieben und du wirst geschoben." When, therefore, we look back at the nineteenth century, which certainly was driven more than it drove, and in most things deviated to an almost ridiculous extent from the paths it had originally intended to pursue, we cannot help feeling a thrill of honest admiration and almost of enthusiasm. In this century

* This famous sentence is only conditionally true; I have submitted it to a thorough criticism in the last chapter, to which I here refer in order to avoid misconceptions.

an enormous amount of work has been done, and that is the foundation of all " growing better and happier " ; this was the morality of our age, if I may so express myself. And while the workshop of great creative ideas was seemingly unproductive, the methods of work were perfected in a manner hitherto undreamt of.

The nineteenth century is the triumph of method. In this more than in any political organisation we see a victory of the democratic principle. Men as a whole rose hereby a step higher, and became more efficient. In former centuries only men of genius, later only highly gifted men could accomplish anything ; now, thanks to method, every one can do so. Compulsory education, followed by the imperative struggle for existence, has provided thousands to-day with the " method " to enable them, without any special gift, to take part in the common work of the human race as technicians, industrials, natural investigators, philologists, historians, mathematicians, psychologists, &c. The mastery of so colossal a material in so short a space of time would otherwise be quite unthinkable. Just consider what was understood by " philology " a hundred years ago ! Where was there such a thing as true " historical investigation " ? We meet with exactly the same spirit in all spheres which lie far remote from science : the national armies are the most universal and simple application of method and the Hohenzollerns are in so far the democrats of the nineteenth century that they set the fashion for others : method in arm and leg movement, but at the same time method in education of the will, of obedience, of duty, of responsibility. Skill and conscientiousness have in consequence—unfortunately not everywhere, but nevertheless in many spheres—decidedly increased : we make greater demands on ourselves and on others than we did of old ; in a sense a general technical improvement has taken place—an improvement which extends even to men's habits of thinking. This amelioration of conditions can hardly fail to have a bearing upon morality: the abolition of human slavery outside Europe—at least in the officially recognised sense of the word—and the beginning of a movement to protect animal slaves are omens of great significance.

And so I believe that in spite of all doubts a just and loving contemplation of the nineteenth century must both "enlighten the understanding" and "awaken enthusiasm." To begin with, we consider only its "Foundations," that is, the "sum of all that has gone before"—that Past out of which the nineteenth century has laboriously but successfully extricated itself.

CONTENTS

FOUNDATIONS OF THE
NINETEENTH CENTURY

FIRST PART

THE ORIGINS

Und keine Zeit und keine Macht zerstückelt
Geprägte Form, die lebend sich entwickelt.

GOETHE.

DIVISION I

THE LEGACY OF THE ANCIENT WORLD

Das Edelste, was wir besitzen, haben wir nicht von uns selbst ; unser Verstand mit seinen Kräften, die Form in welcher wir denken, handeln und sind, ist auf uns gleichsam herabgeerbet.—HERDER.

INTRODUCTORY

HISTORICAL PRINCIPLES

"THE WORLD," says Dr. Martin Luther, "is ruled by God through a few heroes and pre-eminent persons." The mightiest of these ruling heroes are the princes of intellect, men who without sanction of diplomacy or force of arms, without the constraining power of law and police, exercise a defining and transforming influence upon the thought and feeling of many generations, men who may be said to be all the more powerful the less power they have, but who seldom, perhaps never, ascend their throne during their lifetime ; their sway lasts long, but begins late, often very late, especially when we leave out of account the influence which they exercise upon individuals and consider the moment when that which filled their life begins to affect and mould the life of whole peoples. More than two centuries elapsed before

3

the new conception of the Cosmos, which we owe to
Copernicus, and which was bound to revolutionise all
human thought from its foundations, became common
property. Men as important among his contemporaries
as Luther said of Copernicus that he was " a fool who
turned upside down the whole art of astronomia."
Although his system of the world was already taught in
antiquity ; although the works of his direct predecessors,
Regiomontanus and others, had prepared everything
that made the last discovery inevitable, so that one
might safely say that the Copernican system was only
awaiting for its completion the spark of inspiration in
the brain of the " most pre-eminent " ; although it was
here not a question of baffling problems in metaphysics
and morals, but of a simple and, moreover, a demonstrable conception ; although no material interest whatever was threatened by the new doctrine, much time
was needed for this conception, which was in so many
important respects of a revolutionary character, to
travel from the brain of its author into that of a few
other privileged men, and, ever spreading, finally take
possession of the whole of mankind. It is well known
how Voltaire in the first half of the eighteenth century
fought for the recognition of the great triad—Copernicus,
Kepler, Newton—but as late as the year 1779 the worthy
Georg Christoph Lichtenberg felt himself compelled to
undertake a campaign in the *Göttingisches Taschenbuch*,
against the "Tychonians," and it was not till the year
of grace one thousand eight hundred and twenty-two
that the Congregation of the Index authorised the
printing of books which teach that the earth moves!

I make this statement in advance that the reader may
comprehend in what sense the year 1 is here chosen as
the starting-point of our age. It is no random date,
chosen for reasons of convenience, or because the outward
course of political events had stamped this year as

particularly noteworthy; it has been adopted because the simplest logic compels us to trace a new force back to its origin. It is a matter of "history" how slowly or how quickly it grows into an effective power; the actual life of the hero is, and cannot but be, the living source of all subsequent developments.

The birth of Jesus Christ is the most important date in the whole history of mankind.* No battle, no dynastic change, no natural phenomenon, no discovery possesses an importance that could bear comparison with the short earthly life of the Galilean; almost two thousand years of history prove it, and even yet we have hardly crossed the threshold of Christianity. For profoundly intrinsic reasons we are justified in calling that year the "first year," and in reckoning our time from it. In a certain sense we might truly say that "history" in the real sense of the term only begins with the birth of Christ. The peoples that have not yet adopted Christianity—the Chinese, the Indians, the Turks and others—have all so far no true history; all they have is, on the one hand, a chronicle of ruling dynasties, butcheries and the like: on the other the uneventful, humble existence of countless millions living a life of bestial happiness, who disappear in the night of ages leaving no trace behind; whether the kingdom of the Pharaohs was founded in the year 3285 or in the year 32850 is in itself of no consequence; to know Egypt under one Rameses is the same as to know it under all fifteen Ramesides. And so it is with the other pre-Christian nations (with the exception of those three—of which I shall speak presently—that stand in organic relation to our Christian epoch): their culture, their art, their religion, in short their condition may interest us, achievements of their intellect or their

* The fact that this birth did not take place in the year 1, but in all probability some years before, is for us here of no special consequence.

industry may even have become valuable parts of our
own life, as is exemplified by Indian thought, Babylonian
science and Chinese methods; their history, however,
purely as such, lacks moral greatness, in other words,
that force which rouses the individual man to consciousness of his individuality in contrast to the surrounding
world and then—like the ebb and flow of the tide—
makes him employ the world, which he has discovered in
his own breast, to shape that which is without it. The
Aryan Indian, for example, though he unquestionably
possesses the greatest talent for metaphysics of any people
that ever lived, and is in this respect far superior to all
peoples of to-day, does not advance beyond inner enlightenment: he does not shape; he is neither artist
nor reformer, he is content to live calmly and to die
redeemed—he has no history. No more has his opposite,
the Chinaman—that unique representative of Positivism
and Collectivism; what our historical works record as
his "history" is nothing more than an enumeration of
the various robber bands, by which the patient, shrewd
and soulless people, without sacrificing an iota of its
individuality, has allowed itself to be ruled: such enumerations are simply "criminal statistics," not history,
at least not for us: we cannot really judge actions which
awaken no echo in our breast.

Let me give an example. While these lines are being
written [1897], the civilised world is clamorously indignant with Turkey; the European Powers are being
compelled by the voice of public opinion to intervene
for the protection of the Armenians and Cretans; the
final destruction of the Turkish power seems now only
a question of time. This is certainly justified; it was
bound to come to this; nevertheless it is a fact that
Turkey is the last little corner of Europe in which a
whole people lives in undisturbed prosperity and happiness. It knows nothing of social questions, of the bitter

struggle for existence and other such things ; great
fortunes are unknown and pauperism is literally non-
existent ; all form a single harmonious family, and no
one strives after wealth at the expense of his neighbour.
I am not simply repeating what I have read in newspapers
and books, I am testifying to what I have seen with my
own eyes. If the Mohammedan had not practised
tolerance at a time when this idea was unknown to the
rest of Europe, there would now be idyllic peace in the
Balkan States and in Asia Minor. Here it is the
Christian who throws in the leaven of discord ; and with
the cruelty of a ruthlessly reacting power of nature, the
otherwise humane Moslem rises and destroys the dis-
turber of his peace. In fact, the Christian likes neither
the wise fatalism of the Mohammedan nor the prudent
indifferentism of the Chinese. " I come not to bring
peace, but a sword," Christ himself said. The Christian
idea can, in a certain sense, be said to be positively
anti-social. Now that the Christian has become conscious
of a personal dignity otherwise never dreamt of, he is
no longer satisfied with the simple animal instinct of
living with others ; the happiness of the bees and the
ants has now no charm for him. If Christianity be
curtly characterised as the religion of love, its importance
for the history of mankind is but superficially touched
upon. The essential thing is rather this : by Christianity
each individual has received an inestimable, hitherto
unanticipated value—even the " hairs on his head are
all numbered by God " (Matthew x. 30) ; his outward
lot does not correspond to this inner worth ; and thus
it is that life has become tragic, and only by tragedy
does history receive a purely human purport. For
no event is in itself historically tragic ; it is only rendered
tragic by the mind of those who experience it ; otherwise
what affects mankind remains as sublimely indifferent
as all other natural phenomena. I shall return soon to

the Christian idea.   My purpose here has been merely to indicate, first, how deeply and manifestly Christianity revolutionises human feeling and action, of which we still have living proofs before our very eyes ;* secondly, in what sense the non-Christian peoples have no true history, but merely annals.

HELLAS, ROME, JUDEA

History, in the higher sense of the word, means only that past which still lives actively in the consciousness of man and helps to mould him.   In pre-Christian times, therefore, it is only when it concerns peoples which are hastening towards the moral regeneration known as Christianity that history acquires an interest at once scientific and universally human.   Hellas, Rome, Judea alone of the peoples of antiquity are historically important for the living consciousness of the men of the nineteenth century.

Every inch of Hellenic soil is sacred to us, and rightly so.   On the other side of the strait, in Asia, not even the men had or yet have a personality ; here, in Hellas, every river, every stone is animate and individualised, dumb nature awakes to self-consciousness.   And the men by whom this miracle was performed stand before us, from the half-fabulous times of the Trojan War on to the supremacy of Rome, each one with his own incomparable physiognomy :   heroes, rulers, warriors, thinkers, poets, sculptors.   Here man was born :   man capable of becoming a Christian.   Rome presents in many respects the most glaring contrast to Greece ; it is not only geographically but also mentally more distant from Asia, that is, from Semitic, Babylonian and

---

* It is altogether erroneous to think one must attribute such effects not to the awakened soul-life, but merely to race ; the Bosniac of pure Servian descent and the Macedonian of Grecian stock are, as Mohammedans, just as fatalistic and anti-individualistic in their mode of thinking as any Osmanli whatever.

Egyptian influences; it is not so bright and easily satisfied, not so flighty. Possession is the ambition of the people as it is of the individual. The Roman mind turns from the sublimely intuitive in art and philosophy to the intellectual work of organisation. In Greece a single Solon, a single Lycurgus in a way created fundamental laws of State as dilettanti, from purely individual conviction of what was right, while later a whole people of glib amateurs forcibly took the supreme power into their own hands; in Rome there grew up a long-lived community of sober, serious legislators, and while the outward horizon—the Roman Empire and its interests—continually widened, the horizon of internal interests grew most perilously narrower. Morally, however, Rome stands in many respects higher than Greece: the Greek has from the earliest times been what he is to-day, disloyal, unpatriotic, selfish; self-restraint was foreign to him and so he has never been able either to control others or to submit with dignified pride to being controlled. On the other hand, the growth and the longevity of the Roman state point to the shrewd, strong, conscious political spirit of the citizens. The family and the law that protects it are the creations of Rome. And indeed this is true of the family in the narrower sense of an institution laying the foundation of every higher morality, as well as in the extended sense of a power which unites the whole of the citizens into one firm state capable of self-defence; only from the family could a permanent state arise, only through the state could that which to-day we call civilisation become a principle of society capable of development. All the states of Europe are grafts on the Roman stem. And however frequently of old, as to-day, might prevailed over right, the conception of right is our inheritance from the Roman. Meanwhile, just as the day is followed by the night (the sacred night, which reveals to our eye the secret of other worlds, worlds above us in the firmament of heaven and worlds within ourselves, in the depths of our silent hearts), so the glorious positive work of the Greeks and Romans demanded a negative completion ; and this was provided by Israel. To enable us to see the stars, the light of day must be extinguished ; in order to become truly great, to attain that tragic greatness which, as I have said, alone gives vivid purport to history, man had to become conscious not only of his strength but also of his weakness. It was only by clear recognition and unsparing accentuation of the triviality of all human action, the pitiableness of reason in its heavenward flight, the general baseness of human feelings and political motives, that thought was able to take its stand upon a totally new foundation, from which it was to discover in the heart of man capacities and talents, that guided it to the knowledge of something that was sublimer than all else ; Greeks and Romans would never by their methods have reached this sublimest goal ; it would never have occurred to them to attach so great importance to the life of the single individual. If we contemplate the outward history of the people of Israel, it certainly offers at the first glance little that is attractive ; with the exception of some few pleasing features, all the meanness of which men are capable seems concentrated in this one small nation ; not that the Jews were essentially baser than other men, but the grinning mask of vice stares at us from out their history in unveiled nakedness ; in their case no great political sense excuses injustice, no art, no philosophy reconciles us to the horrors of the struggle for existence. Here it was that the negation of the things of this world arose, and with it the vague idea of a higher extra-mundane vocation of mankind. Here men of the people ventured to brand the princes of this earth as " companions of thieves," and to cry out upon the rich, "Woe unto

them that join house to house, that lay field to field till
there be no place, that they may be placed alone in the
midst of the earth." That was a different conception
of right from that of the Romans, to whom nothing
seemed more sacred than property. But the curse
extended not merely to the mighty, but also to "them
that are wise in their own eyes and prudent in their own
sight," and likewise to the joyous heroes, who "drink
wine," and have chosen the world as their sporting
place. So speaks an Isaiah already in the eighth century
before the birth of Christ.* But this first outcry against
what is radically evil in man and in human society
rings louder and louder in the course of the following
centuries from the soul of this strange people : it grows
in earnestness, until Jeremiah cries out, " Woe unto me,
O mother, that thou hast given me birth ! " Finally
the negation becomes a positive principle of life, and
the sublimest of prophets suffers on the cross out of
love. Now it matters not whether we adopt the
attitude of a believing Christian or simply that of the
objective historian ; one thing is certain, that in order
to understand the figure of Christ, we must know the
people who crucified Him. One point of course must be
kept in mind : in the case of the Greeks and Romans
their deeds were their positive and permanent achievement ; in the case of the Jews, on the other hand, it
was the negation of the deeds of this people that was
the only positive achievement for mankind. But this
negation is likewise an historical fact, a fact indeed that
has " grown historically." Even if Jesus Christ, as is
extremely probable, was not descended from the Jewish
people,† nothing but the most superficial partisanship

* *See* Isaiah, chaps. i. and v.

† For the proof that Christ was no Jew (in the sense of Jew by race)
and also for the exposition of his close relation to the moral life of
the real Jewish people, *see* chap. iii. ; chap. v. then deals more fully
with the Jewish people.

can deny the fact that this great and divine figure is
inseparably bound up with the historical development of
that people.

Who could doubt it? The history of Hellas, that of
Rome, and that of Judea have had a moulding influence
upon all centuries of our era and still had a living influence upon the nineteenth century. Indeed they
were not merely living, but also life-retarding influences,
inasmuch as they obstructed our free view into the
purely human sphere in many directions by a fence of
man's height. This is the unavoidable fate of mankind:
what advances him, at the same time fetters him. And
so the history of these peoples must be carefully noted
by any one who proposes to discuss the nineteenth
century.

In the present work a knowledge of pure history, of
the chronology of the world, has been assumed. I can
attempt only one thing here, viz., to define with the greatest
possible brevity what are the most essential distinguishing marks of this "legacy of the old world". This I
shall do in three chapters, the first of which treats of
Hellenic art and philosophy, the second of Roman law,
and the third of the advent of Jesus Christ.

PHILOSOPHY OF HISTORY.

Before concluding these introductory remarks, one
more warning! The expression, this or that "had to"
happen, slipped from my pen a moment ago; perhaps
it will recur in what follows. Thereby I am far from
admitting that the philosophy of history has any right
to dogmatise. The contemplation of the past from the
point of view of the present admits the logical conclusion
that certain events "had to" happen at that time, in
order that the present should become what it has become.
The subtle question as to whether the course of history

might have been different from what it was would be
out of place here. Scared by the dreary clamour of so-
called scientism, most of our modern historians have
handled this subject with timidity. And yet it is clear
that it is only when considered *sub specie necessitatis*
that the present acquires an instructive significance.
Vere scire est per causas scire, says Bacon ; this way of
viewing things is the only scientific one ; but how shall
it be successfully applied if necessity is not everywhere
recognised ? The phrase " had to " expresses the necessary connection of cause and effect, nothing more ; it
is with such examinations as these that we men gild
the main beams of our narrow intellectual sphere,
without imagining that thereby we have flown out into
the open air. The following should, however, be borne
in mind : if necessity be a shaping power, then round
this central point wider and wider circles form themselves,
and no one can blame us if, when our purpose demands
it, we avoid the long circuitous path, in order that we may
take our stand as near as possible to the axis which while
causing motion is itself hardly moved—that point where
what appears to be an arbitrary law almost merges into
undeniable necessity.

FIRST CHAPTER

HELLENIC ART AND PHILOSOPHY

Nur durch den Menschen tritt der Mensch in das Tageslicht
des Lebens ein.—JEAN PAUL FRIEDRICH RICHTER.

MAN BECOMING MAN

MUCH wit has been spent in defining the difference
between man and beast, but the distinction between man
and man seems to me to be even more important, pre-
paring the way, as it does, for the recognition of a fact
of greater significance. The moment a man awakens
to a consciousness of freely creative power, he crosses
a definite boundary and breaks the spell which showed
how closely, in spite of all his talent and all his achievements, he was related even in mind to other living
creatures. Through art a new element, a new form
of existence, enters into the cosmos.

In expressing this as my conviction, I put myself on
the same footing as some of Germany's greatest sons.
This view of the importance of art corresponds, too, if
I am not mistaken, to a specific tendency of the German
mind ; at any rate so clear and precise a formulation
of this thought, as we find in Lessing and Winckelmann,
Schiller and Goethe, Hölderlin, Jean Paul and Novalis,
in Beethoven and Richard Wagner, would hardly be
met with among the other members of the related Indo-
Teutonic group. In order to do justice to this view, we
must in the first place know exactly what is here meant

14

by "art." When Schiller writes, "Nature has formed
creatures only, art has made men," we surely cannot
believe that he was thinking here of flute-playing or
verse-writing ? Whoever reads Schiller's writings (especially of course his *Briefe über die ästhetische Erziehung
des Menschen*) carefully and repeatedly, will recognise
more and more that the idea "art" means to the
poet-philosopher something very vivid, something glowing in him, as it were, and yet a very subtle thing,
which can scarcely be confined within a brief definition.
A man must have misunderstood him if he believes
himself free of such a belief. Let us hear what Schiller
says, for an understanding of this fundamental idea
is indispensable not merely for the purpose of this
chapter, but also for that of the whole book. He writes :
"Nature does not make a better beginning with man
than with her other works : she acts for him, while he
cannot yet act for himself as a free intelligent being. But
what precisely makes him a man is the fact that he does
not stand still as mere nature made him, but is endowed
with the capacity of retracing with the aid of reason the
steps which nature anticipated with him, of transforming the work of necessity into a work of his free
choice and of raising the physical necessity to a moral
one." First and foremost then it is the eager struggle for
freedom which, according to Schiller, betokens the artistic
temperament. Man cannot escape necessity, but he
"transforms" it, and, in so doing, shows himself to be an
artist. As such he employs the elements, which nature offers
him, to create for himself a new world of semblance ; but a
second consideration follows from this, which must not
on any account be overlooked : by placing himself "on
his æsthetic standpoint," as it were, "outside the world
and contemplating it," man for the first time clearly
sees this world, the world outside himself ! The desire
to tear himself away from nature had indeed been a

delusion, but it is this very delusion which is now bringing him to a full and proper consciousness of nature : for " man cannot purge the semblance from the real without at the same time freeing the real of the semblance." It is only when man has begun to invent artistically that he also begins to think consciously, it is only when he himself builds that he begins to perceive the architectonics of the universe. Reality and semblance are at first mixed up in his consciousness ; the conscious, freely creative dealing with the semblance is the first step towards attaining to the freest and purest possible cognition of reality. True science—a science that not only measures and records, but contemplates and perceives—owes its origin, according to Schiller, to the direct influence of the artistic efforts of man. Then for the first time philosophy finds a place in the human intellect ; for it hovers between the two worlds. Philosophy is based at once on art and on science : it is, if I may so express myself, the latest artistic elaboration of a reality which has been sifted and purified. But this does not by any means exhaust the import of Schiller's conception of art. For " beauty " (that freely transformed, new world) is not simply an object, in it rather there is mirrored also " a condition of our subject " : " Beauty is, in truth, form, because we contemplate it, but it is at the same time life, because we feel it. In a word, it is at once a state and an achievement." * To feel artistically, to think artistically denotes then a particular condition of man in general ; it is a phase of feeling, or rather attitude of mind—still better, perhaps, a latent store of power, which must everywhere act as a " freeing," "transforming," " purging " element in the life of the individual man, as well as in the life of a whole nation, even where art,

* Cf. *Aesthetische Erziehung*, Bd. 3, 25, 26. Further particulars in chap. ix. div. 7 of this book (vol. ii.).

science and philosophy are not directly concerned.   Or,
to present this relation to ourselves from a different side,
we can also—and indeed here too with Schiller *—say,
" From being a successful instrument, man became an
unsuccessful artist."   That is the tragedy of which I
spoke in the introductory remarks.

We must, I think, admit that this German
conception of " man becoming man " goes deeper,
embraces more, and throws a brighter light upon that
future of mankind after which we have to strive than
any narrowly scientific or purely utilitarian one.   However that may be, one thing is certain : whether such a
view is to have unconditional or merely conditional
validity, it is of the very greatest service for a study of
the Hellenic world and the sure revelation of its principle
of life ; for though in this subjective formulation it may
be a characteristically German conception, it leads back
in the main to Hellenic art and to Hellenic philosophy,
which embraced natural science, and proves that
Hellenism lived on in the nineteenth century not merely
outwardly and historically, but also as an inherent force
that has helped to mould the future.†

ANIMAL AND MAN

Not every artistic activity is art.   Numerous animals
evince extraordinary skill in the construction of dwellings ;
the song of the nightingale vies successfully with the
natural song of the savage ; capricious imitation we find

* Cf. *Etwas über die erste Menschengesellschaft*, div. 1.

† To avoid misunderstanding, I wish to mention that here at the
beginning of my book I have without further criticism joined hands with
Schiller, to ensure that what follows may be more easily understood ;
only in my final chapter can I establish my view that in the case of the
Teutonic peoples, in contrast to the Hellenes, the turning-point in " man
becoming man " is to be sought not in art, but in religion—this however does not mean a deviation from Schiller's conception of " art "
but purely and simply a particular gradation.

highly developed in the animal kingdom, and that too in the most various spheres—imitation of activity, of sound, of form—and here it must also be remembered that we know next to nothing of the life of the higher apes ; * language, that is, communication of feelings and judgments from one individual to another, is widespread throughout the whole animal kingdom and the means adopted are so incredibly sure that not only anthropologists but also philologists † do not consider it superfluous to warn us against thinking that vibration of the human vocal chords—or for that matter sound in general—is the only thing that can be called language.‡ By instinctively uniting into civic organisations, no matter how complex and intricate they may be, the human race similarly achieves nothing which is in principle an advance on the exceedingly complex animal communities ; modern sociologists, indeed, consider the origin of human society as having a close organic connection with the development of the social instincts in the surrounding animal kingdom.§ If we consider

* *See*, however, the observations of J. G. Romanes in the case of a female chimpanzee, given in fullest detail in *Nature*, vol. xi., p. 160 ff, condensed in the books of the same author. In a short time this ape learned to count up to seven with unfailing accuracy. On the other hand, the Bakairi (South American Indians) are able to count only up to six, and that with great difficulty. (*See* Karl von Steinen : *Unter den Naturvölkern Brasiliens.*)

† *See*, for example, Whitney, *The Life of Language* (Fr. edit. p. 238 f).

‡ Compare especially the instructive remarks of Topinard in his *Anthropologie*, pp. 159–162. It is interesting to know that so great and at the same time so extremely cautious a naturalist as Adolf Bastian, with all his abhorrence of everything fantastic, claims for the articulata (with the tentacles with which they touch each other) a language analogous to ours and in keeping with their nature ; see *Das Beständige in den Menschenrassen*, p. viii. of the preface. In Darwin's *Descent of Man*, chap. iii., we find an exceedingly interesting review of the facts pertaining to this question and an energetic refutation of the paradoxes of Max Müller and others.

§ *See*, for example, the *Principles of Sociology* of the American Professor Franklin H. Giddings (Fr. edit., 1897, p. 189) : "Les bases de l'empire de l'homme furent posées sur les associations zoogéniques des plus humbles formes de la vie consciente."

the civic life of the ants, and see by what daring refinements they ensure the practical efficiency of the social mechanism and the faultless fitting of all parts into each other—as an example I shall mention only the removal of the baneful sexual impulse in a large percentage of the population, and that too not by mutilation, as is the case with our wretched makeshift castration, but by shrewd manipulation of the fecundating germs— then we must admit that the civic instinct of man is not of a high standard ; compared with many animal species we are nothing but political blunderers.* Even in the special exercise of reason we can indeed recognise a peculiar specific feature of man, but hardly a fundamentally new natural phenomenon. Man in his natural condition uses his superior reason exactly as the stag his speed of foot, the tiger his strength, the elephant his weight; it is his finest weapon in the struggle for existence, it takes the place of agility, bulk and so many other things that he lacks. The times are past when men had the effrontery to deny that animals have reason ; not only do the ape, the dog and all higher animals manifest conscious reflection and unerring judgment, but insects have been experimentally proved to do the same : a colony of bees, for example, placed in unaccustomed and absolutely new surroundings, adopts new measures, tries this and that, till it has found what

---

* See Carl Vogt's amusing *Untersuchungen über die Tierstaaten* (1851). In Brehm, *Vom Nordpol zum Aequator* (1890), we find very noteworthy facts concerning the waging of war by baboons ; their tactics change according to the nature of the ground, they divide their forces into definite groups, first line, second line of attack, &c., several work together, so as to roll a large boulder down on the enemy, &c. Perhaps the most amazing social life is that of the farming ants from South America, first reported upon by Belt, *Naturalist in Nicaragua,* then by the German Alfred Möller ; now we can observe these animals in the Zoological Garden in London, where it is especially easy to follow the activity of the large-headed " overseers," which rush forward and shake up the workers whenever they take things easy !

suits it.* There is no doubt that if we investigate with
more care and insight the psychological life—so far

* *Cf.* Huber, *Nouvelles observations sur les abeilles*, ii. 198, and the
fine book by Maurice Maeterlinck, *La vie des abeilles*, 1901. The best
and shortest recent *résumé* of the most important facts pertinent to our
case is probably that by J. G. Romanes, *Essays on Instinct*, 1897 ;
even this distinguished pupil of Darwin is, however, under the constant
necessity of referring to the series of observations of the two Hubers
as being the most brilliant and reliable ; but too little known is another
work, that of J. Traherne Moggridge, *Observations on harvesting
Ants and Trapdoor Spiders* (Reeve, London, 1873) ; in general the
psychologists of the animal kingdom should direct more attention to
the spiders, which beyond doubt are endowed with special gifts of
their own. But *see* H. C. MacCook, *American Spiders* (Philadelphia,
1889), and the various volumes of the invaluable *Souvenirs entomo-
logiques* by Fabre. Among older writings, Kirby's *History, Habits,
and Instincts of Animals* is of lasting value. Of the more philosophic
writings I shall here call attention especially to Wundt's *Vorlesungen
über die Menschen- und Tierseele* and to Fritz Schulze's *Vergleichende
Seelenkunde* (Second Part, " The Psychology of Animals and Plants,"
1897). In this note I should like at the same time to put in an express
caveat, namely, that here and further on I do not fail to recognise
the deep gulf between the intellect of thinking man and that of the animal ;
it was high time that a Wundt with all his intellectual keenness should
openly oppose our almost ineradicable inclination to anthropomorphic
interpretations ; but it seems to me that Wundt himself and with him
Schulze, Lubbock and others fall into the opposite error : they make
indeed a just protest against the uncritical over-estimation of the
thought-life of the animals, yet these learned men, accustomed from
their earliest years to think and speculate unceasingly, do not seem
to have any idea of the minimum of consciousness and reflection
with which mankind as a whole manages to go through life; they are
in general inclined to attach too great importance to " consciousness "
and " reflection " ; this manifests itself in their treatises on the
elementary conditions of the human $\psi\nu\chi\acute{\eta}$ and—perhaps still more
clearly—in their lack of ability to explain the nature of the real act of
creative genius (Art and Philosophy). One Wundt having reduced
the estimate of animal intelligence to its right level, we should need a
second to expose our tendency to overrate enormously our own importance. The following point also seems to me never to have been
properly emphasised : that in our observations of animals we, do what
we will, remain anthropomorphists ; for we cannot even conceive a
sense (I mean a physical instrument for acquiring knowledge of the
surrounding world) if we do not possess it ourselves, and we must
of necessity remain for ever blind and deaf to all manifestations of
feeling and understanding, which are not immediately echoed in our
own intellectual life. It is all very well for Wundt to warn against
" false analogies " ; in this whole sphere no conclusions but those
of analogy are possible. As Clifford has clearly shown (cf. *Seeing and*

practically unknown to us—of animals from remote classes, we shall everywhere find similar things.

Thinking), we can proceed neither purely objectively nor purely subjectively here ; this mixed method of knowing he has therefore termed an "ejective" one. We estimate those animals as most intelligent whose intelligence most closely resembles our own, and is therefore best understood by us, but is not this extremely simple and thoughtless in reference to a cosmic problem such as that of intellect ? Is this not disguised anthropomorphism ? Most certainly. When Wundt therefore maintains, "In this sphere experiment is in a high degree superior to mere observation," one can only very conditionally agree with him ; for experiment is from the outset a reflex of our purely human conceptions, whereas the loving observation of a quite differently organised creature in its own most normal conditions and that with the desire not to criticise its achievements but to understand them—as far as our human narrow intellectual horizon permits us—would be bound to lead to many surprising discoveries. And so old blind Huber has taught us much more about bees than Lubbock in his—nevertheless admirable—book on *Ants, Bees and Wasps* (1883). And so it is that the rough trainers, who demand of each animal only such tricks as they can expect from it on the basis of daily observation of its capabilities, achieve such remarkable results. Here as elsewhere our science of to-day is still in the toils of Helleno-Jewish anthropomorphism, and not least just where it warns us against it. Since the above has been written, the sensational book of Bethe, *Dürfen wir Ameisen und Bienen psychische Qualitäten zuschreiben ?* has appeared, which in its whole argumentation is a classical example of disguised anthropomorphism. By ingenious (though in my opinion by no means conclusive) tests, Bethe has come to the conclusion that ants recognise by smell that they belong to the nest, and their finding of their way depends on the excretion of a chemical substance, &c. The whole is "Chemoreflex," the whole life of these animals "purely mechanical." One is astonished to find such an abyss of philosophical barbarity. Why, is not the whole sense-life as such inevitably mechanical ? Can I recognise my own father without help of a mechanism ? Does not the dog recognise its master almost entirely by smell ? Are Descartes' automata always to rise into life again, as though science and philosophy had stood still for three hundred years ? Here we have the real ineradicable anthropomorphism. In the case of vertebrates their strict analogy with our own structure lets us draw conclusions about psychical processes ; in the insect, on the other hand, a totally strange being is before us, built on a plan which is so fundamentally at variance with that of our body that we are not in a position to explain with certainty even the purely mechanical working of the organs of sense (*see* Gegenbaur, *Vergleichende Anatomie*) and in consequence cannot know at all what a world of sense-impressions and of possibilities of communication, &c., quite closed to us, may surround these creatures. Not to comprehend this fact is to display an ant-like naïveté.—(Addenda of the

Thus the comparatively enormous development of the human brain * gives us after all only a relative superiority. Man does not walk upon earth like a God, but as a creature among other creatures, perhaps it would be no exaggeration to say as *primus inter pares;* for it is difficult to comprehend why a higher differentiation, with its countless disadvantages, should be forthwith regarded as higher " perfection " ; the relative perfection of an organism should be judged, in my opinion, by its suitability to given conditions. Through all the fibres of his nature man is organically and closely connected with his surroundings ; all this is blood of his blood ; if we think him apart from nature, he is a fragment, an uprooted stem.

What now distinguishes man from other beings ? Many will answer, his inventive power : it is the instrument which shows him to be prince among the animals. Yet even with this he still remains an animal among animals. Not only the anthropoid, but also the common

third edition.) In the opening speech of the fourth International Congress of Zoologists on August 23, 1898, Sir John Lubbock violently attacked the automata theory and said, *inter alia :* " Many animals possess organs of sense, the meaning of which is inscrutable to us men. They notice sounds which we cannot hear, they see things which remain invisible to us, they receive impressions of sense, which lie beyond the sphere of our power of conception. The world which we know so well must have for them quite a different physiognomy." Montaigne had already expressed the opinion : " Les bêtes ont plusieurs conditions qui se rapportent aux nôtres ; de celles-là, par comparaison, nous pouvons tirer quelque conjecture : mais ce qu'elles ont en particulier, que savons-nous que c'est ? " The psychiatrician Forel became convinced after thirty years of diligent observation that ants possessed memory, had the capacity of unifying in their brain various impressions of sense and acted with conscious reflection. (Speech delivered on August 13, 1901, at the Congress of Zoologists in Berlin.)

* It is well known that Aristotle has made a serious mistake here, as he often does : man possesses, neither absolutely nor relatively (that is, in relation to weight of body), the largest brain ; the superiority of this apparatus in his case is based on other things. (*See* Ranke, *Der Mensch.*, second edition, I., pp. 551 and 542 f.).

ape, invents simpler instruments (any one can obtain information on this point by referring to Brehm's *Tier-leben*), and the elephant is, if perhaps not in invention, yet in the employment of instruments a real master. (*See* Romanes, *Die geistige Entwickelung im Tierreich*, pp. 389 ff.) The most ingenious dynamo machine does not raise men one inch over the earth-surface which is common to all creatures ; all such things denote merely a new accumulation of strength in the struggle for ex-istence ; man becomes thereby in a way a more highly potentiated animal. Instead of going to bed, he illu-mines with tallow candles, oil, gas or electricity; he thereby gains time and can do more work ; but there are likewise countless animals which procure light for them-selves, many by phosphorescence, others, particularly the deep sea fishes, by electricity ; * we travel by bicycle, by train, and shall perhaps soon travel by airship— the bird of passage and the inhabitant of the sea had brought travelling long ago into fashion, and just like them, men travel in order to subsist. The incalculable superiority of man shows itself certainly in this, that he can invent all these things rationally and can unite individual discoveries, so as to make still further pro-gress. The impulse to imitate and the capacity for assimilation which one certainly finds in all mammals are in his case of so high a standard that the same thing becomes, so to speak, a different thing ; in analo-gous manner we see in chemical substances that fre-quently the addition of a single essentially similar atom,

* Emin Pasha and Stanley tell about chimpanzees which go out at night with torches on their predatory raids.   With Romanes, one would do well to doubt this fact till further information is available. Stanley did not see it himself and Emin Pascha was exceedingly shortsighted.   If apes have really discovered the art of lighting fires, to us men there would remain nevertheless the invention of the figure of Prometheus, and that this, and not that, is what makes man man forms exactly the substance of my remarks.

accordingly a simple numerical addition, fundamentally changes the qualities of the substance in question ; if one adds oxygen to oxygen, a new compound, ozone, is formed ($O_2 + O_1 = O_3$). One should, however, not forget that all human discoveries rest on assimilation and imitation ; man "finds out" (er-findet) what is there and has only awaited his coming, just as he " discovers " what hitherto was covered with a veil ; nature plays at " hide and seek " and " blind man's buff " with him. *Quod invenitur, fuit,* says Tertullian. The fact that he understands this, that he seeks what is hidden, and bit by bit reveals and finds so much, certainly testifies to the possession of incomparable gifts ; but if he did not possess them, he would indeed be the most miserable of creatures, for there he stands weaponless, powerless, wingless ; bitter necessity is his incentive, the faculty of invention his salvation.

Now man becomes truly man, a creature differing from all animals, even human ones, when he reaches the stage of inventing without necessity, when he exercises his incomparable gifts of his own free will and not because nature compels him, or—to use a deeper and more suitable expression—when the necessity which impels him to invent enters his consciousness, no longer from outside, but from his inner self ; when that which was his salvation becomes his sanctuary. The decisive moment is when free invention consciously appears, that is, therefore, when man becomes artist. The study of surrounding nature, as, for example, of the starry heavens, may have made great strides, and a complex cult of gods and spirits have been formed without thereby anything fundamentally new entering into the world. All this proves a latent capacity ; essentially, however, it is nothing more than the half-unconscious exercise of an instinct. It is only when an individual man, like Homer, invents the gods of his own free will as he wishes them to be; it is only when an observer of nature, like Democritus, from free creative power invents the conception of the atom; when a pensive seer, like Plato, with the wilfulness of the genius superior to the world throws overboard all visible nature and puts in its place the realm of ideas that man has created; it is only when a most Sublime Teacher proclaims, "Behold the kingdom of Heaven is within you"—it is only then that a completely new creature is born, that being of whom Plato says, "He has generative power in his soul rather than in his body," it is only then that the macrocosm contains a microcosm. The only thing that deserves to be called culture is the daughter of such "creative freedom," or in a word "art," and with art philosophy—genuine, creative philosophy and science—is so closely related that both must be recognised as two sides of the same being; every great poet has been a philosopher, every philosopher of genius a poet. That which lies outside this microcosmic life of culture is nothing more than "civilisation," that is, a more and more highly potentiated, increasingly more industrious, easier and less free ant-like state-existence, certainly rich in blessing and in so far desirable, nevertheless a gift of the ages, in the case of which it frequently remains exceedingly questionable whether the human race does not pay more for it than it receives from it. Civilisation is in itself nothing, for it denotes something merely relative; a higher civilisation could be regarded as a positive gain (*i.e.*, an "advance") only when it led to an increasingly intensive intellectual and artistic shaping of life and to an inner moral enlightenment. Because this seemed to him not to be the case with us, Goethe, as the most competent judge, could make the melancholy confession, "These times are worse than one thinks." On the other hand, the undying importance of Hellenism lies in this, that it understood how to create for itself an age better than any that we can conceive, an age incomparably better, if I may so express it, than its own backward civilisation deserved. To-day all ethnographists and anthropologists distinguish clearly between morals and religion, and recognise that both in a certain sense are independent of each other ; it would be just as useful to learn to distinguish clearly between culture and civilisation. A highly developed civilisation is compatible with a rudimentary culture : Rome, for example, exemplifies a wonderful civilisation with very insignificant and quite unoriginal culture. Athens, on the other hand (with its free citizens) reveals a stage of culture in comparison with which we Europeans of the nineteenth century are in many respects still barbarians, and this is united with a civilisation which—in comparison with ours—may with perfect justice be termed really barbaric.* Compared with all other phenomena of history, Hellenism represents an exuberantly rich blossoming of the human intellect, and the reason of this is that its whole culture rests on an artistic basis. The freely creative work of human imagination was the starting-point of the infinitely rich life of the Hellenes. Their language, religion, politics, philosophy, science (even mathematics), history and geography, all forms of imaginative invention in words and sounds, their whole public life and the whole inner life of the individual—everything radiates from this work, and everything finds itself in it once more as in a figurative and at the same time organic centre, a centre which reduces the greatest divergencies in characters,

* We have an excellent example of this in the case of the Indo-Aryans in their original home, where the formation of a language, "which surpassed all others, was completely uniform and wonderfully perfect," apart from other intellectual achievements, pointed to a high culture. These men were nevertheless a race of shepherds who walked abroad almost naked and knew neither cities nor metals. (See in particular Jhering, *Vorgeschichte der Indoeuropäer*, p. 2.) For a definite distinction between knowledge, civilisation and culture I refer readers to vol: ii. chap. ix. of this book and the synopsis contained in it.

interests and endeavours to reach a living conscious unity. At this central point stands Homer.

HOMER

The fact that the existence of the poet Homer has been open to doubt will give later generations no very favourable idea of the intellectual acumen of our epoch. It is exactly a century ago since F. A. Wolf published his hypothesis; since that time our neo-Alexandrians have bravely "sniffed and shovelled away," till at last they arrived at the conclusion that Homer was merely a pseudo-mythical collective term and the *Iliad* and the *Odyssey* nothing more than a skilful pasting together and re-editing of all sorts of poems. . . . Pasted together by whom? and by whom so beautifully edited? Well, naturally by learned philologists, the ancestors of the modern ones! The only matter for surprise is that, as we are once more in possession of such an ingenious race of critics, these gentlemen have not taken the trouble to piece together for us poor wretches a new *Iliad*. There is truly no lack of songs, no lack of genuine, beautiful folksongs; is there, perhaps, a lack of paste, of brain-paste? The most competent judges in such a question are clearly the poets, the great poets; the philologist clings to the shell which has been exposed to the caprice of centuries; but the congenial glance of the poet, on the other hand, penetrates to the kernel and perceives the individual creative process. Now Schiller, with his unerring instinct, immediately stigmatised as " simply barbaric " the view that the *Iliad* and the *Odyssey* were not, in all essential points of their construction, the work of a single inspired individual. Indeed, in his excitement, he so far oversteps the mark that he calls Wolf a " stupid Devil "! The opinion of Goethe is almost more interesting. His much-lauded objectivity manifested itself, among other things, in this, that he unreservedly and unresistingly let himself be influenced by an impression ; Wolf's great philological merits and the mass of correct statements which his expositions contained, misled the great man ; he felt convinced and declared this openly. But later, when he again had the opportunity of studying the Homeric poems thoroughly— and viewed them no longer from a philologico-historical but from a purely poetic standpoint—he retracted his over-hasty endorsement of the " subjective trash " (as he now called it), for now his knowledge was precise ; behind these works there stands a " glorious unity, a single, higher poetical sense." * But the philologists too, in their necessarily roundabout way, have come to the same view, and Homer enters the twentieth century, the fourth millennium of his fame, greater than ever.†

* *See*, for example, the small work, *Homer noch einmal*, of the year 1826.

† I must take care to avoid even the slightest assumption of a learning which I do not possess ; a man in my position can only note the results of learned research ; but it is his right and his duty to approach these results as a free man, possessing unexceptionable critical power. Indeed, he must, in my opinion, use his critical power above all in the same way as a monarch whose wisdom has especially to prove itself in the choice of his advisers ; the layman cannot sit in judgment on the value of learned arguments, he can, however, from style, language and train of thoughts very well form an estimate of the individual scholar and distinguish between mason and architect. It is not therefore in the sense of a material proof, but merely in order that the reader himself may be able, in the sense alluded to, to gauge my ability to form a critical judgment, that I now and then refer in the notes to my " authorities." As I have pointed out in the text, I here in the first place hold with Socrates that musicians are the best judges of flute-playing, poets of poetical works. Goethe's opinion with regard to Homer is worth more to me than that of all the philologists together who have lived since the beginning of the world. I have, however, informed myself, as far as a layman can, in regard to the latter, and in so complicated a question this is very essential. The summary accounts of Niese, *Die Entwickelung der Homerischen Poesie*, 1882, and of Jebb, *Homer*, 1888, enable us to follow the course of the discussion up to modern times, but nothing more. On the other hand, in Bergk, *Griechische Litteraturgeschichte*, 1872–84, we have a safe guide. That Bergk was a Hellenist of the first rank is admitted by all Homeric scholars and even the ordinary man is impressed by the comprehensive and penetrating character of his knowledge. com-

For besides many philologising nonentities, Germany has produced an undying race of really great linguistic and literary scholars ; F. A. Wolf himself was one of them ; he never lowered himself to the absurd idea afterwards propounded, that a great work of art could be produced by the united efforts of a number of insignificant men or directly from the vague consciousness of the masses, and he would be the first to learn with satisfaction of the successful issue that finally attended the protracted scientific researches. Even if as great a genius as Homer himself had devoted himself to improving and embellishing Homer's works—this is of course almost a senseless supposition—the history of all art teaches us that genuine individuality defies all imitation ; but the farther the critical investigations of the nineteenth century advanced, the more was every capable investigator compelled to realise that even the most important imitators, completers and restorers of the epics of Homer all differed from him in this, that not one of them approached even in the slightest degree

bined as it is with a moderation which bordered on the jejune ; Bergk is not a fiery spirit; his attitude in this question forms the complement to the lightning intuition of a Schiller. One should read not only the chapter, " Homer an historical personality," but particularly also in the later paragraph, " Homer in modern times," the remarks on the song-theory, of which Bergk says, " The general premisses, from which the advocates of the song-theory proceed, prove themselves on closer examination, especially when one considers the Homeric poems in connection with the whole development of epic poetry, as quite untenable.   This theory could only be formulated by critics by whom the Homeric epic, separated from its surroundings and without any regard to the history of Greek literature, was submitted to their disintegrating criticism " (i. 525).   One should read also his proof that the use of writing was common in Homer's time, and that external as well as internal facts testify that Homer actually left his works in writing (i. 527 ff).—1905.   In the meantime the discoveries in Crete have proved that the use of script was common among the Hellenes long before the Achæans entered the Peloponnese.   In the palace of Minos, the most modern parts of which can be proved to have been built not later than 1550 years before Christ, whole libraries and archives have been discovered (cf. the publications of A. J. Evans in the last volumes of the *Annual of the British School at Athens*).

his commanding genius. Disfigured though they were by countless misconceptions, copyists' mistakes, and still more by the supposed improvements of irrepressible wiseacres and the interpolations of well-meaning followers, the more the patchwork of the present form of these poems was shown up by the polishing work of research, the more they testified to the incomparable divine creative power of the original artist. What marvellous power of beauty must have been possessed by works which could so successfully defy for centuries the stormy social conditions, and for a still longer time the desecrating tempest of narrow-mindedness, mediocrity and pseudo-genius, that even to-day, from the midst of the ruins, the ever youthful charm of artistic perfection greets us like the good fairy of our own culture ! At the same time other investigations, which had gone their own independent way—historical and mythological studies—clearly proved that Homer must have been an historical personage. It has, in fact, been shown that in these poems both saga and myth have been treated very freely and according to definite principles of conscious artistic shaping. To mention only the most essential point : Homer was a remarkable simplifier, he un-ravelled the tangled clue of popular myths, and from the planless medley of popular sagas, which had a different form in every district, he wove certain definite forms in which all Hellenes recognised themselves and their gods, although this very delineation was quite new to them. What we have now discovered after so much toil the ancients knew very well ; I quote in this connection the remarkable passage in *Herodotus :* " From the Pelasgians the Hellenes took their gods. But whence each of the gods comes, whether they were always there, what their form is, we Hellenes only know as it were since yesterday. For it is Hesiod and Homer, in the first place, who created for the Greeks their race of gods, who gave the gods their names, distributed honours and arts among them, and described their forms. The poets, however, who are supposed to have lived before these two men, in my opinion at least, really came after them " (Book II. 53). Hesiod lived about a hundred years after Homer and was directly influenced by him ; with the exception of this little error the simple naive sentence of Herodotus contains all that the gigantic critical work of a century has brought to light. It has been proved that the poets who according to the priestly tradition lived before Homer—*e.g.*, Orpheus, Musæos, Eumolpos from the Thracian school, or Olen and others of the Delian school—in reality lived after him ; * and it is likewise proved that the religious conceptions of the Greeks have been drawn from very different sources ; the Indo-European inheritance forms the main capital ; to this were added all kinds of motley Oriental influences (as Herodotus had also shown in the passage which precedes that above quoted) : upon this chaos a hand was now laid by the one incomparable man with the sovereign authority of the freely creative, poetic genius, and out of it he formed by artistic means a new world ; as Herodotus says : he creates for the Greeks their race of gods.

May I here be permitted to quote the words of Erwin Rohde,† recognised as one of the most learned of living Hellenists : " The Homeric epic can only be called folk-poetry because it is of such a nature that the whole Greek-speaking people willingly took it up and could make it their own, not because the ' people ' in any mystic way were engaged in its production. Many hands have been at work on the two poems, but all in

* *See* in particular Flach, *Geschichte der griechischen Lyrik nach den Quellen dargestellt,* I. pp. 45 ff, 90 ff.

† Since the above was written, German science has had to deplore the death of this extraordinary man.

the direction and in the sense which the greatest poetic
genius among the Greeks, and probably of mankind,
and not the people or the saga, as one certainly hears
maintained, gave to them. In Homer's mirror Greece
appears united and uniform in belief, in dialect, in constitution, customs and morals. One may, however,
boldly maintain that this unity cannot in reality have
existed ; the elements of Panhellenism were doubtless
present, but it was the genius of the poet alone that
collected and fused them together in a merely imaginary
whole."* Bergk, whose whole rich scholastic life was
devoted to the study of Greek poetry formulates the
opinion : " Homer draws chiefly from himself, from his
own inner soul ; he is a truly original spirit, not an imi-
tator, and he practises his art with full consciousness "
(*Griech. Litteraturgesch.*, p. 527). Duncker, too, the
historian, remarks that " what was lacking in the
imitators of Homer—what accordingly distinguished this
one man—was the comprehensive eye of genius."†
And to close these quotations in a worthy manner I
refer to Aristotle, in whom one must admit some com-
petence, so far as critical acumen is concerned. It
is striking and consoling to see that he too discovers
the distinguishing-mark of Homer to be his eye ; in
the eighth chapter of his *Poetics* (he is speaking of the
qualities of poetic action), he says : " But Homer, just as
he is different in other things also, seems here too to have
seen aright, either by art or by nature." A profound
remark ! which prepares us for the surprising outburst
of enthusiasm in the twenty-third chapter of the *Poetics :*
Homer is above all other poets *divine.*

* *Seelenkult und Unsterblichkeitsglaube der Griechen,* pp. 35, 36.
† *Gesch. des Altertums,* v. 566.

Artistic Culture

I have felt bound to prove this, even at the cost of some detail ; not because it is of importance for the subject treated in this book, whether one man named Homer wrote the *Iliad*, or in how far the poem, which to-day is so entitled, may correspond to the original poem ; the special proof is a side issue. It is, on the other hand, essential for my whole work that I should emphasise the incomparable importance of personality in general ; it is likewise essential to recognise the fact that every work of art always and without exception presupposes a strong individual personality,—a great work of art a personality of the first rank, a Genius ; it is, finally, imperative that we should grasp the fact, that the secret of the magic power of Hellenism lies locked in this idea " personality." For indeed if we would understand what Hellenic art and Hellenic thought have meant for the nineteenth century, if we would know the secret of so lasting a power, we must realise especially that it is the power of great personalities that, coming down from that vanished world, still influences us with the freshness of youth.

> Höchstes Glück der Erdenkinder
> Ist nur die Persönlichkeit :

says Goethe ; this greatest gift—*höchstes Glück*—the Greeks possessed as no other people ever did, and it is this very thing that surrounds them with that sunny halo which is peculiarly theirs. Their great poems and their great thoughts are not the work of anonymous commercial companies, as are the so-called art and wisdom of the Egyptians, Assyrians, Chinese, *e tutti quanti ;* the life-principle of this people is heroism ; the individual steps forward alone : boldly crossing the boundary of what is common to all, he leaves behind all that civilisation which has accumulated instinctively, unconsciously and uselessly, and fearlessly hews out a path in the ever-deepening gloom of the primeval forest of accumulated superstitions,—he dares to have Genius! And this daring gives rise to a new conception of manhood; for the first time man has "entered into the daylight of life."

The individual, however, could not accomplish this alone. Personalities can clearly reveal themselves as such, only when surrounded by other personalities; action receives a conscious existence only after reaction has taken place; the genius can breathe only in an atmosphere of genius. If then a single, surpassingly great, incomparably creative personality has undoubtedly been the condition and absolutely indispensable *primum mobile* of the whole Grecian culture, we must recognise as the second characteristic factor in this culture the fact that the surroundings proved themselves worthy of so extraordinary a personality. That which is lasting in Hellenism, that which keeps it alive to-day and has enabled it to be a bright ideal, a consolation and a hope to so many of the best men in the nineteenth century, can be summed up in one word: it is its element of Genius. What would a Homer have availed in Egypt or Phœnicia? The one would have paid no heed to him, the other would have crucified him; yes, even in Rome . . . but here we have the experimental proof before our eyes. Has all the poetry of Greece succeeded in striking even a single spark out of this sober, inartistic heart? Is there among the Romans a single true poetic genius? Is it not pitiful that our schoolmasters are condemned to embitter the fresh years of our childhood by compulsory admiration of these rhetorical, unnatural, soulless, hypocritical imitations of genuine poetry? And is this example alone not

enough to prove—a few poets more or less make really
no difference—how all culture is linked to art ?   What
is one to say to a history which embraces more than
1200 years and does not show a single philosopher,
not even a philosopher in miniature ?   What to a people
which has to conceal its own modest claims in this
respect by the importation of the latter-day persecuted,
anæmic Greeks, who, however, are not philosophers at
all but merely very commonplace moralists ?   How low
must the quality of genius have sunk when a good
Emperor, who wrote maxims in his leisure hours, is
commended to the reverence of coming generations
as a thinker ! *   Where is there a great, creative natural
scientist among the Romans ?   Surely not the industrious
encyclopædist, Pliny ?   Where is there a mathematician

* Lucretius might be named as a man certainly worthy of admiration
both as a thinker and as a poet ; but his thoughts are, as he admits,
always Greek thoughts, and his poetical apparatus is predominantly
Greek.   And withal there lies over his great poem the deadly shadow
of that scepticism, which sooner or later leads to unproductivity, and
which must be carefully distinguished from the deep insight of truly
religious minds, which become aware of the figurative element in
their conceptions, without for that reason doubting the sublime truth
of what they vaguely feel in their hearts but cannot fathom, as when,
for example, the Vedish seer suddenly exclaims :

> From what it has arisen, this creation
> Whether created it has been or not—
> Whoever in the heavens watches o'er it,
> He knows it well !   Or does he too not know ?
>
> *Rigveda*, x. 129.

or as Herodotus in the passage quoted a few pages previously, where
he expresses the opinion that the poet created the gods.   And Epicurus
himself, the " atheist," the man whom Lucretius describes as the
greatest of all mortals, the man from whom he takes his whole system
—do we not learn that in his case " religious feeling must have been
so to speak inborn ? " (*See* the sketch of Epicurus' life by K. L. von
Knebel, which Goethe recommends.)   " Never," exclaimed Diocles
when he found Epicurus in the temple, " never have I seen Zeus
greater than when Epicurus lay at his feet ! "   The Latin fancied he
had spoken the last word of wisdom with his *Primus in orbe deos fecit
timor ;* the Greek, on the other hand, as an enlightened being, knelt
more fervently than ever before the glorious god-image, which heroism
had freely created for itself, and in so doing testified to his own genius.

of importance ? Where a meteorologist, a geographer,
an astronomer ? All that was achieved under the sway
of Rome, in these and other sciences, is derived without
exception from the Greeks. But the poetical fountain
had dried up, and so too, bit by bit, creative thinking
and creative observation were exhausted, even among
the Greeks of the Roman Empire. The life-giving
breath of genius was gone ; neither in Rome nor in
Alexandria was there anything of this manna of the
human spirit for the ever upward-soaring Hellenes ; in
the one city the superstition of utility, in the other,
scientific elephantiasis, gradually choked every movement of life. Learning indeed steadily increased, the
number of known facts multiplied continually, but the
motive-power, instead of increasing, decreased, where
increase was badly needed. Thus the European world,
in spite of its great progress in civilisation, underwent
a gradual decline in culture—sinking down into naked
bestiality. Nothing probably is more dangerous for the
human race than science without poetry, civilisation
without culture.*

In Hellas the course of events was quite different.
So long as art flourished, the torch of genius flashed up
heavenward in all spheres. The power, which in Homer
had fought its way to a dominant individuality,
recognised in him its vocation, narrowed down in
the first instance to the purely artistic creation
of a world of beautiful semblance. Around the
radiant central figure arose a countless army of poets
and a rich gradation of poetical styles. Immediately
after Homer's time and later, originality formed
the hall-mark of Greek creation. Inferior powers
naturally took their direction from those of greater
eminence ; but there were so many of the latter, and

* Compare in vol. ii., chap. ix., the remarks about China, &c.

these had invented so infinitely manifold forms, that
the lesser talent was enabled to choose what was exactly
fitted to it, and thus achieve its highest possibilities. I
am speaking not only of poetry in words wedded to
music, but also of the unexampled glory of the
poetry that delights the eye, which grew up beside the
other, like a dearly beloved younger sister. Architecture,
sculpture, painting, like epic, lyric and dramatic
poetry, like the hymn, the dithyramb, the ode,
the romance, and the epigram, were all rays of that
same sun of art, only differently refracted according
to the individual eye. It is surely ridiculous that
schoolmen cannot distinguish between true culture and
ballast, and should inflict on us interminable lists of
unimportant Greek poets and sculptors; the protest—
ever growing in violence—which began to be made
against this at the end of the nineteenth century, must
be welcome; but before we consign the many superfluous names to a deserved oblivion, we would express
our admiration of the phenomenon as a whole; it gives
evidence of a supremacy of good taste which is always
desirable, of a fineness of judgment never since equalled,
and of a widespread creative impulse. Greek art was a
truly "living" thing, and so it is alive to-day. That which
lives is immortal. It possessed a solid, organic central
point, and obeyed a spontaneous and therefore unerring
impulse, which knitted into one creative artistic whole of
the most varied luxuriance the most trifling fragments,
and even the wildest excrescences. In short—if I
may be forgiven for the apparent tautology—Hellenic art
was an artistic art, and no individual, not even a Homer,
could make it that; it could only become such by the
united efforts of a whole body of artists. Since that
time nothing similar has happened, and so it is that
Greek art not only still lives, works and preaches in
our midst, but the greatest of our artists (of our artistic

creators of actions, sounds, words, figures) have in the nineteenth century as in former ages felt themselves drawn to Greece as to a home. Among us the man of the people has only an indirect knowledge of Greek art ; for him the gods have not, as for Epicurus, ascended a still higher Olympus ; they have been hurled down and dashed to pieces by rude Asiatic scepticism and rude Asiatic superstition ; but he meets them on our fountains and theatre curtains, in the park, whither he resorts on Sundays for fresh air, and in the museums, where sculpture has always had a greater attraction for the masses than painting. The " man of culture " carries fragments of this art in his head as the undigested material of education : names rather than living conceptions ; yet he meets it too frequently at every step, to be able ever to lose sight of it completely ; it has a greater share in the building of his intellect than he himself is aware of. The artist, on the other hand—and here I mean every artistic mind— cannot help turning eyes of longing to Greece, not merely because of the individual works which arose there— for among us too many a glorious thing has been created since the year 1200 : Dante stands alone, Shakespeare is greater and richer than Sophocles, the art of a Bach would have been a complete novelty for a Greek—no, what the artist finds there and misses here is the artistic element, artistic culture. Since the time of the Romans, European life has had a political basis : and now it is gradually becoming economic. Whereas among the Greeks no free man could venture to be a merchant, among us every artist is a born slave : art is for us a luxury, a realm of caprice ; it is not a State necessity, and it does not lay down for our public life the law that the feeling for beauty should pervade everything. Even in Rome it was the caprice of a single Mæcenas that called poetry into life, and

since that time the greatest achievements of the most
glorious minds have depended largely on a Pope's passion
for building, on the conceit of a prince educated in the
classics, or on the extravagant taste of a pompous commercial guild.   Now and then a lifegiving breath was
wafted from higher spheres, as, for example, from the
religious New Birth which the great and saintly Francis
of Assisi tried to bring about—a movement which gave
the first impetus to our modern art of painting—or from
the gradual awakening of the German soul to which we
owe that glorious new art German music.   But what
has become of the pictures ?   The wall-paintings were
covered over with plaster because they were thought
ugly ; the pictures were torn from the sacred places of
worship and hung side by side on the walls of museums ;
and then—because otherwise the evolution up to these
most treasured masterpieces could not have been scientifically explained—the plaster was scratched off, well
or badly as the case might be, the pious monks were
turned out and cloisters and *campi santi* became a second
class of museums.   Music fared little better ; I have
myself been present at a concert where J. S. Bach's
" Passion of Matthew " was given.   It was in one of
the capitals of Europe—which, moreover, is specially
famed for its educated musical taste—and here every
" number " was followed by applause and the Chorale
" O Haupt voll Blut und Wunden " was actually received
with cries of " Da capo " !   We have much that the
Greeks did not possess, but such instances are clear yet
painful proofs of how much is lacking in us that they
possessed.   One can well understand how Hölderlin
could exclaim to the artist of to-day :

> Stirb ! Du suchst auf diesem Erdenrunde,
> Edler Geist, umsonst dein Element !
> (Die!   Thou seekest on this earthly ball,
> In vain, O noble mind, thine element !)

It is not lack of inner strength or of originality that draws the heart of the artist of to-day to Greece, but the consciousness and the experience that the individual, by himself, cannot be really original. For originality is quite different from caprice; originality is the free pursuit of the path involuntarily marked out for itself by the particular nature of the personality in question; but the artist can only find this freedom where he is surrounded by a thoroughly artistic culture; such a culture he cannot find to-day. It would of course be absolutely unjust to deny to our European world of to-day artistic impulses: the interest in music shows that men's minds are in a mighty ferment, and modern painting is laying hold upon well-defined but at the same time extensive circles, and rousing an enthusiasm which amounts to an almost uncanny passion, but all this remains outside the life of the nations, it is a supplement—for hours of leisure and men of leisure; and so fashion and caprice and manifold hypocrisy are predominant, and the atmosphere in which the genuine artist lives lacks all elasticity. Even the most powerful genius is now bound, hemmed in, repelled on many sides. And so Hellenic art lives on in our midst as a lost ideal, which we must strive to recover.

SHAPING

Under a happier star Hellenic philosophy and natural science enjoy with us children of the nineteenth and twentieth centuries a hospitality gladly and gratefully bestowed. Here too it is not a question of mere *lares*, or worship of ancestry; on the contrary, Hellenic philosophy is very much alive among us, and Hellenic science, so helpless on the one hand, and so incredibly powerful in intuition on the other, compels us to take in it not merely an historical but also a living interest. The pure joy excited in us by contemplating Greek thought may be due, to some extent, to the consciousness that we have advanced so much further here than our great ancestors. Our philosophy has become more philosophical, our science more scientific : an advance which, unfortunately, we do not find in the domain of art. So far as philosophy and science are concerned, our modern culture has shown itself worthy of its Hellenic origin ; we have a good conscience.

It cannot pertain to my purpose here to point out connections of which every educated man must be aware. These connections, so far as philosophy is concerned, are purely genetic, since it was only through contact with Greek thought that modern thought awoke, acquiring from it indeed that power of contradiction and independence which was the last to reach maturity : so far as mathematics, the foundation of all science, are concerned, they were equally genetic ; in the case of the sciences of observation * they were less genetic, and in former years rather a hindrance than a help. My one task must be to explain in a few words what secret power gave these old thoughts such a tenacious spirit of life.

How much of what has been done since has passed into everlasting oblivion, while Plato and Aristotle, Democritus, Euclid and Archimedes still live on in our midst, inspiring and teaching us, and while the half-fabulous form of Pythagoras grows greater with every century ! †
And I am of opinion that what gives everlasting youth to the thought of a Democritus, a Plato, a Euclid, an

* With regard to the last point one must, however, remark that many a splendid achievement of Hellenic talent in this sphere remained unknown to us till a short time ago.

† This is a return to a former view. When the Romans were commanded by an oracle to erect a statue to the wisest of the Hellenes, they put up the statue of Pythagoras (Plutarch, *Numa*, chap. xi.).

Aristarchus * is that same spirit, that same mental power which makes Homer and Phidias ever young : it is the creative and—in the widest sense of the word—the really artistic element. For the important thing is that the conception by which man seeks to master the inner world of his Ego, or the outer world, and assimilate them in himself, should be sharply defined and shaped with absolute clearness. If we glance back at about three thousand years of history, we shall see that while the human mind has certainly been broadened by the knowledge of new facts, it has been enriched only by new ideas, that is, by new conceptions. This is that creative power, of which Goethe speaks in the *Wanderjahre*, which "glorifies nature" and without which in his opinion "the outer world would remain cold and lifeless." † But its creations are lasting only when beautiful and perspicuous, that is, artistic.

> As imagination bodies forth
> The forms of things unknown, the poet's pen
> Turns them to shapes.
> SHAKESPEARE.

But only those conceptions which have been transformed into shapes form a lasting possession of human consciousness. The supply of facts is ever changing, hence the centre of gravity of the Actual (if I may so express it) is subject to constant shifting ; besides, about the half of our knowledge or even more is provisional : what was yesterday regarded as true is false to-day ; nor can the future change anything in this respect, since the multiplication of the material of knowledge keeps pace with the extension of knowledge itself.‡ On the other hand, that which man in the capacity of

---

* Aristarchus of Samos, the discoverer of the so-called Copernican system of the world.

† One sees that according to Goethe a creative act of the human mind is necessary, in order that life itself may become "living" !

‡ A general text-book of botany or of zoology of the year 1875 is, for example, useless to-day, and that not solely or even chiefly

artist has formed, the figure into which he has breathed the breath of life, does not decay. I must repeat what I have already said : what lives is immortal. We know that to-day most zoologists teach the theory of immortality—physical immortality—of the germ-plasma ; the gulf between organic and inorganic, that is, between living and dead nature, which at the beginning of the nineteenth century was thought to have been bridged,

because of the new material collected, but because actual relations are viewed differently and exact observations are overthrown by still more exact ones. Trace, for example, the dogma of Imbibition with its endless series of observations from its first appearance in 1838 to its point of highest popularity, about 1868 ; then begins the countermine and in the year 1898 the zealous student hears no more about it. It is particularly interesting to observe how in zoology, in which at the beginning of the nineteenth century great simplification had been considered possible and in which, under Darwin's influence, there had been an effort to reduce, if possible, all animal forms to one single family, now, as our knowledge has gradually increased, an ever greater complication of the original scheme of types has revealed itself. Cuvier thought four " general structure-plans " sufficient. Soon, however, it was necessary to recognise seven different types, all disconnected, and about thirty years ago Carl Claus found that nine was the minimum. But this minimum is not enough. When we disregard all but the convenience and needs of the beginner (Richard Hertwig's well-known and otherwise excellent text-book is an example), when we weigh structural differences against each other without reference to richness of forms and so on—we find now that anatomical knowledge is more thorough, that not less than sixteen different groups, all equally important as types, must be taken into account. (See especially the masterly Lehrbuch der Zoologie, by Fleischmann, 1898.)—At the same time opinions with regard to many fundamental zoological facts have been quite changed by more exact knowledge. For instance, twenty years ago when I studied zoology under Karl Vogt it was considered an established fact that worms stood in direct genetic relation to vertebrates ; even such critically independent Darwinists as Vogt considered this settled and could tell many splendid things about the worm, which had developed as high as man. In the meantime much more accurate and comprehensive investigations on the development of animals in the embryo have led to the recognition of the fact that there are two great groups inside the " metazoa " (which comprises animals that do not consist of simple separable cells), the development of which from the moment of the fecundation of the embryo proceeds on quite different lines, so that every true—not merely apparent—relationship between them is out of the question, not only the genetic relationship which the evolutionists assume, but also the purely architectonic. And behold ! the worms belong to

becomes deeper every day ; * this is not the proper place for a discussion on the subject ; I merely adduce this fact by way of analogy, to justify me in extending to the intellectual sphere the sharp distinction which I have drawn between organised and inorganised conceptions, and in expressing my conviction that nothing which the style of the creative artist has formed into a living figure has ever yet died. Cataclysms may bury

the one group (which reaches its highest point in the insects), and the vertebrates belong to the other and might as well be said to be descended from cuttle-fishes and sea-urchins ! (*Cf.* especially Karl Camillo Schneider : *Grundzüge der tierischen Organisation* in the *Preussische Jahrbücher*, 1900, July number, p. 73 ff.) Such facts serve to prove and confirm what has been said on p. 42, and it is absolutely necessary that the layman, who is ever apt to suppose that the science of his time is perfection, should learn to recognise in it only a transition stage between a past and a future theory.

* *See*, for example, the standard work of the American zoologist, E. B. Wilson (Professor in Columbia) : *The Cell in Development and Inheritance*, 1896, where we read : " The investigation of cell activity has on the whole rather widened than narrowed the great gulf which separates the lowest forms of life from the phenomena of the inorganic world." Privy Councillor Wiesner lately assured me of the absolute correctness of this statement from the standpoint of pure natural science. Wilson's book has in the meantime (1900) appeared in a second enlarged edition. The sentence quoted stands unaltered on p. 434. The whole of the last chapter, *Theories of Inheritance and Development*, is to be recommended to all who desire not mere phrases but real insight into the present state of scientific knowledge with reference to the important facts of the animal form. They will find a chaos. As the author says (p. 434), " The extraordinary dimensions of the problem of development, whether ontogenetic or phylogenetic, have been underestimated." Now it is recognised that every newly discovered phenomenon does not bring enlightenment and simplification, but new confusion and new problems, so that a well-known embryologist (*see* Introduction) lately exclaimed : " Every animal embryo seems to carry its own law in itself ! " Rabl arrives at similar results in his investigations on *Der Bau und die Entwickelung der Linse* (1900) ; he finds that every animal form possesses its specific organs of sense, the differences between which are already conditioned in the embryo cell. And thus by the progress of true science—as distinguished from the nonsense regarding power and matter, with which generations of credulous laymen have been befooled—our view of life became always " more living," and the day is surely not far distant when it will be recognised as more reasonable to try to interpret the dead from the standpoint of the living than the other way about. (I refer to my *Immanuel Kant*, p. 482 f.)

such figures, but centuries later they once more emerge in perpetual youth from their supposed grave ; it frequently occurs also that the children of thought, like their brothers and sisters, the marble statues, become maimed, broken or even completely shattered ; that is, however, a mechanical destruction, not death.   And thus Plato's theory of ideas, more than one thousand years old, has been a living factor in the intellectual life of the nineteenth century, an " origin " of very many thoughts ;   almost every philosophical speculation of importance has been connected with it at one point or another.   In the meantime the spirit of Democritus has been paramount in natural science : fundamental as were the alterations that had to be made on his brilliant theory of atoms in order to adapt it to the knowledge of to-day, he still remains the inventor, the artist.   It is he who, to use the language of Shakespeare, has by the force of his imagination bodied forth "the forms of things unknown," and then "turned them to shapes."

PLATO

Instances of the manner in which Hellenic creative power has given life and efficacy to thought are not difficult to find.   Take Plato's philosophy.   His material is not new ; he does not sit down, like Spinoza, to evolve a logical system of the world out of the depths of his own consciousness ;   nor does he with the splendid simplicity of Descartes reach into the bowels of nature, in the delusion that he will there find as explanation of the world a kind of clockwork ; he rather takes here and there what seems to him the best—from the Eleatics, from Heraclitus, the Pythagoreans, Socrates —and forms out of this no really logical, but certainly an artistic, whole.   The relation of Plato to the former philosophers of Greece is not at all unlike that of Homer

to past and contemporary poets. Homer, too, probably
"invented" nothing, just as little as Shakespeare
did later on; but from various sources he laid hold
of that which suited his purpose and welded it into a
new whole, something thoroughly individual, endowed
with the incomparable qualities of the living individual
and burthened with the limitations, failings, and
peculiarities inseparably bound up with his nature—for
every individual says with the God of the Egyptian
mysteries: "I am who I am," and stands before us
a new, inscrutable, unfathomable thing.* Similar is
Plato's philosophy. Professor Zeller, the famous historian
of Greek philosophy, expresses the opinion that "Plato
is too much of a poet to be quite a philosopher." It
would probably be difficult to extract any definite sense
out of this criticism. Heaven knows what a philosopher
in abstracto may be. Plato was himself, and no one
else, and his example shows us how a mind had to be
fashioned in order that Greek thought might yield its
highest fruit. He is the Homer of this thought. If a
competent man were to analyse the doctrine of Plato in
such a way that we could clearly see what portions are
the original property of the great thinker, not merely
by the process of reproduction through genius but as
entirely new inventions, then the poetical element in
his work would certainly become specially clear. For
Montesquieu, too (in his *Pensées*), calls Plato one of the
four great poets of mankind. Especially that which
is blamed as inconsistent and contradictory would reveal
itself as an artistic necessity. Life is in itself a contradiction : *la vie est l'ensemble des fonctions qui résistent à
la mort*, said the great Bichat; each living thing has
therefore something fragmentary about it, something

* "A genuine work of art is, like a work of nature, always infinite
to our mind ; it is seen, felt ; it produces its effect, but it cannot really
be known, much less can its essence, its merit, be expressed in words."
(Goethe.)

which might be called arbitrary ; the addition which man makes to it—a free, poetical and only conditionally valid addition—is the sole thing that makes the joining of the two ends of the magic girdle possible.   Works of art are no exception.   Homer's *Iliad* is a splendid example of this, Plato's philosophy a second, Democritus' theory of the world a third of equal importance.   And while the philosophies and theories so finely carved by the " logical " method disappear one after the other in the gulf of time, these old ideas take their place in all the freshness of youth, side by side with the most recent. Clearly it is not " objective truth," but the manner in which things receive shape, *l'ensemble des fonctions*, as Bichat would say, that is the decisive thing.

Still another remark in reference to Plato ; again it is only a hint—for the space at my disposal will not allow of lengthy treatment—but enough, I hope, to leave nothing vague.   That Indian thought has exercised an influence of quite a determinative character upon Greek philosophy is now a settled fact ; our Hellenists and philosophers have, it is true, long combated this with the violent obstinacy of prejudiced scholars ; everything was supposed to have originated in Hellas as *autochthon ;* at most the Egyptians and the Semites were allowed to have exercised a moulding influence—whereby philosophy would in truth have had little to gain ; the more modern Indologists, however, have confirmed the conjectures of the oldest (particularly of that genius Sir William Jones).   It has been fully proved in regard to Pythagoras especially that he had a thorough knowledge of Indian doctrines,* and as Pythagoras is being recognised more and more as the ancestor of Greek thought, that in itself means a great deal.   Besides, direct influence upon the Eleatics, Heraclitus, Anaxagoras, Democritus, &c., has been

* *Cf.* on this point Schroeder : *Pythagoras und die Inder* (1884):

shown to be most probable.* In these circumstances it cannot be surprising that so lofty a spirit as Plato forced his way through much misleading extraneous matter and—especially in reference to some essential points in all genuine metaphysics—endorses in every detail some of the sublimest views of Indian thinkers.† But compare Plato and the Indians, his works and their works! Then we shall no longer wonder why Plato lives and influences, while the Indian philosophers live indeed but do not directly affect the wide world and the progress of mankind. Indian thought is unsurpassed in depth and comprehensive many-sidedness; if Professor Zeller thought that Plato was " too much of a poet to be quite a philosopher," we see from the example of the Indian what becomes of a philosopher when a thinker is too " completely " a philosopher to be at the same time something of a poet. This pure thinking of the Indians lacks all capacity of being communicated—and we find this simply but at the same time profoundly expressed by the Indians themselves, for according to their books the highest and final wisdom can be taught only by silence.‡ How different the Greek! Cost what it

* The best summary account of recent times that is known to me is that of Garbe in his *Sâmkhya-Philosophie* (1894), p. 85 f.; there we also find the most important bibliography.

† For the comparison between Plato and the Indians in reference to the recognition of the empirical reality and transcendental ideality of experience *see* specially Max Müller : *Three Lectures on the Vedânta Philosophy* (1894), p. 128 f. Plato's relation to the Eleatics becomes hereby for the first time clear. Fuller information in Deussen's works, especially in his lecture, " On the Philosophy of the Vedânta in Relation to the Metaphysical Doctrines of the West," Bombay, 1893.

‡ " When Bâhva was questioned by Vâshkali, the former explained Brahmanism to him by remaining silent. And Vâshkali said, ' Teach me, O revered one, Brahmanism ! ' But the latter remained quite silent. When now the other for the second or third time asked, he said, ' I am indeed teaching you it, but you do not understand it ; this Brahmanism is silence.' " (Sankara in the *Sûtra's of Vedânta*, iii. 2, 17). And in the *Taittiriya Upanishad* we read (ii. 4) : " From the great joy of knowledge all language and all thought turn away, unable to reach it."

might, he must "body forth the forms of things un-known and give them shape." Read in this connection the laboured explanation in Plato's *Theætetus*, where Socrates ultimately admits that we may possess truth without being able to explain it, but that this is not knowledge; what knowledge is remains certainly un-decided at the end (a proof of Plato's profundity!); however, in the culminating-point of the dialogue it is termed "right conception," and the remark is made that we must be able to give a reasoned explanation of right conception; we should also read in this connection the famous passage in the *Timæus*, where the cosmos is compared to a "living animal." It must be conceived and endowed with shape : that is the secret of the Greek, from Homer to Archimedes. Plato's theory of ideas bears exactly the same relation to metaphysics as De-mocritus' theory of atoms to the physical world : they are creations of a freely creative, shaping power and in them, as in all works of art, there wells up an inexhaustible fountain of symbolical truth. Such creations bear the same relation to material facts as the sun to the flowers. Hellenic influence has not been an unqualified blessing : much that we have received from the Greeks still weighs like a nightmare upon our struggling culture. But the goodly inheritance which we hold from them has been first and foremost this flower-compelling sunshine.

ARISTOTLE

It was under the direct influence of Plato that Aristotle, one of the mightiest sages that the world has ever seen, shot up into the empyrean. The nature of his intellect accounts for the fact that in certain respects he de-veloped as the opposite of Plato : but without Plato he would never have become a philosopher, at any rate not a metaphysician. A critical appreciation of this

great man would take me too far : I could not do it
adequately even if I were to limit myself to the scope
and object of this chapter. I could not, however, pass
him by unnoticed, and I take it for granted that no one
fails to admire the creative power that he revealed in
his logical *Organon*, his *Animal History*, his *Poetics*, &c.
These have been the admiration of all ages. To appropriate a remark of Scotus Erigena : it was in the sphere
of *naturalium rerum discretio* that he achieved unparalleled
results and won the gratitude of the most distant generations. Aristotle's greatness lies not in the fact that he was
right—no man of the first rank has made more frequent
or more flagrant mistakes—but in the fact that he
knew no peace, till he had wrought in all spheres of
human life and evolved order out of chaos.* In so far
he is a genuine Hellene. Certainly we have paid dear
for this " order." Aristotle was less of a poet than
perhaps any of the great philosophers of Greece ; Herder
says of him that he was perhaps the driest writer that
ever used a stylus ; † he must, I fancy, be " philosopher
enough " even for Professor Zeller ; certainly he was
this in a sufficient degree—thanks to his Hellenic creative
power—to sow more persistent error in the world than
any man before or after him. Till a short time ago
he had paralysed the natural sciences at all points ;
philosophy and especially metaphysics have not yet
shaken off his yoke ; our theology is, if I might call it
so, his natural child. In truth, this great and important
legacy of the old world was a two-edged sword. I shall
return shortly in another connection to Aristotle and
Greek philosophy ; here I shall only add that the Greeks
certainly had great need of an Aristotle to lay emphasis

---

* Eucken says in his essay, *Thomas von Aquin und Kant*, p. 30
(*Kantstudien*, 1901, vi. p. 12) : The intellectual work of Aristotle
is " an artistic or more accurately speaking a plastic shaping."
† *Ideen zur Geschichte der Menschheit*, XIII., chap. v.

upon empiric methods and in all things to recommend the golden mean ; in their brilliant exuberance of pride and creative impulse they were inclined to dash upwards and onwards with thoughtless disregard of the serious ground of reality, and this in time was bound to have a baneful influence ; it is nevertheless characteristic that Aristotle, Greek as he was, exercised comparatively little influence, to begin with, on the development of Greek intellectual life ; the healthy instinct of a people that rejoiced in creating rebelled against a reaction which was so fatally violent, and had perhaps a vague feeling that this pretended empiricist brought with him as his curative medicine the poison of dogma. Aristotle was, of course, by profession a doctor—he was a fine example of the doctor who kills to cure. But this first patient of his had a will of his own ; he preferred to save himself by flying to the arms of the neo-Platonic quack. But we, hapless posterity, have inherited as our legacy both doctor and quack, who drench our healthy bodies with their drugs. Heaven help us !

NATURAL SCIENCE

One word more about Hellenic science. It is only natural that the scientific achievements of the Greeks should hardly possess for us anything more than an historical interest. But what cannot be indifferent to us is the perception of the incredible advances which were made in the correct interpretation of nature when newly discovered artistic capacities began to develop and exercise influence. We are involuntarily reminded of Schiller's statement that we cannot separate the phantom from the real without at the same time purging the real of the phantom.

If there is a sphere in which one might expect less than nothing from the Greeks, it is that of geography. What we remember having read in their poems—the

wanderings of Odysseus and of Io, &c.—seemed to us rather
confused and was rendered still more confusing by contradictory commentaries. Moreover, up to the time of
Alexander, the Greeks did not travel far. But if we
glance at Dr. Hugo Berger's *Geschichte der wissenschaft-
lichen Erdkunde der Griechen*, a strictly scientific work,
we shall be lost in amazement. At school we learn
at most something of Ptolemæus, and his geographical
map strikes us as almost as curious as his heavenly
spheres encased in each other ; that, however, is all the
result of a period of decay, of a science wonderfully
perfect, which, however, had become weak in intuition,
the science of a raceless chaos of peoples. Let us, on
the other hand, inquire into the geographical conceptions of the genuine Greeks, from Anaximander to
Eratosthenes, and we shall understand Berger's assertion:
" The achievements of the remarkably gifted Greek nation
in the sphere of scientific geography are indeed worth
investigating. Even to-day we find their traces at every
step and cannot do without the foundations laid by
them " (i. p. vi.). Particularly striking are the comparatively widespread knowledge and the healthy conceptive power possessed by the ancient Ionians. There
was serious falling off later, due especially to the
influence of " the despisers of physics, meteorology and
mathematics, the cautious people, who would believe
only their own eyes or the credible information
gained at first hand by eye-witnesses " (i. 139). Still
later, investigators had further to contend with so
deeply rooted scientific prejudices that the voyages of
the " first North Pole explorer," Pytheas (a contemporary
of Aristotle), with their accurate descriptions of the coasts
of Gaul and Britain, their narratives of the sea of ice,
their decisive observations with regard to the length of
day and night in the northern latitudes were declared
by all scholars of antiquity to be lies (iii. 7, compare the

opinion of men of to-day, iii. 36).   Philipp Paulitschke
in his work, *Die geographische Erforschung des afrikan-
ischen Kontinents* (second edition, p. 9), calls attention
to the fact that Herodotus possessed a more accurate
conception of the outlines of Africa than Ptolemæus.
The latter, however, was considered an " authority."·
Thereby hangs a tale, and it is with genuine regret that
I establish the fact that we have inherited from the
Hellenes not only the results of their " remarkable
ability," as Berger puts it, but also their mania for
creating " authorities " and believing in them.   In this
connection the history of palæontology is specially instructive. With the artless simplicity of unspoiled intuitive
power the ancient Greeks had, long before Plato and
Aristotle, noticed the mussels on mountain-tops, and
recognised even the impressions of fishes for what they
are ; upon these observations men like Xenophanes
and Empedocles had based theories of historical development and geocyclic doctrines.   But the authorities declared this view to be absurd ; when the facts multiplied,
they were simply explained away by the grand theory of
vis plastica ; * and it was not till the year 1517 that a
man ventured once more to express the old opinion,
that the mountain-tops once lay beneath the sea : " in
the year of the Reformation, accordingly, after 1500
years, knowledge had reached the point at which it had
stood in classical antiquity." † Fracastorius' idea received but scant support, and should it be desired to
estimate—it is really very difficult after the advance of
science—how great and venerable a power of truth lay in
the seeing eye of these ancient poets (Xenophanes and
Empedocles were in the first place poets and singers), I
recommend the student to consult the writings of the

* According to Quenstedt this hypothesis is due to Avicenna ; but
it is to be traced back to Aristotle and was taught definitely by Theophrastus (*see* Lyell, *Principles of Geology,* 12th ed., i. 20).

† Quenstedt, *Handbuch der Petrefaktenkunde,* 2nd ed., p. 2.

free-thinker Voltaire and to see what abuse he hurled at the palæontologists even as late as the year 1768.* Just as amusing are the frantic efforts of his scepticism to resist evidence. Oysters had been found on Mont Cenis : Voltaire is of opinion that they fell from the hats of Roman pilgrims ! Hippopotamus bones had been dug up not far from Paris : Voltaire declares *un curieux a eu autrefois dans son cabinet le squelette d'un hippopotame !* Evidently scepticism does not suffice to clear a man's sight.† On the other hand, the oldest poems provide us with examples of peculiar discernment. Even in the *Iliad*, for instance, Poseidon is called the " shaker of the earth," this god, that is, water and especially the sea, is always mentioned as the cause of earthquakes : that is exactly in accordance with the results arrived at by science to-day. However, I wish merely to point to such features as a contrast to the ignorance of those heroes of a pretended " age of enlightenment."—Much more striking examples of the freeing of the real from the phantom are met with in the sphere of astrophysics, especially in the school of Pythagoras. The theory of the spherical shape of the earth is found in the earliest adepts, and even a great deal that is fantastic in the conceptions of these ancients is rich in instruction, because it contains in a manner *in nuce* what afterwards proved to be correct.‡ And so

* See *Des singularités de la Nature*, chaps. xii. to xviii., and *L'Homme aux quarante écus*, chap. vi., both written in the year 1768. Similar remarks in his letters (*see* especially, *Lettre sur un écrit anonyme*, 19.4.1772).

† This same Voltaire had the presumption to describe the great astronomical speculations of the Pythagoreans as " galimatias," on which the famous astronomist Schiaparelli remarks with justice : " Such men do not deserve to understand what great speculative power was necessary to attain to a conception of the spherical form of the earth, of its free floating in space and its mobility : ideas without which we should have had neither a Copernicus nor a Kepler, a Galileo nor a Newton " (*see* the work mentioned below, p. 16).

‡ Zeller, *Die Philosophie der Griechen*, 5th ed., Pt. I., p. 414 ff. More technical, but explained with remarkable lucidity in the work of

in the case of the Pythagoreans, as time went on, to the theory of the earth as a sphere and the inclination of its orbit, there was added that of its revolving on its axis, and that of motion round a central point in space, vouched for from Philolæus, a contemporary of Democritus, onward ; a generation later the hypothetical " central fire " had been replaced by the sun.   Not of course as a philosopher, but as an astronomer, Aristarchus had at a later time (about 250 B.C.) founded the heliocentric system upon clear lines and had undertaken to calculate the distance from sun and moon, and recognised in the sun (1900 years before Giordano Bruno) one of the countless fixed stars.*

Schiaparelli, *Die Vorläufer des Kopernikus im Altertum* (translated into German from the Italian original by the author and M. Curtze, published in the *Altpreussische Monatsschrift*, 1876).   "We are in a position to assert that the development of the physical principles of this school was bound by logical connection of ideas to lead to the theory of the earth's motion" (*see* 5 f.).   More details of the "really revolutionary view, that it is not the earth that occupies the centre of the universe," in the recently published book of Wilhelm Bauer, *Der ältere Pythagoreismus* (1897), p. 54 ff. 64 ff. &c.   The essay too of Ludwig Ideler, *Über das Verhältnis des Kopernikus zum Altertum* in the *Museum für Altertumswissenschaft*, published by Fr. Aug. Wolf, 1810, p. 391 ff., is still worth reading.

* " Aristarchus puts the sun among the number of the fixed stars and makes the earth move through the apparent track of the sun (that, is the ecliptic), and declares that it is eclipsed according to its inclination," says Plutarch. For this and the other evidences in reference to Aristarchus compare the above-mentioned book of Schiaparelli (pp. 121 ff. and 219). This astronomer is moreover convinced that Aristarchus only taught what was already discovered at the time of Aristotle (p. 117), and here too he shows how the method adopted by the Pythagoreans was bound to lead to the correct solution.   But for Aristotle and neo-Platonism the heliocentric system would, even at the time of Christ's birth, have been generally accepted ; in truth, the Stagyrite has honestly deserved his position as official philosopher of the orthodox church !   On the other hand, the story of the Egyptians having contributed something to the solution of the astrophysical problem has been proved to be quite unfounded, like so many other Egyptian stories (Schiaparelli, pp. 105–6). Moreover Copernicus himself tells us in his introduction dedicated to Pope Paul III.: "I first found in Cicero that Nicetus had believed that the earth moved.   Afterwards I found also in Plutarch that some others had likewise been of this opinion.   This was what caused me too to begin to think about the earth's mobility."

What imaginative power, what capacity of bodying forth, as Shakespeare calls it, this presupposes is clearly seen by later history : Bruno had to pay for his imaginative power with his life, Galileo with his freedom ; it was not till the year 1822 (2000 years after Aristarchus) that the Roman Church took the work of Copernicus off the Index and sanctioned the printing of books which taught that the earth moves, without, however, annulling or in any way lessening the validity of the Papal bulls, in which it is forbidden to believe in the motion of the earth.* We must, moreover, always bear in mind that it was the Pythagoreans, who were decried as mystagogues, who led up to this brilliant " purging the real of phantom," and they were supported by the idealist Plato, particularly towards the end of his life, whereas the herald of the sole saving grace of induction, Aristotle, attacked the theory of the motion of the earth with the whole weight of his empiricism. . ".The Pythagoreans," he writes, in reference to the theory of the earth's turning on its axis, which he denied, " do not deduce grounds and causes from phenomena observed, but endeavour to make phenomena harmonise with views and assumptions of their own ; they thus attempt to interfere with the formation of the world " (*De Cælo*, ii. 13). This contrast should certainly give pause to many of our contemporaries ; for we have no lack of natural scientists who still cling to Aristotle, and in our newest scientific theories there is still as much stiff-necked dogmatism as in the Aristotelian and Semitic doctrines grafted upon the Christian Church.†—The progress of mathematics and especially of geometry affords us in quite a different

---

* *Cf.* Franz Xaver Kraus in the *Deutsche Literaturzeitung*, 1900, Nr. 1.
† What the English scientist, John Tyndall, in his well-known speech in Belfast, 1874, said, " Aristotle put words in the place of things ; he preached induction, without practising it," will be considered by later ages as just as apt for many an Ernst Haeckel of the nineteenth century. It should also be mentioned that the system of

form a proof of the life-giving influence of Greek creative power. Pythagoras is the founder of scientific mathematics in Europe ; that he owed his knowledge, especially the so-called " Pythagorean theorem," the idea of irrational magnitudes, and—very probably—also his arithmetic, to the Indians is of course an established fact,* and with regard to abstract arithmetical calculation, the so-called " Arabian cyphers " which we owe to the Aryan Indians, Cantor says, " Algebra attained among the Indians to a height which it has never been able to reach in Greece." † But see to what transparent perfection the Greeks have brought formal mathematics, geometry ! In the school of Plato was educated Euclid, whose *Elements of Geometry* are such a perfect work of art that it would be exceedingly regrettable if the introduction of simplified and more modern methods of teaching were to remove such a jewel from the horizon of educated people. Perhaps I should be expressing my partiality for mathematics too simply if I confessed that Euclid's *Elements* seem to me almost as fine as Homer's *Iliad*. At any rate I may look upon it as no accident that the incomparable geometrician was also an enthusiastic musician, whose *Elements of Music*, if we possessed them in the original form, would perhaps form a worthy counterpart to his *Elements of Geometry*. And here I may recognise the cognate poetical spirit, that power of bodying forth and of giving an artistic form to conceptions. This sunbeam will not readily be extinguished. Let me here make a remark which is of the highest importance for our subject : it was the almost pure poetry of arithmetical theory and geometry that caused the Greeks at a later

Tycho de Brahe is also of Hellenic origin ; *see* details in Schiaparelli, (p. 107 ff. and especially p. 115) ; no possible combination could indeed escape the richness of this imagination.
  * *See* Leopold von Schroeder : *Pythagoras und die Inder*, p. 39 ff.
  † Cantor : *Vorlesungen über Geschichte der Mathematik*, i. 511 (quoted from Schroeder, p. 56).

time to become the founders of scientific mechanics. As in the case of everything Hellenic so here too the meditation of many minds received shape and living power in the life-work of one single all-powerful genius : the " century of mechanics " has, I think, every reason to venerate Archimedes as its father.

PUBLIC LIFE

Inasmuch as I am only concerned here with the achievements and the individuality of the Greeks in so far as they were important factors in our modern culture and living elements of the nineteenth century, much must be omitted, though in connection with what has been said, one would be tempted to go into more detail. Rohde told us above that creative art was the unifying force for all Greece. Then we saw art—widening gradually to philosophy and science—laying the foundations of a harmony of thinking, feeling and knowing. This next spread to the sphere of public life. The endless care devoted to the development of beautiful, powerful human frames followed artistic rules; the poet had created the ideals, which people henceforth strove to realise. Every one knows how great importance was attached to music in Greek education; even in rough Sparta it was highly honoured and cultivated. The great statesmen have all a direct connection with art or philosophy : Thales, the politician, the practical man, is at the same time lauded as the first philosopher and the first mathematician and astronomer ; Empedocles, the daring rebel, who deals the death-blow to the supremacy of the aristocracy in his native city, the inventor of public oratory (as Aristotle tells us), is also poet, mystic, philosopher, natural investigator and evolutionist. Solon is essentially a poet and a singer, Lycurgus was the first to collect the Homeric poems and that too " in the interests of the State and of morality."* Pisistratus is another instance : the creator of the Theory of Ideas is statesman and reformer ; it was Cimon who prepared for Polygnotus a suitable sphere of activity, and Pericles did the same for Phidias. As Hesiod puts it, " Justice (Diké) is the maiden daughter of Zeus " † and in this observation is contained a definite philosophy embracing all state relations, a philosophy which though also religious is mainly artistic ; all literature, too, even the most abstruse writings of Aristotle, and even remarks like that of Xenophanes (meant, indeed, as a reproach) that the Greeks were accustomed to derive all their culture from Homer,‡ testify to the same fact. In Egypt, in Judea, and later in Rome we see the law-giver laying down the rules of religion and worship ; among the Teutonic peoples the king decrees what his people shall believe ; § in Hellas the reverse holds good : it is the poet, the " creator of the race of gods," the poetical philosopher (Anaxagoras, Plato, &c.), who understands how to lead all men to profound conceptions of the divine and the moral. And those men who—in the period of its greatness—give the land its laws, have been educated in the school of these same poets and philosophers. When Herodotus gives each separate book of his history the name of a Muse, when Plato makes Socrates deliver his finest speeches only in the most beautiful spots inhabited by nymphs, and represents him as closing dialectical discussions with an invocation to Pan " Oh, grant that I may be inwardly beautiful.

---

* Plutarch, *Life of Lycurgus*, chap. iv.
† *Work and Days*, 256.
‡ Fragment 4 (quoted from Flach, *Geschichte der griechischen Lyrik*, ii. p. 419).
§ The principle introduced at the time of the Reformation " cujus est regio, illius est religio " only expresses the old condition of law as it existed from time immemorial.

and that my outward appearance may be in harmony with the inner ! "—when the oracle at Thespiæ promises a " land rich in fruits of the soil " to those who " obey the agricultural teaching of the poet Hesiod " *—such traits (and we meet them at every step) point to an artistic atmosphere permeating the whole life : the memory of it has descended to us and coloured many an ideal of our time.

HISTORICAL FALSEHOODS

Hitherto I have spoken almost solely of a positive beneficial inheritance. It would, however, be entirely one-sided and dishonest to let the matter rest there. Our life is permeated with Hellenic suggestions and achievements and I fear that we have adopted the baneful to a greater extent than the good. If Greek intellectual achievements have enabled us to enter the daylight of human life, Greek achievements have, on the other hand—thanks perhaps to the artistic creative power of this remarkable people—also played a great part in casting a mist over the light of day and hiding the sun behind a jealous mask of clouds. Some items of the Hellenic inheritance which we have dragged into the nineteenth century, but which we had been better without, need not be touched upon until we come to deal with that century ; some other points must, however, be taken up here. And in the first place let us consider what lies on the surface of Greek life.

That to-day, for example,—when so much that is great and important claims our whole attention, when we have piled up endless treasures of thought, of poetry

* French excavation of the year 1890. (*See* Peppmüller : *Hesiodos* 1896, p. 152.) One should note also such passages as Aristophanes, *Frogs*, l. 1037 ff.

and above all of knowledge, of which the wisest Greeks
had not the faintest idea and to a share of which every
child should have a prescriptive right—that to-day we are
still compelled to spend valuable time learning every
detail of the wretched history of the Greeks, to stuff
our poor brains with endless registers of names of
vainglorious heroes in *ades, atos, enes, eiton,* &c., and,
if possible, wax enthusiastic over the political fate of
these cruel, short-sighted democracies, blinded with
self-love, and based upon slavery and idleness, is indeed
a hard destiny, the blame for which, however, if we do
but reflect, lies not with the Greeks but with our own
shortsightedness.* Certainly the Greeks frequently set

* I said " cruel " and in fact this trait is one of the most characteristic
of the Hellenes, common to them and the Semites. Humanity,
generosity, pardon were as foreign to them as love of truth. When
they meet these traits for the first time in the Persians, the Greek historians betray an almost embarrassed astonishment : to spare prisoners,
to give a kingly reception to a conquered prince, to entertain and give
presents to envoys of the enemy, instead of killing them (as the Lace-
dæmonians and Athenians did, Herodotus, vii. 119), indulgence to
criminals, generosity even to spies, the assumption that the first duty
of every man is to speak the truth, ingratitude being regarded as a
crime punishable by the State—all this seems to a Herodotus, a Xenophon, almost as ridiculous as the Persian custom not to spit in presence
of others, and other such rules of etiquette (*cf.* Herodotus i,
133 and 138). How is it possible that in the face of such a mass of
indubitable facts our historians can go on systematically falsifying
history ? Leopold van Ranke, for instance, tells in his *Weltgeschichte*
(Text edition, i. 129) the well-known anecdote of the disgraceful treatment of the corpse of Leonidas, and how Pausanias rejected the proposal
to avenge himself by a similar sin against the corpse of the Persian
commander Mardonius, and continues : " This refusal affords food for
endless thought. The contrast between East and West is here expressed in a manner which henceforth was to remain the tradition."
And yet the whole of Greek history is filled with the mutilation not
only of corpses, but of living people, torture, and every kind of cruelty,
falsehood and treachery. And thus, in order to get in a high-sounding
empty phrase, to remain true to the old absurd proverb of the contrast
between Orient and Occident (how ridiculous in a spherical world !),
in order to retain cherished prejudices and give them a stronger
hold than ever, one of the first historians of the nineteenth
century simply puts aside all the facts of history—facts concerning
which even the most ignorant man can inform himself in Duncker,

an example of heroism, though indeed frequently also
of the opposite ; but courage is the commonest of all
human virtues, and the constitution of such a State as
the Lacedæmonian would lead us rather to conclude
that the Hellenes had to be forced to be brave, than
that they naturally possessed the proud contempt of
death which distinguishes every Gallic circus-fighter,
every Spanish toreador and every Turkish Bashi-bazouk.*
" Greek history," says Goethe, " has in it little that is
gratifying—besides, that of our own days is really great
and stirring ; the battles of Leipzig and Waterloo, for
example, after all throw into the shade Marathon and
others like it.   Our own heroes, too, are not behindhand ;
the French marshals, and Blücher and Wellington may
well be put side by side with those of antiquity." †   But
Goethe does not go nearly far enough.   The traditional
history of Greece is, in many points, a huge mystification :
we see that more clearly every day ; and our modern
teachers—under the influence of a " suggestion " that
has completely paralysed their honesty—have falsified it
worse than the Greeks themselves.   With regard to the
battle of Marathon, for example, Herodotus admits quite
honestly that the Greeks were in this battle put to flight,

Geschichte des Altertums ; Gobineau, *Histoire des Perses ;* Maspero, *Les
premières Mêlées des peuples,* &c.—and the credulous student is forced
to accept a manifest untruth with regard to the moral character of
the different human races, on the basis of a doubtful anecdote.   Such
unscrupulous perfidy can only be explained in the case of such a man
by the supposition of a " suggestion " paralysing all judgment.   As a
matter of fact, from India and Persia we derive the one kind of humanity
and generosity and love of truth, from Judea and Arabia the other
(caused by reaction)—but none from Greece, nor from Rome, that is,
therefore, none from the " Occident."   How far removed Herodotus
is from such designed misrepresentation of history ! for, when he has
told of the mutilation of Leonidas, he adds, " Such treatment is not
the custom among the Persians.   They more than all other nations are
wont to honour brave warriors " (vii. 238).
   * Helvétius remarks exquisitely (*De l'Esprit,* ed. 1772, II. 52) :
" La législation de Lycurgue métamorphosait les hommes en héros."
   † Conversation with Eckermann, Nov. 24, 1824.

where they were opposed by Persians and not Hellenes
(iv. 113) ; how this fact is always explained away by us !
And with what infantile credulity—though we know
quite well how utterly unreliable Greek numbers are—
all our historians still copy from the old stories the
number of 6400 Persian slain and 192 Hoplites who met
their death bravely, but omit to mention what Herodotus
in the same chapter (vi. 117) relates with inimitable
artlessness how an Athenian became blind with fright
in that battle. This " glorious victory " was in reality
an unimportant skirmish, in which the Greeks had rather
the worst than the best of it.* The Persians, who had
come to Greece in Ionian ships, not of their own accord,
but because they were invited by the Greeks, returned
in all tranquillity to Ionia with several thousand prisoners
and rich booty, because these ever fickle allies thought the
moment unfavourable (see Herodotus, vi. 118).† In the
same way the whole description of the later struggle
between Hellas and the Persian empire is falsified,‡
but after all we must not criticise the Greeks too harshly

---

* Since these lines were written, I have received the well known English Hellenist Professor Mahaffy's *A Survey of Greek Civilisation*, 1897, in
which the battle of Marathon is termed "a very unimportant skirmish."

† *See* Gobineau : *Histoire des Perses*, ii. 138-142.

‡ Particularly the famous battle of Salamis, of which one gets a
refreshing description in the above-mentioned work of Count Gobineau,
ii. 205-211): " C'est quand les derniers bataillons de l'arrière-garde
de Xerxès eurent disparu dans la direction de la Béotie et que toute
sa flotte fut partie, que les Grecs prirent d'eux-mêmes et de ce qu'ils
venaient de faire et de ce qu'ils pouvaient en dire l'opinion que la
poésie a si heureusement mise en œuvre. Encore fallut-il que les
alliés apprissent que la flotte ennemie ne s'était pas arrêtée à Phalère
pour qu'ils osassent se mettre en mouvement. Ne sachant où elle
allait—ils restaient comme éperdus. Ils se hasardèrent enfin à sortir
de la baie de Salamine, et se risquèrent jusqu'à la hauteur d'Andros.
C'est ce qu'ils appelèrent plus tard avoir poursuivi les Perses !
Ils se gardèrent cependant d'essayer de les joindre, et rebrous-
sant chemin, ils retournèrent chacun dans leurs patries respectives "
(p. 208). In another place (ii, 360) Gobineau characterises Greek
history as " la plus élaborée des fictions du plus artiste des
peuples."

for this, as the same tendency * has manifested and still manifests itself among all other nations. However, if Hellenic history is really to mould the intellect and the judgment, it would need, one would fancy, to be a true, just history, grasping events by their deepest roots and revealing organic connections, not the immortalisation of half-invented anecdotes and views, which could only be excused by the bitterness of the struggle for existence, and the crass ignorance and infatuation of the Greeks. Glorious indeed is the poetic power by which gifted men in that land sought to inspire with patriotic heroism a fickle, faithless, corruptible people inclined to panic, and —where the discipline was firm enough, as in Sparta— actually succeeded in doing so. Here too we see art as the animating and moving power. But that we should impose as truth upon our children the patriotic lies of the Greeks, and not merely on our children, but also— in works like Grote's—should force them as dogmas upon the judgment of healthy men and let them become an influential factor in the politics of the nineteenth century, is surely an extreme abuse of our Hellenic legacy, after Juvenal 1800 years ago mockingly had said :

creditur quidquid Græcia mendax audet in historia.

Still worse does it seem to me to force us to admire

* The principal thing is clearly not what is found in learned books, but what is taught in school, and here I can speak from experience, for I was first in a French " Lycée," then in an English " college," afterwards I received instruction from the teachers of a Swiss private school, and last of all from a learned Prussian. I testify that in these various countries even the best certified history, that of the last three centuries (since the Reformation), is represented in so absolutely different ways that without exaggerating I may affirm that the principle of historical instruction is still everywhere in Europe systematic misrepresentation. While the achievements of our own country are always emphasised, those of others passed over or suppressed, certain things put always in the brightest light, others left in the deepest shadow, there is formed a general picture which in many parts differs only for the subtlest eye from naked lies. The foundation of all genuine truth : the absolutely disinterested love of justice is almost everywhere absent ; a proof that we are still barbarians !

political conditions, which should rather be held up as
an example to be avoided. It is no business of mine
to take any side, either that of Great Greece or of Little
Greece, of Sparta or of Athens, either (with Mitford
and Curtius) that of the nobility, or (with Grote) of the
Demos ; where the political characters, individually or
as a class, are so pitiful, no lofty political conditions
could exist. The belief that we even received the idea
of freedom from the Hellenes is a delusion ; for freedom
implies patriotism, dignity, sense of duty, self-sacrifice,
but from the beginning of their history to their suppression by Rome, the Hellenic States never cease to
call in the enemies of their common fatherland against
their own brothers ; indeed, within the individual States,
as soon as a statesman is removed from power, away
he hurries, it may be to other Hellenes, or to Persia
or to Egypt, later to the Romans, in order to reduce
his own city to ruin with their help. Numerous are
the complaints of the immorality of the Old Testament ;
to me the history of Greece seems just as immoral ;
for among the Israelites we find, even in their crimes,
character and perseverance, as well as loyalty to their
own people. It is not so with the Greeks. Even a
Solon goes over at last to Pisistratus, denying the work
of his life, and a Themistocles, the " hero of Salamis,"
bargains shortly before the battle about the price for
which he would betray Athens, and later actually lives
at the court of Artaxerxes as " declared enemy of the
Greeks," but rightly regarded by the Persians as a
" crafty Greek serpent " and of little account ; as for
Alcibiades, treachery had become with him so entirely
a life-principle that Plutarch can jokingly say that he
changed colour " quicker than a chameleon." All this
was so much a matter of course with the Hellenes that
their historians do not disturb themselves about it.
Herodotus, for instance. tells us with the greatest tran-

quillity how Miltiades forced on the battle of Marathon by calling the attention of the commander-in-chief to the fact that the Athenian troops were inclined to go over to the Persians, and urging him to attack as soon as possible, that there might not be time to put this "evil design" into execution ; half an hour later, and the "heroes of Marathon" would have marched with the Persians against Athens. I remember nothing like this in Jewish history. In such a soil it is manifest that no admirable political system could flourish. "The Greeks," says Goethe again, "were friends of freedom, yes, but each one only of his own freedom ; and so in every Greek there was a tyrant." If any one wishes to make his way to the light through this primeval forest of prejudices, phrases and lies, which have grown up luxuriantly in the course of centuries, I strongly recommend him to read the monumental work of Julius Schvarcz, *Die Demokratie von Athen,* in which a statesman educated theoretically as well as practically, who is at the same time a philologist, has shown once for all what importance is to be attached to this legend. The closing words of this full and strictly scientific account are : "Inductive political science must now admit that the democracy of Athens does not deserve the position which the delusion of centuries has been good enough to assign to it in the history of mankind " (p. 589).*

One single trait moreover suffices to characterise the whole political economy of the Greeks—the fact that Socrates found it necessary to prove at such length that to be a statesman one must understand something of the business of State ! He was condemned to death for preaching this simple elementary truth. "The cup of poison was given purely and simply to the political

---

* It is the first part (published 1877) of a larger work : *Die Demo-kratie,* the second part of which appeared in two volumes in 1891 and 1898 under the title *Die Römische Massenherrschaft.*

reformer," * not to the atheist. These ever-gossiping
Athenians combined in themselves the worst conceit
of an arrogant aristocracy and the passionate spitefulness
of an ignorant impudent rabble. They had at the same
time the fickleness of an Oriental despot. When, shortly
after the death of Socrates, as the story goes, the tragedy
Palamedes was acted, the assembled spectators burst
into tears over the execution of the noble, wise hero ;
the tyrannical people lamented its mean act of vengeance.†
Not a jot more did it listen to Aristotle and other wise
men, on the contrary it banished them. And these
wise men ! Aristotle is wondrous acute and as a political
philosopher as worthy of our admiration as the great
Hellenes always are, when they rise to artistically philosophical intuition ; he, however, played no part as a statesman, but calmly and contentedly watched the conquests
of Philip, which brought ruin on his native land, but
procured for him the skeletons and skins of rare animals ,
Plato had the success in statesmanship which one would
expect from his fantastic constructions. And even the
real statesmen—a Draco, a Solon, a Lycurgus, yes, even
a Pericles—seem to me, as I said already in the preface
to this chapter, rather clever dilettanti than politicians
who in any sense laid firm foundations. Schiller somewhere characterises Draco as a " beginner " and the
constitution of Lycurgus as " schoolboyish." More
decisive is the judgment of the great teacher of Comparative History of Law, B. W. Leist : " The Greek,
without understanding the historical forces that rule the
life of nations, believed himself to be completely master
of the present. Even in his highest aspirations he
looked upon the actual present of the State as an object

* Schvarcz, *loc. cit.* p. 394 ff.

† According to Gomperz, *Griechische Denker*, ii. 95, this anecdote
is an " empty tale " : but in all such inventions, as in the *eppur si muove*,
&c., there lives an element of higher truth ; they are just the reverse
of " empty."ı

in which the philosopher might freely realise his theory,
taking over from history as a guide only so much as
might suit this theory." *   In this sphere the Greeks
lack all consistency and self-control ; no being is more
immoderate than the Hellene, the preacher of moderation
(Sophrosyne) and the " golden mean " ; we see his various
constitutions sway hither and thither between hyper-
fantastic systems of perfection and purblind prejudice
for the interests of the immediate present. Even
Anacharsis complained, " In the councils of the Greeks it
is the fools who decide."   And so it is clear we should seek
to admire and emulate not Greek history in truth, but
Greek historians, not the heroic acts of the Greeks—which
are paralleled everywhere—but the artistic celebration of
their deeds. It is quite unnecessary to talk nonsense
about Occident and Orient, as if " man " in the true sense
could arise only in a definite longitude ; the Greeks stood
with one foot in Asia and the other in Europe ; most of
their great men are Ionians or Sicilians ; it is ridiculous to
seek to oppose their fictions with the weapons of earnest
scientific method, and to educate our children with
phrases ; 'on the other hand, we shall ever admire and
emulate in Herodotus his grace and naturalness, a higher
veracity, and the victorious eye of the genuine artist.
The Greeks fell, their wretched characteristics ruined
them, their morality was already too old, too subtle and
too corrupt to keep pace with the enlightenment of their
intellect ; the Hellenic intellect, however, won a greater
victory than any other intellect has won ; by it—and by
it alone—" man entered into the daylight of life " ; the
freedom which the Greek hereby won for mankind was not
political freedom—he was and remained a tyrant and a
slave-dealer—it was the freedom to shape not merely
instinctively but with conscious creative power—the
freedom to invent as a poet. This is the freedom of

* *Graeco-italische Rechtsgeschichte*, pp. 589, 595, &c.

which Schiller spoke, a valuable legacy, for which we should be eternally grateful to the Hellenes, one worthy of a much higher civilisation than theirs and of a much purer one than ours.

It has been necessary for me to discuss these matters as paving the way for a last consideration.

DECLINE OF RELIGION

If we realise the fact that the educationist has the power to restore dead bodies to life and to force mummies as models upon an active, industrious generation, then we must on closer investigation see that others can do the same thing in a still higher degree, since among the most living portions of our Hellenic inheritance we find a really considerable part of our Church doctrine—not indeed its bright side, but the deep shade of weird and stupid superstition, as well as the arid thorns of scholastic sophistry, bereft of all the leaves and blossoms of poetry. The angels and devils, the fearful conception of hell, the ghosts of the dead (which in this presumably enlightened nineteenth century set tables in motion to such an extent with knocking and turning), the ecstatically religious delirium, the hypostasis of the Creator and of the Logos, the definition of the Divine, the conception of the Trinity, in fact the whole basis of our Dogmatics we owe to a great extent to the Hellenes or at least to their mediation ; at the same time we are indebted to them for the sophistical manner of treating these things : Aristotle with his theory of the Soul and of the Godhead is the first and greatest of all schoolmen ; his prophet, Thomas Aquinas, was nominated by the infallible Pope official philosopher of the Catholic Church towards the end of the nineteenth century (1879) ; at the same time a large proportion of the logic-chopping

free-thinkers, enemies of all metaphysics and pro-
claimers of a new "religion of reason," like John Stuart
Mill and David Strauss, &c., based their theories
on Aristotle. Here, as is evident, we have to deal with
a legacy of real living force, and it reminds us that
we should speak with humility of the advances made in
our time.

The matter is an exceedingly complicated one; if in
this whole chapter I have had to be satisfied with mere
allusions, I shall here have to confine myself to hinting
at allusions. And yet in this very matter relations
have to be pointed out, which, so far as I know, have
never been revealed in their proper connection. I wish
to do this with all modesty, and yet with the utmost
precision.

It is the common practice to represent the religious
development of the Hellenes as a popular superstitious
polytheism, which in the consciousness of some pre-
eminent men had gradually transformed itself into a purer
and more spiritualised faith in a single God ;—the human
spirit thus advancing from darkness to ever brighter
light. Our reason loves simplifications : this gradual
soaring of the Greek spirit, till it was ripe for a higher
revelation, is very much in tune with our inborn sluggish-
ness of thought. But this conception is in reality utterly
false and proved to be false : the faith in gods, as we
meet it in Homer, is the most elevated and pure feature
of Greek religion. This religious philosophy, though,
like all things human, compassed and limited in many
ways, was suited to the knowledge, thought and feeling
of a definite stage of civilisation, and yet it was in all
probability as beautiful, noble and free as any of which
we have knowledge. The distinguishing-mark of the
Homeric creed was its intellectual and moral freedom—
indeed, as Rohde says, "almost free-thinking"; this
religion is the faith acquired through artistic intuition and

analogy (that is, purely by way of genius) in a cosmos—
an " order of the world," which is everywhere perceived,
but which we are never able to think out or comprehend,
because we after all are ourselves elements of this cosmos
—an order which nevertheless reflects itself of necessity
in everything, and which therefore in Art becomes visible
and directly convincing. The conceptions which are
held by the people, and have been produced by the poetical
and symbolising faculty of each simple mind as yet
innocent of dialectics, are here condensed and made
directly visible, and that, too, by lofty minds, which are
still strong enough in faith to possess the most glowing
fervour and at the same time free enough to fashion
according to their own sovereign artistic judgment.   This
religion is hostile to all faith in ghosts and spirits, to all
clerical formalism ; everything of the nature of popular
soul-cult and the like which occurs in the *Iliad* and the
Odyssey is wonderfully cleared, stripped of all that is
terrible, and raised to the eternal truth of something
symbolical ; it is equally hostile to every kind of
sophistry, to all idle inquiries regarding cause and purpose,
to that rationalistic movement, therefore, which has
subsequently shown itself in its true colours as merely
the other side of superstition. So long as these conceptions, which had found their most perfect expression
in Homer and some other great poets, still lived among
the people, the Greek religion possessed an ideal element ;
later (particularly in Alexandria and Rome) it became an
amalgam of Pyrrhonic, satirical, universal scepticism,
gross superstitious belief in magic and sophistical scholasticism. The fine structure was undermined from two
different quarters, by men who appeared to possess little
in common, who, however, later joined hands like brothers,
when the Homeric Parthenon (*i.e.*, " temple of the
Virgin ") had become a heap of ruins within which a
philological " stone-polishing workshop " had been set

up : it was these two parties that had found no favour with Homer, priestly superstition and hypersubtle hunting after causality.*

The results of anthropological and ethnographic study allow us, I think, to distinguish between superstition and religion.   Superstition we find everywhere, over the whole earth, and that too in definite forms which resemble each other very much in all places and among the most different races, and which are subject to a demonstrable law of development ; superstition cannot in reality be eradicated.   Religion, on the other hand, as being a collective image of the order of the world as it hovers before the imagination, changes very much with times and peoples ; many races (for instance the Chinese) feel little or no religious craving : in others the need is very pronounced ; religion may be metaphysical, materialistic or symbolistic, but it always appears—even where its external elements are all borrowed—in a completely new, individual form according to time and country, and each of its forms is, as history teaches us, altogether transitory.   Religion has something passive in it ; while it lives it reflects a condition of culture ; at the same time it contains arbitrary moments of inestimable consequence ; how much freedom was manifested by the Hellenic poets in their treatment of the material of their faith !   To what an extent did the resolutions of the Council of Trent, as to what Christendom should believe and should not believe, depend on diplomatic moves and the fortune of arms ! This cannot be said of superstition ; its might is assailed in vain by power of Pope and of poets ; it crawls along a thousand hidden paths, slumbers unconsciously in every

* It matters little that in Homer's time there may have been no " philosophers " ;   the fact that in his works nothing is " explained," that not the least attempt at a cosmogony is found, shows the tendency of his mind with sufficient clearness.   Hesiod is already a manifest reaction, but still too magnificently symbolical to find favour with any rationalist.

breast and is every moment ready to burst out into flame ;
it has, as Lippert says, " a tenacity of life which no religion
possesses " ; * it is at the same time a cement for every
new religion and an enemy in the path of every old one.
Almost every man has doubts about his religion, no one
about his superstition ; expelled from the direct consciousness of the so-called " educated " classes, it nestles
in the innermost folds of their brains and plays its tricks
there all the more wantonly, as it reveals itself in the
mummery of authentic learning, or of the noisiest free-
thinking. We have had plenty of opportunity † of
observing all this in our century of Notre Dame de Lourdes,
" Shakers," phrenology, odic force, spirit photographs,
scientific materialism, and " healing priestcraft," ‡ &c.
To understand rightly the Hellenic inheritance we must
learn to make a distinction there too. If we do so, our
eyes will open to the fact that even in Hellas, at the
brilliant epoch of the glorious art-inspired religion, an
undercurrent of superstitions and cults of quite a different
kind had never ceased to flow : at a later period, when
the Greek spirit began to decline and the belief in gods
was a mere form, it broke out in a flood and united with
the rationalistic scholasticism which had in the meantime
been abundantly fed from various sources, till finally
it presented in pseudo-Semitic neo-Platonism the grinning
caricature of lofty, free intellectual achievements. This
stream of popular belief, restrained in the Dionysian cult,
which through tragedy reached the highest artistic perfection, flowed on underground by Delphi and Eleusis ;
the ancient soul-cult, the awe-stricken and reverent remem-

* *Christentum, Volksglaube und Volksbrauch*, p. 379. In the second
part of this book there is an instructive list of pre-Christian customs
and superstitions still prevalent in Europe.

† " Even the most civilised nations do not easily shake off their
belief in magic."—Sir John Lubbock, *The Prehistoric Age* (German
edition, ii. 278).

‡ F. A. Lange used the expression, "*medizinisches Pfaffentum,*"
somewhere in his *Geschichte des Materialismus.*

brance of the dead formed its first and richest source ; with this became gradually associated, by inevitable progression (and in various forms) the belief in the immortality of the soul. Doubtless the Hellenes had brought the original stock of their various superstitions from their former home ; but new elements were constantly added, partly as Semitic * imports from the coasts and islands of Asia Minor, but with more permanent and disturbing influence from that North which the Greeks thought they despised. It was not poets that proclaimed these sacred "redeeming" mysteries but Sibyls, Bacchides, female utterers of Pythian oracles ; ecstatic frenzy took hold of one district after the other, whole nations became mad, the sons of the heroes who had fought before Troy whirled round in circles like the Dervishes of to-day, mothers strangled their children with their own hands. It was these people, however, who fostered the real faith in souls, and even the belief in the immortality of the soul was spread by them from Thrace to Greece.†

* The Semitic peoples in old times do not seem to have believed in the immortality of the individual soul ; but their cults supplied the Hellene, as soon as he grasped this thought, with weighty stimulus. The Phœnician divine system of the Cabiri (*i.e.*, the seven powerful ones) was found by the Greeks on Lemnos, Rhodes and other islands, and with regard to this Duncker writes in his *Geschichte des Altertums*, I⁴, 279, "The myth of Melcart and Astarte, of Astarte who was adopted into the number of these gods, and of Melcart, who finds again the lost goddess of the moon in the land of darkness and returns from there with her to new light and life—gave the Greeks occasion to associate with the secret worship of the Cabiri the conceptions of life after death, which had been growing among them since the beginning of the sixth century."

† We need not be surprised that this belief (according to Herodotus, iv. 93) was prevalent in the Indo-European race of the Getæ and from there found its way into Greece ; it was an old racial possession ; it is very striking, on the other hand, that the Hellene at the period of his greatest strength had lost this belief or rather was quite indifferent to it. "An everlasting life of the soul is neither asserted nor denied from the Homeric standpoint. Indeed, this thought does not come into consideration at all" (Rohde, *Psyche*, p. 195); a remarkable confirmation of Schiller's assertion that the æsthetic man, *i.e.*, he in whom the sensual and the moral are not diametrically opposed in aim "needs no

In the mad Bacchantic dance the soul for the first time
[among the Greek people] separated itself from the body
—that same soul about which Aristotle from the stillness
of his study had so much that was edifying to tell us ; in
the Dionysian ecstasy man felt himself one with the
immortal gods and concluded that his individual human
soul must also be immortal, a conclusion which Aristotle
and others at a later time attempted ingeniously to
justify.*   It seems to me that we are still suffering from
something of this vertigo !   And for that reason let us
attempt to come to a sensible conclusion regarding this
legacy which clings so firmly to us.

   To this belief in a soul Hellenic poetry as such has contributed nothing ; it reverently adapted itself to the conventional—the ceremonious burial of Patroclus, for instance, who otherwise could not enter on his last rest—
the performance of the necessary acts of consecration by
Antigone beside the corpse of her brother—and nothing
more.   It did unconsciously help to promote the belief in
immortality, by maintaining that the gods must be conceived not indeed as uncreated but, for their greater
glorification, as undying—an idea quite foreign to the
Aryan Indians.†   The idea of sempiternity, that is, the

immortality to support and hold him " (Letter to Goethe, August 9, 1796).
Whether or not the Getæ were Goths and so belonged to the Teutonic
peoples, as Jacob Grimm asserted, does not here much matter ; however,
a full discussion of this interesting question is to be found in Wieters-
heim-Dahn, *Geschichte der Völkerwanderung*, i. 597 ; the result of the investigation is against Grimm's view.   The story that the Getic King
Zalmoxis learned the doctrine of immortality from Pythagoras is characterised by Rohde as an " absurd pragmatical tale " (*Psyche*, p. 320).

   * On this very important point, the genesis of the belief in immortality
among the Greeks, *see* especially Rohde, *Psyche*, p. 296.

   † In an old Vedic hymn, which I quoted on p. 35. a verse runs, " The
Gods have arisen on this side of creation " ; in their capacity as individuals, however, they too cannot, according to the Indian conviction, possess " sempiternity," and Çankara says in the *Vedânta
Sutra's*, when speaking of the individual gods, " Such words as Indra, &c.,
signify, like the word ' General,' only occupation of a definite post.
Whoever therefore occupies the post in question bears the title Indra "
(i. 3, 28, p. 170 of Deussen's translation).

immortality of an individual who at some time had come into being, was in consequence familiar to the Greeks as an attribute of their gods ; poetry probably found it already existing, but at any rate it was first raised to a definite reality by the power of poetical imagination. Art had no greater share in it than this. Art rather endeavours as far as possible to remove, to temper, to minimise that " belief in dæmons which has everywhere to be taken as primeval," * the conception of a " lower world," the story of "islands of the blest "—in short, all those elements which, growing up out of the subsoil of superstition, force themselves on the human imagination—and all this in order to gain a free, open field for the given facts of the world and of life, and for their poetically religious, imaginative treatment. Unlike art, popular belief, not being satisfied with a religion so lofty and poetic, preferred the teaching of the barbarous Thracians. Neither was it accepted by philosophy, which held a position inferior to such poetical conceptions, until the day came when it felt itself strong enough to set history against fable, and detailed knowledge against symbol ; but the stimulus in this direction was not drawn by philosophy from itself nor from the results of empiric science, which had nowhere dealt with the doctrines of souls, the entelechies of Aristotle, immortality and the rest ; it was received from the people, partly from Asia (through Pythagoras), partly from Northern Europe (as Orphic or Dionysian cult). The theory of a soul separable from the living body and more or less independent ; the theory easily deduced therefrom of bodiless and yet living souls —those, for example, of the dead, which live on as mere souls, as also of a " soul-possessed " divine principle (quite analogous to the *Nous* of Anaxagoras, that is, of power distinct from matter)—furthermore, the theory of

* Deussen, *Allgemeine Geschichte der Philosophie*, i. 39. *See also* Tylor.

the immortality of this soul—all these are, to begin with, not results of quickened philosophical thought, nor do they form in any sense an evolutional development, a glorification of that Hellenic national religion which had found its highest expression in the poets ; it is rather that people and thinker here put themselves in opposition to poet and religion. And though obeying different impulses, people and thinker played into each other's hands, and together caused the decline and fall of poetry and religion. And when the crisis thus brought about was past, the result was that philosophers had taken the place of artists as the heralds of religion. To begin with, both poets and philosophers had of course derived their material from the people ; but which of the two, I ask, has employed it the better and more wisely ? Which has pointed the way to freedom and beauty, and which to bondage and ugliness ? Which has paved the way for healthy empiric science and which has checked it for almost twenty centuries ? In the meantime, from quite another direction, from the midst of a people that possessed neither art nor philosophy, a religious force had entered the world, so strong that it could bear, without breaking down, the madness of the whirling dance that had been elevated to a system of reason—so full of light that even the dark power of purely abstract logic could never dim its radiance—a religious power, qualified by its very origin to promote civilisation rather than culture ; had that power not arisen, then this supposed elevation to higher ideals would have ended miserably in ignominy, or rather its actual wretchedness would never have remained concealed. If any one doubts this, let him read the literature of the first centuries of our era, when the State-paid, anti-Christian philosophers entitled their theory of knowledge " Theology " (Plotinus, Proclus, &c.), let him see how these worthies in the leisure hours which remained to

them after picking Homer to pieces, commenting on Aristotle, building up Trinities, and discussing the question
whether God had the attribute of life as well as of being,
and other such subtleties, wandered from one place
to another in order that they might be initiated into
mysteries, or admitted as hierophants into Orphic societies
—the foremost thinkers sunk to the grossest belief in
magic. Or if such reading appals him, let him take up
the witty Heinrich Heine of the second century, Lucian,
and complete the information there given by the more
serious but no less interesting writings of his contemporary
Apuleius *—and then say where there is more religion
to be found and where more superstition, where there is
free, sound, creative human power and where fruitless,
slovenly working of the treadmill in a continual circle.
And yet the men who stand in that Homeric circle seem
to us childishly pious and superstitious, these on the
other hand enlightened thinkers ! †

One more example ! We are wont according to old
custom to commend Aristotle more warmly for his
teleological theory of the universe than for anything else,
whereas we reproach Homer with his anthropomorphism.
If we did not suffer from artificially produced atrophy of
the brain, we should be bound to see the absurdity of this.
Teleology, that is, the theory of finality according to the
measure of human reason, is anthropomorphism in its
highest potency. When man can grasp the plan of the
cosmos, when he can say whence the world comes, whither
it goes and what the purpose of each individual thing is,

* *See* particularly in the eleventh book of the *Golden Ass* the initiation
into the mysteries of Isis, Osiris, Serapis and the admission into the
association of the Pastophori. Plutarch's writing *On Isis and Osiris*
should also be read.

† Bussell, *The School of Plato*, 1896, p. 345, writes of this philosophical
period : " The dæmons monopolise a worship, which cannot be devoted
to a mere idea, and philosophy breathes out its life on the steps of
smoking sacrificial altars and amid the incantations and delusions of
prophecy and magic."

then he is really himself God and the whole world is
" human " ; this is expressly stated by the Orphics and
—Aristotle. But the poet's attitude is quite different.
Every one quotes, and has done so even from the times
of Heraclitus and down to those of Ranke, the charge
which Xenophanes made against Homer that he forms the
gods like Hellenes, but that the negroes would invent a
black Zeus and horses would think of the gods as horses.
No remark could be more senseless or superficial.* The
reproach is not even correct in fact, since the gods in
Homer appear in all possible forms. As K. Lehrs says
in his fine but unfortunately almost forgotten book,
Ethik und Religion der Griechen (pp. 136–7) : " The
Greek gods are by no means images of men, but antitypes.
They are neither cosmic potencies (as the philosophers
first regarded them) nor glorified men ! They frequently occur in animal form and only bear as a rule the
human form as being the noblest, most beautiful and
most suitable, but every other form is in itself just as
natural to them." Incomparably more important, however, is the fact that in Homer and the other great poets
all teleology is wanting ; for undeniable anthropomorphism did not appear till this idea did. Why should I
not represent the gods in the image of man ? Should I
introduce them into my poem as sheep or beetles ? Did
not Raphael and Michael Angelo do the very same thing
as Homer ? Has the Christian religion not accepted the
idea that God appeared in human form ? Is the Jehovah
of the Israelites not a prototype of the noble and yet
quarrelsome and revengeful Jew ? It would surely not
be advisable to recommend to the imagination of the
artist the Aristotelian " being without size which thinks

---

* Giordano Bruno, enraged at this fundamentally wrong and pedanti-
cally narrow judgment, writes : " Only *insensate bestie et veri bruti*
would be capable of making such a statement." (*Italienische Schriften*,
ed. Lagarde, p. 534). One should compare also M. W. Visser, *Die
nicht menschengestalligen Götter der Griechen*, Leyden, 1903.

the thing thought." On the other hand, the poetical religion of the Greeks does not presume to give information about the "uncreated" and to "explain according to reason" the future. It gives a picture of the world as in a hollow mirror and thinks thereby to quicken and to purify the spirit of man, and nothing more. Lehrs demonstrates, in the book mentioned above, how the idea of teleology was introduced by the philosophers, from Socrates to Cicero, but found no place in Hellenic poetry. "The idea of beautiful order, harmony, cosmos, which pervades Greek religion, is," he says (p. 117), "a much higher idea than that of teleology, which in every respect has something paltry about it." To bring the matter quite home to us, I ask, Which is the anthropomorphist, Homer or Byron? Homer, whose personal existence could be doubted, or Byron, who so powerfully grasped the strings of the harp and attuned the poetry of our century to the melody, in which Alps and Ocean, Past and Present of the human race only serve to mirror, and form a frame for the individual Ego? I should think it almost impossible for each of us to-day, surrounded as we are by human actions and permeated with the dim idea of an ordered Cosmos to remain to so small a degree anthropomorphic, so very "objective" as Homer.

METAPHYSICS

It is essential to distinguish between philosophy and philosophy, and I think I have above warmly expressed my admiration for the Hellenic philosophy of the great epoch, particularly where it appeared as a creative activity of the human spirit closely related to poetry; in this respect Plato's theory of ideas is unsurpassed, while Aristotle appears to be incomparably great in analysis and method, but at the same time, as a philosopher in the

sense given, the real originator of the decay of the
Hellenic spirit.   But here as elsewhere we must guard
against over-simplification ; we must not attribute to a
single man what was peculiar to his people and only found
in him its most definite expression.   In reality Greek
philosophy from the very beginning contained the germ of
its fatal development later ; the inheritance which still
lies heavily upon us goes back almost to Homer's time.
For it will be found upon reflection, that the old Hylo-
zoists are related to the Neoplatonists : whoever, like
Thales, without further ado " explains " the world as
having arisen from water, will afterwards equally find an
" explanation " of God ; his nearest successor, Anaximander, establishes as principle the " Infinite " (the
Apeiron), the " Unchangeable amid all changes " : here
in truth we are already in the toils of the most unmitigated
scholasticism and can calmly wait till the wheel of time
sets down on the surface of the earth Ramon Lull and
Thomas Aquinas.   The fact that the oldest among the
well-known Greek thinkers believed in the presence of
countless dæmons, but at the same time from the beginning * attacked the gods of the popular religion and of
the poets—Heraclitus would " gladly have scourged " †
Homer—serves only to complete the picture.   However,
one thing must be added : a man like Anaximander, so
subordinate as a thinker, was a naturalist and theorist of
the first rank, a founder of scientific geography, a pro-
moter of astronomy ; all these people are presented to
us as philosophers, but in reality philosophy was for them
something quite apart ; surely we should not reckon
the agnosticism of Charles Darwin or the creed of Claude
Bernard among the philosophical achievements of our

* Authenticated at least from Xenophanes and Heraclitus onwards.
† 1 quote from Gomperz : *Griechische Denker*, i. 50 ; according to
Zeller's account so violent an expression would seem unlikely.   If I
remember rightly, it is Xenophanes who assigns the words to Heraclitus.

century? Here is a characteristic example of the many traditional consecrated confusions; we find the name of Sankara (certainly one of the greatest metaphysicians that ever lived) in no history of philosophy, while on the other hand the worthy olive-farmer Thales is ever paraded as the "first philosopher." And, if the matter be closely investigated, it will be found that almost all so-called philosophers at the zenith of Hellenic greatness are in a similar position : so far as we can judge from contradictory reports, Pythagoras did not found a philosophic school, but a political, social, dietetic and religious brotherhood ; Plato himself, the metaphysician, was a statesman, moralist, practical reformer ; Aristotle was a professional encyclopædist, and the unity of his philosophy is due much more to his character than to his forced, half-traditional, contradictory metaphysics. Without therefore underestimating in any way the achievements of the Greek thinkers, we shall yet, I think, be able to assert (and so put an end to the confusion), that these men have paved the way for our science (including logic and ethics), and for our theology, and that they, through their poetically creative genius, have poured a flood of light upon the paths which speculation and intellectual investigation were afterwards to follow ; as metaphysicians, in the real narrower sense of the word, they were, however, with the sole exception of Plato, comparatively of much less importance.

That nothing may remain obscure in a matter so weighty that it strikes into the depths of our life to-day, I should like briefly to refer to the fact, that in the person of the great Leonardo da Vinci we have an example— closely related to modern thought and feeling—of the deep gulf which separates poetical from abstract perception, religion from theologising philosophy. Leonardo brands the intellectual sciences as "deceptive" (le

bugiarde scientie mentali) ; " all knowledge," he says,
" is vain and erroneous, unless brought into the world
by sense-experience, the mother of all certainty " ;
especially offensive to him are the disputes and proofs regarding the entity of God and of the soul : he is of opinion
that " our senses revolt against " these conceptions, consequently we should not let ourselves be deluded : " where
arguments of reason and clear right are wanting, clamour
takes their place ; in the case of things which are certain,
however, this does not happen " ; and thus he arrives
at the conclusion : " dove si grida non è vera scientia,"
where there is clamour there is no genuine knowledge
(*Libro di pittura*, Part I., Division 33, Heinrich Ludwig's
edition).   This is Leonardo's theology !   Yet it is this
very man—and surely the only one, the greatest not
excepted—who paints a Christ which comes near being
a revelation, "perfect God and perfect man," as the
Athanasian creed puts it.   Here we have close intrinsic
relationship with Homer : all knowledge is derived from
the experience of sense, and from this the Divine, proved
by no subtleties of reasoning, is formed as free creation,
with popular belief as its basis—something everlastingly
true.   Thanks to special circumstances and particular
mental gifts, thanks above all to the advent of men of
great genius who alone give life, this particular faculty
had become so intensely developed in Greece that the
sciences of experience received a new and greater impulse,
as they did later among us through the influence of
Leonardo, whereas the reaction of philosophising abstraction was never able to develop freely and naturally, but
degenerated either into scholasticism or the clouds of
fancy.   The Hellenic artist awoke to life in an atmosphere
which gave him at the same time personal freedom and
the elevating consciousness that he was understood by
all ; the Hellenic philosopher (as soon as he trod the path
of logical abstraction) had not this gift ; on the contrary

he was hemmed in on all sides, outwardly by custom, beliefs and civic institutions, inwardly by his whole personal education, which was principally artistic, by everything that surrounded him during his whole life, by all impressions which eye and ear conveyed to him ; he was not free : because of his talent he did achieve great things, but nothing that satisfied—as his art did—the highest demands of harmony, truth and universal acceptance. In the case of Greek art the national element is comparable to pinions that raise the spirit to lofty heights, where "all men become brothers," where the separating gulf of times and races adds to rather than detracts from the charm ; Hellenic philosophy, on the contrary, is in the limiting sense of the word fettered to a definite national life and consequently hemmed in on all sides.*

It is exceedingly difficult with such a view to prevail against the prejudice of centuries. Even such a man as Rohde calls the Greeks the "most fruitful in thought among nations" and asserts that their philosophers "thought in advance for all mankind" ; † Leopold von Ranke, who has no other epithet for Homeric religion than "idolatry" (!) writes as follows : "What Aristotle says about the distinction between active and passive reason, only the first of which, however, is the true one, autonomous and related to God, I should be inclined to say was the best thing that could be said about the human spirit, with the exception of the Revelation of the Bible. We may say the same, if I am not mistaken, of Plato's doctrine of the soul."‡ Ranke tells us further that the mission of Greek philosophy was to purge the old faith of its idolatrous element, to unite rational and

---

* *Cf.*, further, vol. ii. pp. 135 and 364.

† *Psyche*, p. 104.

‡ *Weltgeschichte* (Text edition), i. 230. This axiom of wisdom reminds one perilously of the well-known story from the nursery : "Whom do you love most, papa or mamma ?—Both !" For though Aristotle starts from Plato, one can hardly imagine anything more

religious truth ; but that the democracy frustrated this
noble design, because it " held fast to idolatry " (i. 230).*
These examples may suffice, though one could quote many
others.   I am convinced that this is all illusion, indeed
baneful illusion, and in essential points the very opposite
of truth.   It is not true that the Greeks have thought
in advance for all mankind : before them, at their time
and after them there has been deeper thinking, more
acute and more correct.   It is not true that the red-tape
theology of Aristotle *ad usum* of the mainstays of society
is " the best thing that could be said " : this Jesuitical
scholastic sophistry has been the black plague of philosophy.   It is not true that Greek thinkers have purified
the old religion : they have rather attacked in it that
very thing that deserved everlasting admiration, namely,
its free, purely artistic beauty ; and while they pretended
to substitute rational for symbolical truth, they in reality
only adopted popular superstition and set it, clad in logical
rags, upon the throne, from which they—in company
with the mob—had hurled down that poetry which
proclaimed an everlasting truth.

As regards the so-called " thinking in advance," it will
suffice to call attention to two circumstances to prove the
erroneous nature of this assertion : in the first place, the
Indians began to think before the Greeks, their thought
was profounder and more consistent, and in their various
systems they have exhausted more possibilities ; in the
second place, our own western European thought only
began on the day when a great man said, " We must
admit that the philosophy which we have received from

different than their theories of the soul (as well as their whole metaphysics).   How then can both have said " the best thing " ?   Schopenhauer has expressed the matter correctly and concisely, " The radical
contrast to Aristotle is Plato."

* O twenty-fourth century ! What sayest thou to this ?   I   for
my part am silent—at least with regard to personalities—and follow
the example of wise Socrates in sacrificing a cock to the idols of my
century !

the Greeks is childish, or at least that it rather encourages talk than acts as a creative stimulus." * To pretend that Locke, Gassendi, Hume, Descartes, Kant, &c., chewed the cud of Greek philosophy is one of the worst sins of Hellenic megalomania against our new culture. Pythagoras, the first great Hellenic thinker, offers a conclusive instance in reference to Hellenic thought. From his Oriental journeys he brought back all kinds of knowledge, significant and trifling, from the idea of re-demption to the conception of the ether and the forbidding of the eating of beans : all of it was Indian ancestral property. One doctrine in particular became the central point of Pythagoreanism, its religious lever, if I may say so : this was the secret doctrine of the transmigration of souls. Plato afterwards robbed it of the aureole of secrecy and gave it a place in public philosophy. But among the Indians the belief in the transmigration of souls long before Pythagoras formed the basis of all ethics ; though much divided in politics, religion and philosophy, and though living in open opposition, the whole people was united in the belief in the never-ending series of rebirths. "In India one never finds the question put, as to whether the soul transmigrates : it is universally and firmly believed." † But there was a class there, a small class, which did not believe in the transmigration of souls, in so far as they considered it to be a symbolical conception, a conception which to those wrapt in the illusions of world-contemplation allegorically conveys a loftier truth to be grasped more correctly by deep metaphysical thinking alone : this small class was (and is to-day) that of the philosophers. "The idea of

* Bacon of Verulam : *Instauratio Magna*, Introduction. " Et de utilitate aperte dicendum est : sapientiam istam, quam a Græcis potissimum hausimus, pueritiam quandam scientiæ videri, atque habere quod proprium est puerorum ; ut ad garriendum prompta, ad generandum invalida et immatura sit. Controversiarum enim ferax, operum effœta est."

† Schroeder, *Indiens Litteratur und Kultur*, p. 252.

the soul transmigrating rests on ignorance, while the soul in the sense of the highest reality is not transmigratory " : such is the teaching of the Indian thinker.* A really " secret doctrine," such as the Greeks following Egyptian example loved, the Indians never knew : men of all castes, even women, could attain to the highest knowledge ; but these profound sages knew very well that metaphysical thought requires special faculties and special development of those faculties ; and so they let the figurative alone.   And this figure, this magnificent conception of the transmigration of souls, which is perhaps indispensable for morals though essentially but a popular belief, while in India it was prevalent among the whole people from the highest to the lowest with the exception of the thinkers alone, became in Greece the most sublime " secret doctrine " of their first great philosopher, never quite disappeared from the highest regions of their philosophical views, and received from Plato the alluring charm of poetical form.   These are the people who are said to have paved the way for us in thought, " the richest in thought of nations " !   No, the Greeks were no great metaphysicians.

THEOLOGY

But they have just as little claim to be considered great moralists and theologians.   Here too one example

---

* Sankara :   *Stra's des Vedânta*, i 2, 11.   Of course Sankara lived long after Pythagoras (about the eighth century of our era) but his teaching is strictly orthodox, he makes no risky assertion which is not based on old canonical Upanishads.   It is clear that an actual "transmigration" was, even at the time of and according to the oldest Upanishads, for the man who truly had insight, a conception only serving popular ends.   Further proof with regard to this matter will be found in Sankara in the introduction to the *Sûtra's* and in i. 1, 4, but especially in the magnificent passage ii. 1, 22, where the Samsâra, in conjunction with the whole creation, is described as an illusion, " which like the illusion of partings and separations by birth and death does not exist in the sense of the highest reality."

instead of many. The belief in dæmons is everywhere current ; the idea of a special intermediate race
of dæmons (between the gods in heaven and men on earth)
was very probably derived by the Greeks from India (by
way of Persia),* but that does not matter ; in philosophy,
or, as it may be called, in " rational religion," these
creatures of superstition were first adopted by Plato.
Rohde writes on this point as follows : † " Plato is the first
of many to write about a whole intermediate hierarchy of
dæmons, entrusted with all that is wrought by invisible
powers but seems beneath the dignity of the sublime
gods. Thus the Divine itself is freed from everything
evil and degrading." So with full consciousness and
for the " rational " and flagrantly anthropomorphic
purpose of " freeing " God of what seems evil to us men,
that superstition which the Hellenes shared with bushmen
and Australian blacks was adorned with a philosophical
and theological aureole, recommended to the noblest
minds by a noble mind and bequeathed to all future
generations as an inheritance. The fortunate Indians
had long before discarded the belief in dæmons ; it
was retained only by the totally uneducated people ;
among the Indians the philosopher was bound no
longer to any religious ceremony ; for without denying
their existence, like the superficial Xenophanes, he had
learned to see in the gods symbols of a higher truth not
able to be grasped by the senses—what use then had
such people for dæmons ? Homer, however, it should
be noticed, had been on the same path. It is true that
the hand of Athene stops the hastily raised arm of
Achilles, and Here inspires the hesitating Diomedes with
courage—with such divine freedom does the poet interpret,
inspiring all ages with poetical thoughts—but genuine

* Colebrooke, *Miscellaneous Essays*, p. 442.
† In a short summary, *Die Religion der Griechen*, published in 1895
in the *Bayreuther Blätter* (also printed separately in 1902).

superstition plays a very subordinate part in Homer, and by his "divine" interpretation he raises it out of the sphere of real dæmonism ; his path was sunnier, more beautiful than that of the Indo-Aryan ; instead of indulging in speculative metaphysics like the latter, he consecrated the empiric world and thereby guided mankind to a glorious goal.* Then came Socrates ;— old, superstitious, advised by Pythian oracles, taught by priestesses, possessed by dæmons, and after him Plato and the others. O Hellenes ! if only you had remained true to the religion of Homer and the artistic culture which it founded ! If you had but trusted your divine poets, and not listened to your Heraclitus and Xenophanes, your Socrates and Plato, and all the rest of them ! Alas for us who have for centuries been plunged into unspeakable sorrow and misery by this belief in dæmons, now raised to sacred orthodoxy, who have been hampered by it in our whole intellectual development, who even to this day are under the delusions of the Thracian peasants ! †

SCHOLASTICISM

Not one whit better is that Hellenic thought which follows neither the path of mysticism nor that of poetical sugges-tion, but openly links itself to natural science and with the

---

* See, for example, in Book XXIV. of the *Iliad* (verse 300 ff.) the appearance " from the right " of the eagle which presages good. Very significant are the words of Priam in the same book with regard to a vision he has seen (verse 990 ff.) : " Had any other of mortal men bidden me believe it, an interpreter of signs or prophet or sacrificial priest, I should have called it deceit and turned from it with contempt." Magnificent, too, is the conception of " spirits " in Hesiod, although he is much nearer to the popular superstition than Homer (*Works and Days*, 124 ff.) : " They defend the right and hinder deeds of impiety : everywhere over the earth they wander, hidden in mist, and scatter blessings ; this is the kingly office which they have received."

† Döllinger calls the " systematic belief in dæmons " one of the " Danaan gifts of Greek imagining " (*Akad. Vorträge*, i. 182).

help of philosophy and rational psychology undertakes
to solve the great problems of existence. Here the Greek
spirit at once falls into scholasticism, as already hinted.
"Words, words, nothing but words!" In this case
detailed treatment would unfortunately go far beyond the
scope of this book. But if any one is shy of the higher
philosophy, let him take up a catechism, he will find
plenty of Aristotle in it. Talk of the Divinity with such
a man, and tell him that it " did not come into existence
and was not created ; that it has been from all time and
is immortal," and he will think that you are quoting from
the creed of an œcumenical council, whereas, as a matter
of fact, it is a quotation from Aristotle! And if you
further say to him that God is " an everlasting, perfect,
unconditioned being, gifted with life, but without bulk,
one who in eternal actuality thinks himself, for (this serves
as explanation) thinking becomes objective to itself by
the thinking of the thing thought, so that thinking
and the thing thought become identical," the poor man
will fancy that you are reading from Thomas Aquinas
or at least from Georg Wilhelm Friedrich Hegel, but
again it is a quotation from Aristotle.* The rational
doctrine of God, the rational doctrine of the soul, above
all the doctrine of a purposed order of the world suitable
to human reason, or teleology (through which Aristotle, by
the way, introduced such grotesque errors into his natural
science), that was the inheritance in this sphere ! How
many centuries did it take till there came a brave man
who threw this ballast overboard and showed that one
cannot prove the existence of God, as Aristotle had made
twenty centuries believe :—till a man came who ventured
to write the words, " Neither experience nor conclusions
of reason adequately inform us whether man possesses
a soul (as a substance dwelling in him, distinct from
body and capable of thinking independently of it and

* *Metaphysics*, Book XII. chap. viii

therefore a spiritual substance), or whether life may not rather be a property of matter." *

But enough. I think I have shown with sufficient clearness that Hellenic philosophy is only genuinely great when we take the word in its widest sense, somewhat in the English sense, according to which a Newton and a Cuvier, or a Jean Jacques Rousseau and a Goethe are called "philosophers." As soon as the Greek left the sphere of intuition—right from Thales onward—he became fatal; he became all the more fatal when he proceeded to use his incomparable plastic power (which is so strikingly absent in the metaphysical Indian) in giving a seductive shape to shadowy chimeras and in emasculating and bowdlerising deep conceptions and ideas that do not lend themselves to any analysis. I do not blame him because he had mystical tendencies and a plainly expressed need of metaphysics, but because he attempted to give shape to mysticism in a way other than the artistically mythical, and, going blindly past the central point of all metaphysics (I always naturally except Plato), tried to solve transcendent questions by prosaic empirical means. If the Greek had continued to develop his faculties on the one hand purely poetically, on the other purely empirically, his influence would have become an unmixed and inexpressible blessing for mankind; but, as it is, that same Greek who in poetry and science had given us an example of what true creative power can effect, and so of the way in which the development of man has taken place, at a later time proved to be a cramping and retarding element in the growth of the human intellect.

Conclusion

It may be that these last remarks rather trespass on the province of a later part of my book. But I had to

* Kant: *Metaphysische Anfangsgründe der Tugendlehre*, Part I., *Ethische Elementarlehre*, § 4.

face the difficulty. Great as has been the influence which the Hellenic inheritance has exercised upon our century, as upon those which preceded it, there has been no little confusion and no lack of misunderstanding concerning it. In order that the sequel might be under-stood, it was necessary that the mental condition of the heirs should be set out as clearly as the many-sided and complex nature of the inheritance which they received.

No summary is needed. Indeed what I have said about our rich Hellenic inheritance, which so deeply penetrates our intellectual life, is of itself a mere summary —a mere indication. If we were to carry this experiment further we should arrive at a point where every concrete idea would become sublimated, where the sinuous lines of Life would shrivel into mere degrees in a scale, and there would remain nothing but a geometrical figure—a construction of the mind—instead of the representation of that manifold truth which has the gift of uniting in itself all contradictions. The philosophy of history, even in the hands of the most distinguished men, such as Herder for example, has a tendency rather to provoke contradiction than to encourage the formation of correct opinions. My object, moreover, is not so far-reaching. It is no part of my plan to pronounce judgment upon or to explain historically the spirit of ancient Greece : it suffices for me to bring home to our consciousness how boundless is the gift which it has brought us, and how actively that gift still works upon our poetry, our thought, our faith, our researches. I could not be exhaustive ;—I have contented myself with the endeavour to give a vivid and truthful picture. In so doing I have inflicted upon my readers some trouble, but this could not be avoided.

SECOND CHAPTER

ROMAN LAW

Von Jugend auf ist mir Anarchie verdriesslicher
gewesen als der Tod.—GOETHE

DISPOSITION

TO define in clear terms what we have inherited from Rome, what out of that vast manufactory of human destinies still exercises a living influence, is certainly impossible, unless we have a clear conception of what Rome was. Even Roman Law in the narrower sense of the word (Private Law), which, as every one knows, forms the chief material on which all juristical minds are to this day trained, and provides the actual basis even for the freest, most divergent and more modern systems of law, cannot be judged in a way that will give a proper estimate of its peculiar value, if it be simply regarded as a kind of lay Bible, a canon, which has taken a permanent place, hallowed by tens of centuries. If this blind attachment to Roman legal dicta is the result of a superficial historical appreciation, the same may be said of the violent reaction against Roman Law. Whoever studies this law and its slow tedious development, even if only in general outlines, will certainly form a different judgment. For then he will see how the Indo-European races * even in earliest times possessed certain clearly expressed

* In another place I shall have to recur to the difficult question of races (see chap. iv.). I shall here only insert a very important remark :

fundamental legal convictions, which developed in
different ways in the different races, without ever being
able to attain to any full development ; he will see that
they could not do so because no branch could succeed
in founding a free and at the same time a lasting State ;
then he will be surprised to perceive how this small nation
of men of strong character, the Romans, established both
State and Law—the State by every one desiring permanently to establish his own personal right, the Law by
every one possessing the self-control to make the necessary
sacrifices and to be absolutely loyal to the common weal ;
and whoever gains this insight will certainly never
speak except with the greatest reverence of Roman
Law as one of the most valuable possessions of mankind.
At the same time he will certainly perceive that the
highest quality of Roman Law and the one most worthy
of imitation is its exact suitability to definite conditions
of life. He cannot, however, fail to note that State and
Law—both creations of the " born nation of lawyers " *

while from various sides the existence of an Aryan race is called in
question, while many philologists doubt the validity of the language
criterion (*see* Salomon Reinach, *L'origine des Aryens*) and individual
anthropologists point to the chaotic results of the measuring of skulls
(*e.g.*, Topinard and Ratzel), the investigators in the sphere of history
of law unanimously use the expression Aryans or Indo-Europeans,
because they find a definite conception of law in this group of
linguistically related peoples, who from the beginning and through all
the branchings of a manifold development have fundamentally nothing
in common with certain equally ineradicable legal conceptions prevalent among the Semites, Hamites, &c. (*See* the works of Savigny,
Mommsen, Jhering and Leist.) No measuring of skulls and philological subtleties can get rid of this great simple fact—a result of
painfully accurate, juristical research—and by it the existence of a
moral Aryanism (in contrast to a moral non-Aryanism) is proved, no
matter how varied are the elements of which the peoples of this group
should be composed.

* Jhering : *Entwickelungsgeschichte des römischen Rechts*, p. 81. An
expression which is all the more remarkable as this great authority on
law is wont to deny vigorously that anything is innate in a people ;
he even goes the length in his *Vorgeschichte der Indoeuropäer*
(p. 270) of making the extraordinary statement that the inherited
physical (and with it simultaneously the moral) structure of man—

—are here inseparable, and that we cannot understand either this State or this Law, if we have not a clear conception of the Roman people and its history. This is all the more indispensable, as we have inherited from the Roman idea of State as well as from Roman Private Law a great deal that still lives to-day—not to speak of the political relations actually created by the Roman idea of State, relations to which we owe the very possibility of our existence to-day as civilised nations. Hence it may be opportune to ask ourselves, What kind of people were the Romans ? What is their significance in history ? Naturally only a very hasty sketch can be given here : but it may, I hope, suffice to give us a clear idea of the political achievements of this great people in their essential outlines and to characterise with clearness the somewhat complicated nature of the legacy of politics and of political law that has been handed down to our century. Then and then only will it be feasible and profitable to consider our legacy of private law.

ROMAN HISTORY

One would think that, as the Latin language and the history of Rome play such an important *rôle* in our schools, every educated person would at least possess a clear general conception of the growth and achievements of the Roman people. But this is not the case, and indeed it is not possible with the usual methods of instruction.

for this is surely what the term " race " is intended to designate—has absolutely no influence on his character, but solely the geographical surroundings, so that the Aryan, if transferred to Mesopotamia, would *eo ipso* have become a Semite and *vice versâ*. In comparison with this, Haeckel's pseudo-scientific phantasma of different apes, from each of which a different race of men derives its origin, seems a sensible theory. Of course one must not forget that Jhering had to contend all his life against the mystic dogma of an "innate *corpus juris,*" and that it is his great achievement to have paved a way for true science in this matter ; that explains his exaggerations in the opposite direction.

Of course every person of culture is, to a certain point, at home in Roman history : the legendary Romulus, Numa Pompilius, Brutus, the Horatii and Curiatii, the Gracchi, Marius, Sulla, Cæsar, Pompey, Trajan, Diocletian and countless others, are all at least just as familiar to us (*i.e.*, in regard to names and dates) as our own great men ; a youth who could not give information about the Second Punic War or confused the different Scipios would feel just as ashamed as if he could not explain the advantages of the Roman legions and maniples over the Macedonian phalanx. One must also admit that Roman history, as it is usually presented to us, is a remarkably rich store of interesting anecdotes ; but the knowledge one derives from it is one-sided and absolutely defective. The whole history of Rome almost assumes the appearance of a great and cruel sport, played by politicians and generals, whose pastime it is to conquer the world, whereby they achieve many marvellous results in the art of systematic oppression of foreign peoples and egging on of their own, as well as in the equally noble art of inventing new stratagems of war and of putting them into practice with as large herds of human cattle as possible. There is beyond doubt some truth in this view. There came a time in Rome when those who considered themselves aristocrats chose war and politics as their life-work, instead of taking them up only in time of necessity. Just as with us a short time ago, a man of family could only become an officer, diplomatist or administrative official, so the " upper ten thousand " in later Rome could enter only three professions that did not degrade them socially—*res militaris, juris scientia* and *eloquentia*.* And as the world was still young and the province of science not too large to be covered, a man of ability could master all three ; if in addition he had plenty of money, his qualifications

* *Cf.* Savigny : *Geschichte des römischen Rechtes im Mittelalter.* **chap.** i

for politics were complete. It is only necessary to read over again the letters of Cicero to see from his simple confessions, hopelessly entrammelled as he was in the ideas of his time, and unable to look beyond his own nose, how mighty Rome and its destinies became the play-ball of idle dawdlers and how much truth there is in the assertion that Rome was not made but unmade by its politicians. Politics have their peculiarities in other countries as well as in Rome. From Alexander to Napoleon, one can hardly over-estimate the power of criminal obstinacy in purely political heroes. A brief discussion of this point is all the more appropriate in this chapter, as Rome in particular is rightly regarded as a specifically political State and we may therefore hope to learn from it how and by whom great and successful politics are achieved.

What Gibbon says about kings in general, that " their power is most effective in destruction," is true of almost all politicians—as soon as they possess sufficient power. I am not sure that it was not the wise Solon who made a prosperous development of the Athenian State impossible for all time, by doing away with the historically given composition of the population from various tribes and introducing an artificial class-division according to property. This so-called timocracy (honour to him who has money) comes in, it is true, of its own accord almost everywhere to a smaller or greater extent, and Solon at least took the precaution of making duties increase with increase of wealth ; nevertheless he it was with his constitution that laid the axe to the root, from which—however painfully—the Athenian State had grown.* A less

* Many will think, but unjustly so, that the constitution of Lycurgus is still more arbitrary. For Lycurgus does not undermine the foundations provided by historical development ; on the contrary, he strengthens them. The peoples that had migrated, one after another, into Lacedæmonia, formed layers above each other, the latest comers at the top—and Lycurgus allowed this to remain so. Though the

important man would not have ventured to make such a revolutionary change in the natural course of development, and that would probably have been a blessing. And can we form a different opinion of Julius Cæsar? Of the famous generals in the history of the world as a politician he probably played the greatest part; in the most widely different spheres (think only of the improvement of the calendar, the undertaking of a universal legal code, the founding of the African colony) he revealed a penetrating understanding; as an organising genius he would, I think, not have been surpassed by Napoleon, under equally favourable conditions—and withal he had the inestimable advantage of being not a foreign *condottiere*, like Napoleon or Diocletian, but a good genuine Roman, firmly rooted in his hereditary fatherland, so that his individual arbitrariness (as in the case of Lycurgus) would certainly not have erred far from the plumb-line of what suited his nation. And yet it is this very man and no other who bent the tough tree of life of the Roman con-

Pelasgians (Helots) tilled the land, the Achæans (περίοικοι) engaged in trade and industry, and the Dorians (Spartiatæ) waged war and in consequence ruled, that was no artificial division of labour but the confirmation of a relationship actually existing. I am also convinced that life was in Lacedæmonia for a long time happier than in any other part of Greece; slave-trade was forbidden, the Helots were hereditary tenants, and though not bedded on roses they yet enjoyed considerable independence; the περίοικοι had freedom to move about, even their limited military service being frequently relaxed in the interests of their industries, which were hereditary in the various families; for the Spartiatæ, finally, social intercourse was the principle of their whole life, and in the rooms where they met at their simple meals, there stood resplendent one single statue as protecting deity, that of the god of laughter (Plutarch, *Lycurgus*, xxxvii.). Lycurgus, however, lays himself open to the reproach that he tried to fix these existing and so far sound conditions, and thus robbed the living organism of its necessary elasticity; secondly, that on the substantial and strong foundation he erected a very fantastic structure. Here again we see the theorising politician, the man who tries to decide by way of reasoning how things must be, while as a matter of fact the function of logical reason is to record and not to create. But to the fact that Lycurgus, in spite of everything, took historical data as his starting-point, are due that strength and endurance which his constitution enjoyed above those of the rest of Greece.

stitution and gave it over to inevitable decay and ruin. For the remarkable thing in pre-Cæsarean Rome is not that the city had to experience so many violent internal storms—in the case of a structure so incomparably elastic that is natural, the clash of interests and the never-resting ambition of professional politicians saw to that in Rome as elsewhere—no, what fills us with wonder and admiration is rather the vitality of this constitution. Patricians and Plebeians might periodically be at each other's throats : yet an invisible power held them firmly together ; as soon as new conditions were provided for by a new compromise, the Roman State stood once more stronger than ever.*   Cæsar was born in the midst of one of these severe crises ; but perhaps it appears to us in history worse than all previous ones—both because it is nearer to us in time, and we are therefore more fully

* The expression " Aristocracy and Plebs," which Ranke likes to use for Patricians and Plebeians, is to the layman most misleading. Niebuhr already objected to the confusion of Plebs and *Pöbel* (rabble). Patricians and Plebeians are rather like two powers in the one State, the one certainly privileged politically, the other the reverse in many ways (at least in former times), both, however, composed of free, independent, altogether autonomous yeomen.   And for that reason Sallust can write, even of the oldest times : " The highest authority certainly lay with the Patricians, but the power most assuredly with the Plebeians " (*Letters to Cæsar*, i. 5); we also see the Plebeians from earliest times play a great part in the State, and their families intermarry to a large extent with the Patricians.   The uneducated man among us is therefore quite misled if he receives the idea that in Rome it was a question of an aristocracy and a proletariat.   The peculiarity and the remarkable vitality of the Roman State had its foundation in this, that it contained from the first two differentiable parts (which present in their political efficacy in many points an analogy to Whigs and Tories, only that here it is a question of " born parties "), which, however, had grown up together with the State through exactly the same interests of property, law and freedom ; from this the Romans derived, internally, continuous freshness of life, and in foreign affairs, perpetual unswerving unanimity.   Of the Plebeian portions of the army Cato says, " viri fortissimi et milites strenuissimi " ; they were indeed free-men, who fought for their own homes and hearths.   In ancient Rome, as a matter of fact, only freeholders could serve in the army, and Plebeians held the rank of officer equally with Patricians (*see* Mommsen : *Abriss des römischen Staatsrechtes*, 1893, p. 258 ; and Esmarch : *Römische R   sgeschichte*, 3rd ed., p. 28 ff.).

informed of it, and because we know the issue which Cæsar brought about. I for my part consider the interpretation which the philosophy of history gives to these events a pure abstraction. Neither the rough hand of the impetuous, passionate Plebeian Marius nor the tiger-like cruelty of the coolly calculating Patrician Sulla would have inflicted fatal wounds upon the Roman constitution. Even the most critical danger—the freeing of many thousands of slaves and the bestowing of citizenship on many thousands of those freed-men (and that for political, immoral reasons)—Rome would soon have surmounted. Rome possessed the vitality to ennoble slavery, that is, to give it the definite Roman character. Only a mighty personality, one of those abnormal heroes of will, such as the world scarcely produces once in a thousand years, could ruin such a State. It is said that Cæsar was a saviour of Rome, snatched away too soon, before he could finish his work: this is false. When the great man arrived with his army on the banks of the Rubicon, he is said to have hesitatingly commanded a halt and reflected once more on the far-reaching consequences of his action ; if he did not cross, he himself would be in danger, if he did cross the boundary marked by sacred law, he would involve the whole world (*i.e.*, the Roman State) in danger : he decided for ambition and against Rome. The anecdote may be invented, Cæsar at least lets us see no such inner struggle of conscience in his *Civil War ;* but the situation is exactly described thereby. No matter how great a man may be, he is never free, his past imperatively prescribes the direction of his present ; if once he has chosen the worse part, he must henceforth do harm, whether he wills it or not, and though he raise himself to an autocracy, in the fond hope that he henceforth has it in his power to devote himself wholly to doing what is good, he will experience in himself that " the might of Kings is most effective in destruction." Cæsar had written to Pompey even from Ariminum to the effect that the interests of the republic were nearer his heart than his own life ;* and yet Cæsar had not long been all-powerful to do good, when his faithful friend Sallust had to ask him whether he had really saved or despoiled the republic ?† At the best he had saved it as Virginius did his daughter. Pompey, as several contemporary writers tell us, would allow no one beside him, Cæsar no one over him. Imagine what might have been the result for Rome if two such men, instead of being politicians, had acted as the servants of the Fatherland, as had been Roman custom hitherto !

It is not my business to enter more fully into the subject briefly sketched here ; my only object has been to show what a superficial knowledge we have of a people, if we study only the history of its politicians and generals. This is particularly the case with Rome. Whoever studies Rome merely from this point of view, no matter how industriously he may examine its history, can certainly arrive at no other result than did Herder, whose interpretation therefore will remain classic. To this man of genius Roman history is " the history of demons," Rome a " robbers' cave," what the Romans give to the world " devastating night," their " great noble souls, Cæsars and Scipios," spend their life in murdering, the more men they have slaughtered in their campaigns, the warmer the praise that is paid them.‡ This is from a certain point of view correct ; but the investigations of Niebuhr, Duruy and Mommsen (especially the last), as well as those of the brilliant historians of law in our century—Savigny, Jhering and many others—have brought to light another Rome, to the existence of which Montesquieu had been the first

* *Civil War*, i. 9. Thoroughly Roman, by the way, to use such a commonplace expression at such a time !
† Second Letter to Cæsar.
‡ *Ideen zur Geschichte der Menschheit*, Bk. XIV.

to call attention. Here the important thing was to discover and put in its right light what the old Roman historians, intent on celebrating battles, describing conspiracies, slandering enemies and flattering politicians who paid well, had passed by unnoticed or at any rate had never duly appreciated. A people does not become what the Romans have become in the history of mankind by means of murder and robbery, but in spite of it ; no people produces statesmen and warriors of such admirably strong character as Rome did, if it does not itself supply a broad, firm and sound basis for strength of character. What Herder and so many after him call Rome can therefore be only a part of Rome, and indeed not the most important part. The exposition of Augustine in the fifth book of his *De civitate Dei* is, in my judgment, far happier ; he calls attention particularly to the absence of greed and selfishness among the Romans and says that their whole will proclaimed itself in the one resolution, " either to live free or die bravely " (aut fortiter emori aut liberos vivere) ; and the greatness of the Roman power, as well as its durability, he ascribes to this moral greatness.

In the general introduction to this book I spoke of " anonymous " powers, which shape the life of peoples ; we have a brilliant example of this in Rome. I believe we might say without exaggeration that all Rome's true greatness was such an anonymous " national greatness." If in the case of the Athenians genius unfolded itself in the blossom, here it did so in the trunk and the roots ; Rome was of all nations that with the strongest roots. Hence it was that it defied so many storms, and the history of the world required almost five hundred years to uproot the rotten trunk. Hence too, however, the peculiar grisaille of its history. In the case of the Roman tree everything went to wood, as the gardeners say ; it bore few leaves, still fewer blossoms, but

the trunk was incomparably strong; by its support
later nations raised themselves aloft. The poet and the
philosopher could not prosper in this atmosphere, this
people loved only those personalities in whom it recognised itself, everything unusual aroused its distrust;
" whoever wished to be other than his comrades passed
in Rome for a bad citizen."* The people were right;
the best statesman for Rome was he who did not move
one hair's-breadth from what the people as a whole
wished, a man who understood how to open the safety-
valve now here, now there, to meet the growing forces
by the lengthening of pistons and by suitably arranged
centrifugal balls and throttles, till the machine of State
had quasi-automatically increased its size and perfected
its administrative power; he must be, in short, a reliable
mechanician: that was the ideal politician for this strong,
conscious people whose interests lay entirely in the
practical things of life. As soon as any one overstepped
this limit, he necessarily committed a crime against the
common weal.

Rome, I repeat—for this is the chief point to grasp,
and everything else follows from it—Rome is not the
creation of individual men, but of a whole people; in
contrast to Hellas everything really great is here " anonymous "; none of its great men approaches the greatness
of the Roman people as a whole. And so what Cicero
says in his *Republic* (ii. 1) is very correct and worth
taking to heart: " The constitution of our State is
superior to that of others for the following reason: in
other places it was individual men who by laws and
institutions founded the constitution, as, for example,
Minos in Crete, Lycurgus in Lacedæmonia, in Athens
(where change was frequent) at one time Theseus, at
another Draco, then Solon, Clisthenes and many others;
on the other hand, our Roman Commonwealth is founded

* Mommsen: *Römische Geschichte,* 8th ed., i. 24i

not on the genius of a single man but of many men, nor did the span of a fleeting human life suffice to establish it, it is the work of centuries and successive generations." Even the General in Rome needed only to give free play to the virtues which his whole army possessed—patience, endurance, unselfishness, contempt of death, practical common sense, above all the high consciousness of civic responsibility—and he was sure of victory, if not to-day, then to-morrow. Just as the troops consisted of citizens, their commanders were magistrates who only temporarily changed the office of an administrator or councillor and judge for that of commander-in-chief; in general too it made little difference when in the regular routine of office the one official relieved the other in command; the idea "soldier" came into prominence only in the time of decline. It was not as adventurers but as the most domiciled of citizens and peasants that the Romans conquered the world.

ROMAN IDEALS

The question here forces itself upon us : is it at all admissible to apply the term conquerors to the Romans ? I scarcely think so. The Teutonic peoples, the Arabians and the Turks were conquerors ; the Romans, on the other hand, from the day they enter history as an individual, separate nation are distinguished by their fanatical, warm-hearted, and, perhaps, narrow-minded love for their Fatherland ; they are bound to this spot of earth —not particularly healthy nor uncommonly rich—by inseverable ties of heart, and what drives them to battle and gives them their invincible power is first and foremost the love of home, the desperate resolve to yield up the independent possession of this soil only with their lives. That this principle entailed gradual extension of the State does not prove lust for conquest, it was the natural

outcome of a compulsion. Even to-day might is the
most important factor in international law, and we have
seen how in our century the most peaceful of nations,
like Germany, have had unceasingly to increase their
military power, but only in the interests of their independence. How much more difficult was the position of
Rome, surrounded by a confused chaos of peoples great
and small—close at hand masses of related races constantly warring against each other, farther afield an ever-
threatening unexplored chaos of barbarians, Asiatics
and Africans! Defence did not suffice; if Rome wished
to enjoy peace, she had to spread the work of organisation and administration from one land to the other.
Observe the contemporaries of Rome and see what a
failure those small Hellenic States were owing to the lack
of political foresight; Rome, however, had this quality
as no people before or after. Its leaders did not
act according to theoretical conceptions, as we might
almost be inclined to believe to-day when we see so
strictly logical a development; they rather followed
an almost unerring instinct; this, however, is the surest
of all compasses—happy he who possesses it! We hear
much of Roman hardness, Roman selfishness, Roman
greed; yes! but was it possible to struggle for independence and freedom amid such a world without being
hard? Can we maintain our place in the struggle for
existence without first and foremost thinking of self?
Is possession not power? But one fact has been practically disregarded, viz., that the unexampled success
of the Romans is not to be looked upon as a result of
hardness, selfishness, greed—these raged all around in
at least as high a degree as among the Romans, and
even to-day no great change has taken place—no, the
successes of the Romans are based on intellectual and
moral superiority. In truth a one-sided superiority;
but what is not one-sided in this world? And it cannot
be denied that in certain respects the Romans felt more

intensely and thought more acutely than any other men at any time, and they were in addition peculiar in this, that in their case feeling and thinking worked together and supplemented each other.

I have already mentioned their love of home. That was a fundamental trait of the old Roman character. It was not the purely intellectual love of the Hellenes, bubbling over and rejoicing in song, yet ever prone to yield to the treacherous suggestions of selfishness ; nor was it the verbose love of the Jews : we know how very pathetically the Jews sing of the " Babylonian captivity," but, when sent home full-handed by the magnanimous Cyrus, prefer to submit to fines and force only the poorest to return, rather than leave the foreign land where they are so prosperous ; no, in the case of the Romans it was a true, thoroughly unsentimental love that knew few words, but was ready for any sacrifice ; no man and no woman among them ever hesitated to sacrifice their lives for the Fatherland. How can we explain so unmeasured an affection ? Rome was (in olden times) not a wealthy city ; without crossing the boundaries of Italy one could see much more fruitful regions. But what Rome gave and securely established was a life morally worthy of man. The Romans did not invent marriage, they did not invent law, they did not invent the constitutional freedom-giving State ; all that grows out of human nature and is found everywhere in some form and to some degree ; but what the Aryan races had conceived under these notions as the bases of all morality and culture had nowhere been firmly established till the Romans established it.* Had the Hellenes got too

---

* For the Aryan peoples in particular, see Leist's excellent *Gräco-italienische Rechtsgeschichte* (1884) and his *Altarisches Jus civile* (1896), also Jhering's *Vorgeschichte der Indoeuropäer.* The ethnical investigations of the last years have, however, shown more and more that marriage, law and State exist in some form everywhere, even among the savages of least mental development. And this must be strongly emphasised, for the evolution mania and the pseudo-scientific dogma-

near Asia ?   Were they too suddenly civilised ?   Had the
Celts, who were by nature endowed with almost as much

tism of our century have brought into most of our popular books
absolutely invented descriptions, which are very difficult to remove
from them, in spite of the sure results of exact research; and
from here these descriptions also force their way into valuable
and serious books.   In Lamprecht's famous *Deutsche Geschichte*,
vol. i., for instance, we find what is supposed to be a description
of the social conditions of the old Teutonic peoples, sketched
" under the auspices of comparative ethnology "; here we are told of
a time when among these peoples a " community of sex limited by
no differences of any kind prevailed, all brothers and sisters were
husbands and wives to each other and all their children brothers and
sisters, &c.": the first progress from this state, as we are to suppose,
was the establishment of the mother's right, the so-called *Matriarchate*—
and so the tale continues for pages; one fancies one is listening to the
first stuttering of a new mythology.   As far as the mother-right is
concerned (*i.e.*, family name and right of inheritance after the mother,
as the fatherhood was always a common one), Jhering has convincingly
shown that even the oldest Aryans, before the breaking off of a Teutonic branch, knew nothing of it (*Vorgeschichte*, p. 61 ff.), and the very
oldest parts of the Aryan language point already to the " supreme
position of the husband and father of the household " (Leist, *Gräco-
ital. Rechtsgeschichte*, p. 58); that supposition therefore lacks every
scientific basis.   [This was meantime confirmed by Otto Schrader,
Reallexicon der indogermanischen Altertumskunde, 1901, p. xxxiii.]   It is
still more important to establish the fact that the " comparative ethnography " appealed to by Lamprecht has found community of sex
nowhere in the world among human beings.   In the year 1896 a small
book appeared which summarises in strictly objective fashion all
the researches that refer to this, Ernst Grosse's *Die Formen der Familie
und die Formen der Wirtschaft*, and there we see how the so-called
empirical philosophers, with Herbert Spencer at their head, and the so-
called strictly empirical anthropologists and ethnologists, honoured as
" authorities " (with praiseworthy exceptions like Lubbock), simply
started from the *à priori* supposition that there must be community
of sex among simpler peoples, since the law of evolution demands it,
and then everywhere discovered facts to confirm this.   But more exact
and unprejudiced investigations now prove for one race after the
other that community of sex does not exist there, and Grosse may
put down the apodictic assertion : " There is, in fact, no single primitive people whose sexual relations approached a condition of promiscuity or even hinted at such a thing.   The firmly knit individual
family is by no means a late achievement of civilisation, it exists in
the lowest stages of culture as a rule without exception " (p. 42).
Exact proofs are to be found in Grosse ; besides, all anthropological
and ethnological accounts of recent years testify how very much we
have undervalued the so-called savages, how superficially we have
observed and how thoughtlessly we have drawn conclusions about
primitive conditions, of which we know absolutely nothing with surety,

fire, become so savage in the wild North that they were no longer able to construct anything, to organise anything,

[Lately Heinrich Schurtz, in his *Altersklassen und Männerbunde, eine Darstellung der Grundformen der Gesellschaft*, 1902, has fully shown that the arguments for promiscuity in early times, which are wont to be drawn from phenomena of " free love " to-day, are to be interpreted quite differently, and that, on the contrary, " with the most primitive races marriage, and in connection with it the formation of society on a purely sexual basis, is more strongly developed " (p. 200).] As this subject is essentially of the greatest importance and throws a peculiar and very noteworthy sidelight upon scientific modes of thought and power of thought in our century, I should like to add one more instruc- tive example. The original inhabitants of central Australia are, as is well known, supposed to belong to the most backward, intellectually, of all peoples ; Lubbock calls them " wretched savages, who cannot count their own fingers, not even the fingers of one hand " (*The Pre- historic Age*, Germ. trans., ii. 151). One can imagine with what con- tempt the traveller Eyre wrote of the " remarkably peculiar cases where marriage is forbidden " in this wretched race, " where a man may not marry a woman who has the same name as he, even though she be by no means related to him." Strange ! And how could these people come to have such inexplicable caprices when it would have been their duty, according to the theory of evolution, to have lived in abso- lute promiscuity ? Since that time two English officials, who lived for years among these savages and gained their confidence, have given us a detailed account of them (*Royal Society of Victoria*, April 1897, summary in *Nature*, June 10, 1897), and it appears that their whole intellectual life, their " conceptive life " (if I may say so) is so in- credibly complicated that it is almost impossible for one of us to comprehend it. These people, for example, who are supposed not to be able to count up to five, have a more complicated belief than Plato with regard to the transmigration of souls, and this faith forms the basis of their religion. Now as to their marriage laws. In the par- ticular district spoken of here there lives an ethnically uniform race, the Aruntas. Every marriage union with strange races is forbidden ; thereby the race is kept pure. But the extremely baneful effects of long-continued inbreeding (Lamprecht's Teutons would long have become Cretins before ever they entered into history !) are prevented by the Australian blacks by the following ingenious system : they divide (mentally) the whole race into four groups ; for simplicity I designate them *a b c d.* A youth from the group *a* may only marry a girl from group *d*, the male *b* only the female *c*, the male *c* only the female *b*, the male *d* only the female *a*. The children of *a* and *d* form once more the group *b*, those of *b* and *c* the group *a*, those of *c* and *b* the group *d*, those of *d* and *a* the group *c*. I simplify very much and give only the skeleton, for I fear my European reader would otherwise soon reach the stage of likewise not being able to count up to five. That such a system imposes important restrictions on the rights of the heart cannot be denied, but I ask, how could a scientifically trained selector have hit upon a more ingenious expedient to satisfy the two laws of breeding

or to found a State ?*   Or was it not rather that blood-
mixtures within the common mother race, and at the
same time the artificial selection necessitated by geographical and historical conditions tended to produce
abnormal gifts (naturally with accompanying phenomena
of reversion) ?†   I do not know.   Certain it is, however,
that previous to the Romans there was no sacred, worthy
and at the same time practical regulation of matters
which are established by strict observation, namely, (1) the race must
be kept pure, (2) continuous inbreeding is to be avoided ? (*see* chap.
iv.).   Such a phenomenon calls for reverence and silence.   When contemplating it one gladly keeps silent regarding such systems as those
already mentioned as belonging to the end of the nineteenth century.   But
what must we feel when we turn our glance from the extremely laboured
efforts of these worthy Australian Aruntas to Rome and behold here,
in the middle of a frightful world, the sacredness of marriage, the
legal status of the family, the freedom of the head of the household
rising up out of the heart of the people, for it was at a much later
period that it was engraved on bronze tables ?

   * Thierry, Mommsen, &c.

   † Till a short time ago it was a favourite practice to represent the
population of Rome as a kind of medley of peoples living side by
side ; it was supposed to have borrowed its traditions from Hellenic
units, its administration from Etruscan ones, its law from Sabines, and
its intellect from Samnites, &c.   Thus Rome would have in a way been a
mere word, a name, the common designation of an international trysting-
place.   This soap-bubble, too, which rose from the brain foam of pale professors, has burst, like so many others, in Mommsen's hands.   Facts and
reason both prove the absurdity of such a hypothesis, " which attempts
to change the people, which, as few others, has developed its language,
state, and religion purely and popularly, into a confused rubble of
Etruscan, Sabine, Hellenic, and unfortunately even Pelasgic ruins "
(*Röm. Gesch.*, i. 43).   The fact, however, that this thoroughly uniform
and peculiar people originated from a crossing of various related races
is undeniable, and Mommsen himself clearly shows this ; he admits
two Latin and one Sabellian race ; at a later time all kinds of elements
were added, but only after the Roman national character was firmly
developed so that it assimilated the foreign portion.   It would, however, be ridiculous to " assign Rome to the number of mixed peoples "
(*see* p. 44).   It is quite a different thing to establish the fact that the
most extraordinary and most individual talents and the sturdiest power
are produced by crossing.   Athens was a brilliant example, Rome
another, Italy and Spain in the Middle Ages equally so, just as Prussia
and England prove it at the present day (more details in chap. 4).   In
this respect the Hellenic myth that the Latins were descended from
Hercules and a Hyperborean maiden is very noteworthy as one of those
incomprehensible traits of innate wisdom ; whereas the desperate
efforts of Dionysius of Halicarnassus (who lived at the time of the

relating to marriage and family ; no more was there a
rational law resting on a sure foundation capable of being
widened, or a political organisation able to resist the
storms of a chaotic time. Though the simply constructed mechanism of the old Roman State might
frequently be awkward in its working and require
thorough repairs, it was yet a splendid structure well
adapted to the time and to its purpose. In Rome, from
the first, the idea of Law had been finely conceived and
finely carried into effect ; moreover its limitations were in
keeping with the conditions. Still more was this the case
with the family. This institution was to be found in
Rome alone—and in a form more beautiful than the
world has ever since seen ! Every Roman citizen,
whether Patrician or Plebeian, was lord, yea, king in
his house : his will extended even beyond death by the
unconditional freedom of bequest, and the sanctity of
the last testament ; his home was assured against
official interference by more solid rights than ours ;
in contrast to the Semitic patriarchate he had introduced the principle of agnation* and thereby swept
entirely aside the interference of mothers-in-law and
women as a whole ; on the other hand, the materfamilias
was honoured, treasured, loved like a queen. Where
was there anything to compare with this in the world
at that time ? Outside of civilisation perhaps ; inside
it nowhere. And so it was that the Roman loved his
home with such enduring love and gave his heart's blood
for it. Rome was for him the family and the law, a
rocky eminence of human dignity in the midst of a
surging sea.

birth of Christ) to prove the descent of the Romans from Hellenes,
" as they could not possibly be of barbarian origin," shows with
touching simplicity how dangerous a conjunction of great learning
with preconceived opinions and conclusions of reason can become !

* The family resting upon relationship to the father alone, so that only
descent from the father's side by males, and not that from the mother's
side, establishes relationship at law. Only a marriage contracted in
the right forms produces children who belong to the agnate family.

Let no one fancy that anything great can be achieved in this world unless a purely ideal power is at work. The idea alone will of course not suffice ; there must also be a tangible interest, even should it be, as in the case of the martyrs, an interest pertaining to the other world ; without an additional ideal element the struggle for gain alone possesses little power of resistance ; higher power of achievement is supplied only by a " faith," and that is what I call an " ideal impulse " in contrast to the direct interest of the moment—be that last possession or anything else whatever. As Dionysius says of the ancient Romans, " they thought highly of themselves and could not therefore venture to do anything unworthy of their ancestors " (i. 6) ; in other words, they kept before their eyes an ideal of themselves. I do not mean the word " ideal " in the degenerate, vague sense of the " blue flower " of Romance, but in the sense of that power which impelled the Hellenic sculptor to form the god from out the stone, and which taught the Roman to look upon his freedom, his rights, his union with a woman in marriage, his union with other men for the common weal, as something sacred, as the most valuable gift that life can give. A rock, as I said, not an Aristophanic Cloud-cuckoo-land. As a dream, the same feeling existed more or less among all Indo-Europeans : we meet with a certain holy awe and earnestness in various forms among all the members of this family ; the persevering power to realise things practically was, however, given to no one so much as to the Roman. Do not believe that " robbers " can achieve results such as the Roman State, to the salvation of the world, achieved. And when once you have recognised the absurdity of such a view, search deeper and you will see that these Romans were unsurpassed as a civilising power, and that they could only be that because, though they had great faults and glaring intellectual deficiencies, they yet possessed high mental and moral qualities.

The Struggle against the Semites

Mommsen tells (i. 321) of the alliance between the Babylonians and the Phœnicians to subdue Greece and Italy, and is of opinion that " at one stroke freedom and civilisation would have been swept off the face of the earth." We should weigh carefully what these words mean when uttered by a man who commands the whole field as no one else does ; freedom and civilisation (I should rather have said culture, for how can one deny civilisation to the Babylonians and Phœnicians, or even to the Chinese ?) would have been destroyed, blotted out for ever ! And then take up the books which give a detailed and scientific account of the Phœnician and Babylonian civilisation, in order to see clearly what foundation there is for such a far-reaching statement. It will not be difficult to see what distinguishes a Hellenic " Colony " from a Phœnician Factory : and from the difference between Rome and Carthage we shall readily understand what an ideal power is, even in the sphere of the driest, most selfish politics of interest. How suggestive is that distinction which Jhering (*Vorgeschichte*, p. 176) teaches us to draw between the " commercial highways " of the Semites and the " military roads " of the Romans : the former the outcome of the tendency to expansion and possession ; the latter the result of the need of concentrating their power and defending the homeland. We shall also learn to distinguish between authentic " robbers," who only civilise in as far as they understand how to take up and utilise with enviable intelligence all discoveries that have a practical worth and to encourage in the interests of their commerce artificial needs in foreign peoples, but who otherwise rob even their nearest relations of every human right— who nowhere organise anything but taxes and absolute slavery, who in general, no matter where they plant their foot, never seek to rule a country as a whole under systematic government, and, being alive only to their commercial interests, leave everything as barbarous as they find it : we shall, as I say, learn to distinguish between such genuine robbers and the Romans, who, in order to retain the blessings that attend the order reigning in their midst, are compelled—beginning from that unchanging centre, the home—slowly and surely to extend their ordering and clearing influence all round ; they never really conquer (when they can help it) ; they spare and respect every individuality ; but withal they organise so excellently that people approach them with the prayer to be allowed to share in the blessings of their system ;* their own splendid " Roman law " they generously make accessible to ever-increasing numbers, and they at the same time unite the various foreign legal systems, taking the Roman as a basis, in order gradually to evolve therefrom a " universal international law."† This is surely not how robbers act. Here we have rather to recognise the first steps towards the permanent establishment of Indo-European ideals of freedom and civilisation.

* One of the last instances are the Jews who (about the year 1] came to Rome with the urgent request that it should deliver them from their Semitic sovereigns and make them into a Roman province. It is well known what gratitude they afterwards showed to Rome, which ruled them so mildly and generously.

† Esmarch, in his *Römische Rechtsgeschichte*, 3rd ed., p. 185, writes as follows on the frequently very vaguely developed and defined *jus gentium :* " This law in the Roman sense is to be regarded neither as an aggregate of accidentally common clauses, formed from a comparison of the laws that were valid among all the nations known to the Romans, nor as an objectively existing commercial law recognised and adopted by the Roman State ; it should be regarded, according to its essential substance, as a system of order for the application of private law to international relations, evolved out of the heart of Roman popular consciousness." Within the several countries the conditions of law were as little changed as possible by the Romans, one of the surprising proofs of the great respect which in the period of their true greatness they paid to all individuality.

Livy says with justice : " It was not only by our weapons but also by our Roman legislation that we won our far-reaching influence."

It is clear that the commonly accepted view of Rome as the conquering nation above all others is very one-sided. Indeed even after Rome had broken with its own traditions, or rather when the Roman people had in fact disappeared from the earth, and only the idea of it still hovered over its grave, even then it could not depart far from this great principle of its life : even the rough soldier-emperors were unable to break this tradition. And thus it is that the real military hero—as individual phenomenon—does not occur at all among the Romans. I will not make any comparisons with Alexander, Charles XII. or Napoleon ; I ask, however, whether the one man Hannibal, as an inventive, audacious, arbitrary prince of war, has not displayed more real genius than all the Roman imperators taken together.

It need scarcely be stated that Rome fought neither for a Europe of the future nor in the interests of a far-reaching mission of culture, but simply for itself ; but thanks to this very fact, that it fought for its own interests with the reckless energy of a morally strong people, it has preserved from sure destruction that " intellectual development of mankind which depends upon the Indo-Teutonic race." This is best seen clearly in the most decisive of all its struggles, that with Carthage. If Rome's political development had not been so strictly logical up till then, if it had not betimes subdued and disciplined the rest of Italy, the deadly blow to freedom and civilisation mentioned above would assuredly have been dealt by the allied Asiatics and Carthaginians. And how little a single hero can do in the face of such situations of world-wide historical moment, although he alone, it may be, has taken a comprehensive view of them, is shown by the fate of Alexander, who having destroyed

Tyre meditated embarking on a campaign against Carthage, but at his early death left nothing behind but the memory of his genius. The long-lived Roman people, on the other hand, was equal to that great task, which it finally summed up in the monumental sentence, *delenda est Carthago.*

What laments and moralisings we have had on the destruction of Carthage by the Romans, from Polybius to Mommsen! It is refreshing to meet a writer who, like Bossuet, simply says : " Carthage was taken and destroyed by Scipio, who in this showed himself worthy of his great ancestor," without any moral indignation, without the well-worn phrase that all the suffering which later befell Rome was a retribution for this misdeed. I am not writing a history of Rome and do not therefore require to sit in judgment on the Romans ; but one thing is as clear as the noonday sun ; if the Phœnician people had not been destroyed, if its survivors had not been deprived of a rallying-point by the complete destruction of their last city, and compelled to merge in other nations, mankind would never have seen this nineteenth century, upon which, with all due recognition of our weaknesses and follies, we yet look back with pride, justified in our hopes for the future. The least mercy shown to a race of such unparalleled tenacity as the Semites would have sufficed to enable the Phœnician nation to rise once more ; in a Carthage only half-burned the torch of life would have glimmered beneath the ashes, to burst again into flame as soon as the Roman Empire began to approach its dissolution. We are not yet free of peril from the Arabs,* who long seriously threatened our existence, and their

* The struggle which in late years raged in Central Africa between the Congo Free State and the Arabs (without being much heeded in Europe) is a new chapter in the old war between Semites and Indo-Europeans for the supremacy of the world. It is only in the last fifty years that the Arabs have been advancing from the East Coast of Africa into the interior and almost up to the Atlantic Ocean ; the famous Hamed ben Mohammed ben Juna, called Tippu-Tib, was for a long time absolute ruler of an immense realm which reached almost

creation, Mohammedanism, is the greatest of all hindrances
to every progress of civilisation, hanging like a sword
of Damocles over our slowly and laboriously rising culture
in Europe, Asia and Africa ; the Jews stand morally
so high above all other Semites that one may hardly
name them in conjunction with these (their ancestral
enemies in any case from time immemorial), and yet
we should need to be blind or dishonest, not to confess that the problem of Judaism in our midst is one
of the most difficult and dangerous questions of the
day ; now imagine in addition a Phœnician nation,
holding from the earliest times all harbours in their
possession, monopolising all trade, in possession of the
richest capitals in the world and of an ancestral
national religion (Jews so to speak who had never known
Prophets) . . .! It is no fantastic philosophising on
history but an objectively demonstrable fact that, under
such conditions, that which we to-day call Europe could
never have arisen. Once more I refer to the learned
works on the Phœnicians, but above all, because available
to every one, to the splendid summary in Mommsen's
Römische Geschichte, Book III. chap. i., " Carthage."

straight across all Africa with a breadth of about 20 degrees. Countless tribes which Livingstone in his time found happy and peace-
loving have since then in some cases been destroyed entirely—since
the slave-trade to foreign parts is the chief occupation of the Arabs
and never, in the history of mankind, was carried on to such an extent
as in the second half of the nineteenth century—in other cases the
natives have undergone a remarkable moral change by contact with
Semitic masters ; they have become cannibals, great stupid children
changed to wild beasts. It is, however, noteworthy that the Arabs,
where they found it paid them, have revealed their culture, knowledge
and shrewdness in laying out magnificent stretches of cultivated land,
so that parts of the Congo river district are almost as beautifully
farmed as an Alsatian estate. In Kassongo, the capital of this rich
country, the Belgian troops found magnificent Arabian houses with silk
curtains, bed-covers of satin, splendidly carved furniture, silver ware, &c.;
but the aboriginal inhabitants of this district had in the meantime degenerated into slaves and cannibals. A real tangible instance of the
difference between civilising and spreading culture. (*See* especially
Dr. Hinde: *The Fall of the Congo Arabs*, 1897, p. 66 ff. 184 ff., &c.)

The intellectual barrenness of this people **was really** horrifying. Although destiny made the Phœnicians brokers of civilisation, yet this never inspired them to invent anything whatever ; civilisation remained for them altogether something absolutely external ; of what we call " culture " they had not the least notion, even to the last : clad in magnificent garments, surrounded by works of art, in possession of all the knowledge of their time, they continued as before to practise sorcery, offered human sacrifices and lived in such a pit of unspeakable vice that the most degraded Orientals turned in disgust from them. With regard to their share in the spread of civilisation Mommsen says : " This they have done more as the bird scatters the seed * than as the sower sows the corn. The Phœnicians absolutely lacked the power, possessed by the Hellenes and even the Italic peoples, of civilising and assimilating the nations capable of being educated, with whom they came in contact. In the sphere of Roman conquest the Iberian and Celtic languages have disappeared before the Romance tongue ; the Berbers of Africa speak the same language to-day as they did at the time of Hanno and the Barcidæ. But the Phœnicians like all Aramaic peoples, in contrast to the Indo-Teutonic, lack above all the impulse to form States—the brilliant idea of freedom that is self-governing." Where the Phœnicians settled, their constitution was, fundamentally, merely a " government of capitalists, consisting on the one hand of a city mob, without property, living from hand to mouth, treating the conquered people in the country districts as mere slave-cattle without rights, and on the other hand of merchant princes, plantation-owners and aristocratic governors." These are the men, this the fatal branch of the Semitic family, from which we have been saved by the brutal

* Every reader knows by what automatic process the bird unwittingly contributes to the spread of plant life.

delenda est Carthago. And even if it should be true that the Romans in this case listened more than was their wont to the mean promptings of revenge, perhaps even of jealousy, all the more am I bound to admire the unerring certainty of instinct which induced them, even where they were blinded by evil passions, to strike down that which any cool, calculating politician gifted with the eye of the prophet would have been bound to urge them to destroy for the salvation of mankind.*

A second Roman *delenda* has for the history of the world an almost equally inestimable importance : the *delenda est Hierosolyma.* Had it not been for this achievement (which we certainly owe as much to the Jews who have at all times rebelled against every system of government as to the long-suffering Romans) Christianity would hardly ever have freed itself from Judaism, but

* Mommsen, who feels bound strongly to condemn the action of the Romans against Carthage, admits at a later point (v. 623) that it was in his opinion neither lust of empire nor of possession but fear and jealousy that prompted it. This very distinction is of importance for our reasoned view of the part played by Rome in the history of the world. If in a world which recognises might alone as the norm of international law, we can say with certainty of a people that it was not greedy of possessions or power, it seems to me that we have given it a testimonial to its moral character which makes it tower high above all contemporary peoples. As regards "fear," it was thoroughly justified, and it is surely permitted to think that the Roman senate formed a more correct judgment of the situation than Mommsen.—The arbitrary Cæsar, of whom even his zealous friend Celius must say that he sacrifices the interests of the State to his personal ends, built Carthage again at a later time. And what did it become ? The most notorious pit of vice in the world, where all whose destiny cast them thither—Romans, Greeks, Vandals—degenerated to the very marrow of their bones. Such devastat ng magic was still possessed by the curse which rested on the spot where Phœnician horrors had reigned supreme for five hundred years ! From its houses of evil repute there arose a mighty cry of indignation against everything called civilisation : That it bore Tertullian and Augustine is the only merit that we can attribute to this shortsighted and shortlived creation of Cæsar.—To characterise the nineteenth century, let me quote the opinion of one who is among its so-called greatest historians. Professor Leopold von Ranke says : "The Phœnician element has by means of commerce, colonisation and, finally, also by war, in the main exercised a quickening influence upon the Occident" (*Weltgeschichte,* i. 542).

would have remained, in the first instance, a sect among sects. The might of the religious idea, however, would have prevailed in the end ; as to that there can be no question : the enormous and increasing spread of the Jewish Diaspora * before the time of Christ proves it ;

* Diaspora is the name given to the widened Jewish community. Originally the term was applied to those Jews who had preferred not to return from the Babylonian captivity, because they were better off there than in their home. Soon there was no prosperous city in the world without a Jewish community ; nothing is more erroneous than the widespread belief that it was the destruction of Jerusalem that first scattered the Jews over the world. In Alexandria and its neighbourhood alone there were reckoned to be under the first Roman emperors a million Jews, and Tiberius already recognised the great danger of this theocratic State in the midst of the legal State. The men of the Diaspora were keen and successful propagandists, and their considerate adoption of men as " half Jews " under remission of the painful initiatory ceremony, helped them greatly ; in addition, material advantages contributed to their success, since the Jews pleaded their religion as an excuse for exemption from military service and a series of other burdensome civic duties ; but the Hebrew missionaries had the greatest success with women. Now it is a noteworthy fact that this international community, which contained Hebrews and non-Hebrews, and in which all shades of faith were represented, from the most bigoted Pharisaism to open scoffing irreligion, held together like one man as soon as it was a question of the privileges and interests of the common Jewry ; the Jewish freethinker would not for the world have omitted to send in his yearly contribution to Jerusalem for the temple-offerings ; Philo, the famous Neoplatonist, who believed in Jahve as little as in Jupiter, nevertheless represented the Jewish community of Alexandria in Rome in favour of the synagogues threatened by Caligula ; Poppæa Sabina, the mistress and later the wife of Nero, though no Hebrew but a keen member of the Jewish Diaspora, supported the prayers of the Jewish actor Alityrus, the favourite of Nero, to root out the sect of the Christians, and thereby became very probably morally responsible for that frightful persecution of the year 64, in which it is said that the apostles Peter and Paul met their death. The fact that the Romans, who otherwise at that time could not distinguish Christians from orthodox Jews, were on this occasion able to do so accurately, is regarded by Renan as conclusive proof of this charge, which was made against the Diaspora even in the first century (in Tertullian's *Apologeticus*, chap. xxi., for example, somewhat reserved but yet clear ; *see also* Renan, *L'Antéchrist*, chap. vii.). Newer convincing proofs that up to Domitian's time, and so till long after Nero's death, the Romans regarded the Christians as a Jewish sect, are to be found in Neumand : *Der römische Staat und die allgemeine Kirche* (1890), pp. 5 ff. and 14 ff. That Tacitus distinguished clearly between Jews and Christians manifestly proves nothing in this matter, as he wrote fifty years after Nero's persecu-

we should therefore have received a Judaism reformed
by Christian influence and ruling the world. Perhaps
the objection may be urged that that has come to pass,
and that it correctly describes our Christian Church.
Certainly, the objection is in part justifiable; no rightly
thinking man will deny the share that Judaism has in it.
But when we see how in earliest times the followers of
Christ demanded the strict observance of the Jewish
"law," how they, less liberal than the Jews of the Diaspora, took into their community no "heathens" who had
not submitted to the mark of circumcision common to
all Semites; when we think of the struggles which
the Apostle Paul (the Apostle of the heathen) had to
wage till his death with the Jew-Christians, and that
even much later, in the *Revelation of St. John* (iii. 9) he
and his followers are scorned as being "of the synagogue
of Satan which say they are Jews and are not, but do
lie"; when we see the authority of Jerusalem and
its temple continue to be simply invincible, even inside
the Pauline Christendom, so long as both actually did
stand intact,* then we cannot doubt that the religion
of the civilised world would have pined under the purely
Jewish primacy of the city of Jerusalem, if Jerusalem
had not been destroyed by the Romans. Ernst Renan,
certainly no enemy of the Jews, has in his *Origines du
Christianisme* (iv. chap. xx.) eloquently shown what
an "immense danger" would have lain therein.† Still
worse than the commercial monopoly of the Phœnicians
would have been the religious monopoly of the Jews;
under the leaden weight of these born dogmatists and
fanatics all freedom of thought and faith would have

tion and in his narrative transferred the knowledge of a later time to an
earlier. (*See*, too, in connection with the "Jewish jealousy," Paul Allard:
Le Christianisme et l'Empire romain de Néron à Théodose (1897), chap. i.)
   * *Cf.* on this, Graetz, *Volksth. Geschichte der Juden*, i. 653.
   † In his *Discours et Conférences*, 3rd ed., p. 350, he calls the destruc-
tion of Jerusalem "un immense bonheur."

disappeared from the world ; the flatly materialistic view
of God would have been our religion, pettifoggery our
philosophy. This too is no imaginary picture, only too
many facts speak for it ; for what is that rigid, illiberal,
intellectually narrow dogmatising of the Christian Church
—a thing undreamt of by the Aryan—what is that
disgraceful, bloodthirsty fanaticism which runs through
all the ages down to our own nineteenth century, that
curse of hatred that has clung to the religion of love
from the beginning and from which Greeks and Romans,
Indians and Chinese, Persians and Teutonic peoples turn
with horror ? What is it, if not the shadow of that temple,
in which sacrifices were offered to the god of anger and vengeance, a dark shadow cast over the youth of the heroic race
" that from out the darkness strives to reach the light " ?

Without Rome it is certain that Europe would have
remained a mere continuation of the Asiatic chaos.
Greece always gravitated towards Asia, till Rome tore
it away. It is the work of Rome that the centre of
gravity of culture has been once and for all removed to
the west, that the Semitic-Asiatic spell has been broken
and at least partly cast aside, that the predominantly
Indo-Teutonic Europe became henceforth the beating
heart and thinking brain of all mankind. While this
State fought for its own practical (but, as we saw, not
unideal) interests without the least regard for others—
often cruelly, always sternly, but seldom ignobly—it has
put the house in readiness, the strong citadel in which
our race, after long aimless wanderings, was to settle down
and organise itself for the salvation of mankind.

For the accomplishment of Rome's work so many centuries were necessary, and in addition so high a degree of
that unerring, self-willed instinct, which hits the mark,
even where it seems to be going senselessly astray,
doing good even where its will is baneful, that it was
not the fleeting existence of pre-eminent individuals but

the dogged unity of a steel-hardened people, working
almost like a force of nature, that was the right and
only efficacious thing. Hence it is that so-called
" political history," that history which tries to build
up the life of a people from the biographies of famous
men, the annals of war and diplomatic archives, is
so inappropriate here; it not only distorts, but fails to
reveal in any way those things that are the most essential. For what we, looking back and philosophising,
regard as the office or vocation of Rome in the history
of the world, is surely nothing else than an expression
for the bird's-eye view of the character of this people
as a whole. And here we must admit that the politics of
Rome moved in a straight and—as later times have
shown—perfectly correct line, so long as they were not
in the hands of professional politicians. Cæsar's period
was the most confused and most productive of evil;
both people and instinct were then dead, but the work
continued to exist, and, embodied with it, the idea of
the work, but it was nowhere capable of being set apart
as a formula and as a law for future actions, for the
simple reason that the work had not been reasoned,
considered and conscious, but unconscious and accomplished of necessity.

ROME UNDER THE EMPIRE

After the fall of the true Roman people this idea
—the idea of the Roman State—came again to life in
very different ways in the brains of individuals who were
called to power. Augustus, for example, seems really
to have been of the opinion that he had restored the
Roman republic, otherwise Horace would certainly not
have gone the length of praising him for it. Tiberius,
who transformed " the insult to the majesty of the
Roman people," the *crimen majestatis*, which was punished

even in former times, into quite a new crime, viz., " the insult to his own Cæsarean person," took thereby a very great step towards dissipating into a mere idea the actual free State created by the people of Rome—a step from which in the nineteenth century we have not yet gone back. But so firmly was the Roman idea planted in every heart that a Nero took his own life, because the Senate had branded him an " enemy of the republic." Soon, however, the proud assembly of Patricians found itself face to face with men who did not tremble before the magic words *senatus populusque Romanus :* the soldiers chose the bearer of the Roman Imperium ; it was not long before Romans, and Italians as well, were excluded for ever from this dignity : Spaniards, Gauls, Africans, Syrians, Goths, Arabs, Illyrians followed one another ; not one of them probably was even distantly related to those men who with sure instinct had created the Roman State. And yet the idea lived on ; in the Spaniard Trajan it even reached a climax of brilliancy. Under him and his immediate followers it worked so expressly as an ordering civilising power, resorting to conquest only where the consolidation of peace unconditionally demanded it, that we are justified in saying that during the Antonine century Roman imperialism—which had lived in the people previously only as an impulse, not as an end in view—came to be conscious of itself, and that in a manner which was only possible in the minds of nobly thinking foreigners, who found themselves face to face with a strange idea, which they henceforth embraced with full objectivity, in order to set it in operation with loyalty and understanding. This period had a great influence on all future time ; wherever with noble purpose the idea of a Roman Empire was again taken as a starting-point, it was done under the influence and in imitation of Trajan, Hadrian, Antoninus Pius and Marcus Aurelius. And yet there is a peculiar soullessness in this whole period. Here the sway of understanding is supreme, the heart is dumb; the passionless mechanism affects even the soul, which does right not from love but from reason: Marcus Aurelius' " Monologues " are the mirror of this attitude of mind, and the inevitable reaction appears in the sexual aberrations of his wife Faustina. The root of Rome, the passionate love of the family, of the home, was torn out; not even the famous law against bachelors, with premiums for children (Lex Julia et Papia Poppæa) could again make marriage popular. Where the heart does not command, nothing is enduring. And now other foreigners usurped supreme power, this time men full of passion but devoid of understanding, African half-breeds, soldier Emperors, who saw in the Roman State nothing more than a gigantic barracks, and had no idea why Rome in particular should be the permanent headquarters. The second of them, Caracalla, even extended the Roman franchise to all the inhabitants of the Empire: thereby Rome ceased to be Rome. For exactly a thousand years the citizens of Rome (with whom those of the other cities of Italy and of other specially deserving States had gradually been put on an equal footing) had enjoyed certain privileges, but they had gained them by burden-some responsibility as well as by restless, incomparably successful, hard work; from now onward Rome was everywhere, that is, nowhere. Wherever the Emperor happened to be was the centre of the Roman Empire. Diocletian transferred his residence to Sirmium, Constantine to Byzantium, and even when a separate Western Roman Empire arose, the imperial capital was Ravenna or Milan, Paris, Aachen, Vienna, never again Rome. The extension of the franchise to all had another result: there were no longer any citizens. Caracalla,* the murderous, pseudo-Punic savage, used

* For an understanding of the character of Caracalla and his motives

to be commended for his action and even to-day he has
his admirers (*see* Leopold von Ranke, *Weltgeschichte*, ii.
195). In reality, however, he had, by cutting the last
thread of historical tradition, *i.e.*, of historical truth,
destroyed also the last trace of that freedom, the in-
domitable, self-sacrificing and thoroughly ideal power
of which had created the city of Rome and with it Europe.
Political law was, of course, henceforth the same for
all ; it was the equality of absolute lawlessness. The
word citizen (*civis*) gave way now to the term subject (*subjectus*) : all the more remarkable, as the idea of being subject was as strange to all branches of the Indo-Europeans
as that of supreme kingship, so that we see in this one
transformation of the legal idea the incontestable proof
of Semitic influence (according to Leist, *Graco-italische
Rechtsgeschichte*, pp. 106, 108). The Roman idea certainly still lived on, but it had concentrated itself or,
so to speak, become merged in one person the Emperor ; the privileges of the Romans and their summary

I recommend the little book of Prof. Dr. Rudolf Leonhard, *Roms
Vergangenheit und Deutschlands Recht*, 1889, pp. 93–99. He shows
in the course of a few pages how this Syrian, "a descendant of the
Carthaginian human butchers and the countrymen of those priests of
Baal who were wont to throw their enemies into hot ovens" (the Jews
did the same ; *see* 2 *Samuel*, xii. 31), had adopted as his aim in life
the annihilation of Rome and the destruction of the still living remains
of Hellenic culture, and at the same time the flooding of the cultured
European world with the pseudo-Semitic refuse of his home. This
was all done systematically, maliciously and under cover of such
phrases as universal franchise and religion of mankind. Thus in one
single day he succeeded in destroying Rome for ever ; thus unsuspecting
Alexandria, the centre of art and science, became a victim of the raceless,
homeless bestiality that tore down all barriers. Let us never—never for
a moment forget that the spirit of Caracalla is among us and waiting for
its chance ! Instead of repeating by rote the deceptive phrases about
humanity which were the fashion even 1800 years ago in the Semitic
salons in Rome, we should do better to say with Goethe :

> Du musst steigen oder sinken,
> Du musst herrschen und gewinnen,
> Oder dienen und verlieren,
> Leiden oder triumphieren,
> Amboss oder Hammer sein

powers had not disappeared from the world, they had all been delegated to a single man : that is the course of events from Augustus to Diocletian and Constantine. The first Cæsar had been satisfied with uniting in his own hands all the most important offices of State,* and that had been granted to him only for one definite object limited in respect of time, namely, to restore legal order in the civilised world (*restauratio orbis*) ; within three centuries things had come to this, that a single individual was invested not only with all offices but with all the rights of all the citizens. Just as in early times (at the time of the first successor to Augustus) the " majesty of the people " had become the " majesty " of one man, so gradually each and every power, each and every right passed over to him. Augustus had, like every other citizen, still given his vote in the Comitia ; now there sits a monarch on the throne, whom one may only approach " reverentially " on one's knees, and before him all men are alike, for all, from the foremost statesman to the lowest peasant, are his subjects. And while thus the " great king " and with him all that belonged to his Court continually increased in riches and dignity, the rest sank ever lower : the citizen could no longer even choose his profession ; the peasant, formerly the free proprietor of his ancestral estate, was the bondman of a master and bound to the soil ; but death looses all bonds, and the day came when the tax-collector had to mark what were formerly the most fertile parts of the Empire in their papers as *agri deserti*.

* Augustus was at once : (1) *Princeps*, that is, first citizen, at that time really only a title of honour ; (2) *Imperator*, commander-in-chief ; (3) tribune of the people for life ; (4) *Pontifex maximus*—the highest religious office, an office for life from earliest times ; (5) *Consul*—not, it is true, for life, but still in continuous possession of consular power ; (6) likewise of proconsular power which embraced the government of all the provinces ; and (7) likewise of censorial power, which embraced the control of morals, the right to appoint and remove from the list senators, knights, &c.

It is not my intention to trace further through history the idea of the Roman State; something will still have to be said on this matter in a later chapter; I shall restrict myself to reminding the reader that a Roman Empire—in idea a direct continuation of the old Imperium—legally existed till August 6, 1806, and that the oldest Roman office, that of *Pontifex maximus*, which was held by Numa Pompilius himself, is still in existence; the Papal stool is the last remnant of the old heathen world which has continued to live to the present day.* If what I have briefly pointed out is known to all, it has been brought forward in the hope that I might be able to demonstrate more vividly and suggestively than could be done by theoretical analysis the peculiarly complicated form of the political legacy which our century received from Rome. Here as elsewhere in this book learned considerations have no place; these are to be found in histories of constitutional law; here I bring forward only general observations, which are accessible and stimulating to all. In purely political matters we have inherited from Rome not a simple idea, not even anything so simple as what is embraced by the phrase "Hellenic art," however full of meaning that may be, but on the other hand there has come down to us a remarkable mixture of possessions of the greatest reality —civilisation, law, organisation, administration, &c.; and at the same time of ideas which, though we may not comprehend them, are yet all-powerful; of notions which no one can fully grasp and which, nevertheless, for good and for evil, still influence our public life. We certainly cannot understand our own century thoroughly and critically, if we have not clear conceptions regarding this double political legacy.

* Details in vol; ii. chap. viii

THE LEGACY OF CONSTITUTIONAL LAW

Now that we have discussed political matters in the narrower sense, let us, before passing on to the consideration of Private Law, cast a glance at the constitutional and ideal legacy in general.

So long as Rome was effectively engaged in positively creative work—more than five hundred years before Cæsar and then for more than a century in its agony *—it might seem to us totally destitute of ideas; it only creates, it does not think. It creates Europe and destroys, as far as possible, Europe's nearest and most dangerous enemies. That is the positive legacy of this time. The countries, too, which Rome never subdued, as for example the greatest part of Germany, have received from Rome all the germs of constitutional order, as the fundamental condition of every civilisation. Our languages still show us that all administration goes back to Roman teaching or suggestion. We live to-day in conditions so securely established by order that we can scarcely conceive that it was ever otherwise ; not one among ten thousand of us has the faintest idea of the organisation of the machine of State ; everything seems to us necessary and natural, law, morals, religion, even State itself. And yet the establishment of this, the ordered, secure State, worthy of free citizens, was—as all history proves—a task extremely difficult to accomplish ; India had a most noble religion, Athens perfect art, Babylonia a wondrous civilisation —everything had been achieved by the founding of a free and at the same time stable State that guaranteed conditions of law ; for this Herculean task an individual hero did not suffice, a whole nation of heroes was necessary—each one strong enough to command, each one

* The issue of the *Edictum perpetuum* by Hadrian is perhaps the last great creative benefaction.

proud enough to obey, all unanimous, each one standing up for his own personal right. When I read Roman history I feel compelled to turn away with horror; but when I contemplate the two incomparable creations of this people, the ordered State and private law, I can only bow in silent reverence before such intellectual greatness.

But this heroic people died out, and after its complete extinction there came, as we saw, a second period of Roman politics. Foreigners occupied the supreme power and foreign lawyers became the masters of public law and constitutional law as well as of the incomparable private law which had grown like a living thing, and which they preserved, so to speak, in alcohol, in the wise conviction that it could not be made more perfect but at most might degenerate. These advisers of the crown were mostly natives of Asia Minor, Greeks and Semites, that is to say, the recognised masters in the handling of abstractions and in juristic subtleties. And now there came an episode of the Roman constitution in which, if nothing absolutely new was invented, there were many new interpretations, which were sublimated to principles, and then crystallised into rigid dogmas. The process is very analogous to that described in the passage dealing with Hellenic art and philosophy. The Roman republic had been a living organism, in which the people was constantly and industriously introducing improvements; the formal question of leading "principles" had never arisen, the present had never wished to hold the future in bondage. That went so far that the highest officials of the law-court, the prætors, nominated for a year, each issued on his entry into office a so-called "prætorian edict," in which he published the principles which he intended to follow in his administration of the law; and thus it became possible to adapt the existing code to changing

times and conditions. Similarly everything in this
State was elastic, everything remained in touch with the
needs of life. But exactly as the poetical inspirations
of the Greek philosophers and their mystical interpretations of the Inscrutable had been transformed in Helleno-
Semitic Alexandria to dogmas of faith, so here State and
law were changed to dogmas, and pretty much by the
same people. We have inherited these dogmas, and
it is important that we should know whence they come
and how they arose.

For example, our idea of the monarch is derived neither
from the Teutonic nations, nor from the Oriental despots,
but from the learned Jurists who were in the service
of the Illyrian shepherd Diocletian, of the Illyrian cowboy Galerius and of the Illyrian swineherd Maximinus,
and is a direct parody—if the truth must be told—
of the greatest State-ideas of Rome. "The State-idea
among the Romans," writes Mommsen, "rests upon the
ideal transmission of the individual's capacity for action
to the whole body of citizens, the *populus*, and upon the
submission on the part of each physical member of the
community of his individual will to this universal will.
The repression of individual independence in favour
of the collective will is the criterion of a constitutional
community." * To picture to oneself what is implied
by this "transmission," this "repression of individual
independence," one must recall to memory the un-
controllable, individual love of freedom characteristic
of each Roman. Of the oldest legal monument of the
Romans, the famous twelve bronze tables (450 B.C.),
Esmarch says, "The most pregnant expressions in these
tables are the guarantees of the autocracy of the private
rights of Roman citizens," † and when three hundred
and fifty years later the first detailed system of law was

* I quote from the abridged edition of his Roman Constitutional
Law in Binding's *Systematisches Handbuch der deutschen Rechtswissen-
schaft*, p. 81 ff.
† *Römische Rechtsgeschichte*, 3rd ed., p. 218.

compiled and written down, all the storms of the inter-
vening period had caused no difference in this one
point.* As a free self-governing man the Roman accordingly transmits to the collective will, whose spontaneous
member he is, as much of his freedom as is necessary
for the defence of that freedom. "The collective will is
now in itself, if one is permitted to apply to it an
expression of Roman private law, a fiction of constitutional
law. Representation is in fact required for it. The
action of will of the one man who represents it in
the special case is equivalent constitutionally to the
action of the collective will. The constitutional act of
will in Rome is always the act of one man, since will and
action in themselves are inseparable ; collective action
by majority of votes is from the Roman point of view
a *contradictio in adjecto*." In every clause of this Roman
constitutional law one sees a nation of strong, free men :
the representation of the common cause, that is, of
the State, is entrusted for a definite time to individual
men (consuls, prætors, censors) ; they have absolutely
plenary power and bear full responsibility. In case
of need this conferring of absolute power goes so far
that the citizens nominate a dictator, all in the
interest of the common weal and in order that the
freedom of each individual may remain unimpaired.—
Now the later emperors, or rather their advisers, did not,
as one might have expected, overthrow this constitutional idea ; no, they made it the legal foundation for
monarchical autocracy, a thing unprecedented in history.
Elsewhere despots had ruled as the sons of gods, as
for instance in Egypt and even at the present day in
Japan—others, in former times and to-day, as representatives of God (I need only mention the Jewish kings
and the Khalifs)—others again by the so-called *jus
gladii*, the right of the sword. But the soldiers who

---

* **Certain** limitations of the freedom of leaving property by will
formed certainly a first indication of future times.

had usurped what had once been the Roman Empire founded their claims to rule as absolute autocrats upon Roman constitutional law ! They had not in their opinion usurped the power like a Greek tyrant and overthrown the constitutional order ; on the contrary, the all-powerful monarch was the flower, the perfection of the whole legal development of Rome : this the Oriental jurists had by their subtlety contrived to establish. With the help of the transmission theory just explained, the trick had been accomplished—in the main as follows. One of the main pillars of Roman constitutional law is that no enactment has the force of law, if it is not approved by the people. Under the first emperors appearances were still maintained in this respect. But after Caracalla " Rome " had come to mean the whole civilised world. And now all rights of the people were " transmitted " to the Senate to simplify the issuing of new laws, &c. In the *Corpus juris* it stands thus : " As the Roman people has grown to such an extent that it would be difficult to call it together to one spot for the purpose of approving laws, it was held to be right to consult the Senate instead of the people." As we now speak of a Viceroy, so the Senate was called henceforth *vice populi*. The approval of the Senate too had become purely a matter of form— once in possession of so beautiful an abstract principle, there was no stopping half-way ; and so the text continues : " but that also which it pleases the Prince to decree has the power of law, for the people has transmitted to him its whole plenitude of power and all its rights." * We

* Secs. 5 and 6, J. *de jure naturali*, i. 2. The last words of the second excerpt I have had to translate somewhat freely. The original is : " omne suum imperium et potestatem "; how difficult it is to give these words the exact legal sense of ancient Rome can be seen in Mommsen, p. 85. *Imperium* means originally " utterance of the will of the community " ; hence the bearer of this absolute will was called *imperator ;* more limited and defining rather the sphere of private law is *potestas.* Therefore I have translated them by plenitude of power and rights (German *Machtfülle* and *Rechte*), and think I have thereby expressed the sense.

have here accordingly the strictly legal derivation of an absolute monarchy and that too in the way in which it certainly could be developed from the Roman constitution alone—with its rejection of the principle of majority and with its system of transmitting supreme power to individual men.*   And this Roman " principate," as it is called, for the title of King was borne by no Cæsar, forms to the present day the basis of all European kingships.   By the introduction of constitutionalism, but still more by the manipulation of the law there is at present in many countries a movement back to the free standpoint of the ancient Romans ; but everywhere " monarchical rule " is still in principle what the legal authorities of the fallen Roman State had made it, an institution which stands in direct contradiction to the true spirit of genuine Rome.   The army is not even at the present day the army of the people, defending the home of that people, it is everywhere (even in England) called the army of the king ; the officials are not appointed and invested with authority by the collective will, they are servants of the king.   That is all Roman, but, as has been said, Roman of the cowboy, shepherd and swineherd age.   I unfortunately cannot go into greater detail here, but must refer my readers to the classical works of Savigny, *Geschichte des römischen Rechtes im Mittelalter*, and Sybel, *Entstehung des deutschen Königtums*, as also to Schulte, *Deutsche Reichs- und Rechtsgeschichte*.   Among us the absolute monarchy has everywhere arisen through contact with the Roman Empire.   Formerly the Teutonic Kings had everywhere limited rights ; the touchstone of high treason was either not recognised as a crime or punished simply by a " wergild " (Sybel, 2nd ed., p. 352) ; the nomination of counts as officials of the king does not

---

* As a not unimportant fact, I may be allowed to mention that rule by majority is just as little Teutonic or Greek as it was Roman, (*See* Leist, *Gräco-italische Rechtsgeschichte*, pp. 129, 133 ff., 727.)

occur till the conquest of Roman lands, in fact there is a long period in which the Teutonic kings have greater authority over their Roman subjects than over their free Franks (Savigny, I., chap. iv. div. 3).—Above all the idea of a subject, the Roman *subjectus*, is a legacy which still clings fast to us, and which should let us see very clearly what to this day connects us with the Roman Empire at the time of its fall, and how much still separates us from the genuine heroic people of Rome.

In all this I have no wish to moralise in the interests of any tendency. The old Roman forms of government would not have been applicable to new conditions and new men ; indeed they no longer sufficed even for Rome itself when once it had extended its boundaries. Add to this that Christianity had arisen, making the suppression of slavery an obvious command. All that made a strong kingdom a necessity. But for the kings, slavery would never have been abolished in Europe, the nobles would never have set their slaves free, they would rather have made free-born men their bondmen. The strengthening of the kingly office has everywhere for a thousand years been the first condition of the strengthening of an ordered state of society and civic freedom, and even to-day there is probably no country in Europe where an absolutely free plebiscite would proclaim as the will of the people any other form of government than the monarchical. Public consciousness, too, is penetrating through the deceptive veils which sophists and pettifoggers have hung round it; and is recognising the genuine legal meaning of the King, namely, the old Roman view of the first official of State; glorified by that sacred element which finds a not unsuitable mystical expression in the words, " by the Grace of God." Many things which we have noticed around us in the nineteenth century justify us in believing that without a kingship and without a special grace of God we could not, even to-day, rule ourselves.

For that possibly not only the virtues but also the faults of the Romans, and above all their excessive intellectual sobriety, were necessary.

However that may be, we see that the legacy of political and constitutional law which Rome has given us forms a complicated and confused mass, and that principally for two reasons : first of all, because Rome, instead of flourishing like Athens for a short time and then disappearing altogether, lived on for 2500 years, first as a world-ruling State, later as a mighty State-idea, whereby what had been a single impulse broke up into a whole series, which frequently neutralised each other ; in the second place, because the work of an incomparably energetic, Indo-European race was revised and manipulated by the subtlest minds of the West-Asiatic mixed races, this again leading to the obliteration of unity of character.

I hope that these brief allusions with regard to the extraordinarily complicated conditions of universal history have sufficed to guide the reader. For clear thinking and lucid conception it is above all indispensable to separate rightly and to connect rightly. This has been my endeavour, and to this I must needs confine myself.

Jurisprudence as a Technical Art

Besides this legacy which we have more or less unconsciously carried along with us, we Europeans possess an inheritance from Rome that has become more than any other inheritance from antiquity an essential element in our life and science, viz., Roman law. By that we have to understand public law (*jus publicum*) and private law (*jus privatum*).* To write about this is an

* That the public law of the Romans has not exercised upon us moderns the same influence as the private does not justify us in leaving it unmentioned, since a model of private law could not come into existence without an excellent public law.

easy task, inasmuch as this law is available to us in a very late codification, that of the Emperor Justinian, dating from the middle of the sixth century A.D.   Besides, the efforts of jurists and historians have succeeded in tracing far back the growth of this law, and in recent years they have even been able on the one hand to demonstrate the connection of its origins with old Aryan law, and on the other to follow its fate in the various countries of Europe through centuries of vague ferment up to the present day.   Here we have accordingly definite and clearly sifted material, and a legal expert can easily prove how much Roman law is contained in the lawbooks of our States to-day; it must also be easy for him to prove that the thorough knowledge of Roman law will for indefinite ages remain the canon of all strictly juridical thought.   Here too in the Roman legacy we have to distinguish between two things : actual legal tenets, which have stood for centuries and to some extent are still valid, and besides this a treasure of ideas and methods.   The legal expert can explain all this easily, but only when he is speaking to those who know law.   Now I am no authority on law (though I have industriously and lovingly studied its fundamental principles and the general course of its history), nor am I entitled to suppose that my readers are informed on the subject ; my task is therefore different and quite clearly defined by the purpose of this book.   It is only from a summary and universally human standpoint that I can venture briefly to indicate in what sense Roman law was in the history of the Indo-European nations a factor of such unparalleled significance that it has remained a part of our culture to the present day.

Why is it utterly impossible to speak of jurisprudence except to an audience equipped with a large store of technical juristical knowledge ?   This preliminary question will lead us at once to the heart of our subject, and will point the way to a perhaps not detailed, but at any rate accurate, analysis of what the Romans have accomplished in this department.

Law is a technical subject : that is the whole answer. Like medicine, it is neither pure science nor pure art ; and while every science in its results and every art by the impression which it makes can be communicated to all and so is in its essentialities common property, a technical subject remains accessible only to the expert. Cicero indeed compares jurisprudence with astronomy and geometry and expresses the opinion that " all these studies are in pursuit of the truth,"* but this is a perfect example of a logically false comparison. For astronomy and geometry investigate actual, fixed, unchangeable conditions, some outside of, others inside the mind,† whereas legal decisions are derived first of all from the observation of variable, contradictory and ever undefinable tendencies, habits, customs and opinions, and jurisprudence as a discipline must according to the nature of things confine itself to the subject before it, formulating it more definitely, expressing it more exactly, making it more intelligible by comparison, and—above all—classifying it accurately by the finest analysis and adapting it to practical needs. Law is, like the State, a human, artificial creation, a new systematic arrangement of the conditions arising out of the nature of man and his social instincts. The progress of jurisprudence does not imply by any means an increase of knowledge (which must surely be the object of science), but merely a perfecting of the technical art ; that is, however, a great deal and may presuppose high gifts. An abundant material is thus consistently and with

* *De Officiis*, i. 6.
† I say this without any metaphysical *arrière-pensée ;* whether mathematical conceptions are judgments *à priori* (as Kant asserts) or not, every one will admit that geometry is the purely formal activity of the mind, in contrast to the investigation of the heavens.

increasing skill employed by the human will in working
out the life-purpose of man.

I shall introduce a comparison to make this clearer.

How conditional and, consequently, how little to the
purpose would be the statement that the God who formed
iron also caused the smithy to be built !   In a certain
sense the remark would be undeniably correct : without
definite tendencies which impelled him to search further
and further, without definite capacities for invention and
manipulation, man would never have attained to the
working of iron ; he did live long on the earth before he
reached that stage.   By acuteness and patience he at last
succeeded : he learnt how to make the hard metal pliant
and serviceable to himself.   But here we have clearly not
to deal with the discovery of any eternal truth, as in the
case of astronomy and every genuine science, but on the
one hand with patience and skill, on the other hand with
suitability to practical purposes ; in short, working iron
is no science but, in the true sense of the Greek word,
a technique, *i.e.*, a matter of skill.   And the conditions
of this technique, since they depend on the human will
(showing their relationship with art), vary with the times,
with the tendencies and the habits of races, just as
on the other hand they are influenced by the progress of
knowledge (showing their relationship with science). In the
nineteenth century, for example, the working of iron has
passed through great changes which would have been
inconceivable but for the progress of chemistry, physics,
mechanics and mathematics ; a practical art may thus
demand manifold scientific knowledge from those who
pursue it—but it does not for all that cease to be a practical art.   And because it is a practical art, it can be
learnęd by any one, however poor his mental endowments, provided only he has some skill, whereas on the
other hand it is a dead letter even for the more gifted of
men if he has not made himself familiar with its methods

For while science and art contain something which is of interest to every intelligent person, an applied art is merely a method, a procedure, a manipulation, something artificial and not artistic, an application of knowledge, not really knowledge itself, a power, yet not a creative power, and so only that which is produced by it, *i.e.*, the finished object, in which there is nothing technical left, can claim universal interest.

It is exactly the same with jurisprudence, with this one difference, that the material here to be worked up is purely intellectual. In principle jurisprudence is and remains an applied art, and many an almost ineradicable misunderstanding would have been avoided if the legal authorities had not lost sight of this simple fundamental truth. From Cicero to the present day* excellent jurists have only too often looked upon it as their duty to claim for their branch of study the designation " science," cost what it might ; they seem to fear that they will be degraded if their claims are held to be absurd. Naturally people will continue to speak of a " science of law " ; but only in the derived sense ; the mass of the material on law, history of law, &c., is so gigantic that it, so to speak, forms a little world for itself, in which research is made and this research is called science (*Wissenschaft*). But this is obviously an improper use of the word. The root " vid " denotes in Sanscrit to find ; if language is not to pale into colourless ambiguity, we must see to it that a knowing (*Wissen*) always denotes a finding. Now a finding presupposes two things : in the first place, an object which is and exists before we find it ; and secondly, the fact that this object has not yet been found and discovered ; neither of the two things can be said of jurisprudence ; for " law " does not exist till men make it, nor does it exist as a subject outside of our consciousness ; besides, the science

* *See*, for example, Holland ; *Jurisprudence*, 6th ed., p. 5.

of law does not reveal or find anything but itself. And so those ancient authorities were perfectly right who, instead of speaking of *juris scientia*, preferred to say *juris notitia, juris peritia, juris prudentia*, that is, practically, knowledge, skill, experience in the manipulation of law.

NATURAL LAW

This difference is of far-reaching importance. For it is only when we have recognised what law essentially is, that we can follow its history intelligently and comprehend the decisive importance of Rome in the development of this applied art. Now and now only can we not merely cut but untie that Gordian knot, the question of natural law. This great question, which has been the subject of dispute for centuries, arises solely and simply from a misunderstanding of the nature of law ; whether we answer it by yes or no does not help us out of the maze. Cicero, in the confused manner peculiar to him, has used all sorts of oratorical flourishes on this subject ; at one time he writes : in order to explain law, one must investigate the nature of man—there he seemed to be on the right track ; immediately after he says that law is a " sublime reason " which exists outside of us and is " implanted in us " ; then again we hear that law " arises out of the nature of things " ; finally, that it was " born simultaneously with God, older than mankind." * I do not know why these quibbling platitudes are quoted everywhere ; I do so merely lest I should be reproached with having heedlessly passed by so famous a fount of wisdom ; however, I would draw the reader's attention to Mommsen's verdict : " Cicero was a journalist in the worst sense of the term, over-rich in words, as he himself confesses, and beyond all imagination poor in thoughts."† It was worse when

---

* *De legibus*, i. 5 and 6, ii. 4, &c.   † *Römische Geschichte*, iii. 620.

their Asiatic love of dogmatism and stickling for principle induced the really important legal teachers of the so-called "classical jurisprudence" to formulate clearly the quite un-Roman idea of a natural law and to introduce it systematically. Ulpian calls natural law that " which is common to animals and men." A monstrous thought ! Not merely in art is man a free creator, in law too he proves himself a magnificent inventor, an incomparably skilled, thoughtful workman, the forger of his own fate. Roman law is as characteristic a creation of the one individual human spirit as Hellenic art. What would be said of me if I were to speak of a " natural art " and then tried to draw an analogy, however far-fetched, between the spontaneous chirping of a bird and a tragedy of Sophocles ? Because the jurists form a technical guild, many of them have for centuries talked nonsense like this without the world noticing it. Gaius, another classical authority whom the Jews claim as their countryman and who, history tells us, was "not deep but very popular," gives a less extravagant but equally invalid definition of natural law : he identifies it with the so-called *jus gentium*, that is, with the " common law " which grew out of the legal codes of the various races of the Roman provinces ; in ambiguous words he explains that this law was common to " all nations of the earth " : a fearful assertion, since the *jus gentium* is just as much the work of Rome as its own *jus civile* and represents only the result of the systematising activity of Roman jurisprudence amidst the confusion of contradictory and antagonistic codes.* The very existence of the *jus gentium* beside and in contrast to the Roman *jus civile*, as well as the confused history of the origin of this " Law of nations," should have made clear to the dullest eye that there is not one law but many ; also that law is not an entity, which can be

* *See* p. 113.

scientifically investigated, but a product of human skill, which can be viewed and carried out in very different ways. But the ghost of natural law still merrily haunts certain brains ; for example, legal theorists, as far apart as Hobbes and Rousseau, agree in this one idea ; but the greatest achievement was the famous Hugo Grotius' division in natural, historical, and divine law, which makes one ask whether then the divine law was un-natural ? or the natural a work of the devil ? It needed the brilliant intellect and the outspoken impertinence of a Voltaire to venture to write: "Rien ne contribue peut-être plus à rendre un esprit faux, obscur, confus, incertain, que la lecture de Grotius et de Pufendorf."* In the nineteenth century, however, this pale abstraction has been sharply attacked; the historians of law, and with them the brilliant theorist Jhering, have dealt the finishing blow. For this all that was really necessary was to understand that law is an applied art.

Considered from this point of view it is easy to comprehend that in reality the idea "natural law" (*jus naturæ*) contains a flagrant *contradictio in adjecto*. As soon as a legal agreement is come to among men—it does not at all need to be written, a convention silent or by word of mouth is in principle the same thing as a bulky civil code of law—for the state of nature has ceased ; but if the pure natural impulse still prevails, *eo ipso* there is no law. For even if men in a natural state were to live together in association, no matter how mild and humane they might be towards one another, there would be no law, no *jus ;* there would be just as little law as if the brutal power of the fist were the decisive factor with them. Law is a regulation of the relations of an individual to others, artificially arranged and enforced upon him by the community. It is an em-

* *Dictionnaire philosophique.* J. J. Rousseau, too, calls Grotius "un enfant, et qui pis est, un enfant de mauvaise foi " (*Emile,* v.).

ployment or these instincts which impel man to live
together in societies, and, at the same time, of that
necessity which forces him *nolens volens* to unite with
his like : love and fear, friendship and enmity. If
we read in the dogmatic metaphysicians, " Law is
the abstract expression of the general will, existing
of its own accord and for its own benefit,"* we feel
that we are getting air instead of bread to eat ; when
the great Kant says, " Law is the essence of the
conditions under which the arbitrary will of the
one can be harmonised with that of the other according to a universal law of freedom,"† we must at
once see that this is the definition of an ideal, the
definition of a possible or at least thinkable state
of law, but not an all-embracing definition of law in
general, as it presents itself to us ; besides, it contains
a dangerous error. It is indeed a fallacy to suppose
arbitrary will in the soul of the individual and then to
construe law into a reaction against it ; rather every individual manifestly acts according to the necessity of his
nature, and the element of arbitrariness only comes in
with the measures whereby this natural action is restricted ; it is not the natural man that is arbitrary, it is
the man of law. If we wished to attempt a definition with
Kant's ideas as basis, we should have to say : Law is the
essence of the arbitrary conditions, which are introduced
into a human society, in order that the necessary action
of one man may be counterbalanced by the necessary
action of another and so harmonised as to give as large an
amount of freedom as possible. The simplest formulation
of the idea would be as follows : Arbitrariness in place of
instinct in the relations of men to men is law. And by
way of explanation it would have to be added that the
non plus ultra of arbitrariness consists in declaring an
arbitrarily established form (for punishment, buying,

* Hegel, *Propädeutik*, Kursus i. § 26.
† *Metaphysische Anfangsgründe der Rechtslehre* Einleitung, § B.

marriage, testaments, &c.,) to be henceforth and for ever unchangeable, so that all actions thereby covered are invalid and have no legal support, whenever the prescribed form is not observed. Law is accordingly the lasting rule of definite arbitrary relations between men. Moreover, it is unnecessary to enter into speculations with regard to quite unknown prehistoric times, in order to see *jus* in simple forms, where this central element of arbitrariness clearly appears ; we need only to look at the inhabitants of the Congo State to-day. Every little tribe has its chief ; he alone decides matters of law and his decision is irrevocable. The legal disputes which occupy him are under such simple conditions of a very simple nature ; they have to deal mostly with crimes against life and property ; the penalty is death, seldom slavery ; if the chief by motion of hand has given his decision against the accused, the latter is hacked into a hundred pieces by the bystanders and then eaten. The ideas of law therefore are very elementary on the Congo ; and yet the idea of law is there ; the natural man, that is, the man acting instinctively, would himself kill the supposed murderer or thief ; here he does not do that, the criminal is dragged to the place of assembly and judged. Similarly the chief decides disputes of inheritance and the regulation of boundaries. The unlimited arbitrary power of the chief is accordingly the " law " of the land, it is the cement by which society is held together, instead of falling to pieces in a lawless condition of nature.* The progress of law lies in the practical development and the ethical clarification of this arbitrary element.†

* I have no doubt that there, too, certain rules are rendered sacred by custom and binding also on the chief, but legally he is quite free ; only the fear of being roasted and eaten himself can restrain him from any arbitrary procedure.

† In reference to law as a " living power," as the product of " the creative thoughts of great individualities," in contrast to all the dogmatics of the supposed law of nature, read the interesting lecture of

ROMAN LAW

I think we have now sufficient material to enable us without technical discussions, and at the same time without phrase-making, to understand the special merits of the Roman people in regard to law, or at least the special character of those merits. The nature of our legacy will at the same time be exactly characterised.

If law is not an inborn principle nor an exact science capable of investigation, but a useful adaptation of human capabilities to the building up of a society fitted for civilisation, then it is clear from the first that there will be and must be codes of law varying very much in value. Fundamentally a law will be influenced principally by two forces from which it will receive its characteristic colouring : first, by the moral character of the people in whose midst it comes into force, and, secondly, by the analytical acuteness of that people. By the happy union of both—a union occurring only once in the history of the world—the Roman people found themselves in a position to build up a legal code of great perfection.* Mere egoism, the greed of possession, will never suffice to found

Prof. Eugen Ehrlich, *Freie Rechtsfindung und freie Rechtswissenschaft,* Leipzig, 1903.

* The assertion that history constantly repeats itself belongs to the countless untruths which are in circulation as wisdom among the " nonocentists." Never in history—as far as our knowledge goes—has anything repeated itself, never ! Where is the repetition of Athens and Sparta ? of Rome ? of Egypt ? Where has the second Alexander flourished ? where a second Homer ? Neither nations nor their great men return again. And so mankind does not become wiser by " experience " ; the past offers it no paradigm for the present to form its judgment ; it is made worse or better, wiser or more foolish, simply by the influences that are brought to bear on its intellect and character. Gutzkow's Ben Akiba was fundamentally wrong in his famous remark, " All has occurred before " ! Such an ass as he himself never lived before, and, it is to be hoped, will never appear again. And even if this were so, it would only be the repetition of the individual who under new circumstances would commit new follies for our amusement.

a lasting code of law; we have rather learned from the Romans that the inviolable respect for the claims of others to freedom and possession is the moral foundation upon which alone we can build for all time. One of the most important authorities on the Roman law and people, Karl Esmarch, writes : " The conscience of the Italian Aryans in regard to right and wrong is strong and unadulterated ; in self-control and, when necessary, self-sacrifice, that virtue of theirs which springs from inner impulse and is supported by a most profound inner nature reaches its culmination." Because he knew how to rule himself the Roman was qualified to rule the world and to develop a strong idea of the State ; by the fact that he could sacrifice his own interests to the universal weal, he proved his capacity to establish valid principles in regard to the rights of private property and of individual freedom. But these high moral qualities had to be supported by exceptional intellectual qualities. The Romans, quite insignificant in philosophy, were the greatest masters in the abstraction of firm principles from the experiences of life—a mastery which becomes specially remarkable when we compare other nations with them, as, for example, the Athenians, who, though marvellously gifted, and delighting in legal quarrels and sophistical law riddles, never were anything but blunderers in this branch of thought.* This peculiar capacity, to elevate definite practical relations to clearly defined principles implies a great intellectual achievement ; for the first time order and lucidity of arrangement were brought into social conditions, just as language, by the formation of abstract collective words, had made higher systematic thinking possible. It is no longer a question of vague instincts nor of obscure and changing conceptions of justice and injustice ; all relations stand definitely grouped before our

* *Cf.* Leist, *Graeco-italische Rechtsgeschichte,* p. 694, and for the following quotation, p. 682.

eyes, and these relations are to be regulated by the invention of new legal rules or the further development
of those already existing. And since life gradually
widens experience, or itself assumes more complicated
forms, the Roman acuteness little by little inside the
individual " groups " discovers the " species." " In point
of fine, carefully pondered ideas of right, Roman law
is and will remain the permanent teacher of the civilised
world," says Professor Leist, the very man who has done
more than any other to prove that the Universities
should give up the present one-sided Roman standpoint
of history of law and should teach students to recognise
Roman law as a link in the chain, as one of the steps
" which the Aryan mind has mounted in the clearing up
of legal conceptions." The more carefully we study
the numerous attempts at legislation previous to and
contemporary with the Roman, the more we recognise
what incomparable services were rendered by Roman law
and realise that it did not fall from heaven but was the
creation of the intellects of grand and sturdy men. One
thing must not be overlooked : in addition to the qualities of self-control, of abstraction, and the finest analysis,
the Roman possessed a special gift of plastic shaping. Here
appears their relationship to Hellenism, which we seek in
vain elsewhere. The Roman too is an artist of mighty creative power—an artist in the clear, plastic shaping of the
complicated machine of State. No theorist in the world
could have thought out such an organism of State, which
perhaps should rather be pointed to as a work of art
than as a work of reason. He is still more an artist in
the plastic working out of his conceptions of law.
Highly characteristic too is the manner in which the
Roman strives to give visible expression to his artistically
moulded conceptions even in legal actions, everywhere
" to give an outward expression to the inner diversity,
to bring what is inward, so to speak, to the sur-

face." * Here we have a decidedly artistic instinct, the
outcome of specifically Indo-European tendencies. In
this artistic element too lies the magic power of the Roman
legacy ; that is the indestructible and ever incomparable part of it.

On one point indeed we must be quite clear ;—
Roman law is just as incomparable and inimitable as
Hellenic art. Our ridiculous Germanomania will make no
change in that. People tell marvels about a" German
law," supposed to have been stolen from us by the introduction of the Roman ; but there never was a German
law, but merely a chaos of rude contradictory laws, a
special one for each tribe. It is also absolutely in-
accurate to speak of " adopting " Roman law between
the thirteenth and the sixteenth centuries ; for the
Teutonic peoples have " adopted " continuously from
the time when they first came into contact with the
Roman Empire. Burgundians and East Goths as
early as the fifth century of the Christian era (or at the
very beginning of the sixth) introduced modified (cor-
rupted) forms of Roman law,† and the oldest sources of
Saxon, Frankish, Bavarian and Alemannic law, &c., are
so interlarded with Latin words and half-understood
principles, that the need of a reasoned codification of
law is only too apparent. One might well relegate
German law as an ideal to the future, but to seek it in
the past is hypocritical twaddle.‡ Another hindrance

---

* For examples, read the splendid chapter *Plastik des Rechtes*
in Jhering's *Geist des römischen Rechtes*, § 23. Of the modern
undramatic life of law, Jhering says : " One would have liked to give
law, instead of a sword, a quill as its attribute, for the feathers were
scarcely more necessary to the bird than to it, except that in the case
of law the attribute produced the opposite effects and speed stood
in converse relation to the amount of feathers employed."

† Savigny, *Geschichte des römischen Rechtes im Mittelalter*, chap. i.

‡ I know no more conclusive proof of the original incapacity of the
Teutonic peoples to judge acutely in questions of law than that such
a man as Otto the Great could not decide, otherwise than by a duel,
the fundamental question whether descendants should inherit or not :

to the proper estimation of Roman law is due to the
frenzy produced by the dogma of evolution, which has
led to such confusion of thought in the nineteenth century.
The feeling for the Individual, the established view that
the Individual alone has everlasting importance, has been
seriously injured by it. Although the only effective
powers that history reveals are absolutely individualised
nations and great personalities that never recur, the
theory of evolution leads to the idea that capacities and
beginnings were everywhere identical and that essentially
analogous structures must " develop " from these same
germs. The fact that this never happens and that
Roman law, for example, came into being once for all, does
not disturb our dogmatists in the least. With this is con
nected the further conception of unceasing progress
towards " perfection," in consequence of which our law
must as a matter of course surpass the Roman, because
it is later, and yet nature never offers an example of
development taking place in anything living without
entailing a corresponding loss.* Our civilisation stands
high above the Roman ; in respect of the vividness of
our legal sense, on the other hand, an educated man
of the nineteenth century can certainly not come up
to a Roman peasant of the year 500 B.C. No one who
has any thinking power and knowledge will dispute
that. I said in relation to law, not to justice. When
Leist writes, " The unprejudiced inquirer will not find
that the present age as compared with the Roman
has made such glorious advance in the practice or even
in the knowledge of real justice," † he makes a remark
well worth taking to heart ; but I quote these words

this judgment of Heaven was then adopted as a piece of law for good
by a *pactum sempiternum !* (*See* Grimm, *Rechtsaltertümer,* 3rd ed.,
p. 471.]
 * The detailed proof that the ideas of a progress and decline of
humanity have no concrete significance will be found in the ninth
chapter. † *Gräco-italische Rechtsgeschichte,* p. 441*

to make it clear that I do not here speak of justice, but of law, and to ensure that the difference between the two may be obvious. Our noble conception of the duties of humanity points, I am sure, to more enlightened ideas with regard to justice; the legal sense is, however, quite a different thing and is neither proved nor promoted even by the possession of the most perfect and yet imported systems of law.

To understand how incomparable was the achievement of the Romans, one circumstance must certainly not be overlooked : the Justinian *corpus juris* with which we are familiar is only the embalmed corpse of Roman law.* For centuries skilled legal authorities kept in it a semblance of life by galvanic means ; now all civilised nations have worked out a law of their own ; but this would not have been possible without the Roman, we all lack the necessary talent. A single observation will suffice to show the cleft between the Romans and ourselves : Roman law of the real heroic period was firm as a rock but nevertheless incredibly elastic— "incredibly," I mean, to our modern, timid conceptions, for we have taken everything from that law, except its living character. The Roman law was always "in a state of growth," and capable, thanks to certain brilliant contrivances, of adapting itself to the changing needs of the times. The law, which in the fifth century B.C. was in its general outlines engraved in bronze tables by the decemvirs nominated for that purpose, was not a new and improvised code, nor one which from that time forth was immutable, but was more or less a codification of already existing laws which had grown up historically ; the Romans knew how to invent ways and means to keep it even then from crys-

* Francis Bacon points out how inferior the *corpus juris* of Justinian is to the genuine Roman law, and blames so " dark an age " for taking the liberty of laying hands upon the work of so " brilliant an age " in order to improve it. (*See* the dedication of the *Law Tracts.*)

tallising. In dealing with the Twelve Tables, for example, the officials did good service by their acumen in " interpreting "—not with the object of twisting the statutes to suit some special purpose, but of adapting them half-automatically to wider conditions ; brilliant inventions—as, for example, that of the legal "fiction," by which means were found (if I may express myself as a layman) of putting to use existing legal norms to forestall others that were not yet existent—and constitutional arrangements, like those of the Prætors, by which a place was assured to that law of custom which is so necessary in a living organism, till the best law has been provided by practice, arrangements by means of which the *jus gentium* also gradually developed in close touch with the narrower Roman *jus civile*—all these things brought about a fresh pulsating life in law—a life which no one can appreciate unless he has studied law, inasmuch as we have nothing of the kind, absolutely nothing.* Moreover, in order to estimate the gulf between us and the Romans, we must remember that real scholarly and trained jurists did not come into existence till the end of the republic, and that this splendid, and in most parts most delicately chiselled product of legal applied art is the work of peasants and rude warriors. The reader should try to make clear to an average philistine of the present day the juristical difference between property and possession, to bring home to him that a thief is the legal possessor of the stolen object, and as such enjoys legal protection for his possession, as does also the pawnbroker and the hereditary landlord ; he will not succeed, I know it from experience ; I purposely choose this as a simple example. The Roman peasant, on the other hand, who could neither read

---

* Especially of the year's edicts of the Prætors. Leist says that they had become " the principal moment in the finer development of Roman law " (as quoted above, p. 622).

nor write, knew all this quite accurately five hundred years before Christ.* He certainly did not know much more, but his law he knew and employed with as exact knowledge as he did his plough or his oxen ; and by knowing it and thinking about it,† by striving to obtain for himself, his possessions, and his relatives an ever firmer and more definite legal protection, he built up that legal structure, under which at a later time other races found shelter in stormy days, and which we at the present day with more or less success, with more or less changes, seek to extend, finish and perfect. No people but the Romans could of themselves have created and built it up, for nowhere else was there present the necessary conjunction of qualities of character and of intellect, and this law had to be lived before it was thought, before the arrival of those worthies who could tell us so much that was edifying in regard to a " natural law," and thought it comparable to the geometry which the scholar puzzles out in his lonely room.

In later times Hellenes and Semites have rendered great services as dogmatists and advocates, Italians as teachers of law, Frenchmen as systematisers, Germans as historians ; in none of the races mentioned, however, could one have found the soil that could bring that tree to maturity. In the case of the Semites, for instance, the moral subsoil was wanting, in the case of the Germans acumen. The Semites have great moral qualities, but not those from which a law for civilised nations could have been developed. For the disregard of the legal claims and the freedom of others is a feature that ever reappears in all races strongly imbued with Semitic blood. Already in ancient Babylon they had a finely worked out law of commerce and obligations ; but even in this limited

* *See* the clear distinction between property and possession in Table VII., clause 11.

† In Cicero's time every boy still learned the Twelve Tables by heart.

branch nothing was done to suppress the frightful exaction
of usury, and as for safeguarding personal rights, that
of freedom, for instance, no one ever even thought of it.*
But even under more favourable circumstances, for
instance, among the Jews, there is not even the beginning
of a genuine formation of law; strange as that may
appear, a single glance at the legal clauses of the greatest
Jewish thinker, Spinoza, solves the riddle. In his
Political Tractate (ii. 4 and 8) we read, " The right of
each one is in proportion to his power." Here we might
of course imagine that it was merely a question of establishing actual relations, for this second chapter bears
the title " On Natural Law."† However, in his *Ethics*
(Part IV., Supplement, 8) we find in black and white;
" According to the highest law of nature every man
has unlimited power to do that which in his opinion
will be in his interest ": and in the treatise *On True
Freedom* we find the words: " To obtain that which
we demand for our salvation and our peace, we need
no other principle than this, to lay to heart what is
for our own interests." ‡ That it does not disconcert
so honest a man to build up a pure theory of morals
upon such foundations is the finest testimony to his
inborn casuistical gifts; but it proves that Roman
law could never have grown on Jewish soil. No, there

* Compare the very minute information in Jhering's *Vorgeschichet
der Indoeuropäer*, p. 233 ff. The usual rate of interest in Babylon was
20 to 25 per cent. Jhering asserts that interest was a Babylonian, a
Semitic (not a Sumarian) invention; he says, " all other peoples owe
their acquaintance with it to the Babylonians." Honour to whom
honour is due! Also the subtlest form of interest, for instance, the
favourite plan of lending money without interest, by immediately
taking it from the capital, was well known in ancient Babylon, even
before Homer had begun to write verses. When, then, shall we be
spared the old fiction that it was only in recent centuries that the Semites
were forced by the persecution of Christians to become usurers?

† How astonished Cicero and Seneca, Scævola and Papinian would
have been at such a conception of natural law!

‡ The resemblance between the principles (not the conclusions) of
Spinoza and of Nietzsche is striking enough to claim our attention.

would have been at the most a simplified code, such as King Tippu Tib, for instance, may use on the Congo.* It was only on the foundation of a law invented and worked out in detail by Indo-Europeans that the Jew could display his astonishing juristical abilities.—The drawbacks in the case of the German lie in quite a different direction. Self-sacrifice, the impulse " to build from within outwards," the emphasising of the ethical moment, the unswerving love of freedom, in short, all the requisite moral qualities they would have possessed in abundance ;—not the intellectual ones. Acumen was never a national possession of the Teutons ; that is so manifest that it requires no proof. Schopenhauer asserts that " the real national characteristic of the German is dull-wittedness (*Schwerfälligkeit*)." Moreover, the peculiar gifts of the Germans are a hindrance in the formation of law—his incomparable fancy (in contrast to the flat empiricism of the Roman imagination), the creative passion of his mind (in contrast to the cool sobriety of the Roman), his scientific depth (in contrast to the practical political tendencies of the born legal race), his lively sense of fairness (in social relations always a weak reed in comparison with the strictly legal attitude of the Roman). No, this people could never have brought the applied art

* A few years ago I met in society an educated Jew, an owner of petroleum wells and a member of the notorious petroleum-ring. No argument could convince the honest man, who would not have harmed a fly, how morally condemnable such a ring was ; his constant answer was, " I can, and therefore I may ! " Spinoza word for word, as one can see.—This brings up the grave question as to whether in Teutonic countries men of Jewish race should be appointed judges. Without any passion or prejudice, without doubting the knowledge and the spotless honour of those in question, one ought to ask oneself, on the ground of historical and ethical data, whether it should be taken for granted that these men are capable of completely assimilating a conception of law which is so thoroughly in opposition to their natural tendencies ; whether they really understand and feel this law which they use so masterfully. Whoever has come to recognise the clearly marked individuality of the various races of mankind can bring up such a question in all seriousness and without any ill-will.

of law to high perfection; it resembles too closely the Indo-Aryans, whose " complete lack of the juristical power of distinguishing " is demonstrated by Jhering in his *Vorgeschichte der Indoeuropäer*, § 15.

THE FAMILY

I should like to introduce another national comparison with regard to the formation of law, that between the Hellenes and the Romans. It reveals the essence of Roman law, the one point to which I may call special attention in this book. At the same time it will make us feel how deeply our civilisation is indebted to the Roman legacy. My discussion will be brief, and though it deals with the simple beginnings of the remote past, it will also introduce us to the burning questions of the immediate present.

Every educated person knows that the Greeks were not only great politicians but at the same time great theorists in law. The " lawsuit about the shadow of the ass " * is an ancient Attic witticism, which satirises excellently the love of this thoughtless, litigious people for actions at law. I recall too the *Wasps* of Aristophanes with the heartrending prayers of Philocleon when shut in by his son : " Let me out, let me out—to judge ! " But we should look further around. Homer has a court scene represented on the shield of Achilles (*Iliad*, xviii. 497 ff.), Plato's largest works are on politics and the theory of law (the *Republic* and the *Laws*), Aristotle's *Rhetoric* is in parts simply a handbook for advocates beginning their profession ; notice, for example, how in chap. xv. of the first book he expounds a detailed theory of deceptive sophistry for hedge-lawyers, gives them

* An Athenian hires an ass to carry his baggage to Megara. At a resting-place he sits down in the shadow of it ; the driver will not permit this without extra payment, as he had hired the ass but not its shadow.

hints how to twist the law to the advantage of their clients, and advises them to let their clients swear false oaths in court, whenever it is to their advantage.* . . . We see that, except in Sparta (where according to Plutarch's assurance there were absolutely no cases), the Hellenic atmosphere was charged with questions of law. The Romans, always ready to recognise the merits of others, had, from time immemorial, recourse to the Greeks, particularly to the Athenians, for advice in the development of their law. Even when they were about to fix their fundamental legal principles (in the Twelve Tables) for the first time, they sent a commission to Greece, and in the final editing of this earliest monument, an Ephesian, Hermodorus, who was banished from his native city, is said to have been of considerable service. Time made no change in this. The great authorities on law, a Mucius Scævola, a Servius Sulpicius, have a thorough knowledge of Hellenic legal enactments ; Cicero, and all that this name stands for, derives his obscure remarks on divine justice, natural law, &c., from Greek philosophers : in the pseudo-Platonic *Minos* he might have read that law is the discovery of an objective thing, not a human invention, and from Aristotle he quotes the words, " The universal law, because it is the natural law, never changes, but the written law, on the other hand, often does." † In the later period of the imperial decay, when the

---

* This belongs, according to the great philosopher, to " the means of persuasion that lie outside of art."

† Up to the present day one finds this passage quoted in juristical works, but with little justification, as Aristotle is here giving merely a rhetorical trick for use in court and on the next page teaches the use of the opposite assertion. Still less to the point is the passage from the *Nicomachean Ethics*, v. 7, which culminates in the sentence, " Law is the mean between a certain advantage and a certain disadvantage." How great does Democritus show himself here as always when he says, with that clear insight characteristic of him, that " laws are the fruits of human thinking in contrast to the things of nature " (Diogenes Laertius, ix. 45).

Roman people had disappeared from the face of the earth, the so-called "classical jurisprudence" was founded and put into shape almost entirely by Greeks more or less of Semitic descent. There is a remarkable want of information with regard to the antecedents and history of the most famous teachers of law in the later Roman ages ; all of a sudden they appear in office and dignity, no one knowing whence they have come.* But at the beginning of the Imperial rule with its inevitable influence upon the life of law the passionate struggle between Labeo, the irrepressible, free old plebeian, and Capito the upstart, who is striving for wealth and honour, is truly pathetic ; it is the struggle for organic free development in opposition to the faith in authority and dogma. And dogma conquered in the legal sphere as in that of religion.—But in the meantime, as we have said, the practical Romans had learned a great deal in Greece, especially from Solon, who had, as a builder of States, achieved little that lasted, but accomplished all the more in the sphere of law. Whether Solon was the originator of written legislation and the momentous principle of *actiones* (the division of suits according to definite principles), or whether he merely systematised and fixed them—I know not : at any rate both are derived from Athens.† This I mention only as an instance of the great importance of Greece in the development of Roman law. Later, when all Hellenic countries were under Roman administration, the Greek cities contributed most to the formation of the *jus gentium* and in that way to the perfecting of Roman law. Here we may ask, how is it that the Hellenes, so superior intellectually to the Romans, created nothing

* With regard to the predominantly Semitic and Syrian race-connection of the later codifiers and embalmers of the Roman law, for whom we have shown too much admiration, *see* p. 91 ff. of the address of Leonhard quoted on p. 125.

† Leist, *Gräco-italische Rechtsgeschichte*, p. 585.

in the branch of knowledge that was lasting or perfect, but shared in the great civilising work of the formation of law solely through the medium of the Romans ?

A single but fatal mistake was at the bottom of it : the Roman started from the family, on which basis he erected State and law ; the Greek, on the other hand, took as his starting-point the State, his ideal being always the organisation of the " polis," while family and law remained subordinate. All Greek history and literature prove the correctness of this assertion, and the fact that the greatest Hellene of post-Homeric times, Plato, considered the complete abolition of the family in the upper classes a desirable aim, shows to what fatal confusions such a fundamental error must in time lead. With perfect right Giordano Bruno says (I forget where), " The very smallest mistake in the way in which a thing is attacked leads finally to the very greatest erroneous discrepancies ; thus the most trifling mistake in the ramification of thought can grow as an acorn does into an oak." * And this was not " the very smallest mistake " but a very great one. Herein lies all the misery of the Hellenic peoples ; here we have to seek the reason of their inability to develop either State or Law in a lasting and ideal manner. If we take up a careful individual account, for example Aristotle's book *The Athenian Constitution,* discovered a few years ago, this succession of constitutions, all different and all breathing an essentially different spirit, makes us giddy : the pre-Draconian, those of Draco, Solon, Cleisthenes, Aristeides, Pericles, the Four Hundred, &c. &c., all within two hundred and fifty years ! Such a state of things would have been impossible where there existed a firmly knit family life. Without that it was easy for the Greeks to arrive at that characteristically

---

* The above words are perhaps from one of the very free translations by Kuhlenbeck. In Bruno's *De Immenso et Innumerabilibus* 1 found the following remark (Bk. II. chap. i.] : "Parvus error in principio, magnus in fine est."

unhistorical view of theirs, that law was a subject for
free speculation; and so they lost all feeling for the
fact that in order to live, law must grow out of actual
conditions.*　And how striking it is that even the most
important questions of family law are regarded as subordinate, that Solon, for example, the most prominent
Athenian as a lawyer, leaves the law of inheritance
so obscure, that it is left to the caprice of the law-
courts to interpret it (Aristotle, as above, division IX).
—With Rome it was different. The strong tendency to
discipline here finds its first expression in the firm organisation of the family. The sons remain under the control
of the father, not merely till their fourteenth year, as
in Greece, but till the death of the father; by the exclusion of relationship on the mother's side, by the
legal recognition of the unlimited power of the *pater-
familias*, even in regard to the life and death of his children,
(although his son might have risen in the meantime to
the highest offices in the State), by the greatest freedom
and the most accurate individual enactments in reference
to the law of wills and legacies, by the strictest protection
of all the father's rights of property and legal claims (for
he alone possessed a right to property and was a *persona
sui juris, i.e.*, a person with full rights at law)—by these
things and many more the family became in Rome an
impregnably firm, indissoluble unity, and it is essentially to this that we are indebted for the particular
form of the Roman State and Roman law. One can
easily imagine how such a strict conception of the family
must affect the whole life, the morals of the men, the
character of the children, the anxiety to retain and to
bequeath what had been acquired, the love of country,
which did not need to be artificially nourished, as in

---

* J. Jacques Rousseau makes an excellent remark in this connection:
"Si quelquefois les lois influent sur les mœurs, c'est quand elles en
tirent leur force" (*Lettre à d'Alembert*).

Greece : for the citizen fought for what was assured to him for ever, he fought for his sacred home, for the future of his children, for peace and order.

MARRIAGE

The intimate conception of marriage and the position of women in society are naturally connected with all this. Here we have evidently the positive element in the formation of the Roman family, that which could not be fixed by law but which on the contrary determined the forms of law. Among old Aryans marriage was already regarded as a " divine institution," and when the young wife crossed the threshold of her new home she was received with the cry, " Come into the house of thy husband, that thou mayest be called mistress ; be therein as one who commands ! "* In this very point, Greeks and Romans, otherwise so manifoldly related, differed from one another. In Homer's time we certainly see the woman highly respected by the Greeks, and the comrade of the man ; but the Ionians who emigrated to Asia Minor took strange wives, " who did not venture to call the Greek husband by his name, but addressed him as master—this degeneration of the Asiatic Ionians has reacted on Athens."† The Roman, on the other hand; regarded his wife as his companion and equal, his life's mate, one who shared everything, divine as well as human, with him. The wife has, however, this position in Rome not because she is wife, but because she is a woman, *i.e.*, because of the respect which the Roman pays to the female sex as such. In all relations where the natural difference of sex does not make a distinction necessary, the Roman puts woman on an equality with himself. There is no more convincing proof of this than the old Roman law of inheritance,

* Zimmer, *Indisches Leben*, p. 313 ff.
† Etfried Müller, *Dorier*, 2nd ed., i. 78, ii. 282 (quoted from Leist).

which makes absolutely no difference between the two sexes : the daughter receives exactly the same as the son, the kinswoman the same as the kinsman ; if there are no children, the widow receives the whole inheritance and excludes the male line ; the sister does the same when there is no widow. We must be acquainted with the slighting treatment to which the female sex is subjected in the laws of so many other nations to understand the significance of this point ; in Greece, for instance, the nearer male relation excluded the wife altogether, and the lot of a daughter was indeed lamentable, the nearest male relation having the power to take her from her husband.* The Roman wife was honoured in her house as princess, *princeps familiæ,* and the Roman law speaks of the *matronarum sanctitas,* the sacredness of wives who are blessed with children. Children who in any way sinned against their parents fell under the ban of gods and men ; no penalty was enacted for the murder of a father, because, as Plutarch tells us, this crime was considered unthinkable—in fact it was more than five hundred years before a case of parricide occurred.† To form a right conception of this old Roman family, we must keep one other fact in view : that in Roman

* Jhering : *Entwickelungsgeschichte des römischen Rechtes,* p. 55.‡ Among the Teutons it was no better. " The right of inheritance is in the oldest German laws either restricted or denied to women altogether," says Grimm, *Deutsche Rechtsaltertümer,* 3rd ed. p. 407. The concessions gradually granted are to be traced to Roman influence. Where this was little or not at all felt, the German legal books, even in the Middle Ages, still show the "complete inequality of women." In the extreme North, in Scandinavia and in oldest Frisia, a woman could inherit nothing at all, neither movable nor fixed property ; " the man enters into inheritance, the woman leaves it." Not till the thirteenth century did women receive a limited right of inheritance (Grimm, p. 473). These are the conditions of law to which the Germanomaniacs longingly desire to return !

† (*Romulus,* xxix.) It may be mentioned by way of contrast that it was the custom among the Germans till the introduction of Christianity (among the Wends even till the seventeenth century) to kill old weak parents ! (*See* Grimm ; *Rechtsaltertümer,* pp. 486–90.)

life the sacred element, that is, the reverence for divine commands, played a great part. While the pater-familias was, according to human law, an absolute despot in his house, the divine command forbade him to abuse this power.* The home was indeed a sanctuary, the hearth comparable to an altar ; and while it is somewhat revolting to our feelings to-day to hear that parents in very great poverty sometimes sold their children as slaves, yet all histories of law give one the firm impression that any cruelty, according to ideas of that age, towards wife or children was almost or quite unknown. Indeed at law the wife is in relation to her husband *filiæ loco* (equal to a daughter) in relation to her own children *sororis loco* (equal to a sister) : but this is done in the interests of the unity of the family, and in order that, in constitutional as well as in private law relations, the family may appear as a sharply defined, autonomous, organic entity, represented at law by a single person, not as a more or less firm conglomerate of merely individual fragments. We have already seen in the political part of this chapter that the Roman loved to transmit power to single individuals, confident that from freedom united to responsibility, both focussed, so to speak, in a personality conscious of its individuality, moderate, and at the same time energetic and wise action would result. It is the same principle that prevails here. Later this family life degenerated ; cunning means were invented to bring into usage substitutes for genuine marriage, in order that the wife should no longer come into the legal power of the husband ; " marriage became a money matter like everything else ; not in order to found families, but to improve shattered fortunes by means of dowries, were marriages contracted, and existing ones

---

* Besides he was subject to the censorial power, as much for too great strictness in the exercise of his paternal rights as for carelessness therein ; *see* Jher ng ; *Geist des römischen Rechtes*, § 32.

dissolved, in order to form new unions " ; * but in spite
of this Publius Syrus could in Cæsar's time still express
the Roman conception of marriage by the line :

Perenne animus conjugium, non corpus facit.

The soul, not the body, makes marriage eternal.

WOMAN

This is the central point of Roman law ; the contrast
with Greece (and with Germany) gives us an idea of the
importance of such an organic central point. Here too
the Roman proves himself far from unideal, though he
is absolutely without sentiment and almost painfully devoid of phantasy. Indeed, his " idea " is so strong, that
what he really in his heart desired never again altogether
disappeared. We have already seen in the preceding
section that ideas are immortal, and though the Roman
State was destroyed, yet the idea of it lived on through
the centuries, a still powerful influence ; at the end of the
nineteenth century four mighty monarchs of Europe
still bear the title of Cæsar, and the idea of *res publica*
is still moulding the greatest State of the new world.
But Roman law does not live on merely as a Justinian
mummy or a technical secret, revealed only to members
of the craft ; no, I believe that the life-giving germ
from which that law had fundamentally grown was never
totally destroyed, but continues to live on among us as a
most valuable possession, in spite of the darkness of dis-
gracefully wicked centuries and the disintegrating ferment
that followed them. We still talk of the sacredness of the
family ; any one who, like certain Socialists, denies it is
struck from the list of politicians capable of forming a
judgment, and even those who are not pious Catholics will
a hundred times rather become reconciled to the concep-

* Esmarch: *Römische Rechtsgeschichte,* p. 317.

tion that marriage is a religious sacrament (as it indeed
was in ancient Rome; the Pontificate in this as in so
much else being directly based on old Roman Pontifical
law and proving itself the last official representative of
Heathendom), than admit that marriage is, as the
learned Anarchist leader Elisée Reclus elegantly says,
" merely legal prostitution." That we feel thus is
a Roman legacy. The high position of woman too,
which makes our civilisation rank far above the
Hellenic and the various degenerate Semitic and
Asiatic types, is not, as Schopenhauer and so many
others have taught, a " Christian-Teutonic," but a
Roman creation. As far as one can judge, the old
Teutons cannot have treated their women particularly
well; here Roman influence appears to have first brought
about a change; the oldest German lawbooks are, in
reference to the legal position of the wife, full of phrases
taken literally from Roman law (*see* Grimm: *Deutsche
Rechtsaltertümer*, II. chap. i., B. 7 and ff.). It was the
work of the Romans to give woman a firm, secure, legal
position in Europe. The " fair sex " was indeed first
glorified in song by Germans, Italians, French, English
and Spaniards; the Roman people had not thought of
that.* But I ask, whether without the keen penetration and sense of justice, above all without the incomparable State-building instinct of the Romans, we should
ever have advanced so far as to take woman into our
political system as our life's comrade and the corner-
stone of the family? I think I may answer a decided
no. Christianity in no wise signifies a strengthening of the
idea of the family. On the contrary, its real essence
is to destroy all political and legal bonds and make every
single individual rely upon himself. And it was from

* I speak of the true, chaste woman; for the adulteress and the
courtesan were loudly celebrated by the most popular of degenerate
Rome's poets, Catullus and Virgil especially.

the Christian Emperor Constantine, who annulled the
sovereignty of the *paterfamilias*, that the Roman family
in fact received its death-blow. Christianity, moreover,
being derived from Judaism, is from the first an anarchic,
anti-political power. That the Catholic Church followed
a different road and became a political power of the
greatest magnitude, is to be attributed simply to the
fact that it denied the clear teaching of Christ and adopted
instead the Roman State-idea—though it was only the
idea of the degenerate Roman State. The Church did
more than any other power for the maintenance of
Roman law; * Pope Gregory IX., for instance, aspired
solely to the title of a " Justinian of the Church "; this
recognition of his juristical services lay nearer his
heart than sanctification.† Though the motives that
impelled the Church and the Kings to retain and forcibly
introduce Roman law in its degenerate Byzantine form
were not particularly noble ones, yet that could not
prevent many very noble Roman thoughts from being
saved at the same time. And just as the tradition of
Roman law never died, so, too, the Roman conception
of the dignity of woman and of the political importance
of the family never quite disappeared from the consciousness of men. For several centuries (here as in so many
things the thirteenth century is with Petrus Lombardus
the almost exact border-line) we have come nearer and
nearer to the old Roman conception, particularly since
the Council of Trent and Martin Luther simultaneously
emphasised the sacredness of marriage. That this
approach is in many respects a purely ideal one does
not matter; a perfectly new civilisation cannot too
thoroughly free itself from old forms; as it is, we pour far
too much new wine into old bottles; but I do not think

---

* *See* particularly Savigny: *Geschichte des römischen Rechtes im
Mittelalter,* chaps. iii. xv. xxii., &c.
† Bryce: *The Holy Roman Empire,* p. 131 of the French edition.

that any unprejudiced man will deny that the Roman family is one of the most glorious achievements of the human mind, one of those heights which cannot be scaled twice, and to which the most distant generations will look up in admiration, making sure at the same time that they themselves are not straying too far from the right path. In every study of the nineteenth century, *e.g.*, when discussing the burning question of the emancipation of women or when forming an opinion with regard to those socialistic theories which, in contrast to Rome, culminate in the formula, "No family, all State," the contemplation of this lofty height will be of invaluable service.

POETRY AND LANGUAGE

I have attempted a somewhat difficult task—that of speaking untechnically on a technical subject. I have had to confine myself to proving the peculiar fitness of the Romans for bringing to perfection this practical art ; what I have tried to emphasise as their most far-reaching achievement for human society—the strong legal establishment of the family—is, as will have been noticed, similar in essence to the original impelling force from which the technical mastery had gradually grown up. All that lies between, that is, the whole real practical art, had to be neglected, and equally all discussion of the advantages and disadvantages of the preponderating influence of Roman law in the nineteenth century in its purely technical connection. And without needing to tread upon such dangerous quicksands, there are plenty of suggestive considerations for us laymen.

I have intentionally confined myself to politics and law. What did not come down to us as a legacy does not fall within the scope of this book, and many things that have been preserved to us, as, for example, the works of

Latin poets, claim the attention of the scholar and the
dilettante, but do not form a living part of our life. To
put Greek and Latin poetry together and call them
" classical literature " is a proof of incredible barbarism in taste and of a regrettable ignorance of the
essence and value of the art of genius. Whenever
Roman poetry attempts the sublime, as in Virgil and
Ovid, it clings with a correct sense of its own hopeless
unoriginality as slavishly as possible to Hellenic models.
As Treitschke says, " Roman literature is Greek literature
written in Latin."* What are our unhappy boys to
think when in the forenoon the *Iliad* of the greatest
poetical genius of all times is expounded to them and in
the afternoon that servile epic the *Æneid*, written by
imperial command—both as classical models ? The
genuine and the false, the glorious, free creation arising
out of the greatest creative necessity and the finely
formed technique in the service of gold and dilettantism,
genius and talent, presented as two flowers from the
same stem, differing but little ! As long as that pale
abstraction, the idea of " classical literature," lives on
among us as dogma, so long will the night of the chaos
of races overshadow us, so long will our schools be sterilising institutions destroying every creative impulse.
Hellenic poetry was a beginning—a dawn—it created
a people, it lavished upon them all that the highest
beauty can impart to make life sacred, all that poetry
can do to elevate hapless, tortured human souls and to
fill them with a feeling of invisible friendly powers—
and this fount of life wells on and never again dries up :
one century after the other is refreshed by it, one people
after another draws from its waters the power of inspiration to create beauty themselves ; for genius is like
God : it indeed reveals itself at a definite time and under

* With regard to the great Lucretius as an exception, *see* the note
on p. 35.

distinct conditions, but in its essence it is free from conditions ; what becomes a fetter to others is the material
out of which it makes for itself pinions, it rises out of time
and time's death-shadow, and passes in all the glow of life
into eternity. In Rome, on the other hand, one may
boldly assert, genius was altogether forbidden. Rome
has no poetry till it begins to decline. It is not till the
night sets in, when the Roman people is no longer there
to hear, that the singers of Rome raise their voices ; they
are night flutterers ; they write for the boudoirs of lasci-
vious ladies, for the amusement of men of the world and
for the court. Although Hellenes were close neighbours
and from the earliest times scattered the seeds of Hellenic
art, philosophy and science (for all culture in Rome was
from the first of Greek origin), not a single grain took root.
Five hundred years before the birth of Christ the Romans
sent to Athens, to glean accurate information regarding
Greek law ; their ambassadors met Æschylus in the
fulness of his powers and Sophocles already active as a
creative artist ; what an artistic splendour must have
sprung up in the all-vigorous Rome after such contact,
if even the slightest talent had been there ! But it did
not. As Mommsen says, " The development of the arts
of the Muse in Latium was rather a drying up than a
growing up." The Latins until their decline had no word
for poet, the idea was strange to them !—If now their
poets were without exception devoid of genius, wherein
lay the importance of those among them who, like Horace
and Juvenal, have always excited the admiration of the
linguistic artists ? Manifestly, as with everything that
comes from Rome, their importance lay in their art.
The Romans were great builders—of sewers and aque-
ducts ; * magnificent painters—of room-decorations ; great

* And yet not inventors even here ; see Hueppe's investigations
into the waterworks of the ancient Greeks, *Rassenhygiene der Griechen,*
p. 37.

manufacturers—of objects belonging to the industrial
arts ; in their circuses, masters of the art of fighting
fought for money and professional charioteers drove
on the racecourse. The Roman could be a virtuoso,
not an artist ; all virtuosity interested him, but no
art. The poems of Horace are technical masterpieces.
Apart from their historically picturesque interest as
descriptions of a life that has vanished, the virtuosity
alone in these poems attracts us. The " wisdom of
life," some one suggests by way of reproach ? Yes,
if such a matter-of-fact and prosaic wisdom were not
better anywhere else than in the fairy realm of art, the
wide-open, childlike eyes of which proclaim from every
Hellenic work of poetry quite a different wisdom from that
which occurs to Horace and his friends between cheese
and dessert. One of the most truly poetical natures that
ever lived, Byron, says of Horace :

> It is a curse
> To understand, not feel thy lyric flow,
> To comprehend, but never love thy verse,

What kind of art is that which speaks to the intelligence,
never to the heart ? It can only be an artificial work, an
applied art ; if it came from the heart it would go to the
heart. In truth we still stand in this matter under French
tutelage as the French stand under Syrian-Jewish
(Boileau—pseudo-Longinus) ; and though little of this inheritance has come into modern life, we should cast it off
once for all in favour of our own poets in words and music,
divinely inspired men, whose works tower high as the
heavens above all that shot up in unhealthy haste like
etiolated plants without root and without sap on the
ruins of fallen Rome.*

* Of the very considerable literature which in the last years has
been written on this question, and with which I have but little acquaintance, I recommend especially the small work of Prof. Albert Heintze,
Latein und Deutsch, 1902, which is written with as much knowledge
as it is to the point and devoid of passion.

In the hands of the specialist, *i.e.*, of the philologist, Latin poetry will be as surely and suitably preserved as the *corpus juris* in those of the investigators of law. If, however, the Latin tongue is to be retained at all costs as the universal trainer of the mind (instead of teaching Greek alone but more thoroughly), then let it be seen at work where it accomplishes wonders, where it, in accordance with the particular tendency of the Roman people and with its historical development, does what no other language ever did or will be able to do—in the plastic moulding of legal notions. People say that the Latin language educates the logical sense ; I will believe it, although I cannot help remarking that it was this very language in which during the scholastic centuries, in spite of all logic, more nonsense was written than in any other at any time ; but whereby has the Latin language acquired a character of such conciseness and definiteness ? By the fact that it was built up solely as the language of business, administration and law. This the most unpoetical of all languages is a magnificent monument of the momentous struggle of free men to obtain a sure code of law. Let our boys see it at work here. The great law-teachers of Rome have *eo ipso* written the finest Latin ; that, and not verse-writing, was the business of the language ; the faultlessly transparent formation of sentences, which shut out every possibility of misconstruction, was an important instrument of juristical applied art. From the study of law alone Cicero has taken his qualities of style. Mommsen says even of the oldest documents of the language of business and law that they were distinguished by " acumen and definiteness," * and philologists are of opinion that in the language of Papinian, one of the last great teachers of law (in the time of Marcus Aurelius), we have " the culmination of the capacity always to find the

* *Römische Geschichte*, i. 471.

expression which fully answers to the depth and clearness of the thought " ; his sentences, they say, stand as though chiselled out of marble : " not a word too much, not one too few, every word in the absolutely right place, thus rendering, as far as this is feasible with language, every ambiguity impossible." * Intercourse with such men would indeed be a valuable addition to our education. And it seems to me that when every Roman boy knew the Twelve Tables by heart, it would be appropriate and intellectually beneficial to our youths to leave school not merely as stupid, learned *subjecti*, but with some accurate conceptions of private and constitutional law, thinking not merely according to formal logic, but also reasonably and practically, and steeled against all empty raving about " German law " and such-like. In the meantime, because of the position we take up in reference to the Latin language, this legacy is badly administered and consequently of but little profit.

SUMMARY

We men of the nineteenth century should not be what we are if a rich legacy from these two cultures, the Hellenic and the Roman, had not come down to us. And so we cannot in the least judge what we truly are, and confess with modesty how little that is, if we do not form a quite clear conception of the nature of these inheritances. I hope that my endeavours in this direction will not have been quite fruitless and I hope also that the reader will especially have noticed that the legacy of Rome is utterly and fundamentally different from that of Greece.

In Hellas the personality of genius had been the decisive factor : whether on this side or on that of the Adriatic and the Ægean Seas, the Greeks were great so long as they

* Esmarch ; *Römische Rechtsgeschichte*, p. 400.

possessed great men. In Rome, on the other hand, there were only great individualities in so far and so long as the people was great, and it was great as long as it physically and morally remained genuinely Roman. Rome is the extreme example of a great corporate national power, which works unconsciously but all the more surely. For that reason, however, it is less attractive than Hellas, and hence what Rome did for our civilisation is seldom justly estimated. And yet Rome commands our admiration and gratitude ; its gifts were moral, not intellectual ; but by this very fact it was capable of achieving great things. Not the death of a Leonidas could save Europe from the Asiatic peril, upholding man's dignity with man's freedom, and handing it over to future ages to cultivate in peace and consolidate ; this could only be accomplished by a long-lived State, unbending and inexorably consistent in its politics. But neither theory nor fanaticism nor speculation could create this long-lived State ; it had to be rooted in the character of the citizen. This character was hard and self-seeking, but great by reason of its high sense of duty, by its capacity for making sacrifices and by its devotion to the family. The Roman, by erecting amidst the chaos of contemporary attempts at State-building a strong and solid State of his own, provided a model for all ages to come. By bringing his law to a technical perfection previously unknown, he laid the foundations of jurisprudence for all mankind. By following his natural inclination and making the family the centre of State and law, by, in fact, almost assigning extravagant importance to this conception, he raised woman to equality with man and transformed the union of the sexes into the sacredness of marriage. While our artistic and scientific culture is in many essential points derived from Greece, our social culture leads us back to Rome. I am not speaking

here of material civilisation, which is derived from many
countries and epochs and especially from the inventive
industry of recent centuries, but of the secure moral
foundations of a dignified social life ; the laying of
these was a great work of culture.

THIRD CHAPTER

THE REVELATION OF CHRIST

By the virtue of One all have been truly saved.

Mahâbhârata.

INTRODUCTORY

BEFORE our eyes there stands a vision, distinct, incomparable. This picture which we behold is the inheritance which we have received from our Fathers. Without an accurate appreciation of this vision, we cannot measure and rightly judge the historical significance of Christianity. The converse, on the other hand, does not hold good, for the figure of Jesus Christ has, by the historical development of the Churches, been dimmed and relegated to the background, rather than unveiled to the clear sight of our eyes. To look upon this Figure solely by the light of a church doctrine, narrowed both in respect of place and of time, is voluntarily to put on blinkers and to narrow our view of the eternally Divine. The vision of Christ, moreover, is hardly touched upon by the dogmas of the Church. They are all so abstract that they afford nothing upon which either our understanding or our feelings can lay hold. We may apply to them in general what an artless witness, St. Augustine, said of the Dogma of the Trinity: "But we speak of three Persons, not because we fancy that in so doing we have uttered something, but simply because we cannot be silent."* Surely we are guilty of no outrage upon due reverence if we say, it is not the Churches that constitute the might of Christianity, for that might is drawn solely from the fountain head from which the churches themselves derive all their power— the contemplation of the Son of Man upon the Cross.

Let us therefore separate the vision of Christ upon earth from the whole history of Christianity.

What after all are our nineteen centuries for the conscious acceptance of such an experience—for the transformation which forces itself through all the strata of humanity by the power of a fundamentally new aspect of life's problems ? We should remember that more than two thousand years were needed before the structure of the Kosmos, capable as it is of mathematical proof and of demonstration to the senses, became the fixed, common possession of human knowledge. Is not the understanding with its gift of sight and its infallible formula of $2 \times 2 = 4$ easier to mould than the heart, blind and ever befooled by self-seeking ? Here is a man born into the world and living a life through which the conception of the moral significance of man, the whole philosophy of life, undergoes a complete transformation —through which the relation of the individual to himself, to the rest of mankind, and to the nature by which he is surrounded, is of necessity illuminated by a new and hitherto unsuspected light, so that all motives of action, all ideals, all heart's-desires and hopes must be remoulded and built up anew from their very foundations. Is it to be believed that this can be the work of a few centuries ? Is it to be believed that this can be brought about by misunderstandings and lies, by political intrigues and œcumenical councils, at the word of command of kings maddened by ambition, or of greedy priests,

* " Dictum est tamen tres personæ, non ut aliquid diceretur, sed ne taceretur."—*De Trinitate*, V. chap. ix.

by three thousand volumes of scholastic disputations, by the fanatical faith of narrow-minded peasants and the noble zeal of a small number of superior persons, by war, murder and the stake, by civic codes of law and social intolerance? For my part I disclaim any such belief. I believe that we are still far, very far, from the moment when the transforming might of the vision of Christ will make itself felt to its utmost extent by civilised mankind. Even if our churches in their present form should come to an end, the idea of Christianity would only stand out with all the more force. In the ninth chapter I shall show how our new Teuton philosophy is pushing in that direction. Even now, Christianity is not yet firm upon its childish feet : its maturity is hardly dawning upon our dim vision. Who knows but a day may come when the bloody church-history of the first eighteen centuries of our era may be looked upon as the history of the infantile diseases of Christianity?

In considering the vision of Christ, then, let us not allow our judgment to be darkened by any historical delusions, or by the ephemeral views of our century. We may be sure that up to the present we have only entered upon the smallest portion of this same inheritance, and if we wish to know what is its significance for all of us, be we Christians or Jews, believers or unbelievers, whether we are conscious of our privilege or not—then must we in the first place stop our ears against the chaos of creeds and of blasphemies which beshame humanity, and in the next place raise our eyes up to the most incomparable vision of all times.

In this section I shall be forced critically to glance at much that forms the intellectual foundation of various religions. But just as I leave untouched that which is hidden in the Holy of Holies of my own heart, so I hope to steer clear of giving offence to any other sensible man. It is as easy to separate the historic vision of

Christ from all the supernatural significance which dwells in it as it must be to treat Physics upon a purely material basis without imagining that in so doing we have dethroned Metaphysics.

Christ indeed can hardly be spoken of without now and again crossing the boundary ; still belief, as such, need not be touched, and if I as historian proceed logically and convincingly, I can bear with any refutation which the reader may bring forward as a question of feeling, as apart from understanding. With this consciousness I shall speak as frankly in the following chapters as I have done in those which have gone before.

THE RELIGION OF EXPERIENCE

The religious faith of more than two-thirds of all the inhabitants of the earth to-day starts from the life on earth of two men, Christ and Buddha, men who lived only a few centuries ago. We have historical proofs of their having actually existed, and that the traditions regarding them, though containing much that is fabulous and uncertain, obscure and contradictory, nevertheless give us a faithful picture of the main features of their real lives. Even apart from this sure result of the scientific investigations of the nineteenth century,* men of acute and sound judgment will never have doubted the actual existence of these great moral heroes : for although the historical and chronological material regarding them is extremely scanty and imperfect, yet their moral and intellectual individuality stands out so clearly and brilliantly before our eyes, and this individuality is so incomparable, that it could not be

---

* The existence of Christ was denied even in the second century of our era, and Buddha till twenty-five years ago was regarded by many theologians as a mythical figure. *See*, for example, the books of Sénart and Kern.

an invention of the imagination. The imagination of
man is very narrowly circumscribed; the creative mind
can work only with given facts: it was men that Homer
had to enthrone on Olympus, for even his imagination
could not transcend the impassable boundary of what
he saw and experienced; the very fact that he makes
his gods so very human, that he does not permit his
imagination to soar to the realm of the Extraordinary and
Inconceivable (because never seen), that he rather keeps
it in subjection, in order to employ its undivided force
to create what will be poetical and visible, is one of a
thousand proofs, and not the least important one, that
intellectually he was a great man. We are not capable
of inventing even a plant or animal form; when we try
it, the most we do is to put together a monstrosity composed of fragments of all kinds of creatures known to us.
Nature, however, the inexhaustibly inventive, shows us
a new thing whenever it so pleases her; and this new
thing is for our consciousness henceforth just as indestructible as it formerly was undiscoverable. The figure
of Buddha, much less that of Jesus Christ, could not be
invented by any human poetical power, neither that of
an individual nor that of a whole people; nowhere can
we discover even the slightest approach to such a thing.
Neither poets, nor philosophers, nor prophets have been
able even in their dreams to conceive such a phenomenon.
Plato is certainly often mentioned in connection with
Jesus Christ; there are whole books on the supposed
relation between the two; it is said that the Greek
philosopher was a forerunner who proclaimed the new
gospel. In reality, however, the great Plato is a quite
irreligious genius, a metaphysician and politician,
an investigator and an aristocrat. And Socrates!
The clever author of grammar and logic, the honest
preacher of a morality for philistines, the noble gossip
of the Athenian gymnasia,—is he not in every respect

the direct contrast to the divine proclaimer of a Heaven of them " that are poor in spirit " ? In India it was the same : the figure of a Buddha was not anticipated nor conjured up by the magic of men's longing. All such assertions belong to the wide province of that delusive historic philosophy which constructs after the event. If Christ and Christianity had been an historical necessity, as the neoscholastic Hegel asserts, and Pfleiderer and others would have us believe to-day, we should inevitably have seen not one Christ but a thousand Christs arise ; I should really like to know in what century a Jesus would not have been just as " necessary " as our daily bread ?* Let us therefore discard these views that are tinged with the paleness of abstraction. The only effect they have is to obscure the one decisive and pregnant thing, namely, the importance of the living, individual, incomparable personality. One is ever and anon forced to quote Goethe's great saying :

> Höchstes Glück der Erdenkinder
> Ist nur die Persönlichkeit !

The circumstances in which the personality is placed— a knowledge of its general conditions in respect of time and space—will certainly contribute very much towards making it clearly understood. Such a knowledge will enable us to distinguish between the important and

---

* Hegel in his *Philosophie der Geschichte*, Th. III., A. 3, chap. ii., says about Christ : " He was born as this one man, in abstract subjectivity, but so that conversely finiteness is only the form of his appearance, the essence and content of which is rather infiniteness and absolute being-for-self. . . . The nature of God, to be pure spirit, becomes in the Christian religion manifest to man. But what is the spirit ? It is the One, the unchanging infinity, the pure identity, which in the second place separates itself from itself, as its second self, as the being-for-itself and being-in-itself in opposition to the Universal. But this separation is annulled by this, that the atomistic subjectivity, as the simple relativity to itself, is itself the Universal, Identical with itself." What will future centuries say to this clatter of words ? For two-thirds of the nineteenth it was considered the highest wisdom.

the unimportant, between the characteristically individual and the locally conventional. It will, in short, give us an increasingly clearer view of the personality. But to explain it, to try to show it as a logical necessity, is an idle, foolish task ; every figure—even that of a beetle—is to the human understanding a " wonder " ; the human personality is, however, the *mysterium magnum* of life, and the more a great personality is stripped by criticism of all legendary rags and tatters, and the more successful that criticism is in representing each step in its career as something fore-ordained in the nature of things, the more incomprehensible the mystery becomes. This indeed is the final result of the criticism to which the life of Jesus has been submitted in the nineteenth century. This century has been called an irreligious one ; but never yet, since the first Christian centuries, has the interest of mankind concentrated so passionately around the person of Jesus Christ as in the last seventy years ; the works of Darwin, however widespread they were, were not bought to one-tenth the extent of those of Strauss and Renan. And the result of it all is, that the actual earthly life of Jesus Christ has become more and more concrete, and we have been compelled to recognise more and more distinctly that the origin of the Christian religion is fundamentally to be traced to the absolutely unexampled impression which this one personality had made and left upon those who knew Him. So it is that to-day this revelation stands before our eyes more definite and for that very reason more unfathomable than ever.

This is the first point to be established. It is in accordance with the whole tendency of our times, that we can grow enthusiastic only in regard to what is concrete and living. At the beginning of the nineteenth century it was different ; the Romantic movement threw its shadows on all sides, and so it had become fashionable

to explain everything "mythically." In the year 1835
David Strauss, following the example proffered on all
sides, presented as a key to the gospels "the idea of the
myth"!* Every one now recognises that this so-called
key was nothing more than a new, mistily vague para-
phrase of a still-unsolved problem, and that not an
"idea," but only an actually lived existence, only the
unique impression of a personality, whose like the world
had never before known, supplies the "key" to the
origin of Christianity. The greater the amount of
such useless ballast that was manifest on the one hand in
the shape of pseudo-mythical (or rather pseudo-historical)
legend-making, on the other in the form of philosophically
dogmatic speculation, the greater is the power of life
and resistance that must be attributed to the original
impelling and creating force   The most modern, strictly
philological criticism has proved the unexpected antiquity
of the gospels and the extensive authenticity of the
manuscripts which we possess ; we have now succeeded
in tracing, almost step for step, the very earliest records

---

* *See* first edition, i. 70 ff., and the popular edition (ninth) p. 191 ff.
Strauss never had the least notion what a myth is, what mythology
means, how it is produced by the confusion and mingling of popular
myths, poetry and legends. That, however, is another story. Posterity
will really not be able to understand the reception given to such dreary
productions as those of Strauss : they are learned, but destitute of all
deeper insight and of any trace of genius. Just as bees and ants
require in their communities whole cohorts of sexless workers, so it
seems as if we human beings could not get along without the industry
and the widespread but ephemeral influence of such minds, marked with
the stamp of sterility, as flourished in such profusion about the middle of
the nineteenth century. The progress of historico-critical research on
the one hand, and on the other the increasing tendency to direct attention
not to the theological and subordinate, but to that which is living and
decisive, causes one to look upon the mythological standpoint of Strauss
as so unintelligent that one cannot turn over the leaves of this honest
man's writings without yawning. And yet one must admit that such
men as he and Renan (two concave mirrors which distort all lines, the
one by lengthening, the other by broadening) have accomplished an
important work—by drawing the attention of thousands to the great
miracle of the fact of Christ and thus creating a public for profounder
thinkers and wiser men.

of Christianity in a strictly historical manner.* But all this when considered from the universal human standpoint is of much less importance than the one fact, that in consequence of these researches the figure of the one Divine Man has been brought into relief, so that the unbeliever as well as the believer is bound to recognise it as the centre and source of Christianity, taking the word in the most comprehensive sense possible.

BUDDHA AND CHRIST

A few pages back I placed Buddha and Christ in juxtaposition. The kernel of the religious conceptions of all the more gifted races of mankind (with the two exceptions of the small family of the Jews on the one hand and their antipodes the Brahman Indians on the other) has been for the past few thousand years not the need for an explanation of the world, nor mythological Nature-symbolism, nor meditative transcendentalism, but the experience of great characters. The delusion of a "rational religion" still haunts us ; occasionally too in recent years there has been talk of a "replacing of religion by something higher," and on the hilltops of certain German districts new "worshippers of Wotan" have offered up sacrifice at the time of the solstice ; but none of these movements have exercised the slightest influence upon the world. For ideas are immortal—I have said so already and shall have to repeat it constantly—and in such figures as Buddha and Christ an idea—that is, a definite conception of human existence—acquires such a living bodily form, becomes so thoroughly an experience of life, is placed so clearly before the eyes of all men, that it can never more disappear from their conscious-

* Later there came a dark period upon which light has still to be thrown.

ness.   Many a man may never have seen the Crucified One
with his eyes; many a man may constantly have passed
this revelation carelessly by; thousands of men, even
among ourselves, lack what one might call the inner sense
to perceive Christ at all; on the other hand, having
once seen Jesus Christ—even if it be with half-veiled
eyes—we cannot forget Him; it does not lie within
our power to remove the object of experience from our
minds.   We are not Christians because we were brought
up in this or in that Church, because we want to be
Christians; if we are Christians, it is because we cannot
help it, because neither the chaotic bustle of life nor the
delirium of selfishness, nor artificial training of thought
can dispel the vision of the Man of Sorrow when once
it has been seen.   On the evening before His death, when
His Apostles were questioning Him as to the significance
of one of His actions, He replied, "I have given you an
example."   That is the meaning not only of the one
action but of His whole life and death.   Even so strict an
ecclesiastic as Martin Luther writes: "The example of
our Lord Jesus Christ is at the same time a sacrament,
it is strong in us, it does not, like the examples of the
fathers, merely teach, no, it also effects what it teaches,
it gives life, resurrection and redemption from death."
The power of Buddha over the world rests on similar foundations.   The true source of all religion is, I repeat, in the
case of the great majority of living people not a doctrine
but a life.   It is a different question, of course, how far we,
with our weak capability, can or cannot follow the example; the ideal is there, clear, unmistakable, and for
centuries it has been moulding with incomparable power
the thoughts and actions of men, even of unbelievers.

I shall return to this point later in another connection.
If I have introduced Buddha here, where only the figure
of Christ concerns me, I have done so for this reason,
that nothing shows up a figure so well as comparison.

The comparison, however, must be an appropriate one, and I do not know any other than Buddha in the history of the world whom we could compare with Christ. Both are characterised by their divine earnestness ; they have in common the longing to point out to all mankind the way of redemption ; they have both incomparably magnetic personalities. And yet if one places these two figures side by side, it can only be to emphasise the contrast and not to draw a parallel between them. Christ and Buddha are opposites. What unites them is their sublimity of character. From that source have sprung lives of unsurpassed loveliness, lives which wielded an influence such as the world had never before experienced. Otherwise they differ almost in every point, and the neo-Buddhism which has been paraded during recent years in certain social circles in Europe —in the closest relation, it is said, to Christianity and even going beyond it—is but a new proof of the widespread superficiality of thought among us. For Buddha's life and thought present a direct contrast to the thought and life of Christ : they form what the logician calls the " antithesis," what to the natural scientist is the " opposite pole."

BUDDHA

Buddha represents the senile decay of a culture which has reached the limit of its possibilities. A Prince, highly educated, gifted with a rich fulness of power, recognises the vanity of that education and that power. He professes what to the rest of the world seems to be the Highest, but with the vision of truth before him, this possession melts away to nothing. Indian culture, the outcome of the meditative contemplation incident to a pastoral life, had thrown itself with all the weight of its lofty gifts into the development of the one attribute peculiar to mankind—Reason with the power of combination : so it came to pass that connection with the surrounding world—childlike observation with its practical adaptation to business—languished, at any rate among the men of higher culture. Everything was systematically directed to the development of the power of thought : every educated youth knew by heart, word for word, a whole literature charged with matter so subtle that even to this day few Europeans are capable of following it : even geometry, the most abstract of all methods of representing the concrete world, was too obvious for the Indians, and so they came instead to revel in an arithmetic which goes beyond all possibility of presentation: the man who questioned himself as to his aim in life, the man who had been gifted by nature with the desire to strive for some highest goal, found on the one side a religious system in which symbolism had grown to such mad dimensions that it needed some thirty years to find oneself at home in it, and on the other side a philosophy leading up to heights so giddy that whoso wished to climb the last rungs of this heavenly ladder must take refuge from the world for ever in the deep silence of the primeval forest. Clearly here the eye and the heart had lost their rights. Like the scorching simoom of the desert, the spirit of abstraction had swept with withering force over all other gifts of this rich human nature. The senses indeed still lived—desires of tropical heat : but on the other side was the negation of the whole world of sense : between these nothing, no compromise, only war, war between human perception and human nature, between thought and being. And so Buddha must hate what he loved ; children, parents, wife, all that is beautiful and joyous—for what were these but veils darkening perception, bonds chaining him to a dream-life of lies and desire ? and what had he to do with all the wisdom of the Brahmans ? Sacrificial ceremonies which no

human being understood, and which the priests themselves explained as being purely symbolical and to the
initiated futile :—beyond this a redemption by perception accessible to scarcely one man in a hundred
thousand. Thus it was that Buddha not only cast away
from him his kingdom and his knowledge, but tore
from his heart all that bound him as man to man, all
love, all hope : at one blow he destroyed the religion
of his fathers, drove their gods from the temple of the
world, and rejected as a vain phantom even that most
sublime conception of Indian metaphysics, that of a one
and only God, indescribable, unthinkable, having no part
in space or time, and therefore inaccessible to thought,
and yet by thought dimly imagined. There is nothing in
life but suffering, this was Buddha's experience and consequently his teaching. The one object worth striving
for is "redemption from suffering." This redemption
is death, the entering into annihilation. But to every
Indian the transmigration of souls, that is the eternal
reincarnation of the same individual, was believed in
as a manifest fact, not even to be called in question.
Death then, in its ordinary shape, cannot give redemption : it is the gift of that death only upon which
no reincarnation follows : and this redeeming death can
only be attained in one way, namely, that man shall
have died during his life and therefore of his own free
will : that is to say, that he shall have cut off and annihilated all that ties him to life, all love, all hope, all desire,
all possession : in short, as we should say with Schopenhauer, that he shall have denied the will to live. If man
lives in this wise, if while yet alive he makes himself into
a moving corpse, then can the reaper Death harvest no
seed for a reincarnation. A living Death ! that is the
essence of Buddhism ! We may describe Buddhism
as the lived suicide. It is suicide in its highest potentiality : for Buddha lives solely and only to die, to be

dead definitely and beyond recall, to enter into Nirvana
—extinction.*

CHRIST

What greater contrast could there be to this figure
than that of Christ, whose death signifies entrance into
eternal life ?   Christ perceives divine Providence in the
whole world ; not a sparrow falls to the ground, not a hair
on the head of a man can be injured, without the permission of the Heavenly Father.   And far from hating this
earthly existence, which is lived by the will and under
the eye of God, Christ praises it as the entry into eternity,
as the narrow gate through which we pass into the
Kingdom of God.   And this Kingdom of God, what is it ?
A Nirvana ? a Dream-Paradise ?   a future reward for
deeds done here below ?   Christ gives the answer in one
word, which has undoubtedly been authentically handed
down to us, for it had never been uttered before, and no
one of His disciples evidently understood it; much less
invented it ; indeed, this eagle thought flashed so far
in front of the slow unfolding of human knowledge that
even to the present day few have seen the meaning of it
—as I said before, Christianity is still in its infancy—
Christ's answer was, " The Kingdom of God cometh not
with observation : neither shall they say, Lo here or lo
there.   For behold, the Kingdom of God is within you."
This is what Christ himself calls the " mystery " ; it
cannot be expressed in words, it cannot be defined ; and
ever and ever again the Saviour endeavours to bring home

* I have translated *das nichts* by *extinction,* which is the rendering
of Nirvana by Rhys Davids.   He says : " What then is Nirvana, which
means simply *going out, extinction* "; and then he goes on to say that
it ought to be translated "Holiness."   But that will not do here,
nor is it altogether incapable of being argued.   Extinction gives
Chamberlain's meaning better than " nothingness," which is not quite
satisfactory.   Perhaps " Holy Extinction " comes near to the Buddhist
conception.   The idea of Rhys Davids would thus not be lost.   (Trans
lator's Note.)

His great message of salvation by means of parables : the
Kingdom of God is like a grain of mustard seed in the
field, " the least of all seeds," but if it is tended by the
husbandman, it grows to a tree, " so·that the birds of
the air come and lodge under its branches " ; the Kingdom
of God is like the leaven among the flour, if the housewife
take but a little, it leavens the whole lump ; but the
following figure speaks most plainly : " the Kingdom
of God is like unto a treasure hid in a field." * That
the field means the world, Christ expressly says (see
Matthew xiii. 38) ; in this world, that is, in this life,
the treasure lies concealed ; the Kingdom of God is
buried within us ! That is the " mystery of the Kingdom
of God," as Christ says ; at the same time it is the secret
of His own life, the secret of His personality. An estrange-
ment from life, as in the case of Buddha, is not to be
found in Christ, there is, however, a "conversion" of the
direction of life, if I may so call it, as, for example, when
Christ says to His disciples, " Verily I say unto you,
Except ye be converted, ye shall not enter into the Kingdom of God."† At a later period this so easily grasped
" conversion " received—perhaps from a strange hand—
the more mystical expression, " Except a man be born
again, he cannot see the Kingdom of God." The words
do not matter, what is important is the conception
underlying them, and this conception stands out lumi-
nously clear, because it gives form to the whole life of

* The expression Uranos or " Kingdom of Heaven " occurs only in
Matthew and is certainly not the right translation into Greek of any
expression used by Christ. The other evangelists always say " Kingdom
of God." (*Cf.* my collection of the *Worte Christi*, large edition,
p. 260, small edition, p. 279, and for more learned and definite explanation *see* H. H. Wendt's *Lehre Jesu*, 1886, pp. 48 and 58.)

† The emphasis clearly does not lie on the additional clause " and
become as little children " ; this is rather an explanation of the
conversion. What is it that distinguishes children ? Unalloyed joy
in life and the unspoilt power of throwing a glamour over it by their
temperaments.

Christ.   Here we do not find a doctrine like that of Buddha with a logical arithmetical development ; nor is there, as has so frequently been asserted by the superficial, any organic connection with Jewish wisdom : read the words of Jesus Sirach, who is most frequently compared with Christ, and ask yourselves whether that is " Spirit of the same Spirit " ?   Sirach speaks like a Jewish Marcus Aurelius and even his finest sayings, such as " Seek wisdom until death, and God will fight for you," or, " The heart of the fool lies upon his tongue, but the tongue of the wise man dwells within his heart," are as a sound from another world when put beside the sayings of Christ : " Blessed are the meek, for they shall inherit the earth ; blessed are the pure in heart, for they shall see God ; take my yoke upon you and learn of me, for I am meek and lowly of heart, and you will find rest unto your souls, for my yoke is easy and my burden is light."   No one had ever spoken like that before, and no one has spoken so since.   These words of Christ have, however, as we can see, never the character of a doctrine, but just as the tone of a voice supplements by a mysterious inexpressible something—which is the most personal element in the personality—what we already know about a man from his features and his actions, so do we seem to hear in them his voice ; what he exactly said we do not know, but an unmistakable, unforgettable tone strikes our ear and from our ear enters our heart. And then we open our eyes and see this figure, this life. Down through the ages we hear the words, " Learn of me," and we understand what they mean : to be as Christ was, to live as Christ lived, to die as Christ died, that is the Kingdom of God, that is eternal life.

In the nineteenth century, the ideas of pessimism and negation of the will, which have become so common, have been frequently applied to Christ ; but though they fit Buddha and certain features of the Christian churches and their dogmas, Christ's life is their denial. If the Kingdom of God dwells in us, if it is embraced in this life like a hidden treasure, what becomes of the sense of pessimism ? * How can man be a wretch born only for grief, if the divinity lies in his breast ? How can this world be the worst of all possible worlds (see Schopenhauer: *Die Welt als Wille und Vorstellung*, vol. ii. chap. xlvi.) if it contains Heaven ? For Christ these were all delusive fallacies ; woe to you, He said of the learned, " who shut up the Kingdom of God against men ; for ye neither go in yourselves neither suffer ye them that would enter to go in," and He praised God that He had " revealed to babes and sucklings what He had hidden from the wise and prudent " ; Christ, as one of the greatest men of the nineteenth century has said, was " not wise, but divine ";† that is a mighty difference; and because He was divine, Christ did not turn away from life, but to life. This is eloquently vouched for by the impression which Christ made and left upon those who knew Him ; they call Him the tree of life, the bread of life, the water of life, the light of life, the light of the world, a light from above sent to lighten those that sit in darkness and in the shadow of death ; Christ is for them the rock, the foundation upon which we are to build our lives, &c. &c. Everything is positive, constructive, affirmative. Whether Christ really brought the dead to life may be doubted by any one who will ; but such a one must estimate all the more highly the life-giving impression which radiated from this figure, for wherever Christ went people believed that they saw the dead come to life and the sick rise healed from their beds. Everywhere He sought out the suffering, the poor, those laden with sorrow,

* I need scarcely say that I take the word pessimism, which is capable of such a variety of interpretations, in the popular, superficial sense of a moral frame of mind, not a philosophical cognition.

† Diderot also, to whom one cannot attribute orthodox faith, says in the *Encyclopédie :* " *Christ ne fut point un philosophe, ce fut un Dieu.*"

and bidding them " weep not," consoled them with words
of life.   From inner Asia came the idea of flight from
the world to the cloister.   Buddhism had not in truth invented it, but gave it its greatest impulse.   Christianity,
too, imitated it later, closely following the Egyptian
example.   This idea had already advanced to the very
neighbourhood of the Galilean ; yet where does one
find Christ preaching monastic doctrines of seclusion
from the world ?   Many founders of religion have imposed penance in respect of food upon themselves and
their disciples ; not so Christ ; He emphasises particularly
that He had not fasted like John, but had so lived that
men called Him a "glutton and a winebibber."   All the
following expressions which we know so well from the
Bible—that the thoughts of men are vain, that the life
of man is vanity, he passes away like a shadow, the
work of man is vain, all is vanity—come from the Old,
not from the New Testament.   Indeed such words as
those, for example, of the preacher Solomon, " One generation passeth away and another generation cometh, but
the earth abideth for ever," are derived from a view of
life which is directly contrary to that of Christ ; because
according to the latter Heaven and earth pass away,
while the human breast conceals in its depths the only
thing that is everlasting.   It is true that Jesus Christ
offers the example of an absolute renunciation of much
that makes up the life of the greater proportion of mankind ; but it is done for the sake of life ; this renunciation
is the " conversion " which, we are told, leads to the
Kingdom of Heaven, and it is not outward but purely
inward.   What Buddha eaches is, so to speak, a physical process, it is the actual extinction of the physical
and intellectual being ; whoever wishes to be redeemed
must take the three vows of chastity, poverty and obedience.   In the case of Christ we find nothing similar :
He attends marriages, He declares wedlock to be a holy

ordinance of God, and even the errors of the flesh he judges so leniently that He Himself has not a word of condemnation for the adulteress ; He indeed speaks of wealth as rendering the " conversion " of the will more difficult—as, for example, when He says that it is more difficult for a rich man to enter into that kingdom of God which lies within us than for a camel to go through the eye of a needle, but He immediately adds—and this is the characteristic and decisive part—" the things which are impossible with men are possible with God." This is again one of those passages which cannot be invention, for nowhere in the whole world do we find anything like it. There had been enough and to spare of diatribes against wealth before (one need only read the Jewish Prophets), they were repeated later (read, for instance, the *Epistle of James*, chap. ii. ; according to Christ, how-ever, wealth is a mere accessory, the possession of which may or may not be a hindrance, for the one thing which concerns Him is the inner and spiritual conversion. And this it was that, in dealing with this very case, by far the greatest of the Apostles amplified so beau-tifully ; for while Christ had advised the rich young man, " Sell all that thou hast and give it to the poor," Paul completes the saying by the remark, " and though I bestow all my goods to feed the poor and have not charity it profiteth me nothing." The Buddhist who is steering for death may be satisfied with poverty, chastity, and obedience ; he who chooses life has other things to think of.

And here it is necessary to call attention to one more point, in which the living essence of Christ's personality and example manifests itself freshly and convincingly ; I refer to His combativeness. The sayings of Christ on humility and patience, His exhortation that we should love our enemies and bless those that curse us, find almost

exact parallels in the sayings of Buddha ; but they spring
from quite a different motive.   For Buddha every injustice
endured is an extinction, for Christ it is a means of advancing the new view of life : " Blessed are they which
are persecuted for righteousness' sake, for theirs is the
Kingdom of God " (that kingdom which lies hidden like a
treasure in the field of life).   But if we pass to the inner
being, if that one fundamental question of the direction of
will is brought up, then we hear words of quite a different
kind : " Suppose ye that I am come to give peace on
earth ?   I tell you, Nay, but rather division !   For from
henceforth there shall be five in one house divided, two
against three, and three against two. . . . For I am come
to stir up the son against his father, and the daughter
against her mother, and the daughter-in-law against the
mother-in-law ; and the man's enemies shall be they of
his own household."   Not peace but the sword : that is a
voice to which we cannot shut our ears, if we wish to
understand the revelation of Christ.   The life of Jesus
Christ is an open declaration of war, not against the forms
of civilisation, culture and religion, which He found around
Him—He observes the Jewish law of religion and teaches
us to give to Cæsar what is Cæsar's—but certainly against
the inner spirit of mankind, against the motives which
underlie their actions, against the goal which they set
for themselves in the future life and in the present.
The coming of Christ signifies, from the point of view
of the world's history, the coming of a new human species.
Linnæus distinguished as many human species as there
are colours of skin ; but a new colouring of the will goes
really deeper into the organism than a difference in the
pigment of the epidermis !   And the Lord of this new
human species, the " new Adam," as the Scripture
so well describes Him, will have no compromise ; He
puts the choice : God or mammon.   Whoever chooses

conversion, whoever obeys the warning of Christ, " Follow me ! " must also when necessary leave father and mother, wife and child ; but he does not leave them, like the disciples of Buddha, to find death, but to find life. Here is no room for pity : whom we have lost we have lost, and with the ancient hardness of the heroic spirit not a tear is shed over those who are gone: " Let the dead bury their dead." Not every one is capable of understanding the word of Christ, He in fact tells us, " Many are called but few are chosen," and here again Paul has given drastic expression to this fact : " The preaching of the Cross is to them that perish foolishness ; but unto us which are saved it is the power of God." So far as outward forms go Christ has no preferences, but where the direction of the will is concerned, whether it is directed to the Eternal or the Temporal, whether it advances or hinders the unfolding of that immeasurable power of life in the heart of man, whether it aims at the quickening of that " Kingdom of God within us " or, on the other hand, scatters for ever the one treasure of " them that are chosen "—there is with Him no question of tolerance and never can be. In this very connection much has been done since the eighteenth century to rob the sublime countenance of the Son of Man of all its mighty features. We have had represented to us as Christianity a strange delusive picture of boundless tolerance, of universally gentle passivity, a kind of milk-and-water religion ; in the last few years we have actually witnessed " interconfessional religious congresses," where all the priests of the world shake hands as brothers, and many Christians welcome this as particularly " Christlike." It may be ecclesiastical, it may be right and good, but Christ would never have sent an apostle to such a congress. Either the word of the Cross is " foolishness " or it is " a divine power " ; between the two Christ himself has torn open the yawning gulf of "division," and, to prevent any possibility of its being bridged, has drawn the flaming "sword." Whoever understands the revelation of Christ cannot be surprised. The tolerance of Christ is that of a spirit which soars high as Heaven above all forms that divide the world ; a combination of these forms could not have the slightest importance for Him—that would mean only the rise of a new form ; He, on the other hand, considers only the "spirit and the truth." And when Christ teaches, "Whosoever shall smite thee on thy right cheek turn to him the other also, and if any man will take away thy coat let him have thy cloak also "—a doctrine to which His example on the Cross gave everlasting significance—who does not understand that this is closely related to what follows, "Love your enemies, do good to them that hate you," and that here that inner "conversion" is expressed, not passively, but in the highest possible form of living action ? If I offer the impudent striker my left cheek, I do not do so for his sake ; if I love my enemy and show him kindness, it is not for his sake ; after the conversion of the will it is simply inevitable and therefore I do it. The old law, an eye for an eye, hatred for hatred, is just as natural a reflex action as that which causes the legs of a dead frog to kick when the nerves are stimulated. In sooth it must be a "new Adam " who has gained such complete mastery over his "old Adam " that he does not obey this impulse. However, it is not merely self-control—for if Buddha forms the one opposite pole to Christ, the Stoic forms the other ; but that conversion of the will, that entry into the hidden kingdom of God, that being born again, which makes up the sum of Christ's example, demands a complete conversion of the feelings. This, in fact, is the new thing. Till Christ blood-vengeance was the sacred law of all men of the most different races ; but from the Cross there

came the cry, " Father, forgive them, for they know not
what they do!" Whoever takes the divine voice
of pity for weak humanitarianism has not understood
a single feature of the advent of Christ. The voice which
here speaks comes from that Kingdom of God which is
within us ; pain and death have lost their power over
it ; they affect him who is born again just as little as
the stroke on the cheek or the theft of the coat ; everything that drives, constrains and compels the human
half-ape — selfishness, superstition, prejudice, envy,
hatred—breaks on such a will as this like sea-foam
on a granite cliff ; in face of death Christ scarcely notices
His own pain and tribulation, He sees only that men are
crucifying what is divine in them, and they are treading
under foot the seed of the Kingdom of God and scattering
the " treasure in the field," and thus it is that, full of pity,
He calls out, " They know not what they do ! " Search
the history of the world and you will not find a word to
equal this for sublime pride. Here speaks a discernment
that has penetrated farther than the Indian mind, here
speaks at the same time the strongest will, the surest
consciousness of self.

Just as we children of a modern age have discovered
in the whole world a power which before only from
time to time flashed forth in fleeting clouds as the lightning, a power hidden, invisible, perceived by no sense,
to be explained by no hypothesis, but all-present and
almighty, and in the same way as we are driven to trace
the complete transformation of our outward conditions of
life to this power—so Christ pointed to a hidden power in
the unfathomed and unfathomable depths of the human
heart, a power capable of completely transforming
man, capable of making a sorrow-trodden wretch mighty
and blessed. The lightning had hitherto been only
a destroyer ; the power which it taught us to discover is

now the servant of peaceful work and comfort; in like manner the human will, from the beginning of time the seed of all the misfortune and misery that descended upon the human race, was henceforth to minister to the new birth of this race, to the rise of a new human species. Hence, as I have pointed out in the introduction to this book, the incomparable significance of the life of Christ for the world's history. No political revolution can compare with it.

From the point of view of universal history we have every reason to put the achievement of Christ on a parallel with the achievements of the Hellenes. In the first chapter I have described in how far Homer, Democritus, Plato, &c. &c. are to be considered as real " creators," and I added, " then and then only is a new creature born, then only does the macrocosm contain a microcosm. The only thing that deserves to be called culture is the daughter of such creative freedom."* What Greece did for the intellect, Christ did for the moral life : man had not a moral culture till He gave it. I should rather say, the possibility of a moral culture ; for the motive power of culture is that inner, creative process, the voluntary masterful conversion of the will, and this very motive power was with rare exceptions quite overlooked ; Christianity became an essentially historical religion, and at the altars of its churches all the superstitions of antiquity and of Judaism found a consecrated place of refuge. Yet we have in the revelation of Christ the one foundation of all moral culture, and the moral culture of our nations is greater or smaller in proportion to the extent to which his personality is able more or less clearly to prevail.

It is in this connection that we can with truth assert that the appearance of Christ upon earth has divided

* See p. 25.

mankind into two classes. It created for the first time true nobility, and indeed true nobility of birth, for only he who is chosen can be a Christian. But at the same time it sowed in the hearts of the chosen the seed of new and bitter suffering : it separated them from father and mother, it made them lonely wanderers among men who did not understand them, it stamped them as martyrs. And who after all is really master ? Who has entirely conquered his slavish instincts ? Discord from now onward rent the individual soul. And now that the individual, who hitherto in the tumultuous struggle of life had scarcely attained to a consciousness of his " Ego," was awakened to an unexpectedly high conception of his dignity, inner significance and power, how often was his heart bound to fail him in the consciousness of his weakness and unworthiness ? Now and now only did life become truly tragical. This was brought about by man's own free act in rising against his animal nature. " From a perfect pupil of nature man became an imperfect moral being, from a good instrument a bad artist," says Schiller. But man will no longer be an instrument ; and as Homer had created gods such as he wished them, so now man rebelled against the moral tyranny of nature and created a sublime morality such as he desired ; he would no longer obey blind impulses, beautifully constrained and restricted as they might be by legal paragraphs ; his own law of morals would henceforth be his only standard. In Christ man awakens to consciousness of his moral calling, but thereby at the same time to the necessity of an inner struggle that is reckoned in tens of centuries. Under the heading Philosophy in the ninth chapter (vol. ii.), I shall show that after an anti-Christian reaction lasting for many centuries we have with Kant returned again to exactly the same path. The humanitarian Deists of the eighteenth century who turned away from Christ thought the proper course was a " return to nature " : on the contrary, it is emancipation from nature, without which we can achieve nothing, but which we are determined to make subject to ourselves. In Art and Philosophy man becomes conscious of himself, in contrast to nature, as an intellectual being ; in marriage and law he becomes conscious of himself as a social being, in Christ as a moral being. He throws down the gauntlet for a fight in which there is no place for humility ; whoever will follow Christ requires above all courage, courage in its purest form, that inner courage, which is steeled and hardened anew every day, which proves itself not merely in the intoxicating clash of battle, but in bearing and enduring, and in the silent, soundless struggle of every hour in the individual breast. The example is given. For in the advent of Christ we find the grandest example of heroism. Moral heroism is in Him so sublime that the much-extolled physical courage of heroes seems as nothing ; certain it is that only heroic souls—only " masters "—can in the true sense of the word be Christians. And when Christ says, " I am meek," we well understand that this is the meekness of the hero sure of victory ; and when He says, " I am lowly of heart," we know that this is not the humility of the slave, but the humility of the master, who from the fulness of his power bows down to the weak.

On one occasion when Jesus was addressed not simply as Lord or Master, but as " good master," He rejected the appellation : " Why callest thou Me good : there is none good." This should make us think, and should convince us that it is a mistaken view of Christ which forces His heavenly goodness, His humility and longsuffering, into the foreground of His character ; they do not form its basis, but are like fragrant flowers on a strong stem. What was the basis of the world-power of

Buddha ? Not his doctrine, but his example, his heroic achievement; it was the revelation of an almost supernatural will-power which held and still holds millions in its spell. But in Christ a still higher will revealed itself; He did not need to flee from the world; He did not avoid the beautiful, He praised the use of the costly—which His disciples called "prodigality"; He did not retire to the wilderness, from the wilderness He came and entered into life, a victor, who had a message of good news to proclaim—not death, but redemption! I said that Buddha represented the senile decay of a culture which had strayed into wrong paths: Christ, on the other hand, represents the morning of a new day; He won from the old human nature a new youth, and thus became the God of the young, vigorous Indo-Europeans, and under the sign of His cross there slowly arose upon the ruins of the old world a new culture—a culture at which we have still to toil long and laboriously until some day in the distant future it may deserve the appellation " Christ-like."

THE GALILEANS

Were I to follow my own inclination, I should close this chapter here. But it is necessary in the interest of many points to be discussed later to consider the personality of Christ not only in its pure isolated individuality but also in its relation to its surroundings. Otherwise there are many important phenomena in the past and the present which remain incomprehensible. It is by no means a matter of indifference whether by close analysis we have formed exact ideas as to what in this figure is Jewish and what is not. On this point there has been from the beginning of the Christian era to the present day and from the lowest depths of the intellectual world to its greatest heights, enormous confusion. Not merely was so sublime a figure not easy for any one to comprehend and to contemplate in its organic relations to the contemporary world, but everything concurred to dim and falsify its true features : Jewish religious idiosyncrasy, Syrian mysticism, Egyptian asceticism, Hellenic metaphysics, soon too Roman traditions of State and Pontifex, as also the superstitions of the barbarians ; every form of misunderstanding and stupidity had a share in the work.   In the nineteenth century many have devoted themselves to the unravelling of this tangle, but, so far as I know, no one has succeeded in separating from the mass of facts the few essential points and putting them clearly before the eyes of all.   In fact even honest learning does not protect us against prejudice and partiality.   We shall here try, unfortunately indeed without the specialist's knowledge, but also without prejudice, to find out how far Christ belonged to His surroundings and employed their forms for viewing things, how far He differed from them and rose high as the heavens above them ; only in this way can we free His personality from all accidental circumstances and show its full autonomous dignity.

Let us therefore first ask ourselves, was Christ a Jew by race ?

The question seems at the first glance somewhat childish.   In the presence of such a personality peculiarities of race shrink into nothingness.   An Isaiah, however much he may tower above his contemporaries, remains a thorough Jew ; not a word did he utter that did not spring from the history and spirit of his people ; even where he mercilessly exposes and condemns what is characteristically Jewish, he proves himself—especially in this—the Jew ; in the case of Christ there is not a trace of this. Take again Homer ! He awakens the Hellenic people for the first time to consciousness of itself ; to be able to do that, he had to harbour in his own bosom the quintessence of all Hellenism. But where is the people, which, awakened by Christ to life, has gained for itself the precious right—of calling Christ its own? Certainly not in Judea!—To the believer Jesus is the Son of God, not of a human being; for the unbeliever it will be difficult to find a formula to characterise so briefly and yet so expressively the undeniable fact of this incomparable and inexplicable personality. After all there are phenomena which cannot be placed in the complex of our intellectual conceptions without a symbol. So much in regard to the question of principle, and in order to remove from myself all suspicion of being taken in tow by that superficial " historical " school, which undertakes to explain the inexplicable. It is another matter to seek to gain all possible information regarding the historical surroundings of a personality for the simple purpose of obtaining a clearer and better view of it. If we do attempt this, the answer to the question, Was Christ a Jew? is by no means a simple one. In religion and education He was so undoubtedly; in race—in the narrower and real sense of the word " Jew " —most probably not.

The name Galilee (from *Gelil haggoyim*) means " district of the heathen." It seems that this part of the country, so far removed from the intellectual centre, had never kept itself altogether pure, even in the earliest times when Israel was still strong and united, and it had served as home for the tribes Naphtali and Zebulon. Of the tribe Naphtali we are told that it was from the first " of very mixed origin," and while the non-Israelitic aborigines continued to dwell in the whole of Palestine as before, this was the case " nowhere in so great a degree as in the northern districts."* There was, however,

---

* Wellhausen: *Israelitische und jüdische Geschichte*, 3rd ed., 1897, pp. 16 and 74. *Cf.* too, *Judges*, i. 30 and 33, and further on in this book, chap. v.

another additional circumstance. While the rest of
Palestine remained, owing to its geographical position,
isolated as it were from the world, there was, even at
the time when the Israelites took possession of the land,
a road leading from the lake of Gennesareth to Damascus,
and from that point Tyre and Sidon were more accessible than Jerusalem. Thus we find that Solomon ceded
a considerable part of this district of the heathen
(as it was already called, 1 *Kings*, ix. 11), with twenty
cities to the King of Tyre in payment of his deliveries
of cedar- and pine-trees, as well as for the one hundred
and twenty hundredweights of gold which the latter
had contributed towards the building of the temple ; so
little interest had the King of Judea in this land, half
inhabited as it was by heathens. The Tyrian King Hiram
must in fact have found it sparsely populated, as he
profited by the opportunity to settle various foreign tribes
in Galilee.* Then came, as every one knows, the division
into two kingdoms, and since that time, that is, since
about a thousand years before Christ (!) only now and
again, and then but for a short time, had there been any
comparatively close political connection between Galilee
and Judea, and it is only this, not community of religious
faith, that furthers a fusion of races. In Christ's time,
too, Galilee was politically quite separate from Judea, so
that it stood to the latter in the relation " of a foreign
country "† In the meantime, however, something had
happened, which must have destroyed almost completely

---

* Graetz : *Volkstümliche Geschichte der Juden*, i. 88.

† *Ibid.* i. 567. Galilee and Perea had together a tetrarch who ruled
independently, while Judea, Samaria and Idumea were under a Roman
procurator. Graetz adds at this point, " Owing to the enmity of
the Samaritans whose land lay like a wedge between Judea and
Galilee and round [*sic*] both, there was all the less intercourse between
the two separated districts." I have here for simplicity refrained
from mentioning the further fact that we have no right to identify
the genuine " Israelites " of the North with the real " Jews " of the
South ; but *cf.* chap. v.

for all time the Israelitish character of this northern district : seven hundred and twenty years before Christ (that is about one hundred and fifty years before the Babylonian captivity of the Jews) the northern kingdom of Israel was laid waste by the Assyrians, and its population—it is said to a man, at all events to a large extent—deported into different and distant parts of the Empire, where it soon fused with the rest of the inhabitants and in consequence completely disappeared.* At the same time strange races from remote districts were transported to Palestine to settle there. The authorities indeed suppose (without being able to vouch for it) that a considerable portion of the former mixed Israelitish population had remained in the land ; at any rate this remnant did not keep apart from the strangers, but became merged in the medley of races.† The fate of these districts was consequently quite different from that of Judea. For when the Judeans at a later time were also led into captivity, their land remained so to speak empty, inhabited only by a few peasants who moreover belonged to the country, so that when they returned from the Babylonian captivity, during which they had kept their race pure, they were able without difficulty to maintain that purity. Galilee, on the other hand, and

---

* So completely disappeared that many theologians, who had leisure, puzzled their brains even in the nineteenth century to discover what had become of the Israelites, as they could not believe that five-sixths of the people to whom Jehovah had promised the whole world should have simply vanished off the face of the earth. An ingenious brain actually arrived at the conclusion that the ten tribes believed to be lost were the English of to-day·! He was not at a loss for the moral of this discovery either : in this way the British possess by right five-sixths of the whole earth ; the remaining sixth the Jews. *Cf.* H. L. : *Lost Israel, where are they to be found ?* (Edinburgh, 6th ed., 1877). In this pamphlet another work is named, Wilson, *Our Israelitish Origin.* There are, according to these authorities, honest Anglo-Saxons who have traced their genealogy back to Moses !

† Robertson Smith : *The Prophets of Israel* (1895), p. 153, informs us to what an extent " the distinguishing character of the Israelitish nation was lost."

the neighbouring districts had, as already mentioned, been systematically colonised by the Assyrians, and, as it appears from the Biblical account, from very different parts of that gigantic empire, among others from the northerly mountainous Syria. Then in the centuries before the birth of Christ many Phœnicians and Greeks had also migrated thither.* This last fact would lead one to assume that purely Aryan blood also was transplanted thither ; at any rate it is certain that a promiscuous mixture of the most different races took place, and that the foreigners in all probability settled in largest numbers in the more accessible and at the same time more fertile Galilee. The Old Testament itself tells with artless simplicity how these strangers originally came to be acquainted with the worship of Jehovah (2 *Kings*, xvii. 24 ff.) : in the depopulated land beasts of prey multiplied ; this plague was held to be the vengeance of the neglected " God of the Land " (verse 26) ; but there was no one who knew how the latter should be worshipped ; and so the colonists sent to the King of Assyria and begged for an Israelitish priest from the captivity, and he came and " taught them the manner of the God of the land." In this way the inhabitants of Northern Palestine, from Samaria downward, became Jews in faith, even those of them who had not a drop of Israelitish blood in their veins. In later times many genuine Jews may certainly have settled there ; but probably only as strangers in the larger cities, for one of the most admirable characteristics of the Jews—particularly since their return from captivity where the clearly circumscribed term " Jew " first appears as the designation of a religion (see *Zechariah*, viii. 23)—was their care to keep the race pure ; marriage between Jew and Galilean was unthinkable. However,

---

* Albert Réville : *Jésus de Nazareth*, i. 416. One should remember also that Alexander the Great had peopled neighbouring Samaria with Macedonians after the revolt of the year 311.

even these Jewish elements in the midst of the strange population were completely removed from Galilee not very long before the birth of Christ! It was Simon Tharsi, one of the Maccabeans, who, after a successful campaign in Galilee against the Syrians, "gathered together the Jews who lived there and bade them emigrate and settle bag and baggage in Judea."* Moreover the prejudice against Galilee remained so strong among the Jews that, when Herod Antipas during Christ's youth had built the city of Tiberias and tried to get Jews to settle there, neither promises nor threats were of any avail.† There is, accordingly, as we see, not the slightest foundation for the supposition that Christ's parents were of Jewish descent.

In the further course of historical development an event took place which has many parallels in history: among the inhabitants of the more southerly Samaria (which directly bordered on Judea)—a people which beyond doubt was much more closely related to the real Jews by blood and intercourse than the Galileans were—the North-Israelitish tradition of hatred and jealousy of the Jews was kept up; the Samaritans did not recognise the ecclesiastical supremacy of Jerusalem and were therefore, as being "heterodox," so hated by the Jews that no kind of intercourse with them was permitted: not even a piece of bread could the faithful take from their hand; that was considered as great a sin as eating pork.‡ The Galileans, on the other hand, who were to the Jews simply "foreigners," and as such of course despised and excluded from many religious observances, were yet strictly orthodox and frequently fanatical

---

* Graetz, as above, i. 400. *See also* 1 *Maccabees*, v. 23.

† Graetz, as above, i. 568. Compare *Josephus*, Book XVIII., ;hap. iii.

‡ Quoted by Renan from the Mishna: s. *Vie de Jésus*, 23rd edition, p. 242.

" Jews." To see in that a proof of descent is absurd. It is just the same as if one were to identify the genuinely Slav population of Bosnia or the purest Indo-Aryans of Afghanistan ethnologically with the " Turks," because they are strict Mohammedans, much more pious and fanatical than the genuine Osmans. The term Jew is applicable to a definite, remarkably pure race, and only in a secondary and very inexact sense to the members of a religious community. It is moreover far from correct to identify the term " Jew " with the term " Semite," as has so frequently been done of late years ; the national character of the Arabs, for instance, is quite different from that of the Jews. I return to this point in the fifth chapter ; in the meantime, I must point out that the national character of the Galileans was essentially different from that of the Jews. Open any history of the Jews that you will, that of Ewald or Graetz or Renan, everywhere you will find that in character the Galileans present a direct contrast to the rest of the inhabitants of Palestine ; they are described as hot-heads, energetic idealists, men of action. In the long struggles with Rome, before and after the time of Christ, the Galileans are mostly the ringleaders—an element which death alone could overcome. While the great colonies of genuine Jews in Rome and Alexandria lived on excellent terms with the heathen Empire, where they enjoyed great prosperity as interpreters of dreams,* dealers in second-hand goods, pedlars, money-lenders, actors, law-agents, merchants, teachers, &c., in distant Galilee Hezekiah ventured, even in the lifetime of Cæsar, to raise the standard of religious revolt. He was followed by the famous Judas the Galilean with the motto, " God alone is master, death does not matter, freedom is all

* Juvenal says :

Aere minuto
Qualiacunque voles Judæi somnia vendunt ı ı ı

in all ! " * In Galilee was formed the Sicarian party
(*i.e.*, men of the knife), not unlike the Indian Thugs
of to-day ; their most influential leader, the Galilean
Menaham, in Nero's time destroyed the Roman garri-
son of Jerusalem, and as a reward the Jews themselves
executed him, under the pretext that he wished to proclaim himself the Messias ; the sons of Judas also were
crucified as politically dangerous revolutionaries (and
that too by a Jewish procurator) ; John of Giscala,
a city on the extreme northern boundary of Galilee,
headed the desperate defence of Jerusalem against Titus
—and the series of Galilean heroes was completed by
Eleazar, who years after the destruction of Jerusalem
maintained with a small troop a fortified position in the
mountains, where he and his followers, when the last hope
was lost, killed first their wives and children and then
themselves.† In these things, as every one will probably
admit, a peculiar, distinct national character reveals
itself. There are many reports too of the special beauty
of the women of Galilee ; moreover, the Christians
of the first centuries speak of their great kindness, and
contrast their friendliness to those of a different faith
with the haughty contemptuous treatment they met with
at the hands of genuine Jewesses. Their peculiar national
character unmistakably betrayed itself in another way,
viz., their language. In Judea and the neighbouring
lands Aramaic was spoken at the time of Christ ; Hebrew
was already a dead language, preserved only in the sacred
writings. We are now informed that the Galileans
spoke so peculiar and strange a dialect of Aramaic that
one recognised them from the first word ; " thy language
betrayeth thee " the servants of the High Priest cry to

* Mommsen, *Römische Geschichte*, v. 515.
† Later, too, the inhabitants of Galilee were a peculiar race distinguished for strength and courage, as is proved by their taking part
in the campaign under the Persian Scharbarza and in the taking of
Jerusalem in the year 614.

Peter.* The acquisition of Hebrew is said to have been utterly impossible to them, the gutturals especially presenting insuperable difficulties, so that they could not be allowed, for example, to pray before the people, as their " wretched accent made every one laugh."† This fact points to a physical difference in the form of the larynx and would alone lead us to suppose that a strong admixture of non-Semitic blood had taken place ; for the profusion of gutturals and facility in using them are features common to all Semites.‡

I have thought it necessary to enter with some fulness into this question—was Christ a Jew in race ?—because in not a single work have I found the facts that pertain to it clearly put together. Even in an objectively scientific work like that of Albert Réville,§ which is influenced by no theological motives—Réville is the well-known Professor of Comparative Religions at the Collège de France—the word Jew is sometimes used to signify the Jewish race, sometimes the Jewish religion.

* As a matter of fact sufficient evidence of the difference between the Galileans and the real Jews could be gathered from the gospels. In *John* especially " the Jews " are always spoken of as something alien, and the Jews on their part exclaim, " Out of Galilee ariseth no prophet" (7, 52).

† *Cf.*, for example, Graetz, as above, i. 975. With regard to the peculiarity of the speech of the Galileans and their incapacity to pronounce the Semitic gutturals properly, *see* Renan : *Langues sémitiques*, 5th ed., p. 230.

‡ *See*, for example, the comparative table in Max Müller : *Science of Language*, 9th ed., p. 169, and in each separate volume of the *Sacred Books of the East*. The Sanscrit language has only six genuine " gutturals," the Hebrew ten ; most striking, however, is the difference in the guttural aspirate h, for which the Indo-Teutonic languages from time immemorial have known only one sound, the Semitic, on the other hand, five different sounds. Again, we find in Sanscrit seven different lingual consonants, in Hebrew only two. How exceedingly difficult it is for such inherited linguistic marks of race to disappear altogether is well known to us all through the example of the Jews living among us ; a perfect mastery of the lingual sounds is just as impossible for them as the mastery of the gutturals for us.

§ *Jésus de Nazareth, études critiques sur les antécédents de l'histoire évangélique et la vie de Jésus*, vol. ii. 1897.

We read, for example (i. 416), " Galilee was chiefly inhabited by Jews, but Syrian, Phœnician and Greek heathens also made their home there." Here accordingly Jew means one who worships the God of the land of Judea, no matter of what race he may claim to be. On the very next page, however, he speaks of an " Aryan race," in opposition to a " Jewish nation " ; here consequently Jew denotes a definite, limited race which has kept itself pure for centuries. And now follows the profound remark : " The question whether Christ is of Aryan descent is idle. A man belongs to the nation in whose midst he has grown up." This is what people called " science " in the year of grace 1896 ! To think that at the close of the nineteenth century a professor could still be ignorant that the form of the head and the structure of the brain exercise quite decisive influence upon the form and structure of the thoughts, so that the influence of the surroundings, however great it may be estimated to be, is yet by this initial fact of the physical tendencies confined to definite capacities and possibilities, in other words, has definite paths marked out for it to follow ! To think that he could fail to know that the shape of the skull in particular is one of those characteristics which are inherited with ineradicable persistency, so that races are distinguished by craniological measurements, and, in the case of mixed races, the original elements which occur by atavism become still manifest to the investigator ! He could believe that the so-called soul has its abode outside the body, and leads the latter like a puppet by the nose. O Middle Ages ! when will your night leave us ? When will men understand that form is not an unimportant accident, a mere chance, but an expression of the innermost being ? that in this very point the two worlds, the inner and the outer, the visible and the invisible, touch ? I have spoken of the human personality as the *mysterium magnum* of existence ; now this inscrutable wonder shows itself in its visible form to the eye and the investigating understanding. And exactly as the possible forms of a building are determined and limited in essential points by the nature of the building material, so the possible form of a human being, his inner and his outer, are defined in decisively essential points by the inherited material of which this new personality is composed. It certainly may happen that too much importance is attached to the idea of race : we detract thereby from the autonomy of personality and run the risk of undervaluing the great power of ideas ; besides, this whole question of race is infinitely more complicated than the layman imagines ; it belongs wholly to the sphere of anthropological anatomy and cannot be solved by any dicta of the authorities on language and history. Yet it will not do simply to put race aside as a negligible quantity ; still less will it do to proclaim anything directly false about race and to let such an historical lie crystallise into an indisputable dogma. Whoever makes the assertion that Christ was a Jew is either ignorant or insincere : ignorant when he confuses religion and race, insincere when he knows the history of Galilee and partly conceals, partly distorts the very entangled facts in favour of his religious prejudices or, it may be, to curry favour with the Jews.* The probability that Christ was no Jew, that He had not a drop of genuinely Jewish

* How is one, for example, to explain the fact that Renan, who in his *Vie de Jésus*, published in 1863, says it is impossible even to make suppositions about the race to which Christ by blood belonged (*see* chap. ii.), in the fifth volume of his *Histoire du Peuple d'Israël*, finished in 1891, makes the categorical assertion, " Jésus était un Juif," and attacks with unwonted bitterness those who dare doubt the fact ? Is it to be supposed that the *Alliance Israélite*, with which Renan was so closely connected in the last years of his life, had not had something to do with this ? In the nineteenth century we have heard so much fine talk about the freedom of speech, the freedom of science, &c. ; in reality, however, we have been worse enslaved than in the eighteenth century ; for in addition to the tyrants who have really never been disarmed, new and worse ones have arisen. The former tyranny could, with all its bitter injustice, strengthen the character : the new, which is a tyranny proceeding from and aiming at money, degrades to the lowest depth of bondage.

blood in his veins, is so great that it is almost equivalent to a certainty.   To what race did He belong ?   This is a question that cannot be answered at all.   Since the land lay between Phœnicia and Syria, which in its south-western portion was strongly imbued with Semitic blood, and in addition had never been quite cleared of its former mixed-Israelitish (but at no time Jewish) population, the probability of a descent principally Semitic is very great. But whoever has even casually glanced at the race-babel of the Assyrian empire* and then learns that colonists from all parts of this empire settled in that former home of Israel, will be baffled by the question.   It is indeed possible that in some of these groups of colonists there prevailed a tradition of marrying among themselves, where-by a tribe would have kept itself pure ; that this, how-ever, should have been kept up more than five hundred years is almost unthinkable ; the very conversion to the Jewish faith had gradually obliterated those tribal differ-ences which at first had been maintained by religious customs brought from their old homes (2 *Kings*, xvii. 29).   We hear that in later times Greeks too migrated thither ; in any case they belonged to the poorest classes, and accepted immediately the " god of the country " ! Only one assertion can therefore be made on a sound historical basis : in that whole region there was only one single pure race, a race which by painfully scrupulous measures protected itself from all mingling with other nations—the Jewish ; that Jesus Christ did not belong to it can be regarded as certain.   Every further state-ment is hypothetical.

This result, though essentially negative, is of great value ; it means an important contribution to the right knowledge of the personality of Christ, and at the same time to the understanding of its effectiveness up to the present day as well as to the disentanglement of the

---

* *Cf.* Hugo Winckler: *Die Völker Vorderasiens,* 1900.

wildly confused clue of contradictory ideas and false conceptions, which has wound itself around the simple, transparent truth. It is time to go deeper. The outward connection is less important than the inner; now and now only do we come to the decisive question: how far does Christ as a moral fact belong to Judaism and how far does He not ? To fix this once for all, we shall have to make a series of important distinctions, for which I beg the fullest attention of the reader.

RELIGION

Christ is, quite generally—indeed, perhaps universally —represented as the perfecter of Judaism, that is to say, of the religious ideas of the Jews.* Even the orthodox Jews, though they cannot exactly honour Him as the perfecter, behold in Him an offshoot from their tree and proudly regard all Christianity as an appendix to Judaism. That, I am firmly convinced, is a mistake; it is an inherited delusion, one of those opinions that we drink in with our mother's milk and about which in consequence the free-thinker never comes to his senses any more than the strictly orthodox Churchman. Certainly Christ stood in direct relation to Judaism, and the influence of Judaism, in the first place upon the moulding of His personality and in a still higher degree upon the development and history of Christianity is so great, definite and essential, that every attempt to deny it must lead to nonsensical results; but this influence is only in the smallest degree a religious one. Therein lies the heart of the error.

We are accustomed to regard the Jewish people as the religious people above all others : as a matter of fact in

---

* The great legal authority Jhering is a praiseworthy exception. In his *Vorgeschichte der Indoeuropäer*, p. 300, he says: "The doctrine of Christ did not spring from his native soil, Christianity is rather an overcoming of Judaism; there is even in his origin something of the Aryan in Christ."

comparison with the Indo-European races it is quite stunted in its religious growth. In this respect what Darwin calls " arrest of development " has taken place in the case of the Jews, an arrest of the growth of the faculties, a dying in the bud. Moreover all the branches of the Semitic stem, though otherwise rich in talents, were extraordinarily poor in religious instinct; this is the " hardheartedness " of which the more important men among them constantly complain.* How different the Aryan! Even the oldest documents (which go back far beyond the Jewish) present him to us as earnestly following a vague impulse which forces him to investigate in his own heart. He is joyous, full of animal spirits, ambitious, thoughtless, he drinks and gambles, he hunts and robs; but suddenly he begins to think: the great riddle of existence holds him absolutely spellbound, not, however, as a purely rationalistic problem—whence is this world? whence came I? questions to which a purely logical and therefore unsatisfactory answer would require to be given—but as a direct compelling need of life. Not to understand, but to be, that is the point to which he is impelled. Not the past with its litany of cause and effect, but the present, the everlasting present holds his astonished mind spellbound. And he feels that it is only when he has bridged the gulf between himself and all that surrounds him, when he recognises himself—the one thing that he directly knows—in every phenomenon and finds again every phenomenon in himself, when he has, so to speak, put the world and himself in harmony, that he can hope to listen with his own ear to the weaving of the everlasting work and hear in his own heart the mysterious music of existence. And in order that he may find this harmony, he utters

---

* " The Semites have much superstition, but little religion," says Robertson Smith, one of the greatest authorities. (See *The Prophets of Israel*, p. 33.)

his own song, tries it in all tones, practises all melodies ;
then he listens with reverence.   And not unanswered
is his call : he hears mysterious voices ; all nature becomes alive, everything in her that is related to man begins
to stir.   He sinks in reverence upon his knees, does not
fancy that he is wise, does not believe that he knows the
origin and finality of the world, yet has faint forebodings
of a loftier vocation, discovers in himself the germ of
immeasurable destinies, " the seed of immortality."
This is, however, no mere dream, but a living conviction,
a faith, and like everything living, it in its turn begets life.
The heroes of his race and his holy men he sees as " super-
men " (as Goethe says) hovering high above the earth ;
he wills to be like them, for he too is impelled onward
and upward, and now he knows from what a deep inner
well they drew the strength to be great.——Now this
glance into the unfathomable depths of his own soul,
this longing to soar upwards, this is religion.   Religion
has primarily nothing to do either with superstition or
with morals ; it is a state of mind.   And because the
religious man is in direct contact with a world beyond
reason, he is thinker and poet : he appears consciously as
a creator ; he toils unremittingly at the noble Sisyphus
work of giving visible shape to the Invisible, of making
the Unthinkable capable of being thought ;* we never find
with him a hard and fast chronological cosmogony and
theogony, he has inherited too lively a feeling of the Infinite
for that ; his conceptions remain in flux and never grow
rigid ; old ones are replaced by new ; gods, honoured in
one century, are in another scarcely known by name.
Yet the great facts of knowledge, once firmly acquired, are

* Herder says well, " Man alone is in opposition to himself and the
earth ; for the most fully developed creature among all her organisations
is at the same time the least developed in his own new capacity. ↲ ↲ ↲
He represents therefore two worlds at once and this causes the apparent
duplicity of his being."—*Ideen zur Geschichte der Menschheit*, Teil I.,
Buch V., Abschnitt 6.

never again lost, and more than all that fundamental
truth which the Rigveda centuries and centuries before
Christ tried thus to express, " The root of existence,
the wise found in the heart "—a conviction which in the
nineteenth century has been almost identically expressed
by Goethe :

> *Ist nicht der Kern der Natur
> Menschen im Herzen ?

That is religion !—Now this very tendency, this state of
mind, this instinct, " to seek the core of nature
in the heart," the Jews lack to a startling degree.
They are born rationalists. Reason is strong in them,
the will enormously developed, their imaginative and
creative powers, on the other hand, peculiarly limited.
Their scanty mythically religious conceptions, indeed
even their commandments, customs and ordinances of
worship, they borrowed without exception from abroad,
they reduced everything to a minimum † which they
kept rigidly unaltered; the creative element, the real
inner life is almost totally wanting in them; at the best
it bears, in relation to the infinitely rich religious life
of the Aryans, which includes all the highest thought
and poetical invention of these peoples, like the lingual
sounds referred to above, a ratio of 2 to 7. Consider
what a luxuriant growth of magnificent religious conceptions and ideas, and in addition, what art and philosophy,
thanks to the Greeks and Teutonic races, sprang up
upon the soil of Christianity and then ask with what
images and thoughts the so-called religious nation of
the Jews has in the same space of time enriched mankind !
Spinoza's *Geometric Ethics* (a false, still-born adaptation
of a brilliant and pregnant thought of Descartes) seems
to me in reality the most cruel mockery of the Talmud

> * Is not the core of nature
> In the heart of man ?
> † For details, *see* chap. v.

morality and has in any case still less to do with religion than the Ten Commandments of Moses, which were probably derived from Egypt.* No, the power of Judaism which commands respect lies in quite another sphere ; I shall speak of it immediately.

But how then was it possible to let our judgment be so befogged as to consider the Jews a religious people ?

In the first place it was the Jews themselves, who from time immemorial assured us with the greatest vehemence and volubility, that they were " God's people " ; even a free-thinking Jew like the philosopher Philo makes the bold assertion that the Israelites alone were " men in the true sense " ; † the good stupid Indo-Teutonic peoples believed them. But how difficult it became for them to do so is proved by the course of history and the statements of all their most important men. This credulity was only rendered possible by the Christian interpreters of the Script making the whole history of Judah a Theodicy, in which the crucifixion of Christ forms the culminating point. Even Schiller (*Die Sendung Moses*) seems to think that Providence broke up the Jewish nation, as soon as it had accomplished the work given it to do ! Here the authorities overlooked the telling fact that Judaism paid not the slightest attention to the existence of Christ, that the oldest Jewish historians do not once mention His name ; and to this has now to be added the fact that this peculiar people after two thousand years still lives and manifests great prosperity ; never, not even in Alexandria, has the lot of the Jews been so bright as it is to-day. Finally a third prejudice, derived fundamentally from the philosophic workshops of Greece, had some influence ; according to it monotheism, *i.e.*, the idea of a single inseparable God, was supposed to be the symptom

---

* *See* chap. cxxv. of the *Book of the Dead.*
† Quoted by Graetz, as above, i. 634, without indication of the passage.

of a higher religion; that is altogether a rationalistic conclusion; arithmetic has nothing to do with religion; monotheism can signify an impoverishment as well as an ennobling of religious life. Besides, two objections may be urged against this fatal prejudice, which has contributed perhaps more than anything else to the delusion of a religious superiority of the Jews; in the first place, the fact that the Jews, as long as they formed a nation and their religion still possessed a spark of fresh life, were not monotheists but polytheists, for whom every little land and every little tribe had its own God; secondly, that the Indo-Europeans by purely religious ways had attained to conceptions of an individual Divinity that were infinitely more sublime than the painfully stunted idea which the Jews had formed of the Creator of the world.*

* I do not require to adduce evidence of the polytheism of the Jews; one finds it in every scientific work and besides on every other page of the Old Testament; see chap. v. Even in the *Psalms* " all the Gods" are called upon to worship Jehovah; Jehovah is only in so far the " one God" for later Jews, as the Jews (as Philo just told us) are " the only men in the real sense." Robertson Smith, whose *History of the Semites* is regarded as a scientific and fundamental book, testifies that monotheism did not proceed from an original religious tendency of the Semitic spirit, but is essentially a political result ! ! (*See* p. 74 of the work quoted.)—With regard to the monotheism of the Indo-Europeans I make the following brief remarks. The Brahman of the Indian philosophers is beyond doubt the greatest religious thought ever conceived; with regard to the pure monotheism of the Persians we can obtain information in Darmesteter (*The Zend-Avesta*, I. lxxxii. ff.); the Greek had however been on the same path, as Ernst Curtius testifies, "I have learned much that is new, particularly what a stronghold of the monotheistic view of God Olympia was and what a moral world-power the Zeus of Phidias has been" (Letter to Gelzer of Jan. 1, 1896, published in the *Deutsche Revue*, 1897, p. 241). Besides we can refer here to the best of all witnesses. The Apostle Paul says (*Romans*, i. 21): "The Romans knew that there is one God"; and the church-father Augustine shows, in the eleventh chapter of the 4th book of his *De civitate Dei*, that according to the views of the educated Romans of his time, the *magni doctores paganorum*, Jupiter was the one and only God, while the other divinities only demonstrated some of his "virtutes." Augustine employed the view which was already prevalent, to make it clear to the heathens that it would be no trouble for them to adopt the belief in a single God and to give up the others. *Hæc si ita sint, quid perderent si unum Deum colerent prudentiore compendio ?* (the

I shall have repeated occasion to return to these questions, particularly in the sections dealing with the entry of the Jews into western history and with the origin of the Christian Church. In the meantime I hope I have succeeded in removing to some extent the preconceived opinion of the special religiousness of Judaism. I think the reader of the orthodox Christian Neander will henceforth shake his head sceptically when he finds the assertion that the advent of Christ forms the " central point " of the religious life of the Jews, that

recommendation to believe in a single God " because it simplifies matters " is a touching feature of the golden childhood of the Christian Church !). And what Augustine demonstrates in the case of the educated heathen, Tertullian asserts of the uneducated people in general. " Everybody," he says, " believes only in a single God, and one never hears the Gods invoked in the plural, but only as ' Great God ' ! ' Good God ' ! ' As God will ' ! ' God be with you ' ! ' God bless you ' ! " This Tertullian regards as the evidence of a fundamentally monotheistic soul : " O testimonium animæ naturaliter Christianæ ! " (Apologeticus, xvii]. [Giordano Bruno in his Spaccio de la bestia trionfante, ed. Lagarde, p. 532, has some beautiful remarks on the monotheism of the ancients.]—In order that in a matter of such significance nothing may remain obscure, I must add that Curtius, Paul, Augustine and Tertullian are all four labouring under a thorough delusion, when they see in these things a proof of monotheism in the sense of Semitic materialism ; their judgment is here dimmed by the influence of Christian ideas. The conception " the Divine " which we see in the Sanscrit neuter Brahman and in the Greek neuter θεῖον, as well as in the German neuter Gott, which only at a later time in consequence of Christian influence was regarded as a masculine (see Kluge's Etymologisches Wörterbuch), cannot be identified at all with the personal world-creator of the Jews. In this case one can say of all the Aryans who are not influenced by the Semitic spirit what Professor Erwin Rohde proves for the Hellenes : " The view that the Greeks had a tendency to monotheism (in the Jewish sense) is based on a wrong interpretation. . . . It is not a unity of the divine person, but a uniformity of divine entity, a divinity living uniformly in many Gods, something universally divine in the presence of which the Greek stands when he enters into religious contact with the Gods " (Die Religion der Griechen in the Bayreuther Blätter, 1895, p. 213]. Very characteristic are the words of Luther in this connection, " In creation and in works (to reckon from without to the creature] we Christians are at one with the Turks ; for we say too that there is not more than one single God. But we say, this is not enough, that we only believe that there is one single God."

" in the whole organism of this religion and people's history it was of inner necessity determined," &c. &c.*
As for the oratorical flourishes of the free-thinker Renan : *Le Christianisme est le chef-d'œuvre` du judaïsme, sa gloire, le résumé de son évolution. . . . Jésus est tout entier dans Isaïe*, &c.,† he will smile over them with just a shade of indignation ; and I fear he will burst into Homeric laughter when the orthodox Jew Graetz assures him that the teaching of Christ is the " old Jewish doctrine in a new dress," that " the time had now come when the fundamental truths of Judaism . . . the wealth of lofty thoughts concerning God and a holy life for the individual and the community should flow in upon the emptiness of the rest of the world, filling it with a rich endowment."‡

* *Allgemeine Geschichte der christlichen Religion*, 4th ed. i. 46.

† *Histoire du Peuple d'Israël*, v. 415, ii. 539, &c. The enormity of the assertion in regard to Isaiah becomes clear from the fact that Renan himself describes and praises this prophet as a " littérateur " and a " journaliste," and that he proves in detail what a purely political *rôle* this important man played. " Not a line from his pen, which was not in the service of a question of the day or an interest of the moment " (ii. 481). And we are to believe that in this very man the whole personality of Jesus Christ is inherent ? It is quite as unjustifiable (unfortunately in others as well as in Renan) to quote single verses from *Isaiah*, to make it appear as if Judaism had aimed at a universal religion. Thus xlix. 6, is quoted, where Jehovah says to Israel, " I will also give thee for a light to the Gentiles, that thou mayest be my salvation unto the end of the earth," and nothing is said of the fact that in the course of the chapter the explanation is given that the Gentiles shall become the slaves of the Jews and their Kings and Princesses shall " bow down to them with their face toward the earth " and " lick up the dust of their feet." And this we are to regard as a sublime universal religion ! Exactly the same is the case with the constantly quoted chapter lx. where we find first the words, " The Gentiles shall come to thy light," but afterwards with an honesty for which one is thankful, " The nation and kingdom that will not serve thee shall perish, yea, those nations shall be utterly wasted " ! Moreover the Gentiles are told in this passage to bring all their gold and treasures to Jerusalem, for the Jews shall " inherit the land for ever." To think of any one venturing to put such political pamphleteering on a parallel with the teaching of Christ !

‡ As above, i. 570. It has often been asserted that the Jews have little sense of humour : that seems to be true, at least of individuals ;

CHRIST NOT A JEW

Whoever wishes to see the revelation of Christ must passionately tear this darkest of veils from his eyes. His advent is not the perfecting of the Jewish religion but its negation. It was in the very place where feelings played the least part in religious conceptions that a new religious ideal appeared, which—unlike the other great attempts further to explain the inner life, by thoughts or by images—laid the whole burthen of this " life in spirit and in truth " upon the feelings. The relation to the Jewish religion could at most be regarded as a reaction ; the feelings are, as we have said, the fountain head of all genuine religion ; this spring which the Jews had well-nigh choked with their formalism and hard-hearted rationalism Christ opened up. Few things let us see so deeply into the divine heart of Christ as His attitude towards the Jewish religious ordinances. He observed them, but without zeal and without laying any stress upon them ; at best they are but a vessel, which, holding nothing, would remain empty ; and as soon as an ordinance bars His road, He breaks it without the least scruple, but at the same time calmly and without anger : for what has all this to do with religion ?   " Man* is Lord

just imagine the " wealth" of these crassly ignorant unimaginative scribes and the " emptiness " of the Hellenes !   Graetz has not much regard for the personality of Christ ; the highest appreciation to which he deigns to rise is as follows : " Jesus may also have possessed a sympathetic nature that won hearts, whereby His words could make an impression " (i. 576). The learned Professor of Breslau regards the crucifixion as the result of a " misunderstanding." With regard to the Jews who afterwards went over to Christianity Graetz is of opinion that it was done for their material advantages and because the belief in the Crucified One " was taken into the bargain as something unessential " (ii. 30). Is that still true ?   We knew from the Old Testament that the covenant with Jehovah was a contract with obligations on both sides, but what can be " bargained " in regard to Christ I cannot understand.
    * The following information about the expression " son of man " is important : " The Messianic interpretation of the expression ' son

222 FOUNDATIONS OF THE XIXTH CENTURY

also of the Sabbath " : for the Jew Jehovah alone had been
Lord—man his slave. With regard to the Jewish laws in
relation to food (so important a point in their religion
that the quarrel with regard to its obligatoriness continued
on into the early Christian times) Christ says : " Not that
which goeth into the mouth defileth a man but that
which cometh out of the mouth, this defileth a man.
For those things which proceed out of the mouth come
forth from the heart : and they defile the man." * In
this connection consider too how Christ uses Holy
Scripture. He speaks of it with reverence but without
fanaticism. It is indeed very remarkable how He makes
Scripture serve His purpose; over it too He feels Himself
" Lord " and transforms it, when necessary, into its opposite. His doctrine is that the " whole law and the prophets " may be summed up in the one command : Love
God and thy neighbour. That sounds almost like sublime
irony, especially when we consider that Christ on this
occasion never once mentions " the fear of God," which
(and not the love of God) forms the basis of the whole
Jewish religion. " The fear of the Lord is the beginning of
wisdom," sings the Psalmist. " Hide thee in the dust
for fear of the Lord, and for the glory of His majesty,"
Isaiah calls to the Israelites, and even Jeremiah seemed
to have forgotten that there is a law according to which
man " shall love God with all his heart, with all his
soul, with all his strength, and with all his mind,"†

of man ' originated from the Greek translators of the Gospel. As
Jesus spoke Aramaic, He said not ὁ υἱὸς τοῦ ἀνθρώπου but barnascha.
But that means man and nothing more ; the Arameans had no other
expression for the idea " (Wellhausen : *Israelitische und jüdische
Geschichte*, 3rd ed. p. 381).

* " If man is impure, he is so because he speaks what is untrue,"
said the sacrificial ordinances of the Aryan Indians, one thousand years
before Christ (Satapatha-Brâhmana), 1st verse of the 1st division of
the 1st book.

† In the fifth book of Moses (*Deuteronomy* vi. 5) are to be found
words similar to these quoted from Christ's sayings (from *Matthew*
xxii. 37), but—we must look at the context ! Before the command-

and had represented Jehovah as saying to His people, " I will put my fear in their hearts that they shall not depart from me ; they shall fear me for ever " ; it is only when the Jews fear Him that He " will not turn away from them to do them good," &c. We find that Christ also frequently changes the meaning of the words of Scripture in a similar manner. Now if we see on the one hand a God of mercy and on the other a hard-hearted Jehovah,* on the one hand the doctrine which teaches us to love our " heavenly Father " with all our heart and on the other " servants," who are enjoined " to fear the lord " as their

ment to love (to our mind a peculiar conception—to love by command) stands as the first and most important commandment (verse 2), " Thou shalt fear the Lord, thy God, to keep all his statutes and his commandments" ; the commandment to love is only one among other commandments which the Jew shall observe and immediately after it comes the reward for this love (verse 10 ff.): " I shall give thee great and goodly cities, which thou buildedst not, and houses full of all good things which thou filledst not, and wells digged which thou diggedst not, vineyards and olive-trees, which thou plantedst not, &c." That kind of love may be compared to the love which underlies so many marriages at the present day ! In any case the " love of one's neighbour " would appear in a peculiar light, if one did not know that according to the Jewish law only the Jew is a " neighbour " of the Jew ; as is expressed in the same place, chap. vii. 16, " Thou shalt consume all the peoples which the Lord thy God shall deliver thee ! " This commentary to the commandment to " love one's neighbour " makes every further remark superfluous. But in order that no one may be in doubt as to what the Jews later meant by the command to love God with the whole heart, I shall quote the commentary of the *Talmud* (*Jomah*, Div. 8) to that part of the law, *Deuteronomy*, vi. 5 : " The teaching of this is : thy behaviour shall be such that the name of God shall be loved through you; man shall in fact occupy himself with the study of Holy Scripture and of the Mishna and have intercourse with learned and wise men ; his language shall be gentle, his other conduct proper, and in commerce and business with his fellow men he shall strive after honesty and uprightness. What will people then say ? Hail to this man who has devoted himself to the study of the sacred doctrine ! " In the book *Sota* of the Jerusalem Talmud (v. 5) one finds a somewhat more reasonable but no less prosaic commentary.—This is the orthodox Jewish interpretation of the commandment, " Thou shalt love the Lord with all thy heart " ! Is it not the most unworthy playing with words to assert that Christ taught the same doctrine as the *Thora* ?

* The orthodox Jew Montefiore, *Religion of the Ancient Hebrews* (1893), p. 442, admits that the thought, " God is love," does not occur in any purely Hebrew work of any time.

first duty,* we may well ask what meaning can there be in characterising the one personal philosophy as the work, as the perfection of the other? This is sophistry, not truth. Christ himself has said in plain words, "Whoever is not with me is against me"; no fact in the world is so completely against Him as the Jewish religion, indeed the whole Jewish conception of religion—from earliest times to the present day.

And yet the Jewish religion has in this connection formed a fine soil, better than any other, for the growth of a new religious ideal, that is, for a new conception of God.

What meant poverty for others became in fact for Christ a source of the richest gifts. For example, the fearful, to us almost inconceivable, dreariness of Jewish life—without art, without philosophy, without science —from which the more gifted Jews fled in crowds to foreign parts, was an absolutely indispensable element for his simple, holy life. The Jewish life offered almost nothing—nothing but the family life—to the feelings of the individual. And thus the richest mind that ever lived could sink into itself, and find nourishment only in its own inmost depths. "Blessed are the poor in spirit, for theirs is the Kingdom of Heaven." Perhaps it was only in these dreary surroundings that it was possible to discover that conversion of will as the first step towards a new ideal of mankind; only here where the "Lord of hosts" ruled without pity, that the heavenly presentiment God is love could be elevated to a certainty.

The following is, however, the most important point in this discussion.

The peculiar mental characteristic of the Jews, their

* Montefiore and others dispute the statement that the relation of Israel to Jehovah was that of servants to their master, but Scripture says so clearly in many places, *e.g.*, *Leviticus* xxv. 55: "The children of Israel are servants, they are my servants whom I brought forth out of the land of Egypt," and the literal translation of the Hebrew text would be slave! (*Cf.* the literal translation by Louis Segond.)

lack of imagination, brought about by the tyrannical predominance of the will, had led them to a strange abstract materialism. Being materialists, the Jews were most prone, like all Semites, to crass idolatry; we see them ever and anon setting up images and bowing down before them; the moral struggle which their great men for centuries waged against it is an heroic page in the history of the human power of will. But the will which was not balanced by imagination shot as usual far beyond the mark; every image, in fact frequently everything that is at all the " work of hands," contains for the Jew of the Old Testament the danger of becoming a worshipped idol Not even the coins may bear a human head or an allegorical figure, not even the flags an emblem. And so all non-Jews are to the Jews " worshippers of idols." And from this fact again arose, by the way, a Christian misconception which was not dissipated till the last years of the nineteenth century, and then only for the specialist, not for the mass of the educated. As a matter of fact, the Semites are probably the only people in the whole earth who ever were and could be genuine idolators. In no branch of the Indo-European family has there ever been idolatry. The unmixed Aryan Indians, as also the Eranians, had never either image or temple; they would have been incapable even of understanding the crassly materialistic sediment of Semitic idolatry in the Jewish ark of the covenant with its Egyptian sphinxes; neither the Teutons nor the Celts nor the Slavs worshipped images. And where did the Hellenic Zeus live ? Where Athene ? In poetry, in the imagination, up in cloud-capped Olympus, but never in this or that temple. In honour of the god Phidias created his immortal work, in honour of the gods the numerous little images were made which adorned every house and filled it with the living conception of higher beings. To the Jew, however, that seemed idolatry ! The will being with them predominant, they regarded each thing only from the point of view of its utility ; it was incomprehensible to them that a man should put anything beautiful before his eyes, to elevate and console himself therewith, to provide food for his mind, to awaken his religious sense. Similarly, too, the Christians have at a later time looked upon images of Buddha as idols : but the Buddhists recognise no God, much less an idol ; these statues served as a stimulus to contemplation and alienation from the world. Indeed ethnologers have lately been beginning to question the possibility of there ever being a people so primitive as to worship so-called fetishes as idols. Formerly this was simply taken for granted ; now it is being found in more and more cases that these children of nature attach the most complicated symbolical conceptions to their fetishes. It seems as if the Semites were the only human race that had succeeded in making golden calves, iron serpents, &c., and then worshipping them.* And as the Israelites even at that time were much more highly developed than the Australasian negroes of to-day, we conclude that such aberrations on their part must be put down not to immaturity of judgment, but to some one-sidedness of their intellect : this onesidedness was the enormous predominance of will. The will as such lacks not merely all imagination, but all reflection ; to it only one thing is natural, to precipitate itself upon, and to grasp the present. And so for no people was it so difficult as it was for the people of Israel, to rise to a high conception of the Divine, and for none was it so hard to keep this conception pure. But strength is steeled in the fray : the most unreligious people in the world created in its need the foundation of a new and most sublime conception

---

* It is scarcely necessary to call the reader's attention to the fact that the Egyptian and Syrian forms of worship from which the Jews took the idea of the ox and the serpent were purely symbolical.

of God, which has become the common property of all
civilised mankind. For on this foundation Christ built ;
He could do so, thanks to that "abstract materialism"
which He found around Him. Elsewhere religions were
choked by the richness of their mythologies ; here there
was no mythology at all. Elsewhere every god possessed
so distinct a physiognomy, had been made by poetry and
the plastic arts so thoroughly individual, that no one
could have changed him over night ; or, on the other
hand (as is the case with Brahman in India) the
conception of him had been gradually so sublimated
that nothing remained from which to create a new living
form. Neither of these two things had happened with
the Jews : Jehovah was in truth a remarkably concrete,
indeed an altogether historical conception, and in so
far a much more tangible figure than the imaginative
Aryan had ever possessed ; at the same time it was forbidden to represent Him either by image or word.* Hence
the religious genius of mankind found here a *tabula rasa*.
Christ required to destroy the historical Jehovah just
as little as the Jewish " law " ; neither the one nor the
other has an immediate relation to real religion ; but just
as He in point of fact by that inner " conversion " transformed the so-called law into a fundamentally new law, so
He used the concrete abstraction of the Jewish God
in order to give the world a quite new conception of God.
We speak of anthropomorphism ! Can then man act
and think otherwise than as an anthropos ? This new
conception of the Godhead differed, however, from other
sublime intuitions in this, that the image was created not
with the brilliant colours of symbolism nor with the etch-
ing-needle of thought, but was caught as it were on a mirror

---

* When at a very late period the Jews could not quite resist the
impulse to presentation, they sought to conceal the want of imaginative power by Oriental verbiage. We can see an example of it in
chap. i. of *Ezekiel*.

in the innermost mind, and became henceforth a direct individual experience to every one that had eyes to see.— Certain it is that this new ideal could not have been set up in any other place than where the conception of God had been fanatically clung to, and yet left totally undeveloped.

Hitherto we have directed our attention to what separates or at least distinguishes Christ from Judaism ; it would be one-sided to leave it at that alone. His fate and the main tendency of His thought are both closely connected with genuine Jewish life and character. He towers above His surroundings, but yet He belongs to them. Here we have to consider especially two fundamental features of the Jewish national character : the historical view of religion and the predominance of the will. These two features are, as we shall immediately see, genetically related. The former has strongly influenced Christ's life and His memory after death ; in the latter is rooted His doctrine of morals. A study of these two points will throw light on many of the deepest and most difficult questions in the history of Christianity, as well as on many of the inexplicable inner contradictions of our religious tendencies up to the present day.

HISTORICAL RELIGION

Of the many Semitic peoples one only, and that one politically one of the smallest and weakest, has maintained itself as a national unity ; this small nation has defied all storms and stands to-day a unique fact among men—without fatherland, without a supreme head, scattered all over the world, enrolled among the most different nationalities, and yet united and conscious of unity. This miracle is the work of a book, the *Thora*, with all that has been added to it by way of supplement up to the present day. But this book must be regarded as evidence of a peculiar national soul, which at a critical

moment was guided in this direction by individual eminent and far-seeing men.   In the next chapter but one I
shall have to enter more fully into the origin and importance of these canonical writings.   In the meantime, I shall
merely call attention to the fact that the Old Testament is
a purely historical work.   If we leave out of account a
few late and altogether unessential additions (like the so-
called *Proverbs of Solomon*), every sentence of these books
is historical ; the whole legislation too which they contain
is based on history, or has at least a chronological connection with the events described : " The Lord spake unto
Moses," Aaron's burnt-offering is accepted by the Lord,
Aaron's sons are killed during the proclamation of the
law, &c. &c. ; and if it is a question of inventing something, the narrator either links it on to a fictitious story,
as in the book of *Job,* or to a daring falsification of history,
as in the book of *Esther*.   By this predominance of the
chronological element the Bible differs from all other
known sacred books.   The religion it contains is an element in the historical narrative and not *vice versâ ;* its
moral commandments do not grow with inherent necessity out of the depths of the human heart, they are
" laws," which were promulgated under definite conditions
on fixed days, and which can be repealed at any time.
Compare for a moment the Aryan Indians ; they often
stumbled upon questions concerning the origin of the
world, the whence and the whither, but these were not
essential to the uplifting of their souls to God ; this
question concerning causes has nothing to do with their
religion : indeed, far from attaching importance to it, the
hymnists exclaim almost ironically :

> Who hath perceived from whence creation comes ?
> He who in Heaven's light upon it looks,
> He who has made or has not made it all,
> He knows it !   Or does he too know it not ? *

Goethe, who is often called the " great Heathen," but

* *Rigveda,* x. 129, 7.

who might with greater justice be termed the "great
Aryan," gave expression to exactly the same view when
he said, "Animated inquiry into cause does great harm."
Similarly the German natural scientist of to-day says
"In the Infinite no new end and no beginning can be
sought. However far back we set the origin, the question
still remains open as to the first of the first, the beginning
of the beginning." * The Jew felt quite differently.
He knew as accurately about the creation of the world as
do the wild Indians of South America or the Australian
blacks to-day. That, however, was not due—as is the
case with these—to want of enlightenment, but to the
fact that the Aryan shepherd's profound, melancholy
mark of interrogation was never allowed a place in
Jewish literature ; his tyrannous will forbade it, and it
was the same will that immediately silenced by fanatical
dogmatism the scepticism that could not fail to assert
itself among so gifted a people (*see* the *Koheleth*, or Book
of the Preacher). Whoever would completely possess
the "to-day" must also grasp the "yesterday"
out of which it grew. Materialism suffers shipwreck
as soon as it is not consistent ; the Jew was taught
that by his unerring instinct ; and just as accurately
as our materialists know to day how thinking arises out
of the motion of atoms, did he know how God had created
the world and made man from a clod of earth. Creation,
however, is the least thing of all ; the Jew took the myths
with which he became acquainted on his journeys,
stripped them as far as possible of everything mythological and pruned them down to concrete historical
events.† But then, and not till then, came his master-
piece : from the scanty material common to all Semites ‡

* Adolf Bastian, the eminent ethnologist, in his work : *Das Beständ-
ige in den Menschenrassen* (1868), p. 28.
† "*Les mythologies étrangères se transforment entre les mains des
Sémites en récits platement historiques*" (Renan, *Israël*, i. 49).
‡ *Cf.* the history of creation by the Phœnician Sanchuniathon.

the Jew constructed a whole history of the world of which
he made himself the centre ; and from this moment,
that is, the moment when Jehovah makes the covenant
with Abraham, the fate of Israel forms the history of the
world, indeed, the history of the whole cosmos, the one
thing about which the Creator of the world troubles
himself. It is as if the circles always became narrower ;
at last only the central point remains—the " Ego," the
will has prevailed. That indeed was not the work of
a day ; it came about gradually ; genuine Judaism,
that is, the Old Testament in its present form, shaped
and established itself only after the return of the Jews
from the Babyloniah captivity.* And now what formerly
had been effected with unconscious genius was applied
and perfected consciously : the union of the past and the
future with the present in such a way that each individual
moment formed a centre on the perfectly straight path,
which the Jewish people had to follow and from which it
henceforth could not deviate either to right or to left.
In the past divine miracles in favour of the Jews and in
the future expectation of the Messiah and world-empire :
these were the two mutually complementary elements of
this view of history. The passing moment received a
peculiarly living importance from the fact that it was seen
growing out of the past, as reward or punishment, and
that it was believed to have been exactly foretold in
prophecies. By this the future itself acquired unexampled reality : it seemed to be something tangible.
Even should countless promises and prophecies not
come true,† that could always be easily explained. Will
looks not too close, but what it holds it does not let go,

* *See* chap. v. In order to give a fixed point and to reveal drastically
the differences of mental tendencies, I may mention that this was
about three hundred years after Homer, scarcely a century before
Herodotus.

† For example, the promise to Abraham in reference to Canaan,
" To thee will I give it, and to thy seed for ever."

even if it be but a phantom ; the less the past had given the richer appeared the future ; and so much was possessed in black and white (particularly in the legend of the *Exodus*), that doubt could not arise. The so-called Jewish " literal adherence to creed " is surely quite a different thing from the dogmatic faith of the Christians : it is not a faith in abstract inconceivable mysteries and in all kinds of mythological conceptions, but something quite concrete and historical. The relation of the Jews to their God is from the first political.* Jehovah promises them the empire of the world—under certain conditions ; and their historical work is such a marvel of ingenious structure that the Jews see their past in the most glowing colours, and everywhere perceive the protecting hand of God extended over His chosen people, " over the only men in the true sense of the word " ; and this in spite of the fact that theirs has been the most wretched and pitiful fate as a people that the annals of the world can show; for only once under David and Solomon did they enjoy half a century of relative prosperity and settled conditions : thus they possess on all hands proofs of the truth of their faith, and from this they draw the assurance that what was promised to Abraham many centuries before will one day take place in all its fulness. But the divine promise was, as I have said, dependent upon conditions. Men could not move about in the house, could not eat and drink or walk in the fields, without thinking of hundreds of commandments, upon the ful- filment of which the fate of the nation depended. As the Psalmist sings of the Jew (*Psalm* i. 2) :

> He placeth his delight
> Upon God's law, and meditates
> On his law day and night.†

* *See* Rob. Smith : *The Prophets of Israel*, pp. 70 and 133.
† In the *Sippurim*, a collection of Jewish popular sagas and stories, it is frequently mentioned that the ordinary uneducated Jew has 613 commandments to learn by heart. But the *Talmud* teaches 13,600

Every few years each of us throws a voting-paper into the box ; otherwise we do not know or hardly know that our life is of national importance ; but the Jew could never forget that. His God had promised him, " No people shall withstand thee, till thou destroyest it," but immediately added, " All the commandments which I command thee, thou shalt keep ! " God was thus always present to consciousness. Practically everything but material possession was forbidden to the Jew ; his mind therefore was directed to property alone ; and it was to God that he had to look for the possession of that property.—The man who has never brought home to himself the conditions here hastily sketched will have difficulty in realising what unanticipated vividness the conception of God acquired under these conditions. The Jew could not indeed represent Jehovah by images ; but His working, His daily intervention in the destiny of the world was, so to speak, a matter of experience ; the whole nation indeed lived upon it ; to meditate upon it was their one intellectual occupation (if not in the Diaspora, at least in Palestine).

It was in these surroundings that Christ grew up ; beyond them He never stepped. Thanks to this peculiar historical sense of the Jews He awoke to consciousness as far as possible from the all-embracing Aryan cult of nature and its confession *tat-tvam-asi* (that thou art also), in the focus of real anthropomorphism, where all creation was but for man, and all men but for this one chosen people, that is, He awoke in the direct presence of God and Divine Providence. He found here what He would have found nowhere else in the world : a complete scaffolding ready for Him, within which His entirely new conception of God and of religion could be built up. After Jesus had lived, nothing remained of the genuinely Jewish

laws, obedience to which is divine command! (*See* Dr. Emanuel Schreiber : *Der Talmud vom Standpunkte des modernen Judentums.*

idea; now that the temple was built the scaffolding
could be removed. But it had served its purpose,
and the building would have been unthinkable without
it. The God to whom we pray to give us our daily bread
could only be thought of where a God had promised to
man the things of this world; men could only pray for
forgiveness of sins to Him who had issued definite commandments.—I almost fear, however, that if I here
enter into details I may be misunderstood; it is enough
if I have succeeded in giving a general conception of the
very peculiar atmosphere of Judea, for that will enable us
to discern that this most ideal religion would not possess
the same life-power if it had not been built upon the
most real, the most materialistic—yes, assuredly the
most materialistic—religion in the world. It is this
and not its supposed higher religiosity that has made
Judaism a religious power of world-wide importance.

The matter becomes still clearer whenever we consider
the influence of this historical faith upon the fate of
Christ.

The most powerful personality can be influential only
when it is understood. This understanding may be very
incomplete, it may indeed frequently be direct misunderstanding, but some community of feeling and
thought must form the link of connection between the
lonely genius and the masses. The thousands that
listened to the Sermon on the Mount certainly did not
understand Christ; how could that have been possible?
They were a poor people, downtrodden and oppressed
by continual war and discord, systematically stupefied
by their priests; but the power of his word awakened
in the heart of the more gifted among them an echo
which it would have been impossible to awaken in any
other part of the world: was this to be the Messiah,
the promised redeemer from their misery and wretchedness?
What immeasurable power lay in the possibility of such

a conception! At once the homely, fleeting present was linked to the remotest past and the most indubitable future, and thereby the present received everlasting importance. It does not matter that the Messiah, whom the Jews expected, had not the character which we Indo-Europeans attach to this conception*; the idea

---

* Even so orthodox an investigator as Stanton admits that the Jewish idea of the Messiah was altogether political (see *The Jewish and the Christian Messiah*, 1886, pp. 122 f., 128, &c.). It is well known that theology has occupied itself much of late years with the history of the conceptions of the Messiah. The principal result of the investigation for us laymen is the proof that the Christians, misled by what were specifically Galilean and Samarian heterodoxies, supplanted the Jewish conception of the coming of the Messiah by a view which the Jews never really held. The Jews who were learned in Scripture were always indignant at the strained interpretations of the Old Prophets; now even the Christians admit that the Prophets before the exile (and these are the greatest) knew nothing of the expectation of a Messiah (*see*, for example, the latest summary account, that of Paul Volz: *Die vorexilische Jahveprophetie und der Messias*, 1897); the Old Testament does not even know the word, and one of the most important theologists of our time, Paul de Lagarde (*Deutsche Schriften*, p. 53), calls attention to the fact that the expression *mâschîach* is not of Hebrew origin at all, but was borrowed at a late time from Assyria or Babylon. It is particularly noteworthy also that this expectation of the Messiah wherever it existed was constantly taking different forms; in one case a second King David was to come, in another the idea was one only of Jewish world-empire in general, then again it is God himself with his heavenly judgment " who will put an end at once to those who have hitherto held sway and give the people of Israel power for ever, an all-embracing empire, in which the just of former times who rise again shall take part, while the rebellious are condemned to everlasting shame " (*cf.* Karl Müller: *Kirchengeschichte*, i. 15); other Jews again dispute whether the Messiah will be a Ben-David or a Ben-Joseph; many believe there would be two of them, others are of the opinion that he would be born in the Roman Diaspora; but nowhere and at no time do we find the idea of a suffering Messiah, who by his death redeems us (*see* Stanton, pp. 122–124). The best, the most cultured and pious Jews have never entertained such apocalyptic delusions. In the Talmud (*Sabbath*, Part 6) we read, " Between the present time and the Messianic there is no difference except that the pressure, under which Israel pines till then, will cease." (Contrast with this the frightful confusion and complete puerility of the Messianic conceptions in the *Sanhedrin* of the Babylonian Talmud.) I think that with these remarks I have touched the root of the matter: in the case of an absolutely historical religion, like the Jewish, the sure possession of the future is just as imperative a necessity as the sure possession of the

was there, the belief founded on history that at any
moment a saviour could and must appear from Heaven.
In no other part of the earth could a single man have
this conception, full of misunderstandings as it was,
of the world-wide importance of Christ. The Saviour
would have remained a man among men. And in so
far I think that the thousands who soon afterwards cried,
" Crucify him, crucify him," showed just as much understanding as those who had piously listened to the Sermon
on the Mount. Pilate, at other times a hard, cruel judge,
could find no fault in Christ ; * in Hellas and in Rome
He would have been honoured as a holy man. But the
Jew lived only in history, to him the " heathen " idea
of morality and sanctity was strange, since he knew
only a " law," and moreover obeyed this law for quite
practical reasons, namely, to stay the wrath of God and to
make sure of his future, and so he judged a phenomenon
like the revelation of Christ from a purely historical
standpoint, and became justly filled with fury, when
the promised kingdom, to win which he had suffered
and endured for centuries—for the sake of possessing
which he had separated himself from all people upon
the earth, and had become hated and despised of all—
when this kingdom, in which he hoped to see all nations
in fetters and all princes upon their knees " licking the
dust," was all at once transformed from an earthly
kingdom into one " not of this world." Jehovah had
often promised his people that he would " not betray "
them ; but to the Jews this was bound to appear be-

---

past ; from the earliest times we see this thought of the future inspiring the Jews and it still inspires them ; this unimaginative
people gave its expectations various forms, according to the varying
influences of surroundings, essential only is the firm ineradicable conviction that the Jews should one day rule the world. This is in fact
an element of their character, the visible bodying-forth of their
innermost nature. It is their substitute for mythology.

* Tertullian makes the charmingly simple remark : " Pilate was
already at heart a Christian " (*Apologeticus* xxi.).

trayal. They executed not one only but many, because they were held to be, or gave themselves out to be, the promised Messiah. And rightly too, for the belief in the future was just as much a pillar of the popular idea as the belief in the past. And now, to crown all, this Galilean heterodoxy! To plant the flag of idealism on this ancient consecrated seat of the most obstinate materialism! To transform, as if by magic, the God of vengeance and of war into a God of love and peace! To teach the stormy will, that stretched out both hands for all the gold of the world, that it should throw away what it possessed and seek the hidden treasure in its own heart! . . . The Jewish Sanhedrim had seen farther than Pilate (and than many thousands of Christian theologists). Not, indeed, with full consciousness, but with that unerring instinct, which pure race gives, it seized Him who undermined the historical basis of Jewish life, by teaching, "Take no heed for the morrow," who in each one of His words and deeds transformed Judaism into its antithesis, and did not release Him till He had breathed His last. And thus only, by death, was destiny fulfilled and the example given. No new faith could be established by doctrines; there was at that time no lack of noble and wise teachers of ethics, but none has had any power over men; a life had to be lived and this life had immediately to receive its place in the great enduring history of the world as a fact of universal moment. Only Jewish surroundings suited these conditions. And just as the life of Christ could only be lived by the help of Judaism, although it was its negation, so too the young Christian Church developed a series of ancient Aryan conceptions—of sin, redemption, rebirth, grace, &c. (things till then and afterwards quite unknown to the Jews)—and gave them a clear and visible form, by introducing them into the Jewish historical scheme.* No one will ever succeed

* The myth of the fall of man stands indeed at the beginning of the first book of *Moses*, but is clearly borrowed, since the Jews never

in quite freeing the revelation of Christ from this Jewish
groundwork ; it was tried in the first centuries of the
Christian era, but without success, since the thousand
features in which the personality had revealed its individuality became thereby blurred, and nothing but an
abstraction remained behind.*

WILL IN THE SEMITIC RACE

Still profounder is the influence of the second trait of
character.

We have seen that what I call the historical instinct
of the Jews rests above all upon the possession of an
abnormally developed will. The will in the case of the
Jew attains such superiority that it enthrals and tyrannises
over all other faculties. And so it is that we find on the
one hand extraordinary achievements, which would be
almost impossible for other men, and on the other, peculiar
limitations. However that may be, it is certain that
we see this very predominance of will in Christ at all
times : frequently un-Jewish in His individual utterances,
quite Jewish, in so far as the will is almost solely emphasised. This feature is like a branching of veins that goes
deep and spreads far : we find it in every word, in every

understood it and did not employ it in their system. He who does
not transgress the law is, in their eyes, free from sin. Just as little
has their expectation of a Messiah to do with our conception of redemption. *See*, further, chap. v. and vol ii. chap. vii.

* That is the tendency of gnosticism as a whole ; this movement finds
its most carefully pondered and noblest expression, as far as I can
venture to express an opinion, in Marcion (middle of the second century),
who was more filled with the absolutely new in the Christian ideal than
perhaps any religious teacher since his time ; but in just such a case
one sees how fatal it is to ignore historical data. (*See* any Church
History. On the other hand I must warn the student that the three
lines which Professor Ranke devotes to this really great man (*Weltgeschichte*, ii. 171) contain not a single word of what should have been
said on this point.) [For a knowledge of Marcion and gnosticism as a
whole Mead's *Fragments of a Faith Forgotten* may be recommended.]

single conception. By a comparison I hope to make my meaning clear and comprehensible.

Consider the Hellenic conception of the Divine and the Human and of their relation to one another. Some Gods fight for Troy, others for the Achæans; while I propitiate one part of the Divine I estrange the other; life is a battle, a game, the noblest may fall, the most miserable gain the victory; morality is in a way a personal affair, man is lord of his own heart but not of his destiny; there is no Providence that protects, punishes and rewards. The Gods themselves are in fact not free; Zeus himself must yield to fate. Herodotus says, " Even a God cannot escape what is destined for him." A nation which produces the *Iliad* will in a later age produce great investigators of nature and great thinkers. For he who looks at nature with open eyes which are not blinded by selfishness will discover everywhere in it the rule of law; the presence of law in the moral sphere is fate for the artist—predestination for the philosopher. For the faithful observer of nature the idea of arbitrariness is, to begin with, simply impossible; do what he will, he cannot make up his mind to impute it even to a God. This philosophical view has been beautifully expressed by Here in Goethe's fragment, *Achilleis*:

> Willkür bleibet ewig verhasst den Göttern und Menschen,
> Wenn sie in Thaten sich zeigt, auch nur in Worten sich kundgiebt*
> Denn so hoch wir auch stehen, so ist der ewigen Götter
> Ewigste Themis * allein, und diese muss dauern und walten.†

---

* Themis has degenerated in modern times to an allegory of impartial jurisdiction, that is, of an altogether arbitrary agreement, and she is appropriately represented with veiled eyes; while mythology lived, she represented the rule of law in all nature, and the old artists gave her particularly large, wide-open eyes.

† Arbitrariness remains ever hateful to gods and men, when it reveals itself in deeds or even in words only. For however high we may stand, the eternal Themis of the eternal Gods alone is, and she must lastingly hold sway.

On the other hand, the Jewish Jehovah can be described as the incarnation of arbitrariness. Certainly this divine conception appears to us in the *Psalms* and in *Isaiah* in altogether sublime form ; it is also—for the chosen people —a source of high and serious morality. But what Jehovah is, He is, because He wills to be so ; He stands above all nature, above every law, the absolute, unlimited autocrat. If it pleases Him to choose out from mankind a small people and to show His favour to it alone, He does so ; if He wishes to vex it, He sends it into slavery ; if he, on the other hand, wishes to give it houses which it has not built and vineyards which it has not planted, He does so and destroys the innocent possessors ; there is no Themis. So too the divine legislation. Beside moral commands which breathe to some extent high morality and humanity, there stand commands which are directly immoral and inhuman ; * others again determine most trivial points : what one may eat and may not eat, how one shall wash, &c., in short, everywhere absolute arbitrariness. He who sees deeper will not fail to note in this the relationship between the old Semitic idolatry and the belief in Jehovah. Considered from the Indo-European standpoint, Jehovah would in reality be called rather an idealised idol, or, if we prefer it, an anti-idol, than a god. And yet this conception of God contains something which could not, any more than arbitrariness, be derived from observation of nature, namely, the idea of a Providence. According to Renan, " the exaggerated belief in a special Providence is the basis of the whole Jewish religion."† Moreover, with

---

* Besides the countless raids involving wholesale slaughter divinely commanded, in which " the heads of the children " are to be " dashed against the stones," note the cases where command is given to attack with felonious intent " the brother, companion, and neighbour " (*Exodus* xxxii. 27), and the disgusting commands such as in *Ezekiel* v. 12–15.

† *Histoire du peuple d'Israël*, ii. p. 3.

this freedom of God another freedom is closely connected, that of the human will.   The *liberum arbitrium* is
decidedly a Semitic conception and in its .full development a specifically Jewish one ; it is inseparably bound
up with the particular idea of God.*   Freedom of will
implies nothing less than " ever repeated acts of creation " ;
carefully considered it will be clear that this supposition
(as soon as it has to do with the world of phenomena) contradicts not merely all physical science, but also all metaphysics, and means a negation of every transcendent religion.   Here cognition and will stand in strict opposition.
Now wherever we find limitations of this idea of
freedom—in Augustine, Luther, Voltaire, Kant, Goethe
—we can be sure that an Indo-European reaction
against the Semitic spirit is taking place. So, for example,
when Calderon in the *Great Zenobia* lets the wild autocratic
Aurelian mock him

who called the will free»

For — though one must certainly be on one's guard
against misusing such formulary simplifications—one can
still make the assertion that the idea of necessity is in all
Indo-European races particularly strongly marked, and
is met with again and again in the most different spheres ;
it points to high power of cognition free from passion ;
on the other hand, the idea of arbitrariness, that is, of an

---

* We can trace in every history of Judaism with what very logical
fanaticism the Rabbis still champion the unconditioned and not
merely metaphysically meant freedom of will.   Diderot says : " *Les
Juifs sont si jaloux de cette liberté d'indifférence, qu'ils s'imaginent qu'il
est impossible de penser sur cette matière autrement qu'eux.*"   And how
closely this idea is connected with the freedom of God and with Providence becomes clear from the commotion which arose when Maimo-
nides wished to limit divine Providence to mankind and maintained
that every leaf was not moved by it nor every worm created by its
will.—Of the so-called " fundamental doctrines " of the famous
Talmudist Rabbi Akiba the two first are as follow : (1) Everything is
supervised by the Providence of God ; (2) Freedom of will is stipulated
(Hirsch Graetz ; *Gnosticismus und Judentum,* 1846, p. 91).

unlimited sway of will, is specifically characteristic of the Jew; he reveals an intelligence which in comparison with his will-power is very limited. It is not a question here of abstract generalisations, but of actual characteristics, which we can still daily observe; in the one case intellect is predominant, in the other the will.

Let me give a tangible example from the present. I knew a Jewish scholar, who, as the competition in his branch prevented him from earning much money, became a manufacturer of soap, and that, too, with great success; but when at a later time foreign competition once more took the ground from beneath his feet, all at once, though ripe in years, he became dramatic poet and Man of Letters and made a fortune at it. There was no question of universal genius in his case; he was of moderate intellectual abilities and devoid of all originality; but with this intellect the will achieved whatever it wished.

The abnormally developed will of the Semites can lead to two extremes: either to rigidity, as in the case of Mohammed, where the idea of the unlimited divine caprice is predominant; or, as is the case with the Jews, to phenomenal elasticity, which is produced by the conception of their own human arbitrariness. To the Indo-European both paths are closed. In nature he observes everywhere the rule of law, and of himself he knows that he can only achieve his highest when he obeys inner need. Of course his will, too, can achieve the heroic, but only when his cognition has grasped some idea—religious, artistic, philosophic, or one which aims at conquest, command, enrichment, perhaps crime; at any rate, in his case the will obeys, it does not command. Therefore it is that a moderately gifted Indo-European is so peculiarly characterless in comparison with the most poorly gifted Jew. Of ourselves, we should certainly never have arrived at the conception of a free almighty God and of what may be called an " arbitrary Providence," a Providence, that is, which can decree something in one way, and then in answer to prayers or from other motives decide in a contrary direction.*   We do not find that, outside of Judaism, man ever came to the conception of a quite intimate and continual personal relation between God and mankind—to the conception of a God who would almost seem to be there only for the sake of man.   In truth the old Indo-Aryan Gods are benevolent, friendly, we might almost say genial powers ; man is their child, not their slave ; he approaches them without fear ; when sacrificing he " grasps the right hand of God " ; † the want of humility in presence of God has indeed filled many a one with horror : yet as we have seen nowhere do we find the conception of capricious autocracy.   And with this goes hand in hand remarkable infidelity ; now this, now that God is worshipped, or, if the Divine is viewed as a unified principle, then the one school has this idea of it, the other that (I remind the reader of the six great philosophically religious systems of India, all six of which passed as orthodox); the brain in fact works irresistibly on, producing new images and new shapes, the Infinite is its home, freedom its element and creative power its joy.   Just consider the beginning of the following hymn from the *Rigveda* (6, 9) :

> My ear is opened and my eye alert,
> The light awakes within my heart !
> My spirit flies to search in distant realms :
> What shall I say ? of what shall my verse sing ?

---

* In the case of the Indo-Europeans the Gods are never "creators of the world " ; where the Divine is viewed as creator, as in the case of the Brahman of the Indians, that refers to a freely metaphysical cognition, not to an historical and mechanical process, as in *Genesis* i. ; in other cases the Gods are viewed as originating " on this side of creation," their birth and death are spoken of.

† Oldenberg: *Die Religion des Veda*, p. 310.

and compare it with the first verses of any Psalm, for instance, the 76th :

> In Judah is God known : His name is great in Israel.
> In Salem also is His tabernacle, and His dwelling-place in Sion.

We see what an important element of faith the will is. While the Aryan, rich in cognition, " flies to search in distant realms," the strong-willed Jew makes God pitch His tent once for all in his own midst. The power of his will to live has not only forged for the Jew an anchor of faith, which holds him fast to the ground of historical tradition, but it has also inspired him with unshakable confidence in a personal, directly present God, who is almighty to give and to destroy ; and it has brought him, the man, into a moral relation to this God, in that God in His all-powerfulness issued commands, which man is free to follow or neglect.*

THE PROPHET

There is another matter which must not be omitted in this connection : the one-sided predominance of the will makes the chronicles of the Jewish people in general

---

* If this were the place for it, I should gladly prove in greater detail that this Jewish conception of the almighty God who rules as free Providence inevitably determines the historical view of this God and that every genuine Aryan mind revolts again and again against this. This has caused, for instance, the whole tragic mental life of Peter Abelard : in spite of the most intense longing for orthodoxy, he cannot adapt his spirit to the religious materialism of the Jews. Ever and anon, for example, he comes to the conclusion that God does what he does of necessity (and here he could refer for support to the earlier writings of Augustine, especially his *De libero arbitrio*) ; this is intellectual anti-Semitism in the highest degree ! He denies also every action, every motion in the case of God ; the working of God is for him the coming to pass of an everlasting determination of will : " with God there is no sequence of time." (*See* A. Hausrath : *Peter Abelard*, p. 201 f.) With this Providence disappears.—However, what is the use of seeking for learned proofs ? The noble Don

dreary and ugly; and yet in this atmosphere there grew up a series of important men, whose peculiar greatness makes it impossible to compare them with other intellectual heroes. In the introduction to this division I have already spoken of those "disavowers" of the Jewish character, who themselves remained the while such out and out Jews, from the crown of their heads to the soles of their feet, that they contributed more than anything else to the growth of the most rigid Hebraism; in chap. v. I shall return to them; only so much must here be said: these men, in grasping religious materialism by its most abstract side, raised it morally to a very great height; their work has paved the way historically in essential points for Christ's view of the relation between God and man. Moreover, an important feature, which is essentially rooted in Judaism, shows itself most clearly in them: the historical religion of this people lays emphasis not upon the individual, but upon the whole nation; the individual can benefit or injure the whole community, but otherwise he is of little moment; from this resulted of necessity a markedly socialistic feature which the Prophets often powerfully express. The individual who attains to prosperity and wealth, while his brothers starve, falls under the ban of God. While Christ in one way represents exactly the opposite principle, namely, that of extreme individualism, the redeeming of the individual by regeneration, His life and His teaching, on the other hand, point unmistakably to a condition of things which can only be realised by having all things common. The communism of "one flock and one shepherd" is certainly different from the entirely politically coloured, theocratic communism of the Prophets;

Quixote explains with pathetic simplicity to his faithful Sancho, "for God there is no past and no future, all is present" (Book IX. chap. viii.): hereby the immortal Cervantes expresses briefly and correctly the unhistorical standpoint of all non-Semites.

but here again the basis is solely and characteristically Jewish.

CHRIST A JEW

Whatever one may be inclined to think of these various Jewish conceptions, no one will deny their greatness, or their capacity to exercise an almost inestimable influence upon the moulding of the life of mankind. Nor will any one deny that the belief in divine almightiness, in divine Providence and in the freedom of the human will,* as well as the almost exclusive emphasising of the moral nature of men and their equality before God (" the last shall be first ") are essential elements of the personality of Christ. Far more than the fact that He starts from the Prophets, far more than His respect for Jewish legal enactments, do these fundamental views show us that Christ belonged morally to the Jews. Indeed, when we penetrate farther to that central point in Christ's teaching, to that " conversion of the will," then we must recognise—as I have already hinted at the beginning of this chapter in the comparison with Buddha —that here is something Jewish in contrast to the Aryan negation of the will. The latter is a fruit of perception, of too great perception ; Christ, on the other hand, addresses Himself to men, in whom the will—not the thought, is supreme ; what He sees around Him is the insatiable, ever-covetous Jewish will that is always stretching out both hands ; He recognises the might of this will and commands it—not to be silent, but to take a new direction. Here we must say, Christ is a Jew, and He can only be understood when we have learned to grasp critically these peculiarly Jewish views which He found and made His own.

* The latter, however, as it appears, with important limitations, since the Aryan idea of grace more than once clearly appears in Christ's words.

I said just now that Christ belonged "morally" to the Jews. This somewhat ambiguous word "moral" must here be taken in a narrow sense. For it is just in the moral application of these conceptions of God's almightiness and providence, of the direct relations between man and God following therefrom, and of the employment of the free human will, that the Saviour departed *in toto* from the doctrines of Judaism; that is clear to every one, and I have, moreover, sought to emphasise it in what has gone before; but the conceptions themselves, the frame into which the moral personality fitted itself, and out of which it cannot be moved, the unquestioning acceptance of these premisses regarding God and man, which by no means belong to the human mind as a matter of course but are, on the contrary, the absolutely individual achievement of a definite people in the course of an historical development which lasted for centuries: this is the Jewish element in Christ. In the chapters on Hellenic Art and Roman Law I have already called attention to the power of ideas; here again we have a brilliant example of it. Whoever lived in the Jewish intellectual world was bound to come under the influence of Jewish ideas. And though He brought to the world an entirely new message, though His life was like the dawn of a new morn, though His personality was so divinely great that it revealed to us a power in the human breast, capable—if it ever should be fully realised—of completely changing humanity: yet the personality, the life and the message were none the less chained to the fundamental ideas of Judaism; only in these could they reveal, exercise and proclaim themselves.

THE NINETEENTH CENTURY

I hope I have attained my purpose. Proceeding from the consideration of the personality in its individual, autonomous import, I have gradually widened the circle, to reveal the threads of life which connect it with its surroundings. In this a certain amplification was unavoidable ; the sole subject of this book, the foundations of the nineteenth century, I have nevertheless not lost sight of for a single moment. For how could I, an individual, venture to approach that age either as chronicler or encyclopædist ? May the Muses keep me from such madness ! On the other hand, I shall attempt to trace as far as possible the leading ideas, the moulding thoughts of our age; but these ideas do not fall from Heaven, they link on to the past ; new wine is very often indeed poured into old bottles, and very old, sour wine, which nobody would taste, if he knew its origin, into quite new ones ; and as a matter of fact the curse of confusion weighs heavily upon a culture born so late as ours, especially in an age of breathless haste, where men have to learn too much to be able to think much. If we wish to become clear about ourselves, we must, above all, be quite clear about the fundamental thoughts and conceptions which we have inherited from our ancestors. I hope I have brought it home to the reader how very complex is the Hellenic legacy, how peculiarly contradictory the Roman, but at the same time how profoundly they affect our life and thought to-day. Now we have seen that even the advent of Christ, on the threshold between the old and the new age, does not present itself to our distant eye in so simple a form that we can easily free it from the labyrinth of prejudices, falsehoods and errors. And yet nothing is more necessary than to see this revelation of Christ clearly in the light of truth. For—

however unworthy we may show ourselves of this—our whole culture, thank God, still stands under the sign of the Cross upon Golgotha.   We do see this Cross ; but who sees the Crucified One ?   Yet He, and He alone is the living well of all Christianity, of the intolerantly dogmatic as well as of that which gives itself out to be quite unbelieving.   In later ages it will be an eloquent testimony to the childishness of our judgment that we have ever doubted it, and that the nineteenth century has reared itself on books, which demonstrated that Christianity originated by chance, at haphazard, as a " mythological paroxysm," as a " dialectical antithesis," as a necessary result of Judaism, and I know not what else.   The importance of genius cannot be reckoned high enough : who ventures to estimate the influence of Homer upon the mind of man ?   But Christ was still greater. And like the everlasting " hearth-fire " of the Aryans, so the torch of truth which He kindled for us can never be extinguished ; though at times a shadow of night may wrap manhood far and wide in the folds of darkness, yet all that is wanted is one single glowing heart, in order that thousands and millions may once more blaze under the bright light of day. . . . Here, however, we can and must ask with Christ, " But if the light that is in thee be darkness, how great is that darkness ? " Even the origin of the Christian Church leads us into the profoundest gloom, and its further history gives us rather the impression of a groping about in darkness than of clear seeing in the sunlight.   How then shall we be able to distinguish what in so-called Christianity is spirit of Christ's spirit, and what, on the other hand, is imported from Hellenic, Jewish, Roman and Egyptian sources, if we have never come to see this revelation of Christ in its sublime simplicity ?   How shall we speak about what is Christian in our present confessions, in our literatures and arts, in our philosophy and politics, in our social institutions and ideals, how shall we separate what is Christian from what is anti-Christian, and be able with certainty to decide, what in the movements of the nineteenth century can be traced back to Christ and what not, or in how far it is Christian, whether merely in the form or also in the content, or perhaps in content, *i.e.*, in its general tendency, but not with regard to the characteristically Jewish form—how shall we, above all, be able to sift and separate from the " bread of life " this specifically Jewish element which is so threateningly perilous to our spirit, if the revelation of Christ does not stand conspicuously before our eyes in its general outlines, and if we are not able clearly to distinguish in this image the purely personal from its historical conditions. This is certainly a most important and indispensable foundation for the formation of our judgments and appreciations.

To pave, to some modest degree, the way for that result has been the purpose of this chapter.

DIVISION II

THE HEIRS

Der hohe Sinn, das Rühmliche
Von dem Gerühmten rein zu unterscheiden
GOETHE.

INTRODUCTORY

WHO were the heirs of antiquity? This question is at least as important as that concerning the legacy itself and, if possible, more difficult to answer. For it introduces us to the study of race problems, which science during the last quarter of a century, so far from solving, has rather revealed in all their intricacy. And yet all true comprehension of the nineteenth century depends on the clear answering of this question. Here, then, we must be at once daring and cautious if we are to remember the warning of the preface, and steer safely between the Scylla of a science almost unattainable, and so far most problematic in its results, and the Charybdis of unstable and baseless generalisations. Necessity compels us to make the bold attempt.

THE CHAOS

Rome had transterred the centre of gravity of civilisation to the West. This proved to be one of those unconsciously

251

accomplished acts of world-wide importance which no
power can undo. The West of Europe, remote from
Asia, was to be the focus of all further civilisation and
culture. But that happened only gradually. At first
it was politics alone which turned ever more and more
towards the West and North; intellectually Rome
itself long remained very dependent upon the former
centre of culture in the East. In the first centuries of
our era, with the exception of Rome itself, only what lies
South and East of it is intellectually of any importance;
Alexandria, Ephesus, Antioch, in fact all Syria, then
Greece with Byzantium, as well as Carthage and the other
towns of ancient Africa, are the districts where the legacy
was taken up and long administered, and the inhabitants
of these places then handed it on to later times and other
races. And these very countries were at that time, like
Rome itself, no longer inhabited by a definite people,
but by an inextricable confusion of the most different
races and peoples. It was a chaos. And this chaos did
not by any means disappear at a later time. In many
places this chaotic element was pressed back by the
advance of pure races, in others it fell out of the list
of those that count through its own weakness and want
of character, yet for all that it has beyond doubt maintained itself in the South and East; moreover fresh
influx of blood has frequently given it new strength.
That is a first point of far-reaching importance. Consider, for example, that all the foundations for the structure of historical Christianity were laid and built up by
this mongrel population! With the exception of some
Greeks, all of whom, however, with Origenes at their
head, disseminated highly unorthodox, directly anti-
Jewish doctrines which had no success,* one can scarcely
even conjecture to what nationality any of the Church

* Origenes, for example, was confessedly a pessimist (in the metaphysical sense of the word), by which in itself he proved his Indo-
European descent; he saw suffering everywhere in the world and con-

fathers actually belonged. The same may be said of the *corpus juris;* here, too, it was the Chaos (according to Hellenic ideas the mother of Erebus and Nox, of darkness and night), to which the task fell of perfecting and transforming the living work of a living people to an international dogma. Under the same influence, art ever more and more lost its personal, freely creative power and became transformed into an hieratically formulary exercise, while the lofty, philosophical speculation of the Hellenes was displaced by its caricature, the cabalistic phantoms of demiurges, angels and daemons—conceptions which could not be designated by a higher name than "airy materialism."* We must therefore, to begin with, turn our attention to this Chaos of Peoples.

THE JEWS

Out of the midst of the chaos towers, like a sharply defined rock amid the formless ocean, one single people, a numerically insignificant people—the Jews. This one race has established as its guiding principle the purity of the blood ; it alone possesses, therefore, physiognomy and character. If we contemplate the southern and eastern centres of culture in the world-empire in its down-

cluded from that that its chief end was not the enjoyment of a god-given happiness but the prevention of an evil (compare Christ's chief doctrine, that of the "conversion of will," *cf.* p. 188). Augustine, the African mestizo, found it easy to refute him ; he appealed to the first chapter of the first book of the Jewish *Thora,* to prove beyond dispute that everything is good and that " the world exists for no other reason than because it has been pleasing to a good God to create the absolutely good." (*See* the very instructive discussion in the *De civitate Dei,* xi. 23.) Augustine triumphantly introduces another argument in this place : if Origenes were right, then the most sinful creatures would have the heaviest bodies and devils would be visible, but devils have airy, invisible shapes, and so, &c. Thus thoughts that arose in the Chaos prevailed over metaphysical religion. (The same arguments are to be found, word for word, in the *Führer der Irrenden* of the Jew Maimuni.)

* Bürger calls it *Luftiges Gesindel* (airy rabble) in his *Lenore.*

fall, and let no sympathies or antipathies pervert our judgment, we must confess that the Jews were at that time the only people deserving respect. We may well apply to them the words of Goethe, " the faith broad, narrow the thought." In comparison with Rome and still more so with Hellas their intellectual horizon appears so narrow, their mental capacities so limited, that we seem to have before us an entirely new type of being ; but the narrowness and want of originality in thought are fully counterbalanced by the power of faith, a faith which might be very simply defined as " faith in self." And since this faith in self included faith in a higher being, it did not lack ethical significance. However poor the Jewish " law " may appear, when compared with the religious creations of the various Indo-European peoples, it possessed a unique advantage in the fallen Roman Empire of that time : it was, in fact, a law ; a law which men humbly obeyed, and this very obedience was bound to be of great ethical import in a world of such lawlessness. Here, as everywhere, we shall find that the influence of the Jews—for good and for evil— lies in their character, not in their intellectual achievements.* Certain historians of the nineteenth century, even men so intellectually pre-eminent as Count Gobineau, have supported the view that Judaism has always had merely a disintegrating influence upon all peoples. I cannot share this conviction. In truth, where the Jews become very numerous in a strange land, they may make it their object to fulfil the promises of their Prophets and with the best will and conscience to " consume the strange peoples " ; did they not say of themselves, even in the lifetime of Moses, that they were "like locusts"? However, we must distinguish between Judaism and the Jews and admit that Judaism as an idea is one of the most conservative ideas in the world. The idea of physical race-unity and race-purity, which is the very

* See p. 238 f.

essence of Judaism, signifies the recognition of a fundamental physiological fact of life ; wherever we observe
life, from the hyphomycetes to the noble horse, we see the
importance of " race " ; Judaism made this law of nature
sacred. And this is the reason why it triumphantly prevailed at that critical moment in the history of the
world, when a rich legacy was waiting in vain for worthy
heirs. It did not further, but rather put a stop to,
universal disintegration. The Jewish dogma was like a
sharp acid which is poured into a liquid which is being
decomposed in order to clear it and keep it from further
decomposition. Though this acid may not be to the
taste of every one, yet it has played so decisive a part in
the history of the epoch of culture to which we belong
that we ought to be grateful to the giver : instead of
being indignant about it, we shall do better to inform
ourselves thoroughly concerning the significance of this
" entrance of the Jews into the history of the West," an
event which in any case exercised inestimable influence
upon our whole culture, and which has not yet reached
its full growth.

Another word of explanation. I am speaking of Jews,
not of Semites in general : not because I fail to recognise
the part played by the latter in the history of the world,
but because my task is limited both in respect of time and
space. Indeed for many centuries other branches of the
Semitic race had founded powerful kingdoms on the
South and East coasts of the Mediterranean and had
established commercial depots as far as the coasts of the
Atlantic Ocean ; doubtless they had also been stimulative
in other ways, and had spread knowledge and accomplishments of many kinds ; but nowhere had there been a
close intellectual connection between them and the other
inhabitants of future Europe. The Jews first brought
this about, not by the millions of Jews who lived in the
Diaspora, but first and foremost by the Christian idea.
It was only when the Jews crucified Christ that they

unconsciously broke the spell which had hitherto isolated them in the pride of ignorance.—At a later time, indeed, a Semitic flood swept once more across the European, Asiatic and African world, a flood such as, but for the destruction of Carthage by Rome, would have swept over Europe a thousand years before, with results which would have been decisive and permanent.* But here, too, the Semitic idea—" faith wide, narrow the thought " —proved itself more powerful than its bearers ; the Arabs were gradually thrown back and, in contrast to the Jews, not one of them remained on European soil ; but where their abstract idolatry † had obtained a foothold all possibility of a culture disappeared ; the Semitic dogma of materialism, which in this case and in contrast to Christianity had kept itself free of all Aryan admixtures, deprived noble human races of all soul, and excluded them for ever from the " race that strives to reach the light."—Of the Semites only the Jews, as we see, have positively furthered our culture and also shared, as far as their extremely assimilative nature permitted them, in the legacy of antiquity.

THE TEUTONIC RACES

The entrance of the Teutonic races into the history of the world forms the counterpart to the spread of this diminutive and yet so influential people. There, too, we see what pure race signifies, at the same time, however, what variety of races is—that great natural principle of many-sidedness, and of dissimilarity of mental gifts, which shallow, venal, ignorant babblers of the present day would fain deny, slavish souls sprung from the chaos of peoples, who feel at ease only in a confused atmosphere of characterlessness and absence of individuality. To this day these two powers—Jews and Teutonic

* *See* p. 115.   † *See* p. 240.

races—stand, wherever the recent spread of the Chaos has not blurred their features, now as friendly, now as hostile, but always as alien forces face to face.

In this book I understand by " Teutonic peoples " the different North-European races, which appear in history as Celts, Teutons (Germanen) and Slavs, and from whom— mostly by indeterminable mingling—the peoples of modern Europe are descended. It is certain that they belonged originally to a single family, as I shall prove in the sixth chapter; but the Teuton in the narrower Taci- tean sense of the word has proved himself so intellectually, morally and physically pre-eminent among his kins- men, that we are entitled to make his name summarily represent the whole family. The Teuton is the soul of our culture. Europe of to-day, with its many branches over the whole world, represents the chequered result of an infinitely manifold mingling of races : what binds us all together and makes an organic unity of us is "Teutonic" blood. If we look around, we see that the importance of each nation as a living power to-day is dependent upon the proportion of genuinely Teutonic blood in its population. Only Teutons sit on the thrones of Europe.—What preceded in the history of the world we may regard as Prolegomena ; true history, the history which still controls the rhythm of our hearts and circulates in our veins, inspiring us to new hope and new creation, begins at the moment when the Teuton with his masterful hand lays his grip upon the legacy of antiquity.

FOURTH CHAPTER

THE CHAOS

So viel ist wohl mit Wahrscheinlichkeit zu urteilen: dass die Vermischung der Stämme, welche nach und nach die Charaktere auslöscht, dem Menschengeschlecht, alles vorgeblichen Philanthropismus ungeachtet, nicht zuträglich sei.

IMMANUEL KANT.

SCIENTIFIC CONFUSION

THE remarks which I made in the introduction to the second division will suffice as a general preface to this chapter on the chaos of peoples in the dying Roman Empire; they explain to what time and what countries I refer in speaking of the "chaos of peoples." Here, as elsewhere, I presuppose historical knowledge, at least in general outline, and as I should not like to write a single line in this whole book which did not originate from the need of comprehending and of judging the nineteenth century better, I think I should use the subject before us especially to discuss and answer the important question: Is nation, is race a mere word? Is it the case, as the ethnographer Ratzel asserts, that the fusion of all mankind should be kept before us as our "aim and duty, hope and wish"? Or do we not rather deduce from the example of Hellas and Rome, on the one hand, and of the pseudo-Roman empire on the other, as well as from many other examples in history, that man can only attain his zenith within those limits in which sharply defined, individualistic national types are produced? Is the present condition of things in

258

Europe with its many fully formed idioms, each with its
own peculiar poetry and literature, each the expression of
a definite, characteristic national soul—is this state of
things really a retrograde step in comparison with the
time, when Latin and Greek, as a kind of twin Volapuk,
formed a bond of union between all those Roman subjects
who had no fatherland to call their own ?   Is community
of blood nothing ?   Can community of memory and of
faith be replaced by abstract ideals ?   Above all, is the
question one to be settled by each as he pleases, is there
no clearly distinguishable natural law, according to which
we must fit our judgment ?   Do not the biological
sciences teach us that in the whole animal and vegetable
kingdoms pre-eminently noble races—that is, races
endowed with exceptional strength and vitality—are
produced only under definite conditions, which restrict
the begetting of new individuals ?   Is it not possible,
in view of all these human and non-human phenomena,
to find a clear answer to the question, What is race ?
And shall we not be able, from the consciousness of
what race is, to say at once what the absence of definite
races must mean for history ?   When we look at those
direct heirs of the great legacy, these questions force
themselves upon us.   Let us in the first place discuss
races quite generally ; then, and then only, shall we be
able to discuss with advantage the conditions prevailing
in this special case, their importance in the course of history, and consequently in the nineteenth century.

   There is perhaps no question about which such absolute
ignorance prevails among highly cultured, indeed learned,
men, as the question of the essence and the significance
of the idea of " race."   What are pure races ? Whence
do they come ?   Have they any historical importance ?
Is the idea to be taken in a broad or a narrow sense ?
Do we know anything on the subject or not ?   What is the
relation of the ideas of race and of nation to one another ?

I confess that all I have ever read or heard on this subject has been disconnected and contradictory: some
specialists among the natural investigators form an
exception, but even they very rarely apply their clear
and detailed knowledge to the human race. Not a
year passes without our being assured at international congresses, by authoritative national economists, ministers,
bishops, natural scientists, that there is no difference and
no inequality between nations. Teutons, who emphasise the importance of race-relationship, Jews, who
do not feel at ease among us and long to get back to
their Asiatic home, are by none so slightingly and scorn-
fully spoken of as by men of science. Professor Virchow,
for instance, says * that the stirrings of consciousness of
race among us are only to be explained by the " loss of
sound common sense ": moreover, that it is " all a riddle
to us, and no one knows what it really means in this age of
equal rights." Nevertheless, this learned man closes his
address with the expression of a desire for " beautiful
self-dependent personalities." As if all history were not
there to show us how personality and race are most
closely connected, how the nature of the personality is
determined by the nature of its race, and the power of
the personality dependent upon certain conditions of
its blood ! And as if the scientific rearing of animals and
plants did not afford us an extremely rich and reliable
material, whereby we may become acquainted not only
with the conditions but with the importance of " race " !
Are the so-called (and rightly so-called) " noble " animal
races, the draught-horses of Limousin, the American
trotter, the Irish hunter, the absolutely reliable sporting

* Der Übergang aus dem philosophischen in das naturwissenschaftliche
Zeitalter, Rektoratsrede, 1893, p. 30. I choose this example from
hundreds, since Virchow, being one of the most ardent anthropologists
and ethnographers of the nineteenth century, and in addition, a man
of great learning and experience, ought to have been well informed
on the subject.

dogs, produced by chance and promiscuity ?   Do we get
them by giving the animals equality of rights, by throwing
the same food to them and whipping them with the same
whip ?   No, they are produced by artificial selection and
strict maintenance of the purity of the race.   Horses
and especially dogs give us every chance of observing that
the intellectual gifts go hand in hand with the physical ;
this is specially true of the moral qualities : a
mongrel is frequently very clever, but never reliable ;
morally he is always a weed.   Continual promiscuity
between two pre-eminent animal races leads without
exception to the destruction of the pre-eminent characteristics of both.*   Why should the human race form an
exception ?   A father of the Church might imagine that
it does, but is it becoming in a renowned natural investigator to throw the weight of his great influence into the
scale of mediæval ignorance and superstition ?   Truly
one could wish that these scientific authorities of ours,
who are so utterly lacking in philosophy, had followed a
course of logic under Thomas Aquinas ; it could only be
beneficial to them.   In spite of the broad common foundation, the human races are, in reality, as different from
one another in character, qualities, and above all, in the
degree of their individual capacities, as greyhound, bull-
dog, poodle and Newfoundland dog.   Inequality is a
state towards which nature inclines in all spheres ; nothing
extraordinary is produced without " specialisation " ;
in the case of men, as of animals, it is this specialisation
that produces noble races ; history and ethnology reveal
this secret to the dullest eye.   Has not every genuine
race its own glorious, incomparable physiognomy ?
How could Hellenic art have arisen without Hellenes ?

* *See* especially Darwin's *Plants and Animals under Domestication*,
chaps. xv. xix. " Free crossing obliterates characters." For the
" superstitious care with which the Arabs keep their horses pure bred "
see interesting details in Gibbon's *Roman Empire*, chap. 50.   *See also*
Burton's *Mecca*, chap. xxix.

How quickly has the jealous hostility between the different cities of the small country of Greece given each part its sharply defined individuality within its own family type! How quickly this was blurred again, when Macedonians and Romans with their levelling hand swept over the land! And how everything which had given an everlasting significance to the word "Hellenic" gradually disappeared when from North, East and West new bands of unrelated peoples kept flocking to the country and mingled with genuine Hellenes! The equality, before which Professor Virchow bows the knee, was now there, all walls were razed to the ground, all boundaries became meaningless; the philosophy, too, with which Virchow in the same lecture breaks so keen a lance, was destroyed, and its place taken by the very soundest "common sense"; but the beautiful Hellenic personality, but for which all of us would to-day be merely more or less civilised barbarians, had disappeared, disappeared for ever. *"Crossing obliterates characters."*

If the men who should be the most competent to pronounce an opinion on the essence and significance of Race show such an incredible lack of judgment—if in dealing with a subject where wide experience is necessary for sure perception, they bring to bear upon it nothing but hollow political phrases—how can we wonder that the unlearned should talk nonsense even when their instinct points out the true path? For the subject has in these days aroused interest in widely various strata of society, and where the learned refuse to teach, the unlearned must shift for themselves. When in the fifties Count Gobineau published his brilliant work on the inequality of the races of mankind, it passed unnoticed: no one seemed to know what it all meant. Like poor Virchow men stood puzzled before a riddle. Now that the Century has come to an end things have changed: the more passionate, more impulsive element in the

nations pays great and direct attention to this question.
But in what a maze of contradiction, errors and delusions
public opinion moves ! Notice how Gobineau bases his
account—so astonishingly rich in intuitive ideas which
have later been verified and in historical knowledge—
upon the dogmatic supposition that the world was
peopled by Shem, Ham and Japhet. Such a gaping void
in capacity of judgment in the author suffices, in spite
of all his documentary support, to relegate his work to
the hybrid class of scientific phantasmagorias. With
this is connected Gobineau's further fantastic idea, that
the originally " pure " noble races crossed with each other
in the course of history, and with every crossing became
irrevocably less pure and less noble. From this we
must of necessity derive a hopelessly pessimistic view
of the future of the human race. But this supposition
rests upon total ignorance of the physiological importance
of what we have to understand by " race." A noble
race does not fall from Heaven, it becomes noble gradually, just like fruit-trees, and this gradual process can
begin anew at any moment, as soon as accident of geography and history or a fixed plan (as in the case of the
Jews) creates the conditions. We meet similar absurdities
at every step. We have, for example, a powerful Anti-
Semitic movement: are we to consider the Jews as identical
with the rest of the Semites ? Have not the Jews by their
very development made themselves a peculiar, pure
race profoundly different from the others ? Is it certain
that an important crossing did not precede the birth
of this people ? And what is an Aryan ? We hear so
many and so definite pronouncements on this head.
We contrast the Aryan with the " Semite," by whom we
ordinarily understand " the Jew " and nothing more,
and that is at least a thoroughly concrete conception based
upon experience. But what kind of man is the Aryan ?
What concrete conception does he correspond to ? Only

he who knows nothing of ethnography can give a definite
answer to this question. As soon as we do not limit this
expression to the Indo-Eranians who are doubtless inter-
related, we get into the sphere of uncertain hypotheses.*
The peoples whom we have learned to classify together as
" Aryans " differ physically very much from each other ;
they reveal the most different structure of skull, also
different colour of skin, eyes and hair ; and even granted
that there was cnce a common ancestral Indo-European
race, what evidence can we offer against the daily increasing sum of facts which make it probable that other
absolutely unrelated types have also been from time
immemorial richly represented in our so-called Aryan
nations of to-day, so that we can never apply the term
" Aryan " to a whole people, but, at most, to single
individuals ? Relationship of language is no conclusive
proof of community of blood ; the theory of the immigration of the so-called Indo-Europeans from Asia,
which rests upon very slight grounds, encounters the
grave difficulty that investigators are finding more and
more reason to believe that the population which we are
accustomed to call Indo-European was settled in Europe
from time immemorial ; † for the opposite hypothesis

* Even with this very qualified statement, derived from the best
books I know, I seem to have presupposed more than science
can with certainty assert ; for I read in a specialised treatise, *Les
Aryens au nord et au sud de l'Hindou-Kousch*, by Charles de Ujfalvi
(Paris, 1896, p. 15), " Le terme d'aryen est de pure convention ; les
peuples éraniens au nord et les tribus hindoues au sud du Caucase
indien, diffèrent absolument comme type et descendent, sans aucun
doute, de deux races différentes."

† G. Schrader (*Sprachvergleichung und Urgeschichte*), who has studied
the question more from the linguistic standpoint, comes to the conclusion, " It is proved that the Indo-Teutonic peoples were settled in
Europe at a very ancient period " ; Johannes Ranke (*Der Mensch*)
is of opinion that it is now an established fact that at least a great
part of the population of Europe were Aryans as early as the stone
age ; and Virchow, whose authority is all the greater in the sphere
of anthropology because he shows unconditional respect for facts and,

of a colonisation of India from Europe there are not the
slightest grounds . . . in short, this question is what
miners call "swimming land"; he who 'knows the
danger sets foot on it as little as possible. The more we
study the specialists, the less certain we become. It was
originally the philologists who established the collective
idea "Aryans." Then came the anatomical anthropologists; the inadmissibility of conclusions drawn
from mere philology was demonstrated, and now skull-
measuring began; craniometry became a profession,
and it did provide a mass of extremely interesting material;
lately, however, the same fate is overtaking this so-called
"somatic anthropology" that formerly overtook philology: ethnographers have begun to travel and to make
scientifically systematic observations from living man,
and in this way have been able to prove that the measuring of bones by no means deserves the importance that
was wont to be attached to it; one of the greatest of
Virchow's pupils has become convinced that the idea
of solving problems of ethnology by the measurement
of skulls is fruitless.* All these advances have been
made in the second half of the nineteenth century;
who knows what will be taught about "Aryans" †
in the year 1950? At present, at any rate, the
layman can say nothing on the subject. If he turns
up one of the well-known authorities, he will be told that
the Aryans "are an invention of the study and not a

unlike Huxley and many others, builds no Darwinian castles in the air,
says that from anatomical discoveries one may assert that "the
oldest troglodytes of Europe were of Aryan descent!" (quoted from
Ranke, *Der Mensch*, ii. 578].

* Ehrenreich: *Anthropologische Studien über die Urbewohner
Brasiliens*, 1897.

† When I use the word Aryan in this book, I take it in the sense
of the original Sanscrit "ârya," which means "belonging to the
friends," without binding myself to any hypothesis. The relationship
in thought and feeling signifies in any case an homogeneousness. *Cf.*
the note on p. 93.

primeval people," * if he seeks information from another, he receives the answer that the common characteristics of the Indo-Europeans, from the Atlantic Ocean to India, suffice to put the actual blood-relationship beyond all doubt.†

I hope I have clearly illustrated in these two paragraphs the great confusion which is prevalent among us to-day in regard to the idea " race." This confusion is not necessary, that is, with practical, active men who belong to life as we do. And it is unnecessary for this reason, that we, in order to interpret the lessons of history and to comprehend our present age in connection therewith, do not in any way need to seek for hidden origins and causes. In the former division I have already quoted the words

* R. Hartmann: *Die Negritier* (1876), p. 185. Similarly Luschan and many investigators. Salomon Reinach, for instance, writes in *L'Origine des Aryens*, 1892, p. 90 : " Parler d'une race aryenne d'il y a trois mille ans, c'est émettre une hypothèse gratuite : en parler comme si elle existait aujourd'hui, c'est dire tout simplement une absurdité."

† Friedrich Ratzel, Johannes Ranke, Paul Ehrenreich, &c., in fact the more modern, widely travelled ethnographers. But they hold the view with many variations, since the relationship does not necessarily rest upon common origin, but might have been produced by crossing. Ratzel, for instance, who in one place positively asserts the uniformity of the whole Indo-European race (*Litterarisches Centralblatt*, 1897, p. 1295), says in another (*Völkerkunde*, 1895, ii. 751), " the supposition that all these peoples have a uniform origin is not necessary or probable."—It is worth remarking that even those who deny the fact of an Aryan race still constantly speak of it ; they cannot do without it as a " working hypothesis." Even Reinach, after proving that there never was an Aryan race, speaks in an unguarded moment (*loc. cit.* p. 98) of the " common origin of the Semites and the Aryans." Ujfalvi, quoted above, has after profound study arrived at the opposite conclusion and believes in a " grande famille aryenne." In fact anthropologists, ethnographers and even historians, theologians, philologists and legal authorities find the idea " Aryan" more and more indispensable every year. And yet if one of us makes even the most cautious and strictly limited use of the conception, he is scorned and slandered by academic scribes and nameless newspaper reviewers. May the reader of this book trust science more than the official simplifiers and levellers and the professional anti-Aryan confusion-makers. Though it were proved that there never was an Aryan race in the past, yet we desire that in the future there may be one. That is the decisive standpoint for men for action.

of Goethe, "Animated inquiry into cause does great harm." What is clear to every eye suffices, if not for science, at least for life. Science must, of course, ever wander on its thorny but fascinating path; it is like a mountain climber, who every moment imagines that he will reach the highest peak, but soon discovers behind it a higher one still. But life is only indirectly interested in these changing hypotheses. One of the most fatal errors of our time is that which impels us to give too great weight in our judgments to the so-called "results" of science. Knowledge can certainly have an illuminating effect; but it is not always so, and especially for this reason, that knowledge always stands upon tottering feet. For how can intelligent men doubt but that much which we think we know to-day will be laughed at as crass ignorance, one hundred, two hundred, five hundred years hence? Many facts may, indeed, be looked upon to-day as finally established; but new knowledge places these same facts in quite a new light, unites them to figures never thought of before, or changes their perspective; to regulate our judgments by the contemporary state of science may be compared to an artist's viewing the world through a transparent, ever-changing kaleidoscope, instead of with the naked eye. Pure science (in contrast to industrial science) is a noble plaything; its great intellectual and moral worth rests in no small degree upon the fact that it is not "useful"; in this respect it is quite analogous to art, it signifies the application of thought to the outward world; and since nature is inexhaustibly rich, she thereby ever brings new material to the mind, enriches its inventory of conceptions and gives the imagination a new dream-world to replace the gradually fading old one.* Life,

* The physical scientist Lichtenberg makes a similar remark: "The teaching of nature is, for me at least, a kind of sinking fund for religion, when overbold reason falls into debt" (*Fragmentarische Bemerkungen über physikalische Gegenstände,* 15).

on the other hand, purely as such, is something different from systematic knowledge, something much more stable, more firmly founded, more comprehensive ; it is in fact the essence of all reality, whereas even the most precise science represents the thinned, generalised, no longer direct reality. Here I understand by " life " what is otherwise also called " nature," as when, for instance, modern medicine teaches us that nature encourages by means of fever the change of matter and defends man against the illness which has seized him. Nature is in fact what we call " automatic," its roots go very much deeper than knowledge will ever be able to follow. And so it is my conviction that we—who as thinking, well-informed, boldly dreaming and investigating beings are certainly just such integral parts of nature as all other beings and things, and as our own bodies—may entrust ourselves to this nature—to this " life "—with great confidence. Though science leaves us in the lurch at many points, though she, fickle as a modern parliamentarian, laughs to-day at what she yesterday taught as everlasting truth, let this not lead us astray ; what we require for life, we shall certainly learn. On the whole science is a splendid but somewhat dangerous friend ; she is a great juggler and easily leads the mind astray into wild sentimentality ; science and art are like the steeds attached to Plato's car of the soul ; " sound common sense " (whose loss Professor Virchow lamented) proves its worth not least of all in pulling the reins tight and not permitting these noble animals to bolt with its natural, sound judgment. The very fact that we are living beings gives us an infinitely rich and unfailing capacity of hitting upon the right thing, even without learning, wherever it is necessary. Whoever simply and with open mind questions nature— the " mother " as the old myths called her—can be sure of being answered, as a mother answers her son, not always in blameless logic, but correctly in the main, intelligibly and with a sure instinct for the best interests of the son. So is it, too, in regard to the question of the significance of race : one of the most vital, perhaps the most vital, questions that can confront man.

IMPORTANCE OF RACE

Nothing is so convincing as the consciousness of the possession of Race. The man who belongs to a distinct, pure race, never loses the sense of it. The guardian angel of his lineage is ever at his side, supporting him where he loses his foothold, warning him like the Socratic Daemon where he is in danger of going astray, compelling obedience, and forcing him to undertakings which, deeming them impossible, he would never have dared to attempt. Weak and erring like all that is human, a man of this stamp recognises himself, as others recognise him, by the sureness of his character, and by the fact that his actions are marked by a certain simple and peculiar greatness, which finds its explanation in his distinctly typical and super-personal qualities. Race lifts a man above himself : it endows him with extraordinary—I might almost say supernatural—powers, so entirely does it distinguish him from the individual who springs from the chaotic jumble of peoples drawn from all parts of the world : and should this man of pure origin be perchance gifted above his fellows, then the fact of Race strengthens and elevates him on every hand, and he becomes a genius towering over the rest of mankind, not because he has been thrown upon the earth like a flaming meteor by a freak of nature, but because he soars heavenward like some strong and stately tree, nourished by thousands and thousands of roots—no solitary individual, but the living sum of untold souls striving for the same goal. He who has eyes to see at once detects Race in animals. It shows itself in the whole habit of the beast, and proclaims itself in a hundred peculiarities which defy analysis : nay more, it proves itself by achievements, for its possession invariably leads to something excessive and out of the common—even to that which is exaggerated and not free from bias. Goethe's dictum, " only that which is extravagant (*überschwänglich*) makes greatness," is well known.* That is the very quality which a thoroughbred race reared from superior materials bestows upon its individual descendants—something " extravagant "—and, indeed, what we learn from every race-horse, every thoroughbred fox-terrier, every Cochin China fowl, is the very lesson which the history of mankind so eloquently teaches us ! Is not the Greek in the fulness of his glory an unparalleled example of this " extravagance " ? And do we not see this " extravagance " first make its appearance when immigration from the North has ceased, and the various strong breeds of men, isolated on the peninsula once for all, begin to fuse into a new race, brighter and more brilliant, where, as in Athens, the racial blood flows from many sources— simpler and more resisting where, as in Lacedæmon, even this mixture of blood had been barred out. Is the race not as it were extinguished, as soon as fate wrests the land from its proud exclusiveness and incorporates it in a greater whole ? † Does not Rome teach us the same

* *Materialien zur Geschichte der Farbenlehre*, the part dealing with Newton's personality.

† It is well known that it was but gradually extinguished, and that in spite of a political situation, which must assuredly have brought speedy destruction on everything Hellenic, had not race qualities here had a decisive influence. Till late in the Christian era Athens remained the centre of intellectual life for mankind ; Alexandria was more talked of, the strong Semitic contingent saw to that ; but any one who wished to study in earnest travelled to Athens, till Christian narrow-mindedness for ever closed the schools there in the year 529, and we learn that as late as this even the man of the people was distinguished in Athens " by the liveliness of his intellect, the correctness of his language and the sureness of his taste " (Gibbon,

lesson ? Has not in this case also a special mixture of blood produced an absolutely new race,* similar in qualities and capacities to no later one, endowed with exuberant power ? And does not victory in this case effect what disaster did in that, but only much more quickly ? Like a cataract the stream of strange blood overflooded the almost depopulated Rome and at once the Romans ceased to be. Would one small tribe from among all the Semites have become a world-embracing power had it not made " purity of race " its inflexible fundamental law ? In days when so much nonsense is talked concerning this question, let Disraeli teach us that the whole significance of Judaism lies in its purity of race, that this alone gives it power and duration, and just as it has outlived the people of antiquity, so, thanks to its knowledge of this law of nature, will it outlive the constantly mingling races of to-day.†

What is the use of detailed scientific investigations as to whether there are distinguishable races ? whether race has a worth ? how this is possible ? and so on. We turn the tables and say : it is evident that there are such races : it is a fact of direct experience that the quality of the race is of vital importance ; your province is only to find out the how and the wherefore, not to deny the facts themselves in order to indulge your ignorance. One of the greatest ethnologists of the present day,

chap. xl.). There is in George Finlay's book, *Mediæval Greece*, chap. i., a complete and very interesting and clear account of the gradual destruction of the Hellenic race by foreign immigration. One after the other colonies of Roman soldiers from all parts of the Empire, then Celts, Teutonic peoples, Slavonians, Bulgarians, Wallachians, Albanesians, &c., had moved into the country and mixed with the original population. The Zaconians, who were numerous even in the fifteenth century, but have now almost died out, are said to be the only pure Hellenes.

  * *Cf.* p. 109, note.

  † *See* the novels *Tancred* and *Coningsby*. In the latter Sidonia says : " Race is everything ; there is no other truth. And every race must fall which carelessly suffers its blood to become mixed."

Adolf Bastian, testifies that, "what we see in history is not a transformation, a passing of one race into another, but entirely new and perfect creations, which the ever-youthful productivity of nature sends forth from the invisible realm of Hades." * Whoever travels the short distance between Calais and Dover, feels almost as if he had reached a different planet, so great is the difference between the English and French, despite their many points of relationship. The observer can also see from this instance the value of purer " inbreeding." England is practically cut off by its insular position : the last (not very extensive) invasion took place 800 years ago ; since then only a few thousands from the Netherlands, and later a few thousand Huguenots have crossed over (all of the same origin), and thus has been reared that race which at the present moment is unquestionably the strongest in Europe.†

Direct experience, however, offers us a series of quite different observations on race, all of which may gradually contribute to the extension of our knowledge as well as to its definiteness. In contrast to the new, growing, Anglo-Saxon race, look, for instance, at the Sephardim, the so-called " Spanish Jews " ; here we find how a genuine race can by purity keep itself noble for centuries and tens of centuries, but at the same time how very necessary it is to distinguish between the nobly reared portions of a nation and the rest. In England, Holland and Italy there are still genuine Sephardim but very few, since

---

* *Das Beständige in den Menschenrassen und die Spielweite ihrer Veränderlichkeit*, 1868, p. 26.

† Mention should also be made of Japan, where likewise a felicitous crossing and afterwards insular isolation have contributed to the production of a very remarkable race, much stronger and (within the Mongoloid sphere of possibility) much more profoundly endowed than most Europeans imagine. Perhaps the only books in which one gets to know the Japanese soul are those of Lafcadio Hearn : *Kokoro, Hints and Echoes of Japanese Inner Life ; Gleanings in Buddha Fields*, and others.

they can scarcely any longer avoid crossing with the Ashkenazim (the so-called "German Jews"). Thus, for example, the Montefiores of the present generation have all without exception married German Jewesses. But every one who has travelled in the East of Europe, where the genuine Sephardim still as far as possible avoid all intercourse with German Jews, for whom they have an almost comical repugnance, will agree with me when I say that it is only when one sees these men and has intercourse with them that one begins to comprehend the significance of Judaism in the history of the world. This is nobility in the fullest sense of the word, genuine nobility of race! Beautiful figures, noble heads, dignity in speech and bearing. The type is Semitic in the same sense as that of certain noble Syrians and Arabs. That out of the midst of such people Prophets and Psalmists could arise—that I understood at the first glance, which I honestly confess that I had never succeeded in doing when I gazed, however carefully, on the many hundred young Jews—"Bochers"—of the Friedrichstrasse in Berlin. When we study the Sacred Books of the Jews we see further that the conversion of this monopolytheistic people to the ever sublime (though according to our ideas mechanical and materialistic) conception of a true cosmic monotheism was not the work of the community, but of a mere fraction of the people; indeed this minority had to wage a continuous warfare against the majority, and was compelled to enforce the acceptance of its more exalted view of life by means of the highest Power to which man is heir, the might of personality. As for the rest of the people, unless the Prophets were guilty of gross exaggeration, they convey the impression of a singularly vulgar crowd, devoid of every higher aim, the rich hard and unbelieving, the poor fickle and ever possessed by the longing to throw themselves into the arms of the wretchedest and filthiest idolatry. The course of Jewish history has provided for a peculiar artificial selection of the morally higher section : by banishments, by continual withdrawals to the Diaspora —a result of the poverty and oppressed condition of the land—only the most faithful (of the better classes) remained behind, and these abhorred every marriage contract—even with Jews !—in which both parties could not show an absolutely pure descent from one of the tribes of Israel and prove their strict orthodoxy beyond all doubt.* There remained then no great choice ; for the nearest neighbours, the Samaritans, were heterodox, and in the remoter parts of the land, except in the case of the Levites who kept apart, the population was to a large extent much mixed. In this way race was here pro- duced. And when at last the final dispersion of the Jews came, all or almost all of these sole genuine Jews were taken to Spain. The shrewd Romans in fact knew well how to draw distinctions, and so they removed these dangerous fanatics, these proud men, whose very glance made the masses obey, from their Eastern home to the farthest West,† while, on the other hand, they did not disturb the Jewish people outside of the narrower Judea more than the Jews of the Diaspora.‡—Here, again, we have a most interesting object-lesson on the origin and worth of " race " ! For of all the men whom we are wont to characterise as Jews, relatively few are descended from these great genuine Hebrews, they are rather the descendants of the Jews of the Diaspora,

* Natural children are not at all taken into the community by orthodox Jews. Among the Sephardim of East Europe to-day, a girl who is known to have gone wrong is immediately taken by the pleni- potentiaries of the community to a strange land and provided for there ; neither she nor her child can venture ever to let anything be heard of them, they are regarded as dead. Thus they provide against blind love introducing strange blood into the tribe.

† See Graetz, as above, chap. ix., on The Period of the Diaspora.

‡ In Tiberias, for example, there was a Rabbi's school which for centuries set the fashion. (Regarding the ennobling of the Sephardim by Gothic blood, see below.)

Jews who did not take part in the last great struggles, who, indeed, to some extent did not even live through the Maccabean age; these and the poor country people who were left behind in Palestine, and who later in Christian ages were banished or fled, are the ancestors of "our Jews" of to-day. Now whoever wishes to see with his own eyes what noble race is, and what it is not, should send for the poorest of the Sephardim from Salonici or Sarajevo (great wealth is very rare among them, for they are men of stainless honour) and put him side by side with any Ashkenazim financier; then will he perceive the difference between the nobility which race bestows and that conferred by a monarch.*

THE FIVE CARDINAL LAWS

It would be easy to multiply examples. But I think that we now have all the material that is necessary for a systematic analysis of our knowledge regarding race, from which we may then derive the cardinal principles of a conscious and appropriate judgment. We are not reasoning from hypothetical conditions in the remote past to possible results, but arguing from sure facts back to their direct causes. The inequality of gifts even in what are manifestly related races is evident; it is, moreover, equally evident to every one who observes more closely that here and there, for a shorter or a longer time, one tribe does not only distinguish itself from the

* The Goths, who in a later age went over to Mohammedanism in great crowds, and became its noblest and most fanatical protagonists, are said to have at an earlier period adopted Judaism in great numbers, and a learned specialist of Vienna University assures me that the moral and intellectual as well as the physical superiority of the so-called "Spanish" and "Portuguese" Jews is to be explained rather by this rich influx of Teutonic blood than by that breeding which I have singled out to emphasise, and the importance of which he too would not incline to underestimate. Whether this view is justifiable or not may remain an open question.

others, but is easily pre-eminent among them because there is something beyond the common in its gifts and capabilities. That this is due to racial breeding I have tried to illustrate graphically by the preceding examples. The results deducible from these examples (and they can be multiplied to any extent) enable us to affirm that the origin of such noble races is dependent upon five natural laws.

(1) The first and fundamental condition is undoubtedly the presence of excellent material. Where there is nothing, the king has no rights. But if I am asked, Whence comes this material ? I must answer, I know not, I am as ignorant in this matter as if I were the greatest of all scholars and I refer the questioner to the words of the great world-seer of the nineteenth century, Goethe, " What no longer originates, we cannot conceive as originating. What has originated we do not comprehend." As far back as our glance can reach, we see human beings, we see that they differ essentially in their gifts and that some show more vigorous powers of growth than others. Only one thing can be asserted without leaving the basis of historical observation : a high state of excellence is only attained gradually and under particular circumstances, it is only forced activity that can bring it about ; under other circumstances it may completely degenerate. The struggle which means destruction for the fundamentally weak race steels the strong ; the same struggle, moreover, by eliminating the weaker elements, tends still further to strengthen the strong. Around the childhood of great races, as we observe, even in the case of the metaphysical Indians, the storm of war always rages.

(2) But the presence of excellent human material is not enough to give birth to the " extravagant " ; such races as the Greeks, the Romans, the Franks, the Swabians, the Italians and Spaniards in the period of their splendour,

the Moors, the English, such abnormal phenomena as the Aryan Indians and the Jews only spring from continued inbreeding. They arise and they pass away before our eyes. Inbreeding means the producing of descendants exclusively in the circle of the related tribesmen, with the avoidance of all foreign mixture of blood. Of this I have already given striking examples.

(3) But inbreeding *pur et simple* does not suffice : along with it there must be selection, or, as the specialists say, "artificial selection." We understand this law best when we study the principles of artificial breeding in the animal and vegetable worlds ; I should recommend every one to do so, for there are few things which so enrich our conceptions of the plastic possibilities of life.* When one has come to understand what miracles are performed by selection, how a racehorse or a Dachshund or a choice chrysanthemum is gradually produced by the careful elimination of everything that is of indifferent quality, one will recognise that the same phenomenon is found in the human race, although of course it can never be seen with the same clearness and definiteness as in the other spheres. I have already advanced the example of the Jews ; the exposure of weak infants is another point and was in any case one of the most beneficial laws of the Greeks, Romans and Teutonic peoples ; hard times, which only the strong man and the hardy woman can survive, have a similar effect.†

(4) There is another fundamental law hitherto little heeded, which seems to me quite clear from history, just as it is a fact of experience in the breeding of animals :

* The literature is very great : for simplicity, comprehensibility and many-sidedness I recommend to every layman especially Darwin's *Animals and Plants under Domestication*. In the *Origin of Species* the same subject is treated rather briefly and with too much bias.

† Jhering demonstrates with particular clearness that the epoch of the migrations, which lasted for many centuries, necessarily had upon the Teutonic peoples the effect of an ever more and more ennobling artificial selection (*Vorgeschichte*, p. 462 f.).

the origin of extraordinary races is, without exception, preceded by a mixture of blood. As that acute thinker, Emerson, says : " we are piqued with pure descent, but nature loves inoculation." Of the Aryan Indians of course we can say nothing as regards this, their previous history being hidden in the misty distance of time ; on the other hand, with regard to the Jews, Hellenes and Romans the facts are perfectly clear, and they are no less so in regard to all the nations of Europe which have distinguished themselves by their national achievements and by the production of a great number of individuals of " extravagant " endowments.   With regard to the Jews I refer the reader to the following chapter, as regards the Hellenes, Romans and English I have often pointed to this fact ; * nevertheless, I would urge the reader not to grudge the labour of carefully reading in Curtius and Mommsen those chapters at the beginning which, on account of the many names and the confusion of detail, are usually rather glanced through than studied.   There has never been so thorough and successful a mixture as in Greece : with the old common stock as basis there have gradually sprung up in the valleys, separated by mountains or seas, characteristically different tribes, composed here of huntsmen, there of peaceful farmers, in other parts of seafarers, &c. ; among these differentiated elements we find a mixing and crossing, so fine that a human brain selecting artificially could not have reasoned the matter out more perfectly.   In the first place we have migrations from East to West, later from West to East over the Ægean Sea ; in the meantime, however, the tribes of the extreme North (in the first place the Dorians) advanced to the extreme South, forcing many of the noblest who would not submit to bondage from the South to that North from which they themselves had just come, or over the sea to

* *See* especially pp. 109, 272, 286 and 293.

the islands and the Hellenic coast of Asia. But every one
of these shiftings meant mixture of blood. Thus, for
example, the Dorians did not all move to the Peloponnese,
portions of them remained at every stopping-place in their
slow wanderings and there fused with the former population. Indeed, these same original Dorians, whose special
unity is such an apparent characteristic, knew in the old
times that they were composed of three different stems,
one of which moreover was called " Pamphyle," that is,
" the stem of people of various descent." The most
exuberant talent showed itself where the crossing had been
happiest—in New Ionia and in Attica. In New Ionia
" Greeks came to Greeks, Ionians returned to their old
home, but they came so transformed that from the
new union of what was originally related, a thoroughly
national development, much improved, rich, and in
its results absolutely new, began in the old Ionian land."
But most instructive is the history of the development
of the Attic and particularly of the Athenian people.
In Attica (just as in Arcadia, but nowhere else) the
original Pelasgic population remained ; it " was never
driven out by the power of the stranger." But the
coastland that belonged to the Archipelago invited
immigration ; and this came from every side ; and
while the alien Phœnicians only founded commercial
stations on the neighbouring islands, the related Greeks
pressed on into the interior from this side and that
side of the sea, and gradually mingled with the former
inhabitants. Now came the time of the already mentioned Dorian migrations and the great and lasting
changes ; Attica alone was spared ; and thither fled
many from all directions, from Bœotia, Achæa, Mes-
senia, Argos and Ægina, &c. ; but these new immi-
grants did not represent whole populations ; in the
great majority of cases they were chosen men, men of
illustrious, often of royal birth. By their influx the one

small land became exceptionally rich in genuine, pure nobility. Then and then only, that is, after a varied crossing, arose that Athens to which humanity owes a greater debt than could ever be reckoned up.*—The least reflection will show that the same law holds good in the case of Germans, French, Italians and Spaniards. The individual Teutonic tribes, for example, are like purely brutal forces of nature, till they begin to mingle with one another; consider how Burgundy, which is rich in great men, owes its peculiar population to a thorough crossing of the Teutonic and the Romance elements, and develops its characteristic individuality by long-continued political isolation; † the Franks grow to their full strength and give the world a new type of humanity where they mingle with the Teutonic tribes who preceded them and with Gallo-Romans, or where they, as in Franconia, form the exact point of union of the most diverse German and Slavonic elements; Swabia, the home of Mozart and Schiller, is inhabited by a half-Celtic race; Saxony, which has given Germany so many of its greatest men, contains a population quickened almost throughout by a mixture of Slavonic blood; and has not Europe seen within the last three centuries how a nation of recent origin—Prussia—in which the

---

* See Curtius: *Griechische Geschichte*, i. 4, and ii. 1 and 2. Count Gobineau asserts that the extraordinary intellectual and above all artistic talent of the Greeks is to be explained by an infiltration of Semitic blood: this shows to what senseless views one is forced by fundamental hypotheses which are false, artificial and contrary to history and natural observation.

† This thorough crossing was caused by the fact that the Burgundians settled individually over the whole land and each of them became the " hospes " of a former inhabitant, of whose cultivated land he received two-thirds, and of his buildings and garden a half, while woods and pastures remained common property. Now though there might not be much sympathy between the new-comer and the old possessor, yet they lived side by side and were solidly united in disputes about boundaries and such-like questions of property; thus crossing could not be long deferred. (*Cf.* especially Savigny, *Geschichte des römischen Rechts im Mittelalter*, chap. v. div. 1.)

mixture of blood was still more thorough, has raised
itself by its pre-eminent power to become the leader of
the whole German Empire ?—It cannot of course be my
task to give a detailed proof of what is here simply pointed
out ; but as I am advocating especially the great importance of purely-bred races, I desire particularly to
emphasise the necessity, or at least the advantage, of
mixture of blood and that not merely to meet the objection of one-sidedness and bias *a priori*, but because it
is my conviction that the advocates of this theory have
injured it very much by disregarding the important
law of crossing. They get then to the mystical conception of a race pure in itself, which is an airy abstraction that retards instead of furthering. Neither history
nor experimental biology has anything to say for such
a view. The race of English thoroughbreds has been
produced by the crossing of Arabian stallions with
ordinary, but of course specially chosen, English mares,
followed by inbreeding, yet in such a way that later
crossing between varieties not far removed, or even with
Arabians, is advisable from time to time ; one of the
noblest creatures that nature possesses, the so-called
" genuine " Newfoundland dog, originated from the
crossing of the Eskimo dog and a French hound ; in
consequence of the isolated position of Newfoundland,
it became by constant inbreeding fixed and " pure,"
it was then brought to Europe by fanciers and raised to
the highest perfection by artificial selection.—Many of
my readers may be amused at my constant references to
the breeding of animals. But it is certain that the laws
of life are great simple laws, embracing and moulding
everything that lives ; we have no reason to look upon
the human race as an exception ; and as we are unfortunately not in a position to make experiments in this
matter with human beings, we must seek counsel from the
experiments made with plants and animals —But I cannot

close my discussion of the fourth law without emphasising another side of this law of crossing ; continued inbreeding within a narrow circle, what one might call " close breeding," leads in time to degeneration and particularly to sterility. Countless experiences in animal breeding prove that. Sometimes in such a case a single crossing, applied, for example, only to single members of a pack of hounds, will suffice to strengthen the weakened race and restore its productivity. In the case of men the attraction of Passion provides sufficiently for this quickening, so that it is only in the highest circles of the nobility and in some royal houses * that we observe increasing mental and physical degeneration in consequence of " close breeding."†

The slightest increase of remoteness in the degree of relationship of those marrying (even within the strict limits of the same type) suffices to give all the great advantages of inbreeding and to prevent its disadvantages. Surely it is manifest that here we have the revelation of a mysterious Law of Life, a Law of Life so urgent that in the vegetable kingdom—where fructification within one and the same blossom seems at the first glance the natural and unavoidable thing—there are in most cases the most complicated arrangements to hinder this and at the same time to see that the pollen, when not borne by the wind, is carried by insects from the one individual flower to the other.‡ When we perceive

---

* *See* the facts in Haeckel: *Natürliche Schöpfungsgeschichte* (lect. 8). Still more detail in a book by P. Jacoby, which I have unfortunately not before me, his *Études sur la sélection dans ses rapports avec l'hérédité chez l'homme.*

† In this connection too we have the well-known evil results of marriage between near relatives : the organs of sense (in fact the whole nervous system) and the sexual organs suffer most frequently from this. (*See* George H. Darwin's lectures, *Die Ehen zwischen Geschwisterkindern und ihre Folgen*, Leipzig, 1876.)

‡ I should recommend the large number of people who unfortunately still keep aloof from natural science, to read carefully Christian Konrad Sprengel's *Das entdeckte Geheimnis der Natur im Bau und in der Befrucht-*

what is so evidently a fundamental law of nature, we
are led to suppose that it is not by mere chance that
pre-eminent races have sprung from an original fusing
of different stems, such as we have observed in history ;
the historical facts rather provide still further proof for
the view that mixture of blood supplies particularly
favourable physiological conditions for the origin of
noble races.*

(5) A fifth law must also be mentioned, although it is
restrictive and explanatory rather than contributive of
any new element to the question of race. Only quite
definite, limited mixtures of blood contribute towards
the ennoblement of a race, or, it may be, the origin of a
new one. Here again the clearest and least ambiguous
examples are furnished by animal breeding. The mixture
of blood must be strictly limited as regards time, and
it must, in addition, be appropriate ; not all and any
crossings, but only definite ones can form the basis of
ennoblement. By time-limitation I mean that the
influx of new blood must take place as quickly as possible
and then cease ; continual crossing ruins the strongest
race. To take an extreme example, the most famous

ung der Blumen, 1793. The whole German nation ought to be proud of
this work : since 1893 there has been a facsimile reprint of it (Mayer and
Müller, Berlin) and it can be read by any layman. Of more recent publications Hermann Müller's *Alpenblumen, ihre Befruchtung durch Insekten
und ihre Anpassungen an dieselben* (Engelmann, 1881) is specially
stimulating, clear by reason of the many illustrations, and complete.
A summary account, which includes plants other than European, is
found in the same author's *Blumen und Insekten* in Trewendt's
Encyklopädie der Naturwissenschaften. There are certainly few speculations that introduce us so directly to the most mysterious wonders
of nature as this revelation of the mutual relations of the plant and
animal worlds. What are all our knowledge and hypotheses in comparison with such phenomena ? They teach us to observe faithfully
and to be satisfied with the circle of things attainable. (During the
printing of this book Knuth's *Handbuch der Blütenbiologie*, published
by Engelmann, began to appear.)

* For this question of the mixture of blood indispensable to the
origin of pre-eminently gifted races Reibmayr's book, *Inzucht und
Vermischung beim Menschen*, 1897, should be consulted.

pack of greyhounds in England was crossed once only
with bulldogs, whereby it gained in courage and endurance,
but further experiments prove that when such a crossing
is continued, the characters of both races disappear and
quite characterless mongrels remain behind.* *Crossing
obliterates characters.* The limitation to definitely appropriate crossings means that only certain crossings,
not all, ennoble. There are crossings which, far from
having an ennobling influence, ruin both races, and
moreover, it frequently happens that the definite, valuable
characters of two different types cannot fuse at all ;
in the latter case some of the descendants take after
the one parent, others after the other, but naturally
with mingled characteristics, or again, genuine real
mongrels may appear, creatures whose bodies give the
impression of being screwed together from parts that do
not fit, and whose intellectual qualities correspond exactly
to the physical.† Here too it should be remarked that
the union of mongrel with mongrel brings about with
startling rapidity the total destruction of all and every
pre-eminent quality of race. It is therefore an entirely
mistaken idea that mixture of blood between different
stems invariably ennobles the race, and adds new qualities
to the old. It does so only with the strictest limitations
and under rare and definite conditions ; as a rule mixture
of blood leads to degeneration. One thing is perfectly
clear : that the crossing of two very different types
contributes to the formation of a noble race only when
it takes place very seldom and is followed by strict
inbreeding (as in the case of the English thoroughbred
and the Newfoundland dog) ; in all other cases crossing
is a success only when it takes place between those closely
related, *i.e.*, between those that belong to the same funda-

---

* Darwin, *Animals and Plants*, chap. xv.
† For this too there are numerous examples in Darwin. As regards
dogs in particular, examples will occur to every one.

mental type.—Here too no one who knows the detailed results of animal breeding can doubt that the history of mankind before us and around us obeys the same law. Naturally, it does not appear with the same clearness in the one case as in the other; we are not in a position to shut in a number of human beings and make experiments with them for several generations; moreover, while the horse excels in swiftness, the dog in remarkable and plastic flexibility of body, man excels in mind: here all his vigour is concentrated, here too, therefore, is concentrated all his variability, and it is just these differences in character and intelligence that are not visible to the eye.* But history has carried out experiments on a large scale, and every one whose eye is not blinded by details, but has learned to survey great complexes, every one who studies the soul-life of nations, will discover any amount of proofs of the law here mentioned. While, for example, the "extravagantly" gifted Attics and the uniquely shrewd and strong Roman race are produced by the fusion of several stems, they are nevertheless nearly related and noble, pure stems, and these elements are then, by the formation of States, isolated for centuries, so that they have time to amalgamate into a new solid unity; when, on the other hand, these States are thrown open to every stranger, the race is ruined, in Athens slowly, because owing to the political situation there was not much to get there, and the mixing in consequence only took place gradually

---

* We must, however, not overlook the fact that, if we could make experiments in breeding with men, very great differences in physique also could certainly be achieved in regard to size, hair, proportions, &c. Place a dwarf from the primeval forest of the Middle Congo, little more than 3 feet high, the whole body covered with hair, beside a Prussian Grenadier of the Guards: one will see what plastic possibilities slumber in the human body.—As far as the dog is concerned, we must remember also that the various breeds "certainly originate from more than one wild species" (Claus, *Zoologie*, 4th edit. ii. 458); hence its almost alarming polymorphism.

and then for the most part with Indo-European peoples,* in Rome with frightful rapidity, after Marius and Sulla had, by murdering the flower of the genuine Roman youth, dammed the source of noble blood and at the same time, by the freeing of slaves, brought into the nation perfect floods of African and Asiatic blood, thus transforming Rome into the *cloaca gentium*, the trysting-place of all the mongrels of the world.† We observe the same on all sides. We see the English race arising out of a mutual fusion of separated but closely related Teutonic tribes ; the Norman invasion provides in this case the last brilliant touch ; on the other hand, geographical and historical conditions have so wrought that the somewhat more distantly related Celts remained by themselves, and even to-day only gradually mingle with the ruling race. How manifestly stimulating and refreshing, even to the present day, is the influence of the immigration of French Huguenots into Berlin ! They were alien enough to enrich the life there with new elements and related enough to produce with their Prussian hosts not " mongrels that seem screwed together " but men of strong character and rare gifts. To see the opposite, we need only look over to South America. Where is there a more pitiful sight than that of the mestizo States there ? The so-called savages of Central Australia lead a much more harmonious, dignified and, let us say, more " holy " life than these unhappy Peruvians, Paraguayans, &c., mongrels from two and often more than two incongruous races, from two cultures

---

* It is very instructive to observe, on the other hand, that the Hellenes in Ionia, who were subject to every kind of mongrel crossing, disappeared much more quickly.

† Long before me Gibbon had recognised the physical degeneration of the Roman race as the cause of the decline of the Roman Empire ; now that is more fully demonstrated by O. Seeck in his *Geschichte der Unterganges der antiken Welt*. It was only the immigration of the vigorous Teutonic peoples that kept the chaotic empire artificially alive for a few centuries longer.

with nothing in common, from two stages of development, too different in age and form to be able to form a marriage union—children of an unnatural incest. Any one who earnestly desires to know what race signifies can learn much from the example of these States ; let him but consult the statistics, he will find the most different relations between the pure European or pure Indian population and the half-caste, and he will see that relative degeneration goes exactly hand in hand with the mixture of blood. I take the two extreme examples, Chile and Peru. In Chile, the only one of these States * that can make a modest claim to true culture and that can also point to comparatively well-ordered political conditions, about 30 per cent. of the inhabitants are still of pure Spanish origin, and this third is sufficient to check moral disintegration.† On the other hand, in Peru, which, as is well known, gave the first example to the other republics of a total moral and material bankruptcy, there are almost no Europeans of pure race left ; with the exception of the still uncivilised Indians in the interior the whole population consists of Cholos, Musties, Fusties, Tercerones, Quarterones, &c., crossings between Indians and Spaniards, between Indians and Negroes, Spaniards and Negroes, further between the different races and those mestizos or crosses of the mestizo species among each other ; in recent years many thousands of Chinese have been added . . . here we see the promiscuity longed for by Ratzel and Virchow in progress, and we observe what the result is ! Of course it is an extreme example, but all the more instructive. If the enormous force of surrounding civilisation did not artificially support such a State on all sides, if by any chance it were isolated and left to itself, it would in a short time fall a prey to total

* In Portugese Brazil the conditions are essentially different.
† According to Albrecht Wirth, *Volkstum und Weltmacht in der Geschichte*, 1901, p. 159, the Chilians also derive advantage from the fact that their Indians—the Araucani—are of particularly noble race.

barbarism—not human, but bestial barbarism. All these
States are moving towards a similar fate.*—Here too I
leave it to the reader to think over the matter and to
collect evidence with regard to this fifth law, which shows
us that every crossing is a dangerous matter and can
only help to ennoble the race when definite conditions
are observed, as also that many possible crossings are
absolutely detrimental and destructive ; once the eyes
of the reader are opened, he will find everywhere both
in the past and in the present proofs of this law as well as
of the other four.†

These then are the five principles which seem to me
to be fundamental : the quality of the material, inbreeding, artificial selection, the necessity of crossings,
the necessity of strictly limiting these crossings both in
respect of choice and of time. From these principles
we further deduce the conclusion that the origin of a
very noble human race depends among other things
upon definite historical and geographical conditions ;
it is these that unconsciously bring about the ennobling
of the original material, the in-breeding and the artificial
selection, it is these too—when a happy star shines over
the birthplace of a new people—that produce happy
tribal marriages and prevent the prostitution of the noble
in the arms of the ignoble. The fact that there was a
time in the nineteenth century when learned investigators,
with Buckle at their head, could assert that geographical
conditions produced the races, we may now appropriately

---

* As is well known, very similar conditions prevail in the Spanish
colonies. The island of Porto Rico forms the sole exception : here the
native Caribbees were exterminated, and the result is a pure Indo-
European population, distinguished for industry, shrewdness and love
of order : a striking example of the significance of race !

† In his book *Altersklassen und Männerb nde* (p. 23), Heinrich Schurtz
comes to the conclusion that, " Successful crossings are possible and
advantageous only within a certain sphere of relationship. If the
relationship is too close, really near blood-relationship, sickly tendencies
are not counterbalanced but increased ; if it is too remote, no felicitous
mixing of the qualities is possible."

mention with the scant honour of a paraleipsis ; for that
doctrine is a blow in the face of all history and all observation. On the other hand, every single one of the
laws enumerated, and in addition the examples of Rome,
Greece, England, Judea and South America in particular,
let us see so clearly in how far the historical and geographical conditions not only contribute to the origin
and the decline of a race but are actually decisive factors
therein, that I can refrain from further discussion of the
matter.*

OTHER INFLUENCES

Is the question of race now exhausted ? Far from it !
These biological problems are remarkably complex.
They embrace, for example, the still so mysterious subject
of heredity, in regard to the fundamental principles of which
the most important specialists are more at variance every
day.† Besides, many other circumstances which profounder
study reveals would have to be taken into account.
Nature is in fact inexhaustible ; however deep we sink
the plummet, we never reach the bottom. Whoever
would make a study of these matters must not, for
example, overlook the fact that small numbers of foreign
elements are wont in a short time to be entirely absorbed
by a strong race, but that there is, as the chemists say, a
definite capacity, a definite power of absorption, beyond

* If, for example, the climate of Attica had been the decisive thing,
as is often asserted, it would be impossible to understand why the
genius of its inhabitants was produced only under certain racial conditions and disappeared for ever with the removal of these conditions ;
on the other hand, the importance of the geographical and historical
conditions becomes quite clear, when we observe that they isolated
Attica for centuries from the ceaseless changes brought about by the
migrations, but at the same time contributed to the influx of a
select, noble population from different but related tribes, which mingled
to form a new race.

† The reader will find an interesting summary of the different
opinions of modern times in Friedrich Rohde's *Entstehung und Vererbung
individueller Eigenschaften,* 1895.

which a loss of the purity of the blood, revealed by the diminution of the characteristic qualities, is involved. We have an instance of this in Italy, where the proudly passionate and brilliant families of strong Teutons, who had kept their blood pure till the fourteenth century, later gradually mingled with absolutely mongrel Italians and Italiots and so entirely disappeared (*see* chaps. vi. and ix.): *crossing obliterates characters*. The careful observer will further notice that in crossings between human stems, which are not closely related, the relative generative power is a factor which can prevail after centuries and gradually bring about the decline of the nobler portion of a mixed people, because in fact this generative power often stands in inverse relation to the nobility of the race.* In Europe at the present day we

* Professor August Forel, the well-known psychiatrist, has made interesting studies in the United States and the West Indian islands, on the victory of intellectually inferior races over higher ones because of their greater virility. "Though the brain of the negro is weaker than that of the white, yet his generative power and the predominance of his qualities in the descendants are all greater than those of the whites. The white race isolates itself (therefore) from them more and more strictly, not only in sexual but in all relations, because it has at last recognised that crossing means its own destruction." Forel shows by numerous examples how impossible it is for the negro to assimilate our civilisation more than skin-deep, and how so soon as he is left to himself he everywhere degenerates into the "most absolute primitive African savagery." (For more detail on this subject, *see* the interesting book of Hesketh Pritchard, *Where Black rules White*, Hayti, 1900; any one who has been reared on phrases of the equality of mankind, &c., will shudder when he learns how matters really stand so soon as the blacks in a State get the upper hand.) And Forel, who as scientist is educated in the dogma of the one, everywhere equal, humanity, comes to the conclusion: "Even for their own good the blacks must be treated as what they are, an absolutely subordinate, inferior, lower type of men, incapable themselves of culture. That must once for all be clearly and openly stated." (*See* the account of his journey in Harden's *Zukunft*, February 17, 1900.)—For this question of race-crossings and the constant victory of the inferior race over the superior, *see also* the work of Ferdinand Hueppe, which is equally rich in facts and perceptions, *Über die modernen Kolonisationsbestrebungen und die Anpassungsmöglichkeit der Europäer an die Tropen* (*Berliner klinische Wochenschrift*, 1901). In Australia, for example, a process of sifting is quietly but very quickly going on, whereby the tall

have an example of this : the short round skulls are constantly increasing in numbers and so gradually superseding the narrow " dolichocephali," of which, according to the unanimous testimony of excavated tombs, almost the whole of the genuine old Teutonic, Slavonic and Celtic races consisted ; in this we see the growing predominance of an alien race which had been conquered by the Indo-Teutonic (to-day it is mostly called " Turanic "), and which by animal force gradually overpowers the mentally superior race.* In this connection too perhaps should be mentioned the peculiar fact that dark eyes are becoming so much more prevalent than grey and blue, because in marriages between people with differently coloured eyes the dark are almost without exception much more frequently represented in the descendants than the light.†

If I were minded to follow up this argument it would land us in one of the thorniest branches of modern science. This, however, is absolutely unnecessary for my purpose. Without troubling myself about any definition, I have given a picture of Race as it is exhibited in the individual character, in the mighty achievements of genius, in the most brilliant pages of the history of man : in the next

fair Teuton—so strongly represented in the English blood—is disappearing, while the added element of the *homo alpinus* is gaining the upper hand.

* There is a clear and simple summary in Johannes Ranke, *Der Mensch*, ii. 296 ff. The discussion of all these questions in Topinard's *L'Anthropologie*, Part II., is more thorough, but for that reason much more difficult to follow. It is remarkable that the latter only uses the word " race " to denote a hypothetical entity, the actual existence of which at any time cannot be proved. *Il n'y a plus de races pures.* Who seeks to prove that there ever were any in this *a priori* sense of anthropological presuppositions ? Pure animal races are obtained only by breeding and on the fundamental basis of crossing ; why should the opposite hold of men ?—Besides, this whole " Turanic " hypothesis is, like all these things, still very much of an airy abstraction. *See* further details in chap. vi.

† Alphonse de Candolle : *Histoire des Sciences et des Savants depuis deux Siècles*, 2e éd., p. 576.

place I have called attention to the most important conditions which scientific observation has pointed out as laying the foundation for the origin of noble races. That the introduction of contrary conditions must be followed by degeneration, or at any rate by the retarding of the development of noble qualities, seems to be in the highest degree probable, and might be proved in many ways by reference both to the past and the present. I have purposely exercised caution and self-restraint. In such labyrinthine tangles the narrowest path is the safest. The only task which I have proposed to myself has been to call into being a really vivid representation of what Race is, of what it has meant for mankind in the past and still means in the present.

THE NATION

There is one point which I have not expressly formulated, but it is self-evident from all that I have said; the conception of Race has nothing in it unless we take it in the narrowest and not in the widest sense : if we follow the usual custom and use the word to denote far remote hypothetical races, it ends by becoming little more than a colourless synonym for " mankind "— possibly including the long-tailed and short-tailed apes : Race only has a meaning when it relates to the experiences of the past and the events of the present.

Here we begin to understand what nation signifies for race. It is almost always the nation, as a political structure, that creates the conditions for the formation of race or at least leads to the highest and most individual activities of race. Wherever, as in India, nations are not formed, the stock of strength that has been gathered by race decays. But the confusion which prevails with regard to the idea of race hinders even the most learned from understanding this great significance of

nations, whereby they are at the same time prevented
from understanding the fundamental facts of history.
For, in fact, what is it that our historians to-day teach
us concerning the relation of race to nation ?

I take up any book by chance—Renan's discourse, *What
is a Nation?* In hundreds of others we find the same
doctrines. The thesis is clearly formulated by Renan :
" The fact of race," he writes, " originally of decisive
importance, loses significance every day." * On what
does he base this assertion ? By pointing to the fact that
the most capable nations of Europe are of mixed blood.
What a mass of delusive conclusions this one sentence
contains, what incapacity to be taught by what is evident
to the eye ! Nature and history do not furnish a single
example of pre-eminently noble races with individual
physiognomies, which were not produced by crossing :
and now we are to believe that a nation of such distinct
individuality as the English does not represent a race,
because it originated from a mixture of Anglo-Saxon,
Danish and Norman blood (stems moreover that were
closely related) ! I am to deny the clearest evidence
which shows me that the Englishman is at least as markedly
unique a being as the Greek and the Roman of the most
brilliant epochs, and that in favour of an arbitrary,
eternally indemonstrable abstraction, in favour of the
presupposed, original " pure race." Two pages before,
Renan himself had stated on the basis of anthropological
discoveries that among the oldest Aryans, Semites,
Turanians (*les groupes aryen primitif, sémitique primitif,
touranien primitif*) one finds men of very different build
of body, some with long, others with short skulls, so
that they too had possessed no common " physiological
unity." What delusions will not arise, as soon as man
seeks for supposed " origins " ! Again and again I must

---

* Renan : *Discours et Conférences*, 3e éd., p. 297, " Le fait de la
race, capital à l'origine, va donc toujours perdant de son importance."

quote Goethe's great remark : " Animated inquiry into
cause does infinite harm." Instead of taking the given
fact, the discoverable as it is, and contenting ourselves
with the knowledge of the nearest, demonstrable conditions, we ever and again fancy we must start from
absolutely hypothetical causes and suppositions lying as
far back as possible, and to these we sacrifice without
hesitation that which is present and beyond doubt. That
is what our " empiricists " are like. That they do not see
further than their own noses, we gladly believe from their
own confession, but unfortunately they do not see even so
far, but run up against solid facts and complain then about
the said facts, not about their own shortsightedness.
What kind of thing is this originally " physiologically
uniform race " of which Renan speaks ? Probably a
near relation of Haeckel's human apes. And in favour
of this hypothetical beast I am to deny that the English
people, the Prussians, the Spaniards have a definite and
absolutely individual character ! Renan misses physiological unity : does he not comprehend that physiological
unity is brought about by marriage ? Who then tells him
that the hypothetical aboriginal Aryans were not also the
result of gradual development ? We know nothing about
it : but what we do know entitles us to suppose it from
analogy. There were among them narrow heads and
broad ones : who knows but this crossing was necessary
to produce one very noble race ? The common English
horse and the Arabian horse (which doubtless was produced originally by some crossing) were also " physiologically " very different, and yet from their union was
produced in the course of time the most physiologically
uniform and noblest race of animals in the world, the
English thoroughbred. Now the great scholar Renan
sees the English human thoroughbred, so to speak, arising
before his eyes : the ages of history are before him. What
does he deduce therefrom ? He says : since the English-

man of to-day is neither the Celt of Cæsar's time nor the
Anglo-Saxon of Hengist, nor the Dane of Knut, nor the
Norman of the Conqueror, but the outcome of a crossing
of all four, one cannot speak of an English race at all.
That is to say because the English race, like every other
race of which we have any knowledge, has grown historically, because it is something peculiar and absolutely
new, therefore it does not exist !   In truth, nothing beats
the logic of the scholar !

> Was ihr nicht rechnet
> Glaubt ihr, sei nicht wahr.*

Our opinion concerning the importance of nationality in
the formation of race must be quite different.   The Roman
Empire in the imperial period was the materialisation of
the anti-national principle ; this principle led to racelessness and simultaneously to intellectual and moral
chaos ; mankind was only rescued from this chaos by
the more and more decisive development of the opposite or national principle.†   Political nationality has
not always played the same *rôle* in the production of
individual races as it has in our modern culture ; I
need only refer to India, Greece and the Israelites ;
but the problem was nowhere solved so beautifully,
successfully and as it appears so lastingly, as by the
Teutonic peoples.   As though conjured up out of the soil
there arose in this small corner of Europe a number of
absolutely new, differentiated national organisms.   Renan
is of opinion that race existed only in the old " polis,"
because it was only there that the numerical limitation
had permitted community of blood ; this is absolutely
false ; one need only reckon back a few centuries, and
every one has a hundred thousand ancestors ; what, therefore, in the narrow circle of Athens took place in a com-

---

* What you do not reckon,
  You fancy, is not true.

† This forms the subject of the eighth chapter (vol. ii.)¿

paratively short time, namely, the physiological union, took place in our case in the course of several centuries and is still continued. Race formation, far from decreasing in our nations, must daily increase. The longer a definite group of countries remains politically united, the closer does the "physiological unity" which is demanded become, and the more quickly and thoroughly does it assimilate strange elements. Our anthropologists and historians simply presuppose that in their hypothetical primitive races the specific distinguishing characteristics were highly developed, but that they are now progressively decreasing; there is consequently, they aver, a movement from original complexity to increasing simplicity. This supposition is contrary to all experience, which rather teaches us that individualisation is a result of growing differentiation and separation. The whole science of biology contradicts the supposition that an organic creature first appears with clearly marked characteristics, which then gradually disappear; it actually forces us to the very opposite hypothesis that the early human race was a variable, comparatively colourless aggregate, from which the individual types have developed with increasing divergence and increasingly distinct individuality; a hypothesis which all history confirms. The sound and normal evolution of man is therefore not from race to racelessness but on the contrary from racelessness to ever clearer distinctness of race. The enrichment of life by new individualities seems everywhere to be one of the highest laws of inscrutable nature. Now here in the case of man the nation plays a most important part, because it almost always brings about crossing, followed by inbreeding. All Europe proves this. Renan shows how many Slavs have united with the Teutonic peoples, and asks somewhat sneeringly whether we have any right to call the Germans of to-day "Teutonic": well, we need not quarrel about names in such a case—what the Germans are to-day Renan has been able to learn in the year 1870; he has been taught it too by the German specialists, to whose industry he owes nine-tenths of his knowledge. That is the valuable result of the creation of race by nation-building. And since race is not a mere word, but an organic living thing, it follows as a matter of course that it never remains stationary; it is ennobled or it degenerates, it develops in this or that direction and lets this or that quality decay. This is a law of all individual life. But the firm national union is the surest protection against going astray: it signifies common memory, common hope, common intellectual nourishment; it fixes firmly the existing bond of blood and impels us to make it ever closer.

THE HERO

Just as important as the clear comprehension of the organic relation of race to nation is that of the organic relation of race to its quintessence, the hero or genius. We are apt to fancy we must choose between hero-worship and the opposite. But the one as well as the other testifies to poverty of insight. What I have said in the general introduction need not be repeated; but here, where the question of race is in the forefront, this problem takes a particularly clear form, and with some power of intuition we must surely perceive that the influence of intellectually pre-eminent units in a race, like the human, the individuality of which depends upon the development of its intellectual faculties, is immeasurable, for good and for evil; these units are the feet that carry and the hands that mould, they are the countenance on which we others gaze, they are the eye which beholds the rest of the world in a definite way and then commu nicates what it has seen to the rest of the organism.

But they are produced by the whole corporation ; they can arise only from its vital action, only in it and from it do they gain importance. What is the use of the hand if it does not grow out of a strong arm as part and parcel of it ?   What is the use of the eye if the radiant forms which it has seen are not reflected in a dark, almost amorphous brain mass lying behind it ?   Phenomena only gain significance when they are united to other phenomena.   The richer the blood that courses invisibly through the veins, the more luxuriant will be the blossoms of life that spring forth. The assertion that Homer created Greece is indeed literally true, but remains onesided and misleading as long as we do not add : only an incomparable people, only a quite definite, ennobled race could produce this man, only a race in which the seeing and shaping eye had been "extravagantly" developed.* Without Homer Greece would not have become Greece, without the Hellenes Homer would never have been born.   It was the same race which gave birth to the great seer of forms that produced the inventive seer of figures, Euclid, the lynx-eyed arranger of ideas, Aristotle, the man who first perceived the system of the cosmos, Aristarchus, and so on ad infinitum. Nature is not so simple as scholastic wisdom fancies : if great personality is our " most precious gift," communal greatness is the only soil on which it can grow. It is the whole race, for instance, that creates the language, and therewith at the same time definite artistic, philosophical, religious, in fact even practical possibilities, but also insuperable limitations.   No philosopher could ever arise on Hebrew soil, because the spirit of the Hebrew language makes the interpretation of metaphysical thoughts absolutely impossible ; for the same reason no Semitic people could possess a mythology in the same sense

---

* Any one who wants to gain a vivid conception of the extraordinary strength of these races, capable of serving as basis for a Homer, should read the description of the strongholds of Tiryns and Mycenæ from the Atridean time, as they still stand to-day after tens of centuries,

as the Indians and the Teutonic peoples. One sees what
definite paths are marked out even for the greatest men
by the common achievements of the whole race.* But
it is not a question of language alone. Homer had to find
the myths in existence in order to be able to mould them
into shape ; Shakespeare put upon the stage the history
which the English people had made ; Bach and Beethoven spring from races which had attracted the attention
of the ancients by their singing. And Mohammed ?
Could he have made the Arabs a world-power, had they
not as one of the purest bred races in the world possessed
definite " extravagant " qualities ? But for the new
Prussian race, could the Great Elector have begun, the
Great Frederick have extended, and the Great William
have completed the structure which is now United
Germany ?

The Raceless Chaos

The first task set us in this chapter is now fulfilled ;
we have got a clear concrete idea of what race is and what
it signifies for mankind ; we have seen too, from some
examples of the present time, how fatal the absence of
race, that is, the chaos of unindividualised, speciesless
human agglomerates, is. Any one who perceives this and
ponders over it will gradually realise what it signifies for
our Teutonic culture that the inherited culture of antiquity,
which at important points still not only forms the foundations but also the walls of the structure, was not transmitted to us by a definite people but by a nationless
mixture without physiognomy, in which mongrels held
the whip-hand, namely, by the racial chaos of the decaying
Roman Empire. Our whole intellectual development
is still under the curse of this unfortunate intermediate

* According to Renan (*Israël*, i. 102) the Hebrew language is
utterly incapable of expressing a philosophical thought, a mythological
conception, the feeling of the Infinite, the emotions of the human soul
or even pure observation of nature.

stage; it is this that supplied weapons to the anti-national, anti-racial powers even in the nineteenth century.

Even before Julius Cæsar, the Chaos begins to appear; through Caracalla it is elevated to the official principle of the Roman Empire.* Throughout the whole extent of the Empire there was thorough mixing of blood, but in such a way that real bastardising, that is, the crossing of unrelated or of noble and ignoble races occurred almost wholly in the most southern and eastern parts, where the Semites met the Indo-Europeans—that is to say, in the capitals Rome and Constantinople, along the whole north coast of Africa (as well as on the coasts of Spain and Gaul), above all in Egypt, Syria and Asia Minor.

It is as easy as it is important to form an idea of the area of this complicated geographical condition. The Danube and the Rhine almost meet at their source. The two river-districts fit so closely into each other that there is, it is said, in the neighbourhood of the Albula Pass a small lake, which when there is high water flows on the one side into the Albula and the Rhine, on the other into the Inn and the Danube. Now if we follow the courses of these rivers, up the Rhine from the mouth of the old Rhine near Leyden and down the Danube till it falls into the Black Sea, we get an unbroken line crossing the Continent from north-west to south-east; this, roughly speaking, forms the northern boundary of the Roman Empire for a long period of time; except in parts of Dacia (the Roumania of to-day) the Romans never asserted themselves for long north and east of this line.†

* *See* p. 124.

† The Roman fortified boundary did indeed include a considerable portion north of the Danube and east of the Rhine, because the *limes* branched off westwards above Regensberg, came near Stuttgart, then north again till it met the Maine west of Würzburg. But this tithe-land, as it was called, was not colonised by Italians, but, as Tacitus tells us, by "the most fickle of the Gauls" (*Cf.* Wietersheim, *Völkerwanderung*, i. 161 ff.).

This line divides Europe (if we include the African and Asian possessions of Rome) into two almost equal parts. In the south the great transfusion of blood (as the doctors call the injecting of strange blood into an organism) took place.   If Maspero in his history of the peoples of the Classical East entitles one volume " The First Chaos of Races," then we may well speak here of a second chaos. In Britain, in Rhetia, in the extreme north of Gaul, &c., it seems indeed that in spite of the Roman sway there was no thorough fusion ; in the rest of Gaul too, as well as in Spain, the newly imported elements from Rome had at least several centuries of comparative isolation to mingle with the former inhabitants before other elements came, a circumstance which rendered possible the formation of a new and very characteristic race, the Gallo-Roman.   In the south-east, on the other hand, and especially in all centres of culture (which, as already pointed out, all lay in the south and the east), there was a medley all the more fundamentally pernicious in that those who came in streams from the Levant were themselves nothing but half-castes.   For example, we must not imagine that the Syrians of that time were a definite nation, a people, a race : they were rather a motley agglomeration of pseudo-Hittite, pseudo-Semitic,   pseudo-Hellenic,   pseudo-Persian,   pseudo-Scythian mongrels.   What the French call *un charme troublant*—superficial cleverness combined with a peculiar sort of beauty—is often the characteristic of the half-caste ; one can observe this daily at the present day in cities like Vienna, where people of all nations meet ; but the peculiar unsteadiness, the small power of resistance, the want of character, in short, the moral degeneracy of these people is equally marked.   I name the Syrian because I prefer examples to wordy enumerations ; he was the very pattern of the bastard sundered from all national relationship, and for that very reason, up to the time of the Teutonic invasion, and even later, he played a leading part. We find Syrians upon the imperial throne ; Caracalla belongs to them, and Heliogabalus, that monster robed in silk and gold, tricked out like a dancing girl, was imported direct from Syria ; we find them in all administrative offices and prefectures ; they, like their counterpart, the African mongrels, have great influence in the codification of the Law and an absolute casting-vote in the constitution of the universal Roman Church. Let us look more closely at one of these men ; we shall in that way gain a lively picture of the civilised fraction of the Empire of that day with its pushing culture-mongers, and at the same time obtain an insight into the soul of the Chaos of Peoples.

LUCIAN

Every one, I fancy, knows the author Lucian, at least by name ; his exceptional talents force him upon our notice. Born on the banks of the Euphrates, not far from the first spurs of the Tauric mountain range (in which energetic races of Indo-European descent still lived), in addition to the Syrian *patois*, the boy begins to learn to murder Greek. Having shown a talent for drawing and sculpture he is apprenticed to a sculptor, but only after a family council has been held to decide how the boy may as speedily as possible make a fortune. During his whole life, in spite of the amount of his subsequent wealth, this desire for money remains the guiding star—no, that is too fine an expression—the driving impulse of this gifted Syrian ; in his *Nigrinus* he admits with enviable frankness that money and fame are the things dearest to him in the world, and even as an old man he writes expressly, that he accepts the high official position offered by the Gladiator-Emperor Commodus for the sake of the money. But in art he makes no progress. In a famous book *The Dream*,* which, however, as far as I know, is not appreciated according to its true purport by any historian, Lucian tells us why he gave up art and preferred to become a jurist and belles-lettrist. In a dream two women had appeared to him : the one " looked like work," had hard hands, her dress covered over and over with plaster ; the other was elegantly dressed and stood calmly there ; the one was Art, the other—he who does not know will never guess, the other was—Culture.† Poor Art tries to inspire her new disciple with zeal by the example of Phidias and Polycletus, of Myron and Praxiteles, but in vain ; for Culture proves convincingly that Art is an " ignoble occupation " ; that the artist remains the whole day bent over his work in a dirty smockfrock, like a slave ; even Phidias was only " a common workman," who " lived from the toil of his hands " ; whoever, on the other hand, chooses Culture instead of Art, has the prospect of riches and high offices, and when he goes for a walk in the street, the people will nudge each other and say, " See, there goes that famous man ! " ‡ Quickly making up his mind Lucian sprang to his feet ; " I left the ugly toilsome life and went over to Culture." To-day sculptor, to-morrow advocate ; he who is born without a definite calling can choose any ; § whoever seeks gold and fame does not need to look aloft and runs no risk of falling into the well, like the hero of the German fairy

---

* Not to be confused with the *Dream of the Shoemaker Micyllus*!

† Greek word παιδεία German *Bildung ;* so the best translators. It is not a question of the education of children, and "Science" would imply too much. The possible objection that the first woman does not introduce herself as "Art" simply, but as the "Art of cutting Hermæ" may be met by the rejoinder that later she is described as τέχνη and that the appeal to Phidias and other artists admits no doubt about the intention.

‡ The faint echo we have heard in the nineteenth century : "When the best names are named, mine too will be mentioned" (Heine).

§ *Cf.* p. 242.

tale. Do not imagine that *The Dream* is a satire ; Lucian gave it as a lecture in his native town, when he visited it later, honoured and wealthy ; he himself tells us that he set up his life as an example to the youth of Samosata. Such men, otherwise so clever, never understand what a bitter satire their fate is on the life of the really great ; how otherwise could a Heine have placed himself on the same plane as a Goethe ? Lucian had chosen Culture, and to acquire it he went to Antioch. Athens was indeed still the great high school of knowledge and taste, but was considered old-fashioned ; Syrian Antioch and the so-called " Hellenic " Ephesus, which nevertheless was even in the second century thoroughly saturated with alien elements, offered much greater attractions to the cosmopolitan youth of the Roman Empire. There Lucian studied law and eloquence. But to him as an intelligent man the abuse of the Greek language by his teachers was painful ; he guessed the value of a pure style and moved to Athens. It is characteristic that he ventured after a short spell of study to appear there as advocate and orator ; in the meantime he had learned everything, except propriety ; the Athenians taught him this, they laughed at the " barbarian " with his pedantic tags of strange culture and thereby gave him a valuable hint ; he disappeared to a place where taste was not so indispensable, to Marseilles. This seaport of the Phœnician Diaspora had just received by the arrival of thousands of Jews from Palestine such a clearly marked character that it was simply called " the city of the Jews " ; but Gauls, Romans, Spaniards, Ligurians, all conceivable races met there. Here, in New Athens, as the inhabitants, with a delicate recognition of their own intellectual worth, called it, Lucian lived for many years and became a rich man ; he gave up the profession of advocate, for which he would have needed to learn Latin thoroughly ; besides, there was great competition, and even in Antioch he had not had great success

as a pleader; what these mushroom plutocrats chiefly
wanted was Culture, modern Culture and rules of etiquette. Had not "Culture" been Lucian's ideal, his
dream? Had he not studied in Antioch and "spoken
openly" even in Athens? Accordingly he gave lectures;
but the listeners did not laugh at him, as in Athens, but
paid any entrance fee that he cared to ask. Besides, he
travelled over all Gaul as professional orator, at that time
a very profitable business: to-day commemorating the
virtues of a dead person, whom he had never seen in life,
to-morrow taking part in the celebration of a religious
festival that was given in honour of some local Gallo-
Roman divinity, whose name a Syrian could not even
pronounce. Any one who wishes to get an idea of this
oratory should look at the *Florida* of Apuleius, a contemporary but African mestizo; * this is a collection of
shorter and longer oratorical passages written for effect,
to be put into any speech whatever, in order that the
audience might think it a sudden inspiration, and be
startled and carried away by the great knowledge, wit
and pathos of the orator; there it is all in stock; the
profound, the pointed, the clever anecdote, the devoutly
submissive, the proud claims of freedom, even the
excuse for being unprepared and the thanks for the
statues that might be offered to the orator as a surprise!
Just such things are pictures of a man and not of a man
only, but of a whole Culture or, to use Lucian's word,
of a whole παιδεία. Any one who has seen Prince
Bismarck in one of his great speeches struggling to
express himself will understand what I mean.—When
forty years of age Lucian turned his back on Gaul; to
settle in a definite place, to link his life perpetually
with that of any country never occurs to him; besides

---

* Apuleius boasts expressly of his mixed origin. He too studied
in Syria and Egypt and travelled in Greece, hence had practically
the same educational course as Lucian.

there were no nations; if Lucian returns for a short
visit to his native place it is not from heartlonging
but, as he himself honestly confesses, to show his rich
garments to those who knew him when poor.* Then
he settles in Athens for a considerable period, but keeps
silent this time and industriously studies philosophy
and science in the honest endeavour to find at last what
lies concealed behind this lauded Hellenic culture.
That this man, who for twenty years had taught " Hellenic culture " and gained riches and honour from it,
suddenly notices that he never understood even the
elements of this culture, is an almost pathetic trait
and a proof of exceptional gifts. For that reason I
have chosen him in particular. In his writings one finds,
alongside of puns and many good jokes and in addition
to fine narrative, many a sharp and sometimes pathetic
remark. But what could be the result of this study ?
Little or nothing. We men are not pieces in a game
of draughts; there was just as little possibility of
becoming a different person by learned instruction in
Athens as there is to-day of becoming a " beautiful
personality " in Berlin, as Professor Virchow hopes from
the influence of the University there—if one is not
already such at matriculation. With nothing is a man's
knowledge so intimately bound up as with his Being, in
other words, with his definite individuality, his definite
organisation. Plato expressed the opinion that knowledge
was remembrance; modern biology gives the word
a slightly different interpretation but agrees with the
philosopher. In a perfectly significant sense we can say
that each man can only know, what he is. Lucian himself

* The *Fliegende Blätter* of 1896 has a picture which shows
a Counsellor of Commerce and his wife just entering their
carriage :
  " *She :* Where shall we drive to to-day ?
  " *He :* Of course through the town ; to make the people envy us ! "
That is exactly the same stage of culture.

felt that all that he had learned and taught hitherto was mere tinsel—matters of fact, not the soul from which these facts grow : the covering but without the body, the shell but without the kernel.   And when at last he understood this and broke the shell, what did he find ?   Nothing. Of course nothing   Nature has first to produce the kernel, the shell is a later accrescence ; the body must be born before it can be clothed ; the hero's heart must beat before heroic deeds can be achieved.   The only kernel Lucian could find was himself ; as soon as he tore from his body the rags of Roman Law and Hellenic poetry, he revealed a clever Syrian mestizo, a bastard born of fifty unrecorded crossings, the man who, with the unerring instinct of youth, had despised Phidias as a workman, and had chosen the career that with the least possible trouble would earn for him most money and the applause of the vulgar herd.   All the philologists in the world may assure me that Lucian's remarks about religion and philosophy are profound, that he was a daring opponent of superstition, &c., I shall never believe it.   Lucian was utterly incapable of knowing what religion and philosophy are.   In many of his writings he enumerates all possible " systems " one after another ; for example, in *Icaromenippus*, in the *Selling of Philosophical Characters*, &c. ; it is always only the most superficial element that he comprehends, the formal motive power, without which the utterance of a thought is not possible, but which in truth must not be confused with the thought itself.   So, too, in regard to religion.   Aristophanes had scoffed as Voltaire did in later days ; but the satire of both these men had its origin in a positive, constructive thought, and everywhere one sees the flash of fanatical love for the people of the homeland, for the firm, definite, related community, which embraced and supported each one of them with its traditions, its faith and its great men ; Lucian, on the other hand, scoffs like Heine,* he has no noble aim, no profound conviction, no thorough understanding ; he drifts about aimlessly like a wreck on the ocean, nowhere at home, not without noble impulses, but without any definite object to which he might devote himself, learned, but yet one of those monsters of learning who, Calderon says,

know everything and understand nothing.

But one thing he understood and therein lies for us his whole importance as a writer ; he understood the spirit that he resembled, namely, the totally bastardised, depraved and degenerate world around him ; he pictures it and scourges it, as only one who himself belonged to it could, one who knew its motives and methods from his own experience. Here the kernel was not lacking. Hence his delightful satires on the Homeric critics, on the learned professions which were rotten to the core, on religious swindlers, on puffed-up, rude and ignorant millionaires, on medical quacks, &c. Here his talent and his knowledge of the world together contributed to the accomplishment of great things.—And in order that my description may not be incomplete, I may add that the second stay in Athens, if it did not teach Lucian the meaning of mythology, or of metaphysics, or of the heroic character, yet became for him a new source of money-making. Here he turned his attention industriously to authorship, wrote his *Conversations of the Gods*, his *Conversations of the Dead*, in all probability most of his best things. He invented a light form of dialogue (for which he gave himself the title of " Prometheus the author " !) ; at bottom they are good feuilletons, of the kind which the philistine to this day likes to read in

* The one fault in this second comparison is that Heine did belong to a definite people and in consequence possessed a more definite physiognomy.

the morning with his coffee. They brought him in considerable sums of money, when he began to travel again and delivered them in public as lectures. But this fashion also passed, or perhaps with age he had tired of a vagabond life. He discarded the one legacy, Hellenic art and philosophy, and turned to the other—Roman Law; he became State Advocate (as some say) or President of the Court (as others say) in Egypt and died in this office.

I think that a single career such as this shows us, more clearly than many a learned exposition, what the mental chaos was, which at that time lay sheltered beneath the uniform mantle of the tyrannical Roman Empire. We cannot say of a man like Lucian that he was immoral; no, what we learn from such an example is that morality and arbitrariness are two contradictory ideas. Men who do not inherit definite ideals with their blood are neither moral nor immoral, they are simply " without morals." If I may be allowed to use a current phrase to explain my meaning, I should say they are neither good nor bad, equally they are neither beautiful nor ugly, deep nor shallow. The individual in fact cannot make for himself an ideal of life and a moral law; these very things can only exist as a gradual growth. For this reason it was very wise of Lucian, in spite of his talent, to give up in time his idea of emulating Phidias. He could become an orator for the Massillians, and a President of Court for the Egyptians, even, if you will, a feuilletonist for all time, but an artist or a thinker never.

AUGUSTINE

We may be met by the objection that out of the old Chaos of Peoples there arose men of great importance, whose influence has made itself felt upon succeeding generations, until this day, in a far more penetrating sense. This presents no difficulty for the irrefutable acceptance of the importance of race to humanity. In the midst of a chaos single individuals may still be of perfectly pure race, or they may at least belong principally to one definite race. Such a man, for example, as Ambrosius must surely be of genuine, noble descent, of that strong race which had made Rome great; I cannot indeed prove it, for in the confusion of those times history is unable to furnish exact information as to the pedigree of any man of importance. At the same time no one can prove the contrary, so the personality of the individual must decide the question. Moreover, it must not be overlooked that, unless crossing without plan or method goes on with wild recklessness, the qualities of a dominant race will remain conspicuous for generations, though maybe in a much weakened condition, and that they are capable of flashing up again as atavism in single individuals. The breeding of animals furnishes numerous examples of this. Take a piece of paper and sketch a genealogical tree; we shall see that, as soon as we go back only four generations, an individual has already thirty ancestors, whose blood flows in his veins. If we now suppose two races A and B, such a table will clearly show how very different the hybridisation in the case of a crossing of peoples must be, from the full hybrid directly composed of A and B to the individual of whose sixteen ancestors only one was a hybrid. Besides, experience daily teaches us that exceptionally gifted and beautiful human beings are frequently produced by crossing; it is, however, as I have said, not a question of the individual only, but of his relation to other individuals, to a uniform complex; if this single mongrel enters into a definite race-centre, he may have a very quickening effect upon it; if he falls among a mere heap of beings, he is, like Lucian, only a stick among sticks, not a branch on a living tree. The immeasurable power of ideas must also be reckoned with. They are indeed misconstrued, mishandled and abused by illegitimate successors—as we saw in the case of pseudo-Roman law and Platonic philosophy—but they continue to have a formative influence. What was it if not the death-agony of the old genuine imperial idea that held together this agglomeration of peoples till the strong Dietrich of Berne came to set them free ? Whence did those men of the chaos derive their thoughts and their religion ? Not from themselves, but only from Jews and Hellenes. And so all that held them together, all upon which their very existence depended, was drawn from the inheritance of noble races. Take any of the greatest men of the chaotic period, for example the venerable Augustine, distinguished alike by temperament and ability. To be unbiased, let us leave our own purely religious standpoint and ask ourselves whether there was not a hopeless chaos in the brain of this eminent man ? In the world of his imagination we find the Jewish belief in Jehovah, the mythology of Greece, Alexandrine Neoplatonism, Romish priestcraft, the Pauline conception of God, and the contemplation of the Crucified Lord, all jumbled together in heterogeneous confusion. Augustine has to reject, in deference to Hebraic materialism, many incomparably loftier religious thoughts —loftier because pure and genuinely racial thoughts— which Origenes held, but at the same time he introduces into theology as predestination the ancient Aryan conception of necessity, whereby the old dogma of all Judaism, the unconditional arbitrariness of will, goes to the wall.*

* Augustine is indeed extremely cautious ; he says, for example, of the prescience of God and the contradictory view, the free will of man : " We embrace both convictions, we confess to both, truly and honestly ; to the one that we may believe rightly, to the other that we may live rightly " (illud, ut bene credamus ; hoc, ut bene vivamus) ; cf. De Civ. Dei, v. 10. With this is closely connected that further question, whether God himself is free or stands under the law ; the intellect inclines clearly in the case of Augustine to

He spends twelve years writing a book against the heathen gods, but himself believes in their existence in so tangible and fetichist a sense as no cultured Greek for a thousand years before him ; he looks upon them in fact as daemons and therefore creations of God ; but one must not, he thinks, regard them as creators (" *immundos spiritus esse et perniciosa daemonia, vel certe creaturas non Creatorem, veritas Christiana convincit* "). In his chief work, *De Civitate Dei*, Augustine disputes in chapter after chapter with his countryman Apuleius regarding the nature of the daemons and other good and bad spirits, endeavouring, if not to deny their existence, at least to reduce them to an unimportant and un-influential element and thus to replace crass super-stition by genuine religion ; nevertheless, he inclines in all earnest to the belief that Apuleius himself was changed by the unguent of the Thessalian witch into an ass, and this is all the more comical to us, because Apuleius, although he wrote a great deal about daemons, never thought of representing this transformation as an actual occurrence when he wrote his novel, *The Metamorphoses or the Golden Ass*.* I cannot of course enter more fully into this matter here, that would take me too far ; it would deserve a whole book to itself ; and yet the detailed characterisa-tion of the intellectual condition of the noble among these sons of the chaos would be the right complement to the sketch of the frivolous Lucian.† We should see

the latter view, his dogmatic creed to the former. Is an action bad because God has forbidden it, or had he to forbid it because it is bad ? In his *Contra Mendacium*, chap. xv., Augustine takes the second alter-native ; in other writings the former.

* This story seems to have been in vogue at the time ; for Lucian too has a *Lucius or the Enchanted Ass*, which looks indeed as if it were translated from fragments of the Apuleian one. Augustine says of the transformation " *aut finxit, aut indicavit*," but he clearly inclines to the latter view.

† The irreconcilable contradictions in the religious thought and feeling of Augustine are fully discussed in the seventh chapter (vol. ii.) and the gap here left is thus to some extent filled.

that everywhere the equilibrium is disturbed. In Lucian
the unfettered intellect is uppermost and lack of moral
strength ruins the finest qualities ; in Augustine, character
wrestles with intellect in a tussle of doubtful issue, and
does not rest until intellect is thrown and put in fetters.

Such were the men who handed down to us the legacy
of antiquity. " We are like shipwrecked sailors thrown
on the shore by the wild breakers," Ambrosius exclaims
in pain. Philosophy and law, ideas of State, freedom,
human dignity passed through their hands ; it was they
who raised to the dignity of acknowledged dogmas
the superstition (belief in daemons, witchcraft, &c.) which
formerly was found only among the most ignorant scum
of the population ; it was they who forged a new religion
out of the most incompatible elements, who gave to the
world the gift of the Roman Church, a kind of changeling
born of the Roman imperial idea ; at the same time it
was they who with the fanaticism of the weak destroyed
everything beautiful belonging to the past on which
they could lay their hands, every memory of great
generations. Hatred and disdain of every great achieve
ment of the pure races were taught ; a Lucian scoffs
at the great thinkers, an Augustine reviles the heroes
of Rome's heroic age, a Tertullian calls Homer " a liar."
As soon as the orthodox emperors—Constantius, Theodosius, and others—ascend the throne (without exceptions
mongrels in race, the great Diocletian being the last
Emperor of pure blood *) the systematic destruction of
all the monuments of antiquity begins. At the same
time is introduced the deliberate lie that is supposed to
further truth : such eminent Church fathers as Hieronymus
and Chrysostomus encourage the *pia fraus*, the pious
deception ; immediately upon this follows the foundation
of the might and right of the Roman see, not by courage
and conquest, but by the colossal forgery of documents.

* *Cf.* also what is said on p. 129 f.

Even so respectable an historian as Eusebius has the simplicity worthy of a better cause to confess that he remodels history wherever he sees the opportunity of furthering " the good cause." In very truth this chaos which arose out of race fusion and the universal craze for anti-nationalism is an appalling spectacle !

ASCETIC DELUSION

Perhaps the fact has never yet been pointed out—1 at least know of no book where it is—that the epidemic of asceticism which broke out at that time was directly connected with the feeling of disgust for that frightful condition of the world ; some would fain see in it an unexampled religious awakening, others a religious disease ; but that is interpreting the facts allegorically, for religion and asceticism are not necessarily connected. Nothing in the example of Christ could encourage asceticism ; the early Christians knew it not ; two hundred years after Christ Tertullian still wrote : " We Christians are not like the Brahmans and Gymnosophists of India, we do not live in forests or in banishment from the society of men : we feel that we owe God the Lord and Creator thanks for everything and we forbid the enjoyment of none of his works ; we only practise moderation in order that we may not enjoy these things more than is good for us or make a bad use of them " (*Apologeticus*, chap. xlii.). Why now did un-Christian asceticism all at once enter into Christianity ? I for my part believe that we have here to deal with physical reasons. Even before the birth of Christ asceticism had taken its rise in the altogether bastardised Syria and Egypt ; wherever blood was most mixed, it had taken a firm hold. Pachomius, the founder of the first Christian cloister, the author of the first monkish rule, is a servant of Serapis from Upper Egypt, who transferred to Christianity

what he had learned in the societies of the fasting and
self-chastising ascetics of Serapis.*   Any one who still
possessed a spark of noble impulse in that world of
the unnational chaos was bound in fact to be disgusted
with himself.   Nowhere, where sound conditions prevailed, has unconditional asceticism been preached ; on
the contrary, the ancient peoples—Aryans, Semites,
Mongolians—led by a marvellous instinct, are at one
in regarding the begetting of children as one of the
most sacred duties ; whoever died without a son was
laden with a curse.   In Ancient India, of course, there were
ascetics ; but they might not disappear into the solitude of
the forest till the son of their son was born ; here the
intention and fundamental idea are almost diametrically
opposed to the asceticism of the Syrian Christians.
To-day we understand this ; for we see that only one
thing contributes to the ennobling of man : the begetting of pure races, the founding of definite nations.   To
beget sons, sons of the right kind, is without question
the most sacred duty of the individual towards society ;
whatever else he may achieve, nothing will have such
a lasting and indelible influence as the contribution to
the increasing ennoblement of the race.   From the
limited, false standpoint of Gobineau it certainly does not
much matter, for we can only decline and fall sooner or
later ; still less correct are they who appear to contradict him, but adopt the same hypothetical acceptation of
aboriginal pure nations ; but any one who understands how
noble races are in reality produced, knows that they can
arise again at any moment ; that depends on us ; here
nature has clearly pointed out to us a great duty.   Those
men of the chaos therefore, who considered begetting a sin,
and complete abstinence therefrom the highest of all
virtues, committed a crime against the most sacred law
of nature, they tried to prevent all good, noble men

* *Cf*: Otto Zöckler :   *skese und Mönchtum*, 1897, i. 193 ff.

and women from leaving descendants, thus promoting the increase of the evil only, which meant of course that they did their best to bring about the deterioration of the human race. A Schopenhauer may joyfully collect from the Church fathers their pronouncements against marriage and see therein a confirmation of his pessimism ; for me the connection is quite different : this sudden horror of the most natural impulses of man, their transformation from the most sacred duty to the most disgraceful sin, has a deeper foundation in those incomprehensible sources of our existence, where the physical and the metaphysical are not yet separated. After wars and pestilences, statistics tell us, births increase to an abnormal degree—nature helps herself ; in that chaos which threatened all culture with eternal destruction, the births had to be retarded as much as possible ; with horror the noble turned away from that world of sin, buried themselves in the deserts or in the caves of the hills, perched themselves on high pillars, chastised themselves and did penance. Childless they passed away.* Even where human society is in a state of disintegration, we see in fact a great connection ; what each man by himself thinks and does always admits of a double interpretation—the subjective or individual, and the objective interpretation in relation to the world at large.

* In the fourth century the Roman Empire numbered hundreds of thousands of monks and nuns. It was not unusual for an abbot to have 10,000 monks in one cloister and in the year 373 the one single Egyptian town Oxyrynchus had 20,000 nuns and 10,000 monks ! Now consider the total numbers of the population of that time, and it will be clear what a great influence this ascetic epidemic must have had upon the non-multiplication of the bastard races. (*See* further details in Lecky's *History of European Morals*, 11th ed. ii. 105 ff.)

SACREDNESS OF PURE RACE

Here we touch upon a deep scientific fact; we are touching upon the revelation of the most important secret of all human history. Every one comprehends that man can in the true sense of the word only become "man" in connection with others. Many, too, have grasped the meaning of Jean Paul's profound remark, which I prefixed as motto to a former chapter, that "only through man does man enter into the light of day"; few, however, have realised the fact that this attainment of manhood—this entry into the light of life—depends in degree upon definite organic conditions, conditions which in old days were observed instinctively and unconsciously, but which, now that owing to the increase of knowledge and the development of thought the impulses of instinct have lost their power, it becomes our duty consciously to recognise and respect. This study of the Roman Chaos of Peoples teaches us that race, and nationality which renders possible the formation of race, possess a significance which is not only physical and intellectual but also moral. Here there is before us something which we can characterise as a sacred law, the sacred law in accordance with which we enter upon the rights and duties of manhood: a "law," since it is found everywhere in nature, "sacred," in so far as it is left to our free will to ennoble ourselves or to degenerate as we please. This law teaches us to look upon the physical constitution as the basis of all that ennobles. For what is the moral apart from the physical? What would a soul be without body? I do not know. If our breast conceals something that is immortal, if we men reach with our thoughts to something transcendent, which we, like the blind, touch with longing hands without ever being able to see it, if our heart is the battlefield between the finite and the infinite, then the constitution of this body—breast, brain, heart—must be of immeasurable consequence. " However the great dark background of things may in truth be constituted, the entrance to it is open to us only in this poor life of ours, and so even our ephemeral actions contain this earnest, deep, and inevitable significance," says Solon in the beautiful dialogue of Heinrich von Stein.* " Only in this life ! " But wherewith do we live if not with our body ? Indeed, we do not need to look forth into any world beyond (which will appear problematic to many people), as Solon does in the passage quoted; the entrance even to this earthly life is solely and only open to us through our body and this life will be for us poor or rich, ugly or beautiful, insipid or precious, according to the constitution of this our one, all-embracing organ of life. I have already shown from examples taken from methodical animal breeding and from human history how race arises and is gradually ennobled, also how it degenerates ; what then is this race if not a collective term for a number of individual bodies ? It is no arbitrary idea, no abstraction ; these individualities are linked with one another by an invisible but absolutely real power resting upon material facts. Of course the race consists of individuals ; but the individual himself can only attain to the full and noblest development of his qualities within definite conditions which are embraced in the word " race." This is based upon a simple law, but it points simultaneously in two directions. All organic nature, vegetable as well as animal, proves that the choice of the two parents is of decisive influence upon the individual that is born ; but besides this it proves that the principle prevailing here is a collective and progressive one, because in the first place a common parent-stock must gradually be formed, from

* *Helden und Welt : dramatische Bilder* (Chemnitz, 1883).

which then, similarly step by step, are produced individuals who are on an average superior to those outside such a union, and among these again numerous individuals with really transcendent qualities. That is a fact of nature, just in the same sense as any other, but here, as in all phenomena of life, we are far from being able to analyse and explain it. Now what must not be lost sight of in the case of the human race is the circumstance that the moral and intellectual qualities are of preponderating importance. That is why in men any want of organic racial consistency, or fitness in the parent stock, means above all things a lack of all moral and intellectual coherence. The man who starts from nowhence reaches nowhither. The individual life is too short to be able to fix the eye on a goal and to reach it. The life of a whole people, too, would be too short if unity of race did not stamp it with a definite, limited character, if the transcendent splendour of many-sided and varying gifts were not concentrated by unity of stem, which permits a gradual ripening, a gradual development in definite directions, and finally enables the most gifted individual to live for a super-individual purpose.

Race, as it arises and maintains itself in space and time, might be compared to the so-called range of power of a magnet. If a magnet be brought near to a heap of iron filings, they assume definite directions, so that a figure is formed with a clearly marked centre, from which lines radiate in all directions ; the nearer we bring the magnet the more distinct and more mathematical does the figure become ; very few pieces have placed themselves in exactly the same direction, but all have united into a practical and at the same time ideal unity by the possession of a common centre, and by the fact that the relative position of each individual to all the others is not arbitrary but obedient to a fixed law. It has ceased to be a heap, it has become a form. In the same way a human race, a genuine nation, is distinguished from a mere congeries of men. The character of the race becoming more and more pronounced by pure breeding is like the approach of the magnet. The individual members of the nation may have ever so different qualities, the direction of their activities may be utterly divergent, yet together they form a moulded unity, and the power—or let us say rather the importance—of every individual is multiplied a thousandfold by his organic connection with countless others.

I have shown above how Lucian with all his gifts absolutely squandered his life; I have shown Augustine helplessly swaying to and fro like a pendulum between the loftiest thoughts and the crassest and silliest superstition : such men as these, cut off from all racial belongings; mongrels among mongrels, are in a position almost as unnatural as a hapless ant, carried and set down ten miles from its own nest. The ant, however, would suffer at least only through outward circumstances, but these men are by their own inner constitution barred from all genuine community of life.

The consideration of these facts teaches us that whatever may be our opinion as to the *causa finalis* of existence, man cannot fulfil his highest destiny as an isolated individual, as a mere exchangeable pawn, but only as a portion of an organic whole, as a member of a specific race.*

THE TEUTONIC PEOPLES

There is no doubt about it ! The raceless and nationless chaos of the late Roman Empire was a pernicious and fatal condition, a sin against nature. Only one ray of light shone over that degenerate world. It came from the north. *Ex septentrione Lux !* If we take up a map, the Europe of the fourth century certainly seems at the

---

* "The individuals and the whole are identical," the Indian thinkers had taught (*see* Garbe's *Sâmkhya-Philosophie*, p. 158).

first glance to be more or less in a state of chaos even north
of the Imperial boundary ; we see quite a number of
races established side by side, incessantly forcing their
way in different directions : the Alemanni, the Marcomanni, the Saxons, the Franks, the Burgundians, the
Goths, the Vandals, the Slavs, the Huns and many others.
But it is only the political relations that are chaotic
there ; the nations are genuine, pure-bred races, men
who carry with them their nobility as their only possession wherever destiny drives them.   In one of the next
chapters I shall have to speak of them.   In the meantime
I should like merely to warn those whose reading is less
wide, against the idea that the " barbarians " suddenly
" broke into " the highly civilised Roman Empire.
This view, which is widespread among the superficially
educated, is just as little in accordance with the facts as
the further view that the " night of the Middle Ages " came
down upon men because of this inroad of the barbarians.

It is this historical lie which veils the annihilating
influence of that nationless time, and which turns into
a destroyer the deliverer, the slayer of the laidly worm.
For centuries the Teutons had been forcing their way
into the Roman Empire, and though they often came
as foes, they ended by becoming the sole principle of
life and of might.   Their gradual penetration into
the Imperium, their gradual rise to a decisive power
had taken place little by little just as their gradual
civilisation had done ; * already in the fourth century
one could count numerous colonies of soldiers from
entirely different Teutonic tribes (Batavians, Franks,
Suevians, &c.) in the whole European extent of the

* Hermann is a Roman cavalier, speaks Latin fluently and has
thoroughly studied the Roman art of administration.   So, too,
most of the Teutonic princes.   Their troops, too, were at home in
the whole Roman empire and so acquainted with the customs of so-
called civilised men, long before they immigrated with all their goods
and chattels into these lands.

Roman Empire ; * in Spain, in Gaul, in Italy, in Thrace, indeed often even in Asia Minor, it is Teutons in the main that finally fight against Teutons. It was Teutonic peoples that so often heroically warded off the Asiatic peril from the Eastern Empire ; it was Teutonic peoples that on the Catalaunian fields saved the Western Empire from being laid waste by the Huns. Early in the third century a bold Gothic shepherd had been already proclaimed Emperor. One need only look at the map of the end of the fifth century to see at once what a uniquely beneficent moulding power had here begun to assert itself. Very noteworthy too is the difference which reveals itself here in a hundred ways, between the innate decency, taste and intuition of rough but pure, noble races and the mental barbarism of civilised mestizos. Theodosius, his tools (the Christian fanatics) and his successors had done their best to destroy the monuments of art ; on the other hand, the first care of Theodoric, the Eastern Goth, was to take strong measures for the protection and restoration of the Roman monuments. This man could not write, to sign his name he had to use a metal stencil, but the Beautiful, which the bastard souls in their "Culture," in their hunting after offices and distinctions, in their greed of gold had passed by unheeded, the Beautiful, which to the nobler souls among the Chaos of Peoples was a hateful work of the devil, the Goth at once knew how to appreciate ; the sculptures of Rome excited his admiration to such a degree that he appointed a special official to protect them. Religious toleration, too, appeared for a time wherever the still unspoiled Teuton became master. Soon also there came upon the scene the great Christian missionaries from the highlands of the north, men who convinced not by means of " pious lies " but by the purity of their hearts.

It is nothing but a false conception of the Middle Ages,

* See Gobineau : *Inequality of the Human Races*, Bk. VI. chap. ·

in conjunction with ignorance as to the significance of
race, which is responsible for the regrettable delusion
that the entry upon the scene of the rough Teutons
meant the falling of a pall of night over Europe. It is
inconceivable that such hallucinations should be so long-
lived. If we wish to know to what lengths the bastard
culture of the Empire might have led, we must study the
history, the science and the literature of the later Byzantium, a study to which our historians are devoting
themselves to-day with a patience worthy of a better
subject. It is a sorry spectacle. The capture of the
Western Roman Empire by the Barbarians, on the
contrary, works like the command of the Bible, " Let there
be Light." It is admitted that its influence was mainly in
the direction of politics rather than of civilisation ; and
a difficult task it was one that is even now not wholly
accomplished. But was it a small matter ? Whence
does Europe draw its physiognomy and its significance—
whence its intellectual and moral preponderance, if not
from the foundation and development of Nations ?
This work was in very truth the redemption from chaos.
If we are something to-day if we may hope perhaps some
day to become something more—we owe it in the first
instance to that political upheaval which, after long
preparation, began in the fifth century, and from which
were born in the fulness of time new noble races, new
beautiful languages, and a new culture entitling us to
nourish the keenest hopes for the future. Dietrich of
Berne, the strong wise man, the unlearned friend of art
and science, the tolerant representative of Freedom of
Conscience in the midst of a world in which Christians
were tearing one another to pieces like hyenas, was as
it were a pledge that Day might once more break upon
this poor earth. In the time of wild struggle that followed, during that fever by means of which alone European humanity could recover and awaken from the hideous

dream of the degenerate curse-laden centuries of a chaos with a veneer of order to a fresh, healthy, stormily pulsing national life—in such a time learning and art and the tinsel of a so-called civilisation might well be almost forgotten, but this, we may swear, did not mean Night, but the breaking of a new Day. It is hard to say what authority the scribblers have for honouring only their own weapons. Our European world is first and foremost the work not of philosophers and book-writers and painters, but of the great Teuton Princes, the work of warriors and statesmen. The progress of development—obviously the political development out of which our modern nations have sprung—is the one fundamental and decisive matter. We must not, however, overlook the fact that to these true and noble men we equally owe everything else that is worth possessing. Every one of those centuries, the seventh, the eighth, the ninth, produced great scholars ; but the men who protected and encouraged them were the Princes. It is the fashion to say that it was the Church that was the saviour of science and of culture ; that is only true in a restricted sense. As I shall show in the next division of the first part of this book, we must not look upon the Early Christian Church as a simple, uniform organism, not even within the limits of the Roman union in Western Europe ; the centralisation and obedience to Rome which we have lived to see to-day, were in earlier centuries absolutely unknown. We must admit that almost all learning and art were the property of the Church ; her cloisters and schools were the retreats and nurseries in which in those rough times peaceful intellectual work sought refuge ; but the entry into the Church as monk or secular priest meant little more than being accepted into a privileged and specially protected class, which imposed upon the favoured individual hardly any return in the way of special duties. Until the thirteenth century every educated man, every teacher and student, every physician and professor of jurisprudence belonged to the clergy : but this was a matter of pure formality, founded exclusively upon certain legal conditions ; and it was out of this very class, that is, out of the men who best knew the Church, that every revolution against her arose—it was the Universities that became the high-schools of national emancipation. The Princes protected the Church, the learned clerics on the contrary attacked her. That is the reason why the Church waged unceasing war against the great intellects which, that they might work in peace, had sought refuge with her ; had she had her way, science and culture would never again have been fledged. But the same Princes who protected the Church also protected the scholars whom she persecuted. No later than the ninth century there arose in the far north (out of the schools of England, which even in those early days were rich in important men) the great Scotus Erigena : the Church did all that she could to extinguish this brilliant light, but Charles the Bald, the same man who was supposed to have sent great tribute to the Pope of Rome, stretched his princely hand over Scotus ; when this became insufficient, Alfred bade him to England where he raised the school of Oxford to a pinnacle of success, till he was stabbed to death by monks at the bidding of the central government of the Church. From the ninth century to the nineteenth, from the murder of Scotus to the issue of the Syllabus, it has been the same story. A final judgment shows the intellectual renaissance to be the work of Race in opposition to the universal Church which knows no Race, the work of the Teuton's thirst for knowledge, of the Teuton's national struggle for freedom. Great men in uninterrupted succession have arisen from the bosom of the Catholic Church ; men to whom, as we must acknowledge, the peculiar catholic order of thought with its all-embracing

greatness, its harmonious structure, its symbolical
wealth and beauty has given birth, making them greater
than they could have become without it; but the Church
of Rome, purely as such, that is to say, as an organised
secular theocracy, has always behaved as the daughter
of the fallen Empire, as the last representative of the
universal, anti-national Principle. Charlemagne by
himself did more for the diffusion of education and
knowledge than all the monks in the world. He caused
a complete collection to be made of the national poetry
of the Teutons. The Church destroyed it. I spoke a
little while ago of Alfred. What Prince of the Church,
what schoolman, ever did so much for the awakening
of new intellectual powers, for the clearing up of living
idioms, for the encouragement of national consciousness
(so necessary at that time), as this one Prince? The
most important recent historian of England has summed
up the personality of this great Teuton in the one sentence: " Alfred was in truth an artist."* Where, in the
Chaos of Peoples, was the man of whom the same could be
said? In those so-called dark centuries the farther we
travel northward, that is to say, the farther from the
focus of a baleful " culture," and the purer the races
with which we meet, the more activity do we find in the
intellectual life. A literature of the noblest character,
side by side with a freedom and order worthy of the
dignity of man, develops itself from the ninth to the
thirteenth century in the far-away republic of Iceland;
in the same way, in remote England, during the seventh,
eighth and ninth centuries we find a true popular poetry
flourishing as it seldom has done since.† The passionate
love of music which then came to light touches us as
though we heard the beating of the wings of a guardian
angel sent down from heaven, an angel heralding the

---

* Green: *History of the English People*, Bk. I. c. iii.
† Olive F. Emerson: *History of the English Language*, p. 54

future. When we hear King Alfred taking part in the songs of his chosen choir—when a century later we see the passionate scholar and statesman Dunstan never, whether on horseback or in the Council Chamber, parted from his harp: then we call to mind the old Grecian legend that Harmonia was the daughter of Ares the God of War. Fighting, in lieu of a sham order, was what our wild ancestors brought with them, but at the same time they brought creative power instead of dreary barrenness. And as a matter of fact in all the more important Princes of that time we find a specially developed power of imagination: they were essentially fashioners. We should be perfectly justified were we to compare what Charlemagne was and did at the end of the eighth and beginning of the ninth centuries, with what Goethe did at the end of the eighteenth and beginning of the nineteenth centuries. Both rode a tilt against the Powers of Chaos, both were artists; both " avowed themselves as belonging to the race which out of darkness is striving to reach the light."

No! and a thousand times no! The annihilation of that monstrosity, a State without a nation, of that empty form, of that soulless congeries of humanity, that union of mongrels bound together only by a community of taxes and superstitions, not by a common origin and a common heart-beat, of that crime against the race of mankind which we have summed up in the definition " Chaos of Peoples "—that does not mean the falling darkness of night, but the salvation of a great inheritance from unworthy hands, the dawn of a new day.

Yet even to this hour we have not succeeded in purging our blood of all the poisons of that Chaos. In wide domains the Chaos ended by retaining the upper hand. Wherever the Teuton had not a sufficient majority physically to dominate the rest of the inhabitants by assimilation, as, for instance, in the south, there the

chaotic element asserted itself more and more. We
have but to look at our present position to see where
power exists and where it is wanting, and how this depends
upon the composition of races. I am not aware whether
any one has already observed with what peculiar exactitude
the modern boundary of the universal Church of Rome
corresponds with what I have pointed out as the general
boundary of the Roman Imperium, and consequently of
the chaotic mongreldom. To the east I admit that the
line does not hold good, because here in Servia, Bosnia,
&c., the Slavonic invaders of the eighth century and the
Bulgarians annihilated everything foreign; in few
districts of modern Europe is Race so uncontaminated,
and the pure Slavs have never accepted the Church of
Rome. In other places too there have been encroach-
ments on both sides of the old boundary-line, but these
have been unimportant, and moreover easily explained
by political relations. On the whole the agreement is
sufficiently striking to give rise to serious thought:
Spain, Italy, Gaul, the Rhenish provinces, and the
countries south of the Danube! It is still morning, and
the powers of darkness are ever stretching out their
polypus arms, clinging to us with their powers of suction
in a hundred places, and trying to drag us back into the
Night out of which we were striving to escape. We can
arrive at a judgment upon these apparently confused,
but really transparent, conditions, not so much by
poring over the details of chronicles, as by obtaining a
clear insight into the fundamental historical facts which
I have set out in this chapter.

FIFTH CHAPTER

THE ENTRANCE OF THE JEWS INTO THE HISTORY OF THE WEST

"Let us forget whence we spring. No more talk of 'German,' or of 'Portuguese' Jews. Though scattered over the earth we are nevertheless a single people."—RABBI SALOMON LIPMANN-CERFBERR in the opening speech delivered on July 26, 1806, at the meeting preparatory to the Synedrium of 1807 which Napoleon called together.

THE JEWISH QUESTION

HAD I been writing a hundred years ago, I should hardly have felt compelled at this point to devote a special chapter to the entrance of the Jews into Western history. Of course the share they had in the rise of Christianity, on account of the peculiar and absolutely un-Aryan spirit which they instilled into it, would have deserved our full attention, as well as also the economic part which they played in all Christian countries; but an occasional mention of these things would have sufficed; anything more would have been superfluous. Herder wrote at that time: " Jewish history takes up more room in our history and more attention than it probably deserves in itself." *   In the meantime, however, a great change has taken place: the Jews play in Europe, ánd wherever European influence extends, a different part to-day from that which they played a hundred years ago; as Viktor Hehn expresses it, we live

* *Von den deutsch-orientalischen Dichtern.* Div. 2.

329

to-day in a "Jewish age"; * we may think what we
like about the past history of the Jews, their present
history actually takes up so much room in our own history
that we cannot possibly refuse to notice them. Herder
in spite of his outspoken humanism had expressed the
opinion that " the Jewish people is and remains in Europe
an Asiatic people alien to our part of the world, bound
to that old law which it received in a distant climate, and
which according to its own confession it cannot do away
with." † Quite correct. But this alien people, everlastingly alien, because—as Herder well remarks—
it is indissolubly bound to an alien law that is hostile
to all other peoples—this alien people has become
precisely in the course of the nineteenth century a dis-
proportionately important and in many spheres actually
dominant constituent of our life. Even a hundred years
ago that same witness had sadly to confess that the
" ruder nations of Europe " were " willing slaves of
Jewish usury "; to-day he could say the same of by far
the greatest part of the civilised world. The possession of
money in itself is, however, of least account ; our govern-
ments, our law, our science, our commerce, our literature,
our art . . . practically all branches of our life have
become more or less willing slaves of the Jews, and drag the
feudal fetter if not yet on two, at least on one leg. In the
meantime the "alien" element emphasised by Herder
has become more and more prominent ; a hundred years
ago it was rather indistinctly and vaguely felt ; now it
has asserted and proved itself, and so forced itself on the
attention of even the most inattentive. The Indo-
European, moved by ideal motives, opened the gates in

* *Gedanken über Goethe*, 3rd ed. p. 40. The passage as it stands
reads, " From the day of Goethe's death, the 22nd March, 1832, Börne
dated the freedom of Germany. In reality, however, one epoch
was with that day closed and the Jewish age in which we live
began."

† *Bekehrung der Juden.* Abschnitt 7 of the *Untersuchungen des
vergangenen Jahrhunderts zur Beförderung eines geistigen Reiches.*

friendship : the Jew rushed in like an enemy, stormed all positions and planted the flag of his, to us, alien nature—I will not say on the ruins, but on the breaches of our genuine individuality.

Are we for that reason to revile the Jews ? That would be as ignoble as it is unworthy and senseless. The Jews deserve admiration, for they have acted with absolute consistency according to the logic and truth of their own individuality, and never for a moment have they allowed themselves to forget the sacredness of physical laws because of foolish humanitarian day-dreams which they shared only when such a policy was to their advantage. Consider with what mastery they use the law of blood to extend their power : the principal stem remains spotless, not a drop of strange blood comes in ; as it stands in the *Thora*, " A bastard shall not enter into the congregation of the Lord ; even to his tenth generation shall he not enter into the congregation of the Lord " (*Deuteronomy* xxiii. 2) ; in the meantime, however, thousands of side branches are cut off and employed to infect the Indo-Europeans with Jewish blood. If that were to go on for a few centuries, there would be in Europe only one single people of pure race, that of the Jews, all the rest would be a herd of pseudo-Hebraic mestizos, a people beyond all doubt degenerate physically, mentally and morally. For even the great friend of the Jews, Ernest Renan, admits, " *Je suis le premier à reconnaître que la race sémitique, comparée à la race indo-européenne, représente réellement une combinaison inférieure de la nature humaine.*" * And in one of his best but unfortunately little-known writings he says again, " *L'épouvantable simplicité de l'esprit sémitique rétrécit le cerveau humain, le ferme à toute idée délicate, à tout sentiment fin, à toute*

---

* *Histoire générale et système comparé des langues sémitiques,* 5ᵉ éd. p. 4. It will make little difference to this view when I show, as I shall do immediately, that the Jews are not pure Semites but half Syrians.

recherche rationelle, pour le mettre en face d'une éternelle tautologie : Dieu est Dieu." ; * and he demonstrates that culture could have no future unless Christian religion should move farther away from the spirit of Judaism and the " Indo-European genius " assert itself more and more in every domain. That mixture then undoubtedly signifies a degeneration : degeneration of the Jew, whose character is much too alien, firm and strong to be quickened and ennobled by Teutonic blood, degeneration of the European who can naturally only lose by crossing with an " inferior type "—or, as I should prefer to say, with so different a type. While the mixture is taking place, the great chief stem of the pure unmixed Jews remains unimpaired. When Napoleon, at the beginning of the nineteenth century, dissatisfied that the Jews, in spite of their emancipation, should remain in proud isolation, angry with them for continuing to devour with their shameful usury the whole of his Alsace, although every career was now open to them, sent an ultimatum to the council of their elders demanding the unreserved fusion of the Jews with the rest of the nation—the delegates of the French Jews adopted all the articles prescribed but one, namely, that which aimed at absolute freedom of marriage with Christians. Their daughters might marry outside the Israelite people, but not their sons ; the dictator of Europe had to yield.† This is the admirable law by which real Judaism was founded. Indeed, the law in its strictest form forbids marriage altogether between Jews and non-Jews ; in *Deuteronomy* vii. 3, we read, " Thy daughter thou shalt not give unto his son nor his daughter shalt thou take unto thy son " ; but, as a rule, emphasis is laid only on the last clause ; for example, in *Exodus*

* *De la part des peuples sémitiques dans l'histoire de la civilisation,* p. 39.
† In the second book I shall find it necessary to give more details concerning this famous synedrium and its casuistic distinction between religious and civil law—a distinction which neither *Talmud* nor *Thora* recognises.

xxxiv. 16, the sons alone are forbidden to take strange daughters, not the daughters to take strange sons, and in *Nehemiah* xiii., after both sides have been forbidden to marry outside the race, only the marriage of a son with a foreign wife is described as a " sin against God." That is also a perfectly correct view. By the marriage of a daughter with a Goy, the purity of the Jewish stem is in no way altered, while this stem thereby gets a footing in the strange camp ; on the other hand, the marriage of a son with a Goya " makes the holy seed common " as the book of *Ezra* ix. 2, drastically expresses it.* The possible conversion of the Goya to Judaism would not help matters : the idea of such a conversion was rightly quite strange to the older law—for the question is one of physical conditions of descent—but the newer law says, with enviable discernment · " Proselytes are as injurious to Judaism as ulcers to a sound body."† Thus was the Jewish race kept pure in the past and it is still kept so : daughters of the house of Rothschild have married barons, counts, dukes, princes, they submit to baptism without demur ; no son has ever married a European ; if he did so he would have to leave the house of his fathers and the community of his people.‡

* In the new literal translation of Professor Louis Segond the passage reads, " the sacred race defiled by mixture with strange peoples"; in the translation of De Wette it is, " they have mingled the holy seed with the peoples of the earth."

† From the *Talmud*, according to Döllinger, *Vorträge* i. 237. In another place the *Talmud* calls the proselytes a " burden." (*See* the Jew Philippson : *Israelitische Religionslehre*, 1861, ii. 189.)

‡ How pure the Jewish race still is, has been shown by Virchow's great anthropological examination of all the school children of Germany ; Ranke gives details in his book, *Der Mensch*, 2nd ed. ii. 293 : " The purer the race, the smaller is the number of mixed forms. In this connection it is certainly a very important fact that the smallest number of mixed forms was found among the Jews, whereby their decided isolation as a race from the Teutonic peoples, among which they live, is shown most clearly."—Measurements in America have, according to the *American Anthropologist*, vol. iv., in the meantime led to the conviction that there too the Jewish race " has kept itself absolutely pure." (Quoted from the *Politisch-anthropologische Revue*, 1904, March, p. 1003.)

These details are somewhat premature; they really belong to a later portion of the book; but my object has been at once and by the shortest way to meet the objection—which unfortunately is still to be expected from many sides—that there is no "Jewish question," from which would follow that the entrance of the Jews into our history had no significance. Others, again, talk of religion : it is a question, they say, of religious differences only. Whoever says this overlooks the fact that there would be no Jewish religion if there were no Jewish nation. But there is one. The Jewish nomocracy (that is, rule of the law) unites the Jews, no matter how scattered they may be over all the lands of the world, into a firm, uniform and absolutely political organism, in which community of blood testifies to a common past and gives a guarantee for a common future. Though it has many elements not purely Jewish in the narrower sense of the word, yet the power of this blood, united with the incomparable power of the Jewish idea, is so great that these alien elements have long ago been assimilated ; for nearly two thousand years have passed since the time when the Jews gave up their temporary inclination to proselytising. Of course, I must, as I showed in the preceding chapter, distinguish between Jews of noble and of less noble birth ; but what binds together the incompatible parts is (apart from gradual fusing) the tenacity of life which their national idea possesses. This national idea culminates in the unshakable confidence in the universal empire of the Jews, which Jehovah promised. "Simple people who have been born Christians" (as Auerbach expresses it in his sketch of Spinoza's life) fancy that the Jews have given up that hope, but they are very wrong ; for "the existence of Judaism depends upon the clinging to the Messianic hope," as one of the very moderate and liberal Jews lately wrote.* The whole Jewish religion is in fact founded on

---

* Skreinka : *Entwickelungsgeschichte der jüdischen Dogmen*, p. 75.

this hope. The Jewish faith in God, that which can and may be called "religion" in their case, for it has become since the source of a fine morality, is a part of this national idea, not *vice versâ*. To assert that there is a Jewish religion but no Jewish nation is simply nonsense.*

The entry of the Jews into the history of the West signifies therefore beyond doubt the entrance of a definite element, quite different from and in a way opposed to all European races, an element which remained essentially the same, while the nations of Europe went through the most various phases; in the course of a hard and often cruel history it never had the weakness to entertain proposals of fraternity, but, possessed as it was of its national idea, its national past, and its national future, felt and still feels all contact with others as a pollution; thanks also to the certainty of its instinct, which springs from strict uniformity of national feeling, it has always been able to

* At the Jewish congress held in Basle in 1898, Dr. Mandelstam, Professor in the University of Kiev, said in the chief speech of the sitting of August 29, " The Jews energetically reject the idea of fusion with the other nationalities and cling firmly to their historical hope, *i.e.*, of world empire " (from a report of one who took part in the congress in *Le Temps*, Sept. 2, 1898). The Vienna newspapers of July 30 and 31, 1901, report a speech on Zionism which the Vienna Rabbi, Dr. Leopold Kahn, delivered in a room of the orthodox Jewish school in Pressburg. In this speech Dr. Kahn made the following admission : " the Jew will never be able to assimilate himself ; he will never adopt the customs and ways of other peoples. The Jew remains Jew under all circumstances. Every assimilation is purely exterior." Words well worth laying to heart ! In the *Festschrift zum 70: Geburtstage A. Berliner's*, 1903, Dr. B. Felsenthal publishes a series of *Jewish Theses* in which he supports with all his energy the thesis that Jewry is a people, not a religion, " Judaism is a special stem, and every Jew is born into this stem." This stem is, according to him, " one of the ethnically purest peoples that exist." Felsenthal reckons that from Theodosius to the year 1800, " perhaps not quite 300 non-Semites were adopted into the Jewish race," and it is characteristic that he denies proselytes the right of looking upon themselves as full-blooded Jews. " The Jewish people, the Jewish stem is the given fact, the constant thing, the necessary substratum, the substantial kernel. The Jewish religion is something attached to this kernel, a quality—an accident, as it is called in the language of the philosophical schools." I quote from the special impression, made by Itzkowski, Berlin.

exercise a powerful influence upon others, while the Jews themselves have been influenced but skin-deep by our intellectual and cultural development. To characterise this most peculiar situation from the standpoint of the European, we must repeat the words of Herder : the Jewish people is and remains alien to our part of the world ; from the standpoint of the Jew the same fact is formulated somewhat differently ; we know from a former chapter how the great free-thinking philosopher Philo put it : " only the Israelites are men in the true sense of the word." *
What the Jew here says in the intolerant tone of racial pride was more politely expressed by Goethe, when he disputed the community of descent of Jews and Indo-Europeans, no matter how far back the origin was put :
" We will not dispute with the chosen people the honour of its descent from Adam. We others, however, have certainly had other ancestors as well." †

THE " ALIEN PEOPLE "

These considerations make it our right and our duty to look upon the Jew in our midst as a peculiar and, in fact, alien element. Outwardly his inheritance was the same as ours ; inwardly it was not so : he inherited quite a different spirit. One single trait is all that is necessary to reveal in an almost alarming manner to our consciousness the yawning gulf which here separates soul from soul : the revelation of Christ has no significance for the Jew ! I do not here speak of pious orthodoxy at all. But read, for example, in Diderot, the notorious free-thinker, the wonderful words on the Crucified One, see how Diderot represents man in his greatest sorrow turning to the

* See p. 217.
† Conversations with Eckermann, October 7, 1828. Giordano Bruno made a similar assertion, viz., that only the Jews were descended from Adam and Eve, the rest of mankind were of much older origin. (See Lo spaccio della bestia trionfante.)

Divine One, and makes us feel that the Christian religion is the only religion in the world. " *Quelle profonde sagesse il y a dans ce que l'aveugle philosophie appelle la folie de la croix ! Dans l'état ou j'étais, de quoi m'aurait servi l'image d'un legislateur heureux et comblé de gloire ? Je voyais l'innocent, le flanc percé, le front couronné d'épines, les mains et les pieds percés de clous, et expirant dans les souffrances ; et je me disais : Voilà mon Dieu, et j'ose me plaindre !* " I have searched through a whole library of Jewish books in the expectation of finding similar words —naturally not belief in the divinity of Christ, nor the idea of redemption, but the purely human feeling for the greatness of a suffering saviour—but in vain. A Jew who feels that is in fact no longer a Jew, but a denier of Judaism. And while we find even in Mohammed's *Koran* at least a vague conception of the importance of Christ and profound reverence for His personality, a cultured, leading Jew of the nineteenth century calls Christ " the new birth with the death-mask," which inflicted new and painful wounds upon the Jewish people ; he cannot see anything else in Him.* In view of the cross he assures us that " the Jews do not require this convulsive emotion for their spiritual improvement," and adds, " particularly not among the middle classes of the inhabitants of the cities." His comprehension goes no further. In a book, republished in 1880 (!), by a Spanish Jew (Mose de Leon) Jesus Christ is called a " dead dog " that lies " buried in a dung-hill." Besides, the Jews have taken care to issue in the latter part of the nineteenth century several editions (naturally in Hebrew) of the so-called " censured passages " from the *Talmud*, those passages usually omitted in which Christ is exposed to our scorn and hatred as a " fool," " sorcerer," " profane person," " idolater," " dog," " bastard," " child of lust," &c. ; so, too, his sublime

* Graetz : *Volkstümliche Geschichte der Juden*, i. 591

mother.* We certainly do the Jews no injustice when we say that the revelation of Christ is simply something incomprehensible and hateful to them. Although he apparently sprang from their midst, he embodies nevertheless the negation of their whole nature—a matter in which the Jews are far more sensitive than we. This clear demonstration of the deep cleft that separates us Europeans from the Jew is by no means given in order to let religious prejudice with its dangerous bias settle the matter, but because I think that the perception of two so fundamentally different natures reveals a real gulf ; it is well to look once into this gulf, so that on other occasions, where the two sides seem likely to unite each other, we may not be blind to the deep abyss which separates them.

When we understand what a chasm there is between us we are forced to a further conclusion. The Jew does not understand us, that is certain ; can we hope to understand him, to do him justice ? Perhaps, if we are really intellectually and morally superior to him, as Renan insisted in the passage quoted above, and as other perhaps more reliable scholars have likewise said.† But we should

---

* See Laible: *Jesus Christus im Talmud*, p. 2 ff. (*Schriften des Institutum Judaicum in Berlin*, No. 10 ; in the supplement the original Hebrew texts are given.) This absolutely impartial scholar, who is, moreover, a friend of the Jews, says : " The hatred and scorn of the Jews was always directed in the first place against the person of Jesus " (p. 25). " The Jesus-hatred of the Jews is a firmly established fact, but they want to show it as little as possible " (p. 3). Hatred of Christ is described by the same scholar as the " most national trait of Judaism " (p. 86) ; he says, " at the approach of Christianity the Jews were seized ever and again with a fury and hatred that were akin to madness " (p. 72). Even to-day no orthodox Jew may use the name of Christ either in speech or in writing (pp. 3 and 32) ; the most common cryptonyms are " the bastard," " the hanged," often, too, " Bileam."

† See especially the famous passage in Lassen's *Indische Altertumskunde*, where the great Orientalist proves in detail his view that the Indo-European race is " more highly and more fully gifted," that in it alone there is " perfect symmetry of all mental powers." (*See* i. 414, of the 1847 edition.)

then have to judge him from the lofty heights of our
superiority, not from the low depths of hatred and
superstition, and still less from the swampy shallows of
misunderstanding in which our religious teachers have
been wading for the last two thousand years. It is
surely an evident injustice to ascribe to the Jew thoughts
which he never had, to glorify him as the possessor of
the most sublime religious intuitions, which were perhaps more alien to him than to any one else in the world,
and at best are to be found only in the hearts of a few
scattered individuals as a cry of revolt against the special
hardness of heart of this people—and then to condemn
him for being to-day quite different from what he should
be according to such fictitious conceptions. It is not only
unfair, but as regards public feeling, regrettably misleading;
for through his connection with our religious life—a connection which is entirely fictitious—his head seems enve-
loped in a kind of nimbus, and then we are greatly incensed
when we find no holy person under this sham halo.
We expect more of the Jews than of ourselves, who are
merely the children of the heathen. But the Jewish testimony is very different and more correct; it leads us to
expect so little that every noble trait discovered later
and every explanation found for Jewish failings gives us
genuine pleasure. Jehovah, for instance, is never tired
of explaining, " I have seen this people and behold it is
a stiff-necked people," * and Jeremiah gives such a
characterisation of the moral constitution of the Jews
that Monsieur Edouard Drumont could not wish it to
be more richly coloured, " And they will deceive every
one his neighbour, and will not speak the truth : they
have taught their tongue to speak lies, and weary themselves to commit iniquity." † Little wonder, after
this description, that Jeremiah calls the Jews " an

* *Exodus* xxxii. 9, xxxiv. 9 ; *Deuteronomy* ix. 13, &c.
† ix. 5.

assembly of treacherous men," and knows only one
desire, "Oh that I had in the wilderness a lodging-place
of wayfaring men ; that I might leave my people and
go from them." For our incredible ignorance of the
Jewish nature we are ourselves solely to blame ; never
did a people give so comprehensive and honest a picture
of its own personality as the Hebrew has done in his
Bible, a picture which (so far as I can judge from fragments) is made more complete by the *Talmud*, though in
faded colours. Without, therefore, denying that it must
be very difficult for us who are " descended from other
ancestors " to form a correct judgment of the " alien
Asiatic people," we must clearly see that the Jews from
time immemorial have done their best to inform the
unprejudiced about themselves, a circumstance which
entitles us to hope that we may gain a thorough knowledge of their nature. As a matter of fact, the events
which take place before our eyes should be sufficient for
that. Is it possible to read the daily papers without
becoming acquainted with Jewish ways of thinking,
Jewish taste, Jewish morals, Jewish aims ? A few annual
volumes of the *Archives israélites* teach us in fact more
than a whole anti-Semitic library, and indeed not only
about the less admirable, but also about the excellent
qualities of the Jewish character. But here, in this chapter,
I shall leave the present out of account. If we are to form
a practical and true judgment concerning the significance
of the Jew as joint-heir and fellow-worker in the nineteenth
century, we must above all become clear as to what he
is. From what a man is by nature follows of strict necessity what he will do under certain conditions ; the philosopher says : *operari sequitur esse ;* an old German
proverb expresses the same thing in a more homely way,
" Only what a man is, can one get out of him."

HISTORICAL BIRD'S-EYE VIEW

Pure history in this case does not bring us either quickly or surely to our goal, and besides it is not my task to furnish a history of the Jews. As in other chapters, so here too I have a horror of copying what has been written before. Every one, of course, knows how and when the Jews entered into Western history : first by the Diaspora, then by being scattered. Their changing fortunes in various lands and times are likewise no secret to us, although, indeed, much that we know is absolutely untrue, and of much that we ought to know we are entirely ignorant. But I do not need to tell any one that throughout the Christian centuries the Jews played an important though at times circumscribed *rôle*. Even in the earliest Western Gothic times they understood how to acquire influence and power as slave-dealers and financial agents. Though they were not everywhere, as they were among the Spanish Moors, powerful Ministers of State, who, following the example of Mardochai, filled the most lucrative posts with "their many brothers," though they did not attain everywhere, as they did in Catholic Spain, to the rank of Bishop and Archbishop,* yet their influence was always and everywhere great. The Babenberg princes as early as the thirteenth century set their successors the example of letting Jews manage the finances of their States and honouring these administrators with titles of distinction ; † the great Pope Innocent III. gave important posts at his Court to Jews ; ‡ the knights of France had to pledge their

---

* *See* the book of the Jew, David Mocatta, *The Jews in Spain and Portugal*, where a detailed account is given of how there were in Spain "generations and generations of secret Jews who mingled with all classes of society and were in possession of every post in the State and especially in the Church ! "

† Graetz, ii. 503.

‡ Israel Abrahams : *Jewish Life in the Middle Ages.*

goods with the Jews, in order to be able to take part in
the Crusades; * Rudolf von Habsburg favoured the
Jews in every way; he vindicated them " as servants
of his imperial exchequer," and by freeing them from
being subject to ordinary justice he made it very difficult
indeed for any action brought against them to be carried
through; † in short, what I call the entrance of the
Jews into Western history has never ceased to make
itself felt at all times and places. If any one were
qualified to study history for the sole purpose of dis-
entangling the question of Jewish influence, he would,
I think, bring to light some unexpected facts. Without
this detailed study the fact of this influence can only be
established clearly and beyond doubt where the Jews
were in considerable numbers. In the second century, for
example, the Jews on the island of Cyprus are more
numerous than the other inhabitants; they resolve to
found a national State and with this intent follow the
procedure known from the Old Testament : they slay
in one day all the other inhabitants, 240,000 in number ;
and in order that this island State may not be without
support on the mainland, they at the same time slay the
220,000 non-Jewish inhabitants of Cyrene.‡ In Spain they
pursue the same policy with greater caution and astonishing perseverance. Under the rule of that thoroughly
Western Gothic king, who had showered benefits on
them, they invite their kinsmen, the Arabs, to come over
from Africa, and, not out of any ill-feeling, but simply because they hope to profit thereby, they betray their noble
protector ; under the Kalifs they then acquire gradually
an even larger share in the government; " they concentrated," their great supporter the historian Heman
writes, " the intellectual and the material powers al-

* André Réville: *Les payans au Moyen-Age*, 1896, p. 3.
† *See* among others Realis: *Die Juden und die Judenstadt in Wien*,
1846, p. 18, &c.
‡ Mommsen: *Röm. Gesch.*, v. 543.

together in their own hands " ; the prosperous Moorish
State was, it is true, thereby intellectually and materially
ruined : but this was a matter of indifference to the
Jews, as they had already obtained as firm a footing in
the Christian State of the Spaniards which was destined
to take the place of the Moorish one. " The movable
wealth of the land was here absolutely in their power ;
the heritable property they made gradually theirs
by usury and the purchase of mortgaged estates of
nobles. From the offices of Secretary of State and
Minister of Finance downwards all the offices which had
to do with taxes and money were in Jewish hands.
Through usury almost all Aragon was mortgaged to
them. In the cities they formed the majority of the
wealthy population." * But here, as elsewhere, they
were not always shrewd ; they had employed their power
to obtain all kinds of privileges ; for example, the oath
of a single Jew sufficed to prove debt claims against
Christians (the same was the case in the Archduchy of
Austria and in many places), while the testimony of a
Christian against a Jew had no weight before a tribunal,
and so on ; these privileges they abused so outrageously
that the people finally revolted. The same would probably have happened in Germany if the Church and intelligent statesmen had not put a stop to the evil in time.
Charlemagne had written to Italy for Jews to manage his
finances ; soon, as farmers of taxes, they secured for themselves wealth and influence in every direction, and used
these to get important concessions for their people, such as
commercial privileges, less severe punishment for crime
and the like ; the whole population was even forced to
make Sunday their market day, as Saturday, the custo-
mary market day, did not suit the Jews because it was

* Heman : *Die historische Weltstellung der Juden*, 1882, p. 24 ff.
For a somewhat differently tinged account which, however, in actual
facts is entirely at one with this, *see* Graetz : *Volksth. Gesch. d. Juden*,
ii. 344 ff.

their Sabbath ; it was at that time fashionable for courtiers to visit the synagogues !   But the reaction set in soon and strongly, and not only, as the historians are wont to represent it, as the result of priestly agitation—such things belong to the shell, not to the kernel of history— but in the first place because the Teuton is in fact just as much a born merchant and industrialist as he is a born warrior, and because, as soon as the growth of cities awakened these instincts in him, he saw the game of his unfair rival, and, full of violent indignation, demanded his removal.   And so, if such were the purpose of this chapter, we could trace the ebb and flow of Jewish influence to the present day, when all the wars of the nineteenth century are so peculiarly connected with Jewish financial operations, from Napoleon's Russian campaign and Nathan Rothschild's *rôle* of spectator at the Battle of Waterloo to the consulting of the Bleichröders on the German side and of Alphonse Rothschild on the French side at the peace transactions of the year 1871, and to the "Commune," which from the beginning was looked upon by all intelligent people as a Jewish-Napoleonic machination.

Consensus Ingeniorum

Now this political and social influence of the Jews has been very variously judged, but the greatest politicians of all times have regarded it as pernicious.   Cicero, for example (no great politician but an experienced statesman), displays a genuine fear of the Jews ; where a legal trans- action encroaches on their interest, he speaks so low that only the judges hear him, for he is well aware, as he says, that all the Jews hold together and that they know how to ruin the one who opposes them ; while he thunders the most vehement charges against Greeks, against Romans, against the most powerful men of his time, he advises caution in dealing with the Jews ; they are to him an

uncanny power and he passes with the greatest haste
over that city of " suspicion and slander," Jerusalem :
such was the opinion of a Cicero during the consulate of
a Julius Cæsar ! * Even before the destruction of Jerusalem the Emperor Tiberius, who was, according to many
historians, the best ruler that the Roman Imperium
ever possessed, recognised a national danger in the immigration of the Jews. Even Frederick the Second, the
Hohenstauffen, certainly one of the most brilliant men
that ever wore a crown or carried a sword, a more free-
thinking man than any monarch of the nineteenth century, an enthusiastic admirer of the East and a generous
supporter of Hebrew scholars, nevertheless held it to
be his duty, contrary to the custom of his contemporaries, to debar the Jews from all public offices, and
pointed warningly to the fact that wherever the Jews
are admitted to power, they abuse it ; the very same
doctrine was taught by the other great Frederick the
Second, the Hohenzollern, who gave universal freedom,
but not to the Jews ; similar were the words of Bismarck,
while he still could speak openly, in the Landtag (1847)
and the great historian Mommsen speaks of Judaism as
of a " State inside the State."—As regards the social
influence in particular, I will only quote two wise and
fair authorities, whose judgment cannot be suspected
even by the Jews, namely, Herder and Goethe. The
former says, " A ministry, in which the Jew is supreme,
a household, in which a Jew has the key of the wardrobe
and the management of the finances, a department or
commissariat, in which Jews do the principal business . . .
are Pontine marshes that cannot be drained " ; and he
expresses the opinion that the presence of an indefinite
number of Jews is so pernicious to the welfare of a
European State, that we " dare not be influenced by
general humane principles " ; it is a national question,

* *See* the *Defence of Lucius Flaccus,* xxviii.

and it is the duty of every State to decide " how
many of this alien people can be tolerated without
injury to the true citizens ? " *   Goethe goes still deeper :
" How should we let the Jews share in our highest culture,
when they deny its origin and source ? "   And he became " violently enraged " when the law of 1823 permitted
marriage between Jews and Germans, prophesying the
" worst and most frightful consequences," particularly
the " undermining of all moral feelings " and declaring
that the bribery of the " all-powerful Rothschild " must
be the cause of this " folly." †   Goethe and Herder have
exactly the same opinion as the great Hohenstauffen,
the great Hohenzollern, and all great men before and after
them : without superstitiously reproaching the Jews
with their peculiar individuality, they consider them an
actual danger to our civilisation and our culture ; they
would not give them an active part in our life. We
cannot proceed with our discussion and simply pass
over such a *consensus ingeniorum*. For to these well-
weighed, serious judgments derived from the fulness of
experience and the insight of the greatest intellects we
have nothing to oppose but the empty phrases of the
droits de l'homme—a parliamentary clap-trap.‡

* Adrastea : *Bekehrung der Juden.*
† Wilhelm Meister's *Wanderjahre*, iii. 11, and the conversation with
von Müller on September 23, 1823.
‡ I have intentionally limited my quotations. But I cannot refrain
from defending in a note the great Voltaire against the almost established
myth that he was altogether favourable and as superficial in his humanitarian judgment of the influence of the Jews upon our culture, as is the
modern fashion. Even Jews of such broad culture as James Darmesteter
(*Peuple Juif*, 2e éd. p. 17) print the name Voltaire in thick type and
represent him as one of the intellectual originators of their emancipation. The opposite is true ; more than once Voltaire advises that the
Jews be sent back to Palestine. Voltaire is one of the authors whom I
know best, because I prefer interesting books to wearisome ones, and
I think I could easily collect a hundred quotations of a most aggressive
nature against the Jews. In the essay of the *Dictionnaire Philosophique*
(end of Section 1) he says : " *Vous ne trouverez dans les Juifs qu'un
peuple ignorant et barbare, qui joint depuis longtemps la plus sordide
avarice à la plus détestable superstition et à la plus invincible haine pour*

PRINCES AND NOBILITY

On the other hand, it is certain and must be carefully observed that, if the Jews are responsible for many a shocking historical development, for the fall of many heroic, powerful peoples, still greater is the responsibility of those Europeans who have always from the most base motives encouraged, protected and fostered the disintegrating activity of the Jews, and these are primarily the Princes and the nobility—and that too from the first century of our era to the present day. Open the history of any European nation you like wherever the Jews are numerous and begin to realise their strength, you will always hear bitter complaints against them from the people, from the commercial classes, from the circles of the learned and the poets; everywhere and at all times it is the Princes and the nobility that protect them: the Princes because they need money for their wars, the nobility because they live extravagantly.

tous les peuples qui les tolèrent et qui les enrichissent." In *Dieu et les hommes* (chap. x.) he calls the Jews *" La plus haïssable et la plus honteuse des petites nations."* Enough has surely been said to make his attitude clear! But this opinion should have all the more force, since Voltaire himself in many long treatises has made a thorough study of Jewish history and the Jewish character (so thorough that he who has been decried as a "superficial dilettante" is occasionally quoted to-day by a scholar of the first rank like Wellhausen). And so it is note-worthy when he writes (*Essai sur les Mœurs*, chap. xlii.): *" La nation juive ose étaler une haine irréconciliable contre toutes les nations, elle se révolte contra tous les maîtres ; toujours superstitieuse, toujours avide du bien d'autrui, toujours barbare—rampante dans le malheur et insolente dans la prospérité."* His judgment of their mental qualities is brief and apodeictic, *" Les Juifs n'ont jamais rien inventé "* (*La défense de mon oncle*, chap. vii.), and in the *Essai sur les Mœurs* he shows in several chapters that the Jews had always learned from other nations but had never taught others anything ; even their music, which is generally praised, Voltaire cannot endure : *" Retournez en Judée le plus tôt que vous pourrez . . . vous y exécuterez à plaisir dans votre détestable jargon votre détestable musique "* (6ᵐᵉ *lettre du Dictionnaire*). He explains elsewhere this remarkable mental sterility of the Jews by their in_ordinate lust for money : *" L'argent fut l'objet de leur conduite dans tous*

Edmund Burke * tells us, for example, of William the Conqueror that, as the income from "talliage" and all kinds of other oppressive taxes did not satisfy him, he from time to time either confiscated the notes of hand of the Jews or forced them to hand them over for next to nothing, and, as almost the whole Anglo-Norman nobility of the eleventh century was under the thumb of Jewish usury, the King himself became the pitiless creditor of his most illustrious subjects. In the meantime he protected the Jews and gave them privileges of various kinds. This one example may stand for thousands and thousands.† If then

les temps" (Dieu et les hommes, xxix.). Voltaire scoffs at the Jews in a hundred places; for instance, in Zadig (chap. x.), where the Jew utters a solemn prayer of thankfulness to God for a successful piece of fraud ; the most biting satire against the Jews that exists is beyond doubt the treatise Un Chrétien contre six Juifs. And yet in all these utterances there was a certain reserve, as they were destined for publication ; on the other hand, in a letter to the Chevalier de Lisle on December 15, 1773 (that is, at the end of his life, not in the heat of youth), he could speak his opinion freely: " Que ces déprépucés d'Israël se disent de la tribu de Naphthali ou d'Issachar, cela est fort peu important ; ils n'en sont pas moins les plus grands gueux qui aient jamais souillé la face du globe." Evidently this fiery Frenchman had just the same to say of the Jews as any fanatical Bishop ; he differs at most in the addition which he occasionally makes to his bitterest attacks, " Il ne faut pourtant pas les brûler." There is a further difference in the fact that it is a humane, tolerant and learned man that utters this very sharp judgment. But how, in a man of such open mind, can we explain the existence of a view so pitilessly one-sided and so ruthlessly intolerant, a view which in its utter lack of moderation compares very unfavourably with the words of the German sages quoted above ? Our age could learn much here, if it wished to ! For we see that the Gallic love of equality and freedom is not based upon love of justice nor respect for the individual ; and we may draw the further conclusion : understanding is not got from principles, and universal humanity does not ensure the possibility of living together in dignified peace, it is only the frank recognition of what separates our own kind and our own interests from those of others that can make us just towards an alien nature and alien interests.

　* An Abridgment of English History, iii. 2.

　† The famous economist Dr. W. Cunningham, in his book The Growth of English Industry and Commerce during the Early and Middle Ages (3rd ed., 1896, p. 201), compares the activity of the Jews in England from the tenth century onward to a sponge, which sucks up all the wealth of the land and thereby hinders all economic development. Interesting,

the Jews have exercised a great and historically baneful influence, it is to no small degree due to the complicity of these Princes and nobles who so shamefully persecuted and at the same time utilised the Jews. And in fact *this* lasts until the nineteenth century : Count Mirabeau was in closest touch with the Jews even before the Revolution,* Count Talleyrand, in opposition to the delegates from the middle classes, supported in the Constituante their unconditional emancipation ; Napoleon protected them, when after such a short time bitter complaints and entreaties for protection against them were sent in to the Government from all France, and he did so although he himself had exclaimed in the Council of State, " These Jews are locusts and caterpillars, they devour my France !" —he needed their money. Prince Dalberg sold to the Frankfort Jews, in defiance of the united citizens, the full civic rights for half a million Gulden (1811), the Hardenbergs and Metternichs at the Vienna Congress fell into the snare of the Rothschild bank, and, in opposition to the votes of all the representatives of the Bund, they supported the interests of the Jews to the disadvantage of the Germans and finally gained their point, in fact, the two most conservative States which they represented were the first to raise to hereditary nobility—an honour which was never conferred on honest and deserving Jews—those members of the

too, is the proof that even at this early period the Government did everything in its power to make the Jews take up decent trades and honest work and thereby at the same time amalgamate with the rest of the population, but all to no purpose.

* With regard to Mirabeau's being influenced by " the shrewd women of the Jews " (as Gentz says) and his connection with essentially Jewish secret societies, *see* besides Graetz, *Volks. Geschichte der Juden* (iii. 600, 610 ff.), particularly L'Abbé Lémann, *L'entrée des Israélites dans la société française*, iii. chap. 7 ; as converted Jew this author understands what others do not, and at the same time he tells what Jewish authors keep secret. The important thing in Mirabeau's case was probably that from youth he was deeply in debt to the Jews (Carlyle : *Essay on Mirabeau*).

'alien Asiatic people" who, in the years of general
suffering and misery, had by the vilest means acquired
immense wealth.* If then the Jews were for us pernicious
neighbours, justice requires us to admit that they acted
according to the nature of their instincts and gifts, and
showed at the same time a really admirable example of
loyalty to self, to their own nation and to the faith of
their fathers; the tempters and the traitors were not
the Jews but we ourselves. We were the criminal
abettors of the Jews, and it is so to-day, as it was in the
past; and we were false to that which the lowest inhabitant of the Ghetto considered sacred, the purity of
inherited blood; that, too, was formerly the case, and
to-day it is more so than ever. The Christian Church
alone of all the great powers seems to have acted on
the whole justly and wisely (of course we must dis-
count the Bishops who were really secular Princes, as
well as some of the Popes). The Church has kept the
Jews in check, treated them as aliens, but at the same
time protected them from persecution. Every seemingly
"ecclesiastical" persecution has its source really in
economic conditions that have become unbearable; we
see that nowhere more clearly than in Spain. To-day,
when public opinion is so fearfully misled by the active,
irreconcilable antagonism of the Jews, especially to every
manifestation of the Christian faith, it may be well to
remind the reader that the last act of the preparatory
meeting to the first Synedrium summoned in our times,
that of 1807, was a spontaneous utterance of thanks to
the ministers of the various Christian Churches for the
protection extended to them throughout the centuries.†

* This is, of course, an old custom of Princes, by which not only
the Jews but others also profit; Martin Luther even had to write:
" The Princes have thieves hanged, who have stolen a Gulden or half
a one, and yet make transactions with those who rob everybody and
steal more than all others " (*Von Kaufhandlung und Wucher*).

† Diogène Tama: *Collection des actes de l'Assemblée des Israélites de
France et du royaume d'Italie* (Paris, 1807, pp. 327, 328; the author is a

INNER CONTACT

Here we must end these hastily sketched historical fragments. They show that " the entrance of the Jews " has exercised a large, and in many ways an undoubtedly fatal, influence upon the course of European history since the first century. But that tells us little about the Jew himself; the fact that the North American Indian dies out from contact with the Indo-European does not prove that the latter is evil and pernicious ; that the Jew injures or benefits us is a judgment which is conditional in too many ways to permit of our forming a true estimate of his nature. In fact, for nineteen centuries the Jew has had not merely an outer relationship with our culture as a more or less welcome guest, but also an inner contact. As Kant rightly says, the preservation of Judaism is primarily the work of Christianity.* From its midst—if not from its stem and its spirit—Jesus Christ and the earliest members of the Christian Church arose. Jewish history, Jewish conceptions, Jewish thought and poetry became important elements in our mental life. It cannot be right to separate the outward friction entirely from the inner penetration. If we had not ceremoniously adopted the Jew into our family circle, he would no more have found a home

Jew and was Secretary of the Jewish deputy of Bouches-du-Rhône, M. Constantini). After a detailed proof the document closes with the following : " Les députés israélites arrêtent : Que l'expression de ces sentiments sera consignée dans le procès-verbal de ce jour pour qu'elle demeure à jamais comme un témoignage authentique de la gratitude des Israélites de cette Assemblée pour les bienfaits que les générations qui les ont précédés ont reçus des ecclésiastiques des divers pays d'Europe." The proposal was moved by Mr. Isaac Samuel Avigdor, representative of the Jews of the Alpes-Maritimes. Tama adds that the speech of Avigdor was received with applause and its insertion in the minutes in extenso adopted.—The Jewish historians of to-day do not say a word concerning this important event. Not only Graetz passes it over in silence, but Bédarride also in his Les Juifs en France, 1859, although he seems as if he were reporting in full from the minutes.

* Die Religion, general note to third chapter.

among us than the Saracen or the other wrecks of half-Semitic peoples who saved their existence—but not their individuality—by unconditional amalgamation with the nations of South Europe. The Jew, however, was proof against this ; though now and then one of them might be dragged to the stake, the very fact that they had crucified Jesus Christ surrounded them with a solemn, awe-inspiring nimbus. And while the people were thus fascinated, the scholars and holy men spent their days and nights in studying the books of the Hebrews : struck down by the commands of Jewish shepherds like Amos and Micah, the monuments of an art, whose like the world has never since seen, fell to the ground ; through the scorn of Jewish priests science sank into contempt ; Olympus and Walhalla became depopulated, because the Jews so wished it ; Jehovah, who had said to the Israelites, " Ye are my people and I am your God," now became the God of the Indo-Europeans ; from the Jews we adopted the fatal doctrine of unconditional religious intolerance. But at the same time we adopted very great and sublime spiritual impulses ; we were taught by prophets, who preached such strict and pure morals as could have been found nowhere else save on the distant shores of India ; we became acquainted with such a living and life-moulding faith in a higher divine power that it inevitably changed our spirit and gave it a new direction. Though Christ was the master-builder, we got the architecture from the Jews. Isaiah, Jeremiah, the Psalmists became, and still are, living powers in our spiritual life.

Who is the Jew ?

And now, when this inner contact is beginning to grow weaker, while the outer friction referred to above is being daily more felt, now, when he cannot any longer rid ourselves of the presence of Jews, it is not sufficient for us to know that almost all pre-eminent and free men, from Tiberius to Bismarck, have looked upon the presence of the Jew in our midst as a social and political danger, we must be in a position to form definite judgments on the basis of adequate knowledge of facts and to act accordingly. There have been published Anti-Semitic catechisms, in which opinions of well-known men have been collected in hundreds; but apart from the fact that many a remark when taken apart from the context does not give quite fairly the intention of the writer, and that out of many others it is merely ignorant blind prejudice that speaks, a single opinion of our own is manifestly worth more than two hundred quotations. Moreover I do not know how we can form a competent judgment, if we do not learn to take a higher standpoint than that of political considerations, and I do not know how we can arrive at this standpoint except through history, not, however, modern history—for there we should be judge and suitor at the same time—but through the history of the growth of the Jewish people. There is no lack of documents; in the nineteenth century especially they have been tested, critically sifted and historically classified by the devoted work of learned men, mostly Germans, but also distinguished Frenchmen, Dutchmen and Englishmen; much remains to be done, but enough has already been accomplished to enable us to survey clearly and surely in its general features one of the most remarkable pages of human history. This Jew, who appears so eternally unchangeable, so constant, as Goethe says, really grew into what he is, grew slowly, even artificially. And of a surety he will pass away like all that has grown. This fact already brings him nearer to us as a human being. What a " Semite " is, no one can tell. A hundred years ago science thought it knew what it meant; Semites

were the sons of Shem; now the answer becomes more
and more vague; it was thought that the criterion of
language was decisive: a very great error! The idea
"Semite" indeed remains indispensable because it embraces collectively a many-sided complex of historical
phenomena; but there is absolutely no sure boundary-
line; at the periphery this ethnographical conception
merges into others. Finally "Semite" remains as the
name of an original race, like "Aryan," one of those
counters without which one could not make oneself
understood, but which one must beware of accepting
as good coin. The real genuine coins are those empirically given, historically developed national individualities, of which I have spoken in the former chapter, such
individualities as the Jews for example. Race is not
an original phenomenon, it is produced; physiologically
by characteristic mixture of blood, followed by inbreeding; psychically by the influence which long-
lasting historical and geographical conditions exercise
upon that special, specific, physiological foundation.*
If we wish then (and I think that must be the principal
task of this chapter) to ask the Jew: Who art thou?
we must first try to discover whether there was not a
definite mixture of blood underlying the fact of this so
clearly marked race, and then—if the answer is in the
affirmative—trace how the peculiar soul, which thus
was produced, differentiated itself more and more.
Nowhere can we trace this process as we can in the Jew:
for the whole national history of the Jews is like a continuous process of elimination; the character of the
Jewish people ever becomes more individual, more
outspoken, more simple; finally there remains in a
way nothing of the whole being but the central skeleton; the slowly ripened fruit is robbed of its downy,
fresh-coloured covering and of its juicy flesh, for these

* *Cf.* p. 288. For the Semites, *see also* p. 361.

might become spotted and worm-eaten ; the stony kernel alone remains, shrivelled and dry, it is true, but defying time. However, as I have pointed out, this was not always the case. That which has been transferred from the sacred books of the Hebrews to the Christian religion does not come down from the senility of real Judaism, but partly from the youth of the much wider and more imaginative " Israelite " people, partly from the mature years of the Judean, just after he had separated from Israel and when he had not yet proudly isolated himself from the other nations of the earth. The Jew whom we now know and see at work has become Jew gradually ; not, however, as pseudo-history would have us believe, in the course of the Christian Middle Ages, but on his national soil, in the course of his independent history ; the Jew moulded his own destiny ; in Jerusalem stood the first Ghetto, the high wall which separated the orthodox and the pure born from the Goyim, and prevented the latter from entering the real city. Neither Jacob, nor Solomon, nor Isaiah would recognise his posterity in Rabbi Akiba (the great scribe of the *Talmud*) much less in Baron Hirsch or the diamond king Barnato.*

Let us therefore try by the shortest way, *i.e.*, by the greatest possible simplification, to make plain the essential features of this peculiar national soul, as it gradually became more clearly and one-sidedly developed. This needs no great learning ; for to the question : Who

---

* For the Messianic period the dream of the later Jews (in contrast to the more free-thinking Israelites of former centuries) was to keep strangers out of Jerusalem altogether: read *Joel* iii. 2 ; and as this very late prophet—from the Hellenic period—says at the same time that God will always dwell in Jerusalem and only in Jerusalem, this command means the banishment of all peoples from God's presence. Such was the tolerance of the Jews !—It is only logical that most of the Rabbis excluded all non-Jews from a future world, while others endured them there as a despised throng (*see* Tractate *Gittin*, fol. 57*a* of the *Babylonian Talmud*, and Weber, *System der altsynagogalen palästinischen Theologie*, p. 372, from Laible) ; the comical thing is the assertion of the Jews to-day that their religion is the " religion of humanity ! "

art thou ? the Jew himself, as I have said, and his ancestor the Israelite have given from the first the clearest of answers : then we have the mass of scientific work, from Ewald to Wellhausen and Ramsay, from De Wette and Reuss to Duhm and Cheyne ; we have only to make out the sum total, as the practical man needs it, who, in the midst of the stormy bustle of the world, wishes to be able to base his judgment upon definite ascertained facts.

I have only two more remarks to make, about method pure and simple. Having already, particularly in the chapter on the Revelation of Christ, discussed the Jew in detail and as this theme will probably come up again, I may here confine myself to the central question and refer the reader for much information on other points to what has been said or will be said elsewhere in my book. As regards the authors consulted, I could not help using, in addition to the Bible and some thoroughly competent modern Jewish writers, also some scholars who are not Jews ; this was quite necessary for our knowledge of the prophets and the correct interpretation of historical events ; but these scholars, even the most free-thinking of them, are all men who display great—perhaps exaggerated—admiration of the Jewish nation, at least in its earlier form, and who are all inclined to look upon this people as in some sense a " chosen " one, so far as religion is concerned. I have, however, in the interests of the exposition entirely disregarded those writers who are avowedly Anti-Semitic.

Systematic Arrangement of the Investigation

There is one point—in my opinion a very important one—upon which the science of the last years has shed a good deal of light, namely, the anthropogeny of the

Israelites, that is, the history of the physical development
of this special national race. Of course here, as everywhere, there is a past which is closed to our knowledge,
and beyond doubt much that daring archæologists have
felt and guessed with the feelers of their wonderfully
trained instinct rather than seen with their own eyes,
will yet be essentially corrected by newer investigations
and discoveries. But that makes no difference to
us here. The important thing—the great, solid achievement of history—is, first, the fact that the Israelite
people represents the product of manifold mixing, and
that, too, not between related races (as the ancient
Greeks, or the English of to-day) but between types
that morally and physically are absolutely distinct; and
secondly, the fact that genuine Semitic blood (if this makeshift word is to have a sense at all) makes up, I suppose,
hardly the half of this mixture. These are certain results
of exact anatomical anthropology and of historical investigation, two branches of knowledge which here extend
to each other a helping hand. A third point completes
those just named; for it we are indebted to the critical
endeavours of Biblical archæology, which has at last
thrown light upon the very complicated chronology of
the books of the Old Testament, which belong to entirely
different centuries and were put together quite arbitrarily,
though not without a plan: these teach us that the
real Jew is not to be identified with the Israelite in the
wider sense of the word, that the house of Judah, even
at the time of its settling in Palestine, was through
blood-mixture and character distinct in several points
from the house of Joseph (which embraced the other
tribes): the Judean stood in fact in a kind of intellectual
dependence upon the Josephite, and only at a relatively
late time, after the violent separation from his brothers,
did he begin to go his own way, the way that led to
Judaism, and which very soon afterwards by the elevation

of inbreeding to a religious principle isolated him from the whole world. The Jew can be called an Israelite in so far as he is an offshoot of that family; the Israelites, on the other hand, even those of the tribe of Judah, were not Jews; the Jew began to develop only after the more powerful tribes of the North had been destroyed by the Assyrians. In order to ascertain who the Jew is, we have therefore first of all to establish who the Israelite was and then to ask how the Israelite of the tribes of Judah and Benjamin became a Jew. And here we must be careful how we use our sources of information. For it was only after the Babylonian captivity that the specifically Jewish character was artificially brought into the Bible, by whole books being invented and ascribed to Moses and frequently by the introduction in verse after verse of interpolations and corrections which obliterated the wider views of old Israel and replaced them by the narrow Jerusalemic cult of Jehovah, giving the impression that this cult had existed from time immemorial and had been directly ordained by God. This has long prevented us from clearly understanding the gradual and perfectly human historical development of the Jewish national character. Now at last light has been thrown on this sphere too. Here also we can say: we hold in our hand a sure and lasting result of scientific investigation. Whether later investigations prove this or that sentence of the Hexateuch, which to-day is ascribed to the "jahvistic" text, to belong to the "elohistic," or to have been inserted by the later "editor," whether a definite utterance was made by Isaiah himself or by the so-called second Isaiah—all these are certainly important questions, but their solution will never in any way alter the established fact that real Judaism, with the special Jehovah faith and the exclusive pre-dominance of priestly law, is due to a demonstrable and very peculiar historical sequence of events and to the active intervention of certain far-sighted and clear-headed men.

These three facts form the essential basis of all knowledge of the Jewish character ; they must not remain the possession of a learned minority but must be incorporated in the consciousness of all educated people. I repeat them in preciser form :

(1) The Israelite people has arisen from the crossing of quite different human types ;

(2) The Semitic element may well have been the stronger morally, but physically it contributed scarcely one-half to the composition of the new ethnological individuality ; it is therefore wrong shortly to call the Israelites " Semites," for the part played by the various human types in the formation of the Israelite race demands a quantitative and qualitative analysis ;

(3) The real Jew only developed in the course of centuries by gradual physical separation from the rest of the Israelite family, as also by progressive development of certain mental qualities and systematic starving of others ; he is not the result of a normal national life, but in a way an artificial product, produced by a priestly caste, which forced, with the help of alien rulers, a priestly legislation and a priestly faith upon a people that did not want them.

This furnishes us with the arrangement of the following discussion. I shall first of all consult history and anthropology, in order that we may learn from what races the new Israelite race (as the foundation of the Jewish) was descended ; then the part played by these various human types must be analysed with regard to their physical and particularly their moral significance, and here our attention must be directed especially to their religious views : for the basis of Judaism is the faith which it teaches and we cannot judge the Jew correctly either in history or in our midst, if we are not quite clear about his religion ; last of all I shall try to show how under the influence of remarkable historical events specific Judaism was established and stamped for ever with its peculiar and incomparable individuality. In this way we shall perhaps attain the object of this chapter, as I have defined it ; for the Jewish race—though later at certain times it adopted not a few alien elements—remained on the whole purer than any other, and the Jewish nation has been from the first an essentially " ideal " one, that is, one resting on faith in a definite national idea, not on the possession of a free State of its own, nor on communal life and work on the soil of that State : and this idea is the same to-day as it was two thousand years ago. Now race and ideal make up the personality of the human being ; they answer the question : Who art thou ?

ORIGIN OF THE ISRAELITE

The Israelites * sprang from the crossing of three (perhaps even four) different human types : the Semitic, the Syrian (or, more correctly, Hittite) and the Indo-European. Possibly Turanian blood, or, as it is more frequently called in Germany, Sumero-Accadian blood, also flowed in the veins of the original ancestors.

In order that the reader may clearly understand how this crossing took place, I must first give a brief historical sketch. It will freshen the memory in regard to familiar facts and help to make the history of the origin of the Jewish race comprehensible.

Although the term " Semite," as applied to a pure autonomous race existing since the beginning of time,

---

* And not they only but also their relatives, the Ammonites, the Moabites and the Edomites. These four make up the family of the " Hebrews," a name usually—but wrongly—applied to the Israelites alone or sometimes even to the Jews. *See* Wellhausen : *Israelitische und jüdische Geschichte*, 3rd ed. p. 7. To the same family belong likewise the Midianites and the Ishmaelites (Maspero: *Histoire ancienne*, 1895, ii. 65.)

a special creation of God, so to speak, is certainly a mere
abstraction, yet it is not so hazardous as the word
" Aryan " : for there still exists to-day a people which
is supposed to represent the pure, untarnished type of
the primeval Semite, viz., the Bedouin of the Arabian
desert.* Let us discard the hazy Semite and confine ourselves to the Bedouin of flesh and blood. It is supposed,
and there are good grounds for the supposition, that some
thousands of years before Christ, human beings, very
closely resembling the Bedouins of to-day, migrated from
Arabia in an almost unbroken stream to east and north
into the land of the two rivers. Arabia is healthy, so
its population increases ; its soil is extremely poor, so a
portion of its inhabitants must seek sustenance elsewhere.
It seems that sometimes great migratory hordes composed
of armed men had thus wandered forth ; in such cases the
surplus population had been cast out with irresistible
force from their home, and left as conquerors upon the
neighbouring countries ; in other cases single families
with their herds wandered peacefully over the indefinitely
marked boundary from one grazing-place to another :
if they did not at once turn off to the west, as many
of them did, it might happen that they advanced as far as
the Euphrates and so, following the stream, worked their
way into the north. In historical times (under the Romans
and subsequent to Mohammed) we have memorable
instances of this summary manner of getting rid of superfluous population ; † in the great civilised States between

* This seems to be unanimously asserted by all writers. I have
quoted Burckhardt in the course of this chapter. Here I shall only refer
to a more modern, universally recognised authority—W Robertson
Smith. In his *Religion of the Semites* (1894, p. 8) he says : " It can be
taken for granted that the Arabs of the desert have from time immemorial been an unmixed race." The same author points out that it is
inadmissible to put the Babylonians, Phœnicians, &c., down as
" Semites " : the only established fact is the relationship of the
languages, and all these so-called " Semitic " nations have sprung from
a decided mixture of blood.

† The last example was in the end of the nineteenth century, when the

the Tigris and the Euphrates, Semitisation was also the work of great, though more peaceful, masses. Wherever, in fact, as in Babylonian Accadia, the Semites came into contact with a ripe, strong, self-reliant culture, they prevailed over it by fusion with the people—a process which in the case of the Babylonians we can now trace almost step by step.* The Beni Israel, on the other hand, emigrated as simple shepherds in small groups and had, in order to secure the safety of their cattle, to avoid all warlike operations, of which their small number would have rendered them incapable in any case.† The Bible narrative naturally gives us only the faint reflection of primeval oral traditions concerning the earliest wanderings of this Bedouin family; they are in addition much falsified by the misconceptions, theories and purposes of late-born scribes; still there is no reason to doubt the correctness of the general details given, all the less so as they contain nothing that is improbable. Everything is indeed much abbreviated: whole families have dwindled into a single person (a universal Semitic custom, " such as we find only in the case of the Semites," says Wellhausen); other pretended ancestors are simply the names of the places in the neighbourhood of which the Israelites had long stayed; movements which required several generations to accomplish are accredited to a

Arabs, who from time immemorial had migrated not only to north and east, but also to west and south, completely devastated a great part of Central Africa. Immense kingdoms, which in the year 1880 were densely populated and entirely under cultivation, have since become a desert. Stanley tells us of a single Arab chieftain who laid waste a region of two thousand square miles! (*See* the books of Stanley, Wissman, Hinde, &c., and the short summary in Ratzel: *Völkerkunde*, 2nd ed. ii. 430.) *Cf. also* p. 115, note.

* *See* Hummel, Sayce, Budge and Maspero with regard to the lost race of the Accadians or Sumerians, the creators of the magnificent Babylonian culture, and their gradual Semitisation.

† To complete and correct what follows, *see* the interesting and excellent book of Carl Steuernagel: *Die Einwanderung der israelitischen Stämme in Kanaan*, Berlin, 1901.

single individual. This need of simplifying the complex, of pressing together what lies far apart, is just as natural to this people as it is to the poet who consciously creates. Thus, for example, the Bible represents Abraham, when already a married man, as emigrating from the district of Ur, on the lower course of the Euphrates, to northern Mesopotamia, at the foot of the Armenian mountain range, to that Paddan-Aram, of which the book of *Genesis* so often speaks and which lies beyond the Euphrates, between it and the tributary Khabur, in a straight line about 375 miles, but following the valley and the line of grazing-tracts at least 937 miles from Ur (*cf.* the map on p. 365); but more than that, this same Abraham is said to have moved later from Paddan-Aram towards the south-west, to the land of Canaan, from there to Egypt and finally (for I leave his shorter journeys out of account) from Egypt to Canaan again and all this accompanied by so numerous herds of cattle that he was forced, in order to find sufficient grazing land for them, to separate from his nearest relatives (*Genesis* xiii.). In spite of this compression the old Hebrew tradition contains all we require to know, particularly in places where the oldest tradition is before us in almost unfalsified form, and Biblical criticism already gives us full information with regard to it.* From this tradition we learn that the Bedouin family in question first of all wandered into the valley of the southern Euphrates and stayed a considerable time in the neighbourhood of the city of Ur. This city lay to the south of the great river and formed the farthest outpost of Chaldea. Here for the first time the nomads came into touch with civilisation. The shepherds could not indeed enter into this district itself, since magnificent cities and a highly developed agriculture required every inch of ground available, but here they

---

* *Cf.* especially Gunkel's *Handkommentar zur Genesis*, 1901 (now published in a second improved edition).

received imperishable impressions and instruction (to which I shall refer later) ; it was here too that they first became acquainted with such names as Abraham and Sarah, which their love of punning make them translate later into Hebrew (*Genesis* xvii. 1–6). They could not stay long in the vicinity of such high culture, or perhaps they were pushed forward by sons of the desert who were pressing on behind. And thus we see them moving ever farther and farther towards the north,* to the then sparsely populated Paddan-Aram,† where they must have stayed for a long time—at the very least for several centuries. When, however, the pasture of Mesopotamia was no longer sufficient for the increased number of human beings and cattle, a portion of them moved from that north-eastern corner of Syria, Paddan-Aram, to the south-western corner nearest Egypt, to Canaan, where they were hospitably received by a settled agricultural people and received permission to pasture their herds on the mountains. But Paddan-Aram lived long in the memory of the descendants of Abraham as their genuine home. Jehovah himself calls Paddan-Aram Abraham's " country " (*Genesis* xii. 1), and the mythical Abraham still speaks, long after he has settled in Canaan, with longing of his distant " country " and sends messengers to his " land " (*Genesis* xxiv. 4 and 7), in order to get in touch again with the relatives who had remained

* The direction was marked out for them ; from Ur they could choose no other course ; for the wilderness runs for several hundred miles parallel to the Euphrates, only a small stretch of watered land separating the two ; but suddenly, exactly at the 35th degree, the wilderness ceases and the land of Syria opens up to west, south and north. Syria stretches southwards to Egypt, westwards to the Mediterranean Sea, northwards to the Taurus, in the east it is bounded to-day by the Euphrates, but according to former conditions and ideas it embraced Mesopotamia, which lies beyond the middle Euphrates, and here the children of Abraham had their home for centuries.

† At a later time Mesopotamia was for long an artificially-watered and consequently richly-cultivated region ; in former times, however, it was, as it is to-day, a poor land, where only nomadic shepherds could find a living (*cf.* Maspero : *Histoire ancienne*, i. 563).

there. And thus the sons of Abraham, although already settled in Canaan, remained half Mesopotamians during all the long years which have been compressed and represented under the pseudo-mythical names Isaac

SKETCH-MAP

and Jacob; it is a perpetual coming and going; the southern branch feeling that it belongs to one principal northern stem.* But the moment came when they had to move farther towards the south; in dry years the pastures of Canaan were no longer sufficient, and perhaps

* This period, during which " Father Jacob developed into the people of Israel," Wellhausen describes as an interval of several centuries' duration (*Israelitische und jüdische Geschichte*, p. 11).

too the Canaanites felt the burden of their increasing numbers ; so at the time when the friendly half-Semitic Hyksos were in power, they wandered away to the land of Goshen, belonging to Egypt.   It was this long stay in Egypt * that first broke off all connection between them and their kinsmen, so that, when the Israelites once more returned to Palestine, they still recognised the Moabites, Edomites and the other Hebrews as distant blood-relations, but felt for them no longer love but hatred and contempt, a state of feeling which received a refreshingly artless expression in the genealogies of the Bible, according to which some of these races owe their origin to incest, while others are descended from harlots.

We can only speak of Israelites in the historical sense of the word from the moment when, as a not very numerous, but yet firmly united people, they forcibly took possession of Canaan on their flight from Egypt, and founded there a State that experienced many different but mostly very sad strokes of fortune, but which, in spite of the fact that it lay (like the rest of Syria) between hammer and anvil, that is, between warring "great Powers," continued to stand as an independent kingdom for almost seven hundred years. We must emphasise the fact that these Israelites were not very numerous ; it is important from an historical as well as from an anthropological point of view ; for to this circumstance we must ascribe the fact that the former and really domiciled inhabitants of Canaan (a mixture of

---

* According to Genesis xv. four hundred years, which is naturally not to be taken literally but simply as an expression for an almost unthinkably long time.   The number forty was among the Hebrews the expression for an indefinitely large number, four hundred *a fortiori*. Renan is of opinion that the stay of the Israelites in Egypt did not last more than one hundred years and that only the Josephites (probably only very distant relations with a strong mixture of Egyptian blood) were settled there for very long (*Histoire du peuple d'Israël*, 13ᵉ éd. i. pp. 112, 141, 142).

Hittites and Indo-European Amorites) were never destroyed and always formed and even still form the stock of the population.* The mingling of races, of which I shall immediately speak, and which had begun as soon as the Israelites entered Syrian territory, continued in the autonomous State of Israel, that is, in Palestine, and came to a sudden stop only after the Babylonian exile, and that in Judea alone, by the introduction of a new law. The fact that the Jews at a later time separated as an ethnological unity from the rest of the Israelites is purely and simply due to this, that the inhabitants of Judea by energetic enactments at last put a stop to the continual fusion (see *Ezra* ix. and x.).

The reader who would like further information on this matter may supplement the knowledge he has derived from this hasty sketch by consulting Wellhausen's concise *Israelitische und jüdische Geschichte*, Stade's *Geschichte des Volkes Israel*, Renan's detailed and yet lightly written *Histoire du peuple d'Israël*, and Maspero's comprehensive and luminous *Histoire ancienne des peuples de l'Orient classique ;* † in the meantime my sketch may suffice to show the origin of the Israelites in broad outline and to impress upon the memory in the simplest form the seemingly complicated facts of the case. I shall now attempt to show how the original, purely Semitic

* Sayce : *The Races of the Old Testament*, 2nd ed. pp. 76, 113. " The Roman drove the Jew out of the land that his fathers had conquered ; the Jews, on the other hand, had never succeeded in driving out the genuine possessors of Canaan. . . . The Jew held Jerusalem and Hebron, as well as the surrounding cities and villages, otherwise (even in Judea itself) he formed only a fraction of the population. As soon as the Jew was removed, for example, at the time of the Babylonian exile or after the destruction of Jerusalem by the Romans, the original population, freed from the pressure, increased . . . and the Jewish colonies in Palestine are to-day just as much foreigners as the German colonies there."

† I name only the latest, most important and most reliable books, written by real scholars but accessible to the unlearned. Of the older ones Duncker's *Geschichte des Altertums* also remains unsurpassed in many respects for the history of Israel.

emigrant became by crossing first of all a Hebrew and then an Israelite.

THE GENUINE SEMITE

The preceding historical sketch shows us a Bedouin family as the starting-point.* Let us first of all establish the one fact : this pure Semite, the original emigrant from the deserts of Arabia, is and remains the impelling power, the principle of life, the soul of the new ethnical unity of the Israelites which arose out of manifold crossing. No matter how much, in consequence not only of their destiny but above all of crossing with absolutely different human types, his descendants might differ in course of time morally and physically from the original Bedouin, yet in many points, good as well as bad, he remained their *spiritus rector*. Of the two or three souls which had their home in the breast of the later Israelites, this was the most obtrusive and long-lived. However, we can only congratulate this Bedouin family on their crossing, for any change in the manner of living is said to have a very bad effect on the high qualities of the genuine and purely Semitic nomads. The learned Sayce, one of the greatest advocates of the Jews at the present day, writes : " If the Bedouin of the desert chooses a settled life, he, as a rule, unites in himself all the vices of the nomad and of the

* As a matter of fact the current opinion is that the Semite and even that purest Bedouin type are the most absolute mongrels imaginable, the product of a cross between negro and white man ! Gobineau preached this doctrine fifty years ago, and was laughed at; to-day his opinion is the orthodox one ; Ranke defines it thus in his *Völkerkunde* (ii. 399) : " The Semites belong to the mulatto class, a transition stage between black and white." But I think that caution is here necessary. What is taking place before our eyes is not warranted to strengthen the belief that from mulattoes there could spring a firm, unchangeable type that would survive the storms of time : quicksand is not more fickle and changeable than this half-caste ; here, then, in defiance of all experience we should have to suppose that the unthinkable, the unexampled had taken place in the case of the Bedouins, (*Cf.*, too, August Forel's remarks, 1900).

peasant. Lazy, deceitful, cruel, greedy, cowardly, he is rightly regarded by all nations as the scum of mankind." *
But long before they settled down, this Bedouin family, the Beni Israel, had fortunately escaped such a cruel fate by manifold crossing with non-Semites.

We saw that the original Bedouin family first stayed for a considerable time on the Southern Euphrates in the neighbourhood of the city of Ur : did crossing take place at this stage ? It has been asserted that it did. And since fairly genuine Sumero-Accadians presumably formed the basis of the population of the Babylonian Empire at that time—for the Semites had merely annexed this State and its high civilisation without performing either the mental work or the manual †—it is assumed that the stock of Abraham was quickened by Sumero-Accadian blood. The occurrence of such strange names as Abraham (this was the name of the first legendary founder and king of Ur among the Sumerians) has given weight to this view, as also the fragments of half-understood Turanian ‡ wisdom and mythology, of which the first chapters of *Genesis* are composed. But such assumptions are purely hypothetical and hence, to begin with, hardly merit serious consideration. Not even probability speaks for this view. The poor shepherds had hardly touched the hem of civilisation, what people then would have entered into family relations with them ? And as regards the adoption of such meagre cosmogonic conceptions as we find in the Bible, intercourse with other Hebrews is sufficient to explain that ; for the mythology, the science and the culture of the Sumerians (in which we still share, thanks

* *The Races of the Old Testament*, p. 106.
† *See* especially Sayce : *Assyria*, p. 24 ff., and *Social Life among the Assyrians and Babylonians ;* also Winckler : *Die Völker Vorderasiens* (1900), p. 8.
‡ The word " Turanian " has escaped my pen, because many autho regard the Sumero-Accadians as Turanians. *See* Hommel : *Gesch. Babyloniens und Assyriens*, pp. 125, 244 f.

to the idea of creation and of the fall of man, the division of the week and the year, the foundation of geometry, and the invention of writing) had spread far and wide; Egypt was their pupil,* and the Semite, incapable of such deep intuition as the Egyptian, had long ago, before the Beni Israel began their wanderings, adopted as much of Egyptian culture as seemed advantageous and practical and had, as active mediators, spread it wherever they went. The crossing with Sumero-Accadians is therefore just as improbable as it is unproved.

We are, however, on sure ground, as soon as the emigrants move to north and west. For now they are in the heart of Syria and they never again leave it (except at the time of their short stay on the borders of Egypt). Here, in Syria, our purely Semitic Bedouin family has been changed by crossing, here its members became Hebrews by mingling with an absolutely different type, the Syrian—as so many a Bedouin colony before and after them. At a later period part of the family was forced to emigrate from Mesopotamia, which lay in the northeast corner, to Canaan, in the extreme south-west, where similar race-moulding influences, to which quite new ones were also added, asserted themselves in a still more definite way. It was only here, in Canaan, that the Abrahamide Hebrews changed gradually into genuine Israelites. To this very Canaan the Israelites, now increased in numbers, returned as conquerors, after their sojourn in Egypt; and here they received, in addition to alien blood, a new culture, which transformed them from nomads into settled farmers and city-dwellers.

We can, therefore, without making any mistake, distinguish two anthropogenetic spheres of influence, which successively came into prominence, a more general one, provided by the entrance into Syria and in particular

* See Hommel: *Der babylonische Ursprung der ägyptischen Kultur* (1892).

by the long stay in Mesopotamia, in regard to which we have no very definite historical dates, but which we may and must deduce from the known ethnological facts ; in the second place, a more particular Canaanite influence, which we can prove from the detailed testimony of the Bible. Let us discuss first the more general sphere of influence and then the more particular one.

THE SYRIAN

If we turn up a text-book of geography or an encyclopædia, we shall find it stated that the present population of Syria is "to the greatest extent Semitic." This is false ; just as false as the statement we find in the same sources, that the Armenians are "Aryans." Here again we see the widespread confusion of language and race ; we should, on the same footing, logically have to maintain that the negroes of the United States were Anglo-Saxons. Scientific anthropology has in recent years, by thorough investigation of an enormous amount of material, irrefutably proved that from the most remote times to which prehistoric discoveries reach back, the main population of Syria has been formed from a type which is absolutely different, physically and morally, from the Semitic, as it is from everything which we are wont to comprise under the term " Aryan " ; and this applies not to the population of Syria alone, but also to that of all Asia Minor and the extensive region which we call Armenia at the present day. There are races which have an inborn tendency to restless wandering (e.g., the Bedouin, the Laplander, &c.), others which possess a rare power of expansion (e.g., the Teutonic races) ; but this inhabitant of Syria and Asia Minor seems to have been distinguished and still to be distinguished by his obstinate attachment to his native soil and the invincible power of his physical constancy. His original home was the trysting-place of nations, he himself almost always being vanquished, and the great battles of the world being fought over him—yet he survived them all and his blood asserted itself to such an extent that the Syrian Semite of to-day should be called Semite in language rather than in race, and the so-called Aryan Armenian, of Phrygian origin, has perhaps not 10 per cent. of Indo-European blood in his veins. On the other hand, the so-called " Syrian " of to-day, the Jew and the Armenian can hardly be distinguished from one another, and this is easily explained, since the primal race which unites all three makes them daily more and more like each other. We may most appropriately apply a quotation from Schiller's *Braut von Messina* to this Syrian stem :

Die fremden Eroberer kommen und gehen:
Wir gehorchen, aber wir bleiben stehen.

Now the people which enters history at a later time under the name of Israelites was subject to this powerful ethnical influence for many centuries, at least for over ten centuries. That is what I called the general sphere of influence by which our genuine Semitic Bedouin family became a group of the so-called " Hebrews." Hebrews are, in fact, a cross between Semite and Syrian. It must not be thought that the nomad shepherds immediately crossed with the strange race, the process was rather as follows : on the one hand they found a considerable number of half and quarter Hebrews, who formed the point of connection; on the other hand they doubtless subdued the original inhabitants (as the predominance of the Semitic languages, Hebrew, Aramaic, &c., proves) and begot sons and daughters with their Syrian slaves·; later (in half-historical times) we see them voluntarily inter-marrying with the independent families of the alien people, and this had beyond doubt been for centuries the custom. However, no matter what theories we

may hold about the process of fusion, certain it is that
it did take place.

To be able to speak of that other Syrian type it would
be convenient to have a name for him. Hommel, the
well-known Munich scholar, calls him the *Alarodian* ; *
he thinks he may ascribe to him considerable expansion
even over Southern Europe and finds him in the Iberians
and Basques of to-day. But the layman must be very
discreet in his use of such hypotheses ; before this book is
printed, the Alarodians may have been thrown among
the scrap-iron of science. The example of the French
zoologist and anthropologist, G. de Lapouge, is worthy of
imitation ; he does not trouble himself about history and
origin, but gives names to the various physical types
according to the Linnean method, such as *Homo europæus,
Homo Afer, Homo contractus,* &c. So far as formation of skull
is concerned, this type from Asia Minor would correspond
pretty exactly to Lapouge's *Homo alpinus ;* † but here
we may safely and simply call him *Homo syriacus,* the
primeval inhabitant of Syria. And just as we found a
point of support for the Semitic type in the Bedouin, so
we find in the Hittite tribe a peculiarly characteristic
representative of the Syrian type, and moreover the one
with which the Israelites in Palestine were closely connected ; it no longer, of course, exists among us as a
national individuality, but it is daily becoming better
known from history and from manifold surviving representations.‡ This Syrian type is distinguished by the
prevalence of a particular anatomical characteristic

* He takes the name from a tribe mentioned by Herodotus as living
at the foot of Mount Ararat.

† Lapouge: *La dépopulation de la France, Revue d'Anthropologie,*
1888, p. 79. F. von Luschan has definitely pointed out the resemblance
of the Syrian to the Savoyard.

‡ A summary of our knowledge of the Hittites will be found in
Winckler's *Die Völker Vorderasiens,* 1900, p. 18 ff. The expression
" Hittite" in this book signifies the same to me as the *x* to a mathe-
matician in a properly stated but not yet numerically solved equation

he is round-headed, or, as the natural scientists say,
"brachycephalous," that is, with a short skull, the
breadth of which is nearly equal to the length.*
The Bedouin, on the other hand, and also every
Semite whose blood is not strongly mixed with
foreign elements, is decidedly "dolichocephalic."
"Long, narrow heads," writes von Luschan, "are a

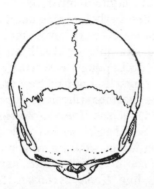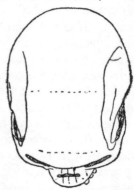

SHORT SKULL (brachycephalous)   LONG SKULL (dolichocephalous)
(After de Mortillet)

striking characteristic of the Bedouin to-day, and we
should have to claim the same for the oldest Arabs were
it not proved from numerous illustrations on the old
Egyptian monuments fortunately preserved." † Naturally
there is more than this one anatomical criterion; corresponding to the round head there is the thick-set body;

* The skull is regarded as particularly long when the relation of
breadth to length is not over 75 to 100, particularly short when it is
80 or more.   When I studied anthropology with Carl Vogt, all the
students were measured craniometrically; in the case of one the rare
relation of 92 to 100 was established, that is, his head was almost quite
round; he was an Armenian, a typical representative of the Syrian
type of skull.

† F. v. Luschan: *Die anthropologische Stellung der Juden* (Lecture
delivered in the General Meeting of the German Anthropological Society
of the year 1892).   This lecture is to be found in the *Correspondenzblatt*
of the Society for 1892, Nos. 9 and 10.   It summarises extensive
researches and I shall often quote from it further on.

it is the expression of a complete and peculiar physiological character. But the skull is the most convenient part óf the skeleton for making comparative studies regarding extinct races, and it is also the most expressive, and no matter how endless the variation in the individuals, it maintains the typical forms with great constancy. But the Hittite had another and much more striking anatomical distinguishing feature, a very

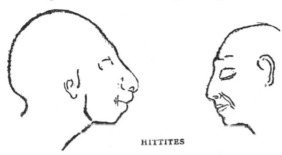

HITTITES

ephemeral one, it is true, since cartilage and not bone went to form it, but it has been splendidly preserved in pictures and so is well known to us to-day—the nose. The so-called " Jewish nose " is a Hittite legacy. The genuine Arab, the pure Bedouin, has usually " a short, small nose little bent " (I quote von Luschan and refer to the illustrations given) and even when the nose is more of the eagle type, it never possesses an " extinguisher " (as Philip von Zesen, the language-reformer, called it) of the specific, unmistakable Jewish and Armenian form. Now by continuous crossing with the round-headed type of the alien people the Israelite has gradually lost his narrow, long Bedouin head, receiving as compensation the so-called Jewish nose. Certainly the long head still occurred, maintaining itself especially among the nobler families; even among the Jews of to-day we find a small percentage of genuine long heads; but the long head disappeared more and more. The nose alone is no reliable proof of Jewish descent; the reason is clear; this Syrian legacy is common to all peoples who have Syrian blood in their veins. In the case of this anthropological discovery we have to do with no hypothetical assertions, such as too frequently occur in theological and critical or historical works; it is the sure result of thorough scientific investigation of a sufficiently large material; * this material

TRUE BEDOUIN OF THE PRESENT DAY †

extends from a very ancient time down to the present, and is excellently supported by the numerous representations found in Egypt and Syria, and gradually assigned to their proper period. We can in a way trace the process by which the Israelite "became Jew" by the Egyptian monuments, although, in fact, even in the oldest of them (which do not go far back into Israelite history, since it was only in Solomon's time that the Jewish people became known beyond their borders) there is little of the genuine Semitic type revealed. Genuine Hittites and half-Hittites are here represented as Israelite soldiers; only the leaders (*see,* for instance, the so-called portrait of

* Von Luschan's *Mitteilungen* of the year 1892 have 60,000 measurements to support them.

† From a photograph in Ratzel's *Völkerkunde*. The other typical pictures are from well-known reliefs on Egyptian monuments.

King Rehoboam, Solomon's son) remind us of Bedouin types, but even they sometimes rather resemble good European countenances.

With these last remarks we pass from the general prehistoric sphere of influence to that of Canaan, which likewise continued for over a thousand years and provides us with plenty of sure facts to go upon. For before the Hebrew Israelites had the honour of

AMORITISH ISRAELITE (portrait of a son of Solomon)

being immortalised by the art of Egyptian painters, they had moved from Mesopotamia to Canaan. We must distinguish between their first appearance in Canaan and their second : in the former case they remained there as nomadic shepherds on the best terms with the rightful inhabitants of the cities and the owners of the tracts under cultivation ; in the second case they entered the country as conquerors. In the former case, in fact, they were not numerous, in the second they were a whole nation. However uncertain and disputed many historical details still may be, one fact is certain : when they entered the land first the Israelites found the Hittites living there, those Hittites who formed a most important stem of the *Homo syriacus*. Abraham says to the inhabitants of Hebron, to the " children of Heth," as he expressly calls them : " I am a stranger and a sojourner

with you" (*Genesis* xxiii. 4), and he begs, as only a
stranger on suffrance could beg, a "burying-place"
for his wife Sarah. Isaac's eldest son, Esau, has only
daughters of Heth as his wives (*Genesis* xxvi. 34); the
younger son, Jacob, is sent to distant Mesopotamia,
that he may take a Hebrew woman as his wife, and from
this we must conclude that there was none in Palestine,
no Hebrew girl at least, who would as regards wealth have
been a suitable match for him. Isaac would not have
insisted upon it, a well-to-do Hittite would have pleased
him, but Rebecca, his Mesopotamian wife, had no
love for her Hittite daughters-in-law, the wives of Esau,
and said she would rather die than let any more such
come into the house (*Genesis* xxvii. 46). Among the sons
of Jacob it is again specially mentioned of Judah that he
married Hittite wives (1 *Chronicles* ii. 3). These popular
tales are a source of historical information; we see that
the Israelites had a clear recollection of having, as a
very limited number of shepherds, lived among a strange,
cultured and friendly people that dwelt in cities; the
rich elders of the race could indulge in the luxury of
sending for wives for their sons from their former home;
but these sons themselves like to follow their direct
inclination rather than the principle of exclusiveness:
they married the maidens whom they saw around them—
unless they were such heartless mercenary match-makers
as Jacob; the poorer classes, of course, selected wives
where they found them. In addition there was the
begetting of children with slave girls. Of Jacob's twelve
sons, for instance, four are the sons of slave girls and they
enjoy the same rights as the others.—All this refers to
the earliest contact with the Hittites of Canaan which
the Bible mentions. Now there followed, according to
legend, the long stay on the borders of Egypt, in the
land of Goshen. But here, too, the Israelites were surrounded by Hittites. For the Hittites extended to the

borders of Egypt, where at that time their kinsmen, the Hyksos, held the sceptre ; the city of Tanis, which was the rallying-point for the Israelites in Goshen, was essentially a Hittite city ; from the earliest times it had been in the closest contact with Hebron ; when the Israelites moved with their flocks from Hebron to the district of Tanis, they accordingly remained in the same ethnical surroundings.* And when they afterwards returned to Canaan as conquerors, they, indeed, gradually overthrew the Canaanites, who consisted mostly of Hittites, but they also, for the first time, entered into close intercourse with them. For, as I insisted above, the Canaanite did not disappear. We need only read the first chapter of the *Book of Judges* to see what Wellhausen too attests : " The Israelites did not conquer the former population systematically, but made their way among them . . . it is impossible to speak of a complete conquest of the land of Palestine." And with regard to the manner in which this alien non-Semitic blood permeated the Hebrew blood more and more, the same author says, " The most important event in the period of Judges took place fairly quietly, namely, the fusion of the new Israelite population of the land with the old population. The Israelites of the time of the Kings had a strong Canaanite admixture in their blood ; they were by no means pure descendants of those who once had immigrated from Egypt. . . . If the Israelites had destroyed the old settled inhabitants, they would have made a desert of the land and robbed themselves of the prize of victory. By sparing them and, as it were, grafting themselves upon them, they grew into their culture. They made themselves at home in houses which they had not built, in fields and gardens which they had not laid out and cultivated. Everywhere, like lucky heirs, they reaped the fruits of

* *Cf.* Renan : *Israël* i. chap. 10.

the labour of their predecessors. Thus they themselves underwent an inner transformation fraught with many consequences; they grew quickly into a cultured people."* At an earlier time, in Hebron or Tanis, the Israelites had learned from the Hittites the art of writing; † now they learned from them how to cultivate crops and vines, how to build and to manage cities—in short, through them they became a civilised people; and through them also they became for the first time a State. Never could the various tribes, living as they did in constant jealousy, in suspicious isolation, have formed themselves into a unity but for the Canaanite element, the cement of the State. And what is more, their religious conceptions, too, received their special colouring and organisation from the Canaanites : Baal, the God of agriculture and of peaceful work, coalesced with Jehovah, the God of armies and of raids. We see how much Baal was honoured among the Israelites (in spite of later corrections on the part of the Jews) from facts such as this, that the first Israelite hero on the soil of Palestine is called Jerubbaal,‡ and, moreover, takes to wife a Hittite : that the first King, Saul, calls one of his sons Ishbaal, David one of his Baaliada, Jonathan his only son Meribbaal, &c. The Israelite borrowed from the Canaanite the whole tradition of Prophets, as also the whole outward cult and the tradition of the sacred places.§ I need not discuss in detail what every one can find in the Bible (sometimes certainly obscured by so many strange-sounding names that one needs an expert guide), namely, the great part played by the Hittites and by their relatives the Philistines in the history of Israel. Till the fusion

---

* *Israel. u. jüd. Geschichte*, 3rd ed. pp. 37, 46 and 48.

† Renan : *Israël* i. 136.

‡ A fact which the later edition of the Bible sought to conceal (*Judges* vi. 32) while the older editors thought nothing of it (1 *Samuel* xii. 11).

§ *Cf.* Wellhausen, as above, pp. 45 f., 102 f. ; concerning the sacred places *see* his *Prolegomena zur Geschichte Israels*, 4th ed. p. 18 f.

has far advanced and the difference in names had disappeared, we find them everywhere, particularly among
the best soldiers ; and how many details in this connection must have disappeared after the later editing of
the Bible by the Jews, who endeavoured to cut out all
that was alien to them and to introduce the fiction of a
pure descent from Abraham ! David's bodyguard is
composed if not wholly yet to a great extent of men who
do not belong to Israel ; Hittites and Gittites hold important posts as officers ; the bulk of the soldiers were
Cerethites and Pelethites, Philistines and all other kinds
of aliens, partly Syrian, partly almost purely European,
some of Hellenic race.* David, in fact, won the throne
only by the help of the Philistines—and probably as their
vassal ; † he even did everything in his power to encourage the fusion of the Israelites with their neighbours,
and himself set the example by marrying women of
Syrian and Indo-European descent.

THE AMORITES

Since the word " Indo-European " has slipped from
my pen I must here dwell upon a fact which I have as yet
scarcely mentioned. The Canaanites consisted principally,
but not solely, of Hittites ; the Amorites lived in close
connection with them, but they were often settled in
separate districts, and thus kept their race relatively
pure. These Amorites were tall, fair, blue-eyed men
of ruddy complexion ; they were " from the north,"
that is, from Europe ; the Egyptians, therefore, called

* There were also Arabs, Hebrews from non-Israelite stems, Arameans
and all kinds of pseudo-Semitic aliens. As there are said to have been
1,300,000 men in Israel and Judah capable of bearing arms according
to the (certainly very false) popular account (2 Samuel xxiv.), we
get the impression that the Israelites themselves were not very warlike.
See especially Renan : Israël ii. livre 3, chap. i.

† Wellhausen : Israelitisce und jüdische Geschichte (3 Ausg.), p. 58.

them Tamehu, the "North men," and moreover they
seem, though this is of course problematic, not to have
reached Palestine very long before the return of the
Israelites from Egypt.* To the east of the Jordan
they had founded mighty kingdoms with which the
Israelites later had to wage many wars ; another portion
had entered Palestine and lived there in the closest friendship with the Hittites ; † others had joined the Philistines,
and that in such large numbers, increased perhaps by
direct immigration from the purely Hellenic West, that
many historians have regarded the Philistines as predominantly Aryan-European.‡ These, our own kinsfolk,
are those children of Anak, the " men of great stature "
who inspired the Israelites with such terror, when
the latter first secretly entered Southern Palestine on a
scouting expedition (*Numbers* xiii.) ; to them belonged the
brave Goliath, who challenges the Israelites to a knightly
combat but is killed by the treacherously slung stone ; §
to them belong those " Rephaims " who carry gigantic
spears and heavy mail of iron (1 *Samuel* xvii. 5 ff.,
2 *Samuel* xxi. 16 ff.). And while the Bible relates in

* The fact that the book of *Genesis* (xiv. 13) represents Abraham as
already living in peaceful alliance with three Amorites in the plain
of Hebron has naturally no claim to historical validity.

† *See* especially Sayce : *The Races of the Old Testament*, p. 110 ff.

‡ *Cf.* Renan : *Israël* ii. livre 3, chap. 3. For the Hellenic origin
of a considerable proportion of the Philistines and the introduction of
a number of Greek words through them into Hebrew, *see* Renan :
Israël, i. p. 157 note, and Maspero, ii. p. 698. As a matter of fact the
question of the origin of the Philistines and Amorites is still very
hotly debated ; we can calmly leave the dispute to historians and
theologians ; the anthropological results are results of exact science,
and philology must follow them, not *vice versâ*. Certain it is that the
Amorites and at least a portion of the Philistines were tall, fair,
blue-eyed dolichocephali : thus they belong to the type *homo europæus*. That is sufficient for us laymen.

§ The legend which ascribes this cowardly act to David is a late
interpretation ; the original account is given in 2 *Samuel* xxi. 19
(*cf.* Stade : *Geschichte des Volkes Israel* i. 225 ff.). It is important
to know this when forming an estimate of David's character. *See*
p. 385.

great detail the heroic deeds of the Israelites against these tall fair men, it could not, on the other hand, conceal the fact that it was from them (the still very savage pure Indo-European tribe of the Gittites) that David drew his best and most reliable soldiers. It was only by the Philistines that the Philistines were conquered, only by the Amorites the Amorites. The Gittites, for example, were not conquered by David, but followed him of their own accord (2 *Samuel* xv. 19 ff.) from their love of war ;

AMORITE

their leader, Ittai, was appointed commander of a third of the Israelite army (2 *Samuel* xviii. 2). Of this "Aryan corps," as he calls it, Renan says : " It was as brave as the Arabian but excelled it in reliability ; to establish anything permanently its support was necessary. . . . It was this that frustrated the treacherous plans of Absalom, of Sebah, of Adonijah ; it was this that saved the threatened throne of Solomon . . . it supplied the cement of the Israelite kingdom." * But these men were not only brave and faithful soldiers, but also builders of cities ; their cities were the best built and the strongest (*Deuteronomy* i. 28) ; † one of them in particular became

* Renan : *Israël* ii. 30–32.
† Sayce (*Races of the Old Testament,* p. 112) gives an account of Flinders Petrie's recent excavations of Amorite cities with walls 2½ metres thick.

world-famous : not far from Hebron, the chief city of their Hittite friends, the Amorites founded a new city, Jerusalem. The King of Jerusalem who marches against Joshua is an Amorite (*Joshua* x. 5), and even though the narrative says that he was defeated and slain with all the other kings, one must take that and the whole book of Joshua *cum grano salis;* for the conquest of Palestine in reality cost the Israelites a great deal of trouble, and was accomplished only very slowly and by the help of foreigners ; * at any rate the city of Jerusalem was till David's time an Amorite city, mixed with much Hittite blood, a mixed population which the Bible calls Jebusites, but it remained free from Israelites ; it was only in the eighth year of his reign that David with his alien mercenaries won this fortress and, because of its strength, chose it as his residence. But the Amorite-Hittite population continued to be of importance by reason of their numbers and position ; † David has to buy ground from a well-to-do Amorite, to erect an altar thereon (2 *Samuel* xxiv. 18 ff.), and it is with a Gittite, one of his most trusted leaders, that he deposits the sacred ark of the covenant, after he has transferred it to Jerusalem (2 *Samuel* iv. 10).‡ Thus, too, the prophet Ezekiel represents God as calling to the city of Jerusalem : " Thy birth and thy nativity is of the land of Canaan ; thy father was an Amorite, and thy mother an Hittite ! " (*Ezekiel* xvi. 3). And then he reproaches the Israelite inhabitants with mixing with these alien elements : " Thou playedst the harlot and pouredst out thy fornications on every one that passed by " (*Ezekiel*

---

* *See* especially Wellhausen's *Prolegomena,* in many passages.

† In *Joshua* xv. 63 we read : " As for the Jebusites, the inhabitants of Jerusalem, the children of Judah could not drive them out ; the Jebusites dwell with the children of Judah at Jerusalem unto this day."

‡ Wellhausen proves (*Prolegomena,* p. 43] that Obededom was really, as the passage quoted says, a Gittite and not a Levite, as the later version gives it (1 *Chronicles* xvi. 18).

xvi. 15)—a piece of simplicity on the part of the pious Jew, since the great men of his race had not been sparing with the example, and he himself, as a Jerusalemite, was the child of this threefold crossing ; Ezekiel, the real inventor of specific Judaism, had already before his mind that paradoxical idea of a Jew of pure race, which is a *contradictio in adjecto*. The Judean, in fact, had adopted more Amorite blood than any other Israelite, and that for the simple reason that the Amorites were pretty numerous in the south of Palestine, the districts of Simeon, Judah and Benjamin, whereas they were less numerous in the north. The Egyptian monuments, on which the various peoples are most characteristically represented, prove incontestably that at the time of Solomon and his successors the inhabitants of Southern Israel, especially the leaders of the army, were distinguished by the predominance of the clearly marked Amorite, that is Indo-European, type.

Indeed it has been sometimes questioned whether David himself was not half or three-quarters Amorite. The Bible emphasises in several places his fairness, and, as Virchow has proved by countless statistics, " the skin with all that belongs to it is even more constant than the skull " ; now fair complexion and light hair never occurred among the Hebrews and the members of the Syrian group, these characteristics of the European being first brought into the land by the Amorites and the Hellenes ; that is why David's fairness was so striking.* In these circumstances it is probably not

* Luther had translated the passages in question (2 *Samuel* xvi. 12, xvii. 42) by the word "brownish"; Genesius, on the other hand, in his dictionary translates the Hebrew word by "red," and while admitting that it usually refers to the hair, he takes great pains to prove that David must have been black-haired and that "red" here refers to the complexion (in the 1899 edition this apologetic attempt is dropped); the best scientific translators to-day look upon the word as meaning "fair-haired," and it seems pretty certain that David was distinctly fair-haired.

too daring to suppose that a shepherd born in Bethlehem (that is, in the district most thickly populated by Amorites) may have had an Amorite mother. His character, its great faults as well as its fascinating qualities, his daring, his spirit of adventure, his carelessness, his fanciful nature, distinguish David, it seems to me, from all the heroes of Israel; equally so his endeavour to organise the kingdom and to unite the scattered tribes into one whole, which drew upon him the hatred of the Israelites. His outspoken predilection for the Philistines, too, among whom he had gladly served as a soldier (*see*, for example, 2 *Samuel* xxi. 3), is a striking feature, as also the remarkable fact, pointed out by Renan (*Israël*, ii. 35), that he treated the Philistines generously in war, but the Hebrew peoples with frightful cruelty, as though they were repugnant to him. Should there be any truth in this supposition, Solomon could hardly be called an Israelite; for it is very unlikely that his mother Bathsheba, the wife of the Hittite Uriah, was an Israelite.* Thus we should have an explanation of the peculiar incompatibility between Solomon's nature and aims and the character of Israel and Judah. Renan says it openly: " *Salomon n'entendait rien à la vraie vocation de sa race* "; † he was a stranger with all a stranger's wishes and a stranger's aims in the midst of the people he thought to make great. And thus this short period of splendour in the history of the Israelite people—David, Solomon—would in reality be nothing else but an " episode " brought about by the exultant strength of an entirely different blood, but soon crushed by the unbending will of the Syro-Semite, who was not inclined to follow in those paths, nor indeed capable of doing so.

* Renan: *Israël* ii. 97. † *Ibid.* ii. 174

COMPARATIVE NUMBERS

Concerning that which I previously termed the special sphere of influence, we possess, as can be seen, sufficient historical material. If my purpose were not limited to describing the origin of the Jews I might add a great deal more—for example, that the tribe of Joseph, the most gifted and energetic of all Israelites from whom are descended Joshua, Samuel, Jerubbaal, &c., and the great dynasty of the Omrides, were half-Egyptians, as *Genesis* xli. 45 tells us with the brevity of such folk-lore, in that Joseph marries the daughter of a priest from Heliopolis, who bears him Ephraim and Manasseh . . . but this fact is of little or no importance in fixing the Jewish line of descent ; for marriages between the different tribes of Israel were made almost impossible by law, and were particularly improbable owing to the persistent antipathy of the children of Joseph to those of Judah. It is just as unnecessary to speak of their contact with many other Hebrew families. The later admixture of negro blood with the Jewish in the Diaspora of Alexandria —of which many a man of Jewish persuasion at this day offers living proof—is also a matter of little importance. What I have said is detailed enough to enable every one to picture to himself the anthropogeny of the Jew in its broad outlines. We have seen that there cannot be the least doubt that the historical Israelite, from whom the real " Jew " later separated himself, is the product of a mixture. He even enters history as a half-caste, namely, as a Hebrew, this Hebrew then contracts marriages with alien non-Semitic women : first of all with the Hittites, a special stem of the widespread and clearly marked *homo syriacus ;* in the second place with the tall, fair, blue-eyed Amorites from the Indo-European group. Now this historical testimony is confirmed in an irrefutable manner by that of science. F. von Luschan thus sum-

marises the evidence in the paper already quoted : " The
Jews are descended, first from real Semites, secondly
from Aryan Amorites, thirdly and chiefly from the
descendants of the old Hittites. These are the three
most important elements in the Jew, and in comparison
other mixtures are of very little account."   This diagnosis
—let it be noted—refers to the Jews at the time when they
were separated from Israel, and it is equally applicable
to-day ; the measurements have been made on old
material and on the very newest, and that with the result
that the various adoptions of aliens (Spaniards, Southern
French, &c.) into Judaism, on which feuilletonists and
unctuous moralists are wont to lay much emphasis, have
remained absolutely without influence ; a race so characteristically composed and then kept so strictly pure
immediately absorbs such drops of water.

The first point is thus settled : the Israelite people is
descended from the crossing of absolutely different
human types. The second point, in which the relation of
the different races to each other has to be discussed, will
require only one paragraph as far as pure statistics are
concerned ; but what would be the use of figures if
they did not give us distinct conceptions ? That would
be purely and simply the x, y, z of elementary algebra ;
the problem is correctly solved, but does not mean anything, as all the figures are unknown ; the quality
of the different races will therefore detain our attention
longer than the quantity.

Now as far as the quantitative composition of the
Israelite blood is concerned, we must not forget that
even 60,000 measurements are little in comparison with
the millions that have lived in the course of centuries ;
it would be wrong to apply them to the single individual ;
statistics of masses cannot lift even the hem of the veil
which envelops the personality. Nevertheless, we should
also remember that beyond the individuality of the person

there is the individuality of the whole people ; and numbers can be much better applied to this more abstract personality. I cannot tell simply from the race of an individual what he will do in a definite case ; but I can, for example, with great certainty prophesy how a large number of Italians, as a collective body, or an equal number of Norwegians will act in a definite case. For our knowledge of the character of a people anthropological figures are therefore of real value. Now these figures give the following results with regard to the Jews (of former times and to-day, in east and in west) ; 50 per cent. show clear evidence of belonging to the type *homo syriacus* (short heads, characteristic, so-called " Jewish " noses, inclination to stoutness, &c.) ; only 5 per cent. have the features and the anatomical structure of the genuine Semite (the Bedouin of the desert) ; in the case of 10 per cent. we find a colour of skin and hair, often too of complexion, which points to the Amorite of Indo-European descent ; 35 per cent. represent indefinable mixed forms, something of the nature of Lombroso's " combined photographs," where countenances occur in which the one feature contradicts the other : skulls which are neither long like those of the genuine Semite, nor half-long like those of the Amorite, nor round like those of the Syrian, noses which are neither Hittite, nor Aryan, nor Semitic, or, again, the Syrian nose, but without the head that belongs to it, and so on *ad infinitum.* The chief result of this anatomical survey is that the Jewish race is in truth a permanent but at the same time a mongrel race which always retains this mongrel character. In the former chapter I have tried to make clear the difference between mixed and mongrel races. All historically great races and nations have been produced by mixing ; but wherever the difference of type is too great to be bridged over, then we have mongrels. That is the case here. The crossing between Bedouin and Syrian was—from an anatomical point of view—probably worse than that between Spaniard and South American Indian. And to this was added later the ferment of a European-Aryan element .

CONSCIOUSNESS OF SIN AGAINST RACE

It is very proper to lay strong emphasis on this; for such a process, however unconsciously it may go on, is an incestuous crime against nature; it can only be followed by a miserable or a tragical fate.   The rest of the Hebrews, and with them the Josephites, had a wretched end; like the families of the more important pseudo-Semitic mestizos (the Phœnicians, Babylonians, &c.) they disappeared and left no trace behind; the Jew, on the other hand, chose the tragic fate ; that proves his greatness, and that *is* his greatness.   I shall soon return to this theme, since this resolve on his part means the founding of Judaism;   I shall only add one remark, for it is appropriate here and has never yet, so far as I know, been made, namely, that this deep consciousness of sin, which weighed upon * the Jewish nation in its heroic days, and which has found pathetic expression in the words of its chosen men, is rooted in these physical relations.   Naturally the intelligence, and the vanity which is common to us all, explained it quite differently, but the instinct went deeper than the understanding, and as soon as the destruction of the Israelites and their own captivity had awakened the conscience of the Jew, his first act was to put an end to that incest (as I called it above, using the very word of Ezekiel) by the strict prohibition of every crossing, even with nearly related tribes.   An inexplicable contradiction has been found in the fact that it was the Jews who brought into our

* " Since the exile the consciousness of sin was (in the case of the Jews), so to say, permanent," says Wellhausen in his *Prolegomena*, 4th ed p. 431.

bright world the ever-threatening conception of sin,
and that they nevertheless understand by sin something
quite different from us. Sin is for them a national thing,
whereas the individual is " just " when he does not transgress the " law " ; * redemption is not the moral redemption of the individual, but the redemption of the State ; †
that is difficult for us to understand. But there is
something more : the sin unconsciously committed is
the same to the Jew as a conscious sin ; ‡ " the notion
of sin has for the Jew no necessary reference to the
conscience of the sinner, it does not necessarily involve
the conception of a moral badness, but points to a legal
responsibility." § Montefiore also expressly declares that
according to the view of the postexilic legislators " sin was
looked upon not as a contamination of the individual
soul, but as a pollution of the physical purity, a disturb-
ance of that untroubled purity of the land and its inhabitants which is the one condition under which God
can continue to dwell among His people and in His sanctuary " (p. 326). Wellhausen expresses himself thus :
" In the case of the Jews . . . there is no inner connection
between the good man and that which is good ; the action
of the hands and the desire of the heart are severed."‖
I am, as I said, convinced that the key to this remarkable
and contradictory conception is to be found in the history
of the physical growth of this people : their existence is

* See *Matthew* xix. 20. The Jew Graetz even to-day approves fully
of the utterance of the rich man and shows that the demand " to repent
of his sins " has no meaning for the Jew (*Volkstümliche Geschichte der
Juden* i. 577).

† W. Robertson Smith: *The Prophets of Israel and their Place in
History*, 1895, p. 247.

‡ *Ibid.* p. 102 ; Montefiore: *Religion of the Ancient Hebrews*, 2nd ed.
p. 558 (supplement by Rabbi Schechter).

§ W. Robertson Smith: *The Prophets of Israel and their Place in
History*, p. 103. In another place he writes : " Sin is to the Hebrew
every action that puts a man in the wrong with one who has the power
to punish him for it " (p. 246).

‖ *Israel. und jüdische Geschichte*, 3rd ed. p. 380.

sin, their existence is a crime against the holy laws of life ; this, at any rate, is felt by the Jew himself in the moments when destiny knocks heavily at his door. Not the individual but the whole people had to be washed clean, and not of a conscious but of an unconscious crime ; and that is impossible, "though thou wash thee with nitre, and take thee much soap," as Jeremiah (ii. 22) says to his people. And in order to wipe out the irretrievable past, in order to fuse that past with the present, in which wisdom and the power of will should set a limit to sin and make a place for purity—the whole Jewish history from the beginning had to be falsified, and the Jews represented as a people chosen above all other peoples by God and of stainlessly pure race, protected by Draconian laws against every crossing. Those who brought that about were not liars, as has probably been supposed, but men who acted under the pressure of that necessity which alone raises us above ourselves and makes us ignorant instruments of mighty dispensations of fate.* If anything is calculated to free us from the blindness of our times and the phrase-making of our authorities †

* The words of Jeremiah, " The pen of the Scribes is in vain " (viii. 8), have been applied to the then recent introduction of *Deuteronomy* and to the recasting and extension of the so-called Law of Moses (of the existence of which none of the Prophets had known anything). This is the view of the orthodox Jew Montefiore (*Religion of the Ancient Hebrews*, 201, 202), and is probably correct.

† Herr von Luschan also, as one can perceive from the conclusion of his work on the ethnographical position of the Jews which is so valuable from a statistical point of view, sees our salvation in the complete amalgamation and fusion of the various human races. One cannot believe one's eyes and ears when these men of the school of Virchow pass from facts to thoughts. The whole history of mankind shows us that progress is conditioned by differentiation and individualisation ; we find life and activity only where clearly marked national personalities stand side by side opposed to each other (as in Europe to-day), the best qualities degenerate under the influence of uniformity of race (as in China), the crossing of incompatible types leads, as we see in all organic spheres, to sterility and monstrosity . . . and yet " amalgamation " is to be our ideal ! Do they not see that uniformity and chaos are the same ?   " Ich liebte mir dafür das Ewigleere ! "

and to open our eyes to the law of nature, that great peoples result only from the ennoblement of the race and that this can only take place under definite conditions, the neglect of which brings in its train degeneration and sterility, it is the sight of this sublimely planned and desperate struggle of the Jews who had become conscious of their racial sin.

HOMO SYRIACUS

If we now return to racial statistics, we find ourselves face to face with a difficult theme ; we may measure skulls and count noses, but how do these results reveal themselves in the inner nature of the Jew ? We hold the bone of the skull in the hand, it is what Carlyle calls " a hard fact." This skull, indeed, symbolises a whole world ; any one with the skill to weigh the mass of it rightly, and to interpret its lines in their mutual relations, could tell us much about the individual : he would see possibilities of which the race in question becomes conscious only after generations, and recognise limitations which separate one man from the other from the very first. On looking at the two skulls on p. 374, the long one and the round one, we seem to see two microcosms. But the power of interpretation is denied us ; we judge men by their deeds, that is really indirectly and according to a fragmentary method, for these deeds are determined only by definite circumstances. Everything remains piecework here. Now the protoplasm of a one-celled alga is such an extremely complicated structure that the chemists do not yet know how many atoms they must suppose in the molecule, and how they can unite them under a symbolical formula that is at all acceptable ; who would presume to find the formula for a human being or a whole people ? The following characterisation of the Hittites, the Amorites and the Semites can only serve to give a very general conception.

On the Egyptian pictures the Hittites look anything but intelligent. The exaggerated " Jewish " nose is continued upwards by a retreating brow and downwards by a still more retreating chin.* Perhaps the *homo syriacus* was not really distinguished by the possession of great and brilliant gifts ; I cannot say that he has given any signs of it in modern times in places where he is supposed to predominate. But he unquestionably possessed good qualities. That his race predominated and still predominates in the various crossings shows great physical power. Moreover, he possessed corresponding endurance and diligence. To judge from the few pictures he must also have been shrewd, in fact extremely cunning (which of course has nothing to do with brilliant intellect, on the contrary). His history, too, shows him to be shrewd : he has known how to rule and how to submit to an alien power where the conditions were favourable. He put barren districts under cultivation, and when the population increased, he built cities and was such a capable merchant that in the Bible the same word served to denote merchant and Canaanite. That he could face death bravely is proved by the long struggle with Egypt † and the occurrence of such characters as Uriah.‡ A feature of kindliness is evident in all the otherwise very different portraits. We can form a vivid mental picture of how these men—equally remote

* *See* especially the figures on a Hittite monument near Aintab (Sayce : *Hittites*, p. 62), and the types from Egyptian monuments on p. 375.

† The Hittites seem for a long time to have ruled all Syria and probably all Asia Minor ; their power was as great as that of Egypt in its splendour (*see* Wright : *Empire of the Hittites*, 1886 ; and Sayce : *The Hittites*, 1892). But one should be cautious, for the Hittite script is not yet deciphered, and though Hittite physiognomy, dress, art and writing form a definite idea for science, the history of this people, of whom nothing was known a few years ago, is still to a large extent wrapt in mystery.

‡ *See* (2 *Samuel* xi.) in what a noble, manly way Uriah acts. This stern undemonstrative devotion to duty presents an agreeable contrast to David's criminal levity.

from symbolical mythology and from fanatical Bedouin delusion—could introduce that simple cult, which the Israelites found in Palestine and adopted—the festival of the vintage (it was New Year also to them, and the Jews later called it the Feast of the Tabernacle), the festival of spring (Easter, transformed later by the Jews into Passover) with the offering of the first-born of cattle and sheep, the festival of the finished harvest (Pentecost, called by the Jews " Festival of the Weeks "), nothing but joyful festivals of a long-settled agricultural people, not those of a nomadic race, festivals without any deeper connection with the spiritual life of man, a simple nature-religion such as may have suited and still certainly would suit simple, industrious and " tolerably honest " people.* As we find human sacrifice only where (as in Phœnicia) the Semitic element strongly predominated,† we may assume that a Semitic and not a Hittite custom reveals itself in the cases where the Canaanite service of Baal permits such horrors at the festival : they are, however, exceptional and probably occur only when alien princesses have come by marriage into the land.‡ . . On the whole the Hittites give us the impression of a respectable

* *Cf.* the details in Wellhausen : *Israel. und jüd. Geschichte*, chap. vi. In spite of the later careful expurgation we find still here and there in the Thora mention of this joyful nature-cult, as, for example, the festival of the vintage in the house of God at Sichem (*Judges* ix. 27). *See*, too, how the ark of the covenant is brought by David to Jerusalem " amid joy and exultation," with music, song and dance (2 *Samuel* vi. 12–15).

† Von Luschan has, by numerous measurements, established the fact that the Phœnician type " was closely related to the Arabian."

‡ Concerning the much more complicated cult in the former capital of the Hittite kingdom, Carchemish (Mabug), see Sayce : *The Hittites*, chap. vi. But I consider Lucian, whom he quotes, a very late and unreliable witness. On the other hand, it is interesting to see how far the lack of imagination went in the case of the Hebrews. Even in the laying out of the Jewish temple, of the outer and inner court, of the curtain before the Holy of Holies, as also the privilege of the High Priest to enter this place : all these (said to have been dictated by God to Moses on Mount Sinai) are exact imitations of the primeval Hittite cult.

mediocrity with great vitality rather than of any special capacity for extraordinary achievements, they possess more endurance than power. Goethe says somewhere that there is no greatness without something extravagant ; according to this definition of Goethe the Hittites can hardly lay claim to greatness.

HOMO EUROPÆUS

On the other hand, in the Amorites—" tall as cedars and strong as oaks " (*Amos* ii. 9), with their bold challenges, their unbridled love of adventure, their insane loyalty even to death towards alien, self-imposed masters, their thick city walls, from which they loved to make forays in the mountains,—the element of extravagance seems to me to be peculiarly characteristic. It was a wild, cruel extravagance, but capable of the very highest things. We seem to catch a glimpse of quite another being when on the Egyptian monuments among the countless number of physiognomies we suddenly see before us this free, frank, open countenance so full of character and intelligence. Like the eye of genius amid the common throng of men, so these features appear to us amid the mass of cunning and bad, stupid and evil countenances, amid this whole riffraff of Babylonians, Hebrews, Hittites, Nubians and all the rest of them. *O homo europæus!* how couldst thou stray among such company ? Yes, thou seemst to me like an eye that looks into a divine transcendental world. And fain would I call to thee : follow not the advice of the learned anthropologists, do not amalgamate with that crowd, mingle not with the Asiatic rabble, obey the great poet of thy race, remain true to thyself . . . but I am 3000 years too late. The Hittite remained, the Amorite disappeared. This is one among the many differences between noble and ignoble : nobility is more difficult to

maintain. Though giants in form these men are nevertheless very delicate in their inner organisation. No
people degenerates so quickly as Lapouge's *homo europæus;* how rapidly, for instance, the Greeks became
barbarians, *in Syros, Parthos, Ægyptos degenerarunt,* as
Livy himself testifies (38, 17, 11). He completely loses
his peculiar qualities, that which is his alone he seems
incapable of giving to others, the others do not possess
the vessel to hold it ; he, on the other hand, possesses
a fatal capacity of assimilating all that is alien. People,
it is true, talk to-day of the fair-haired Syrians, we hear
too that 10 per cent. of the Jews are fair ; but Virchow has
told us that skin and hair endure longer than the skull,
and it is probable that the skull would last longer than
the brain ; I do not know, but I really believe that the
Indo-European left in Asia, as elsewhere, beyond the
memory of his deeds, little more than skin and hair. I
have looked for him in the Talmud, but in vain.*

HOMO ARABICUS

It seems to me very difficult to say anything about the
third of this group, the genuine Semite ; for it is characteristic of this *homo arabicus* not to enter into or influence
human history until he has ceased to be a genuine Semite.
So long as he remains in his wilderness (and for his peace
and greatness of soul he should always remain there),
he really does not belong to history at all ; it is also
very difficult, indeed wellnigh impossible, to get definite

* Yet one Teuton actually occurs there (Tractate *Schabbeth,* vi. 8,
fol. 23*a* of the *Jerusalem Talmud*). He is the slave of a Jew. Ordered
to accompany home Rabbi Hila, a friend of his master, he saved him
from death by inducing a mad dog that rushed at the latter to attack
himself, and he was fatally bitten. But this loyalty does not induce
the pious Jew to utter one word of admiration or thanks. He merely
quotes *Isaiah* xliii. 4 : " Since thou wast precious, O Israel, in my sight,
thou hast been honourable, and I have loved thee : therefore I will
give men for thee and people for thy life."

particulars concerning him there; we merely hear that
he is brave, hospitable, pious, also revengeful and cruel
—these are mere elements of character, there is nothing
to give us a clue to his intellectual gifts. Burckhardt,
who travelled for years in Arabia, represents the Bedouin
as absolutely dormant intellectually, so long as love or
war does not stretch the slack bow—and then he at once
goes to extremes.* But if he breaks into the civilised
world, it is to murder and burn, as under Abu Bekr and
Omar, or to-day in Central Africa.† As soon as he has
laid waste everything far and wide, the genuine Semite
disappears, we hear nothing more of him; wherever
he appears in the history of civilisation crossing has in
the meantime taken place—for no type seems to mix
more quickly and more successfully than that which
has sprung from a compulsory inbreeding of thousands
of years' duration. The noble Moor of Spain is anything
but a pure Arab of the desert, he is half a Berber (from
the Aryan family) and his veins are so full of Gothic blood
that even at the present day noble inhabitants of Morocco
can trace their descent back to Teutonic ancestors.
That is why Harun-al-Raschid's reign is such a bright
moment in a dark, sad history, because the pure Persian
family of the Barmecides, which remained true to the
Iranian religion of Zarathustra,‡ stands by the side of the
Khalif as a civilising and refining influence. Not a single
one of the so-called " Semitic " civilised States of
antiquity is purely Semitic,—no, not one: neither

* *Beduinen und Wahaby*, Weimar, 1831.

† Note how the famous Moorish historian of the fourteenth century,
Mohammed Ibn Khaldun, considered by many the founder of scientific
history and himself half Arab, speaks: " Cast your eyes around,
look at all lands, which have been conquered by the inhabitants of
Arabia since the earliest times ! The civilisation and population disappeared, the soil itself seemed to change and become unfruitful at
their touch " (*Prolegomena zur Weltgeschichte*) 2nd Part; I quote
from Robert Flint: *History of the Philosophy of History*, 1893, p. 166.

‡ Renan: *L'islamisme et la science* (*Discours et Conférences*, 3e éd,
p. 382).

the Babylonian nor the Assyrian nor the Phœnician. History tells us so and anthropology supports the statement. We still hear " wonders and fairy tales " about the rich blessing poured upon us by this civilising work of the so-called Semites : but when we look more closely we always find that the genuine Semitic is simply "grafted" upon the really creative element (as Wellhausen said of the Israelites), and so it is very difficult to decide how much and what in particular is to be ascribed to the Semite as such, and what, on the other hand, to his host.* We know to-day, for example, that the Semites did not invent writing with letters any more than they did the so-called " Arabian ciphers"; it is from the Hittites that the pretended " Phœnician " or " Semitic "

* See Jhering's suggestive but very fanciful *Vorgeschichte der Indoeuropäer*, in which the author characterises the whole Babylonian culture as Semitic, although he admits that the Semites " took it over " and although he points out that the Sumero-Accadians were an influential and vigorous force even in late times (pp. 133, 243, &c.). So, too, von Luschan in the essay mentioned, where he takes the trouble at the end to blow the trumpet of the " Semites " although in the same lecture he has already proved that the most famous Semitic peoples had but little Semitic blood in their veins . . . O logic of the scientists ! And finally he dishes up the old story of how Arabian science flourished luxuriantly in Spain and what it meant for us—a tale the foolishness of which no other than Renan had exposed years ago. " The Semitic spirit," he writes, " is fundamentally antiphilosophical and antiscientific . . . there is much talk of an Arabian science and an Arabian philosophy, and certainly the Arabs were our teachers during one or two centuries ; but that was the case simply because the original Hellenic writings were yet undiscovered. This whole Arabian science and philosophy was nothing but a wretched translation of Hellenic thought and knowledge. As soon as authentic Greece stepped forth from the shadow, these poor products fell into nothing, and it is not without reason that all the authorities on the Renaissance undertake a real crusade against them. Moreover we find on closer examination that this Arabian science was in no respect Arabian. Not only was its basis purely Hellenic, but among those who devoted their energies to the introduction and spread of knowledge, there was not a single genuine Semite ; they were Spaniards and (in Bagdad) Persians, who made use of the prevailing Arabian tongue. It is exactly the same with the philosophical part ascribed to the Jews in the Middle Ages ; they translated from foreign tongues, nothing more. Jewish philosophy is Arabian philosophy ; not a single new thought is added. One page of Roger Bacon possesses

writing * is derived, and " the legend of the handing
down of the alphabet to the Aryans by the Phœnicians
is now discarded for good," since much older letters have
been found than the oldest pseudo-Semitic ones—letters
which prove the existence of a " primitive Aryan-European script, which only at a later period was somewhat
influenced, in the east, by the Asiatic writings.†—We
see, on the other hand, that where the Semitic will prevailed in the pure sphere of religion (not of property)
it forced and commanded mental sterility : we see it in
the Jews after the Babylonian captivity (for the victory
of the religious party is unquestionably a victory of the
Semitic element) and we see it in Mohammedanism.
" Jewish life was, after the exile, devoid of all intellectual
and mental interests except the religious . . . the typical
Jew interested himself neither in politics, literature,
philosophy nor art. . . . The Bible really formed his
whole literature, and its study was his only mental and

more scientific value than the whole of this borrowed Jewish wisdom,
which we must, of course, respect, but which is absolutely devoid of
originality." (*De la part des peuples sémitiques dans l'histoire de la
civilisation*, éd. 1875, p. 22ff.). Renan treats the same subject in
more detail in his lecture of the year 1883 : *L'islamisme et la science* :
" Not only are these thinkers and scholars not of Arabian descent,"
he says there, " but the tendency of their minds is altogether non-
Arabian."

* Renan: *Israël*, i. 134 ff.

† Professor Hueppe: *Zur Rassen- und Sozialhygiene der Griechen*,
1897, p. 26. All authorities at the present day admit that the so-
called " Phœnician " letters were not the invention of Semitic genius :
Halévy supposes an Egyptian origin, Hommel (with more probability)
a Babylonian, that is Sumarian, origin. Delitzsch thinks that the
Syrian half-Semites had formed their alphabet by the fusion of two
different ones, the Babylonian and the Egyptian ; the last investigator of this matter, however, arrives at the conclusion that the alphabet
is altogether an invention of the Europeans, and was first brought to
Asia by the Hellenic Myceneans (*see* H. Kluge: *Die Schrift der Mykenier*,
1897). With regard to the Mycenean letters which have now become
quite well known, a reliable authority, Salomon Reinach, writes (*L'Anthropologie*, 1902, xiii. 34) : *Une chose est certaine : c'est que l'écriture
linéaire des tablettes ne dérive ni de l'Assyrie ni de l'Egypte, qu'elle pré-
sente un caractère nettement européen, qu'elle offre comme une image
anticipée de l'épigraphie hellénique.*

intellectual interest"; this is written by an unprejudiced critic, the Jewish scholar C. G. Montefiore (pp. 419 and 543). An equally reliable witness, Hirsch Graetz, quotes a remark of Rabbi Akiba: "Whoever devotes himself to reading exoteric writings (that is, to any study but the sacred Jewish Thora) has lost his right to future life." * The Mishna teaches, "to have one's son taught Greek science is as accursed as to engage in the breeding of swine." † That the Hittites, who form, as we have seen, the half of the Jewish blood, always protested against such doctrines and devoted their attention by preference to everything "exoteric," is a different matter; I am here trying to define the "Semite" only. As regards the sterilising influence of the most genuine Semitic religion, the Mohammedan, it is too obvious to require proof. We stand here then, to begin with, before a mass of negative and very few positive facts; any one who is not content with phrases will find it difficult to get a clear conception of the personality of the genuine Semite, and yet for our purpose the answering of the question, Who is the Jew? is so important that we must strive to get that conception. Let us call the learned to our aid!

If I consult the work of the most eminent and consequently most reliable of all ethnographists in Germany, Oskar Peschel, I shall find no answer to this question; he was a prudent man. Ratzel writes as follows: The Semite has greater intensity, or, so to say, one-sidedness of religious feeling than either the Hamite or the Indo-Teuton; violence, exclusiveness, in short fanaticism, is his distinguishing mark; religious extravagances, including human sacrifices, are nowhere so widespread as in his midst; the general of the Mahdi even

* *Gnosticismus und Judentum* (Krotoschin, 1846, p. 99). The meaning of the word "exoteric," which is not quite clear in this connection, is explained when we compare other passages, where, for example, the reading of Greek poets is called an "exoteric" occupation (p. 62).

† Quoted from Renan: *L'Origine du Christianisme*, i. 35.

in 1883 had prisoners roasted alive in ovens; the Semite is individualistic, he clings more to family and religion than to the State; since he is not a good soldier, foreign mercenaries had to win his victories for him; in the oldest times the Semite may have done great things for science, but it is possible that these achievements are of foreign origin—later at any rate he does not accomplish much in this sphere, his best work being in religion.* This characterisation seems to me to be very unsatisfactory and scrappy; it says very little, and besides is in certain respects false. It is all very fine to roast one's enemies in ovens—from China to the artistic Netherlands of the sixteenth century where do we not find cruelty?— but to see in that a " higher intensity of religious feeling " is silly, especially when one places the Semite in this respect above the profoundly religious and wonderfully creative Egyptian, and also above the Indo-Teuton, whose religious literature is by far the greatest in the world, and whose "religious feeling" has from time immemorial revealed itself in the fact that thousands and millions of human existences were dedicated and sacrificed to religion alone. When the Brahman, in one of the oldest Upanishads (at least 800 or 1000 years before Christ †) teaches that man should regard every inhalation and exhalation by day and by night as a continual sacrifice to God,‡ does that not represent " the greatest intensity of religious feeling " that the world has ever known? And what is the meaning of the phrase, the Semite is individualistic? As far as we can judge, wherever religion came under Semitic influence,

* *Völkerkunde*, ii. 391 ; summarised from Ratzel's own words.

† *Cf.* Leopold von Schröder: *Indiens Litteratur und Kultur* (1887), 20th Lecture.

‡ *Kaushîtaki-Upanishad*, ii. 5; Deussen, the greatest living authority, gives the following gloss to this passage : The Brahman means, " Religion shall not consist in outward worship but in devoting one's whole life with every breath to its service " (*Sechzig Upanishad's des Veda*, p. 31).

it differed from the Indo-Teutonic (and East-Asiatic) creed in becoming national. The individual, except as member of the community, shrunk almost to a negligible quantity (*cf.* p. 245) ; and the pseudo-Semitic States have, without exception, deprived the individual of all freedom. It seems to me that there is more individualism among Teutonic than among Semitic peoples ; at any rate the assertion that the Semite is individualistic could only be made with many qualifications. Much more profound are the remarks of that thorough scholar Christian Lassen, who knew more of souls than of skulls. Although his characterisation of the Semite dates from the fourth decade of last century, when the half-Semites were not yet clearly distinguished from the genuine stem, he seizes upon points which reveal the intellectual kernel of the Semitic personality. He writes : " The Semitic way of looking at things is subjective and egoistical. His poetry is lyrical, hence subjective, his soul pours out its joys and sorrows, its love and hatred, its admiration and its contempt ; . . . the epic, in which the Ego of the poet steps into the background, he cannot success-fully treat, still less the drama, which demands from the poet a still greater abandonment of the personal standpoint." [*] Nor does philosophy belong to the Semites ; they have adopted, or rather, only the Arabs

---

[*] Is this individualism after all ? Certainly, but in a quite different sense from the case of the Indo-Teuton. In the case of the Semite, as we see from Lassen's remarks, the individual stands, so to speak, in his own way, hence his achievements are only collective. In the case of Greek and Teuton, each work bears the stamp of a definite personality, of an individual. Fr. von Schack holds exactly the same view as Lassen : " The whole creative activity of the Arabs bears a subjective character. Everywhere it is preferably their own " soul-life " that they express. They draw into it the things of the outer world, and show but little inclination to look straight at reality, and so to represent nature in sharp and definite outlines, or to study the individuality of others, thus representing men and conditions of life in a concrete manner. Accordingly those forms of poetry which demand abandonment of the Ego and imaginative power are least congenial to them " (*Poesie und Kunst der Araber,* i. 99).

have, the philosophy of the Indo-Teutons. Their views and conceptions occupy their minds too much to allow them to rise sufficiently out of themselves to grasp pure thought, and to separate the more general and the necessary from their own individuality and its contingencies.* " In his religion the Semite is selfish and exclusive ; Jehovah is merely the God of the Hebrews, and they acknowledge no other than him : all other Gods are absolutely false and have neither share nor part in the truth ; Allah wishes to be not only the God of the Arabs, but to conquer the whole world, and his nature is as egoistic as that of Jehovah ; he, too, denies every iota of truth to all other Gods, but it is of no use to acknowledge Allah, unless you serve him under the exclusive form which proclaims Mohammed his prophet. According to their doctrine the Semites were bound to be intolerant and inclined to fanaticism, as also to stubborn clinging to their religious law. Tolerance appears most pronounced in the case of the Indo-Teutonic peoples ; this tolerance is the result of greater freedom of thought, which does not bind itself exclusively to mere form. . . . The qualities of the Semitic spirit, the passionate temperament, the stubborn will, the firm belief in exclusive justification, their whole egoistical nature—were bound to make their possessors in the highest degree capable of great and daring deeds." † Lassen then proceeds to discuss the pseudo-Semitic States, with regard to which he says that these magnificently planned structures all went to ruin because " here, too, the intractable arbitrariness of the

---

* Concerning science in particular, Grau writes in his well-known philo-Semitic work, *Semiten und Indogermanen* (2nd ed. p. 33) : " The Hebrews, like all Semites, are much too subjective to allow the pure impulse of knowledge to become a power in them. Natural science, in the objective sense which it has among the Indo-Teutons, viz., that nature should retain her own essence and character, while man is merely her interpreter, is unknown to the Hebrew." On p. 50 Grau says : " Everything objective is strange to the Hebrew."

† *Indische Altertumskunde* (ed. 1847), i. 414-416.

stubborn selfish will interfered as a hindering power." *
From this characterisation we have really learned something, almost everything indeed, but the facts must be
polished and pointed before a clear and transparent
conception enters our consciousness. I shall try to do
this. Lassen shows us that the will is the predominant
power in the soul of the Semite ; it is at the root of all
his actions. This will impels, but it also retards. It
makes its possessor capable of great and daring deeds :
it stands in his way wherever the spirit soars to a loftier
activity. The result is a character that is passionate
and eager for great deeds, coupled with an intellect
which is by no means adequate to this impulse, since
it can never unfold itself by reason of the impetuousness
of the will. In this being the will is at the head, the
mind stands next, and lowest of all the understanding.
Lassen especially emphasises the egoism of the Semite,
he repeatedly refers to it. In his poetry, his philosophy,
his religion, his politics, everywhere he sees an " egoistical
nature " at work. That is an unavoidable consequence
of that hierarchy of qualities. Selfishness is rooted in
will ; the only things that can keep it from excess are
the gifts of feeling and understanding—a warm heart,
profound knowledge of the system of the universe, artistic-
creative work, the noble thirst after knowledge. But,
as Lassen hints, as soon as the stormy will with its selfishness predominates, even beautiful qualities remain undeveloped : religion degenerates into fanaticism, thinking
becomes magic or caprice, art expresses only the love

* It is interesting and important to note how the organ of the mind—
language—is suited to and expresses this special Semitic type. Renan
writes : " A quiver full of steel arrows, a firmly wound cable, an iron
trumpet, whose few strident notes rend the air : that is the Hebrew
language. This language is incapable of expressing a philosophical
thought, a scientific result, a doubt, or even the feeling of the Infinite. It can say but little, but what it does say is like the blow of the
hammer on the anvil" (Israel i. 102). Is that not the language of
stubborn will ?

and the hatred of the moment, it is expression but not creation, science becomes industry.

This Semite would seem, then, to be the right counterpart to the Hittite ; in the case of the one we have the beautiful harmony of a nature developed on all sides with moderation, tenacious constancy of will united with prudence and a genial view of life ; in the other we find a leaning towards the Immoderate and the Arbitrary, a character in which the balance is disturbed, one in which the most necessary and at the same time the most dangerous gift of man—the will—has been abnormally developed. Those who do not believe that the so-called " races " fell ready-made from heaven, who refuse, like me, to pay heed to the delusion of supposed primeval beginnings (since growth is only a phase of existence, not *vice versâ*), will probably surmise that this unexampled development of the one quality with the corresponding neglect of the others is the result of a life in the desert for thousands of years, during which the intellect was starved and the feelings confined to a narrow circle, while the will—the will of this individual who had to stand entirely on his own feet, who though in the midst of the unbroken silence of nature was surrounded day and night by foes and danger—was bound to demand all the sap of the body for its service, and constantly to strain to the utmost the powers of the intellect. Be that as it may, such a character has assuredly in it the possibility of true greatness. The extravagance which we missed in the Hittite is here present. And as a matter of fact now that we have carried the analysis to the inner being of the Semite, we are able to lay our finger on the only point where greatness can be expected : clearly only in the sphere of will and in all those achievements which result from the predominance of will over other qualities. That Ibn Khaldun who asserts that " the Semite is utterly incapable of establishing anything permanent," praises as incomparable the simplicity of his needs (lack of imagination), the instinct which makes him cling to his family and separates him from others (impoverished feelings), the ease with which he can be exalted by a prophet to the delirium of ecstasy, obeying the divine command in deep humility (bad judgment in consequence of the non-development of the reasoning faculty). In this sentence I have commented on each assertion of Ibn Khaldun, but my motive has been in no way to undervalue the merits of contentedness, loyalty to family, and obedience to God, but merely to show how each one of the qualities named means the triumph of the power of will. The important thing, however, is to distinguish—this is, in fact, altogether the most important task of the thinker ; and to understand rightly what a genuine Semite is, we must comprehend that the contentedness of an Omar, for whom nothing in the world has any interest, is not the same thing as that of an Immanuel Kant, who desires no outward gifts simply because his all-embracing mind possesses the whole world ; that loyalty to one's own blood is something quite different from the loyalty of the Amorites, for example, to their self-imposed master—the one is simply an instinctive expansion of the egoistical circle of the will, the other a free, personal decision of the individual, a kind of lived poetry ; above all we must, or rather we ought to, learn (I dare not hope to live to see it) to distinguish between true religion and an insane belief in some God, and also not to confuse monolatry with monotheism. That does not at all prevent us from acknowledging the specifically Semitic greatness. Though Mohammedanism may be the worst of all religions, as Schopenhauer asserts, who can repress a thrill of almost uncanny admiration when he sees a Mohammedan go to his death as calmly as if he were going for a walk ? And this power of the Semitic will is so great that it forces itself, as in the case mentioned, upon peoples who have not a drop of Arab blood in their veins. By contact with this will man becomes transformed; there is in it such a power of suggestion that it fascinates us as the eye of the serpent does the bird, and at its command we seem to lose the power of song and flight. And thus it was that the Semite became a power of the first moment in the history of the world. Like a blind power of nature—for the will is blind—he hurled himself upon other races; he disappeared in them, they took him in; it was obvious what these races had given him, not what he had given them; for what he gave possessed no physiognomy, no form, it was only will: an increased energy which often impelled to great achievements, an excitability difficult to control, and an unquenchable thirst after possession which often led to destruction, in short, a definite direction of will; wherever he settled, the Semite had, to begin with, only adopted and assimilated what he found, but he had changed the character of the people.

Homo Judæus

Cursory as may have been this attempt to illustrate clearly some distinguishing characteristics of the Hittites, the Amorites and the Semites, I believe that it will contribute to a sensible and true discernment of the Israelite and Jewish character. We must in any case approach such a task with modesty and self-effacement. At any rate clear pictures of living men and their deeds will give a more vivid conception than figures, though figures are better than phrases. But with every step we must become more cautious, and if we look back at those figures, we shall not be inclined to "construct" the Israelite from percentages of Semites, Amorites and Hittites, somewhat as the cook makes a pudding from a recipe; that would be childish folly. But that dis-

cussion of the matter brings many points more humanly
home to us. Whatever, for instance, in a national
character is inexplicable contradiction—and the Jewish
people is fuller of contradictions than any other—confuses
us to begin with, often indeed distresses us; but this
impression passes away when we know the organic cause
of the contradiction. Thus it is at once apparent that
from the crossing of Hebrews and Hittites contradictory
tendencies must result; for while the Hebrews physically
grafted themselves upon the Hittites, they were in-
oculated with a culture which morally and intellectually
did not belong to them, which had not sprung naturally
from their own need, from an inventive richness of their
own mind; it was taking possession in contrast to original
possession. As a matter of fact the Hebrews obtained
a real title to this culture by adopting the blood of the
creative Hittites and becoming Israelites; but by this
very act contrast and inner discord were henceforth
assured. The two types were fundamentally too different
to amalgamate completely, and this became evident
especially in the contrast between Judah and Israel
which soon manifested itself; for in the north the
Syrian was predominant and the crossing had been much
more rapid and thorough; * in the south, on the other
hand, the Amorites were more numerous, and an almost
constant infiltration of genuine Semitic blood from
Arabia continued. What here took place between tribe
and tribe repeated itself inside the narrower unity: so
long as Jerusalem stood, those of weak faith and the
worldly-minded continually withdrew; they fled from
the home of strict law and unadorned life. The same
phenomenon is seen to-day, but not so clearly. I think
that without straining a point we may fairly say that
we can trace here the lasting influence of the *homo*

* The Hittites were more numerous in the north, the Amorites in
the south. (*See* Sayce: *Hittites*, pp. 13 and 17.)

syriacus on the one hand, and of the *homo arabicus* on the other.

I leave it to the reader to make further observations of this kind on the contributions of the various types to the formation of this particular human race, and turn my attention at once to the most vital point—the influence of the Semitic spirit upon religion. That is clearly the essential question, if we are to understand the origin and character of Judaism ; and while the special business talent is perhaps rather a Hittite than a Semitic legacy, in the sphere of religion the Semitic element probably strongly predominates.* I prefer to discuss this matter at once, and from the general standpoint, rather than later, when the Jewish religion as a particular phenomenon will occupy our attention ; for the wider horizon will give us a broader view, and if we ask ourselves how the special Semitic spirit, the predominant feature of which we now know to be Will, everywhere and of

* In regard to business aptitude a proof is given us by the Armenians, in whose veins there is much more " alarodic," that is, Syrian blood (about 80 per cent. according to a communication by letter from Professor Hueppe), but apart from that only Indo-European, Phrygian and not Semitic blood, and who—without the characteristic " Jewish nose," the Hittite legacy—show the same greed, the same business cunning and the same passionate fondness for usury as the Jews, but all to a much higher degree, so that there is a proverb in the Levant that an Armenian is a match for three Jews.   In David Hogarth's book, *A Wandering Scholar in the Levant* (1896, p. 147 ff.), we find interesting details concerning the character of the Armenians, especially their genius for intrigue and incitement.   It is true that Burckhardt in his famous book, *Über die Beduinen und Wahaby* (Weimar, 1831), represents the genuine Semites, too, as evil, over-cunning business people.   " In their private dealings the Arabs cheat each other as much as possible," he says, " they practise usury, too, whenever they have an opportunity " (p. 149, 154).   But after Burckhardt had lived longer among the Bedouins he somewhat modified his judgment, and while admitting that " greed of gain " is one of their chief characteristics, declared that the inclination to cheating originated from their contact with the cities and the thieving population settled there (p. 292).   Whoever lies has lost his honour among them (296) and Burckhardt can assert that " with all their faults the Bedouins are one of the noblest nations with which I ever had occasion to be acquainted " (288).—In regard to this not unimportant question the recent experiences of the French in

necessity affects the religious sentiment of peoples, the answer to that question will enlighten us regarding the case in hand, and will in addition considerably facilitate the task we have set ourselves in the further course of this work. For it is a question of a power which is still at work in our midst, and which presumably will make itself felt in future, distant centuries—a power which we cannot fathom by the exclusive consideration of limited, specific Judaism.

EXCURSUS ON SEMITIC RELIGION

I have said that the Semite changed the character of nations. The change of character is most evident in the sphere of religion. While in other spheres it is difficult to define the share of the specifically Semitic spirit in mixed races, here we clearly and unmistakably see its influence; for here its tyrannical will extends to cosmic dimensions and changes the whole view of "religion." Schopenhauer says in one place: "Religion is the metaphysics of the people." Now consider what kind of religion men can have whose most outstanding characteristic is the absolute lack of every metaphysical emotion, every philosophical capacity!* This one sentence expresses the profound contrast between Semite and Indo-European. It would be inexplicable how one could see in the Semite the religious man $\kappa\alpha\tau$ ' $\dot{\epsilon}\xi\dot{o}\chi\eta\nu$, if

Algiers are of interest: the Kabyles gladly return to civilisation, whereas the pure Arabian stems have little inclination thereto and demand from the world freedom and nothing more; they reveal themselves as an element absolutely hostile to culture. They prefer to give rather than to sell, to steal than to bargain, they prefer licence to any law. In all these points the contrast to the Hittites, as we see them in history, is very striking. The immoderate will of the Semites, their greed of gain, of which Burckhardt speaks, will have quickened very much the Syrian talent for business, nevertheless this capacity seems to be a Syrian, not a Semitic legacy.

* Renan: *Histoire des langues sémitiques*, p. 18, "L'abstraction est inconnue dans les langues sémitiques, la métaphysique impossible."

we were not still living in the dense mist of inherited
historical prejudices and superstition ; it is certain at
any rate that wherever Semitic influence penetrated,
the conception of religion underwent a great change.*
For everywhere else in the whole world, even among
savage peoples, religion is interwoven with the mysterious.
Plato says that in the other world the soul "will be
initiated into a mystery, which one may name the perfect
bliss." † Jesus Christ says of the doctrine which is the
essence of His religion, that it is a "mystery." ‡ What
here has been most sublimely expressed, we find in all
stages of the human hierarchy except among the Semites.
Schopenhauer calls this, from his standpoint as a philosopher, "metaphysics" ; we may, I think, simply say
that in the world of feeling as of thought man everywhere meets inexplicable contradictions ; this attracts his
attention, and he begins to have a feeling that his understanding is only adequate to a portion of existence,
that what his five senses convey to him and what his
combinative logic constructs therefrom neither exhaust
the essence of the world outside himself nor his own
being ; he conjectures that besides the perceptible cosmos
there is an imperceptible, besides the thinkable an unthinkable ; the simple world extends and becomes a
"double kingdom." § The sight of death itself points
to an unknown world, and birth seems to him like
a message from the same realm. At every step we see
only "miracles" ; the greatest wonders for us are ourselves. How simply the savage wonders and everywhere
suspects the existence of another world is from travellers'
accounts well known to us ; of Goethe, on the other hand,
perhaps the most finely organised brain that humanity
has produced, Carlyle says : "Before his eye lies the
whole world extended and transparent, as though melted

---

* *See* p. 213 ff.   † *Phædrus*, 250.   ‡ *See* p. 187.
§ *Faust*, Second Part, Act i., last words of Faust.

to glass, but on every side surrounded by wonders, everything Natural being in truth a Supernatural " ; * and
Voltaire, the so-called scoffer, closes his scientific researches with the words : " *Pour peu qu'on creuse, on
trouve un abîme infini.*" And so all mankind from the
highest to the lowest are agreed : the living feeling of a
great world-secret, the vague realisation that the natural
is " supernatural," is common to all ; it unites the
Australian negro to a Goethe and a Newton. The Semite
alone stands apart. Of the Arab of the desert Renan
says : " No one in the world has so little inclination to
mysticism, no one is more averse to contemplation and
devotion. God is the creator of the world, he has made it,
that is sufficient to him as an explanation.† This is pure
materialism in contrast to what other men call religion,
by which they all understand " something unthinkable
and inexpressible." Thus Montefiore can proudly say of
the religion of his fathers, in which the Semitic impulse
has found its highest and most perfect form, that it
contains nothing esoteric, not the least inner incompre-
hensibility ; and that hence this religion, which knows
neither superstition nor secret, has become the teacher of
nations.‡ The same Jewish author is never tired of
pointing out with admiration that the Semites never
knew anything of the Fall, of justification by faith, of
redemption, of grace ; § by this he merely shows that
they have scarcely any idea of what the rest of the world
calls religion. In Dr. Ludwig Philippson's *Israelitische
Religionslehre* (Leipzig, 1861), an orthodox Jewish work

* In the essay *Goethe's Works*, towards the end.
† *L'islamisme et la science*, p. 380. Here there is evidently an
intellectual want, as Renan elsewhere admits when he writes : " The
Semitic people almost totally lack the questioning thirst after know-
ledge ; nothing excites their wonder " (*Langues sémitiques*, p. 10).
According to Hume the lack of wonder is the characteristic token of
inferior intellectual power.
‡ Cf. *Religion of the Ancient Hebrews*, p. 160.
§ Pp. 514, 524, 544, and many other places.

dedicated to the " future of the Israelite religion," we find, as one of the three " distinguishing features " of this religion, the sentence, " The Israelite religion has and knows no secrets, no mysteries " (i. 34). Renan, too, in a moment of reckless honesty, admits that " the Semitic faith (monotheism) is in reality the product of a human race whose religious needs are very few. It signifies a minimum of religion." * An important and true remark which has only failed to have effect because Renan did not show in how far and for what compelling reasons the Semite, who is famed for the glow of his faith, yet possesses a minimum of true religion. The explanation is easy for us : where understanding and imagination are under the yoke of blind will, there cannot and must not be any miracle, anything unreachable, any " path into the untrodden, and the not-to-be-trodden," † nothing which the hand cannot grasp and the moment (even if it be but as a clearly conceivable hope) cannot possess. Even such a great mind as the second Isaiah looks upon religious faith as something which is based on empiric foundation and which can be tested, as it were, by a legal process : " Let the people bring forth their witnesses that they may be justified ; or let them hear and say, It is truth " (xliii. 9). We read exactly the same in the second Sura of the *Koran :* " Call your witnesses if you speak the truth." The Jewish teacher Philippson, mentioned above, tells in detail how the Jew " believes solely what he has seen with his eyes," a " blind faith " being unknown to him ; and in a long note he quotes all the passages in the Bible where " faith in God " is mentioned, and asserts that this expression occurs without exception only where

---

* *Nouvelles considérations sur les peuples sémitiques* (*Journal asiatique,* 1859, p. 254). Also Robertson Smith (*The Prophets of Israel,* p. 33) testifies that the genuine Semite has " little religion."

† Or as the *Brihadâranyaka-Upanishad* renders the same conception, " the path of the universe, which one has to follow, to get from the part into the whole universe " (I, 4, 7).

" visible proofs have gone before." * It is always, therefore, a question of outward experience, not of inner ; the conceptions are always thoroughly concrete, material ; as Montefiore assures us, even in the advanced Jewish religion there is nothing which the dullest might not immediately understand and fathom to its uttermost depth ; as soon as a man has a feeling of a mystery, as soon as he, for instance, supposes that there can be anything symbolical in the history of the creation, he is a heretic and a gallows-bird.† Even the utterly materialised history of creation given in the book of *Genesis* is so manifestly alien and borrowed that it remains totally isolated amid the Israelitish tradition and without actual connection with it.‡ The will in fact gives little rope to the understanding and the imagination. So it is that the Semite who has begun to doubt at once becomes an atheist ; there is in any case no secret, no mystery : if Allah is not the creator, then must matter be ; as an explanation of the world there is scarcely the shadow of a difference between the two views, for in the case of neither does the Semite feel himself in the presence of an inexplicable riddle, a superhuman mystery.

But if we wish to appreciate the influence of Semiticism upon religion, it will not suffice to speak of understanding and non-understanding, of feeling and non-feeling of the mystery ; we must remember also the creative influence of the imagination, that " all-uniting heavenly companion," as Novalis calls it. Imagination is the handmaid of religion, she is the great mediator ; born, as Shakespeare says, of the wedlock of head and heart, she moves on the frontier of the " double kingdom " of

* Philippson : *Israelitische Religionslehre*, i. 35 ff.
† *See*, for example, in Graetz, *Gnosticismus und Judentum*, the passage on Ben Soma.
‡ Fully discussed by Renan : *Langues sémitiques*, p. 482 ff. *See*, too, the note on p. 485 and my quotation from Darmesteter, p. 421, note. *Cf.*, too, the introduction to the 4th ed. of this book.

Goethe and so unites the one half to the other : her forms signify more than what the eye alone can see in them, her words proclaim more than the ear alone can hear. She has not the power to open up that which is closed, but she raises before us the mystery of mysteries and convinces our eyes that its veil cannot be raised. Symbolism, as the necessary language of the unspeakable mystery of the world, is her work. Plato calls this language a swimming-board that bears us down the stream of life ; it is as widespread as the feeling of this mystery, its vocabulary as varied as the stages of culture and the climates. Thus the inhabitants of the Samoan Islands have represented symbolically to themselves the inexplicable and yet directly felt mystery of the omnipresence of God in the following manner. They represent the body of their God Saveasiuleo as composed of two separable parts ; the upper, humanly shaped part (the real God) dwells in " the home of spirits " among the dead, the under part is an immensely long structure like a sea-serpent that winds itself round all the islands of the great sea, and pays attention to the doings of men.* It is indeed a long way from such a comparatively crude conception to the idea of the omnipresence of God held by Christian theology ; and it is still further removed from the transcendental idealism which is a Sankara's conception of the same mystery, yet I can find no fundamental difference. Moreover we see from many examples how this occupation of the imagination with religious conceptions everywhere gradually leads to very clear ideas. Tylor, the cautious and reliable scholar, asserts that there is probably on the whole African continent, from the Hottentots to the Berbers, not a single tribe which does not believe in a supreme deity, and he shows how this faith gradually arises out of simple animism. But most of them, as, for example, the negroes of the

---

* E. B. Tylor : *The Beginnings of Culture*, Germ. ed., 1873, II. 309.

Gold Coast, think it beneath the dignity of the great spirit of the world to busy himself with the trifling affairs of the world; it is seldom, according to them, that he intervenes. Another tribe, that of the Yorubas (negroes of the Slave coast, at a perceptibly higher stage of civilisation), teaches that " no one can directly approach God, but God has appointed intercessors and mediators between himself and the human race. Sacrifice is not offered to God, because he needs nothing; on the other hand, the mediators, who are very like men, delight in presents of sheep, pigeons and other things." * That seems to me a very high kind of " popular metaphysics," a religion which deserves all respect. On the other hand, we know how the richest mythology in the world, that of the Indian Aryans, in the very oldest hymns (before the immigration to India) teaches that " the many Gods are a single being that is worshipped under different names," † and how this mythology afterwards led to the sublimest conception of the one God in Brahman, in fact to a wonderfully sublime though at the same time one-sided and consequently inferior religion; we further know how from the same root sprang the ever-blossoming garden of the Hellenic Olympus and the admirable ethical teach-ing of the Avesta and of Zoroaster; we know, finally, how all these things, together with the metaphysical speculations pertaining thereto and the ever-active necessity of our inborn creative impulse, saved Christianity from the fate of becoming a mere annex of Judaism, how they give it mythical (*i.e.*, inexhaustible) significance and charm, how they quickened it with the deepest symbols of the Indo-European mind, and made it a sacred vessel for the secrets of the human heart and the human brain, a pathway into " the untrodden and the not-to-be-

---

* Tylor, pp. 348, 349.
† *Rigveda*, i. 164, 46 (quoted from Barth, *Religions de l'Inde* p. 23).

trodden," a " pathway of the universe." * There can
therefore be no doubt of the importance of the part
which imagination plays in religion. Can we say that
the Semite possesses no imagination ? All such unqualified statements are false ; although the necessary
brevity of the written thought often forces us to adopt
this form, we may well presuppose that the reader automatically supplies the necessary correction. The Semite
is a human being like others ; it is merely a question of
degrees of difference, which, however, in this case, thanks
to the extreme character of this human type, come very
near to the borderland of Affirmation and Negation, of
the To be or the Not to be. All who have any claim at
all to speak, testify unanimously that lack—or let us say
poverty—of imagination is a fundamental trait of the
Semite. I have already given weighty proofs, *e.g.*, the
evidence of Lassen, and I could add many more, but the
question is not worth further discussion : Mohammedanism and Judaism are sufficient proofs ; what we hear
of the Bedouins † shows us only the beginning of this
poverty. As Renan happily remarks : " *le sémite a
l'imagination comprimante,*" that is, his imagination
narrows, limits, confines ; a great thought, a deeply
symbolical image returns from his brain small and thin,
" flattened," robbed of its far-reaching significance. " In
the hands of the Semites the mythologies which they
borrowed from strange peoples became flat historical
narratives." ‡ Wellhausen says : " The fading of the
myths is synonymous with their Hebraising." § And
not only did the Semites possess little creative imagination, but they also systematically checked every tendency
in that direction. Just as man must not wonder and
think, so, too, he must not form any conception of things
invisible. Every attempt to conceive the superhuman

* Concerning mythology in Christianity, *see* vol. ii. chap. vii.
† *See* p. 427.   ‡ Renan : *Israël*, i. 49, 77, 78.
§ *Prolegomena,*

is idolatry ; the Saveasiuleo of the Samoans is an idol, the Sistine Madonna of Raphaël is an idol, the symbol of the Cross is an idol.*   I shall not repeat what I have said in a former chapter on this subject, but ask the reader to look at it again (p. 224 f.).   I have there tried to make it clear why the Semite had to hold this view, how his zeal and the particular nature of his faith, springing as it did from the Will, forced it upon him ; I pointed also to the fact that the Semite, wherever he defied this law of his nature, as in Phœnicia, became himself the most horrible, and perhaps the only genuine idolater humanity has ever known.   For while the Indian taught the negation of will, and Christ its " conversion," religion is for the Semite the idolisation of his will, its most glowing, immoderate and fanatical assertion.   If he had not this faith, which makes him the protagonist of fanatical intolerance and at the same time a paragon among sufferers, he would have no religion, or hardly any ; hence the ever-repeated warning of his legislators against "molten gods."

From these details the following conclusions, to begin with, may be drawn : the Semite banishes from religion contemplative wonder, every feeling of a superhuman mystery, and he banishes likewise creative fancy ; of these he admits only the indispensable minimum, that " minimum of religion " of which Renan spoke.   Wherever, therefore, Semitic influence makes itself felt, whether by physical crossing (as in the case of the Jews) or by the mere force of ideas (as in Christianity) we shall meet with these two characteristic endeavours.   We can express both by one single word—materialism.   Schopenhauer, one of the greatest thinkers that ever lived, whose thought, moreover, possessed unexampled symbolical plasticity—unequalled even by Plato—so that his

* That the Cross is to be regarded as the same thing as the idols of Heathendom is said expressly by Professor Graetz : *Volkstümliche Geschichte der Juden*, ii. 218.

philosophy seems in many ways related to religion, has as metaphysician given this definition : "matter is the mere visibility of will . . . what in appearance, that is, for the conception, is matter, is in itself will." * I shall not enter into metaphysics here, nor shall I champion Schopenhauer's speculative symbolism ; but it is striking that in the sphere of purely empiric psychology an analogous relation unavoidably asserts itself. Where the will has enslaved the questioning understanding and the imagination, there can be no other view of life and no other philosophy than the materialistic. I do not use the word in a depreciatory sense. I do not deny the advantages of materialism, I do not dispute that it can be harmonised with morals ; I simply state a fact. Pure materialism is the religious doctrine of the Arab Mohammed, as are also the transitory processes of his revelations from God, and his paradise with eating and drinking and beautiful houris ; pure materialism is the bargain which Jacob enters into with Jehovah (*Genesis* xxviii. 20–22), in which he makes five conditions, or, as the Jurist would say, stipulations, and then concludes : as thou doest this, so thou shalt be my God. The whole history of creation in *Genesis*—which, it appears, all Hebrews, all Syrian and Babylonian Semites possessed in similar form †—is pure materialism ; it was not so originally ; it was the mythical and symbolical conception of an imaginative people (probably the Sumero-Accadians), but, as Renan has taught us, the myth becomes in the hands of the Semite an historical chronicle.‡

* *Die Welt als Wille und Vorstellung*, 2 vol., Book II. chap. xxiv. In no connection with this, but nevertheless interesting as a reflection of the same discernment is the doctrine of the Sâmkhya philosophy (the rationalistic system of the Brahman Indians), according to which willing is not a mental but a physical function. (*Cf*. Garbe : *Die Sâmkhya-Philosophie*, p. 251.)

† *Cf*. Gunkel : *Handkommentar zur Genesis*, p. xli. ff.

‡ The pre-eminent imagination of the Sumero-Accadians is obvious from their scientific achievements, moreover their language is said to

Of all the deep ideas which thoughtful and reflective minds had breathed into this story in their own wonderful way, the Semites perceived nothing, so absolutely nothing that the Jews, for example, first acquired the conception of an evil spirit, opposed to the good, through Zoroaster during the Babylonian captivity ; till then they had regarded the serpent of their bible just as a serpent ! * Why talk of their ignorance of an evil principle, when in spite of their book of *Genesis*, chaps. i. and ii., the idea even of a God, creator of heaven and earth, was quite unknown to the Israelites till the Babylonian captivity ? The thought appears for the first time in the so-called second Isaiah (*see* chaps. xl. to lvi. of the book of *Isaiah*). The

testify to a special tendency to abstraction, for it is richer in abstract ideas than in *nomina concreta* (*see* Delitzsch : *Die Entstehung des ältesten Schrift-systems*, 1898, p. 118). A more direct contrast to the Semitic nature cannot be imagined ; we can easily fancy what a degradation the Sumerian theories of the creation may have suffered under Israelite hands. But it becomes ever more probable that this whole mythology is permeated with old Aryan conceptions, to which, for example, the tree of life, the flood, the Godhead in water (hence baptism), the stories of the temptation belong. Professor Otto Franke (Königsberg) writes in the *Deutsche Literaturzeitung*, 1901, No. 44, col. 2763 : " Such passages in the Semitic tradition always stand isolated and in strange surroundings, but form organic links in whole Aryan systems of thought: they are often bare and artificial in their Semitic setting, whereas in the Aryan they spring forth like foaming streams from full and sparkling springs."

* *Cf.* Montefiore, p. 453. How deeply rooted in the organism of the Semite this incapacity is we see from the fact that a man like James Darmesteter, one of the most frequently named Orientalists of the nineteenth century, a man of universal knowledge, could in the year of grace 1882 write : " The biblical cosmogony, hastily borrowed from an alien source, and all its stories of apples and serpents, concerning which the generations of Christians have passed sleepless nights, have never caused our Israelite scholars the slightest uneasiness or occupied their thoughts." All his knowledge could not enable this absolutely free-thinking Jew—" an honest Jew," as Shakespeare would have said—to understand any more profoundly ; and thus we may well smile when he tells us, after he has finished with the apples, that the cross is already " rotten " and Christianity an " abortive " religion. When we behold such utter want of intelligence the yawning gulf reveals itself to our eyes ! (See *Coup d'œil sur l'histoire du peuple juif*, p. 19 f.)

conception was still strange to the real Isaiah, as also to Jeremiah.* The fantastically scientific ideas in *Genesis* concerning the origin of the organic world, the profound myth of the fall of man, the theory of the development of man up to the first organisation of society . . . all that became " history," and thereby it at the same time lost all significance as religious myth ; for the myth is elastic, inexhaustible, whereas here a simple chronicle of facts, an enumeration of events, lies before us.† That is materialism. Wherever the Semitic spirit has breathed, we shall meet with this materialism. Elsewhere in the whole world religion is an idealistic impulse ; Schopenhauer called it " popular metaphysics " ; I should rather call it popular idealism ; in the case of the Semites, too, we observe this wistful awakening of a feeling of the superhuman (read the life of Mohammed), but the imperious will immediately lays hold of every symbol, every profound divination of reflective thought, and transforms them into hard empirical facts. And thus it is that with this view of religion only practical ends are pursued, no ideal ones. It is to provide for prosperity in this world, and aims particularly at power and wealth, it is moreover to provide for happiness in the future world (where the idea of immortality is present—an idea introduced into the Israelite faith from the Persian and into the Arabian from Christianity). Downright materialism ! as the comparison with the Saveasiuleo of the Samoans and the great world-spirit of the Yorubas has shown.

This then would be a negative influence of Judaism upon all religion : infection with fundamental views of a materialistic kind. Now we must consider the positive influence, which usually is the only one to be taken into

* Even the Jewish scholar Montefiore explicitly admits this : *Religion of the Ancient Hebrews*, p. 269. Further detail on p. 425.

† For further details concerning the Bible as an historical work and ts significance as such for the Jewish people, *see* the chapter on " The Revelation of Christ," p. 228 f. and further on, p. 486.

account. I think we may assert without qualification
that nowhere in the whole world is there to be found a
faith like that of the Semites, so glowing, so unreserved,
so unshakeable. Without them we might perhaps not
have possessed the idea of religious faith, of *fides*, at all.
The German word *Glaube* is very ambiguous; fundamentally it is almost as near doubt as conviction, the
original meaning is merely to approve (*gutheissen*).*
When we go to the Latin we are no better off, for in truth
fides means trust and nothing more; † the *bona fides*
of legal agreements shows the word in its original significance, the latter *fides salvifica* is a makeshift. Characteristically, in Sanscrit also the word *çraddhâ*, faith, is
distinguished from the Semitic " faith " by the colourless-
ness and uncertainty of its significance ; we get the
impression, which is strengthened when we carefully
survey the events of history, that we have here to deal
with two different things.‡ It may frequently happen
that an increase of the quantity altogether alters the
quality § ; that seems to be the case here too. The
genuinely Semitic faith can be destroyed by nothing, can
be injured by nothing ; it resists every experience, every
evidence. Here Will triumphs, and in fact—this should
be noted, for here we have the psychological explanation
of this remarkable phenomenon—it triumphs not merely
because of its uncommon strength, but at the same time
in consequence of the impoverishment of the understanding and the imagination : opposed to a minimum of religion we find a maximum of unconditional, unshakeable
capacity of faith, of need of faith that stretches out like

* Kluge : *Etymologisches Wörterbuch.*
† Similarly the Greek πίστις.
‡ *Çraddhâ* denotes " trust, confidence, faith, also fidelity, honesty,"
the verb Çrad-dhâ, " to trust, to consider true." But the idea has
something vague and colourless about it, and above all we must carefully note the fact that the word *Çraddhâ* plays a very unimportant
part in the life of this pre-eminently religious people.
§ *See* p. 23.

an avaricious hand—a faith that will and must give to
the believer the whole world as his own, but to him
personally and alone, to the exclusion of all others. It
is characteristic of the absolutism of this " faith-will "
(if I may coin the phrase) that originally every tribe,
every little group of the Semites has its own God. The
Semite would never wish to share with another ; his will
is unconditional, he alone must possess all ; and his faith
is as boundless as his will : these two expressions are for
him almost synonymous. Religion does not appear to
be present, so to speak, for its own sake, but as a means to
an end, as an instrument, to widen as much as possible
the sphere of what can be attained by Will.* The view
that the Semite from the first was monotheist, to which
Renan's famous phrase " *le désert est monothéiste* " † had
contributed a good deal, has long ago been proved erroneous ; ‡ we see each little tribe of the Hebrews in possession of its own God, who exercises power only over this
tribe and inside this stretch of land. If any one leaves
the circle of the family and enters a new region, he comes
under the jurisdiction of another God ; that is surely
not monotheism. § I consider the idea of divine unity

* Many authors testify that even to-day the genuine Bedouins do not
in reality acknowledge the cosmopolitical God of the Koran. Robertson
Smith, *Religion of the Semites*, p. 71, hints that Mohammedanism is
in a way a religion of the cities in contrast to the religion of the desert.
Similarly Burckhardt : *Beduinen*, p. 156.

† *Langues sémitiques*, éd. 1878, p. 6. These words were originally
uttered by Renan in 1855.

‡ *Cf.* Robertson Smith : *Religion of the Semites*, ed. 1894, p. 75 f. It
is well known what zealous polytheists many pseudo-Semitic nations
were ; of course, that does not justify one in drawing conclusions in
regard to the pure Semites. In the introduction to the first edition of
his *Langues sémitiques* Renan has laid great stress on this reservation,
which is scarcely ever observed.

§ David, when driven by Saul from Palestine, cannot do otherwise
than serve strange gods on strange soil (1 *Samuel* xxvi. 19) ; *cf.* with
this particularly Robertson Smith, *Prophets of Israel* (ed. 1895, p. 44)
and the list of characteristic passages, which reveal the same conception,
in Wellhausen, *Prolegomena*, 4th ed. p. 22. The polytheism appears
in a particularly simple fashion in Moses' song of praise, " Who is like

to be altogether un-Semitic—to be, in fact, anti-Semitic, for this reason, that it can only arise from speculation : in the over-plentiful material which the imagination has heaped out, thought brings about order, and thus arrives at the conception of unity; here, on the other hand, there is neither imagination nor speculation but only history and will : from these the one cosmic world-spirit of the Indians, Persians, Hellenes and Christians could never originate, any more than the "one only" God of the Egyptians.* It can be proved that the idea of the one God of the world only entered Judaism at a very late postexilic period, and beyond all doubt under foreign and especially Persian influence; if we wished to be very exact, we should have to say : this idea never really obtained, for to this day, as three thousand years ago, Jehovah is not the God of the cosmic universe but the God of the Jews ; he has only destroyed the other Gods, consumed them, as he will one day consume other nations, with the exception of those who shall serve the Jews as slaves.† That is really not monotheism but, as I have already remarked, unvarnished monolatry.

unto Thee, O Lord, among the Gods ? " (*Exodus* xv. 11)i In the much later *Deuteronomy* a distinction is drawn between Jehovah and the " strange gods " as quite homonymous beings (xxxii. 12) and it is only on very solemn occasions that the former is addressed as " God of all Gods " (x. 17). Even in the time of the Maccabees (more than five hundred years later) we meet the same expression " God of all Gods " in the book of *Daniel*, xi. 36, and find in Jesus Sirach the conception of " subordinate deities " who are appointed by Jehovah to rule over the different peoples (*Jes. Sir.* xvii. 17).

* There is much needless dispute regarding Egyptian monotheism, for it cannot be doubted, when one reads in *The Book of the Dead* : " Thou art the one, the God from the very beginnings of time, the heir of immortality, self-produced and self-born ; thou didst create the earth and make men. ⁹ ⁹ ." (Introductory hymn to Rā ; *see* the complete translation of the *Book of the Dead* from the Theban text by E. A. W. Budge, 1898.) Budge calls attention to the fact (p. xcviii.) that the formula in *Deuteronomy* iv. 4, " The Lord, our God, is one Lord " is a literal imitation of the Egyptian.

† *See*, for example, the *Apokalypse of Baruch* (lxxii.), a famous Jewish work belonging to the end of the first century after Christ : The men of all nations shall be subject to Israel, but those who have

On the other hand, this consideration teaches us what peculiar and important truth lay in the over-generalised remarks of Renan ; as so often, he had seen rightly, but analysed most superficially. He wrote : " The desert is monotheistic ; the sublimity of its immeasurable mono-tony first revealed to man the conception of the Infinite." How false everything is that follows the semicolon in this sentence is proved by Renan's own remarks in another passage, where he shows that the Semitic lan-guages are " incapable of expressing the feeling of the Infinite " (*see* p. 299). In the dark primeval woods of India the feeling of the Infinite had attained such an intensity that man felt his own Ego merge into the All, whereas the inhabitant of the sun-parched desert, blinded by the excess of light, lost the power of his eyes and saw nothing but himself ; far from feeling the Infinite that reveals itself to us only in the night or in the million voices of thronging life, he felt lonely—lonely and yet en-dangered, lonely yet hardly capable of finding the barest subsistence, utterly incapable of doing so if a second family should desire to join his own. This life was a struggle, a struggle in which only unfeeling egoism could exist. While the Indian, quite lost in thought, had only to stretch out his hand to the trees to still his hunger, the Bedouin was day and night on the alert, and had

---

ruled over you shall be destroyed with the sword " (quoted from Stanton, *The Jewish and the Christian Messiah,* p. 316). We see how merely national this supposed creator of Heaven and earth has remained. Montefiore also admits this when he writes, " Jehovah had certainly gradually come to be the one God of the world, but this God remained still Jehovah. Though he had become the absolute ruler of the universe, he did not cease to be the God of Israel " (p. 422). Robertson Smith, one of the first authorities of the day in these questions, interprets *Isaiah* ii. as a prophecy that Jehovah will gradually make himself God of all humanity through the acknowledg-ment of his virtues as a ruler. Hence we find even in the most sublime phases of the Semitic conception of religion, even where God is spoken of, the predominance of the purely historical, flagrantly anthropomorphic, unconditionally materialistic standpoint.

something else to do than to think of the Infinite—for which he was, moreover, so absolutely devoid of capacity and gifts that his language did not offer him the least help in that direction. On the other hand, we can understand perfectly well how the monotonous poverty of the surroundings could lead to unexampled poverty of mythological conceptions ; for man is quite incapable of feeding his imagination from his own resources ; it is, as Shakespeare says, "born in the eye"; where the eye is offered nothing but monotony, the imagination fades and withers.* And we can also easily understand how such surroundings would tend to develop that absolutely egoistic monotheism, where the one God is not the great spirit that presides over the world, as in the case of the poor negroes of the slave-coast, but a hard task-master, who is there only for me the one—that is, for me and my children—who, when I blindly devote myself to him, gives me lands which I have not planted, full of oil and wine, houses which I have not built, and wells which I have not sunk—all those glorious things which I have seen only occasionally from a distance, when, impelled by hunger, I have left the desert and gone on a foray ; and all these men who revel there in work and wealth— and with joyful song and dance and fat offerings worship Gods who give them all these riches, I will sacrifice to my God of the desert and overturn their altars ; only my God shall henceforth be God, I alone will be master in the world ! This is the monotheism of the desert ; it arises not from the idea of the Infinite but from the poverty of ideas of a poor, hungry, greedy man whose range for thought hardly rises above the conception that possession and power would be the highest bliss.

To make quite clear the very profound change of

---

* Burckhardt, who lived for years in Arabia, testifies that the monotony of the desert life and the lack of all occupation lie like an unbearable burden upon the mind and finally quite paralyse it (*Beduinen und Wahaby*, p. 286].

sentiment that is wrought in the human mind by this
Semitic view of faith, I cannot do better than quote
Goethe. His words are cited everywhere : " The real
and only and most profound theme in the history of
the world and of men, to which all other themes are subordinate, is the conflict between belief and unbelief." *
But more important is the following passage in the fourth
book of *Wahrheit und Dichtung :* " The universal, natural
religion really requires no faith ; for the conviction that
a great, creative, ordering and guiding Being is, as it
were, concealed behind nature, in order to make itself
comprehensible to us, forces itself upon every one, and
even should a man occasionally let go the thread of
this faith which guides him through life, he will nevertheless be able to pick it up again at any time and place. It
is quite a different matter with the particular religion
which tells us that this great Being takes under his care,
by preference and choice, a single individual, a tribe, a
people, a country. This religion is founded on faith,
which must be unshakeable if it is not to be destroyed
altogether. Every doubt about such a religion is fatal
to it. We may return to conviction but not to faith."
This process of reasoning brings us on to the right track ;
it enables us to say exactly what the Semite has in this
case given to the world, or, if we will, forced upon it.
An important question, for in this is contained his world-
affecting significance as an influence upon others, and in
this, too, lies at the present day the particular strength
of Judaism, which Herder and so many other great
minds felt as " alien." Goethe has clearly recognised the
essential point and also hinted, but unfortunately not
in such detail that every one may see it as he does ; for
he distinguishes between a natural religion and another
which is therefore unnatural. Now according to Goethe's
way of thinking, the contrast to the natural is the arbi-

* *Noten zum Westöstlichen Divan* (Israel in the Desert).

trary, that in which Will is the "arbiter," that in
which Will—not pure understanding, and not the
undimmed natural instinct—has decisive influence. And
hereby he not only points out to us that there are essential
differences between religions, so essential that the same
word can mean two different things, but he tells us at
the same time how this difference is fundamentally
explicable—that the religion which he contrasts with the
natural is, in fact, the religion of Will. On the other
hand, the use of the word *Glaube* (faith) by him is
vague and confusing ; he has tried to simplify too much.
Goethe says, " The natural religion really needs no faith,"
but in the non-Semitic religions there is really more
of that which is *believed* than in the Semitic ; the material
of faith is richer ; and *Glaube* is expressly demanded
by them. What is the truth in this matter ? The nature
of faith is in the two cases just as different as the nature
of religion ; to the word " religion " Goethe in the
passage quoted gives two significations, to the word
Glaube only one, hence the misunderstanding. In reality
we nowhere find religion without faith ; certainly without faith in the specifically Semitic sense, but not
without faith of some kind. Faith is everywhere the
invisible soul, religion the visible body. We must therefore proceed further if we wish to develop Goethe's utterance until it becomes quite clear. I shall take an illustration.

So far as I know, dogmatism and the idea of revelation
are nowhere so developed as among the Aryan Brahmans ;
yet the result in their case is quite other than in that of
the Semites. The sacred Vedas of the Indians were
looked upon as divine revelation ; every word of theirs
was for all matters of faith authoritative and indisputable—and in spite of this, from this one complex of
scripts, everywhere recognised as infallible, there sprang
no fewer than six entirely different systems of philo-

sophy,*—systems in which (as is characteristic of the
Indian spirit) philosophy and religion grow up inseparably
connected, so that the view of the nature of the Godhead,
of the relation of the individual to it, of the importance
of redemption, &c., is very different in the different
systems; whereby, of course, not only the philosophy,
but above all the religion of the believer is influenced.
And all these doctrines, which frequently contradict
each other in important points, were, nevertheless,
regarded as orthodox, the one as much as the other.
They all were based on the same scripts, originated in
other words from the same fundamental mythological
images of the hymns, and all gave evidence of the same
reverence for the deep speculations in the precepts of the
cult and in the Upanishads. That was sufficient. There
were no historical dates, no chronicle of the creation and
of generations, in which men should blindly believe; for
anything of that kind was meant from the first merely
as an image, a symbol. Thus, for example, the strictly
orthodox commentator of the sacred writings, Sankara,
says in regard to various images and speculations applied
to the Creation : " The script has no intention to instruct
us in regard to the extension of the world which began
with Creation, because it is neither visible, nor anywhere said, or even thinkable, that anything that is of
importance for man depends upon this." † In the same
way, each one was free to think as he pleased of the relation between spirit and matter. The monist was just as
orthodox as the dualist, the idealist as the materialist.
One comprehends how, with such a conception of religion
and faith, " in India at all times the most absolute

* There were more, but the others can be classified under the six
great systems.

† The *Sûtra's des Vedânta*. (Deussens' translation). Who does not
here think of the great remark of Goethe : " Animated inquiry into cause
does great harm ! " (*see* pp. 230 and 267). Carlyle in his essay on
Diderot well remarks, " Every religious faith, which goes back to
origins, is fruitless, inefficient and impossible."

freedom of thought has prevailed "*—I mean, how it was possible to let orthodoxy and unhampered metaphysical speculation exist side by side. But no! we who to-day live under the influence of the Semitic view of faith, find it very difficult to harmonise these conceptions—the acknowledged infallibility of sacred books of religion and at the same time the most absolute freedom of thought! But we should also note the following carefully, for hereby alone will this illustration be instructive in regard to the nature of faith. Life was much more religious in India that it ever was among us, even in the ecclesiastical age, and the Indian religion as such has borne quite different fruits from Judaism, for example, where religion (as a Jewish author assured us) banished from life science, art, literature, in fact, everything but faith and obedience.† For the enormous intellectual activity of the Indian people, whose poetical literature alone surpasses in extent the whole classical literature of Greece and Italy together,‡ is rooted in their faith; their most important achievements, even in remote spheres, radiate from their profound religious feeling. An example. Pânini's *Grammar of the Sanscrit Language*, written two thousand five hundred years ago, and as the culmination of a long, scientific development reaching back for centuries, is recognised as the greatest philological achievement of mankind. Regarding it Benfey writes: "No language of the world can show such a complete grammar; not even the German, in spite of the remarkable works of the Grimms." Georg von der Gabelentz says in his *Sprachwissenschaft* (2nd ed., 1901,

---

* Richard Garbe: *Die Sâmkhya-Philosophie*, p. 121.

† *See* p. 400. Spinoza too, who in each of his thoughts is so thorough a Jew and anti-Aryan, writes, "*Fidei scopus nihil est præter obedientiam et pietatem*" (*Tract. theol.-pol.*, chap. xiv.); that religion can be a creative element of life is a conception which remained quite incomprehensible to this brain.

‡ Max Müller: *Indien in seiner weltgeschichtlichen Bedeutung* (1884) p. 68.

p. 22), "Pânini's wonderful work is the only really complete grammar which ·any language possesses"; Pânini still forms the corner-stone of his science. What, we may ask, was it that spurred on the Indian thinkers to these high scientific achievements? The longing to awaken to new life the sacred songs of the *Rigvedà*, which in the course of centuries had almost ceased to be understood. It was, as Benfey testifies, no simple aimless enthusiasm for science as science, but deep religious sentiment which gave them strength for the undertaking.* Their eminent achievements in the sphere of mathematics —we know that the Indian Aryans are the inventors of the so-called "Arabian ciphers"—have their origin in religion. The solution of the well-known geometrical problem which gives Pythagoras his title to fame, the Indians had in long past ages discovered, automatically, as a necessary consequence of the measurements pre-scribed for sacrificial ceremonies; here, in these religious calculations, we have the germs of a clear knowledge of irrational quantities, and later of the higher algebra, the theory of numbers, &c.† In what sense, therefore, can Goethe say of a religion which informed the whole public life, and at the same time had such an influence upon mind and imagination, that it really needed no faith? Am I not right in asserting that in that passage from Goethe the word " Faith " refers to two different things —two things as different as the beings whose souls they reflect? Goethe, in fact, holds the Semitic view, and according to this view (in contrast to the Indian) religious belief refers solely to historical dates and material facts. Here God is known from historically certified manifesta-tions, not postulated from inner experience, not found out from the contemplation of nature, and not created by the power of the imagination; here everything is even simpler than Ernst Haeckel's history of creation. The

* *Geschichte der Sprachwissenschaft* (1869), pp. 77, 55.
† *Cf.* Schroeder: *Pythagoras und die Inder*, chap. iii.

one thing that is necessary is blind faith, and in this faith is concentrated the whole power of great leading spirits and of the responsible shepherds of the people : punishments on the one hand, promises on the other ; in addition, historical proofs and preternatural miracles. As a contrast to every unadulterated Semitic creed take the so-called apostolic confession of the Christian Church ! Half of the clauses refer to mysteries that cannot be represented, and of which the theologians themselves say, " The layman cannot understand them " ; but in reality it is so little a question of understanding in the logical and comprehensible meaning of the word, that from this one short creed there have been derived the most diverse and most contradictory doctrines.* And now take the Athanasian symbolism ! Here the material of religious faith consists of the most abstract speculations of the human brain. How could faith in the Semitic sense comprehend ideas to which not one man in a million can attach the faintest conception ? Jesus Christ Himself said, when children were brought to Him, "Of such is the Kingdom of Heaven," but He nevertheless added in the same passage : "All men cannot receive this saying, save they to whom it is given. He that is able to receive it, let him receive it " (*Matthew* xix. 11, 12).†
The Semite is quite different, and hence also his form of faith is different. Even the simple sentence, " I believe in God, Creator of Heaven and Earth," forms no part of his creed ; this circumstance is only casually mentioned in the Koran, and scarcely thrice mentioned in the whole sacred writings of the Jews. On the other hand, the first commandment of Moses is, " I am the Lord, who have brought thee out of the land of Egypt ! " The faith at once attaches itself, as one sees, to historical

---

* *Cf.* Harnack : *Dogmengeschichte* (Grundriss, 2nd ed.), p. 63 f.

† In the Syrian translation of the oldest text it runs thus, " Every one who has the power," so that there is no doubt about the meaning. (*See* Adalbert Merx' translation of the palimpsest, 1897.)

facts, which the people regard as authenticated, and
never does it rise above the level of the ordinary eye.
As Montefiore has taught us, there are no mysteries in
the Jewish religion (*see* p. 413 f.). When we, therefore,
speak of the incomparable power of the Semitic faith,
we must not overlook the fact that this faith refers to
an extremely scanty and limited material, that it intentionally leaves out of account the great wonder of the
world, and that by the imposition of a law (in the
juristical sense of the word), it also reduces the inner life
of the heart to a minimum—whoever obeys the law is
without sin, he need trouble his head no further ; regeneration, grace, redemption, &c., do not exist. Thus we
begin to see that this strong faith presupposes as counter-
condition a minimum of the first condition of faith, a
minimum of religion. Moses Mendelssohn has expressed
this truth intelligently and honestly : " Judaism is not
revealed religion, but revealed legislation." *

" The Semite has really little religion," Robertson
Smith, the greatest authority on the Semitic religion, says
with a sigh. " Yes, but much faith," answers Goethe.
And Renan supplies the commentary : " The mind of the
Semite can embrace extremely little, but this little it
embraces with great power." † I think, however, that
we are beginning to distinguish better between faith
and faith, between religion and religion, than did Smith,
Goethe and Renan ; we shall soon get to the root of the
matter. To make the matter thoroughly clear, I must
once more contrast the Semite and the Indian.

The Aryan Indian can stand as an example of the
extreme contrast to the Semite—a contrast, however,
which clearly reveals itself in all peoples that are devoid
of Semite blood, even in the Australian negroes, and which

---

* *Rettung der Juden,* 1872₁ (I quote from Graetz : *Volks. Gesch.*
iii. 578).
† *Langues sématiques,* p. 11

slumbers in the hearts of all of us.   The mind of the
Hindoo embraces an extraordinary amount—too much
for his earthly happiness ; his feelings are tender and full
of sympathy, his sense pious, his thought metaphysically
the deepest in the world, his imagination as luxuriant as
his primeval forests, as bold as the world's loftiest moun
tain peak, to which his eye is ever drawn upwards.   But
two things he entirely lacks ; he has no historical sense at
all. This people has produced everything, but no history
of its own career—not the trace of a chronicle.   That is
the first want.   The second is the capacity to regulate his
imagination, for want of which the Indian, as hyper-
idealist, loses the right sense of proportion for the things of
this world, and—although there is no one who fears death
less—loses at the same time his position as energetic
moulder of the world's history.   He is not materialist
enough. Far from considering himself, with Semitic
pride, the " one man in the real sense of the word," he
looks upon humanity as a phase of life like other phases,
and teaches as the basis of all wisdom and religion the *tat
tvam asi :* that thou too art, *i.e.*, man shall recognise his
own self in everything living. Here we certainly are far
removed from the little chosen people, in whose favour
the creation of the cosmos was undertaken, for whose advantage alone the rest of humanity lives and suffers ; and
it is at once clear that the divinity, or divinities, as it may
be, of these Indians will not be such as one can carry about
in an ark of the covenant, or can imagine as present in a
stone. Even the *tat tvam asi* itself points to a cosmic
religion,   and   a   cosmic   religion   again   implies—in
contrast to a national faith—a direct relation between the
individual and the divinely superhuman. What a difference
there must have been in the meaning which religion and
faith had for this Aryan Indian and for the Semite.   " In
reality no faith," says the German sage, and the Frenchman echoes with the superficiality of parody : " The

Indo-European peoples have never regarded their faith as the absolute truth." * Ah no! this is surely not possible, and it is splendidly contradicted by the life of the Brahmins. For the Indo-Aryans, too, "bring forward their witnesses," though not quite in the same sense as the second Isaiah and Mohammed meant. When the Aryan bids farewell to wife, child and children's children, in order to devote the last years of his life—void of all possessions, living on herbs, naked, in the loneliness of his forests—to pious contemplation and the redemption of his soul; when he digs his grave with his own hands and on the approach of death lays himself down in it to die, with folded hands, resigned and happy; †—can one say then that "in reality he has no faith"? that he "does not look upon his faith as the truth"? It boots not to dispute over words, but at any rate this man possesses religion, and, as it seems to me, a maximum of religion. In his youth he became acquainted with the most luxuriant mythology; all nature was to his childlike eye alive, inspired; in it there dwelt great friendly forms ‡ which constantly gave fresh scope to his fancy, even being urged to further flights by the new hymns which ceaselessly broke upon his ear. As Carlyle said of Goethe, this Hindoo youth saw himself "surrounded by wonders, everything natural in truth

---

* Renan: *Langues sématiques*, p. 7.

† Even to-day one comes upon fresh graves of this kind in the depths of the woods. Without convulsion or struggle these holy men pass from time into eternity, so that when one sees their corpses one might think that the hand of love had put their limbs aright and closed their eyes. (According to oral communications and sketches from nature.) One can see how living and unchanged, because springing from an inner soil that always remains the same, old Aryan religion even to-day is, from Max Müller's life-history of a holy man of Brahman family who died as recently as 1886, *Râmakrishna, his Life and Sayings*, 1898.

‡ Oldenberg (*Religion des Veda*) testifies that the gods of the Aryan Indians, in contrast to others, were bright, true, friendly forms, without malice, cruelty and perfidy (pp. 30, 92, 302, &c.).

supernatural." The first years of manhood brought something new ; his mind was exercised and strengthened by
the most difficult problems, and an all-embracing symbolism was taught him by the contemplation that attached
to the sacrificial ceremonies—a symbolism which almost
goes beyond our modern powers of conception,* the chief
features of which we can, however, clearly deduce from
their wonderful effect. As his mind ripened he began
more and more to realise, not merely that those mythological forms possessed existence in his brain only, had a
meaning only for his special, limited human spirit—
in other words, were symbols of a something which the
reason could not reach—but also that his whole life, the
world that served him as a stage, the actors that moved
upon this stage, the thoughts that he thought, the love
that intoxicated him, the duties he fulfilled, were to be
regarded as mere symbols ; he did not deny the reality
of these things, but he denied that their significance was
exhausted by the empirically perceptible : "On the
standpoint of the highest reality, all empirical activity
has no existence," say the sacred writings of the Hindoos †
—a fact to which Goethe has given immortal expression
when he says :

> Alles Vergängliche
> Ist nur ein Gleichnis.

And the more deeply this conviction settled in his consciousness, the higher rose the conception of the significance of his individual life; this life at once received a cosmic importance. For the script had taught him that "only
unity is in the highest sense real, complexity is but a
cleft gaping out of false perception." The good works,

---

* Oldenberg, *Religion des Veda :* "The details of sacrifice appealed
to the Hindoos as representing analogous facts in the universe which
were united to them by a mystical tie." We find proofs of this on
every page of the *Satapatha-Brâhmana*, that remarkable code of sacra
ficial ceremonies.

† Cankara : *Vedântesûtra's* II. 1, 14 (also for the following quotation).

which formerly appeared to him as part of the divine command had lost all value; henceforth only the inmost purpose, that is to say the inner life, every movement of the mental faculties, every throb of the heart, was regarded as important. If the Semitic law looked to results, not to intention, here we have the other extreme : all idea of result was excluded and moreover a matter of indifference. The important thing was to bring to perfection the highest act of creation in the reformation of man's own soul ; not to chastise—that would be petty —but to transform the slightest stirrings of foolish personal longing, till the One was merged in the All. This was " redemption." But do not fancy that we have to see in this only a philosophical process ; it was a deeply religious one, for the strength of the individual was not sufficient. The Sanscrit word for the highest and only God is Brahma, *i.e.*, " prayer " ; only by grace could man have a share in redemption, and before he could attain such grace by fervent prayer a man must have proved himself worthy of it by a pious life. This point once reached, then the individual no longer believed that he lived and died for himself alone but for the whole world ; hence the feeling of all-embracing responsibility. The one stood for all : his actions, which the delusion of the past seemed to leave to the almost insignificant decision of his own Will, were now of everlasting importance ; for just as the natural is in truth supernatural, so the moment includes eternity and is but its symbol. This was looked upon by the Aryan Indians as religion, this is what they understood by faith.

By this contrast I hope to have made clear the peculiar and distinctive nature of the Semitic view of religion and faith ; I think I have shown wherein lay that great power which inspired so many daring deeds, so many self-sacrificing thoughts ; also what were its limitations. Nothing more is necessary here; the historical importance which this power and these limitations attained is well known. One would almost be inclined to risk the paradox : religion and faith mutually exclude each other, or at least, when the one increases the other decreases. But that would be playing with words, since religion and faith manifestly have for the Semite a different meaning from that which they have for other men. The matter becomes especially intricate where we meet not the pure Semite or, as in the case of the Jews, the strong one-sided predominance of the Semitic will, but merely an infiltration of the Semitic spirit as in our own European history since the beginning of the Christian era. That gives rise to an almost inextricable confusion of ideas, and for that reason I have had to discuss the theme in considerable detail; for the entrance of the Jews into Western history derived its chief significance from the fact that the Christian Church was founded on a Semitic basis, and that the ideas of " faith " and " religion " were introduced in their Semitic sense into a religion which was fundamentally and also through the life of Christ the direct unconditional negation of the Semitic view, and which besides by its further mythological and philosophical development became altogether Indo-European and un-Semitic. It is impossible to calculate the influence of Judaism upon our whole history from its beginnings to the present day unless we are quite clear in regard to these fundamental ideas " religion " and " faith." I confess that I have not seen a work, no matter of what kind, which has succeeded in making this even approximately plain ; in most cases the problem is not even felt as such. An abstract definition of religion is of little use, it does not clear our judgment ; nor are the learned and extremely interesting researches on the origin of religion and its evolution of any value for our present purpose. It is of more importance to see with our eyes what Semitic, especially Jewish, religion is, and what are its distinguishing marks; we shall then realise how much of the Semitic has entered our own thought. For the character of this religion at once reveals to us the nature of its influence; and as, on the other hand, force of will is peculiarly characteristic of the Semite, we may expect that this influence will be great. Materialism in philosophy, prominence given to the historical motive power as opposed to the ideal, strong emphasis laid upon " justice " in the secular sense of the word, that is, of legal and moral conduct and justification by works, in contrast to every attempt at spiritual conversion and to redemption by metaphysical perception or divine grace,* the limitation of the imagination, the forbidding of freedom of thought, deep-rooted intolerance towards other religions, red-hot fanaticism—these are things that we must expect to meet everywhere to a greater or less extent where Semitic blood or Semitic ideas have gained a footing. We shall meet them frequently in the course of this book, even in the most modern and advanced views of the nineteenth century; for instance, in the teaching of Socialism. As far as intolerance in particular is concerned—this absolutely new element in the life of the Indo-European peoples—I shall postpone what I have to say about the " entrance of the Jews " in this connection to the next chapter but one, where we shall see that the earliest Christians in eloquent language demanded unconditional religious freedom, while those of a later period took from the Old Testament the divine commandment of intolerance.

* Zoroaster gives powerful expression to the Indo-European view in contrast to the Semitic in the following passage: " Secular justice, you miser! you form the whole religion of evil spirits and are the destruction of the religion of God " (*Dinkard* VII.

ISRAEL AND JUDAH

And now I again take up the thread where we left off our discussion of the relation of the various types in the blood of the Israelites and the possible influence of these mixtures upon their character (omitting the religious question just discussed). After all that I have said, it is clear that so far as religion was concerned the Semitic element was bound in time to prevail over the Hittite; but this victory was gained slowly and with difficulty, and, in fact, only in the south, *i.e.*, in Judea (Judah and Benjamin), where a frequent influx of fresh Arabian (*i.e.*, pure Semitic) blood may also have been of some influence.* In Israel (*i.e.*, in the north of the land) the old Syrian cult remained in honour till the last—the feasts on the heights, the pilgrimages to sacred places, the images of Baal, &c.; † even Elijah, who as a prophet was so strict in regard to " strange Gods," had not the slightest objection to the worship of the golden calves; he defended only the " God in Israel " against the strange Gods imported by the daughters of Phœnician kings. From Israel itself Judaism would never have sprung. All the more necessary is it that we should now become acquainted with the Jewish idea—the specifically Jewish in contrast to that of the people of Israel. And so I now pass to the third point, namely, that the real Jew only developed in the course of centuries by gradual physical separation from the rest of the Israelite family, as also by progressive development of some mental qualities and systematic starving of others; he is not the result of a normal national life, but, so to speak, an artificial product—the product of a priestly caste which, with the help of alien priests, forced

* Robertson Smith (*The Prophets of Israel*) lays great stress on this (p. 28); *see also* Wellhausen : *Prolegomena.*
† For details *see* Wellhausen and Robertson Smith (e.g., *The Prophets of Israel*, pp. 63, 96].

upon the people against its will a priestly legislation and a priestly faith as having been given by God (359).

Hurried as my sketch has been, and although for the sake of simplification I have passed over many facts in silence, I think that the reader has received a fairly vivid, and in its essential elements accurate conception of the *mixtum compositum* from which the Israelite people sprang ; he has also noticed that the mixed blood in the south of the country, where Judah and Benjamin lay,* was, from the very first moment of the arrival in Palestine, partly subject to exceptional modifying influences, that is to say, the Semitic element in the south was constantly reinforced by new arrivals. Probably this difference was of older standing. From the beginning we see the great strong tribes of the Josephites, Ephraim and Manasseh, round which most of the other tribes grouped themselves like a family, looking upon Judah† with a certain contempt, or even with distrust. The emigration to Egypt and the conquest of Palestine take place under the leadership of the Josephites ; Moses belongs to them, not to Judah (if he was not altogether an un-Semitic Egyptian) ; ‡ Joshua belongs to them,

---

* The borders of Judah and Judea (to which since David's time Benjamin also belonged) have changed very much in the course of time : the whole southern part was joined to Idumea after the exile; on the other hand, the district was, later, extended somewhat towards the north into the former Ephraimite territory by the annexations of Judas Maccabæus.

† Even in the Old Testament in the later time there is a clear distinction between Judah and Israel : " Then I cut asunder mine other staff, even Bands, that I might break the brotherhood between Judah and Israel " (*Zechariah* xi. 14 ; *see*, too, 1 *Sam.* xviii. 16) ; frequently Israel (that is, the ten tribes besides Judah and Benjamin) is simply called " the house of Joseph " in contrast to the " house of Judah " (thus *Zechariah* x. 6).

‡ Renan says : "*Il faut considérer Moïse presque comme un Égyptien*" (*Israël*, i. 220) ; his name is said to be of Egyptian and not Hebrew origin (p. 160). So too Kuenen : *National Religions and Universal Religions*, 1882, p. 315. According to Egyptian tradition he is a renegade priest from Heliopolis, called Osarsyph (*see* Maspero : *Histoire ancienne* ii. 449). To-day, as a reaction from former exaggerations,

also Jerubbaal; in fact, all the men of importance, including Samuel. Judah plays in former times so modest a part that this tribe is not mentioned in the triumphal song of Deborah. Like Simeon and Levi, Judah was almost destroyed when it entered Palestine, so that it was hardly taken into account ; of the three branches of which it consisted one only remained, and it was only by amalgamation with the settled Hittites and Amorites that Judah gradually received a new lease of life and strength.* With David it steps into the forefront, but only for a time, and that after the Benjaminite Saul, from the closely related tribe of Ephraim, had shifted the centre of influence somewhat towards the south. Immediately after Solomon's death the Kings of Judah fell into a kind of vassal relationship to those of Israel—at least they were their forced and subordinate allies. But here it is a question not merely of political jealousy—that would not deserve our attention—but of a profound difference in talent and in moral nature, a difference which is emphasised in all historical works and which forms the foundation, and a most important one, for the later so peculiar and anti-Israelite development of Judaism. In after times, seven centuries before Christ, Judah was practically isolated and separated from Israel for ever by the carrying off of the latter into captivity ; Judah, however, retained from its brother an intellectual legacy—the history of the people, the bases of its political organisation, of its religion, of its cult, of its law, of its poetry. All this, that is to say, every creative element, is

it is fashionable to deny every Egyptian influence on the Israelite cult ; this question can only be settled by specialists, particularly in so far as it affects ceremonial, priestly dress, &c. ; but we who are not scholars must be struck by the fact that the cardinal virtues of the Egyptian—chastity, pity, justice, humility (see Chantepie de la Saussaye :: Religionsgeschichte i. 305)—which do not at all agree with those of the Canaanites, are the very virtues to which the Mosaic law attaches most importance.

* Wellhausen : Die Komposition des Hexateuchs, 2nd ed. pp. 320, 355.

essentially Israelite work, not the work of Judah. Now, however, Judah alone remained behind and worked up this material in its own way. From this—this activity of the sons of Judah, hitherto like minors under the care of guardians and now suddenly left to themselves—grew Judaism ; and as a natural process from Judaism grew the Jew.

All authors are unanimous in laying stress upon the intellectual superiority of the house of Joseph ; I will quote only one. Robertson Smith writes : " It was the northern kingdom that upheld the standard of Israel. Its whole history is more interesting and richer in heroic elements ; its struggles, its calamities, and its glories were cast into a larger mould . . . if the life of the north was more troubled, it was also larger and more intense. Ephraim took the lead in literature and religion as well as in politics. It was in Ephraim far more than in Judah that the traditions of the past were held sacred, and at the same time it was there that the religious development took place which led the way to new problems and so to the arising of the Prophets. So long as the northern kingdom endured, Judah was content to learn from it for good or for evil. It would be easy to show in detail that every great wave of life and thought in Ephraim awakened an enfeebled echo in the southern kingdom."*
All the history that the old Testament contains prior to the exile, up to David's time, and much that is later, comes from Israel, not from Judah. In order to prove that, I should have to analyse in some detail the results of Biblical criticism, and this would take me too far ; the layman will find the clearest and briefest summary in Renan's *Israël*, Book IV., chaps. ii. and iii. ; the critical works of Dillmann, Wellhausen, &c., offer much

---

* *The Prophets of Israel*, p. 192. Here in a clear manner we have a summary of what the same scholar and others have elsewhere proved in detail.

more detail and therefore profounder insight, if he will
take the trouble to read them. The "Book of the
Wars of the Lord," as it is called in *Numbers* xxi. 14,
and other lost sources, from which not only the historical
parts of the Hexateuch, but also the books of *Samuel*,
of the *Kings*, &c., were later composed, originated in
the house of Joseph and celebrate its glory. Wherever
the tribe of Judah is mentioned, it is manifestly done
with the intention to disparage it ; for instance, in *Genesis*
xxxvii., where Judah alone hits upon the base idea of
selling Joseph for money, and still more in the following
chapter, where this tribe from the first is represented as
devoid of morality and as the children of incest, the
history of the chaste Joseph following as a contrast.
This I give merely as an example. The religious law, too,
in its great and fundamental features is derived from
Israel, not from Judah. There has been much discussion
with regard to the Ten Commandments, especially since
Goethe's discovery—which Wellhausen has rescued from
oblivion and scientifically perfected—that the original
Ten Commandments (*Exodus* xxxiv.) had quite a different
purport from those which were interpolated at a later
time and which referred merely to matters of the cult.*
It is sufficient for us to know that the later decalogue in
Exodus xx., which has found a place in the Christian
catechism, is, in the opinion of so learned and orthodox
a Rabbi as Solomon Schechter, the work of a priest from
the northern kingdom, and not from Judea, a man who may
have lived in the ninth century—that is, at least a hundred
or a hundred and fifty years after Solomon, at the time of
the great dynasty of the Omrides.† This fact is not merely
interesting but even amusing ; for the later purely

* Goethe : *Zwo wichtige, bisher unerörterte biblische Fragen, zum
ersten Mal gründlich beantwortet. Erste Frage : Was stund auf den
Tafeln des Bundes ?*
† *See* Schechter's Appendix to Montefiore : *Religion of the Ancient
Hebrews*, p. 557.

Jewish editors of the sacred books have given themselves
all imaginable trouble to represent the Israelite kingdom
as apostate and heathen, whereas it now appears that
the foundations of the religious law originate from this
tabooed kingdom and not from pious Judah. For the
accurate definition of what is specifically Jewish it is
important to know this : the Jew has never distinguished
himself by creative power, even in the limited sphere of
religious legislation ; indeed, what is most his own is
borrowed. For even the great prophetic movement,
which, well considered, is the only manifestation of the
Hebrew intellect which possesses enduring worth,
originated in the north. Elijah, in many respects the
most remarkable and most imaginative personality
in the whole Israelite history, exercised his influence
there only. The accounts of Elijah are so scanty that
many look upon him as a mythological personage,*
but I agree with Wellhausen in thinking that this is
historically impossible, for Elijah is the man who sets
the stone rolling, the inventor in a way of the true religion of Jehovah, the great mind which has a vague
feeling, though not a clear idea, of the monotheistic
essence of that worship. Here a great personality is at
work, and to work it must have lived. Of special interest
is the one exact piece of information which we possess
regarding him ; according to it he was not an Israelite,
but a " settler with half rights " from the other side of
the Jordan, from the farthest boundaries of the land—
a man, therefore, in whose veins in all probability almost
pure Arabian blood must have flowed.† This is interesting, for it shows the genuine Semitic element at work,
trying to save its religious ideal, which in the south by the
eclecticism of such half-Amorites as David and Amorite-

* See especially Renan : *Israël* ii. 282 f.
† See especially Graetz : *Geschichte der Juden* i. 113 ; also Maspero ·
Histoire ancienne ii. 784.

Hittites as Solomon, and in the north by the secular tolerance of the predominantly Canaanite population, had been seriously threatened. In the north alone, which was favoured by its situation, and the inhabitants of which probably were distinguished by greater industry and talent for commerce, there was already prosperity, and with it luxury and the taste for art had developed ; one of the sins with which Amos reproaches the Israelites is that "they make songs like David." Against this the anti-civilising spirit of the more genuine Semite rebelled. The noble-minded man felt instinctively and powerfully the incompatibility between the alien culture and the mental qualities of his people ; he saw before his feet the pit open, into which in truth all mongrel Semitic kingdoms had quickly sunk and left no trace behind, and, fearless as the Bedouin, he prepared for the struggle. From Elijah onwards this prophetic movement is like a healthy, dry desert wind, which, coming from afar, withers up the blossoms of idleness—but at the same time the buds of beauty and of art. Elisha, too, the successor of Elijah, has his home in Ephraim. Now, however, appears the first great prophet, whose words we still possess. I say "great," though because of the fewness of his writings he is reckoned among the minor prophets ; for Amos is, in point of depth of religious thought and acuteness of political insight, equal to the greatest. This prophet is said to have been born in Judea, but this is doubted by many (*e.g.*, by Graetz) * ; at any rate, he knows the country of Joseph as well as if it were his home, and his warnings are directed solely to this tribe. The next great "lesser" prophet, Hosea, likewise a unique personality, is an Ephraimite ; he, too, is bound up with the destiny of the one house of Joseph ; with all his

---

* Many modern authorities too (*e.g.*, Cheyne) have since proved that the famous passage " The Lord will roar from Zion " (*Amos* i. 2) is a late Jewish interpolation.

heart he devotes himself to his beloved people, and, as is the manner of prophets, he prophesies many things which did not take place—the saving of Israel by almighty Jehovah and the everlasting rule of this people. Here the series closes, here ends the influence of Israel upon Judah ; for presumably in the lifetime of Hosea—at any rate soon after his death—the whole northern people was carried off into captivity by the Assyrians and nevermore returned.

DEVELOPMENT OF THE JEW

It was only now—that is, from the year 721 before Christ—that the true Jew could begin to develop ; up till then, as we have just seen, Judah had politically, socially, and religiously been forced to follow the lead of the much more talented Israel ; now this tribe stood alone, on its own feet. The situation was alarming. With horror and trembling the Jews witnessed the fate of their brothers, who robbed themselves of their only protection ; now the circle of enemies closed in around this small land ; how could it exist in opposition to world-empires ? First it existed as the willing vassal of the Assyrians and enjoyed their protection against its nearest oppressors the inhabitants of Damascus ; then it took advantage of the death-struggle of its mighty protector, in order to make itself free from him ; it intrigued with Egypt, but became again reconciled with the Chaldeans, the new lords of Asia Minor, by the payment of heavy indemnity and the ceding of certain lands . . in short, the kingdom dragged on its somewhat miserable existence for a hundred and twenty years more, till, at last, on the occasion of a new revolt, Nebuchadnezzar lost all patience and bore off the king and 10,000 of the most distinguished personages in captivity to Babylon. Eleven years later, when they persisted in their intrigues, he destroyed

Jerusalem and the temple and had the rest of the free-
men of Judea with their families carried off to Babylonia ;
some of them, among whom was Jeremiah, fled to Egypt
and founded the Diaspora there.   After sixty more years a
portion of the exiles returned, but only a portion ; the
majority of the wealthier preferred to remain in Babylon.
It was more than a century before the small colony
that returned home—which included a comparatively
large number of priests and Levites—organised itself in
Jerusalem and the neighbouring very much shrunken
Jewish district, and once more built up the temple and
the walls of their city ; but for the gracious protection
of the Persian monarchs and the gifts of those Jews
who had quickly grown rich in exile they would never
have succeeded in their task.   There were thus once
more a Jerusalem and a Judea, but from this time
onwards there was never again an independent Jewish
state.*

Thus the development of the Judean into the real Jew
took place under the influence of definite historical
conditions.   One is wont to say that history repeats
itself ; it never does.†   The Jew is a unique phenomenon,
to which no parallel can be offered.   Without definite
historical conditions he would, however, not have become
what he did become ; the particular ethnological mixture
out of which he arose, and his further history to the
isolation from Israel, would not have produced the
abnormal phenomenon of Judaism had not a series of
remarkable circumstances favoured this special development.   These circumstances are easy to enumerate ;
they are five in number, and, like the wheels of a well-

* It was only with the help of the Syrians that the Maccabees
obtained the chief power, and the princes too who sprang from them
and belonged to the Hasmonian house have only acquired now and
then an appearance of independence amid the confusion which preceded the supremacy of Rome.

† See p. 145, note.

made watch, fit into each other—the sudden isolation, the hundred years in which they might develop their individuality, the breaking off of all historical local tradition owing to the exile, the renewing of old associations by a generation born abroad, the condition of political dependence in which the Judeans thenceforth lived. A few remarks on these five influences, which followed each other successively, will make the growth of Judaism absolutely clear to us.

(1) The men of Judah had as *in statu pupillari* been wont to receive all inspiration from the older, stronger and cleverer brother ; now all at once they stood alone, in possession of a tradition which was probably only fragmentary, and compelled henceforth to order their intellectual development themselves. It was a sudden powerful movement, which could have but one kind of reaction, a violent and by no means harmonious one.

(2) If the Assyrians had immediately invaded Judah and scattered the inhabitants, these would unquestionably have vanished as completely as the Israelites. But the Judeans were spared for more than a century, and that in a position which actually compelled them to use to the utmost the last suggestion which they had received from Israel, namely, that which their prophets Amos and Hosea had given them—moral conversion, humility before God, confidence in His almighty power. That was in truth their last anchor of hope ; victory by force over the world-power that was drawing near was out of the question. But the Judeans took a purely materialistic view of the sublime doctrine of Amos. In their need they even went so far as madly to think that Jerusalem, as the dwelling-place of Jehovah, was impregnable.* Sensible people of course shook their heads sceptically, but when the army of Sennacherib, after laying waste the

* See *Isaiah*, chap. xxxvii., particularly the verses 33–37.

surrounding land and beginning the siege of Jerusalem, suddenly had to retire, then the Prophets were in the right; a pestilence had broken out in the camp, said the one; inner dissension, said the other, caused the retreat; * it did not matter, on that morning of the year 702 B.C. upon which the inhabitants of Jerusalem no longer saw the host of Sennacherib underneath their walls, the Jew was born, and with him the Jehovah whom we know from the Bible. That day was the turning-point in the history of Judah. Even the foreign peoples saw in the saving of Jerusalem a divine miracle. All at once the Prophets who had hitherto been despised and persecuted—Isaiah and Micah—became the heroes of the day; the king had to join their party and begin to purify the land from strange gods. The faith in the providence of Jehovah, the confident belief that all prosperity depended upon passive obedience to his commands, that every national calamity came as a trial or punishment, the unshakeable conviction that Judah was the chosen people of God, while the other nations stood far below it—in fact, the whole complex of conceptions which was to form the soul of Judaism—now came into existence, developed rapidly from germs which under normal circumstances would never have produced such results, giving great power of resistance but on the other hand choking much that was sensible, sound and natural until it became a fixed idea. Now for the first time were written the momentous words: "Only the Lord had a delight in thy fathers to love them, and he chose their seed after them, even you above all people, as it is this day" (*Deut.* x. 15). From the year 701 to the year 586, when Jerusalem was destroyed, the Jews

---

* *Cf.* Cheyne: *Introduction to the Book of Isaiah*, p. 231 f. It is interesting to learn from Assyrian accounts that Jerusalem was defended by an army of Arabian mercenaries; Judah had been distinguished from time immemorial for its lack of military capacity.

had more than a hundred years to develop this idea. The Prophets and Priests, who now had their opportunity, made good use of their time. In spite of the liberal reaction of Manasseh, they succeeded first in banishing the other gods and then in introducing by a stroke of genius the mad idea that Jehovah could be worshipped in Jerusalem alone, for which reason Josiah destroyed the " high places " and all the other most holy altars of the people, killed most of the Levites of these sanctuaries which were said to have been founded by the Patriarchs and consecrated by divine manifestations, while the rest he made into subordinate servants of the house of God in Jerusalem ; now there was but one God, one altar, one High Priest ; the world was richer by the idea (though not yet by the word) Church ; the foundation of the present Roman church, with its infallible head, was laid. In order to bring this about, they had to have recourse to a clever fraud, the pattern of many later ones. In the year 622, when the Temple was being repaired, a " book of law " was said to be " found " ; * that it was only then written, there can to-day be not the slightest doubt. *Deuteronomy* or the fifth book of Moses ("a quite superfluous expansion of the Ten Commandments," as Luther called it) was meant to introduce a rule of the priesthood, such as had never existed in Israel or Judah, and to form the legal (and at the same time, as always with the Hebrews, the historical) foundation of the justification of Jerusalem alone—an idea which, as long as the northern kingdom, Israel, stood, never could have been entertained, and which had been quite strange even to Isaiah, in spite of all his fanatical patriotism and love for Jerusalem.† This

* 2 *Kings* xxii.

† R. Smith : *Prophets of Israel*, p. 438. In *Deuteronomy* the foundation of real Judaism is laid. It forms the central point of the New Testament in its present form : " and that is the standpoint from which we can and must push our inquiries backwards and forwards if we are to

was all done, not with an evil intention to deceive, but
in order henceforth to keep pure the cult of the Saviour
God Jehovah, and at the same time as the beginning of
a moral regeneration. There, for example, appears for
the first time, shyly and guardedly, the commandment
that we should love God the Lord ; at the same time this
book contained the fanatically dogmatic assertion that
the Jews alone were the people of God, and along with
this came for the first time the prohibition of mixed
marriages, as also the commandment to " destroy" all
" heathens" wherever Jews dwell, and to stone to
death every Jew, man or woman, who is not orthodox
(xvii. 5) ; two witnesses were to be sufficient to justify
the death sentence : the world was richer by the idea
of religious intolerance. How new this course of thought
was to the people, and under what particular circumstance alone it could obtain a hold—namely, amidst
hourly danger and after the wonderful saving of Jerusalem from the hands of Sennacherib—is shown by the
ever-repeated formula : " The Lord hath commanded
that we should fear him, that it may be well with us
all the days of our life, as it is to-day." Frightful punishments on the one hand, boundless promises on the other
and, in addition, the constant enumeration of the wonders
which Jehovah had done on behalf of Israel—these are
the methods of conviction employed by the book of
Deuteronomy, the first independent work of the Judeans
in the sphere of religion.* Sublime this religious motive
is not ; this I must assert in spite of all Jewish and
Christian commentators ; yet when grasped by a fanatical

have any prospect of rightly understanding the rest," said Reuss
many years ago in his fundamental *Geschichte des Alten Testaments*,
§ 286.

* Chapter xxviii. (which is certainly postexilic) contains the blessings,
" and thou shalt not go aside from any of the words which I command
thee this day," and then the curses, more than a hundred in number,
containing all the horrors which a sickly imagination can picture to
itself, " for God will rejoice over you to destroy you."

faith it is an incomparably powerful one. And henceforth all efforts are directed towards strengthening this faith, and once more the circumstances are favourable to those efforts.

(3) One would have thought that the destruction of Jerusalem and the Captivity would have shaken their trust in Jehovah ; but the finishing blow did not come all at once, and the inspiring strength of such a faith as Jeremiah's had ample time to attune itself to new conditions. In the meantime, among the great ones of the kingdom, moral regeneration had quickly turned into the opposite ; they did evil without fear. But Jeremiah saw the future otherwise ; in the Babylonian this prophet saw the scourge of God, sent to punish Judah for its sins ; just as salvation had proceeded from the love of Jehovah to his chosen people, so was the present chastisement love ; and so Jeremiah, in contradiction to Isaiah, prophesied the destruction of Jerusalem, and for this he was persecuted as a traitor and hireling of the Babylonians. But the Prophet was once more right, the shrewd men of the world wrong ; for the latter relied this time upon Jehovah ; had they not been taught for a century that Jerusalem was impregnable ? And when now destruction came, they said : " Behold the prophet has spoken true ; that is the hand of Jehovah." It is easy to understand the great importance of the Captivity for the further development and strengthening of this delusive conception. Without the banishment the true yet so wonderfully artificial Judaism would never have survived. The kings Hezekiah, Josiah and Zedekiah had been able to overturn the altars and cut down the sacred trees, but the people clung to its old sanctuaries ; now all at once it was torn away from every tradition. The sixty years' sojourn in the Babylonian kingdom cut, so to speak, the thread of history in two. Not a man who had left the land of his fathers at

an age when he could form his own judgment, ever came back. When a single individual leaves his fatherland for fifty years—aye, even for twenty—he returns home to relations and friends as a stranger among strangers; he is unable to accommodate himself once more to the special organic law of the individual growth of this particular people, especially if he has left his fatherland in early youth. In this case a whole nation left its historical home; those who returned later had been born and brought up, almost without exception, in the foreign land; there was, perhaps, not one who consciously remembered Judea. And meanwhile, in Babylon, while the blessed connection with the past (the relation of child to mother) was broken off, the embittered zealots among the exiled were brooding over their fate and making resolves which they could never have thought of in the land of their home.* It was in the captivity that specific Judaism had its foundation, and this was brought about by Ezekiel, a priest of the family of the High Priest; hence it is that Judaism has from the very beginning borne the stamp of the Captivity. Its faith is not the faith of a healthy, free people that is fighting for its existence in honest rivalry; it breathes impotence and thirst for vengeance, and seeks to blind men to the misery of the moment by forecasting an impossible future. The book of *Ezekiel* is the most frightful in the Bible; by its employment of extreme means—horrible threats and the most atrocious promises—this narrow-minded, abstractly formalistic, but noble and patriotic spirit † wished to save the much-

* With regard to the incalculably great influence of Babylon upon all Jewish thought from the first one finds the fullest information in Eberhard Schrader's book, *Die Keilinschriften und das Alte Testament*, 3rd ed., revised by Zimmern and Winckler, 1903 ; a short summary is found in Winckler's *Die politische Entwickelung Babylonien und Assyriens*, p. 17 f.

† Splendidly described in chap. xii. of Duhm's *Theologie der Propheten*. Eduard Meyer says in the *Entstehung des Judentums*, p. 219, " Ezekiel

shaken faith of his brothers, and with it the nation.
Up to his time in Israel religion had been, as in Rome,
Greece, Egypt, a fact among other facts of the national
life, and a priesthood a part of the national organisation. Ezekiel said : " No, Israel is not in the world,
to toil and wage war like other peoples, to do work
and to think, but to be the sanctuary of Jehovah ; let
it observe Jehovah's law, and all will be given to it." The
State was now to be replaced by the rule of the religious
law, the so-called nomocracy. Even *Deuteronomy* had
admitted that other peoples had other gods ; Amos,
as an isolated great mind, had had a vague feeling of the
existence of a cosmic god, who was something more than
the political *deus ex machina* of a special little nation :
Ezekiel now united both views and invented therefrom
the Jehovah of Judaism, monotheism in a frightful,
distorted form. Of a surety Jehovah is the only and
almighty God, but He lives merely for His own glory ;
sympathetically gracious towards the Jews (for through
them He will proclaim His glory and show His power
under the condition that they devote themselves solely
to His service), but to all other peoples of the earth He is
a cruel God, who will visit them with " pestilence and
blood," in order that " He may become glorious, sacred
and known " ! All these other peoples are to be destroyed, and Jehovah commands His prophets to call
together the birds and the animals of the world " that
they may eat the flesh of the strong and drink the blood
of princes." Besides this, the book contains the sketch
of the organisation of a hierarchy and of a new straight-
jacket of worship—just the things in regard to which a
prophet living in exile could indulge his imagination,

was manifestly quite an honest nature, but narrow-minded, and
moreover he had grown up in the narrow views of the priesthood, not
to be named in the same breath with the great figures, with whom
he, by the donning of a very threadbare prophet's mantle, ventured
to put himself side by side."

as he could not have done had he stood in the midst of a
national life, where every new statute would have had
to contend with custom and tradition. But not long
after Ezekiel's death the noble Persian king Cyrus conquered the Babylonian Empire. With the simplicity
of the inexperienced Indo-European he permitted the
return of the Jews and gave them a subsidy for the
rebuilding of the temple. Under the protection of
Aryan tolerance the hearth was erected from which, for
tens of centuries a curse to all that is noblest and an
everlasting disgrace to Christianity, Semitic intolerance
was to spread like a poison over the whole earth. Whoever wishes to give a clear answer to the question, Who
is the Jew ? must never forget the one fact, that the
Jew, thanks to Ezekiel, is the teacher of all intolerance,
of all fanaticism in faith, and of all murder for the sake
of religion ; that he only appealed to toleration where
he felt himself oppressed, that he himself, on the other
hand, never practised it nor dared to practise it, for his
law forbade it as it forbids it to-day and will forbid it
to-morrow.

(4) Ezekiel had dreamt, but by the return from captivity his dream became a reality ; his book—not the
history of Israel, not the voices of the great prophets—
was henceforth the ideal according to which Judaism
was organised. And this again could only take place
thanks to the circumstance that the historical process
began with a new generation, in which even the language
of the fathers was forgotten and only the Priests still
understood it.* It was simply due to the coincidence

* Soon after this, more than four hundred years before Christ, the
Hebrew language died out altogether (Paschal : *Völkerkunde*, 2nd ed.
p. 532) ; its adoption once more many centuries later was artificial
and with the object of separating the Jews from their hosts in Europe.
In consequence we find such strange things happen, as for instance
that the French citizens of " Jewish belief " can only fill their voting
papers in Hebrew, an achievement of which Judas Maccabæus would
have been incapable ! The absolute lack of feeling for language among

of such unusual circumstances that something became now possible of which the history of the world gives no second example ; that a few clever and determined men could force an absolutely fictitious, artificially thought out, and exceedingly complicated history of religion and culture upon a whole people under the guise of time-hallowed tradition. The process is quite different from that of the Christian councils, where it was decided that man must believe this and that, on the ground that it was eternal truth. Dogma in our sense of the word is foreign to the Jew ; for the materialistic view which prevails wherever the Semitic spirit rules even if only, as here, as *spiritus rector*, every conviction must rest on an historical basis. And thus the new Jehovah-faith, the new rules for the temple-cult, the many new religious laws,* were introduced as historical things which had been ordained by God of old and had since then been constantly observed except by apostate sinners. The beginning was made by *Deuteronomy* before the Captivity ; but that had only been a timid attempt, and, in fact, not a very successful one in presence of the still vigorous popular consciousness. Now the situation was quite changed. In the first place the Captivity had, as I have already said, cut the historical thread, and secondly, the exiles who returned consisted chiefly of two classes : on the one hand of the poorest, most ignorant and dependent of the people, on the other of Priests and Levites.† The richer more worldly inclined Jews had preferred to remain in the foreign land ; they felt themselves more comfortable there than in

the Jews to-day is explained by the fact that they are at home in no language—for a dead language cannot receive new life by command— and the Hebrew idiom is just as much abused by them as any other.

* Law and religion, one should never forget, are to the Jew synonymous (*see* Moses Mendelssohn).

† *Cf.* Wellhausen : *Israel. und jüd. Geschichte*, p. 159. The same author writes in his *Prolegomena*, p. 28 : " From the exile the nation did not return, but a religious sect only.".

their own community, but they remained (at least the majority remained) Jews—partly, doubtless, because this faith suited them ; partly because of the privileges which they knew how to assure to themselves everywhere, among the first of which was exemption from military service.* It is easy to see how the priesthood now had both these elements in its hand—the ignorant

---

* From the standpoint of the philosophy of history we should certainly explain this peculiar preference of the Jews for a more or less parasitic condition, by their long dependence upon Israel. It is at any rate very noteworthy that the Judeans did not wait for the Captivity (still less for the so-called scattering) to show their preference for this life. In a number of cities on the banks of the Tigris and the Euphrates Israelite seals of older epochs have been found, and already at the time of Sennacherib, *i.e.*, a hundred years before the first destruction of Jerusalem, the greatest banking house in Babylon was Jewish ; this firm, " Egibi brothers," is said to have occupied in the East a position similar to that of the Rothschilds in Europe. (*Cf.* Sayce : *Assyria, its Princes, Priests and People*, p. 138.) I hope we shall hear no more of the nursery tale that the Jews " by nature " are peasants and only became usurers in spite of themselves during the Middle Ages, because they were cut off from every other occupation ; if we read the prophets carefully we shall see how often they complain of usury, which serves the rich as a means of ruining the peasants; we should call to mind the famous passage in the Talmud : " Whoever has 100 Gulden in commerce can eat flesh every day and drink wine ; whoever has 100 Gulden in agriculture must eat herbs and vegetables, and also dig, be wakeful and in addition make enemies. . . . But we are created that we may serve God : is it then not right that we should nourish ourselves without pain ? " (Herder, from whom I quote the passage, adds, " Without pain certainly ! but not by fraud and cunning," *Adrastea* v. 7). We should also read *Nehemiah*, chap. v., and see how, when the Jews neglected everything to build the destroyed temple again, the councillors and priests took advantage of the solemn moment to practise usury and to sweep in the " fields, vineyards, olive-groves and houses " of their poorer comrades among the people. Nothing in the Aryan Medes is so strange to the Jews as the fact that they do not " regard silver nor delight in gold " (*Isaiah* xiii., 17) ; and among the most fearful curses with which Jehovah threatens his people in case of disobedience there is one which says (*Deut.* xxviii) : " that the Jew will no longer lend money to the stranger " ! We should remember, too, that in the book of *Tobias* (about a hundred years before Christ) an angel is sent from Heaven to enforce the payment of the gold which is invested in the neighbouring countries at compound interest (chaps. v, and ix.). It should be mentioned in this connection that already at the time of Solomon the Jews were the horse-copers of all Syria (Sayce : *Hittites*, p. 13).

colonists who were bound by no tradition, and the educated members of the Diaspora, who were, however, far removed from the one centre of the cult. And thus the priesthood set up the artificial structure : *Deuteronomy* was completed (especially by the first eleven so effective historical chapters), then the so-called " priestly code " was made (the whole book of *Leviticus*, three-fourths of *Numbers*, the half of *Exodus* and about eleven chapters of *Genesis*)* ; besides, the historical books of the Old Testament were collected from various sources and put together in the form in which they have come down to us, naturally only after those sources had been revised, expunged and interpolated in order to push the new hierocracy and the new faith in Jehovah together with the new "law," under which the poor Jews were henceforth to groan. This, however, was a work which was beyond the standard of education at the time, so that contradictions burst forth at all corners and we can see pious caprice at work through the gaps that are left.† This Thora (*i.e.*, "Law") was then gradually completed by selections from the partly very old didactic literature and by carefully worked up collections of the prophetic books, enriched by as many *vaticinia ex eventibus* as possible, but so stupidly edited that it is only with the most unspeakable difficulty that we can find out the intention of the

* *Cf.* Montefiore : *Ancient Hebrews*, p. 315, and for the detailed analytic enumeration, Driver : *Introduction to the Literature of the Old Testament* (1892), p. 150 (printed in Montefiore's book, p. 354).

† The old Christians knew very well that the Old Testament was a late and revised piece of work. Thus, for example, in his answer to the twenty-first question of Heloise, Abelard refers to the Church historian Beda, who at the beginning of the eighth century wrote as follows : " *Ipse Esdras, qui non solum legem, sed etiam, ut communis majorum fama est, omnem sacræ scripturæ seriem, prout sibi videbatur legentibus sufficere, rescripsit . . .* " Thus the most modern " Biblical criticism," which is so opposed by the Protestant as well as by the Catholic orthodox theologians, has been promoted simply by the scientific confirmation of a fact which a thousand years ago was common property and to which not even the most pious soul took exception.

Prophets ; still later some freely invented didactic poems were added, as *Esther, Job, Daniel*, also the *Psalms*, &c. Still, long after the time of Ezra, according to Jewish tradition, a collegium of a hundred and twenty scribes, the " great synagogue," worked at the completion and revision of the canon ; the two books of *Chronicles*, for instance, were written two hundred years later, " after the fall of the Persian Empire, out of the midst of Judaism." * I shall have to return immediately to this religion of Ezekiel ; but first I shall discuss the fifth and last historical condition, without which it would never have been able, in spite of all that had gone before, to obtain a footing.

(5) After the Babylonian captivity the Jews never again formed an independent nation. Herder has rightly dwelt upon one profound influence that this fact must have exercised upon the character of the people : " The Jewish people was spoiled in its education because it never attained to the ripeness of political culture on its own soil, and consequently never to the real feeling of honour and freedom."† It is impossible to assert that at first the Jew was organically wanting in the sense of honour and freedom ; his fate, too, would perhaps not have sufficed to produce such a complete atrophy of these precious qualities had not that faith been added which robbed the individual of every freedom and also completely rooted out the " true feeling of honour " by refusing to concede honour to other and higher nations. But the people of the tribe of Judah would never have

* Wellhausen : *Prolegomena*, p. 170. A simple exposition of the growth of the Old Testament, after the manner of Wellhausen's *Israel. und jüd. Geschichte*, is unknown to me. The fundamental work of Eduard Reuss, *Gesch. der hl. Schriften alten Testaments*, is planned and written for scholars, and Zittel, *Die Entstehung der Bibel* in Reclam's series does not at all correspond to the title and does not satisfy even modest claims, however much interesting matter the book otherwise contains.

† *Ideen zur Geschichte der Menschheit*, P. III. Bk. 12, Div. 3.

allowed this faith to be forced upon them if its political impotence, as a small vassal State endured on sufferance, had not delivered it over bound hand and foot to its religious teachers. Such short episodes of half independence as that under Simon Maccabæus only suffice to show that on entering into the sphere of practical life this faith, as genuine popular faith, must needs have undergone profound modifications; for the Maccabees originally sprang into prosperity because they (the children of distant Modin, in what was formerly the Ephraimite mountains) broke one of the strictest laws, that of the Sabbath.* How impossible it would have been to enforce this priestly faith, this priestly cult, this priestly law upon an independent people, we see from the fact that it was difficult enough even under the given conditions, and would not have succeeded but for the vigorous support of the kings of Babylon. For though the Jews had been cut off from all traditions, yet neither their neighbours nor that original and genuinely Canaanite population which had been left behind in considerable numbers in Judea met with the same fate. And thus in the first period after the return they began to form connections again on all sides. The Hittite-Amorite peasants wished, as worshippers of Jehovah, to take part in the sacrifice as before; they did not feel, and would not admit, that Jehovah, the God of their own land, should henceforth be the monopoly of the Jews; on the other hand, the well-to-do among those Israelites who returned contracted marriages with the neighbouring peoples, not minding whether these worshipped Milkom, Moloch or Baal; just as in our days the nobility, however Anti-Semitic, like to marry Jewesses, so the members of the high priestly caste considered marriage with an Ammonite or an Edomite "conformable to their rank," provided the maiden had sufficient money. How

Maccabees ii. 41.

under such conditions could the faith, as Ezekiel taught it, have been imparted and the new law with its countless prescriptions have become the rule of life ? The un-natural product of an overheated priestly brain would within a generation have been consigned *ad patres*. But the Jews did not form an independent State. They had returned to Jerusalem under the leadership of a half-Persian agent, who undoubtedly had definite instructions to support the priests and on the other hand to put down every movement of political ambition. As soon as the religious party saw the work which had just begun endangered by the events just mentioned, they sent to Babylon for help. In the first place reinforcements consisting of priests and scribes were sent ; those were chosen who, with Ezra—" the clever scribe "—at their head, wished to set up the Thora ; they brought with them also kingly edicts and money.* But even this did not suffice ; a man of action was needed, and so the cup-bearer of King Artaxerxes, Nehemiah, was despatched to Jerusalem, armed with dictatorial power. Energetic measures were at once taken. Those worshippers of Jehovah who did not belong officially to the Jewish people were rejected " with horror " ; not faith but genealogy was henceforth to be the decisive thing ; all Jews who had married non-Jewesses must get a divorce or emigrate ; in the book of *Leviticus* the law was in-serted : " I have severed you from other people that ye should be mine " (xx. 26). Henceforth no Jew was

* Ezra brought from the king in money alone £250,000 ! The authenticity, or at least essential authenticity, of the Persian docu-ments quoted by Ezra has in spite of the views of Wellhausen and others finally been proved by Eduard Meyer : *Die Entstehung des Judentums* (1896), pp. 1–71. This settles one of the most important questions in history. Any one who has read the little but very complete book of Meyer will understand his conclusions : " Judaism originated in the name of the Persian king and by the authority of his Empire, and thus the effects of the Empire of the Achemenides extend with great power, as almost nothing else, directly into our present age."

to marry outside his people, under penalty of death; every man who married a foreign woman committed a sin against God." * Nehemiah also built high walls round Jerusalem and put strong gates at the entrances; then he forbade the stranger to enter, that the people ": might be purified from everything foreign." Wellhausen rightly says: " Ezra and Nehemiah became, by the grace of King Artaxerxes, the definite constructors of Judaism." † What Ezekiel founded they completed; they forced Judaism on the Jew.

These, then, are in my opinion the five historical motive powers by which Judaism was rendered possible and furthered. I shall summarise them once more,, to impress them on the memory; the unexpected, sudden separation from the more gifted Israel; the continuance for a hundred years of the tiny State threatened on all sides, which could hope for help only from a superhuman power; the rending of the historical thread and of all local traditions by the carrying-off of the whole people from their home into a foreign land; the reviving of these associations under a generation which was born abroad and hardly understood the language of their fathers; the condition of political dependence which henceforth existed, and to which the priesthood owed its dominating power.

When Ezra for the first time read to the assembled people from the new law, which was to be the "law of Moses," then "all the people wept when they heard the words of the law"; this is the account of Nehemiah, and we can believe it. But it did not help them, for great Jehovah, "powerful and fearful," had commanded it; ‡ and now the so-called "Old Covenant" was renewed,

---

* *Nehemiah* xiii. 27. *Cf.* the beginning of this chapter, p. 333.

† *Israel. u. jüd. Gesch.*, 3rd ed. p. 173.

‡ According to the Talmud, Jehovah occupies himself on Sunday with reading the Thora! (Wellhausen: *Isr. Gesch.*, p. 297 ; Montefiore, p. 461).

but this time in writing, like a notary's contract. Every priest, Levite, and influential man in the country put his seal under it, also every scribe; they and all other men, "with their wives, sons and daughters," had to "bind themselves by oath to walk in the law of God that is given by Moses, the servant of God." * This was now the "New Covenant." It is probably the first and last time that in this way a religion originated in the world! Fortunately, religious instinct still lived among the people, from the midst of which a short time before a Jeremiah and a second Isaiah had arisen. Human nature does not permit itself to be stamped out and distorted without leaving a trace behind, but in this case all that was possible in that way had been done; and if in consequence the Jews became generally unpopular, the reason is solely to be sought in this artificially constructed and mechanically enforced faith, which gradually grew into an ineradicable national idea and destroyed in the Jewish heart the purely human legacy which is common to us all. In the Canaanite-Israelite nature-cult, quickened by Semitic seriousness and Amorite idealism, there must have been many germs promising the finest blossoms; how otherwise should we be able to trace such a development as that which, starting from the orgiastic dance around the image of the calf, still common in all Israel and Judah before the Captivity, leads up to the God of Amos, who " despises feast-days " and " has no pleasure in burnt-offerings " (v. 21, 22), and to the second Isaiah, who considered every temple building unworthy of God, to whom sacrifice and incense are "a horror," and who writes the almost Hindoo words: "He that killeth an ox is as if he slew a man " (*Isaiah* lxvi. 1-3). But henceforth all development was broken off. And as I must a thousand times repeat—for no one says it, and it is the only thing that has to be said—the only thing that makes

* See *Nehemiah*, chaps. viii.-xi

the position of the Jews among us children of the nineteenth century comprehensible—this so-called reform
of Ezra, which in reality signifies the foundation of
Judaism, this reform which became only possible through
the coincidence of the five historical conditions enumerated, does not betoken a stage in religious development, but is a violent reaction from every development ;
it leaves the tree standing, but cuts away all roots from
below it ; now it may stand and wither, supported by the
13,600 neatly cut stakes of the law, that it may not fall.
When, therefore, so important a scholar as Delitzsch
writes, " The Thora shows how the Mosaic law continued
for a thousand years to develop in the consciousness and
practice of Israel," we must offer the objection that the
Thora on the contrary does everything which it can to
mask the process of development which had hitherto
taken place ; that it does not hesitate to utter any lie in
order to represent the law as absolutely stationary, and
fixed since time immemorial, that it gives even such
manifest absurdities as the story of the Tabernacle and
its arrangement ; and we must assert that the Thora is
directed not only against the so-called " idolatry " (from
which the whole Israelite cult proceeded), but just as
much against the free spirit of genuine religion which
had begun to stir in the Prophets. Not one of these
great men—neither Elijah nor Amos, nor Hosea, nor
Micah, nor Isaiah, nor Jeremiah, nor the second Isaiah
—would have put his seal on that document of the New
Covenant—otherwise he would have had to deny his own
words.

THE PROPHETS

I must pause a moment to discuss the Prophets just
mentioned. For it is particularly from the contrast
between what they aimed at and sought and the teachings
of the Jerusalemite hierocrats that it becomes clear to

what an extent the Jew was made Jew, artificially made (so
to speak) by the conscious, calculated religious politics of
individual men and individual associations, and in opposition to all organic development. It is necessary to emphasise
this in order to judge aright the Israelite character, which
in a way was founded in Judaism. In the New Covenant
the observances of the cult have the first place; the
word "sanctity," which occurs so often, signifies in the
first place absolutely nothing but the strict observance of
all ordinances; * purity of heart is hardly considered,†
" purity of skin and cleanness of vessels are more important," as Reuss says with some exaggeration,‡ and in the
midst of these observances stands as the most sacred of all
—an extraordinarily complicated sacrificial ritual.§ A more
flagrant departure from the prophetic teaching is scarcely
thinkable. Let us see. Hosea had represented God as
saying, " I desired mercy and not sacrifice, and the knowledge of God more than burnt-offerings " (vi. 6). Amos
I have just quoted (p. 465). Micah writes : " Wherewith
shall I come before the Lord, and bow myself before the
high God ? Shall I come before him with burnt-offerings,
with calves of a year old ? (vi. 6). He hath showed thee,
O man, what is good ; and what doth the Lord require of
thee, but to do justly and to love mercy and to walk
humbly with thy God ? " (vi. 8). Isaiah expresses
exactly the same thing, but in greater detail, and as if by
a miracle we have a saying of his preserved, in which he

* Montefiore : *Religion of the Ancient Hebrews*, p. 236.
† Robertson Smith : *Prophets of Israel*, p. 424.
‡ *Geschichte der heiligen Schriften Alten Testaments*, § 379.
§ Whoever wishes to form an idea of this should read, in addition
to the books of *Leviticus, Numbers*, &c., the eleven tractates of the
sacrificial ordinances (Kodaschim) in the *Babylonian Island* (the
Haggadian portions form the fourth volume of the only reliable translation, that of Wünsche). One cannot assert that the Jews have got
rid of this ritual since the destruction of Jerusalem, for they still
study it, and certain things, as killing according to their rites, belong
to it, for which reason an animal killed by a non-Jew is carrion to
the Jew (*see* Treatise *Chullin*, fol. 13b).

says, "God wishes not for the Sabbath" and "your new moons and appointed feasts my soul hateth!" The people should rather occupy itself with other things, "learn to do well, seek judgment, relieve the oppressed, judge the fatherless, plead for the widow" (i. 13–17) Jeremiah, in the impetuous manner characteristic of him, goes still further; he places himself in the doorway of the temple of Jerusalem and cries out to those that enter: "Trust ye not in lying words, saying, Here is the temple of the Lord! Here is the temple of the Lord! But amend your ways and your doings; execute judgment between a man and his neighbour; oppress not the stranger, the fatherless and the widow, and shed not innocent blood in this place" (*i.e.*, do not sacrifice) (vii. 4–6). Jeremiah even wishes to hear no more of the sacred old ark of the covenant, "neither shall it come to mind; neither shall they remember it; neither shall they visit it; neither shall that be done any more" (iii. 16). In the *Psalms*, too, we read: "For thou desirest not sacrifice; thou delightest not in burnt-offerings. The sacrifices of God are a broken spirit! A broken and a contrite heart, O God, thou wilt not despise" (li. 18–19).* That all these utterances are followed by fanatical and national ones, as "Jerusalem is God's throne and all other gods are idols," &c., shows a narrowness appropriate to the time,† but does not annul the fact that all these men aimed at a progressive simplification of the cult and, like the Yoruba negroes on the Slave coast (*see* p. 417), declared the sacrifice of food to be senseless, and demanded the abolition, if possible, of every service in the temple, like that great unknown ‡ who represents God as saying, "The Heaven

---

* *See also* xl. 7 and li 13.

† It has been proved that almost all these passages are interpolations of a later time.

‡ *See* Cheyne's *Introduction to the Book of Isaiah* (1895), and Duhm's *Jesaia* (1892), for information about the writer of chaps. xl-lv. of the

is my throne and the earth is my footstool ; where is
the house that ye build unto me ?   Or what is the place of
my rest ? . . . but to this man will I look, even to him
who is poor and of a contrite spirit and trembleth at my
word " (lxvi. 1, 2).   The contrast to the commandments
of the Thora which were soon afterwards introduced
could hardly be greater.   The whole tendency of the
Prophets, as we see, is directed to inculcating the piety
of the heart ; not he who sacrifices, but he who does good,
not he who observes the Sabbath, but he who protects
the oppressed, is in their opinion good.   One must also
notice that in the case of the Prophets nationalism nowhere
(except in the later interpolations) has the dogmatic and
inhuman character of the later official faith.   Amos, a
noble man whom the great synagogue has cruelly used,
makes perhaps the only humorous remark which the
whole literature of the Bible contains : " Are ye not as
children of the Ethiopians unto me, O children of Israel ?
said the Lord " (ix. 7).   And he expresses the opinion
that just as God led the Israelites out of Egypt, so He
brought the Philistines out of Caphthor and the Syrians
out of Kir.   Micah writes with the same tolerance :
" For all people will walk, every one, in the name of his
God, and we will walk in the name of our God " (iv. 5).
The second Isaiah, the only real and conscious monotheist,
simply says : " God of the whole earth He shall be called "
(liv. 5).   Here too, therefore, a direction is clearly marked
out, which later was violently departed from.   But at
the same time that promising tendency, those longings
and attempts to find a less historical and more genuine

Book of Isaiah, usually designated the Second Isaiah or Deutero-
Isaiah, the only one who now and again reminds one of Christ and
whose name the Jews, in characteristic fashion, forgot as soon as he
died, though in all other cases they follow genealogy till the hundreth
generation.   The second Isaiah wrote during the second half of the
exile, hence a century and a half later than the historical Isaiah.
Cheyne is of opinion that chaps. lvi.-lxvi., which are mostly ascribed
to the second Isaiah, were really written by a still later author.

religion—a religion of the individual soul in contrast
to faith in national destinies—were nipped in the bud;
naturally this tendency sprang up anew again and again
in many individual hearts, but it could not inspire
with life the organism which the priestly code had paralysed, there was no longer room for development.
And yet Jeremiah had made important steps in this
direction; he (or some other in his name) had represented
God as saying, " I the Lord search the heart, I try the
reins, even to give to every man according to his ways "
(xvii. 10). Yes, in absolute contrast to the Judaic
justification by works, which the Roman Catholic Church
adopted from the Jews, we seem to see a faint glimmer
of the conception of grace when Jeremiah fervently cries
out, " Heal me, O Lord, and I shall be healed ! Save me,
and I shall be saved ! " (xvii. 14.) And with the second
Isaiah's beautiful verse, in which God says, " My thoughts
are not your thoughts, neither are your ways my ways,"
we stand on the threshold of a transcendental mystery
where the true religion of the Indian and of Jesus Christ
begins. With what justice does the theologian Duhm
say that the writers of *Deuteronomy* and *Ezekiel*, and
with them Judaism, to the present day, stand " in point
of religion and morals far beneath Jeremiah ! " *

But it seems to me more than doubtful whether the
common Semitic qualities, which reveal themselves in

---

* Duhm : *Die Theologie des Propheten*, p. 251. Jeremiah's divination of grace disappeared immediately, never to return again; even the
noblest, most talented Jews, like Jesus Sirach, teach that " whoever
knows the law is virtuous " ; God has created man and then " left
him to his own counsel " ; from this we can logically draw as conclusion
the doctrine of absolute freedom of will, destitute of all divine assistance :
" Before man stand life and death, he can choose what he will . . .
if thou wilt, thou canst keep the law " (*see*, for example, *Ecclesiasticus*
xv. 12–15). The Essenes alone form an exception, for according to
Josephus they taught the doctrine of predestination (*Jüd. Altertümer*,
520) ; this sect, however, was never recognised but persecuted, and
presumably counted few real Jews among its number ; it is an ephemeral
thing without influence.

these pre-eminent men, would have produced much religion in our sense of the word ; for as these quotations (with the exception of the two last) prove, it is always morals that the Prophets oppose to cult, not a new or reformed ideal of religion.* The Israelite prophets (in addition to whom we must reckon some Psalmists) are great by their moral greatness, not by creative power ; in this they reveal themselves as essentially Semites—in whom the will is always supreme—and their influence in the purely religious sphere is to a great extent merely a reaction from the Canaanite cult ascribed to Moses, and introduced nothing in its place. But to believe that one can take from the people one cult without replacing it by another shows but little insight into the human character ; just as little as it testifies to religious understanding, when the Prophets imagined that faith in a God who had never been conceived and never represented, who revealed himself only in political events, and who must be served with good deeds and humility alone, could satisfy even the most modest demands of the imagination. It was in fact through the sublimity of prophetic feeling, through the passionate glow of prophetic words, that one of those materialistic Syro-Semitic peoples, poor in religious conceptions, first received the revelation of the gulf between God and man, and now this gulf yawned threateningly, and not the slightest attempt was made to bridge it over. And yet what constitutes the essence of religion if not the bridging over of this gulf ? All else is philosophy or morals. We are consequently justified in calling the

* This is still truer of such later phenomena as Jesus Sirach, who, generally speaking, are content with giving very wise, noble rules of life : one must not strive after riches, but generosity, not knowledge, but wisdom, &c. (xxix, xxxi., &c.). The only attempt (and it was owing to Greek influence) on the part of the Jewish spirit to attain to the metaphysical, had a poor ending : the so-called " preacher Solomon " has no better advice to give than that we should think of to-day and enjoy our works—" all is vanity ! "

mythology of Greece a religion, for by furnishing conceptions it brings us nearer the Divine.* Not the thought
of a God, who has created heaven and earth, but the para-
clete hovering between Him and me, represents the essential purport of all religion. Mohammed is scarcely less
than Allah, and Christ is God himself, descended upon
the earth. And here we must admit that Isaiah, who
placarded his prophecies at the street corners ; Jeremiah,
the acutest politician of his time ; the second Isaiah, the
venerable, lovable figure from the Babylonian captivity ;
and Amos, the landed proprietor, who saw a national
danger in the corruption of the leading grades of society ;
Hosea, who considered the priests even more dangerous ;
Micah, the Socialist Democratic peasant, who wishes to wipe
out cities (except Jerusalem) from the face of the earth ;—
these are splendid men, in whom we note with delight
how strong in faith and at the same time generous, how
noble, how vigorously the Israelite spirit moved before
it was bound hand and foot, yet they are by no means
religious geniuses. If they had had that power which
they did not possess, their people would have been spared
their bitter fate ; the people would not have needed
to weep " when it heard the words of the law."

THE RABBIS

What the Prophets had failed to accomplish was
achieved by the priests and scribes. They arranged the
connection between God and man by fixing an invented
but exact historical tradition, by the retention and
further development of the sacrificial service and above
all by the so-called " law," that is, by hundreds of

* It is not unimportant to note here how much more insight into
the essence of religious need is shown by a Socrates, who taught
that not the sacrifice and its costliness pleased the gods, but the
innermost feelings of the sacrificer, though he at the same time considered the offering of the usual sacrifices as a duty (Xenophon : *Memo-
rabilia* i. 3). Similarly Jesus Christ.

directions which hedged in every step of a man the whole day long, and continually accompanied him through all seasons—in the field, at home, asleep and awake, eating and drinking. According to the Talmud tradition, in the days of mourning for the death of Moses three thousand such ordinances were forgotten ; * that marks the tendency. The manifest purpose was to keep the thought of God continually alive among the people, and at the same time the thought that they were the chosen of God and of faith in their own future. The object was noble enough, as every one who judges impartially must admit, and it may well be that this Draconian rule had a more moral life as its result, and that thousands of good souls lived contented and happy in the fulfilment of the law ; and yet what happened here was a stroke of violence against nature. It is contrary to nature to hem in every step of a man ; contrary to nature to plague a whole people with priestly subtleties,† and to forbid it all healthy, free, intellectual nourishment ; contrary to nature to teach pride, hatred and isolation as the bases of our moral relations to our fellow-men ; contrary to nature to transfer all our efforts from the present to the future. To establish Judaism, a religion was killed, and then mummified.

Ambrosius praises in the religious doctrine of the Jews especially "the victory of reason over feeling." ‡ The word reason is perhaps not very happily chosen, Will would be nearer the point ; but he is quite right in regard to the subjection of the feelings, and he here says in simple form something of so great significance that his

* Treatise *Themura*, fol. 16*a* (Wünsche).

† According to the testimony of a contemporary Jew, Rubens, *Der alte und der neue Glaube* (Zürich, 1878, p. 79), the Jew who lives according to the ordinances needs " about half the day for religion alone."¹ God wished, says Rabbi Chanania ben Akasiah, to give Israel opportunity to do good service, therefore he imposed on it a mass of rules and observances.

‡ In his work *Von den Pflichten der Kirchendiener* i. 119*i*.

words will spare me considerable discussion. But whoever wishes to know to what this subjugation of the
feelings leads in the case of a religion should study the
history of the Rabbis and attempt to read through some
of the fragments of the Talmud. He will meet noble
Rabbis and in the Talmud more praiseworthy rules for
a man's daily walk and life (especially in the treatise *Pirke
Aboth*, *i.e.*, sayings of the fathers) than he perhaps expects,
but the whole literature of the world has nothing to show
that is so dreary, so childishly wearisome, so composed of
the desert sand of absolute sterility, as this collection of
the wisest discussions which were held among Jews for
centuries concerning the Thora.* And this spiritless

* Examples teach more than differences of opinion. In regard to
the belief in God's almightiness : " Rabbi Janai was so afraid of insects
that he placed four vessels with water under the feet of his bed. Once
he stretched out his hand and found insects in the bed ; then he said
with reference to *Psalm* cxvi. 6 : Lift the bed from the vessels, I rely
on divine protection " (*Terumoth* viii. 3, 30*a*). In regard to Biblical
exegesis : " Rabbi Ismael has taught "—we find it in *Leviticus* xiv. 9—
" on the seventh day he shall shave all his hair off his head and
beard and his eyebrows, even all his hair he shall shave off " ; all
his hair, that is general ; his head, his beard, his eyebrows, that is
special, and his hair, that is again general. In the case of general,
special and general the rule is that you can only render that which is
like to the special, *i.e.*, as the special is a place which embraces in itself
such a collection of hairs " (*Kidduschin* i. 2, 9*a*). In regard to the
law : " Rabbi Pinchas came to a place where the people complained
to him that the mice devoured their grain. He accustomed the mice
to listen to his call ; they assembled before him and began to squeak.
Do you understand, said the Rabbi to the people, what they are
saying ? No, was their answer. They say, in fact, that you do not
give a tithe of their grain. Thereupon the people said, we are grateful
to you for leading us into better paths. Since then the mice did no
more damage " (*Demai* i. 3, 3*b*). In regard to knowledge of nature :
" According to Rabbi Judah the thickness of the heavens amounts to
a journey of fifty years, and since a man of ordinary strength can go
in one day 40 miles and, till the sun breaks through the sky, 4 miles,
so one can conclude that the time of the breaking through the sky
amounts to the tenth part of a day. But as thick as the sky is also
the earth and the abyss. The proof (!) is got from *Isaiah* xl. 20., *Hi.*
xxii. 14 and *Prov.* viii. 27 " (*Berachoth* i. 1, 4*b*). In regard to daily
life : " Rabbi bar Huna did not breakfast till he had brought his
child to school " (*Kidduschin* Div. 1). That one finds many a fine
saying amid the rubbish of the Talmud must, on the other hand, be

product was held more sacred by later Jews than the
Bible ! (Treatise *Pea* ii. 5). Indeed, they had the impertinence to say, " The words of the elders are more important than the words of the Prophets " ! (*Treatise Bera-*

emphasised, but with the addition that these sayings refer only to
morals ; these collections do not contain beautiful thoughts, in fact
almost nothing that has any family resemblance to a thought. And
the fine moral sayings, too, are often like the poems of Heine : the end
spoils the beginning. An example : " A man should sow peace with
his brothers and relatives and with every one, even with the stranger
upon the street "—up to this point no minister in the pulpit could
give better advice : but now the reason, that is usually the weak
point with the Jews (*see* p. 453) : " that we may be beloved in heaven
and liked on earth " (*Berachoth*, fol. 17a). Or again, we read with
pleasure, " Let a man take heed of the honour of his wife, for blessing
is found in the house of a man only because of his wife "—in truth
not quite correct, but these words testify to a sentiment which we
gladly hear expressed ; but here again the conclusion : " Honour
your wives, that you may become rich ! " (*Baba Mezia*, fol. 59a).
However it must also be mentioned that besides the beautiful moral
sayings there are very ugly and abominable ones ; as, for example,
that a Jew cannot transgress the seventh Commandment with a non-
Jewess : " For the heathen have no lawfully wedded wife, they are not
really their wives " (*Sanhedrin*, fol. 52b and 82a). I give intentionally
only one example, in order that the reader may see the tone, that
suffices : *ab uno disce omnes*. Of course there are Rabbis who dispute
this fearful doctrine ; but where the Rabbis contradict each other,
the Jew can choose for himself, and no casuistry can annul the fact
that this contempt for the non-Jew is one of the bases of the Jewish
faith , it follows logically from their insane over-estimation of themselves ; they represent Jehovah as calling to them " ye are gods "
(*Psalms* lxxxii. 6). Other interpretations, too, of the Ten Commandments show how the idea of morality was only skin-deep in the Semitic
Hittites ; thus the Rabbis (*Sanhedrin*, fol. 86a) utter the doctrine :
" the words of the eighth Commandment, ' thou shalt not steal,' refer
according to the script only to man-stealing " !—and as another
passage quoted by scribes of greater moral sentiment says, " thou
shalt not steal " (*Leviticus* xix. 11), and refers expressly to the Israelites
" the one from the other," so in this case, too, the simple moral command
leads to an ocean of casuistry ; the Talmud does not indeed teach
(as far as I could find from the fragments at my disposal) that " thou
mayest rob the non-Jew," but it nowhere teaches the opposite. Fearful,
too, are the many precepts in the Talmud concerning the persecution
and the destruction of the unorthodox Jews : how individuals are to
be stoned and the people executed with the sword, and still more
frightful are the descriptions of the tortures and executions which
this equally dismal and spiritless book expatiates upon with pleasure ;
here too only one example : " The criminal is placed in dirt up to the

choth, i. 4). So surely had the new covenant led them on the downward religious path. In the " bottomless sea," as they themselves call the Babylonian Island, their nobler religious sentiments were drowned for ever.*

knees ; a hard cloth is then laid in a soft one and wrapped round his neck ; the one witness pulls the one end towards himself and the other the other, till the prisoner opens his mouth. In the meantime the lead is heated and poured into his mouth so that it enters his vitals and burns them up" (*Sanhedrin*, fol. 52a). Then there are learned discussions about such things in the Talmud, thus the extremely pious Rabbi Jehuda thinks it would be advisable to open the poor man's mouth with pincers and to pour the lead down quickly, otherwise he might die of strangulation and then his soul would not be consumed with his body.

This is what one comes to with " the subjection of the feelings to the reason ! "

There is not even yet a complete translation of the Talmud, Many have concluded from this that it must contain things that are fearful and dangerous to the Goyim ; it is asserted that it is the Jews who hitherto frustrated every attempt at a complete translation, a suspicion by which they feel themselves greatly flattered. The historian Graetz grows angry with those of his people who " reveal the weaknesses of Judaism to the eyes of Christian readers," and mutters terrible things about certain writings of Spanish Jews, in which the " weaknesses of the Christian articles of faith and sacraments are so openly represented that one cannot venture to explain the purport wherever Christianity is the prevailing religion " (iii. 8). Now we are not so delicate and sensitive, such " revelations " are indifferent to us ; if the Jews keep their literary products secret, that is their business ; but tragical suspicion is out of place, it is merely a question of a feeling of shame easy to understand. (All the above quoted passages are taken from the only reliable translation, that of Dr. Wünsche, which has been revised by two Rabbis : *Der jerusalemische Talmud*, Zürich, 1880, and *Der babylonische Talmud*, Leipzig, 1886–1889 ; only the quotation concerning Rabbi bar Huna is from Seligman Grünwald's collection of Talmudic sayings in the Jewish *Universal-Bibliothek*. *Cf.*, further, Strack, *Einleitung in den Talmud*, No. 2 of the writings of the Jewish Institute in Berlin, where one will find a complete enumeration of all the fragments translated, p. 106 f. Much clearer and less pedantic is the supplement on the Talmud in the excellent little book of William Rubens, *Der alte und der neue Glaube im Judentum*, 1878.

* To this day every orthodox Jew regards the Rabbinical ordinances as divine and holds fast to the Talmudic sentence : " If the Rabbis call left right and right left, you must believe it " (*see* the book of the anti-Rabbinical Jew, Dr. William Rubens, p. 79). The close connection with Jesuitism (*see* next chapter) is here as in many other things very obvious.

THE MESSIANIC HOPE

All this, however, represents as it were the negative element in the founding of Judaism : of the beautiful legacy—simple and lively memories and popular tales of the Hebrews, impressive religious ordinances belonging to the Canaanites, as also many customs such as the Sabbath which rested on Sumero-Accadian influence and were all common to Western Asiatics—of this legacy the priests had made a rigid law ; by art of magic * they had transformed warm blood into cold metal, and of this they had forged a vice for the soul—an instrument of torture like the iron maid at Nürnberg ; they had tied the arteries of spontaneous feeling, or " of the feelings," as Ambrosius says—the arteries of the instinctive creative activity of a people, by which its faith, its customs, its thoughts, adapt themselves to changing times and by new formations arouse to new life what is eternally true in the old ; but their work would have had no permanence if it had halted half-way and been content with this negative element. If in physiological experiments we cut the connection between brain and heart, we have to arrange for artificial breathing or the functions of life cease ; this the priestly founders of religion did by the introduction of the Messianic kingdom of the future.

I have frequently demonstrated,† and shall not do so again, that a materialistic philosophy is necessarily based on an historical view of things, and moreover, that history, wherever it serves as the basis of a religion, must necessarily embrace the future as well as the present and the past. It is therefore beyond all doubt that thoughts of

---

* It is known that Cabal is a Jewish word and a Jewish thing. The impulse common to all men, which in our case leads to mysticism, leads in the case of the Semite to magic. Always and everywhere the rule of blind will !

† Pp. 229, 244 note, 419, 421 f., 440, &c.

the future formed a very old element of the Hebraic legacy. But how modest, how natural, how completely within the limits of the possible and actual! Canaan alone presented Jehovah to the Israelites, for he was the God of Canaan alone; apart from many unavoidable feuds, until the captivity, the tribe of Judah lived, just like the other tribes, on the best terms with its neighbours; there are immigrations and emigrations (*see* the book of *Ruth*); the God of the country where a man settles is adopted as a matter of course (*Ruth* i. 15, 16); the national pride is scarcely greater than in France or Germany to-day. Of course the future is more definite to the Prophets, in harmony with their other ideas and particularly in view of the extremely dangerous political situation (for Prophets arose only in times of political crisis, never in peace); * as a foil to the moral admonitions and threatened punishments, which form almost the whole purport of their proclamations, they required a bright picture of blessings which would fall to a pious, God-fearing people, but in the genuine writings of the Prophets before the exile there is never a word of universal empire. Even Isaiah does not go farther than the idea that Jerusalem is impregnable and that punishment will fall upon his enemies; then, in the "sure dwelling," "salvation, wisdom, prudence, and fear of the Lord will be the treasure of the inhabitants," and as an especial blessing the great man seems to foresee that "at that time there will be no scribes"! † I have the support of the greatest living authority when I assert that the conception of an especial sanctity of the Jewish people—that conception which is the basis of Jewish faith—was quite unknown to Isaiah.‡ All those passages—as, for instance, chap. iv. 3, "He that is left in Zion shall be called holy";

---

* Wellhausen (from Montefiore, p. 154).
† *See*, for instance, chap. xxxiii.
‡ Cheyne: *Introduction to Isaiah* (ed: 1895), pp: 27 and 53:

chap. lxii. 12, " And they shall call them the holy people,"
&c.—have been proved to be late interpolations, that is to
say, the work of the great synagogues already named ; the
language of a much later century which no longer freely
mastered the Hebrew has betrayed the pious forgers.
Invented are also almost all those " consoling additions "
which are found after most of the threats of Amos, Hosea,
Micah, Isaiah, &c.,* and absolutely forged, from the first
to the last word, are such chapters as *Isaiah* lx., that
famous Messianic prophecy, according to which all the
kings of the world will lie in the dust before the Jews,
and the doors of Jerusalem be open day and night in
order that the treasures † of all people may be carried in.
The genuine Isaiah promised his people " wisdom and
prudence " as their reward, the ideal of the still greater
second Isaiah (the one who would have neither sacrifice nor
temple) was that Judah should be the servant of God,
called to bring consolation everywhere to the weary, the
blind, the poor and the heavily laden. But now things
had changed ; the curse of God is henceforth to smite
him who maintains that " the house of Judah is like
unto all the heathen " (*Ezekiel* xxv. 8), for it shall be a
" kingdom of priests " (*Exodus* xix. 6).‡ The Jews were
now promised the possession of all treasures of the world,
particularly of all gold and all silver.§ " Thy people
shall inherit the land for ever " (*Isaiah* lx. 21) ; that is
henceforth the future which is held out to the Jews. In
humility he shall bow before God, but not in that inner
humility, of which Christ speaks—he bows the head before
Jehovah, because of the promise that by the fulfilment

* Cheyne in his Introduction to Robertson Smith : *Prophets of Israel*,
p. xv. f.
† Luther has " might " by mistake.
‡ Wellhausen, *Composition des Hexateuchs*, pp. 93 and 97, proves
that the passage xix. 3–9 is an interpolation of post-Deuteronomic time.
§ *Isaiah*, the whole of chap. xl. *See*, too, the postexilic Prophet
Haggai, who promises to the Jews " the treasures of all Heathens " :
" The silver is mine, the gold is mine, saith the Lord of hosts " (ii. 8, 9).

of this condition he will put his foot upon the neck of
all the nations of the world and be Lord and possessor
of the whole earth.* This one basis of Jewish religion
includes, therefore, a direct criminal attempt upon all
the peoples of the earth, and the crime cannot be dis-
avowed because hitherto the power has been lacking to carry
it out ; for it is the hope itself which is criminal and
which poisons the heart of the Jew.† To the misunderstanding and intentional falsification of the Prophets
were added other dreams of the future, which, however,
were no better. From the Persians the Jews had during
their captivity for the first time heard vague tales of an
immortality and a future life ; they had also heard of
angels and devils, heaven and hell.‡ On this basis there
was now produced an enormous apocalyptic literature of
which the book of *Daniel,* in spite of its senseless mystery-
mongering, would give a much too favourable idea,
which dealt with the end of the world, the resurrection
of the just, &c., without in any way idealising the Messianic hopes ; at the best it is a case of a resurrection
of the body, which shall give support to the dubious

---

* The absurdity of the idea, that this religion is the stem of Christianity,
Christianity its blossom, must be manifest to the most prejudiced.

† The Jewish apologists reply that they obey the law, not " because it is
by these means that they are to attain to empire, but because Jehovah commands it ; that Jehovah gives the world to the Jews as one sacred people
is done to his own honour not theirs." But this seems to me pure contemptible casuistry. A reliable author, Montefiore, says literally, " Beyond
question the argument—' obey the law, for it will pay you '—forms
the chief and fundamental motive in *Deuteronomy*" (p. 531). That
countless Jews are pious men who fulfil the law and lead a pure noble
life, without thinking of reward, only proves that here as elsewhere
morals and religion do not go together and that in the whole world
there are men who are very much better than their faith. But even
to-day fairly free-thinking Jews still write : " The existence of
Judaism depends upon the clinging to the Messianic hope "—the
definite expectation of world empire thus still forms the soul of Judaism
(*cf.* above, p. 334).

‡ In connection with the borrowing of Zoroastric (half-understood)
conceptions by the founders of Judaism, *see* Montefiore : *Religion of
the Ancient Hebrews,* pp. 373, 429, 453, &c.

assurance "to-day you must obey the law and later you will receive your reward" (Talmud, *Treatise Erubin*, Div. 2), and this Jewish "Kingdom of God" will, as one of the most eminent of Israelite thinkers, Saadia (tenth century), assures us, "be a kingdom on earth." The quotation from the *Apok. of Baruch*, on p. 425, shows what was the Jewish idea of this future world ; it differed from the world of to-day almost solely in the predominant position of the Jewish nation. An interesting trace of this view has by mistake found its way even into the New Testament. According to Matthew the twelve apostles, seated on twelve thrones, will judge the twelve tribes of Israel, which of course assumes that no others than Jews enter into heaven.*

Thus the invented and utterly falsified past is completed by an equally fictitious, Utopian future, and so the Jew, in spite of the materialism of his religion, hovers between dreams and delusions. The mirage of the desert of their fathers conjures up by magic for these half-Semites sweet consolation for their tragic destiny—an airy, empty and delusive consolation ; but by the strength of their will—called faith—it is a sufficiently vigorous living power, and indeed often a dangerous one for others. The power of the idea triumphs here in an alarming fashion ; in a people with good capacities but not pre-eminent physically or mentally it produces the delusive idea of a particular selectness, of a special pleasantness in the sight of God, of an incomparable future ; it isolates them in an insane pride from all the nations of the earth ; forces upon them, as laid

* *Matthew* xix. 28 ; *Luke* xxii. 30. This utterance put in the mouth of Christ directly contradicts what is said in *Matthew* xx. 23. The clinging to the twelve tribes also, although for more than five hundred years there were only two, is genuinely Rabbinical. The Rabbis, too, expressly teach the doctrine : " The non-Jews are as such precluded from admission to a future world " (*cf.* Laible : *Jesus Christus im Talmud*, p. 53). Concerning the Messianic expectations, *see* chap. iii. p. 235 note.

down by God, a law which is senseless, unreasonable, and impossible in practice ; it nourishes them with lying memories and lulls them with criminal hopes ;—and, while it thus raises this people in its own conceit to giddy Babel-like heights, it in truth depresses their souls deeply, weighing so heavily upon their best qualities, isolating them from suffering, striving and creating humanity, confirming them hopelessly in the most unfortunate fixed ideas, and making them in every form (from the extremest orthodoxy to outspoken free-thinking) so inevitably the enemy, open or secret, of every other human being, and a danger to every culture, that at all times and places it has inspired the deepest mistrust in the most highly gifted, and horror in the unerring instincts of the common people. I said just now that orthodoxy and free-thinking could be regarded by us as equivalents here, in fact the question to-day is not so much what a Jew believes as what, to use a paradoxical antithesis, he can believe or is capable of believing. Intellectual endowments and morality are individual qualities. The Jew is, like other men, shrewd or stupid, good or bad ; whoever denies that is not worth talking to ; but there is something which is not individual, namely, *les plis de la pensée*, as the Frenchman says, the inborn tendencies of thought and action, the definite bent, which the mind takes from the habits of generations.* And thus we see to-day Jewish atheists of the most modern type who, by their tendency to regard senseless hypotheses or mere makeshift conceptions of science as material, actual facts, by their total incapacity to rise above the narrow historical standpoint, by their talent for planning impossible

* If we reckon twenty-four years as a generation, which is not exaggerated considering how soon the Jews are mature, the Jew of to-day belongs on an average to the hundredth generation since the return from Babylon and the founding of Judaism. That holds of the male line of descent ; an unbroken female line would be in about the one hundred and fiftieth generation.

socialistic and economic Messianic empires without inquiring whether they thereby destroy the whole of the civilisation and culture which we have so slowly acquired, by their childish belief that with decrees and laws the souls of the people can be changed from to-day to to-morrow, by their lack of understanding for everything genuinely great outside the narrow limits of their own circle of thought, and by their ridiculous overestimation of every Lilliputian intellectual work which has a Jew for its author—we see, I say, such so-called freethinkers who prove themselves to be genuine children of the religion of the Thora and the Talmud in a much more thorough and striking fashion than many a pious Rabbi who exercises the lofty virtues of humility and obedience to the law, united with love to neighbour, sympathy with the poor, tolerance towards the Gentiles, and lives in such a way that he would be an honour to any nation and a glory to any religion.

THE LAW

Now in spite of all, there is greatness in the specifically Jewish theory of life, and I have already hinted in a former part of the chapter what makes this greatness (*see* p. 390 f.). Even if, as Robertson Smith assures us, the purely pecuniary interests of the priestly noble caste and their political ambition may have weighed in the momentous decision to centralise the cult in the one city Jerusalem,* yet I am convinced that barren, critical minds always attach far too much importance to such considerations. We cannot, by purely egoistic consideration of interests, found a nation which survives being scattered; such a belief is an error of judgment.†

* *Prophets of Israel*, p. 365.

† A really classical example of this so-called critical but in reality just as uncritical as inappreciative method is seen in Professor Hermann Oldenberg's *Religion des Veda*, where the symbolism and the mysticism of the Hindoos are represented continuously as priestly swindle!

Neither can we see that Ezekiel, Ezra and Nehemiah, who bore the burden and the danger, had any personal advantage in the matter. In fact idealism was required to leave Babylon for Jerusalem; the more luxurious, worldly-minded men remained in the metropolis on the Euphrates. In aftertimes too the Jew was always better off abroad than at home, and the Rabbi who earned his scanty livelihood by tailoring and cobbling and then devoted all his leisure hours to the study of the script, to teaching and discussion, was anything but a pursuer of pecuniary interests. An egoist certainly, a fanatical egoist, but only for his nation, not for himself personally. Here, therefore, as everywhere the ideal sentiment is the only one which has power to create and to maintain, and even the religion of materialism rests upon it. These men forged; that is beyond question. And forging history is in a sense worse than forging cheques; its consequences may be immeasurable; the many millions who were massacred by or for Christianity,* as well as the many Jews who died for their faith, are all victims of the forgeries of Ezra and the great synagogue. But we cannot suspect the motives of these men. They acted in the greatest despair; they wished to accomplish the impossible—to save their nation from downfall. Certainly a noble goal! They could conquer only by the employment of the most extreme means. It was a delusive but not an ignoble aim, for above all they wished to serve their God. "I shall be sanctified in the sight of the heathen" (*Ezekiel* xxviii. 25); "this people have I formed for myself; they shall show forth my praise" (*Isaiah* xliii. 21, postexilic interpolation). If the Jewish people disappeared, Jehovah remained behind unhonoured. That the founders of Judaism

* Voltaire in his article *Dieu et les hommes* gives a detailed calculation, according to which ten million human beings fell victims to the Christian Church doctrine, but everywhere he has reduced the numbers very much, sometimes by half, so as not to be charged with exaggeration.

thought so purely and unselfishly, that they raised their eyes to a God, was the source of their strength. The idea of isolating the nation by forbidding mixed marriages, and of rearing a noble race from the hopelessly mongrel Israelite, is nothing if not brilliant ; equally so the idea of representing the purity of the race as an historical legacy, as the special, characteristic feature of the Jew. In this connection the whole law should be mentioned ; for it was by this law that they succeeded in banishing every thought but the thought of Jehovah in making the people really " sacred " in the Semitic sense. A Jewish writer informs us that " for the Sabbath alone there are thirty-nine chapters of forbidden occupations, and every chapter had sub-divisions *ad infinitum*." *
Moses is said to have been taught three hundred and sixty-five prohibitions and two hundred and sixty-four commands on Mount Sinai,† and this only provides the preliminary scaffolding for the detailed " law." Montefiore asserts also that the obeying of the law had soon become with the Jew the ruling thought to such an extent that it was for him the *summum bonum*, the best, noblest and sweetest occupation in the world.‡ While memory and taste were thus paralysed, the faculty of judgment was simply broken by the law ; a poor woman who on the Sabbath gathered dry wood for her fire committed, by this transgression of the law, as great a

---

* Montefiore : *Religion of the Ancient Hebrews*, p) 504)

† Talmud, Treatise *Maccoth*, Div. 3 (according to Grünwald))

‡ Montefiore, p. 530. " The huge number of ceremonial prescriptions is the high privilege of Israel," says the Talmud (Montefiore, p. 535), and in *Lamentations* (falsely ascribed to Jeremiah) we read : " It is good for a man that he bear the yoke in his youth. He putteth his mouth in the dust ; if so be there may be hope " (iii. 27, 29). For the opposite view one should read the beautiful remarks in Kant's *Anthropologie*, § 10 *a*, concerning religious obligations, in which the great thinker expresses the opinion that nothing is more difficult for a sensible man than " the commands of a bustling do-nothingness (*Nichts-thuerei*), such as those which Judaism established."

crime as if she had broken her marriage vow.* . . . I say, therefore, that the men who founded Judaism were not impelled by evil, selfish motives, but goaded on by a demoniacal power, such as only honest fanatics can possess ; for the terrible work which they completed is perfect in every point.

THE THORA

The everlasting monument of this perfection is their Thora, the books of the Old Testament. Here history again shapes history ! What scientific work could ever hope to exercise such an influence upon the life of humanity ? It has frequently been asserted that the Jew lacks imaginative power ; the study of this remarkable book must teach us something different. At least they acquired this power in their direst need and created a true work of art, for in this history of the world, which begins with the creation of heaven and earth, to end with the future kingdom of God upon earth, all perspective relations serve to emphasise especially the one central thing—the Jewish people. And wherein lies the strength of this people—that vigour which so far has successfully defied every destiny—wherein, if not in this book ? We have learned that the Israelites in former times were in no way distinguished from the neighbouring Hebrew races ; we saw in the Syrian-Hittites an exceedingly hardy but remarkably " anonymous " human type without physiognomy, the nose being more prominent than anything else. And the Judeans ? They were so unwarlike, so unreliable as soldiers, that their king had to entrust the country and his person to the protection of mercenary troops ; they had so little enterprise that the mere sight of the sea, on which their kinsmen,

* According to the law (see *Num.* xv. 32-36) she must be punished with death.

the Phœnicians, had attained such brilliant fortunes, frightened them ; so little capacity for industry that for every undertaking artists and overseers, and for the finer pieces of work even artisans, had to be procured from the neighbouring lands ; they were so little adapted to agriculture that in this (as is clear from many passages of the Bible and the Talmud) the Canaanites not only remained their teachers but also the labour element in the country.* Indeed, even in purely political matters they were such opponents of all stable, ordered conditions that no sensible form of government could exist long among them, and from first to last they were always most comfortable under the yoke of a foreign Power, which did not, however, prevent them from trying to throw it off. . . . Such a people seems predestined to disappear quickly from the history of the world ; and in fact of the other, much more vigorous, half-Semitic races of that time only the names are now known. What saved the small people of the Jews from the same destiny ? What kept it together when it was scattered over the world ? What made it possible for the new world-principle of Christianity to spring from its midst ? This book alone. It would lead us too far if we were to analyse the distinctive features of this book which has played such a part in history. Goethe writes concerning it in one passage : " These writings are so happily grouped that from the most alien elements a delusive whole presents itself to us. They are complete enough to satisfy us, fragmentary enough to stimulate us, sufficiently barbaric to provoke us, sufficiently tender to soothe us." Herder explains the widespread influence of the Old

* Thence it is that one of the worst threats against the Jews, if they did not keep Jehovah's commandments, was that " they would have to do their own work, instead of getting it done by others " (Talmud, Treatise *Berachoth*, chap. vi., according to Grünwald). The idea that "the sons of the alien shall be the ploughmen and the vine-dressers" is also found (as a prophecy) in *Isaiah* lxi. 5.

Testament principally from the fact that "it satisfied the human craving for knowledge by furnishing for such questions as the age and the creation of the world, the origin of evil, &c., popular answers that every one understands and can easily grasp." Thus we see how this book meets the demands of the educated mind and of the man of the people—of the one, because it admires the daring arbitrariness in the "delusive whole"; of the other, because the mystery of existence is, like Jehovah behind the temple curtain, concealed from his gaze, and he receives to every question "popular answers." This book marks the triumph of materialistic philosophy. In truth no small achievement! It signifies the victory of will over understanding and every further effort of creative imagination. Such a work could be created only by pious sentiment and demoniacal power.

We cannot understand Judaism and its power, as well as its ineradicable tenacity, we cannot form a just and proper estimate of the Jew among ourselves, his character and way of thinking, until we have recognised his demoniacal genius and can explain its growth. Here it is a struggle of one against all; this one has taken upon himself every sacrifice and every shame, in order at some time, no matter when, to enter into the Messianic empire of supreme power, to the eternal glory of Jehovah. The Talmud thus expresses it: "Just as thy oppression will follow from transgressing the law, so obedience to it will be rewarded by the fact that thou thyself wilt one day command" (*Aboth* iv. 5; after Montefiore).

JUDAISM

One more word in conclusion. My reply to the question, Who is the Jew? has been, in the first place, to point out whence he came, what was his physical foundation, and secondly, to reveal the leading idea of Judaism in its origin

and nature. I cannot do more ; for the personality
belongs to the single individual, and nothing is falser than
the widespread procedure of judging a people by individuals. I have brought forward neither the " good "
Jew nor the " bad " Jew ; " no one is good," said Jesus
Christ, and when is a man so utterly despicable that we
would be inclined to call him unconditionally bad ?
Before me are lying several criminal statistics ; the one set
tries to prove that the Jews are the most pious and lamb-
like citizens of Europe, the others assert the opposite.
How both conclusions are juggled out of the same figures
beats me, but I am still more surprised that people should
imagine that this is the way to deal with the psychology
of nations. No one steals for the pleasure of it, unless he
is a kleptomaniac. Is the man who through need or in
consequence of a bad example steals, necessarily a bad
man, and he who has not the least occasion to do so a good
one ? Luther says : " Whoever steals bread from the
baker without being forced by hunger is a thief ; if he is
forced by hunger he acts rightly, for people ought to give
to him." Give me a statistic which shows how many
people who live in direst need, oppression and abandonment, do not become criminals ; from it one might
eventually draw some conclusions—yet no very far-reaching ones. Were not the ancestors of our feudal nobility
highway robbers ? and are their descendants not proud of
it ? Did the Popes not have kings assassinated by hired
murderers ? And in our present civilised society are not
lying and misleading recognised in high diplomacy ?
Let us therefore leave morality alone, as also the almost
equally slippery question of predisposition ; that there
are more Jewish than European lawyers in a country
only proves that law pays there—nothing more ; special
ability has nothing to do with it. . . . In all these things,
especially if they are presented statistically, we can
prove anything. On the other hand, the two facts of

race and ideal are fundamental. There are no good and bad men, at least for us, but only before God, for the word " good " refers to a moral estimation, and this again depends on a knowledge of motive, which can never be revealed. " Who can know the heart ? " was the cry of Jeremiah (xvii. 9).* On the other hand there are certainly good and bad races, for here we have to deal with physical relations, general laws of organic nature, which have been experimentally investigated— relations in which, in contrast to those mentioned above figures provide irrefutable proofs—relations concerning which the history of humanity offers us abundant information. And scarcely less manifest are the leading ideas. In reference to race these must in the first place be looked upon as a consequence ; but one should not underestimate this inner, invisible anatomy, this purely spiritual dolichocephaly and brachycephaly, which as cause also has a wide range of influence. Hence it is that every strong nation has so much power of assimilation. The entrance into a new union in the first place changes not a fibre of the physical structure, and only very slowly, in the course of generations, affects the blood ; but ideas have a more rapid effect, because they direct the whole personality almost at once into new channels. And the Jewish national idea seems to exercise a particularly strong influence, perhaps for the very reason that in this case the nation exists merely as an idea and never, from the beginning of Judaism, was it a " normal " nation, but above all, a thought, a hope. It is therefore quite wrong, in the case of the Jews especially, to lay much weight— as Renan for example was fond of doing in his last years —upon the adoption of alien blood which took place from time to time. Renan knew better than anybody else

* As Kant in his *Critique of Pure Reason* says (in explaining the cosmological idea of freedom) : " The real morality of actions (merit and guilt) remains quite concealed from us, even in the case of our own conduct."

that the conversion of Greeks and Romans to Judaism
was an absolutely unimportant phenomenon. What
were those " Hellenes " from Antioch, of whom he tells
us in his lecture " *Judaïsme, race ou religion* " ? and who
are said to have been converted in crowds to Judaism,
a fact for which we possess only the evidence of a very unreliable Jew, Josephus ? They were Hebrew-Syrian
mongrels, in whose veins probably not a drop of Greek
blood flowed. And those " Romans," for whom Renan
quotes the evidence of Juvenal (*Sat.* xvi. 95 f.) ? The
dregs of the people composed of the freed Asiatic and
African slaves. Let him name one single Roman of importance who became a Jew ! Such assertions are an intentional misleading of the unlearned public. But even
if they were based on truth instead of arising out of bias
and falsification, what would that signify ? Are we to
suppose that the Jewish national idea has not the force
of other national ideas ? On the contrary, it is more
powerful, as I have shown, than any other, and
transforms men to its own image. One does not need
to have the authentic Hittite nose to be a Jew ; the term
Jew rather denotes a special way of thinking and feeling.
A man can very soon become a Jew without being
an Israelite ; often it needs only to have frequent
intercourse with Jews, to read Jewish newspapers, to
accustom himself to Jewish philosophy, literature and
art. On the other hand, it is senseless to call an Israelite
a " Jew," though his descent is beyond question, if he
has succeeded in throwing off the fetters of Ezra and
Nehemiah, and if the law of Moses has no place in his
brain, and contempt of others no place in his heart. "What
a prospect it would be," cries Herder, " to see the Jews
purely humanised in their way of thinking ! " * But a
purely humanised Jew is no longer a Jew because, by
renouncing the idea of Judaism, he *ipso facto* has left

* *Adrastea* 7, Stück V., Abschnitt " Fortsetzung."

that nationality, which is composed and held together by a complex of conceptions, by a " faith." With the apostle Paul we must learn that " he is not a Jew who is one outwardly, but he is a Jew who is one inwardly " (*Rom.* ii. 28–29).

Now such national or religious ideals can exercise their revolutionising influence in two ways, positive or negative. I have shown in the case of the Jews how a handful of men forced a definite national idea upon a people not at all inclined to accept it, and so impressed the stamp of this idea upon it that it would seem impossible for that people to efface it ; but consanguinity and congeniality were necessary for the accomplishment of this. In this case, then, the idea exercised a positively creative influence. Just as remarkable a case is the sudden conversion of the bloodthirsty, wild Mongolians by the adoption of the Buddhist faith to mild, pious men, a third of whom have become monks.* But an idea can also have a purely negative result ; it can lead a man out of his own course without opening up another which is suited to his race. A well-known example is the way in which Mohammedanism has affected the Turkomans : by adopting the fatalistic view of the world this wildly energetic people has gradually sunk into complete passivity. If the Jewish influence were to gain the upper hand in Europe in the intellectual and cultural sphere, we should have one more example of negative, destructive power.

I have thus pointed out the method adopted by me and its chief results ; I cannot otherwise summarise this chapter. Formulæ are mere phrases in respect of organic phenomena. The anecdote *Le voilà, le chameau !* is well known. Such a pretension is ridiculous even in respect of the camel, and it would never occur to me to close this sketch with generalisations and formulæ, as

* *Cf.* Döllinger ; *Akademische Vorträge* i. 8.

if I should say, *Le voilà, le juif !* For the theme is in-exhaustible and unfathomable ; I have scarcely used the twentieth part of my illustrations and notes : But my belief is that every one who reads this chapter will feel qualified to form a sharper and clearer judgment of Judaism and its product, the Jew. From this judg-ment will follow of itself the answer to the question, What is the significance of the entrance of the Jew into the history of the West ? It is not my task to trace this influence century by century. The indirect influence of Judaism on Christianity was and still is immense ; its direct influence on the nineteenth century appears for the first time as a new influence in the history of culture : it thus becomes one of the burning subjects of the day, and I have felt bound therefore to lay a sound foundation for its appreciation. Towards this end neither the passionate assertions of the Anti-Semites, nor the dogmatic platitudes of the humanitarians, nor even the many learned books, theological or archæological, from which I have gathered the materials for this chap-ter, give us any assistance. In the task imposed upon me by necessity, I hope I have not striven in vain to arrive at a clear understanding We have to deal here with a question affecting not only the present, but also the future of the world.

SIXTH CHAPTER

THE ENTRANCE OF THE GERMANIC PEOPLE INTO THE HISTORY OF THE WORLD

Mon devoir est mon Dieu suprême.—FREDERICK THE GREAT,
(Letter to Voltaire on June 12, 1740.)

THE entrance of the Jew into European history had, as Herder said, signified the entrance of an alien element—alien to that which Europe had already achieved, alien to all it was still to accomplish ; but it was the very reverse with the Germanic peoples. This barbarian, who would rush naked to battle, this savage, who suddenly sprang out of woods and marshes to inspire into a civilised and cultivated world the terrors of a violent conquest won by the strong hand alone, was nevertheless the lawful heir of the Hellene and the Roman, blood of their blood and spirit of their spirit. It was his own property which he, unwitting, snatched from the alien hand. But for him the sun of the Indo-European must have set. The Asiatic and African slave had by assassination wormed his way to the very throne of the Roman Empire, the Syrian mongrel had made himself master of the law, the Jew was using the library at Alexandria to adapt Hellenic philosophy to the Mosaic law, the Egyptian to embalm and bury for boundless ages the fresh bloom of natural science in the ostentatious pyramids of scientific systematisation ; soon, too, the beautiful flowers of old Aryan life —Indian thought, Indian poetry—were to be trodden under foot by the savage bloodthirsty Mongolian, and the Bedouin, with his mad delusions bred of the desert, was to reduce to an everlasting wilderness that garden of Eden, Erania, in which for centuries all the symbolism of the world had grown ; art had long since vanished ; there were nothing but replicas for the rich, and for the poor the circus : accordingly, to use that expression of Schiller which I quoted at the beginning of the first chapter, there were no longer men but only creatures.   It was high time for the Saviour to appear.   He certainly did not enter into history in the form in which combining, constructive reason, if consulted, would have chosen for the guardian angel, the harbinger of a new day of humanity ; but to-day, when a glance back over past centuries teaches us wisdom, we have only one thing to regret, that the Teuton did not destroy with more thoroughness, wherever his victorious arm penetrated, and that as a consequence of his moderation the so-called " Latinising," that is, the fusion with the chaos of peoples, once more gradually robbed wide districts of the one quicken-ing influence of pure blood and unbroken youthful vigour, and at the same time deprived them of the rule of those who possessed the highest talents.   At any rate it is only shameful indolence of thought, or disgraceful historical falsehood, that can fail to see in the entrance of the Germanic tribes into the history of the world the rescuing of agonising humanity from the clutches of the everlastingly bestial.

If I here use the word " Germanic," I do so, as I have already remarked in the introduction to this division, for the sake of simplification—a simplification which expresses the truth, which must otherwise remain veiled.   But this expression, whether taken in the wide or the narrow sense, seems somewhat elastic, perhaps inadmissible, particularly so because it was late before any people, at any rate we ourselves, became conscious of such a thing as the specifically "Germanic" character. There never has been a people that called itself "Germanic," and never—from their first appearance on the stage of history to the present day—have the whole of the Germanic peoples unitedly opposed themselves to the non-Germanic; on the contrary, from the beginning we find them continually at feud with one another, displaying towards no one such hostility as towards their own blood. During Christ's lifetime Inguiomer betrays his nearest relative, the great Hermann, to the Marcomanni, and thereby hinders the process of union among the northern tribes and the total destruction of the Roman ; Tiberius already could recommend no safer policy to adopt with the Germans than to " leave them to their own internal quarrels " ; all the great wars of the following age, with the exception of the Crusades, were wars between Germanic princes ; the same thing holds in the main for the nineteenth century. But a foreigner had at once recognised the uniformity of the various tribes, and instead of the indistinguishable babel of names, Chatti, Chanki, Cheruski, Gambrivii, Suevi, Vendales, Goti, Marcomanni, Lugii, Langobardi, Sachsi, Frisii, Hermunduri, &c., he had created for the luxuriant offshoots of this strong race the uniform comprehensive term " Germanic," and that because his eye had at the first glance discerned their common stock. Tacitus, after growing tired of enumerating names, says, " the physical characteristics of all these men are the same " ; this was the correct empiric basis for the second and correct judgment, " I am convinced that the various tribes of Germania, unpolluted by marriages with alien peoples, have from time immemorial been a special, unmixed people, resembling itself alone " (*Germania* 4). It is peculiar how much more clearly the stranger, who is not biased by details, sees the great connection of phenomena, than the man who is directly interested in them !

But to-day it is not merely bias which prevents us from using the word " Germanic " in its geographical and racial sense with the simplicity of Tacitus : those " various Germanic stems " which he regarded as an unmixed, comparatively uniform people have, since his day, like their predecessors, the Hellenes, entered into all kinds of unions among each other, and only a portion remains " unpolluted by marriages with strange peoples " ; moreover in consequence of the great migrations, they have been subjected to particular cultural influences, resulting from geographical position, climatic conditions, the standard of civilisation among the nearest neighbours, and so forth. That alone would have sufficed to break up any unity. But the state of things becomes still more confused when we supplement the teaching of political history, on the one hand by more minute, comparative researches in the department of national psychology, philosophy and the history of art, and on the other by the results of the prehistoric and anthropological investigations of the last fifty years. For then we see that we may and must give a much wider meaning to the word " Germanic " than Tacitus did, but at the same time we notice necessary limitations of which he, with the defective knowledge of his time, could not have dreamt. To understand our past and our present, we must follow the example of Tacitus, and like him, collect material and sift it, but upon the broader basis of our modern knowledge. It is only by the exact definition of a new term " Germanic " that our study of the entrance of these peoples into history acquires practical worth. It is the object of this chapter to give such a descriptive definition as briefly as may be. How far does the stem-relationship extend ?   Where do we meet "Arya " (*i.e.,* those who belong to the friends) ? Where do we first find the alien element, which, according to Goethe, we " must not tolerate " ?

Extension of the Idea

I have said that we must give the expression "Germanic" a wider and at the same time a narrower signification than that of Tacitus. Both the extension and the narrowing are the results of historical and anthropological considerations.

The expression is widened by the knowledge that no clear distinction can be drawn physically and mentally between the "German" of Tacitus and his predecessor in history, the "Celt," or his successor whom we are wont even more audaciously to sum up as the "Slav." In view of their physical characteristics the scientist would not hesitate to look upon these three races as varieties of a common stock. The Gauls who in the year 389 B.C. conquered Rome answer exactly to the description which Tacitus gives of the Germanic race: "bright blue eyes, reddish hair, tall figures"; and, on the other hand, the skulls which have been found in the graves of the oldest heroic Slavonic ages have shown to the astonishment of the whole scientific world that the Slavs from the time of the migrations were just as distinctly dolichocephalous (*i.e.*, long-skulled) and as tall as the other Germanic tribes of that time and those of pure race to-day.* Moreover, Virchow's comprehensive investigations into the colour of hair and of eyes have revealed the fact that the Slavs were originally and still are in certain districts just as fair as the Germanic races. Quite apart, therefore, from the general conception "Indo-European," which is a mere theoretical and hypothetical term, it appears that we have every reason for considerably extending the idea "Germanic" which we

* *Cf.* the summary in Ranke: *Der Mensch*, 2nd ed. ii. 297. It is not possible that these excavations revealed facts limited to the Norman Waregians, since the investigations embrace subjects from the most various places, not only in Russia, but also in Germany.

have got from Tacitus and which we have hitherto for philological reasons been inclined to make narrower and narrower.*

THE CELT

Let us speak first of the Celts.

Misled chiefly by philological considerations, the Celtic languages being supposed to be more nearly related to the Italian and Greek than to the Germanic, we have been used to overlook the very decisive physical, and still more decisive moral influence.† We group the Celt with the Græco-Italians, with whom he is manifestly only distantly connected, while he is intimately related to the Germanic peoples. Though the completely Romanised Gaul may have presented a direct contrast to his conqueror, the Burgundian or Frank, yet that original conqueror of Rome, indeed even the later Gaul who had been settled for centuries in Northern Italy,

---

* In consequence the anthropologists of to-day use the expression *homo europæus* (*see* p. 373) in a much more definite sense than Linnæus had done; but such a nomenclature is much too abstract for the historian, who has therefore hitherto taken no notice of it. In order to awaken intelligent interest in wide circles, one must employ the existing, well-known terminology and suit it to new needs. This is here done by widening the idea " Germanic," a procedure which will justify itself step by step in the course of this work; it is only by this that the history of the last two thousand years and especially of the nineteenth century becomes intelligible. That Celts, Slavs and Teutons are descended from a single pure stock may to-day be regarded as certain in the light of anthropology and ancient history. (*Cf.* the final summary of Dr. G. Beck; *Der Urmensch*, Basel, 1899, p. 46 f.). In addition we have historical evidence of the mutual mixing of these different stems. Thus, for instance, H. d'Arbois de Jubainville, Professor at the Collège de France, arrives in his book *Les Celtes*, 1904, at the conclusion: *Il y a probablement en Allemagne plus de sang Gaulois qu'en France.*

† Schleicher, for instance, in his famous, universally copied genealogy of the Indo-Germanic languages (cf. *Die Deutsche Sprache*, 1861, p. 82) makes one group of the Italo-Celtic languages, which he thinks branched off in very early times from the " North European mother tongue"; also such divergent views as the well-known " wave-theory " of Johannes Schmidt continue to represent the Celt as if he were the furthest removed of all Indo-Europeans from the Germanic peoples.

and whom Florus still describes as "superhuman" (*corpora plus quam humana erant*, ii. 4) clearly resembles the Teuton physically ; but not only physically, for his love of wandering, his delight in war, which leads him (as the Goths at a later time) even to Asia in the service of any master who gives him an opportunity of fighting, his love of song . . . all these things are essential features of this same relationship, whereas one would be at a loss to prove the points of connection with the Græco-Italians. The Germanic peoples in the narrower, Tacitean sense of the word enter history for the first time * mixed with Celts and led by Celts ; the word " Germanic " is Celtic. Do we not still meet those tall figures with blue eyes and reddish hair in North-West Scotland, in Wales, &c., and are they not more like a Teuton than a Southern European? Do we not yet see how the Bretons as daring mariners rival the feats of the old Norsemen ?   But no less an authority than Julius Cæsar has told us, in the first chapter of the first book of his Gallic War, how this wild Celto-Germanic mind becomes everywhere gradually effeminate through contact with Roman civilisation.†

More striking and more decisive for my theory is the relationship of Celt and Teuton in the deeper mental qualities.   History gives us ample proof of this, of the relationship of those finer features that make up individuality. Are we to believe—to dive deeply into the subject—that it is an accident that St. Paul's epistle on redemption by faith, on the gospel of freedom (in contrast to the

---

* At the invasion of the Cimbri and Teutons, 114 B.C.

† Regarding the physical identity of Celts and Germanic peoples Professor Gabriel de Mortillet has lately collected such comprehensive material, anthropological facts, as well as the testimonies of old Roman writers, that it is sufficient if I refer to his *Formation de la nation française*, 1897 (p. 114 f.). His final words are : " *La caractéristique des deux groupes est donc exactement la même et s'applique aussi bien au groupe qui a reçu le nom de Gaulois* (synonymous with Celts, see p. 92) *qu'au groupe qui depuis les invasions des Cimbres a pris le nom de Germains.*"

"slavish yoke" of the Church law), on the importance
of religion as not consisting in works but in regeneration
" to a new creature "—was addressed to the Galatians,
those " Gallic Greeks " of Asia Minor who had
remained almost pure Celts—an epistle in which we
seem to hear a Martin Luther speaking to Germans
credulous indeed but yet incomparably gifted for
understanding the deepest mysteries ? *   I for my
part do not believe that there is any room for chance in
such matters ; I believe it all the less in this case, because
I notice in what a different way the same man speaks,
what endless roundabout paths he chooses when teaching
the same truths to a community of Jews and the children
of the chaos of peoples, as in the *Epistle to the Romans*.
But our judgment does not rest merely on such a hypothetical basis, nor does it rest solely upon the relationship
between old Celtic and old Germanic mythical religion,
but upon observation of the relationship between the
mental qualities generally, to which the whole cultured
history of Europe up to the present day testifies—
wherever the Celt has kept his blood pure. Thus, for
example, we find in the genuinely Celtic parts of Ireland
in former times—taking the five hundred years from the
Celt Scotus Erigena to the Celt Duns Scotus—splendid
theologians with high philosophical gifts, whose independence of thought and keen desire to investigate
brought upon them the persecution of the Roman Church ;
in the heart of Bretagne was born that intellectual pioneer
Peter Abelard, and let it be carefully noted that what distinguishes him, like those others, is not merely independent thought and striving after freedom, but above all
the holy earnestness of his life, a thoroughly " Germanic
quality."   These Celtic minds of former centuries, teeming

* Mommsen testifies that Galatia was " a Celtic island amidst the
floods of the Eastern peoples," in which even the Celtic language
maintained itself for a long time : *Roman History*, 3rd ed. v. 311 f.

with strength, are not merely free, and not merely pious,
any more than the Breton seaman of to-day, but they are
both free and pious, and it is this very combination that
expresses what is specifically " Germanic," as we observe
it from Charlemagne and King Alfred to Cromwell and
Queen Louise, from the daring anti-Roman troubadours
and the Minnesingers so politically independent, to
Schiller and Richard Wagner. And when we see, for
example, Abelard contending from profound religious
conviction against the sale of indulgences (*Theologia
Christiana*), and at the same time putting the Hellenes
in every respect far above the Jews, declaring the morals
of their philosophers to be superior to the Jewish sanctity
of law, Plato's view of life more sublime than that of
Moses—yes, when we actually find him in his *Dialogus
inter philosophum, Judæum et Christianum*, making the
recognition of the transcendental ideality of the conception of space the basis of religious thought, so that man
stands directly before God's countenance not by entering
into an empirical heaven but solely by an inner conversion of mind : are we not forced to recognise that this
mind is characteristically Indo-European in contrast to
the Semitic and the late Roman, and that, moreover, an
individuality here reveals itself, which in every single
one of those *plis de la pensée* (of which I spoke in the
previous chapter) betrays the specifically Germanic character ? I do not say German but Germanic character,
and I am not speaking of to-day, when differentiation has
led to the formation of very clearly defined national
characters, but of a man who lived almost a thousand
years ago ; and I assert that so far as the whole tendency
of his thought and feeling is concerned this Breton might
right well have been born in the heart of Germania. A
typical Celt in the gloomy passionateness of his nature,
a new Tristan in his love, he is flesh of our flesh and blood
of our Teutonic blood ; he is Germanic. Just as Germanic

as these so-called " pure German " populations of Swabia
and the Black Forest, the home of Schiller, Mozart and
many others of the greatest of Germany's sons, who owe
their peculiar character and uncommon poetical gifts to
the strong admixture of Celtic blood.* We recognise
this same spirit of Abelard at work wherever it can
be proved that the Celts were present in large numbers,
as in the home of the unfortunate Albigenses in the
South of France, or as they still are in the homeland of
the Methodists, Wales. We recognise it also in the
so-called typically Catholic country Bretagne, for Catho-
licism and Protestantism are, after all, mere words ; the
religiosity of the Breton is genuine, but in its colour it is
really " heathen " rather than Christian ; primeval
popular religion lived on here under the mask of Catho-
licism ; moreover, who would not see in the ineradicable
loyalty of this people to the throne a Germanic characteristic which is just as common as the love of war and
loyalty to the flag among the Irish, who in politics agitate
against England, but at the same time voluntarily furnish
a large proportion of the English Army, and go abroad to
die for the same alien king, to whom they are so hostile
at home ? But the close relationship between Celts and
Germanic peoples (in the narrower sense of the word)
reveals itself most strikingly in their poetry. From the
first Frankish, German and English poetry were closely
allied to genuine Celtic, not that the former people did not
possess motives of their own, but they adopted the Celtic
ones as being originally akin to them, and in these there is
a something strange, something not quite understood,
because half-forgotten, which lends them increased
piquancy and charm. Celtic poetry is incomparably profound, inexhaustibly rich in symbolical meaning ; it was
manifestly in its far distant origin intimately connected

* Wilhelm Henke : *Der Typus des germanischen Menschen* (Tübingen,
1895). Similarly Treitschke : *Politik* i. 279.

with music, the soul of our Germanic poetry. If we examine the works which were written when the poetic impulse once more awoke to life, about the turn of the twelfth and thirteenth centuries, in all Germanic lands, but above all in the lands of the Franks—when we on the one hand consider the *Geste de Charlemagne*, the *Rolandslied*, the *Berte aus grans piès*, *Ogier le Danois*, &c., all independent efforts of Frankish imaginative power, and on the other hand see Celtic poetry live again in the legends of the *Queste du Graal*, *Artus' Tafelrunde*, *Tristan und Isolde*, *Parzival*, &c., we cannot for a moment doubt where the deeper, richer, more genuine and poetically inexhaustible wealth of imagination and thought is to be found. And this Celtic poetry of the thirteenth century was at a disadvantage, since it appeared not in its own form, but robbed of the wings of song, expanded to romance form, quickened with knightly, Roman and Christian beliefs, its genuine poetical kernel almost as much obscured by alien accrescences as the Norse myths in the German *Nibelungenlied*. The further back we go, the more clearly do we recognise—in spite of all individual differences—the intimate relationship between old Celtic and old Germanic poetical tendency ; from stage to stage backwards something is lost, so that, for example, although Gottfried's *Tristan* as a poem undoubtedly surpasses the French versions of the same subject, yet several of the deepest and finest traits, upon which this incomparable, poetical, mythical and symbolical legend is based, are lacking in it, while the old French romance possesses them and Chrestien de Troyes had at least given a suggestion of them ; the same is true of Wolfram's *Parzival*.* But this relationship reveals itself most convincingly and impressively when we see that in reality it was only

* In this place I have used the results of some of my own studies (cf. *Notes sur Parsifal* and *Notes sur Tristan* in the *Revue Wagnérienne*, 1886 and 1887).

German music that was able to awaken to new life the old Celtic and old Germanic poetry in their original intention and significance ; this we have learnt from the artistic achievements of the nineteenth century, which at the same time revealed the close relationship between both these sources.

THE GERMANIC SLAV

Of the genuine Slav there is less to be said, since we are at a loss where to look for him, and are sure of only one thing, that in his case there has been a transformation of the type, so that the thick-set body, round head, high check-bones, dark hair, which we to-day consider to be typically Slavonic, were certainly not characteristics of the Slav at the time when he entered European history. But even to-day the fair type predominates in the north and east of European Russia, and the Pole, too, is distinguished from the southern Slav by the colour of his skin (Virchow). In Bosnia one is struck with the tallness of the men and the prevalence of fair hair. The so-called Slavonic type which merges into the Mongolian I have not once met in a journey of several months across that country, any more than the characteristic " potato-face " of the Czech peasant ; the same may be said of the splendid race of the Montenegrins.* In spite, therefore, of the universal prejudice, there are, as we see, enough physical indications that the Germanic man, when he entered history, had, in addition to an elder brother in

* On the other hand the shape of the skull has undergone a gradual change : among the present inhabitants of Bosnia we find not quite 1½ per cent. of long heads, while there are, on the other hand, 84 per cent. of distinctly round heads ; the oldest graves show 29 per cent. of long heads and 34 per cent. of round ones, and graves from the time of the Middle Ages 21 per cent. of long heads. (*See* Weisbach : *Altbosnische Schädel, in den Mitteilungen der anthropologischen Gesellschaft in Wien*, 1897.) It is interesting to hear that the formation of the face, in spite of the change of skull, has remained " leptoprosop," *i.e.*, long in shape.

the west, a younger in the east who was not so very unlike himself. But on the other hand it is exceedingly difficult to unravel the confused skein of what was originally Slavonic, owing to the manifest fact that this branch of the Germanic family was at a very early time almost completely destroyed by other tribes, much earlier and more thoroughly and more mysteriously than the Celts ; but this fact should not deter us from recognising and admitting the related features and attempting to sift them out from the mass of what is alien.

But here again our best help will lie in searching the depths of the soul. If I may judge from the one Slavonic language of which I have a slight knowledge, the Servian, I should be inclined to think that a strong family resemblance in poetical gifts to the Celts and Germanic peoples could be proved. The heroic cycle which celebrates the great battle of Kossovopolje (1383), but which beyond doubt goes further back in its poetical motives, reminds one of Celtic and Germanic lyric and epic poetry by the sentiments to which it gives utterance—loyalty unto death, heroic courage, heroic women, as well as the high respect which these enjoy, the contempt for all possessions in comparison with personal honour. I read in histories of literature that such poems, and heroic figures like Marco Kraljevich are common to all popular poetry ; but this is not true, and can only appear so to one whose excess of learning has blinded him to the fine features of individuality. Rama is an essentially different hero from Achilles, and he, again, quite different from Siegfried ; while on the other hand the Celtic Tristan betrays in many features direct relationship to the German Siegfried, and that not merely in the external ornaments of the knightly romance (fights with dragons, &c.), which may to some extent be a later addition, but rather in those old, popular creations where Tristan is still a shepherd and Siegfried not yet a hero at the Burgundian Court. It is here that we see clearly that, apart from extraordinary strength and the magic charm of invincibility and more such general attributes of heroes, definite ideals form the basis of the poems ; and it is in these, not in the former, that the character of a people is reflected. So it is in the case of Tristan and Siegfried : loyalty as the basis of the idea of honour, the significance of maidenhood, victory in downfall (in other words, the true heroism centred in the inner motive, not in the outward success). Such features distinguish a Siegfried, a Tristan, a Parzival not only from a Semitic Samson whose heroism lies in his hair, but equally from the more closely related Achilles. Purity is strange to the Hellenes ; faith is not a principle of honour, but only of love (Patroclos) ; the hero defies death ; he does not overcome it, as we can say of the heroes of whom we have spoken. These are just the traits of true relationship which, in spite of all divergences of form, I find in Servian poetry. The fact alone that their heroic cycle groups itself around, not a victory, but a great defeat, the fatal battle of Kossovo, is of great significance ; for the Servians have won victories enough and had been under Stephan Duschan a powerful State. Here, then, beyond question we find a special tendency of character, and we may with certainty conclude that the rich store of such poetical motives—all referring to destruction, death, everlasting separation of lovers— did not spring up only after that unfortunate battle and under the brutalising rule of Mohammedanism, but is an old legacy, exactly as the Fate of the Nibelungs, "aller Leid Ende," and not the Fortune of the Nibelungs, was the German legacy, and exactly as Celtic and Frankish poets neglected a hundred famous victors to sing of the obscure conquered Roland, and to let primitive poetical inspiration once more live through him, in a half-historical new youth. Such things tell their tale. And just as decisive is the peculiar way in which woman is represented among the Servians—so delicate, brave and chaste—also the very great part which poetry assigns to her. On the other hand, only a specialist can decide whether the two ravens that fly up over Kossovo at the end of the battle, to proclaim to the Servian people its downfall, are related to Wotan's ravens, or whether we have here a general Indo-Germanic motive, a relic of the nature myths, a case of borrowing, a coincidence. And so, too, in reference to a thousand details. But fortunately here, as everywhere, the element that is really important is manifest to every unbiased observer. In Russian poetry we seem to find little but legends, fairy tales and songs of the olden time ; but here too the melancholy on the one hand and on the other the intimate relation to nature, particularly to the animal world (Bodenstedt : *Poetische Ukraine*), are unmistakably Germanic.

It is not my intention to carry this investigation further ; want of space as well as my plan forbids me. Let criticism put to the test the truth of what unerring feeling will reveal to every one who has the sense of poetry ; that is the critic's duty. I must, however, mention the second manifestation of the soul-life by which the Germanic element in the Slav clearly reveals itself—Religion.

In whatever direction we glance, we behold the Slav, especially in early times, distinguished by earnestness and independence in religious matters. And one of the principal features of this religiosity is the fact that it is saturated with patriotic feelings. As early as the ninth century, even before the parting between east and west had taken place for ever, we see the Bulgarians in the interest of questions of dogma maintaining equally friendly relations with Rome and with Constantinople. What they demand is solely the recognition of the independence of their Church ; Rome refuses it, Byzantium grants it. And thus in the first half of the tenth century is founded the first Christian Church which has an independent constitution.* The immense importance of such an event must be immediately manifest to every one. With Michael of Bulgaria it was no question of divergences of faith ; he was a Christian, and ready to believe everything that the priests proclaimed as Christian truth. In his case it was solely a question of constitution ; he wanted to see his Bulgarian Church managed by a Bulgarian Patriarch with complete independence ; no Prince of the Church in Rome or Byzantium should interfere. This may seem to many to be merely an administrative question, but in reality it is the rising of the Germanic spirit of free individuality against the last incorporation of the imperium which was born of the chaos, and represented the anti-national, anti-individual and levelling principle. This is not the place to enter more fully into this subject ; that can be done only in the two following chapters But when we encounter the same process everywhere among the Slavs, we cannot deny its significance as a symptom to aid our judgment of their original character. No sooner had the Servians established their kingdom than they made for themselves an autonomous Church ; and the great Czar Stephan Duschan defended his patriarch against the suzerain pretensions of the Byzantine Church and forced the latter to recognise him legally. There, too, it was not a matter of faith ; for at that time (the middle of the fourteenth century) the schism between Rome and Constantinople was a fact of long standing and the Servians were already as they are to-day, fanatically orthodox members of the Greek Church ; but just as the Bulgarians resisted the interference of Rome, so the Servians resisted that of Constantinople. The principle is the same—the maintenance of nationality. The Russian Church certainly took much

* Cf. Hergenröther : Photius ii. 614.

longer to free itself ; indeed only long after the destruction of the Byzantine Empire did it do so. But Russia
can only in a very qualified and un-Germanic sense be
called a Slavonic land, and yet it and England are the
only pre-eminent nations of modern Europe that possess
an absolutely national Church with a national head. It
is, further, a specially striking fact that the Slavs are the
only Christians (with the exception of the Czechs, who are
subject to German influence) who have never tolerated
divine service in any language but their own ! The great
:" Slavonic apostles " Cyrillus and Methodius had trouble
on this account ; though persecuted by the German pre-
lates who clung to the " three sacred languages " (Greek,
Latin, Hebrew), though denounced as heretics by the
Roman Pope, they yet succeeded in gaining this point as
a special right : the strictly Roman Catholic Slavs had
also their Slavonic Mass, and even in the last years of
the nineteenth century Rome had not succeeded in
wresting this privilege from the Dalmatians. But all
this forms only one side of Slavonic religion, the external
(though hardly external in reality) ; the other side is still
more striking. In Russia, in those parts where we find
the greatest percentage of genuine Slavs (that is in Little
Russia, the home of that beautiful poetry which I have
alluded to above), there manifests itself to-day by the
never-ceasing formation of sects an intensive inner religious life similar to that of Würtemberg and Scandinavia.
The relationship is striking. Of this in the so-called
" Latin " countries there is no trace. It is in such matters
that the inmost nature of the soul is reflected. And
here, too, it is a question of a lasting quality, which
asserted itself in every century despite all blood-mixtures.
The extreme trouble experienced in converting the Slavs
to Christianity is a testimony to their deeply religious
nature : Italians and Gauls were the easiest to convert,
Saxons could be won only by the power of the sword,

but it took long years and fearful cruelties to make the Slavs give up the faith of their fathers.* The notorious persecutions of the heathen lasted, in fact, to the century of Gutenberg. Very characteristic is the attitude here also of those genuine, still almost pure Slavs in Bosnia and Herzogovina. At an earlier period the influential part of the nation adopted the doctrines of Bogumil (allied to those of the Catharists or Patarenes) ; that is, they rejected everything Jewish in Christianity and retained besides the New Testament only the Prophets and the Psalms, they recognised no sacraments and above all no priesthood. Though unceasingly opposed, oppressed and crushed from two sides simultaneously—by the orthodox Servians and the Hungarians who obeyed every sign of the Roman Pope—though they were thus the bloody victims of a double and continuous crusade, this little people nevertheless clung to its faith for centuries ; the graves of the heroic followers of Bogumil still adorn the peaks of the hills, to which the corpses were borne to avoid the danger of desecration. It was the Mohammedans who, by forcible conversion, first did away with this sect. The same spirit, which animated a brave but ignorant people in a remote corner of the earth, in other places bore richer fruits, whereby the Slavonic branch distinguished itself just as much as the other branches of the Germanic family.

THE REFORMATION

The most important event in the nineteen centuries that have passed is undoubtedly the so-called " Reformation " : at the bottom of it there is a double principle, a national and a religious ; common to both is the freeing

* The first division of the sixth book of Neander's *Allgemeine Geschichte der Christlichen Religion und Kirche* shows how difficult it was to convert the Wends and Poles to Christianity.

from the alien yoke, the shaking off of that " dead hand "
of the extinct Roman Empire, which stretched not only
over the goods and money, but also over the thoughts and
feelings and faith and hope of humanity. Nowhere does
the organic unity of Slavonic Germanicism manifest itself
more convincingly than in this revolt against Rome. To
understand this movement from the standpoint of national
psychology, one must, to begin with, pay no attention to
any dogmatic disputes concerning creed ; it is not what
people consider the truth in regard to the nature of the
Communion that is important, it is a question solely of
two directly contradictory principles, freedom and slavery.
The greatest of the reformers points out that so far as he
is concerned he is not contending for political rights, and
he goes on to say, " but in spirit and conscience we are
of all men the most independent : here we believe no one,
trust no one, fear no one, but Christ alone." This signifies
the freeing of the individual as well as of the nation. And
when we have thus learned that the " Reformation "
should be regarded not as a purely ecclesiastical affair but
as a revolt of our whole nature against alien rule, of the
Germanic soul against un-Germanic spiritual tyranny,
we must at the same time admit that the " reform "
began as soon as the Germanic peoples by culture and
leisure had awakened to consciousness, and that this
revolt still goes on.* Scotus Erigena (in the ninth century) is a reformer, since he refuses to obey the commands
of Rome, and prefers to die by the dagger of the assassin
than give up an iota of his " freedom of mind and conscience " ; Abelard in the eleventh century is a reformer,
since with all his orthodoxy he refuses to be deprived of
the freedom of his religious conceptions and attacks in
addition the administration of the Roman Church, the

* The anthropologist Lapouge says in his purely scientific definition
of the *homo europæus : " en religion il est protestant."* See *Dépopulation
de la France*, p. 79.

sale of indulgences, &c. ; and in exactly the same way
such lights of the Catholic Church as Döllinger and
Reusch in the nineteenth century are reformers ; not a
single dogmatic question separated them from Rome,
except the one question, freedom. In this momentous
movement not only the Germanic peoples in the narrower
sense of the word, not only the Celts, but also the Slavs
distinguished themselves. What I said in the last paragraph about their refusing to permit alien interference
in their Church administration, and their regarding the
mother tongue as their most sacred legacy, should be
repeated here ; both signify the denial of the essential
principles of Rome. But these endeavours were more
deeply rooted ; in the depth of their hearts it was a
question of religion, not merely of nation. And as soon
as the Reformation had gained a strong hold—which
happened first in distant England—the Slavonic Catholics
crowded to Oxford, drawn thither by the affinity of the
most sacred feelings. It is quite certain that without
the great Martin Luther the Reformation would never
have become what it did—our most modern historians
may say what they like, nature knows no greater power
than that of one great strong man—but the soil on which
this German could develop his full strength, the atmosphere in which alone his cause could prosper, were
primarily the creations of Bohemia and of England.*
Even a hundred years before the birth of Luther every
third man in England was an anti-Papist, and Wyclif's
translation of the Bible was known throughout the whole
land. Bohemia did not lag behind ; already in the
thirteenth century the New Testament was read in the
Czech language, and at the beginning of the fifteenth
century Hus edited the complete Bible in the language
of the people. But the most quickening influence was

---

* Luther writes to Spalatin, February 1520 : " *Vide monstra, quæso
in quæ venimus sine duce et doctore Bohemico.*"

that of Wyclif ; he was the first to open the eyes of the
Slavs to evangelic truth, so that Hieronymus of Prague
could say of him : " Hitherto we have had only the shell,
Wyclif has revealed the kernel." * We get an altogether
false idea of the Slavonic reformation if we direct attention principally to Hus and the Hussite wars ; the predominance of political combinations, as well as of the enmity
between Czechs and Germans from that time forth confused men's minds and obscured the pure object of their
endeavour which at first had been so clear. Even a
hundred years before Hus lived Milič, who, though an
orthodox Catholic and disinclined by his interest in
practical ministry to all speculation concerning dogma,
invented the expression Antichrist for the Roman Church ;
in the prison at Rome he wrote his treatise, *De Anti-
christo*, in which he shows that the Antichrist will not
come in the future, but is already there, he is heaping up
" clerical " riches, buying prebends and selling sacraments.
Mathias von Janow then expands this thought and thus
paves the way for the real theological Reformation ; he
certainly champions the one sacred Church, but it must be
thoroughly purified and built up anew : " It remains for
us now only to wish that the Reformation may be made
possible by the destruction of the Antichrist ; let us
raise our heads, for salvation is already near at hand ! "
(1389). He is followed by Stanislaus von Znaim, who
defends before the University of Prague the forty-five
theses of Wyclif ; Hus, who makes a clear distinction
between the " Apostolic " and the " Papal " and declares
that he will obey the former, but the latter only in as
far as it agrees with the Apostolic ; Nikolaus von Wele-
nowič, who denies the position of the priests as privileged
intercessors with God ; Hieronymus, that splendid knight
and martyr, who moved even the indifferent Papal
secretary Poggio, who was more interested in Hellenic

* Neander, ix. 314.

literature than in Christianity and chiefly known as a collector and editor of obscene anecdotes, to utter the words, " O what a man, worthy of immortal fame ! " And many others. Clearly we have not the achievement of a single, perhaps erratic mind in all this ; on the contrary it is the soul of a nation—at least everything that was genuine and noble in that people—that expresses itself. It is well known what fate overcame this noble section, how it was wiped off the face of the earth. The Pope and the Roman bishops had bribed the army of international mercenaries, and from them it received its death-blow at the White Mountain.* Nor is it a question of a Czech idiosyncrasy ; the other Catholic Slavs adopted exactly the same attitude. Thus, for example, the hymns of Wyclif were printed in the first Polish printing-press ; Poland sent to the Council of Trent bishops whose sympathies were so distinctly Protestant that the Pope accused them before the king of being rabid heretics, But the Polish Parliament was not intimidated ; it demanded from the King a complete reorganisation of the Polish Church upon the one basis of the Holy Scriptures. At the same time it demanded—*mirabile dictu !*— the " equal rights of all sects." The nobility of Poland and all the intellectual aristocracy were Protestant. But the Jesuits profited by the political confusion, which soon arose, to gain a firm footing in the land, and they were supported by France and Austria ; the process was not " bloody and speedy," as Canisius had demanded, but the Protestants were nevertheless persecuted more and more cruelly and finally banished ; with the downfall of its religion the Polish nation also fell.†

* Döllinger : *Das Haus Wittelsbach*, Akad. Vorträge i. 38.

† Read the exceedingly interesting work of Count Valerian Krasinski : *Geschichte des Ursprungs, Fortschritts und Verfalls der Reformation in Polen*, Leipzig, 1841. Nowhere else, perhaps, is to be found so complete, abundant, convincing and perfectly treated material as in Poland, to see how religious intolerance and especially the influence of the Jesuits completely ruined a land which was advancing

As these facts are not universally known, I have had
to emphasise them in some detail, sufficiently, I hope, to
pave the way for the conviction that the genuine Teuton,
the genuine Celt, and the genuine Slav are originally
and intimately related. At the moment when these
races enter history, we do not find three ethnical souls
side by side, but one uniform soul. Though the Celts
have in many places, but not everywhere as I have shown
above, undergone such physical changes by assimilating
Virchow's hypothetical " Pre-Celts " and elements from
the Latin chaos of peoples, that the so-called Celt of
to-day is the very contrary of the original Celtic type ;
though a like fate may, to a still more regrettable degree,
have overtaken the tall fair Slavs, who remind us of
Norsemen, yet throughout the centuries we have seen the
working of that distinct and thoroughly individual
spirit, which I unhesitatingly call the Germanic, because
the genuine Teuton, in the usual, limited sense of the word,

towards a brilliant future in every intellectual and industrial sphere.
We can best see the attitude of the Poles to Rome before the time of
Luther in the speech delivered by Johann Ostrorog in the assembly
of the States in the year 1459, in which he said, " We cannot object
to the recommending of this land as a Catholic one to the protection
of the Pope, but it is unbecoming to promise him unbounded obedience.
The King of Poland is subject to no one, and only God is over him ;
he is not the vassal of Rome . . . &c. &c." ; then he inveighs against
the shameless simony of the Papal stool, the sale of indulgences, the
greed of the priests and monks, &c. (see p. 36 ff.). This whole Polish
movement is, like the Bohemian, distinguished by a fresh breath of
independence and national feeling and at the same time indifference
to and depreciation of dogmatic questions (the Poles never were
Utraquists) ; and (just as in Bohemia) it is born Germans who contend
for Rome and gain the victory over religious and political freedom.
Hosen (Cardinal Hosius)—the man who sends Cardinal de Guise a
letter of congratulation on the murder of Admiral Coligny and who
" thanks God for the great gift that France has received through the
night of St. Bartholomew and prays that God may look upon Poland with
equal mercy "—this same Hosen is at the head of the anti-national
reaction, he introduces the Jesuits into the land, he forbids the reading
of Holy Scripture, he teaches that the subject has absolutely no rights
in reference to his prince, &c. If such a man is Germanic, and those
champions of freedom are not, then this name is purely and simply
term of reproach.

in spite of all blood crossings, preserved this spirit in its purest and therefore most powerful form. This is not hair-splitting but a question of historical insight in the widest sense ; I have no intention of putting down to the Germanic races, or indeed to the German, achievements which they did not accomplish, or of assigning to them fame which belongs to others. On the contrary, I wish to call to life again the feeling for the great northern brother-hood, and that, too, without binding myself to any racial or prehistoric hypothesis whatever, but solely by relying upon what is clear to every eye. I do not even postulate the blood-relationship ; indeed I believe in it, but I am too well aware of the extreme complexity of this problem, I see too clearly that the true progress of science has here chiefly consisted in the discovery of our boundless ignorance and the inadequacy of all hypotheses hitherto formulated, to have any desire on my own part to continue building new castles in the air, when every genuine scientist is beginning to keep silence. " Every-thing is simpler than we can think, and at the same time more complicated than we can comprehend," as Goethe says. In the meantime we have met with relations in spirit, in sentiment and physical form : that may satisfy us. We have a definite something in hand, and since this something is not a definition, but consists of living men, I refer the reader to the study of the real Celts, Teutons and Slavs, that he may learn what is the true Germanic character.

LIMITATIONS OF THE NOTION

I think I have now shown what is to be understood by the necessary extension of the idea ; but in what does the limitation which I described as equally necessary consist ? Here, too, the answer will be twofold, referring to physical qualities on the one hand, to intellectual on the other ; but fundamentally these two things are really manifestations of the same thing.

The physical consideration must not be undervalued ; indeed it would perhaps be difficult to over-estimate it. I have tried to show the reason, in the discussion of the race question in the previous chapter but one ; besides this fact is one of those which mere instinct—that thin silken thread of connection with the tissue of nature— lets us directly feel, without learned proof. For just as the dissimilarity of human individuals can be read in their physiognomy, so the dissimilarity of human races can be read in the structure of their bones, the colour of their skin, their muscular system and the formation of their skull ; there is perhaps not a single anatomical fact upon which race has not impressed its special distinguishing stamp. As is well known, even our nose, this organ of ours which has grown rigid and frostily motionless and which, according to certain followers of Darwin, is on the way to even greater monumentalisation by complete ossifica- tion—even our nose, which in city life to-day is a dispenser of discomforts rather than of joys, a mere burdensome appendage, stands from the cradle to the grave in the centre of our countenance as a witness to our race ! We must therefore, in the first place, strongly emphasise the fact that these North Europeans—the Celts, Teutons and Slavs—were physically different from the other Indo-Europeans, distinguished from the Southern Euro- peans in stature, " and like to themselves only," * but we must at once make the first limitation here, namely, that whoever does not possess these physical characteristics, no matter though he were born in the very heart of Germania

---

* During the last years the conviction is growing among the learned that the Germanic peoples did not emigrate from Asia to Europe, but were settled in Europe from earliest times (see Wilser : *Stammbaum der arischen Völker*, 1889 (Naturw. Wochenschr.} ; Schrader : *Sprach- vergleichung und Urgeschichte*, 2. Auflage, 1890 ; Taylor : *The Origin of the Aryans*, 1890 : Beck : *Der Urmensch*, 1899, &c.).

speaking a Germanic tongue from childhood, cannot be regarded as genuinely Germanic. The importance of this physical motive power is easier to prove in the case of great national phenomena than in individuals, for it may happen that an especially gifted individual assimilates an alien culture and then, just because of his different nature, achieves something new and profitable ; on the other hand, the particular value of race becomes clear as soon as it is a question of collective achievements, as I can impress at once upon the German reader when I tell him in the words of a recognised authority that " the privileged great statesmen and military leaders of the time of the founding of the new empire are mostly of the purest Germanic descent," like the " storm-tried seamen of the North Sea coast and the keen chamois-hunters of the Alps." * These are facts which should be pondered long and carefully. In their presence the senselessness of the well-known phrases of natural scientists, Parliamentarians, &c., concerning the equality of the human races † becomes so plain that one is almost ashamed of having listened to them even with one ear. They let us also see in what definitely conditional sense the well known remark of that thorough Teuton, Paul de Lagarde, may claim validity, namely, that " Germanism does not lie in the blood, but in the mind." In the case of the individual, the mind may indeed rule the blood, and the idea conquer, but it is not so with the great mass. And in order to measure the importance of the physical element, as well as its limitation, one should remember further that that which may be called the Germanic idea is a very delicately constructed, many-jointed organism. One requires only to look at the Jewish idea by way of comparison, this infancy of art, the whole cunning of which lies in binding the human

* Henke : *Der Typus des germanischen Menschen*, p. 33.
† *See* pp. 259 ff., 392 note 2, 531.

soul as tightly as Chinese ladies do their feet, the only difference being that these ladies can no longer move about, whereas a half-throttled soul is easier to carry and causes the busied body less trouble than a fully developed one, laden with its dreams. In consequence of this it is comparatively easy " to become a Jew," difficult, on the contrary, almost to the verge of impossibility " to become Germanic " ; here as everywhere the power of the idea is supreme ; but one should guard against following a true principle so far as to overlook the connection of natural phenomena. The richer the mind, the more closely and manifoldly is it connected with the substructure of a definitely formed blood. It is self-evident that in the unfolding of human qualities, the further their development has advanced, the higher must the differentiation in the physical substratum of our mental life have become, and the more and more delicate its tissues. Thus we saw in the former chapter how the noble Amorite disappeared from the world : by fusion with unrelated races his physiognomy was, as it were, wiped away, his gigantic form shrunk together, his spirit fled : the simple *homo syriacus* is, on the other hand, the same to-day as he was a thousand years ago and the mongrel Semite has to his perpetual contentment come out of the mixture in the crystallised form of the " Jew." The same has happened everywhere. What a magnificent people the Spaniards were ! For centuries the West Goths were strictly forbidden to marry " Romans " (as the rest of the inhabitants were called), whereby a feeling of race nobility was developed, which long prevented mixing even at a time when such a fusion of the population was desired and enforced by the authorities ; but gradually ever deeper and deeper breaches were made in the dam, and after mingling with Iberians, with the numerous remnants of the Roman chaos of peoples, with Africans of the most various origin, with Arabs and Jews, they lost all that the Germanic people had brought with them : their military superiority, their unconditional loyalty (*see* Calderon !), their high religious ideal, their capacity for organising, their rich artistic creative power ; we see to-day what remained over, when the Germanic " blood," as the physical substratum, was destroyed.* Let us therefore not be in too great a hurry to assert that Germanicism does not lie in blood ; it does lie in it ; not in the sense that this blood guarantees Germanic sentiment and capacity, but that it makes these possible.

This limitation is therefore a very clear one : as a rule that man only is Germanic who is descended from Germanic ancestors.

I must, however, immediately call attention to the necessity of the previous extension of the idea, in order that this limitation may be intelligibly applied. Otherwise we must arrive at such comical conclusions as even Henke is guilty of in the pamphlet already quoted, when he says that Luther was not genuinely Germanic or that the Swabians, who are rightly regarded in the whole world as the finest representatives of pure Germanicism, are likewise not genuinely Germanic ! A man whose descent and countenance prove him to be the product of a mixture

---

* *Cf.* Savigny's *Geschichte des römischen Rechtes im Mittelalter*, i., chaps. iii. v. This keeping of the Germanic race pure for centuries, in the midst of an inferior population, is seen not only in Spain but also in Northern Italy, where the Teutons lived under separate laws into the fourteenth century. *See* details below and in vol. ii: chap. ix: When criticising this book, Professor Dr. Paul Barth wrote in the *Vierteljahrsschrift für wissenschaftliche Philosophie*, 1901, p. 75. " Chamberlain might have gone further than he does into the influence of Semitic blood in Spain. By the addition of Semitic blood the Spaniards have become fanatical, they have carried every idea to its extreme, so that it loses all its reason and sense : religious devotion even to " cadaver-obedience " towards their superiors, politeness which is painful, ceremonious etiquette, honour which has become the most insane sensitiveness, pride which is ridiculous grandezza, so that Spanish in popular speech among us has become almost equivalent to absurd."

of genuine German and genuine Slavonic blood, as Henke demonstrates in Luther's case, is genuinely Germanic, the child of a fortunate union ; the same can be said of the Swabians, in whose case a close union of Celts and Germans has taken place and laid the foundation of rich poetical powers and remarkable strength of character. I have already spoken of the great advantages of crossing between nearly related peoples (chap. iv., pp. 277–283) ; this law proved its validity everywhere in the case of the Teutons : among the French, where the most manifold crossings of Germanic types produced a superabundance of rich talents, and where even to-day, in consequence of the existence of many centres of the most diverse pure race cultures, rich life manifests itself, among the English, the Saxons, the Prussians, &c. Treitschke calls attention to the fact that the " State-building power of Germany " has never lain in the pure German stems. " The true pioneers and promoters of culture in Germany were in the Middle Ages the South Germans, who are mixed with Celtic elements ; in modern history it is the North Germans who are mixed with Slavs.* These results are at the same time a proof of the close relationship of the North Europeans, that human type which we can with Lapouge and Linnæus call the *homo europæus*, but better and more simply the Teuton. Now and only now we learn how in reference to ourselves we should distinguish between crossing and crossing. By crossing with each other Germanic peoples suffer no harm—rather the reverse ; but when they cross with aliens they gradually deteriorate.

FAIR HAIR

But this limitation, which is so clear in the general definition, is unfortunately very difficult to apply in individual cases. For it will be asked : By what physical

* *Politik* i. 279.

characteristics can one recognise the Teuton ? Is, for
example, fairness really a characteristic feature of all
Germanic peoples ? This seems to form a fundamental
dogma, not only for the old historians, but also for the
most modern anthropologists, and yet certain facts make
me doubt it very much.   In the first place there is the
fact, which naturally is ignored by Virchow and his
colleagues, blinded as they are by political prejudice ;
I mean the prevalence of dark colour among the members
of the most genuine old Germanic nobility.   In England
this is quite striking.   Tall, spare-built figures, long
skulls, long countenances, the well-known Moltke type
with the large nose and the clean-cut profile (which
Henke too considers characteristically " pure Germanic "),
genealogies which go back to the Norman period, in short,
beyond doubt genuine Teutons in physique and history
—but black hair.   Eckermann was struck by the brown
eyes of Wellington.*   In Germany I have noted the same
in various families of old hereditary nobility.   Moreover
it has appeared to me remarkable that poets from the
extreme north of Germany pretty frequently speak of
dark hair as a characteristic feature not only of the
nobility but also of the people ; thus, for example, in
Theodor Storm's story, *Hans und Heinz Kirch*, those
genuine defiant Germanic seamen have both " dark
brown hair," and of another daring figure, Hasselfritz,
the poet says that he has brown eyes and brown hair ;
those genuine Teutons therefore resemble Achilles with
his " brown hair."   How often, too, in the folksongs do
" dark brown eyes " occur ! Burns, too, the Scottish
peasant-poet, loves the " nut-brown maidens " of his
home.†   Once while on a voyage in Norway north of the
70th degree I was driven out of my course to a group of
islands rarely visited by strangers, and to my astonishment

* *Gespräche mit Goethe*, 16.2.1826.

† Goethe, too, makes "black hair" and "black eyes" heroic
attributes.

I found among the fair fishing population individuals who corresponded exactly to that type : remarkably finely built men with noble, imposing Viking physiognomy, and in addition almost raven-black hair. Later I met this type in the south-east of Europe, in the German colonies of Slavonia, which, settled there for centuries, have kept their German race stainlessly pure amid the Slavs : the figure, the Moltke type (or, as the English say, the Wellington type), and the black hair distinguish these people from their neighbours, who are chiefly fair and have more or less expressionless countenances. However, we do not require to go so far ; we find this type almost the predominant one in German Tyrol, whose inhabitants Henke says " represent the true type of the primeval Teuton." The same scholar explains their having, for the most part, dark and often black hair by the fact that the " sun has burned them black," and is of opinion that colour is " the quality which changes most easily with time." But Virchow's researches had long ago proved the opposite (*see* p. 385) and we might answer this assertion with a question, Why was David fair ? Why did the Jews take from the Amorites a certain tendency to auburn hair and nothing more ? What sun has darkened the hair of the English nobility and of the Norwegian in the far north, where the sun is not seen for months ? No, certainly we have here to deal with other conditions, which must first be cleared up physiologically, for, so far as I am aware, it has not yet been done.* Just as certain red flowers at certain places or under the influence of conditions which are hidden from human observation grow up blue in colour (sometimes red and blue on the same stem), and black animal species sometimes produce white varieties, so it is not unthinkable that the colour of the hair in a certain

* At least I can find nothing on this point either in the text-books of physiology or in such special works as Waldeyer's.

human type is as a rule light, but may under certain
conditions incline to the opposite extreme of the colour
scale.   What is decisive in this case is that we find
this dark hair in individuals whose genuine Germanic
origin is established beyond doubt, not only in the wider
but also in the narrower Tacitean sense of the word,
and moreover confirmed by their whole outward and
inner personality.   However, as soon as we look around,
we see this very type—tall, spare-built, long-skulled,
with Moltke physiognomy, and a " Germanic nature "—
on the southern slopes of the Maritime Alps, for example ;
we need only go from Cannes and Nice, peopled
with the descendants of the chaos, two hours northwards
to more remote parts of the mountains : here, too, one
finds the black hair.   Are they Celts ?   Are they Goths ?
Are they Langobardians ?   I do not know: they are
at any rate brothers of the races just named.   In the
mountains of Northern Italy one finds them also, alter-
nating with the small, round-skulled un-Aryan *homo
alpinus*.   Regarding the Celts, Virchow has already said
that he is " not disinclined to suppose that the original
Celtic population was not fair-Aryan but brown-
Aryan," and armed with this daring " inclination to
suppose " he declares all dark hair to be a sign of an
admixture of Celtic blood.   But the ancients describe
the original Celts as strikingly fair and " red-haired,"
and we can still see them with our own eyes, in Scotland
and Wales ; this hypothesis stands therefore on but one
leg, that the Celts, besides being fair, may also be
brown—or rather dark-haired, which is not quite the
same thing—and among the pure Celts we can find proofs
enough of this.   We have therefore here exactly the
same phenomenon as in the case of the Germanic peoples.
Of the Slavs I can only say one thing, that Virchow
declares them to have been " originally fair."   But
not only were they fair, they still are so ; we only

need to let a Bosnian regiment file past to be convinced of it. The map showing the result of Virchow's investigations in the case of school children proves that the whole of Posen, as well as Silesia east of the Elbe, shows the same small percentage of dark people (10–15 per cent.) as the countries that lie farther to the west ; the greatest percentage of brown people is found in districts which never a Slav entered, namely, Switzerland, Alsace, and the old German Salzkammergut. Whether or not there are genuine Slavs in whom black hair occurs, I do not know.

From these facts one can draw the irrefutable conclusion that fair hair cannot be arbitrarily assigned to the Teuton, as is so often done ; the most genuine sons of this race may be black-haired. The presence of fair hair will certainly always allow us to conjecture Germanic blood (in the wide sense of the term), even though it be a very distant admixture, but the absence of light colour does not justify the opposite conclusion. One must therefore be careful in the application of this limitation ; the hair alone is not a sufficient criterion, the other physical characteristics must also be taken into consideration.

THE SHAPE OF THE SKULL

This brings us to the further, equally difficult question : that of the form of skull. Here it appears as if a boundary could and must be drawn. For, however complex matters are to-day, in old times they were very simple : the old Germanic peoples of Tacitus, as well as the Slavs, were for the most part distinctly long-skulled ; the long skull and the long face beneath it are such unmistakable marks of race that one may well ask whether he who does not possess them may be regarded as belonging to the race. In the Germanic graves of the time of the Migrations one finds half of the skulls long, that is, with a

breadth which stands to the length in the relation of
75 (or less) to 100, and with few exceptions the rest of the
skulls come near to this artificially chosen proportion ; real
round skulls (*see* p. 374) hardly occur at all.   In the old
Slavonic graves the proportion is still more in favour of
the extremely long skulls.   Little is known regarding
the old Celts ; but the tendency to long skulls among the
Gaels of North Scotland and the Cymbrians of Wales
also lends support to the same supposition in their case.*
Since then this has changed very much, at least in many
countries.   It is not so up in the north, in Scandinavia, in
Northern Germany (excluding the towns) and in England ;
on the contrary, the long skulls seem more prevalent in
Denmark than among the Germanic peoples of the time
of the Migrations : there there are 60 long skulls to the
hundred, only six genuine and short ones.   But the Slavs
of Russia show (according to Kollman) scarcely three long
skulls to the hundred, but 72 short skulls and the remainder
incline to be short.   And the old Bavarians !   Johannes
Ranke found by measuring the skulls of 1000 living
individuals that only one in a hundred possessed the old
Germanic skull, while 95 had genuine short skulls !
Measurements of the Hellenic skulls of the Classical age
and of to-day have produced similar results, but even
in the case of the former the middle form of head was
predominant ; yet a third of them had long skulls, and
in their graves fewer genuine short skulls are found than
in Germanic graves ; to-day, however, more than half
are short skulls.   That in these phenomena we see the
effects of the infiltration of an Un-Germanic race, a race
which does not belong at all to the Indo-European circle,
but to the raceless chaos, can scarcely be doubted.   Much
trouble has been taken to sweep aside this conclusion.
For instance, Kollmann (Professor in Basle) has sought
to emphasise the countenance rather than the skull and to

* *Cf.* Ranke: *Der Mensch* ii. 298.

make the distinction one between long faces and short
ones ; * Johannes Ranke took up the idea and constructed
as the specifically Germanic type a long face under a
short skull ; Henke again would fain believe that there
has here been a gradual development, by which the
length of the front of the head has increased rather than
decreased, while the back has become shorter and shorter ;
that in consequence the long skull is still present in the
case of the Germanic peoples with short skulls, only that
it is concealed, &c.   But however worthy of consideration
all these views may be, the fact still remains that the
Germanic peoples, wherever they have not crossed with
others or only to a small extent, as in the north, are
long-skulled and fair (or, it may be, dark) while this
character disappears, first, the nearer one comes to the
Alps, secondly, wherever it has been historically proved
that there was much crossing with races from the
south or with degenerate Celto-Germanic or Slavo-
Germanic races.

Naturally the crossings known to history had the
quickest influence (Italy, Spain, Southern France, &c.,
are well-known examples) ; but besides these mixtures
—and where they did not occur this was the sole influence
—there was another factor at work, namely, the existence
of one or perhaps several prehistoric races, who never
(or only indefinitely) appeared in history as races, and
who, standing on a lower stage of civilisation, were at
an early time conquered and assimilated by the various
branches of the Indo-Germanic peoples.   This, perhaps,
contributes even at the present day to the process of
ungermanising.   For example, Wilhelm von Humboldt
supposed that formerly the Iberians were spread over
Europe, and this view has lately been championed by
Hommel and others.   Even though only a small portion
saved itself by fleeing to the extreme west, the home of

* *Correspondenzblatt der deut. anthrop. Gesellschaft*, 1883, No. 11.

the Basques to-day, and though the majority of the men
died perhaps by the sword of the enemy, yet one seldom
finds complete extinction of the poor and helpless ; they
are kept as slaves, and the women become the property
of the victors.   In the Alps the same or perhaps a
different race, but at any rate an Un-Germanic and non-
Indo-European one had its abode, or at least fled thither
as to a last place of security ; one is forced to this supposition by the fact that to-day the Alps are the centre
of the Un-Germanic, short-skulled, dark type, and that
from here they radiate to north and south ; the Rhætian
race, which anthropology has shown to be distinct, is
perhaps a fairly genuine remnant of those former lake-
dwellers and perhaps identical with Virchow's pre-Celts.
In the wide districts of Eastern Europe we must also
presuppose a special, probably Mongoloid race, to account
for the specific deformation which so rapidly transforms the
majority of the Germanic Slavs into inferior " Slavonics."
How could we then bring ourselves to regard those
Europeans who are descended from this altogether
Un-Germanic type as " Germanic," simply because they
speak an Indo-European language and have assimilated
Indo-European culture ?   I consider it, on the contrary,
a most important duty to make a clear distinction here,
if we wish to understand past and present history. It is by
distinguishing between peoples that we come to recognise
the ideas in their special individuality.   This is all the
more necessary, as we have among us men who are half,
a quarter, or perhaps a sixth Germanic, &c., and in consequence we have a mass of ideas and ways of thinking which
are Germanic to the extent of a half, a fourth, a sixth, &c.,
or on the other hand are directly Anti-Germanic.   And
only by practice in distinguishing between the pure
Germanic and the absolutely Un-Germanic can we find
our way out of the confusion of this growing chaos.
Chaos is everywhere the most dangerous enemy.   In

facing it thought must develop into action ; towards
this, clearness of conception is the first necessary step ;
and in the sphere in which we are at present, clearness
consists in the recognition that Germanicism to-day
contains a large number of Un-Germanic elements, and
in the endeavour to separate what is pure from that
which contains alien, and in no sense Germanic,
ingredients.

Yet, justifiable as it may be to emphasise anatomical
research, I am afraid that anatomy alone will not suffice
here ; on the contrary, it is just on this point that science
is at present like a helpless barque tossing to and fro on
a troubled sea ; whoever is led away by its illusions is
doomed sooner or later to sink. For that which I have
just demonstrated concerning the various races who
survived in Europe from pre-Aryan times, the Iberians,
Rhætians, &c., although indeed essentially correct,
represents only the most elementary simplification of
the innumerable hypotheses which, at the present moment,
are afloat in the air, and every day the matter becomes
more complicated. Thus—to give the layman only
one example—long and careful researches have led
to the conclusion that in Scotland, in the earliest stone
age, there existed a long-skulled race, but that in the stone
age there appeared another exceedingly broad-headed
race, which after fusion with the former and with mixed
forms was typical of the bronze age ; all this took place
in the remote past, long before the arrival of the Celts ;
when these appeared as the vanguard of the Germanic
peoples, it can scarcely be doubted that they underwent changes through contact with the race settled there
before them, since even to-day, after so many and so
strong waves of immigration have swept over that land,
we find in many individuals characteristics which, an
authority tells us, point back directly and unmistakably
to that prehistoric race of the bronze age which sprang

from the mixing of long skulls and short ones ! *　Now
how can we estimate anatomically the craniological
influence of such long-settled races upon the Germanic
peoples, if they themselves already possessed long skulls,
short skulls, and skulls that are between the two ?　And
why is it that to-day only the short skulls tend to increase ?
But here again come other men of science who sing a
different song : some authorities hold that we have no
strong reason for believing in the immigration of the
Indo-European.　It is their opinion that he was already
there in the stone age, was even then distinguished by
his long skull from another short-skulled race, and
struggled with it for the mastery ; that this Long-skull
of the stone age was no other than the Germanic individual !　Virchow's view, based upon anatomical
material, is, that even the oldest Troglodytes of Europe
might have been of Aryan descent, at least that no
one could prove the contrary.†　But with the younger
school such cautious and hesitating judgments find no
favour ; under the pretext of strictly scientific simplification they wave aloft the standard of the chaos and
degrade the whole history of humanity as lies　These
modern theories have been most clearly expressed by
Professor Kollmann.　He reduces all the peoples living
in Europe to four types :　long skulls with long faces,
long skulls with short faces, short skulls with short faces,
and short skulls with long faces ; these four races he
supposes to have lived with and beside each other for
centuries and to do so still.　And now comes the devil's
hoof : all that history teaches us about the Migrations,
nationalities, mental differences, great creative works of
art, which were executed solely by single national individualities and at best merely taken over by others,

* Sir William Turner : *Early Man in Scotland.* Speech delivered
before the Royal Institution in London on January 13, 1898.
† Ranke : *Der Mensch* ii. 578.

and about the war still waged among us between those elements that advance and those that retard culture . . . all this is put aside as rubbish and we are called upon to believe the following dogma : " The development of culture is manifestly the common achievement of all these types. All European races, so far as we have penetrated into the secret of the nature of race, are equally gifted for every task of culture." * Equally gifted ? One can scarcely believe one's eyes ! " Equally gifted " for " every " task ! I shall have to return to this point soon ; I did not wish to leave the question of craniometry without having pointed out, first, how difficult it is here, too, to separate the Germanic from the non-Germanic by formulas, by the compass and the ruler ; secondly, upon what a dangerous path these worthies take us, when they suddenly interrupt their discussion of " chameprosopic, platyrrhinous, mesoconchic, prognathic, proophryocephalous, ooidic, brachyklito-metopic, hypsistegobregmatic Dolichocephali " in order to link on to it general remarks about history and culture. The layman understands little or nothing of the remainder ; he wades hopelessly about in this barbaric jargon of neo-scholastic natural science ; only the one point is printed in all the newspapers of Europe as the visible result of such a congress : that the most learned gentlemen in Europe have solemnly protocolled the fact that all the races bear an equal share in the development of culture ; there never have been Greeks, Romans, Germanic peoples, Jews, but from time immemorial there have lived peace-fully side by side or, it may be, devouring each other, leptoprosopic Dolichocephali, chameprosopic Dolicho-cephali, leptoprosopic Brachycephali and chameprosopic Brachycephali, " all working unitedly at the furtherance of culture " (sic !). It provokes a smile ! But crimes

* Allgemeine Versammlung der deutschen anthropologischen Gesell. schaft, 1892.

against history are really too serious to be punished merely by being laughed at ; the sound common sense of all intelligent men must step vigorously in and put a stop to this : we must say to these worthies, " Cobbler, stick to your last ! " *

How utterly unscientific such a proceeding as that of Kollmann must be is quite manifest. Far-reaching simplification is a law of artistic creating, but not a law of nature ; the characteristic thing here is rather endless complexity. What should we say of a botanist who wished to class plants in families according to the length and breadth of their leaves, or according to any other one characteristic ? Kollmann's method is a retrograde step as compared with old Theophrastus. As long as men attempted artificial classifications, the systematic knowledge of the plant world did not advance one step ; but then came men of genius of the nature of Ray, Jussieu, De Candolle, who by observation united to creative intuition established the chief families of plants and only then discovered the characteristics—mostly very concealed ones—which enabled us to demonstrate the relationship anatomically as well. The same is true of the animal world. All other procedure is absolutely artificial and consequently mere fooling. And hence in the case of man we cannot, as Kollmann does, build up at the anatomist's bidding a system into which facts then have to be fitted as well as may be ; we must ascertain precisely what groups actually exist as individualised, morally and intellectually distinguishable races, and then see whether there are any anatomical characteristics which will aid us in classification.

* *Cf.* the splendid satire by M. Buchner on modern craniometry in the supplement to the Munich *Allgemeine Zeitung*, 1899, No. 282–284.— In the meantime J. Deniker has proposed a new division of all Europeans into six chief and four subordinate races. Thus the picture changes every year !

RATIONAL ANTHROPOLOGY

This digression into the sphere of anatomical science has had the one good result of revealing to us how little sure help and how little useful or practical instruction we may expect from that source. We are either walking upon sandy and shifting ground or in a quagmire, where we sink at the first step and stick fast, or we must spring from point to point on the exceedingly sharp edges of dogma and at any moment fall into the abyss. The digression has moreover positive advantages : it enriches the material of our knowledge and teaches us to see more clearly. Both history and daily observation teach us that the races are not equally gifted, any more than individuals are ; and anthropology shows us further (in spite of Professor Kollmann) that in the case of races which have achieved certain results, a definite physical conformation predominates. The mistake lies in operating with haphazard numbers of objects of comparison and in measuring according to arbitrarily chosen relations. Thus, for example, it is considered a fixed rule that as soon as the breadth of a skull bears the relation of 75 : 100 or less, then it is " dolichocephalous," with 76 or even $75\frac{1}{4}$ it is " mesocephalous " and from 80 onwards " brachycephalous." Who is the authority ? Why should there be a special magic in the number 75 ? Any other magic than that of my own convenience and laziness ? I understand quite well that we cannot get on in daily practice without *termini technici* and limitations, but what I cannot understand is that they should be taken for anything but arbitrary limits and arbitrary words.*

* Very remarkable in this connection are the researches of Dr. G. Walcher, which show that the position of the head of the new-born child exercises a definite influence upon the shape of the skull. In the case of twins from one embryo by this means the one was developed into a distinct dolichocephalous, the other to a brachycephalous child. (See *Zentralblatt für Gynäkologie*, 1905, No. 7.)

This applies to the high and low countenances just as well as to the long and short skulls ; everywhere it is a question of relations which merge by degrees into each other. But it is the nature of life to be plastically mutable ; the living principle of creation is fundamentally different from the crystalline principle in this, that it does not shape according to unchangeable relations of numbers but that it in a way freely creates, while observing the harmony of parts and retaining the fundamental scheme which is given by the nature of the thing itself. No two individuals are like each other. To survey the physical structure of a race at any given moment, I should require to have before me all the representatives of that race and seek out in this crowd the uniform and uniting idea, the predominant specific tendency of physical conformation, which is peculiar to this race as race ; I should see it with my eyes. If I had had, say at the time of Tacitus, all the Germanic peoples before my eyes : the still unmixed Celts, the Teutons and the Germanic Slavs, I should certainly have seen a harmonious whole, in which a certain law of structure predominated, and round it the most manifold and varying conformations would have grouped themselves. Probably there would not have been a single individual who united in himself all the specific characteristics of this plastic idea of race (in the way in which it would have appeared to my thinking brain) in the highest potentiality and in perfect harmony : the great radiant heavenly eyes, the golden hair, the gigantic stature, the symmetrical muscular development, the lengthened skull (which an ever-active brain, tortured by longing, had changed from the round lines of animal contentedness and extended towards the front), the lofty countenance, required by an elevated spiritual life as the seat of its expression—certainly no single individual would have possessed all these features. Were one feature perfect the other would be merely indicated. Here and there, too, nature, which is ever experimenting and never repeating itself, would have broken the law of harmony, an overgrown giant would swing his club over dull eyes, under too long a skull would be seen a face proportionately too short, glorious eyes would beam from beneath a fine lofty forehead, but in comparison, the body would be strikingly small, &c. &c., *ad infinitum.* In other groups again secret laws of the correlation of growth must have manifested themselves; here, for example, families with black hair, but at the same time with particularly large daring aquiline noses and more slender build, there red hair with remarkably white freckled skin and countenance somewhat broader in the upper part . . . for the slightest change in the conformation causes other changes. Still more numerous must those figures have been from which in their average commonplaceness no specific law of structure could have been derived, if they had not appeared as portions of a large whole, in which their place was definitely fixed, so that we could see from the way in which they fitted in that organically they did belong to it. Darwin himself, who worked all his life with compass, ruler and weighing machine, is always in his studies on artificial breeding calling attention to the fact that the eye of the born and experienced breeder discovers things of which figures give not the slightest confirmation, and which the breeder himself can hardly ever express in words; he notices that this and that distinguishes the one organism from the other, and makes his selection for breeding accordingly; this is an intuition born of ceaseless observation. This power of observation we can acquire only by practice; the survey of the Germanic peoples in the time of Tacitus would have served our purpose. We should certainly not have found that in the case of all these men the breadth of the head bore to the length the proportion of 75 : 100; nature knows no such limitations ; in the unlimited complexity of all thinkable intermediate forms, as well as of forms of greater development towards this or that extreme, we should probably here and there have encountered distinct brachycephali ; discoveries in graves make it probable, and why should the plasticity of creative powers not have brought it about ? We should, moreover, not have seen nothing but "giants" and be able to say that he who did not exceed six feet high was not Germanic : on the other hand, we might quite well have made the seemingly paradoxical statement, that the small men of this group are tall, for they belong to a tall race, and for the same reason those short skulls are long ; if we look more closely we shall soon see that outwardly and inwardly they have specific characteristics of the Germanic people. The hieroglyphs of nature's language are in fact not so logically mathematical, so mechanically explicable as many an investigator likes to fancy. Life is needed to understand life. And here a fact occurs to me which I have received from various sources, viz., that very small children, especially girls, frequently have quite a marked instinct for race. It frequently happens that children who have no conception of what "Jew" means, or that there is any such thing in the world, begin to cry as soon as a genuine Jew or Jewess comes near them ! The learned can frequently not tell a Jew from a non-Jew ; the child that scarcely knows how to speak notices the difference. Is not that something ? To me it seems worth as much as a whole anthropological congress or at least a whole speech of Professor Kollmann. There is still something in the world besides compass and yard-measure. Where the learned fails with his artificial constructions, one single unbiased glance can illuminate the truth like a sunbeam.

> Und was kein Verstand der Verständigen sieht,
> Das übet in Einfalt ein kindlich Gemüt.

We shall not interfere with the craniologists any longer than is necessary ; however, we shall not despise the material collected by their diligence : it will be a valuable addition to our knowledge of what is Germanic and an earnest warning in regard to the intrusion amongst us of that which is non-Germanic.

The very necessary limitation of the name " Germanic " to those who are really Teutons or at least have much Germanic blood in their veins can therefore never be carried out with mathematical exactness, but will always require, as it were, the eye of the breeder and the eye of the child. Much knowledge must, of course, be useful, but seeing and feeling is still more indispensable. And with this we transfer our investigation into the necessary limitation of the word " Germanic " to the mental element, in which history teaches us on every hand to separate the Germanic from the non-Germanic, and at the same time thereby to recognise the physical element and value it at its true worth.

SCIENCE OF PHYSIOGNOMY

The science of physiognomy, which is at once spirit and body, mirror of the soul and anatomical " factum," next claims our attention. Look, for example, at the countenance of Dante Alighieri ; we shall learn as much from it as from his poems.* That is a characteristically

* That Dante is Germanic and not a son of the chaos becomes in my opinion so clear from his personality and his work that proof of it is absolutely superfluous. But it is nevertheless interesting to know that the name Alighieri is Gothic, a corruption of Aldiger ; it belongs to those German proper names, at the basis of which lies the word " ger " = spear, as in Gerhard, Gertrude, &c. (a fact which in reference to Shake-speare might have given the visionaries much to think about !). This name came into the family through Dante's grandmother on the father's side, a Goth from Ferrara, whose name was Aldigiero. With regard to the origin of the paternal grandfather and of the poet's mother only the one fact to-day is known, that the attempt to derive him from Roman families is a pure invention of the Italian biographers who thought it more illustrious to belong to Rome than to Germania :

Germanic countenance ! Not a feature in it reminds us of any Hellenic or Roman type, much less of any of the Asiatic or African physiognomies which the Pyramids have faithfully preserved. A new being has entered into the history of the world ! Nature in the fulness of her

DANTE

power has produced a new soul : look at it, here she reflects herself in a countenance such as never was seen before ! " Above the mental hurricane expressed in the countenance rose nobly the peaceful brow arching like a marble dome." * Yes, yes, Balzac is right. Hurricane and marble dome ! If he had only told us that Dante was a leptoprosopic Dolicho-cephalous, we should not have been much wiser. At any rate we shall never find a second Dante, but a walk through the collection of busts in the Berlin Museum will convince us how firmly established this type was in Northern Italy, which had been thoroughly germanised by Goths, Langobards and Franks.

but since the grandfather was a warrior, knighted by the Emperor Conrad, and Dante himself tells us that he belongs to the petty nobility, then his descent from pure Germanic parentage is as good as proven (*cf.* Franz Xaver Kraus : *Dante*, Berlin, 1897, pp. 21-25). Even to the beginning of the fifteenth century many Italians are described in old documents as Alemanni, Langobardi, &c., *ex alamanorum genere, regibus vivens Langobardorum*, &c. (and that though the majority of them had adopted Roman law, whereby the documentary evidence of their descent usually disappeared) ; so thoroughly saturated with Germanic blood (and that too its sole creative element) was that people which the so-called " Roman Culture " to-day wishes to regard as its source (*see* Savigny : *Geschichte des römischen Rechtes im Mittelalter*, i., chap. iii.).

* Balzac : *Les Proscrits*.

To this day we see the closest unmistakable physiognomical relationship in the German Tyrolese mentioned above, as also in Norway, and individual kindred features wherever genuine Teutons are to be found. However, if we look at the greatest Germanic men, we shall not find one but numerous physiognomic conformations; the daring powerfully curved nose predominates; we find,

LUTHER

however, all thinkable combinations, even to that powerful head which in every particular is the very opposite of Dante's and by this very fact betrays the intimate relationship: I mean the head of Martin Luther. Here the hurricane, of which Balzac spoke, embraces forehead, eyes and nose, no marble dome is arched above it; but this flaming volcano of energy and thoughtfulness rests upon mouth and chin as upon a rock of granite. Even the smallest feature of the powerful face testifies to energy and thirst for achievement; when one looks at this countenance the words of Dante rise to one's memory

Colà dove si puote
Ciò che si vuole.

This man can do what he wills and his whole will is directed to great deeds : in this head there is no studying for mere learning's sake, but to find out truth, truth for life ; the man does not sing to charm the ear, but because song elevates and strengthens the heart ; he could not, like Dante, have lived proudly apart and unknown, trusting his fame to future generations—what does such a countenance care for fame? " Love is the pulse-beat of our life," he said. And where love is strong, there too there is strong hatred. It is absolutely false to say, as Henke does, that such a countenance represents the North German Slavonic type.* So mighty a personality towers high above such specifications ; it shows us the outward expression of one of the astonishingly rich possibilities of development of the Germanic spirit in its highest and richest form. Luther's countenance, like Dante's, belongs to all Germanic peoples. One finds this type in England, where no Slav ever made his abode ; one meets it also among the most active politicians of France. One can picture to oneself this man fifteen hundred years ago, on horseback, swinging his battle-axe to protect his beloved northern home, and then again at his own fireside with his children crowding round him, or at the banquet of the men, draining the horn of mead to the last drop and singing heroic songs in praise of his ancestors. Dante and Luther are the extremes of the rich physiognomical scale of great Germanic men. As Tacitus said : they resemble themselves alone. But every attempt to localise the type, to the north or to the south, to the Celtic west or the Slavonic east, is manifestly futile, futile at least when one looks especially at the more important and therefore more characteristic men, and disregards the chance details of habit, especially of the manner of wearing the beard.

* As above, p. 20. What is here said about Luther has since been verified by the strictly anthropological researches of Dr. Ludwig Woltmann ; see the *Politisch-anthropologische Revue*, 1905, p. 683 f.

Goethe, for example, might be the child of any Germanic stem judging by the cast of his face, as might also Johann Sebastian Bach and Immanuel Kant.

FREEDOM AND LOYALTY

Let us attempt a glance into the depths of the soul. What are the specific intellectual and moral character-istics of this Germanic race? Certain anthropologists would fain teach us that all races are equally gifted; we point to history and answer: that is a lie! The races of mankind are markedly different in the nature and also in the extent of their gifts, and the Germanic races belong to the most highly gifted group, the group usually termed Aryan. Is this human family united and uniform by bonds of blood? Do these stems really all spring from the same root? I do not know and I do not much care; no affinity binds more closely than elective affinity, and in this sense the Indo-European Aryans certainly form a family. In his *Politics* Aristotle writes (i. 5): "If there were men who in physical stature alone were so pre-eminent as the representatives of the Gods, then every one would admit that other men by right must be subject unto them. If this, however, is true in reference to the body, then there is still greater justification for distinguishing between pre-eminent and commonplace souls." Physically and mentally the Aryans are pre-eminent among all peoples; for that reason they are by right, as the Stagirite expresses it, the lords of the world. Aristotle puts the matter still more concisely when he says, "Some men are by nature free, others slaves"; this perfectly expresses the moral aspect. For freedom is by no means an abstract thing, to which every human being has funda-mentally a claim; a right to freedom must evidently depend upon capacity for it, and this again presupposes physical and intellectual power. One may make the assertion, that even the mere conception of freedom is quite unknown to most men. Do we not see the *homo syriacus* develop just as well and as happily in the position of slave as of master? Do the Chinese not show us another example of the same nature? Do not all historians tell us that the Semites and half-Semites, in spite of their great intelligence, never succeeded in founding a State that lasted, and that because every one always endeavoured to grasp all power for himself, thus showing that their capabilities were limited to despotism and anarchy, the two opposites of freedom? * And here we see at once what great gifts a man must have in order that one may say of him, he is "by nature free," for the first condition of this is the power of creating. Only a State-building race can be free; the gifts which make the individual an artist and philosopher are essentially the same as those which, spread through the whole mass as instinct, found States and give to the individual that which hitherto had remained unknown to all nature: the idea of freedom. As soon as we understand this, the near affinity of the Germanic peoples to the Greeks and Romans strikes us, and at the same time we recognise what separates them. In the case of the Greeks the individualistic creative character predominates, even in the forming of constitutions; in the case of the Romans it is communistic legislation and military authority that predominate; the Germanic races, on the other hand, have individually and collectively perhaps less creative power, but they possess a harmony of qualities, maintaining the balance between the instinct of individual freedom, which finds its highest expression in creative art,† and the instinct of public freedom which creates the State; and in this way they prove themselves to be the equals of their great predecessors. Art more perfect in its creations,

* *Cf.* p. 404.   † *See* pp. 14, 25, 33, &c.

so far as form is concerned, there may have been, but no
art has ever been more powerful in its creations than
that which includes the whole range of things human
between the winged pen of Shakespeare and the etching-
tool of Albrecht Dürer, and which in its own special
language—music—penetrates deeper into the heart than
any previous attempt to create immortality out of that
which is mortal—to transform matter into spirit. And
in the meantime the European States, founded by Germanic peoples, in spite of their, so to speak, improvised,
always provisional and changeable character—or rather
perhaps thanks to this character—proved themselves to
be the most enduring as well as the most powerful in the
world.   In spite of all storms of war, in spite of the decep-
tions of that ancestral enemy, the chaos of peoples, which
carried its poison into the very heart of our nation,
Freedom and its correlative, the State, remained, through
all the ages the creating and saving ideal, even though
the balance between the two often seemed to be upset :
we recognise that more clearly to-day than ever.

In order that this might be so, that fundamental and
common " Aryan " capacity of free creative power had
to be supplemented by another quality, the incomparable
and altogether peculiar Germanic loyalty (*Treue*). If
that intellectual and physical development which leads
to the idea of freedom and which produces on the one
hand art, philosophy, science, on the other constitutions
(as well as all the phenomena of culture which this word
implies), is common to the Hellenes and Romans as well
as to the Germanic peoples, so also is the extravagant
conception of loyalty a specific characteristic of the
Teuton.   As the venerable Johann Fischart sings :

> Standhaft und treu, und treu und standhaft,
> Die machen ein recht teutsch Verwandtschaft !

Julius Cæsar at once recognised not only the military
prowess but also the unexampled loyalty of the Teutons

and hired from among them as many cavalrymen as he could possibly get. In the battle of Pharsalus, which was so decisive for the history of the world, they fought for him; the Romanised Gauls had abandoned their commander in the hour of need, the Germanic troops proved themselves as faithful as they were brave. This loyalty to a master chosen of their own free will is the most prominent feature in the Germanic character; from it we can tell whether pure Germanic blood flows in the veins or not. The German mercenary troops have often been made the object of ridicule, but it is in them that the genuine costly metal of this race reveals itself. The very first autocratic Emperor, Augustus, formed his personal bodyguard of Teutons; where else could he have found unconditional loyalty? During the whole time that the Roman Empire in the east and the west lasted, this same post of honour was filled by the same people, but they were always brought from farther and farther north, because with the so-called " Latin culture " the plague of disloyalty had crept more deeply into the country; finally, a thousand years after Augustus, we find Anglo-Saxons and Normans in this post, standing on guard around the throne of Byzantium. Hapless Germanic Lifeguardsman! Of the political principles, which forcibly held together the chaotic world in a semblance of order, he understood just as little as he did of the quarrels concerning the nature of the Trinity, which cost him many a drop of blood: but one thing he understood: to be loyal to the master he had himself chosen. When in the time of Nero the Frisian delegates left the back seats which had been assigned to them in the Circus and proudly sat down on the front benches of the senators among the richly adorned foreign delegates, what was it that gave these poor men, who came to Rome to beg for land to cultivate, such a bold spirit of independence? Of what alone could they boast?

" That no one in the world surpassed the Teuton in loyalty." * Karl Lamprecht has written so beautifully about this great fundamental characteristic of loyalty in its historical significance that I should reproach myself if I did not quote him here. He has just spoken of the " retainers " who in the old German State pledge themselves to their chief to be true unto death and prove so, and then he adds : " In the formation of this body of retainers we see one of the most magnificent features of the specifically Germanic view of life, the feature of loyalty. Not understood by the Roman but indispensable to the Teuton, the need of loyalty existed even at that time, that ever-recurring German need of closest personal attachment, of complete devotion to each other, perfect community of hopes, efforts and destinies. Loyalty never was to our ancestors a special virtue, it was the breath of life of everything good and great ; upon it rested the feudal State of the Early and the co-operative system of the Later Middle Ages, and who could conceive the military monarchy of the present day without loyalty ? . . . Not only were songs sung about loyalty, men lived in it. The retinue of the King of the Franks, the courtiers of the great Karolingians, the civil and military ministers of our mediæval Emperors, the officials of the centres of administration under our Princes since the fourteenth and the fifteenth centuries are merely new forms of the old Germanic conception. For the wonderful vitality of such institutions consisted in this, that they were not rooted in changing political or even moral conditions, but in the primary source of Germanicism itself, the need of loyalty." †

However true and beautiful every word that Lamprecht has here written, I do not think that he has made quite clear the " primary source." Loyalty, though distinguish-

---

* Tacitus : *Annals* xiii. 54.
† Lamprecht : *Deut. Gesch.*, 2nd ed. i. 136.

ing the Teutons from mongrel races, is not altogether
a specific Germanic trait. One finds it in almost all
purely bred races, nowhere more than among the negroes,
for example, and—I would ask—what man could be
more faithful than the noble dog ? No, in order to
reveal that " primary source of Germanicism," we must
show what is the nature of this Germanic loyalty, and
we can only succeed in doing so if we have grasped the
fact that freedom is the intellectual basis of the whole
Germanic nature. For the characteristic feature of this
loyalty is its free self-determination. The human character
resembles the nature of God as the theologians represent
it : complex and yet indiscernible, an inseparable unity.
This loyalty and this freedom do not grow the one out
of the other, they are two manifestations of the same character which reveals itself to us on one occasion more from
the intellectual on another more from the moral side. The
negro and the dog serve their masters, whoever they may be :
that is the morality of the weak, or, as Aristotle says, of
the man who is born to be a slave ; the Teuton chooses his
master, and his loyalty is therefore loyalty to himself : that
is the morality of the man who is born free. But loyalty
as displayed by the Teuton was unexampled. The disloyalty of the extravagantly gifted proclaimer of poetical
and political freedom, *i.e.*, of the Hellene, was proverbial
from time immemorial ; the Roman was loyal only in
the defence of his own, German loyalty remained, Lamprecht says, " incomprehensible to him " ; here, as everywhere in the sphere of morals, we see an affinity with the
Indo-Aryans ; but these latter people so markedly lacked
the artistic sense which urges men on to adventure and
to the establishment of a free life, that their loyalty never
reached that creative importance in the world's history
which the same quality attained under the influence of
the Germanic races. Here again, as before, in the consideration of the feeling of freedom, we find a higher

harmony of character in the Teuton ; hence we may say that no one in the world, not even the greatest, has surpassed him. One thing is certain : if we wish to sum up in a single word the historic greatness of the Teuton— always a perilous undertaking, since everything living is of Protean nature—we must name his loyalty. That is the central point from which we can survey his whole character, or better, his personality. But we must remember that this loyalty is not the primary source, as Lamprecht thinks, not the root but the blossom—the fruit by which we recognise the tree. Hence it is that this loyalty is the finest touchstone for distinguishing between genuine and false Germanicism ; for it is not by the roots but by the fruit that we distinguish the species ; we should not forget that with unfavourable weather many a tree has no blossoms or only poor ones, and this often happens in the case of hard-pressed Teutons. The root of their particular character is beyond all doubt that power of imagination which is common to all Aryans and peculiar to them alone and which appeared in greatest luxuriance among the Hellenes. I spoke of this in the beginning of the chapter on Hellenic art and philosophy (*see* p. 14 f.) ; from that root everything springs, art, philosophy, politics, science ; hence, too, comes the peculiar sap which tinges the flower of loyalty. The stem then is formed by the positive strength—the physical and the intellectual, which can never be separated ; in the case of the Romans, to whom we owe the firm bases of family and State, this stem was powerfully developed. But the real blossoms of such a tree are those which mind and sentiment bring to maturity. Freedom is an expansive power which scatters men, Germanic loyalty is the bond which by its inner power binds men more closely than the fear of the tyrant's sword : freedom signifies thirst after direct self-discovered truth, loyalty the reverence for that which has appeared to our ancestors to be true ; freedom decides its own destiny and loyalty holds that decision unswervingly and for ever. Loyalty to the loved one, to friend, parents, and fatherland we find in many places ; but here, in the case of the Teuton, something is added, which makes the great instinct become a profoundly deep spiritual power, a principle of life. Shakespeare represents the father giving his son as the best advice for his path through life, as the one admonition which includes all others, these words :

This above all : to thine own self be true !

The principle of Germanic loyalty is evidently not the necessity of attachment, as Lamprecht thinks, but on the contrary the necessity of constancy within a man's own autonomous circle ; self-determination testifies to it ; in it freedom proves itself ; by it the vassal, the member of the guild, the official, the officer asserts his independence. For the free man, to serve means to command himself. " It was the Germanic races who first introduced into the world the idea of personal freedom," says Goethe. What in the case of the Hindoos was metaphysics and in so far necessarily negative, seclusive, has been here transferred to life as an ideal of mind, it is the " breath of life of everything great and good," a star in the night, to the weary a spur, to the storm-tossed an anchor of safety.* In the construction of the Germanic character loyalty is the necessary perfection of the personality, which without it falls to pieces. Immanuel Kant has given a daring, genuinely Germanic definition of personality : it is, he says, " freedom and independence of the mechanism of all nature " ; and what it achieves he has summed up as follows : " That which elevates man above himself (as part of the world of sense), attaches him to an order of things which only the understanding can conceive,

* But quite analogous to Indian sentiment, in so far as here the regulative principle is transferred to our inmost hearts.

and which has the whole world of sense subject to it, is Personality." But without loyalty this elevation would be fatal : thanks to it alone the impulse of freedom can develop and bring blessing instead of a curse. Loyalty in this Germanic sense cannot originate without freedom, but it is impossible to see how an unlimited, creative impulse to freedom could exist without loyalty. Childish attachment to nature is a proof of loyalty : it enables man to raise himself above nature, without falling shattered to the ground, like the Hellenic Phaethon. Therefore it is that Goethe writes : " Loyalty preserves personality ! " Germanic loyalty is the girdle that gives immortal beauty to the ephemeral individual, it is the sun without which no knowledge can ripen to wisdom, the charm which alone bestows upon the free individual's passionate action the blessing of permanent achievement.

IDEAL AND PRACTICE

These few simplified remarks should, I think, enable us to understand the essential characteristics, intellectual and moral, of the Germanic races. Simplification might easily fill a whole book and it would only be amplification. If we wish clearly to distinguish the Teuton from his nearest kinsmen we should study the inmost being of both and compare a Kant as an ethical teacher with an Aristotle. For Kant " the autonomy of the will is the highest principle of morality " ; a " moral personality " exists for him only from the moment when " a man is subject to no other laws than those which he gives to himself." And according to what principles shall this autonomous personality give itself laws ? We must suppose that there is an unprovable " realm of impulses—certainly only an ideal ! " An ideal is therefore to determine life ! And in a note to the same book (*Grundlegung zur Metaphysik der Sitten*) Kant in a

few words contrasts this new, specifically Germanic philosophy with the Hellenic : " There the realm of impulses
is a theoretical idea, to explain that which is ; here (in the
case of the Teutons) it is a practical idea to bring about
by our active and passive attitude that which is not,
but yet may be." What daring, to create by our will
a moral realm which is not, to cause it "actually"
to come into existence ! What a dangerous piece of
daring if loyalty were not at work, which is so
thoroughly characteristic of Kant's own mental physiognomy ! And we should carefully note this contrast:
here (in the case of the Teuton) Ideal and at the same
time Practice, there (in the case of the Hellene) sober
Reality and, as its associate, Theory. The great captain
of the powers of the chaos laughed at the German
" ideologists," as he called them : a proof of ignorance,
for they were more practical men than he himself. It
is not the ideal that is in the clouds but theory.
The Ideal is, as Kant here wishes it to be understood,
a practical idea as distinguished from a theoretical one.
And that which we see here, on the heights of metaphysics,
in clear-cut outlines, we find again everywhere : the
Teuton is the most ideal, but at the same time the most
practical, man in the world, and that because here we
have not dissimilarity, but on the contrary identity.
A Teuton writes a *Critique of Pure Reason*, but at the same
time a Teuton invents the railway ; the century of Bessemer
and of Edison is at the same time the century of Beethoven
and of Richard Wagner. Whoever does not feel the
unity of the impulse here, whoever considers it a riddle
that the astronomer Newton should interrupt his mathematical investigations to write a commentary to the
Revelation of St. John, that Crompton invented the spin-
ning machine merely to give himself more leisure for his
beloved music, and that Bismarck, the statesman of
blood and iron, caused Beethoven's sonatas to be played

to him in the decisive moments of his life, understands nothing at all of the nature of the Teuton, and cannot in consequence rightly judge the part he plays in the history of the world in the past and at the present time.

TEUTON AND ANTI-TEUTON

So much for this important subject. We have seen who the Teuton is; * let us now see how he entered into history.

I am not qualified and do not wish in this work to give a history of the Germanic races ; but we cannot understand and value the nineteenth century either in so far as it is a product of the preceding ones nor in its own gigantic expansive power, if we do not possess clear conceptions, not only concerning the nature of the Teuton, but also concerning the conflict which has been raging between him and the non-Teuton for fifteen hundred years. To-day is the child of yesterday: what we have is partly the egacy of pre-Germanic antiquity, what we are is altogether the work of the early Teuton, who is wont to be represented to us as a " barbarian," as if barbarism were a question of relative civilisation and did not simply denote a rudeness of mind. One hundred and fifty years ago Montesquieu brilliantly cleared up this confusion of ideas. After showing that all the States that make up Europe to-day (America, Africa and Australia were then out of the question) were the work of Germanic barbarians who suddenly appeared from unknown wilds, he continues, " But in reality these peoples were not barbarians, since they were free : they became barbarians later when, dominated by the absolute power, they lost their liberty."† In these words we read not only the character

* The whole ninth chapter, which tries to describe Germanic civilisation and culture in its principal lines, forms a supplement to what is as briefly as possible sketched here.

† *Lettres persanes*, chap. cxxxvi.

of the Teutons, but also the fate against which they were destined continually to struggle. For it is not possible to say what uniform and independent culture might have arisen on a purely Germanic soil ; instead of this the Teuton entered into a history which was already perfectly shaped, a history with which he had hitherto not come in contact. As soon as the bare struggle for existence gave him leisure, he grasped with the fervour of passion the two constructive ideas which the " old world " now tumbling to pieces had tried in its last agony to develop : imperialism and Christianity. Was this a piece of luck ? Who will venture to affirm it ? He received no great thoughts of antiquity in pure form, all were transmitted by the sterile, shallow spirits of the chaos that shunned the light and hated freedom. But the Teuton had no choice. In order to live, he had in the first place to assimilate alien customs and thoughts as they were presented to him ; he had to be apprenticed to a civilisation which in truth was no longer worthy to loosen the latchet of his shoes ; the Hellenic creative impulse, Roman legislation, the sublime simple doctrine of Christ, which would have had the greatest affinity to his nature, were completely removed from his eyes, to be dug up centuries later by his own diligence. In his adoption of the alien he was greatly aided by his perilous power of assimilation, and also by that " modesty " which Luther praises as " the sure sign of a pious god-fearing heart," but which in its extravagant estimation of the merit of others leads to many a foolish delusion. Hence it is that a sharp critical eye is needed to separate in the motives and thoughts of those old heroic generations what is genuinely Germanic from that which has been deflected from its natural course, sometimes for ever. Take, for example, the absolute religious toleration of the Goths, when they had become masters of that Roman empire where the principle of intolerance had long been predominant : it is just as characteristic of Germanic sentiment as the protection which they gave to the monuments of art.* We see here at once these two features, freedom and loyalty. Characteristic, too, is the constancy with which the Goths clung to Arianism. Dahn is certainly right in saying that it is a chance that the Goths were induced to join the sect of the Arians and not of the Athanasians ; but chance ceases where loyalty begins. Thanks to the great Wulfila, the Goths possessed the whole Bible in their mother tongue, and Dahn's mockery of the incapacity of these rough men for theological disputes is somewhat out of place in view of the fact that this living book was the source of their religious faith—a thing that not every Christian of the nineteenth century could say of himself.† And now comes the really important matter—not the dreary quarrel about Homo-ousian and Homoi-ousian, which even the Emperor Constantine declared to be idle—but the loyal clinging to what has once been chosen, the emphasising of Germanic individuality, and the right of free-agency in dealing with the foreigner. If the Teutons had been as Dahn represents them, mere barbarians with no will, as ready to adopt the cult of Osiris as any other faith, how does it come that all of them (Longobardians, Goths, Vandals, Burgundians, &c.) in the fourth century adopted Arianism and that, while elsewhere it scarcely survived fifty years,

* *See* above, p. 322, and *cf.* Gibbon : *Roman Empire*, chap. xxxix., and Clarac : *Manuel de l'histoire de l'art chez les Anciens jusqu'à la fin du 6ᵐᵉ siècle de notre ère*, ii. 857 f. The mongrel races destroyed the monuments, partly from religious fanaticism, partly because the statues provided the best lime for building and the temples furnished splendid dressed stones. Where are the true barbarians ?

† We can see in Neander's *Kirchengeschichte*, 4th ed. iii. 199, how characteristic of the Goths was the reading of the Bible. Neander quotes a letter in which Hieronymus expresses his astonishment at the manner in which " the barbaric tongue of the Goths seeks after the pure sense of the Hebraic original," while in the south " no one troubles about the matter." That was already in the year 403 !

they remained true to it for centuries ? I see nothing
theological in this and I do not attach the slightest
importance to those subtleties which can be twisted out
of every little trifle to prove a preconceived thesis ; I
direct my attention solely to the great facts of character
and here again I see loyalty and independence. I see
the Germanic peoples instinctively carrying out the emancipation from Rome a thousand years before Wyclif,
at a time when the religious idea of Rome had not been
clearly separated from the Roman imperialism, and in
such a phenomenon I can see nothing accidental.* It
is clear from Karl Müller's account in his *Kirchengeschichte* (1892, i. 263) how far from unimportant this
phenomenon was ; he says of the Arian Teutons : " Each
Empire has its own Church. There are no Church unions
in the manner of the Catholic Church . . . the new priests
. . . have been component parts of the organisation of
the race and the people. The standard of culture in the
ministry is naturally quite different from that among the
Catholics : purely national and Germanic, without being
influenced by the ecclesiastical and profane culture of the
old world. On the other hand, according to all Christian
testimony the customs and morals of the Teutons are im-
measurably higher than those of the Catholic Romance
peoples. It is the moral purity of a still uncorrupted
people as opposed to an absolutely rotten culture."
Tolerant, evangelical, morally pure : that is what the
Teutons were before they came under the influence of
Rome.

Now it is peculiar that the Teutons at a later period
allowed themselves to be ensnared and created knights
of the Anti-Germanic powers ; I am afraid that this too
is a genuinely Germanic feature, for everything living bears
in itself the germ of its own ruin and death. Certainly
Charlemagne never even in his dreams thought of serving

* Dahn, 2te Auflage von Wietersheim's *Völkerwanderung* ii. 60.

the Bishop of Rome; on the contrary, he wanted to make
the Bishop's power subordinate to his own; he treats
the Pope as a master treats his subject,* he is called by his
contemporaries a " reformer " of the Church and carries
his point against Rome even in matters of dogma, as in
the worship of images, to which he as genuine Teuton
objected.   But all this did not hinder him from strengthening the Papacy by bestowing on the head of the Roman
Church power and dignity, and furthering the amalgamation of the German monarchy with a Roman Christianity,
hitherto unheard of, but which thenceforth weighed like
a nightmare upon Germany.   Imagine how matters would
have developed if the Franks, too, had become Arians
or if they as Catholics had early renounced Rome, say
under Charlemagne, and had founded nationally organised
churches like most of the Slavs! When the Popes
urgently appealed to Charlemagne's predecessors, Charles
Martel and Pépin, for help, Rome's position as a world-
power was lost; the decisive rejection of her pretensions
would have destroyed her influence for ever.   Indeed, if
Charlemagne's efforts to get the Imperial Crown conferred
by Byzantium and not by Rome had been successful, the
ecclesiastical independence of the Teutons would never
have been endangered. Charlemagne's whole activity
testifies to such distinctly German nationalism that we
see that Germanisation was his object, and not only his
object but also his life-work, in spite of all appearances
and many consequences which seem to point to the
contrary; for he is the founder of Germany, the man
who, as the venerable Widukind said, made
quasi una gens of the Germans, and in so far he is the
originator of the no longer " Holy Roman " but " Holy
German " empire of to-day. The Roman Church, on the

---

* That the Pope was actually the subject of the Emperor is proved
by civil and by public law, so that the passionate dissertations for and
against are aimless. (*See* Savigny: *Geschichte des römischen Rechtes
im Mittelalter* i. chap. v.).

other hand, was unavoidably the shield- and armour-bearer of all Anti-Germanic movements; this was the part which it played from the beginning—more and more openly as time went on, so that it never was more Anti-Germanic than at the present day. And yet it owes its existence to the Teutons! I am not speaking of matters of faith at all, but of the Papacy as an ideal, secular power; orthodox Catholics, whom I honour in my heart, have understood and admitted this. To give only one example, which is linked with what I have written above: we have seen that religious toleration is natural to the Teuton as a man who has sentiments of freedom and to whom religion is an inner experience; before the Roman Empire was seized by the Goths persecution had been the order of the day, but then it ceased for a long time, for the Teutons put an end to it. It was only after the doctrines and passions of the races had estranged the Teuton from himself that the Frank began to preach Christianity to the Saxon sword in hand. It was the *De Civitate Dei* which impressed upon Charlemagne the duty of conversion by force,* and to this the Pope, who bestowed on him the title of *Christianissimus Rex* unceasingly urged him; hence it was that the first Thirty Years War raged among Germanic brothers, laying waste, destroying, sowing undying hatred, not because they, but because Rome so wished it. It was exactly the same nine hundred years later in the second Thirty Years War, which in some parts of Germany only a fiftieth part of the population survived—certainly a practical way for getting rid of the Teutons, to make them destroy each other. And in the meantime the doctrine of Augustine, the African half-breed, the dogma of systematic intolerance and of the punishment by death of heterodoxy had entered the Church; and, as soon as the Germanic element had been sufficiently weakened and the Anti-Germanic

* Hodgkin: *Charles the Great*, 1897, pp. 107, 248.

element sufficiently strengthened, that dogma solemnly
declared to be law and to the everlasting disgrace of
humanity was put in practice for five hundred years, in
the midst of a civilisation which otherwise was advancing
everywhere. How does one of the most eminent Catholics
of the nineteenth century judge this remarkable event,
this brutalisation of men, who had formerly shown themselves so humane, in the days when they were supposed to
be barbarians ? " It was," he says, " a victory which
the old Roman Imperial law gained over the Germanic
spirit."*

If we wish to carry out the necessary limitation of the
expression " Germanic," that is, separate the Germanic
from the Un-Germanic, we must in the first place endeavour,
as I did in the beginning of this chapter, to realise the
fundamental qualities of mind and character of the
Teutons, and then, as has just been shown by an example,
we must with a critical eye follow the course of history.
Such " victories over the Germanic spirit " were frequently won, many of them with only temporary success,
many so thorough that noble races falling into a progressive degeneracy disappeared for ever from the German
family. For this Teuton who entered into history under
such complex, contradictory and absolutely obsolete conditions had become estranged from himself. Every
power was set in motion to delude him : not only the
passions, the greed, the lust of power, all the evil vices,
which he had in common with others, even his better
qualities were played upon to serve this purpose : his
mystical tendencies, his thirst for knowledge, his force
of faith, his impulse to create, his high organising abilities,
his noble ambition, his need of ideals—everything
possible was used against himself. The Teuton had
entered history not as a barbarian but as a child—as a

* Döllinger : *Die Geschichte der religiösen Freiheit* (in his Academic
Lectures, iii. 278).

child that falls into the hands of old experienced libertines. Hence it is that we find Un-Germanic qualities nestling in the heart of the best Teutons, where, thanks to Germanic earnestness and loyalty, they often took firmer root than anywhere else ; hence, too, the great difficulty of solving the riddle of our history. Montesquieu told us that the Teuton had become barbarian through the loss of his freedom : but who robbed him of it ? The chaos of races in conjunction with himself. Dietrich of Berne had rejected the title and the crown of Imperator ; he was too proud to wish to be more than King of the East Goths. Later Teutons, on the other hand, imbued as they were by Un-Germanic ideas, were dazzled by the Imperial purple with the power of a magic talisman. For in the meantime the Jurisconsults of the late degenerate Roman law had come and whispered in the ear of the German Princes wonders concerning the kingly prerogatives ; and the Roman Church, which was the most powerful disseminator of Justinian law,* taught that this law was sacred and given by God ; † and down came the Pope declaring himself to be lord and master of all crowns ; he alone, as Christ's representative on earth, could grant or remove,‡ and the emperor as mere *rex regum* was subject to the *servus servorum*. But if the Pope bestowed or ratified regal power, every King was King by the grace of God, and when the legal authorities declared that the bearer of the crown was the rightful owner of the whole land, and had unlimited authority over his subjects, the transformation was complete, and in place of a nation of free men there now stood a nation of slaves. This is what Montesquieu rightly calls barbarism. The Germanic Princes, who had made this

* Savigny : *Geschichte des römischen Rechts* i. chap. iii.
† " The Middle Ages put Roman Law as revealed reason in matters of justice (*ratio scripta*) side by side with Christianity as revealed religion" (Jhering : *Vorgeschichte der Indo-europäer*, p. 302).
‡ Phillips : *Lehrbuch des Kirchenrechtes*, 1881 (!), § 102, &c.

contract not merely from lust of power and wealth, but also out of misunderstanding, had unconsciously sold themselves to the hostile powers; thenceforth they became the pillars of Anti-Germanicism. One more victory had been gained over the Germanic spirit !

I leave to the reader's own study other examples of the way in which the Teuton was estranged from himself. Once he had lost the freedom to act and the freedom to believe, the basis of his particular, incomparable nature was undermined in such a way that only the most violent revolt could save him from complete downfall. How free and daring had been the religious speculation of the first Norse schoolmen, full of personality and life; how enslaved and gagged such speculation appeared subsequently to Thomas Aquinas, who to the present day stands as law to all Catholic schools ! * How touching it is to think of the Goths in possession of their Gothic Bible, listening awestruck to the words of Christ which they but imperfectly understood and which seemed to them the words of some ancestral almost forgotten tale, or perhaps a distant voice penetrating to their ear, and calling them to a beautiful inconceivable future ; so that we find them sinking on their knees in the simply hewn house of God or in the tent that served the same purpose,† and praying with childlike simplicity for all that is nearest and dearest to them ! But now all that had disappeared : the Bible was to be read solely in the Latin vulgate—that is, only by scholars—and was soon so little known to even priests and monks that even Charlemagne had to admonish the bishops to pay more earnest heed to

---

* We must also remember that Thomas Aquinas was descended on his mother's side from the house of Stauffen and early came under the influence of German knowledge and thought (Albertus Magnus). Where would the chaos have achieved anything great—and the achievements of Aquinas deserve our admiration for their strength and greatness—without the help of the Teutons ?

† See Hieronymus : Epist. ad Lætum.

the study of the sacred writings ; * the sacred worship
could henceforth be held only in a language which no
layman understood.† How brilliantly clear, on the

* Döllinger : *Das Kaisertum Karls des Grossen*, Acad. Lectures,
iii. 102.

† It is interesting in this connection to call attention to the fact
that Pope Leo XIII., by the constitution *officiorum numerum* of
January 25, 1897, has " not inconsiderably intensified the strictness "
of the Index of forbidden books (so says the orthodox-Roman commentator Professor Hollweck in his book *Das kirchliche Bücherverbot*, 2nd
ed., 1897, p. 15). The old Germanic spirit of freedom had in fact
begun to assert itself in France and Germany in the nineteenth century ;
ecclesiastical teachers asserted that the Index was not valid for those
countries, bishops demanded great changes in the direction of freedom,
laymen (Coblenz, 1869) united in sending addresses, in which they
demanded the complete abolition of the Index (*see* pp. 13, 14) ; Rome's
answer was to make it stricter than ever, as every layman can find
from the book quoted above, which has the episcopal sanction. According to this law the orthodox Roman Catholic is forbidden to read
practically all the literature of the world, and even such authors as
Dante he can read only in drastically expurgated, "episcopally approved"
editions. It is an interesting fact in connection with the strictness
of the new Index constitution that henceforth not merely books which
touch upon theological questions must be episcopally approved but
also that, according to pp. 42 and 43, such as treat of natural science and
art may not be read by orthodox Catholics *absque prævia Ordinariorum
venia*. But it is specially noteworthy that the reading of the Bible
in a faithful complete edition, even when this has been edited by
Catholics, is forbidden as " grievous sin " ! Only those editions may
be read which have been specially revised, provided with notes and
approved by the Papal stool (p. 29). This care, however, is exercised
only for minds already wavering, for during religious instruction as
well as at other times the young are warned so strongly against reading
the Scriptures that I have lived for twenty years in Catholic countries
without encountering a single Catholic layman who ever had had the
complete Bible even in his hand ; in other cases the *Index librorum
prohibitorum* finds little or no application in practical life ; with unerring instinct Rome has felt that the one really dangerous book for
it is that in which we find the simple figure of Christ. Before the
Council of Trent, *i.e.*, at a time when the later " Protestant " had not
yet visibly separated from the later " Catholics," this was not so in
Germany ; by means of that pioneer of the Reformation, the " German
art " of book-printing, in a short time (and in spite of the then existing
ecclesiastical prohibition), the Bible in " right common German " had
become the most popular book in the land (Janssen : *Geschichte des
deutschen Volkes* i. 20). But the Council of Trent for ever put an
end to this state of affairs by its *Decretum de editione et usu sacrorum
librorum*. Immanuel Kant admired, however, the strong consistency
of the Roman Church and looked upon the prohibition to read the

other hand, does the idea of pure science appear in Roger
Bacon at the beginning of the thirteenth century—
observation of nature, philology to be studied scientifically,
mathematics! But his works are condemned by Rome
and destroyed, he himself in the prime of his life is
imprisoned in a cloister, so that all earnest investigation of nature was held back for centuries and then
opposed at every step. That such lights of science as
Copernicus and Galilei were good Catholics, and such
pioneers of new cosmological and philosophical conceptions as Krebs (Nicolaus of Cusa), Bruno, Campanella and
Gassendi, actually Cardinals, monks and priests, only
proves that in the case of all these men it is not a question
of difference of faith but of the struggle between two philosophies, or better still, between two human natures, the
Germanic and the Anti-Germanic, which also was proved
by the fact that most of these men were persecuted, or
that at least their writings were condemned.* Cardinal
Nicolaus of Cusa, the confidant of Popes, who was fortunate enough to live before the retrograde movement
introduced by the Council of Trent, proved his genuinely
Germanic nature by the fact that he was the first to
reveal the forgery of the Decretalia of Isidor and the
would-be donation of Constantine, and that he as an active
reformer of the Church untiringly, though unsuccessfully,
strove to bring about what had later to be obtained by
force. The man who exposes forgeries cannot possibly
be morally identical with him who commits them. And

Bible as its " corner-stone " (Hasse: *Letzte Aüsserungen Kant's*, 1804,
p. 29). At the same time he was wont to laugh at the Protestants,
" who say: study the Scriptures diligently, but you must not find
anything there but what we find " (Reicke: *Lose Blätter aus Kant's
Nachlass* ii. 34).

* It is very remarkable that such original and free-thinking philosophers
as Bruno and Campanella belong to the extreme south of Italy, where
even to-day, according to anthropological verifications, the Indo-
Germanic, distinct dolichocephalous type is most strongly represented
in the Peninsula (*see* Ranke: *Der Mensch* ii. 299).

so we cannot make religious denominations any more than nationalities the test by which to distinguish between that which is genuinely Germanic and that which is Anti-Germanic. Not only is it difficult before the Council of Trent to distinguish between the Roman Christians and others, inasmuch as many of the great teachers of the Church like Origenes and many Catholic doctors had gone much further than a Luther or a Hus in accepting tenets and views which from that time forth were reckoned to be heretical—but in later times and down to the present day we see pre-eminently German minds remain obedient to Rome from deep conviction and loyal attachment to the great idea of a universal Church, and yet prove themselves most genuine Teutons; while on the other hand the man in whom the revolt against the Anti-Germanic powers was most powerfully expressed, Martin Luther, quotes the testimony of Augustine, to urge the Princes to rebellion, and Calvin burns the great doctor Michel Lervet because of his dogmatic views, receiving for this the approval of the humane Melancthon. We cannot therefore put down individual men as representatives of the Teutons; but as soon as they have become subject to the Non-Germanic influence in education, surroundings, &c.—and who was not so influenced during at least a thousand years?—we must learn to distinguish carefully between that which grows out of the genuine pure Germanic nature, be it for good or for evil, as a living component of the personality, and that which is forcibly grafted on or bound up with it.

It is clear that, in a certain sense, we may regard the intellectual and moral history of Europe from the moment of the entry of the Teuton to the present day as a struggle between Teuton and non-Teuton, between Germanic sentiment and Anti-Germanic disposition, as a struggle which is waged partly externally, philosophy against philosophy, partly internally, in the breast of the Teuton himself. But here I am trespassing upon the following division. What has been said here I shall summarise by referring to the perfect type of the Anti-Germanic ; this is, I think, the most valuable supplement to the positive picture.

IGNATIUS OF LOYOLA

The struggle against the Germanic spirit has in a way embodied itself in one of the most extraordinary men of history ; here as elsewhere a single great personality has, by its example and by the sum of living power which it brought into the world, been able to do more than all the councils and all the solemn resolutions of great societies. And it is a good thing to see our enemy before us in a form which deserves respect, otherwise hatred or contempt is apt to dim our judgment. I do not know who would be justified in refusing honest admiration to Ignatius of Loyola. He bears physical pain like a hero,* is just as fearless morally, his will is of iron, his action direct, his powers of thinking spoiled by no pedantry and artificiality ; he is an acute, practical man, who never stumbles over trifles and yet assures to his influence a far-reaching future, by seizing the needs of the moment and making them the basis of his activity ; he is in addition unassuming, an enemy of phrases, and no comedian ; a soldier and a nobleman ; the priesthood is rather his instrument than his natural vocation. Now this man was a Basque ; not only was he born in the pure Basque part of Spain, but his biographers assure us that he was of genuine unmixed Basque descent, that is, he belonged to a race which was not only Un-Germanic but absolutely distinct from the whole Indo-European

---

* His leg had been shattered in battle and after it was completely healed he had it broken again because it had become shorter than the other and so rendered him unsuitable for military service.

group.*   In Spain since the time of the Celtic immigration
the mixed Celtiberians formed a considerable portion of
the population, but in certain northern parts the Iberian
Basques have remained unmixed to the present day and
Ignatius, really Iñigo, is said to be a " genuine son
of the enigmatical, taciturn, energetic and fantastic stem
of the Basques." †   It is, by the way (as an illustration
of the incomparable importance of race), exceedingly
remarkable that the man, to whom principally must be
ascribed the maintenance of the specifically Romish,
Anti-Germanic influence for centuries to come, was not
himself a child of the chaos but a man of pure descent.
Hence the simplicity and power which strike us as so
wonderful when in the midst of the Babel of the sixteenth
century, just as the Germanic spirit of independence is
being reawakened (the true Renaissance !) and all voices
mingle in the hoarse and confused din of fear, we see
this one man, who, standing apart, calm and unconcerned
about what others decide and endeavour to attain
(except in so far as it affects his plans), goes his own way
and without precipitation, in full control of his natural
passionate temperament, forms the plan of campaign,
fixes the tactics to be employed, drills the troops to the
most carefully conceived and therefore most dangerous
attack that was ever made against Germanicism—or
rather against Aryanism as a whole.   Whoever considers
it a coincidence that this personality was a Basque,
whoever considers it a coincidence that this Basque,
although he soon found capable and perfectly devoted
assistants from all nationalities, yet at the summit of his
power made an intimate, indeed almost inseparable
friend of one sole man, consulted with him, and proclaimed
his will through him, and that this one man was by race

* *See* Bastian: *Das Beständige in den Menschenrassen*, p. 110;
Peschel: *Völkerkunde*, 7th ed. p. 539.
† Gothein: *Ignatius von Loyola und die Gegenreformation*, 1895,
p. 209.

a pure Jew (Polanco) who had been converted to Christianity at a later period of his life—whoever, I say, passes such phenomena by unheeded, has no feeling for the majesty of facts.* If we gain access to the innermost mental life of this remarkable man, as we can easily do by his *Exercitia spiritualia* (a fundamental text-book of the Jesuits to the present day) we seem to be entering an absolutely strange world. At first I felt myself in a Mohammedan atmosphere set out with Christian decorations : † the absolute materialism of the conceptions —for example, that we can feel the stench of hell and the glow of its flames, the idea that sins are transgressions of a " paragraphic " law, so that we can keep an account of them and should do so according to a definitely prescribed scheme, and so on—reminds us of Semitic religions ; but we should be doing the latter an injustice if we identified them with the thinly varnished Fetishism of Loyola. The fundamental principle of the religion of Ignatius is opposition to every kind of symbolism. He has been called a mystic and an attempt has been made to prove the influence of mysticism upon his thought, but this intellect is quite incapable of even grasping the idea of mysticism in the Indo-European sense ; for all mysticism from Yâjñavalkya to Jacob Böhme signifies the attempt to discard the dross of empiricism and surrender to a transcendental, empirically inconceivable untruth,‡ while Loyola's whole endeavour is to represent all mysteries of religion as concrete manifest

* It also deserves mention that the first two men who joined Ignatius and helped to found his Order were likewise not Indo-Europeans : Franz Xavier was a genuine Basque, Faber a genuine, superstitious Savoyard (*see* p. 373 note 2).

† Since the above was written, a book by Hermann Müller has appeared, *Les Origines de la compagnie de Jésus*, in which it is proved that Ignatius had studied very carefully the organisation of the Mohammedan secret leagues and in his *Exercises* in many ways followed Mohammedan views. In truth this man is the personification of all that is Un-Germanic.

‡ *See* chap. ix., Division " Philosophy."

facts in direct contrast to mysticism. We are to see, hear, taste, smell and touch them ! His *Exercitia* are not an introduction to mystical contemplation, but rather the systematic development of the hysterical tendencies present in us all. The purely sensuous element of imagination is developed at the expense of reason and judgment and brought to the point of its greatest capacity ; in this way the animal nature proves victorious over the will and henceforth the will is not broken, as is generally asserted, but fettered. In a normal human being, understanding forms the counterpoise of will ; Loyola's idea directs itself, therefore, first against understanding, as the source of freedom and the creative impulse ; in one of his latest proclamations he expresses it concisely : he characterises the " renunciation of will and the negation of our own judgment " as the " source of the virtues." * In the *Exercitia* also, the first rule of orthodoxy is " the destruction of every judgment of our own " (*see* the *Regulæ ad sentiendum vere cum ecclesia*, reg. i.).†

* *See* the last writing to the Portuguese, analysed and quoted by Gothian, p. 450.

† The Jesuit father Bernhard Duhr has devoted a paragraph of the fourth edition of his well-known book *Jesuiten-Fabeln* to my " Foundations." As the expression of a different point of view is always suggestive and instructive, I would gladly recommend this criticism to my readers, just as I have taken every opportunity to refer to the pamphlet of the Catholic theologian Professor Dr. Albert Ehrhard against these " Foundations " (Heft 4. der *Vorträge der Leogesellschaft*). But I must unfortunately point out that my Jesuit opponent does not hesitate at an untruth, whereby he makes his task indeed easier, but spoils its effect on sensible independently thinking readers. As a refutation point for point would lead me too far, I choose two examples : they will suffice. On page 936 Duhr says (in reference to what I asserted on p. 566) : *Nowhere* in the *Exercitia* is any attempt made to *destroy* the judgment of the individual, on the contrary, a number of directions are given for extending our knowledge and so forming our judgment rightly. In the rule quoted by Chamberlan also all that is said is : " Putting aside our own judgment we must be prepared to obey in everything the true bride of Christ, the Church." Now this interpretation is a frivolous sophism ; for when I " put aside " my own opinion to obey " in everything " the judgment of the Church, then I no longer have an opinion of my own. But in the literal trans-

By this the will is not broken, but only freed from obedience to its natural master, the individual ; but what now controls him is the whip of the *Exercitia*. By these, exactly as in the case of the Fakirs, only in much more carefully planned and therefore more successful manner, a pathological condition of the whole individual is produced (and by yearly repetitions and still more frequent ones in the case of persons whose capacity of resistance is greater, it is always strengthened anew), and this condition has exactly the same effect as every other form of hysteria. Modern medicine sums up these psychopathological conditions in the term " forced neurosis " and well knows that the person affected does not indeed lose his will, but certainly within the circle of the forced conceptions all free control of it ! Naturally I cannot here enter more fully into this highly complex matter,

lation of the Spanish original, published by the Jesuits themselves, *versio literalis ex autographo hispanico*, we read as follows : " *Primo, deposito omni judicio proprio, debemus tenere animum paratum et promptum ad obediendum in omnibus veræ sponsæ Christi domini nostri, quæ est nostra sancta mater ecclesia hierarchia, quæ romana est.*" And in the other passage adduced by me, Loyola's epistle to the Portuguese, the words are (S. 21) : " [*vos ego per Christum dominum nostrum obtestor ut ꞉ . .*] *voluntatem dico atque judicium expugnare et subjicere studeatis.*" Are these words not clear enough ? Do " deponere," " expugnare " and " subjicere " really only mean " to put aside " ? The second nstance is still worse. On page 157 of the second volume I have quoted a sentence of the Jesuit Jouvancy concerning and against occupation with the mother tongue ; Duhr boldly answers, " So foolish an assertion Jouvancy has nowhere made." In refutation of this I beg the reader to take up the following book : *Bibliothek der katholischen Pädagogik*, founded with the assistance of P.C. Dr. L. Kellner, Suffragan Bishop Dr. Knecht, Spiritual Councillor Dr. Hermann Rolfus and published by F. X. Kunz, vol. x., *Der Jesuiten Sacchini, Juvencius und Kropf Erläuterungsschriften zur Studienordnung der Gesellschaft Jesu*, trans. by J. Stier, R. Schwickerath, F. Zorell, members of the same society, Freiburg i. B., Herder, 1898. Pages 209 to 322 contain the translation into German of Jouvancy's Lern- und Lehrmethode. And here we read on p. 229, " We must take this opportunity of calling attention to a cliff which is especially dangerous to young teachers, namely, too much reading of works in the mother tongue, especially poetical ones. This is not only a waste of time but may very easily cause shipwreck to the soul.";

which, especially in the second half of the nineteenth century, has been in so far cleared up by the experiments of Charcot and others as well as by scientific psychology that the problem is now clearly grasped and the fearful power of Physis over Psyche recognised ; * it is sufficient if I have proved the destruction of the physical basis of freedom to have been Loyola's first purpose. This direct attack upon the body of the individual, not for the purpose of subjecting the body to the spirit, but to seize and conquer the spirit by means of the body, reveals a sentiment which is the negation of all that we Indo-Europeans have ever called religion. For Loyola's system has nothing in common with asceticism ; on the contrary, he hates asceticism and forbids it, and rightly so from his standpoint : for asceticism increases the intellectual capacities and culminates, when carried out with absolute consistency, in the complete conquest of the senses ; these may then continue, so to speak, as material for the imagination, to serve the mystical devotion of a Saint Theresa or the mystical metaphysics of the author of Chândogya ; from that time forth they are senses rendered subject to will, elevated and purified by the power of the mind, and this the Hindoo teacher expresses when he writes : " the man of understanding is already in his lifetime bodiless."† On the other hand, as I have said, Loyola's method actually prescribes a gymnastic course for the sensitive faculty, by which, as he himself describes his aim, the will and the judgment may be enslaved. While true asceticism is possible only

* To the most interesting summaries of late years belong the essays of Dr. Siegmund Freud : *Über die Ätiologie der Hysterie* and *Die Sexualität in der Ätiologie der Neurosen* in the Vienna *Klinische Rundschau* in 1896 and 1898. I am convinced that every strong stimulus of the outward activity of sense from purely inner excitement, even when it does not occur in sexual form, is an exacerbation of the sense-life, the seat of which is the brain, and from it results a corresponding paralysis.

† Çankara : *Die Sûtra's des Vedânta* i. 1, 4.

to a few chosen individuals, since moral determination must obviously form the basis and constantly hold the reins in this matter, these so-called " mental exercises " of Loyola, which must never last more than four weeks (but may be shortened or adapted by the teacher to each individual) will find an impressionable subject in almost every one, especially in younger years. The suggestive power of such a grossly mechanical method planned with supreme art for exciting the whole individual is so great that no one can get quite out of it. I too feel my senses tremble when I give myself up to these *Exercitia ;* but it is not the anatomically cut out heart of Jesus that I see (as if the muscular apparatus called " heart " had anything in common with divine love !), I see the ravenous *ursus spelæus* lying in wait for its prey ; and when Loyola speaks of the fear of God and teaches that it is not " childlike fear " that should satisfy us, but that we should tremble with " that other fear, called *timor servilis,*" that is, the tottering fear of helpless slaves, then I hear that mighty bear of the cave roar, and I shudder as did the men of the diluvial age, when poor, naked and defenceless, surrounded by danger day and night, they trembled at that voice.* The whole mental disposition of this Basque points backwards thousands of years ; of the intellectual culture acquired by humanity he has adopted some externals but the inner

---

* *Regulæ ad sentiendum cum ecclesia,* No. 18. It is very remarkable in connection with this fundamental doctrine of Ignatius (and all Jesuitism) that the Church father Augustine considered the *timor servilis* a proof that the man who felt it did not know God ! Of such people he says : " They fear God with that slavish fear which proves the absence of love, for complete love knows no fear "—" *Quoniam timent quidem Deum, sed illo timore servili, qui non est in charitate, quia perfecta charitas foras mittit timorem*" (*De Civitate Dei* xxi. 24). Goethe has clearly expressed in his *Wanderjahre* (Bk. ii. chap. i.) what should be the sacred rule of every Teuton in this matter : " no religion which is based on fear, is respected among us." Diderot makes the fine remark : " *Il y a des gens dont il ne faut pas dire qu'ils craignent Dieu, mais bien qu'ils en ont peur* " (*Pensées philosophiques* viii.).

growing and strengthening, that great emancipation of man from fear, that gradual tearing down of the tyranny of sense, which was formerly a condition of existence and hindered the development of every other quality, that " entrance of mankind into the daylight of life " with the awakening of his freely creative power, that tendency to seek ideals, which one does not first smell and taste in order to believe in them, but which one " really allows to grow up," because man, who has become a moral being, so wills it, that divine doctrine that the kingdom of Heaven comes not with outward signs but is within us like a hidden treasure *—all this left absolutely no impression upon this man ; standing apart from the restlessly hurrying waters which flow together to the great stream of Aryanism, his forefathers have lived since time immemorial, proud of their individuality, organically incapable of ever attaining to an intimate knowledge of that other nature. And do not imagine that Ignatius is in this respect a unique phenomenon ! There are hundreds of thousands of people in Europe who speak our Indo-European tongues, wear the same clothes, take part in our life, and are excellent people in their way, but are just as far removed from us Teutons as if they lived on another planet ; here it is not a question of a cleft such as separates us in many respects from the Jew, and which may be bridged at this point and that, but of a wall which is insurmountable and separates the one land from the other. The exceptional importance of Loyola lies in his pre-eminent greatness of character ; in such a man therefore we see the Un-Germanic and the necessarily Anti-Germanic in a clear and great form, whereas at other times, whether it be owing to apparent unimportance or the indefiniteness of the half-breed character, it is easily overlooked or at least difficult to analyse. I said " greatness of character," for as a matter of

See pp. 187, 188. *

fact other greatness is here out of the question : we note in the case of Loyola neither philosophical nor artistic thoughts and just as little real inventive power ; even his *Exercitia* are in their outlines borrowed from former cloister exercises * and merely " materialised " by him, and his great fundamental principle of uncompromising obedience is an old soldier's thoughtlessly brutal transference of a military virtue of necessity to the domain of mind. His activity as an organiser and agitator bespeaks the subtlest cunning and a precise knowledge of mediocrities (very important or original people he systematically excluded from the Order), but nowhere is there evidence of depth. To prevent misunderstandings and misinterpretations I must add that I do not ascribe to him as an intention what has come to pass as the result of his action. Loyola did not call his order into existence with the object of opposing the Reformation —so at least the Jesuits assure us—much less can the word " Germanic " have been associated in his mind with any definite conception, nor can he have viewed his struggle against Germanicism as a life-purpose. We might just as well assert that that race of the Basques which had been pursued, driven and persecuted ever further and further by the encroachment of the Indo-Europeans had wished to avenge itself on the victor through him. But in this book, where we are occupying ourselves not with chronicles but with the discovery of fundamental facts of history, we should emphasise the amount of truth that lies concealed behind these utterances which are untenable from the point of view of chronology. For it is not in what he wished to do but in what he had to do that the greatness of this extraordinary man lies. Father Bernhard Duhr may assure us, in his most excited tone † that the founding of the Order of

* *See*, too, the above note about the influence of Mohammedanism upon the composition of the *Exercitia*.

† See *Jesuitenfabeln*, 2nd ed. pp. 1-111.

the Jesuits had nothing to do with opposition to Protestantism ; its activity culminated from the very first so manifestly and so successfully in the prosecution of this one aim that even the earliest biographers of Loyola bestow on him the title of honour " Anti-Luther." And whoever says " Anti-Luther " says Anti-Germanic—whether he is conscious of this or not. But with regard to the question of race-revenge, the fact that those physically strong but mentally inferior and Anti-Germanic races, which were never quite destroyed but withdrew into the mountains, are reviving and increasing, is engaging more and more the attention not of visionaries but of the most earnest natural scientists.*

With Ignatius of Loyola I place the type of the Anti-Germanic spirit before the reader and I think I have thereby illustrated the necessary limitation of the Germanic idea which at the beginning of the chapter was taken in as comprehensive a sense as possible. I cannot imagine a definition of the Teuton put down in paragraphs—as we have seen that is not even possible with physical man—but rather as something vividly conceived, which qualifies us to give an independent judgment. Here more than anywhere else we must guard against letting the conception stiffen in the definition.† Such living definitions of ideas are not like mathematical ones : it is not sufficient to say that this or that is so and so, it is only by means of the negative supplement, not so and not

---

* I should perhaps have pointed out more emphatically that from the first the activity of the Jesuits has been exercised chiefly in opposition to the Reformation. Thus, for example, two of the direct pupils and friends of Ignatius, Salmeron and Lainez, took care to arrogate to themselves the decisive positions at the Council of Trent, the one as opener of each debate, the other as the last speaker in each case. Little wonder that the " freedom of the Christian," concerning which Luther had written such beautiful words, was fettered once for all at this Council ! The great Catholic Church already entered upon that course which was gradually to lower it to a Jesuit sect.

† *Cf.* Goethe : *Geschichte der Farbenlehre*, under Scaliger.

so, that the positive representation is put in relief and the idea freed from the fetters of words.

BACKWARD GLANCE

Freedom and loyalty then are the two roots of the Germanic nature, or, if you will, the two pinions that bear it heavenwards. These are not meaningless words, each one of them embraces a wide complex of vivid conceptions, experiences and historical facts. Such a simplification has outwardly only been justified by the fact that we have proved that rich endowments were the inevitable basis of these two things : physical health and strength, great intelligence, luxuriant imagination, untiring impulse to create. And like all true powers of nature, freedom and loyalty flowed into each other: the specifically Germanic loyalty was a manifestation of the most elevated freedom—the maintenance of that freedom, loyalty to our own nature. Here too the specifically Germanic significance of the idea of duty becomes clear. Goethe says in one passage—he is speaking of taste in art, but the remark holds for all spheres : " to maintain courageously our position on the height of our barbarian advantages is our duty." * This is Shakespeare's " to thine own self be true ! " This is Nelson's signal on the morning of the Battle of Trafalgar " England expects every man to do his duty ! " His duty ? Loyalty to himself, the maintenance of his barbarian advantages, *i.e.* (as Montesquieu teaches us), of the freedom that is born in him. In contrast to this we behold a man who proclaims as the highest law the destruction of freedom, *i.e.*, of freedom of will, of understanding, of creative work—and who replaces loyalty (which would be meaningless without freedom) by obedience. The individual shall become —as Loyola says word for word in the constitutions of

* *Anmerkungen zu Rameau's Neffe.*

his Order—" as it were a corpse which lets itself be turned on any side and never resists the hand laid upon it, or like the staff of an old man which everywhere helps him who holds it, no matter how and where he wishes to employ it." * I think it would be impossible to make the contrast to all Aryan thought and feeling more clear than it is in these words : on the one hand sunny, proud, mad delight in creating, men who fearlessly grasp the right hand of the God to whom they pray (p. 243) ; on the other a corpse, upon which the " destruction of all independent judgment " is impressed as the first rule in life and for which " cowering slavish fear " is the basis of all religion.

Forward Glance

I sometimes regret that, in a book like this, moralising would be so out of place as to be almost an offence against good taste. When we see those splendid " barbarians " glowing with youth, free, making their entry into history endowed with all those qualities which fit them for the very highest place ; when next we realise how they, the conquerors, the true " Freeborn " of Aristotle, contaminate their pure blood by mixture with the impure races of the slave-born ; how they accept their schooling from the unworthy descendants of noble progenitors, and force their way with untold toil out of the night of this Chaos towards a new dawn ;—then we have to acknowledge the further fact that every day adds new enemies and new dangers to those which already exist— that these new enemies, like the former ones, are received by the Teutons with open arms, that the voice of warning is carelessly laughed at, and that while every enemy of our race, with full consciousness and the

* " *Perinde ac si cadaver essent, quod quoquoversus ferri, et quacunque ratione tractare se sinit : vel similiter atque senis baculus, qui obicumque et quacumque in re velit eo uti. qui cum manu tenet, ei inservit.*"

perfection of cunning, follows his own designs, we—still great, innocent barbarians—concentrate ourselves upon earthly and heavenly ideals, upon property, discoveries, inventions, brewing, art, metaphysics, love, and heaven knows what else ! and with it all there is ever a tinge of the impossible, of that which cannot be brought to perfection, of the world beyond, otherwise we should remain lying idle on our bear-skins ! Who could help moralising when he sees how we, without weapons, without defence, unconscious of any danger, go on our way, constantly befooled, ever ready to set a high price on what is foreign and to set small store by what is our own—we, the most learned of all men, and yet ignorant beyond all others of the world around us, the greatest discoverers and yet stricken with chronic blindness ! Who could help crying with Ulrich von Hutten : " Oh ! unhappy Germany, unhappy by thine own choice ! thou that with eyes to see seest not, and with clear understanding understandest not ! " But I will not do it. I feel that this is not my business, and to tell the truth this haughty pococurantism is so characteristic a feature that I should regret its loss. The Teuton is no pessimist like the Hindoo, he is no good critic ; he really thinks little in comparison with other Aryans ; his gifts impel him to act and to feel. To call the Germans a " nation of thinkers " is bitter irony ; a nation of soldiers and shop-keepers would certainly be more correct, or of scholars and artists—but of thinkers ?—these are thinly sown.*
Hence it was that Luther went so far as to call the Germans " blind people " ; the rest of the Germanic races are the same in scarcely less degree ; for analytical thought belongs to seeing, and to that again capacity, time, practice. The Teuton is occupied with other things ; he has not yet completed his " entrance into the history

* Herder says (*Journal*, 1769, near the end) : " The Germans think much and nothing."

of the world " ; he must first have taken possession of the whole earth, investigated nature on all sides, made its powers subject to him ; he must first have developed the expression of art to a perfection yet unknown, and have collected an enormous store of historical knowledge—then perhaps he will have time to ask himself what is going on immediately around him. Till then he will continue to walk on the edge of the precipice with the same calmness as on a flowering meadow. That cannot be changed, for this pococurantism is, as I said above, characteristic of the Teuton. The Greeks and the Romans were not unlike this : the former continued to think and invent artistically, the latter to add conquest to conquest without ever becoming conscious of themselves like the Jews, without ever noticing in the least how the course of events was gradually wiping them from off the face of the earth ; they did not fall dead like other nations ; they descended slowly into Hades full of life to the last, vigorous to the last, in the proud consciousness of victory.*

And I, a modest historian, who can neither influence the course of events nor possess the power of looking clearly into the future, must be satisfied if in fulfilling the purpose of this book I have succeeded in showing the distinction between the Germanic and the Non-Germanic. That the Teuton is one of the greatest, perhaps the very greatest power in the history of mankind, no one will wish to deny, but in order to arrive at a correct appreciation of the present time, it behoved us to settle once for all who could and who could not be regarded as Teuton. In the nineteenth century, as in all former centuries, but of course with widely different grouping and with con-

---

* This reminds us of what Goethe called " after all the most magnificent symbol " : a setting sun on a sea, with the legend " even when setting it remains the same" (*Unterhaltungen mit dem Kanzler von Müller*, March 24, 1824 »

stantly changing relative power, there stood side by side in Europe these " Heirs "—the chaos of half-breeds, relics of the former Roman Empire, the Germanising of which is falling off—the Jews—and the Germans, whose contamination by mixture with the half-breeds and the descendants of other Non-Aryan races is on the increase. No arguing about " humanity " can alter the fact that this means a struggle. Where the struggle is not waged with cannon-balls, it goes on silently in the heart of society by marriages, by the annihilation of distances which furthers intercourse, by the varying powers of resistance in the different types of mankind, by the shifting of wealth, by the birth of new influences and the disappearance of others, and by many other motive powers. But this struggle, silent though it be, is above all others a struggle for life and death.

END OF VOL. I